A MODERN HISTORY OF EUROPEAN CITIES

A MODERN HISTORY OF EUROPEAN CITIES

1815 TO THE PRESENT

Rosemary Wakeman

BLOOMSBURY ACADEMIC
LONDON • NEW YORK • OXFORD • NEW DELHI • SYDNEY

BLOOMSBURY ACADEMIC
Bloomsbury Publishing Plc
50 Bedford Square, London, WC1B 3DP, UK
1385 Broadway, New York, NY 10018, USA

BLOOMSBURY, BLOOMSBURY ACADEMIC and the Diana logo are trademarks
of Bloomsbury Publishing Plc

First published in Great Britain 2020

Copyright © Rosemary Wakeman, 2020

Rosemary Wakeman has asserted her right under the Copyright, Designs and Patents Act, 1988,
to be identified as Author of this work.

Cover design by Tjaša Krivec
Cover image: France, circa 1896: Paris Vth district, street merchants, rue Mouffetard, 1886
(© Roger Viollet Collection / Getty Images)

All rights reserved. No part of this publication may be reproduced or transmitted in any form or
by any means, electronic or mechanical, including photocopying, recording, or any information
storage or retrieval system, without prior permission in writing from the publishers.

Bloomsbury Publishing Plc does not have any control over, or responsibility for, any third-party
websites referred to or in this book. All internet addresses given in this book were correct at the
time of going to press. The author and publisher regret any inconvenience caused if addresses
have changed or sites have ceased to exist, but can accept no responsibility for any such changes.

A catalogue record for this book is available from the British Library.

A catalog record for this book is available from the Library of Congress.

ISBN: HB: 978-1-3500-1766-5
PB: 978-1-3500-1765-8
ePDF: 978-1-3500-1767-2
eBook: 978-1-3500-1768-9

Typeset by Deanta Global Publishing Services, Chennai, India

To find out more about our authors and books visit www.bloomsbury.com
and sign up for our newsletters.

CONTENTS

List of Figures — vi
Acknowledgments — ix

Introduction — 1

1 The Grand Tour of Urban Europe (1815) — 9

2 Travels through Industrial Landscapes — 29

3 Entertainments and Romantic Dreamscapes (1815–48) — 53

4 Roaming the Markets — 79

5 Urban Reform and the Planned City — 107

6 Wandering City Streets — 135

7 Sightseeing in the Big City (Fin-de-Siècle) — 165

8 Electric Cities and Avant-Garde Itineraries (1920s–30s) — 195

9 Modernism and the City — 223

10 Searching through the Rubble (1939–50s) — 251

11 Car Trips through the City (1960s–70s) — 275

12 Crossing Urban Boundaries after the Berlin Wall — 301

Conclusion — 325

Notes — 327
Bibliography — 362
Index — 376

FIGURES

1	Political map of Europe with cities	3
2	View of the Grain Market and the Astronomical Column, Paris, eighteenth to nineteenth century, engraved by Mattheaus Deisch	14
3	Jewish merchants of Odessa	21
4	An engraving depicting Manchester as viewed from the London and North Western Railway. Dated nineteenth century	32
5	The interior of the Royal Exchange, Manchester, England, in the nineteenth century	37
6	Slums of Glasgow, Thomas Annan, 1861	39
7	Inside of the Krupp factories, Essen (Germany), circa 1905	42
8	View of Cologne, about 1840, steel engraving created in the nineteenth century, North Rhine-Westphalia	62
9	Early autotype of Marseille, Bouches-du-Rhone, France, historical photo, 1884	73
10	The Beach, Blackpool, Lancashire, 1894–1910	76
11	London Paddington station, antique photography-derived dot print illustration, 1895	84
12	Traffic outside the Bank of England and the Royal Exchange in the City of London, 1896	88
13	Great Exhibition of 1851 held in Hyde Park	93
14	Covent Garden Market, London	98
15	Les Halles, the Central Market of Paris	100
16	The Subalpina Gallery in Turin, Italy, engraving by Ernesto Mancastropa from a drawing by Rodolfo Griffi, from *L'Illustrazione Italiana*, No 1, January 5, 1890	102
17	Interior of Au Bon Marché department store, Paris, illustration from *L'Illustration, Journal Universel*, No 1518, Volume LIX, March 30, 1872	104
18	Plan of Paris, circa 1870, with Georges-Eugène Haussmann's boulevards superimposed in black	121
19	Boulevard Montmartre, spring, 1897. Artist Camille Pissarro	123
20	Plan of Barcelona by Ildefons Cerdà with his planned extension called the Eixample	125
21	Panorama of the Franzring on the Ringstrasse, Vienna	127
22	Budapest, Andrássy Avenue	133
23	Dockers Strike, September 7, 1889. From *The London Graphic*—"Dockers' Strike in the East End of London," published 1889	138

Figures

24	Ragpickers, Porte d'Ivry, Paris, 1910–12. Eugène Atget	141
25	Coburg Street, Glasgow Tenements	143
26	AEG Turbine Hall, Huttenstrasse, Berlin Moabit district, 1950s. Peter Behrens	147
27	View into the parlor of a Berlin worker family in the apartment house Liegnitzer Strasse 9, 1910	148
28	"In front of the milk shop," 1924/25, Heinrich Zille	150
29	Hofbräuhaus in Munich, circa 1886	155
30	The Royal Victoria Coffee Palace and Music Hall, London, Illustration from *The Graphic*, vol. XXIV, no 612, August 20, 1881	158
31	The exit of the Moulin Rouge, circa 1900	160
32	The Diamond Jubilee: Queen Victoria's carriage passing the National Gallery, London, 1897	167
33	The Chateau d'eau and Palace of Electricity at the 1900 Paris Exposition	170
34	Café Central in Budapest about 1910	182
35	A L'Innovation department store, Brussels, Victor Horta, 1901	185
36	Art Nouveau building designed by Mikhail Eisenstein on 4A Strelnieku Street, Riga	187
37	Fiat Lingotto Factory, Turin, 1921–23	201
38	Crossing the Kurfürstendamm, Berlin, 1926	203
39	Alexanderplatz with the train station, Wertheim department store, and the tower of the Red City Hall, Berlin	204
40	Tiller Girls in the Haller Revue, 1927	206
41	View of Warsaw with the Alexandrovski Bridge across the Vistula, 1925	208
42	Zuyev Workers Club by Ilya Golosov, Moscow, 1928	213
43	A procession through Moscow's Red Square to celebrate the annual May Day holiday, 1929	214
44	The market in Sarajevo, 1930s	217
45	Belgrade, Kingdom of Serbia, Croatia, and Slovenia	219
46	Piscine Molitor, Paris, 1930	229
47	Karl-Marx-Hof, Vienna	233
48	A block of flats by German architect Ludwig Mies van der Rohe in the Weissenhof Siedlung Housing Project at Stuttgart, 1927	236
49	Inauguration of Via dell'Impero in Rome, October 28, 1932	240
50	Narrow street in Naples, 1937, Martin Hurlimann	243
51	A view of rubble and ruined buildings covering the streets after the German bombing of Warsaw, 1939	252
52	A group of volunteers working to rebuild Dresden	257
53	Plac Konstytucji, Marszalkowska Street, Warsaw, 1956	260
54	The Royal Festival Hall and other specially-erected buildings at the site of the Festival of Britain on the South Bank of the River Thames, London 1951	264
55	The Housing Estate in Sarcelles, 1963	266

Figures

56	Monoprix store in Caen, Ouchacoff and Bataille architects, about 1960	268
57	Teddy Boys on a Sheffield Street	270
58	Hungarian Uprising. Jubilant insurgents outside the Hungarian Parliament Building, Budapest, October 1956	272
59	Mods ride their scooters along the seafront at Hastings, East Sussex, 1964	279
60	Traffic jams in Paris, 1968	282
61	The Lijnbaan in Rotterdam, 1960	284
62	The Bijlmermeer Housing Estate outside Amsterdam, 1973. Hans Peters	289
63	The Lütten Klein Housing Estate, Rostock, 1969	293
64	Happening of the "Kommune I" on the Kurfürstendamm, Berlin	299
65	Saint Cyril and Methodius University in Skopje, Marko Mušič, 1974	302
66	The Ostankino television and radio tower nears completion in Moscow, July 26, 1967	303
67	Shopping center, Bucharest, Romania	312
68	Tallinn's Old Town, Viru Street and the towers of the medieval Viru Gate	317
69	Frankfurt skyline at the business district	322

ACKNOWLEDGMENTS

Books are always collective endeavors, and a great many people have participated in this voyage into the European urban past. For helping me conceive of this project, Rhodri Mogford at Bloomsbury earns my sincere thanks. A fellowship at the Institute for Advanced Study at Central European University was the foundation for much of the material on east central Europe. It was a privilege to take part in the remarkable intellectual life at IAS and CEU. The IAS conferences on "Migration and the City" and "Globalizing Late Habsburg Central Europe" along with "Migrant Narratives on the City" as well as the Academy of Sciences conference on "Modern Capitals and Historical Peripheries" were models of scholarly interaction. Thank you in particular to Gabor Sonkoly at Eötvös Loránd University for many long conversations on European urban places. For their insightful comments, my genuine gratitude goes to Gábor Gyáni, Sándor Hites, Sándor Horváth, and Balint Vargar at the Hungarian Academy of Sciences, Ágnes Györk at Karoli Gaspar University, and Markian Prokopovych at CEU and Birmingham. The tour of Miskolc with Gergely Kunt of the University of Miskolc was an historian's best adventure, as was the tour of Debrecen with Ágnes Györk and colleagues at the University of Debrecen. I was privileged to tour Riga's splendid art nouveau buildings with Jānis Krastiņš of Riga's Technical University. Thank you as well to Eszter Gantner and Heidi Hein-Kircher at the Herder Institute in Marburg, Germany, for their ideas and keen insights, as well as to Laura Kalbe at the University of Helsinki for generously sharing her knowledge of east European urban history. A stay at the Faculty of Architecture & Built Environment at the Technical University Delft provided the opportunity to examine the bond between European urban form and social processes. Thank you to Carola Heinz for this opportunity and for her perceptive knowledge of European cities. A seminar with Moritz Föllmer and Tim Verlaan at the University of Amsterdam's Centre for Urban History helped flesh out the book's themes. Colleagues and students at the Center for Metropolitan Studies at the Technical University in Berlin have long been a source of intellectual inspiration. Thank you in particular to Dorothee Brantz and Boris Vormann for their friendship and canny observations on this project. Colleagues in Paris have long sustained anything I have ever tried in European urban history. My sincere thanks to Laurent Coudroy de Lille, Thierry Paquot, Loïc Vadelorge, Clément Orillard, Corinne Jaquand, Emmanuel Bellanger, Nathalie Roseau, and Florence Bourillon. Thank you to Catherine Maumi at the Ecole Nationale Supérieure d'Architecture in Grenoble for many penetrating conversations about European urbanization. As always, ongoing discussions with friends Michèle Collin and Thierry Baudouin, with Francis Nordemann and Emeline Bailly kept me on track.

Acknowledgments

My intellectual lifeline goes directly to the Stephen A. Schwarzman Building of the New York Public Library. Its extraordinary resources and assistance, with days squirreled away in the Allen Room, were indispensable for this research. Generous Fordham Faculty Fellowships were a mainstay for the time and energy required for scholarship. My thanks as always to colleagues and students at Fordham for their interest and suggestions. Thank you as well to Charlotte Labbe and the staff at Fordham Library's Interlibrary Loan for digging up any document I ask for. My family sustains me. Nothing happens without them. Tom, Gabrielle, and Jessica willingly dragged around from one European city to another, carried luggage and deciphered maps, and listened to me endlessly while I worked out this book. My deepest thanks go to them.

INTRODUCTION

This book is a history of the European urban experience during the nineteenth and twentieth centuries. It takes the reader on a journey to cities and towns across the continent in search of the patterns of development that shaped the urban landscape as indelibly European. The focus is on the built environment, the social and cultural transformations that mark the patterns of continuity and change, and the transition to modern urban society. The book weaves the story of Europe's cities directly into the broader fabric of history. It begins in 1815 with the end of the Napoleonic Wars and continues through the end of the twentieth century and into the early twenty-first century. In the 1990s, German philosopher Peter Sloterdijk defined Europe as the historical and mental unit that brought about modernity, for all its best and worst features.[1] The nineteenth and twentieth centuries were the key period during which European cities were this crucible of modernity. They form a discrete period of vital importance to understanding European urban society.

European urban history has largely been constructed around a vertical "trickle-down" effect: modern modalities were forged in the great capitals and flowed down through the urban hierarchy. Towns were "recipients" of modernity and measured against the processes that took place in western Europe. The more distant the urban place (from western capitals), the more delayed was the leap into the modern world. Regional variants were treated as peripheral derivatives of western European models of modern life. Beyond that, it has generally been assumed that there is not much of a local story to tell. This book steers away from the perspective that capital cities sparked modern urban society and culture, and peripheral towns or cities outside the west had no local culture worth discussing until modernity arrived. My objective is to break down this narrative and decenter modernity away from Paris, London, and Vienna to a wider urban realm. This recognizes the highly complex, often contradictory nature of modernism as it took shape across geo-historical space, and the ways in which local urban cultures influenced modern transformation. It requires a recharting of European urban processes that treats the cities of the east and south not as closed-off backwaters but as highly productive, globally networked, with their own modernist proclivities. Cities were never static societies entrapped in belief systems imposed upon them—whether Ottoman, communist, or capitalist. Much to the chagrin of historians, those who lived in the past rarely behaved according to the simple categories assigned to them. They were capable of a multiplicity of perspectives and identities, especially when they lived in cities.

Rather than the canonical vertical perspective, I am emphasizing the horizontal and spatial layering of modernism and modernity. These were less monolithic and more mongrel processes that interacted with the intimacy of everyday life in countless ways. Rather than categorizing social and cultural forms as "pre-modern" or "modern" and focusing on "growth," the text highlights the fluidity and complexity of the urban world. It steers away from strict categories of social class and instead highlights fluid social and ethnic landscapes. Even small towns were laboratories of modern transformation. The book examines the back-and-forth sociocultural transmission between cities and the ways in which towns throughout Europe interpreted modernity through the lens of their own vernacular practices and histories. This often produced an uneasy and sometimes contradictory urban amalgam. In this sense, the continuities of European urban culture and society were as important as their metamorphosis. The text seeks to understand the urban forms that modernity attempted to repress, but which lingered and were absorbed into the complexities of social and cultural life. It engages with the debates on memory and modernity and explores the pluralities of urban transformation. The book searches for the ways in which modern urban culture and society took root and flowered as a combination of local experience and the influences coming from the great capital cities, and beyond.

So there is no real homogenous view on urban modernity in this volume. Instead, I am looking for the heterogeneity and contradictory quality of urban modernity and modernization and allowing the urban experience to appear edgy and unstable. There was no undifferentiated urban experience. There was no one, monolithic Europe. Having said this, there was also an internal dynamic characteristic of European urban systems. These characteristics and identities embodied a European urban experience, a deeper structural and historical unity over the *longue durée* that was constantly reinvented in the nineteenth and twentieth centuries.

In this sense, the book asks the questions: Is there a European city, and if so, what are its characteristics? What makes a city "European"? Given the globalizing forces of the early twenty-first century, this is one of the most important questions currently engaging scholars. Clearly there is no single European city type: there are many European cities and a plurality of urban modernities. Taken as a whole, Europe is not an easily definable geography. Its physical landscape of mountains, valleys, rivers was not necessarily contiguous with accepted cultural frontiers. Political borders shifted constantly. Any kind of regional taxonomy is vague and porous. Europe's regional concepts—central Europe, eastern Europe, the Baltic, or the Balkans—are slippery cultural constructions that changed dramatically over time. These places have been named and renamed, their territories expanded and shriveled like the bellows of an accordion. Regional imaginaries are riddled with stereotypes and the weight of social and ethnic inclusion and exclusion. Leaving behind these knotty geographic challenges, even the "idea" of Europe is a continuous invention and the term can be peppered with prejudiced and colonial overtones (Figure 1).

Given these complexities, how do we define the geography of Europe and make out the contours of urban development across the continent? The Cold War vision of the "West" and the "Eastern Bloc" are artifacts that have crumbled along with the Berlin wall. Central Europe and East-Central Europe have now (re)entered the geographic imagination. What role did cities play in defining these landscapes? What, after all, are the urban boundaries of Europe? Should we include St. Petersburg and Moscow among

Figure 1 Political map of Europe with cities.

European cities? Most texts do this. Some also include Istanbul. If we include Odessa and Sebastopol, should we include Tbilisi and Baku as European cities? Is there such a thing as Baltic cities or Mediterranean cities, and can we say that their urbanizing processes were specific to place? This book attempts to bring European urban history to bear on these debates.

I have chosen not to define Europe as a specific geographical entity or European cities in terms of geopolitical borders. Instead, I am looking for the spectrum of relations across European urban systems. This does not mean superimposing some sort of Christaller-like central place theory over a map of Europe. But I am approaching geography at different scales rather than the usual "national" country-by-country treatment. I am focusing on localities, regions, the particularities and relations between places. The book is meant to insert cities deeply into the geography of Europe. My touchstone here is more Braudel in its emphasis on historic regions and regional cultures, language and custom, geography and topography, maritime and river systems, and the connectivity of trade, migration, sociocultural transmission. How did these evolve over the modern period and to what degree did they determine local, European-wide, and global urban networks, and with them urban practices? Related to this more inclusive geographic approach, the book focuses not only on capital cities but also on the dense European urban network that evolved during the modern period. It brings the development of urban regions and the web of medium and small towns, even villages, into the dialogue about European urban life.

Writing in the late nineteenth century, sociologist Max Weber was among the first to define the European city,[2] in his case based on the development of capitalism and its heritage of political autonomy. For Weber, the European city was a political community, a distinct civil society with the *Bürgertum* or *bourgeoisie* at its core. What distinguished the European city was this sense of a world apart from the countryside and the bounds of feudal society. Cities became places of social and cultural innovation because they were independent. They turned into symbols of modernization. For Weber, this transformative capacity declined once they were integrated into nation states. Nonetheless, this heritage of urban civil society acted as a foil against private interests and unbridled liberal capitalism. Municipal governance acted on behalf of the city as a whole.[3] A robust public administration provided for the collective provision of basic services and transportation, for urban planning, for the regulation of land use and construction. These governing structures were clear in the health and sanitation movements and the passion for boulevards in the nineteenth century, and then in the projects of municipal socialism in the twentieth century. Ultimately, this European tradition of urban civil society would be the backbone of the modern welfare state.

My approach incorporates the work of Patrick LeGalès and Arnaldo Bagnasco in *Cities in Contemporary Europe*,[4] which posits characteristics such as the stability and longevity of European urban systems, the density and compactness of the urban fabric, the complex sociopolitical structures of European cities, the heritage of political independence, the shared morphology of urban growth, and the strong tradition of town planning. The relative stability of the urban system constitutes one of the most distinctive features of European cities. Individual cities rose and fell in importance. They grew or shrank because of wars, social and economic dislocation. There was a general shift in development over time from Mediterranean cities to the cities of northern Europe. The fastest growing cities were political capitals. Port cities stood out as vital urban gateways. But the broader European urban system remained nearly unchanged. The largest metropolises, London and Paris, still towered over the rest in the year 2000 just as they had in 1815. Only a few cities, such as Berlin and Warsaw, were upstarts. Medium and small cities and towns had long histories of successful adaptation. They absorbed no end of technological changes, socioeconomic transformations, political upheavals. The European urban system reflects the past. It is extremely consistent. This is reflected in the built environment. Most European cities possessed a clearly identifiable ring pattern of development from the ancient core, to medieval and early modern expansion, and then to modern growth discernible in multistory apartment buildings, tree-lined ring boulevards, train stations, museums, theaters, and opera houses.

The book takes great care to emphasize the urban experience in central and eastern Europe and in southern Europe, which have too long remained peripheral in urban historical scholarship. This opens the field of vision about urban development in Europe. The text asks how the concept and imaginary of the European city changes when we steer away from the narrative of exoticism, of blockages and "detours into stagnation," and instead normalize the eastern and southern European urban experience in its own right, without degrading it to second-hand status.[5] This western geographic perception has a long history that was exacerbated by Cold War rhetoric. Since the "discovery" of eastern Europe in the eighteenth century, the region has been treated only in comparison to the West and described as a region of slow or retarded urban growth, only "catching up" when it exhibited western-style modernization.

This text steers away from static categories of "Eastern Europe" or "Southern Europe" as regions of otherness. It takes into account the invented nature of these spatial definitions and boundaries, and instead maps out a more inclusive, fluid urban geography. It assumes more open relations between regions, especially during the Cold War. East central Europe had strong European and global ties, even during the darkest days of communism. From the longer viewpoint, it fully participated in the momentous events in European history from the 1848 revolutions to the First World War and revolutions of 1918, to post-Second World War reconstruction, the 1968 student revolts, and the fall of communism in 1989. Cities across Europe were exposed to world markets, to migration, to information, and to communication flows.

I have also skirted the typologies of either capitalist or socialist cities. A long debate has ensued among scholars over whether there were characteristics specific to the socialist city and then after its demise, a shift to post-socialist features. The arguments focus on the distinctions between the capitalist west and its primacy of private property against the near monopoly on urban development enjoyed by the state in the east. According to this argument, the political economies of socialism and capitalism stood in stark contrast and shaped the patterns of urban development differently. Even debates around post-socialist cities are framed around whether East-Central Europe is becoming "more like" the West. My goal was to avoid the trap of imagining eastern Europe as separate, remote, an unknown world suddenly open to discovery after the fall of the Berlin Wall.

Instead the book underscores the tradition of governance that guided modernization and urban development across Europe in the nineteenth and twentieth centuries. This public management and regulation, whether in the mixed public-private planning programs in western cities or in the cities under socialism, is what distinguished urban development in Europe. On the one hand, it shaped a homogenous urban fabric that is unmistakable in the nineteenth-century boulevards or the late twentieth-century modernist housing estates. These were signatures of urban progress by social elites in full control of the reins of government. On the other hand, modernization was not a monolithic process. It was uneven and took on distinct features as it interacted with specific political and economic landscapes. Vast programs of urban development took place within the context of empire and globalization, nation-building, and even regional and local narratives. These influences coexisted and interacted on the urban world in synchronous, complex ways. Geography also mattered. There were national versions of the social welfare state in western Europe. Even the monolithic quality of Soviet-led modernization rapidly broke down into various national forms of urban development. Socialism was less a distinct expression of urbanity than a forty-year phase in a longer historical process. What counted—and was part of the deep structural unity in the European urban experience I am looking for—was that elites managed to stay in power that supported modernization and industrialization, large-scale infrastructure programs, public housing, and social agendas. Socialism was largely a variant of the modernizing processes of the late twentieth century.

The challenge is to set this deep structural unity of the European urban experience alongside the plurality and discontinuities evidenced in cities and the multiple regional forms that urban modernity has taken. Once we incorporate eastern and southern Europe more concretely into the fabric of urban history, we can say that the global patterns of trade and migration, and global knowledge and information transfers, were more complex and began earlier than scholars have previously envisioned. Typically, globalization as it relates to Europe's cities has been studied as a phenomenon of British and French (German) colonialism in the late nineteenth and twentieth centuries. Globalization is tied to nation-building. However, cities in eastern and southern Europe were global gateways to the Mediterranean, the East, and beyond early in the nineteenth century. A wide-lens look at urban geography across Europe underscores immigration and the mixing of ethnic groups that have been one of the most significant features of European cities. The melting pot of Europe has a long historical trajectory when seen from this perspective.

The manufacture and trade in goods, food products, and luxury items were dispersed across villages, towns, and cities in, for example, the Balkans or in the Polish territories of the Russian Empire. Urban systems were multi-scaled from local networks to the global ties of trade and empire. This kind of global integration did not necessarily await the arrival of industrialization, railroads, or modern infrastructure, although these clearly had important impacts on both time and space. This means that the transfers and networks of information, ideas, and cultures pulsated through European cities and towns in more complex ways than scholars have suggested. I have put aside the notion that eastern Europe was simply "colonized" by empire. The flow of information, travel, and cultures between the Ottoman, Russian, and Hapsburg empires created rich, hybrid urban places, with a frontier or borderland complexity that was international as well as local. This is true of the western Mediterranean as well.

How did these vibrant urban cultures act as mediums of cosmopolitanism and the fluid identities and allegiances that constructed a "European" disposition? The book argues that the cosmopolitan identities created from trade, from the migration and blend of peoples, from cultural diasporas and entrepreneurial worlds were widespread. Cosmopolitanism was not a feature of sophisticated capital cities and didn't transcend the local. Instead, I have incorporated the perspective on cosmopolitanism of Homi

Bhabha and Dipesh Chakrabarty[6] as a creative mélange and weaving together of identities and traditions to create a hodgepodge of cultures. It was part of a layered consciousness and identity, and social solidarity, that people developed and practiced in a myriad of urban places. People belonged to a web of relationships that were local, regional, and also at the scale of empire and globality. Urbanites were open to transnational allegiances and to living with others. In general, cities in east central and southern Europe exhibited these characteristics earlier and more powerfully than western European cities. They were ahead of the curve, rather than behind it. These kinds of urban environments did not await the arrival of the nation state and capital cities, nor was it limited to social elites, western, or otherwise.

Whatever the circumstances, cities were spaces of encounter. The book has a keen eye for the migratory waves that resulted from political territorial shifts and war, from industrialization, economic and environmental crises as well as from social and ethnic diasporas. Flows of people moved in and out of cities and across borders, facing hostility, merging into the urban firmament. Who belonged in the city, who had the right to live there, were contentious questions that had both social class and ethnic frames. This turmoil, these migratory flows, the practices of inclusion and exclusion were as much a part of urban history as the industrial revolution or urban planning. They were essential to fabricating the hodgepodge cosmopolitanism that scholars such as Bhabha describe, and its breakdown into outright intolerance, that were part of the European urban experience.

The history of Europe's cities in the nineteenth century, in fact up to the First World War, follows themes worked out in an outstanding legacy of historical scholarship. However, the signposts for urban development in the twentieth century are somewhat murkier. Even more, European urban history texts have traditionally only dipped their toes in the urban waters of the post-1945 era.[7] My intention was to equally balance the nineteenth and twentieth century narratives. In doing this, the text expands on urban economic development beyond the usual narrative about the industrial revolution. It moves the discussion of urban economic culture, the patterns of business practices forward into the twentieth century. Much excellent scholarship exists on European cities as sites of consumption in this period. The emphasis in this text is also on cities as sites of production, especially in electricity, automobiles, chemical, and consumer products that radically changed the look of cities and how people experienced everyday urban life. The book also weaves the late twentieth century into the fabric of urban history. This is important because the most momentous wave of urbanization in modern Europe took place after 1945. Lacing it into our comprehensive narrative about Europe's urban development is essential. The traditional urban system expanded. Those regions of Europe that had remained largely rural became urban. The impact was profound, as were the 1968 protests, the fall of the Berlin Wall in 1989, and the reknitting of Europe around a shared urban society and culture. The advent of neoliberalism had profound effects on European urban society, as did decolonization and the media revolution.

The book pays special attention to visual landscape and visual culture. The narrative is woven around the plurality of urban spaces, topography, and the built environment, the visual culture that produced both iconic and lesser known images of the European city. The evolution and lived experience of the city is investigated with reference to these visual markers. They reveal the life stories of the city. Land and water, city walls, market halls and expositions, public buildings and public spaces, street festivals and protests, neighborhoods, factories and warehouses, department stores and cinemas, suburban housing estates, and highways become the mediums for storytelling. My objective is to incorporate the excellent scholarship (especially by a new generation of young scholars) on the complicated and open-ended character of modernism, and to see the built environment and spaces of the city as an opportunity to embrace the variations in this discourse. The accent is on narrative form woven around this visual theater of the imagination and the role it played in our understanding of urban history. Any discussion of this kind needs to be sensitive to the interaction between individual perception and the structures of social class and ethnicity that determine viewpoint.

The book takes as its narrative cue the perspective of the "passant" or the traveler passing through the urban realm. This "way of seeing" the European city, of finding the past in the urban landscape, provides the framework for understanding the transformation of urban culture and society. This is not nineteenth-century *flânerie* nor does it privilege a male, bourgeois point of view. It is not a touristic gaze, nor is it a cataloging of European historic buildings and monuments. The visual register of the "passant" was initially formulated by cultural critic Walter Benjamin in his search for modernity and further developed by literary critic Siegfried Kracauer[8] in looking for the seen and unforeseen in the urban landscape. It allows for the interplay between "then" and "now" and for a critical appraisal of history. The perspective of the "passant" displays the interrelationship between historical continuities and modernity, and the ways the European city has been represented and imagined. It is cultural, aesthetic, ethnographic, and material in content. It has overlapping social, economic, and political dimensions. Visual and literary artifacts give full play to this excavation of the everyday world and particularity of place. I am relying on them for an expression of what it was like for people to "travel" through and live in the city and for the sensory responses these experiences aroused. The position of traveler also allows particular awareness of the networks and flows between cities and the forms of sociocultural transmission across European urban geography.

The book stops action throughout the chapters to inspect the histories of individual cities. I am well aware of the snags in selecting specific places to spend time in and the gaps in the cities treated here. At times the watchfulness in particular urban places intensifies: at times the descriptions have a sketchy, unfinished quality. Hopefully the book avoids the pitfalls of either wandering around Europe skipping into every town's story or delving into the convoluted details of too few micro-histories. My hope is that the number and kinds of cities found in this book help to understand how their histories accumulate and shuffle the way we see the processes of European urbanization as a whole.

CHAPTER 1
THE GRAND TOUR OF URBAN EUROPE (1815)

In the early nineteenth century, the map of Europe was already speckled with urban places. The density of towns and cities was one of the continent's defining characteristics. Villages and hamlets were scattered across the countryside. Small and medium size towns were busy with commerce and exchange. There were administrative towns, royal towns, market towns, and university towns. There were a few large cities, above all London and Paris. Greater London was already a sprawling behemoth on the Thames River with a population of just under one million in 1800. The city of Paris was home to nearly 600,000 inhabitants. Beyond that, the scale of Europe's cities quickly diminished. In central Europe, upstart Berlin had some 170,000 residents. Cities such as Hamburg, Munich, and Breslau (Wrocław) had populations of around 100,000. The five Italian cities of Genoa, Milan, Rome, Naples, and Palermo all had populations over 100,000. Around 230,000 people lived in Vienna, the capital of the Hapsburg Empire. Further east, towns were significantly smaller. Warsaw's population was 64,000 while Kraków's inhabitants numbered around 35,000. Budapest claimed 54,000 inhabitants. In the Ottoman Balkans, 42,000 people lived in Bucharest, and another 60,000 resided in Salonica (Thessaloniki) on the Mediterranean coast. For the most part, the everyday world of most town dwellers was local—even neighborhood—in orientation. Daily life was marked first and foremost by homegrown traditions and historic influences. The church, the town hall, and marketplace were the centers of public life. They were surrounded by a jumble of buildings crowded against each other over time. Local materials and regional building styles determined the look of a town. Stone and brick, timber and thatching, rooflines, windows and entryways were woven into patterns that gave each town a distinctive, monochromatic appearance. Towns in the west of Europe tended toward more durable brick and masonry. In the north and east, timber predominated. Unless they were destroyed in some catastrophe (and time and again, cities built of wood went up in flames), the same buildings stood on the streets for hundreds of years. They were sandwiched cheek by jowl along a mix of ancient paths and byways laid out over the course of time. Only the most symbolic public buildings were endowed with grand architectural panache in stone and marble. Even when new buildings were constructed and architectural styles changed, the traditional urban footprint of lot sizes and sites, streets and street names stayed the same.

The stability of European urban topography was remarkable. Europe's cities were ancient places. Even under the impact of formidable social and economic changes, cities adapted to circumstance and hung on to their power and influence. The urban order steadily reproduced itself. The imprint of the past was profound. Europe's biggest cities maintained their place at the apex and would do so throughout the nineteenth and twentieth centuries. Regional cities and smaller towns continued to play roles as industrial centers, administrative and cultural seats, and market centers. Each town had its own way of doing things, its own traditions and habits of mind that made life comprehensible. Local customs, dialects, and costumes were still very much in evidence in the early nineteenth century along with the rhythms that had long defined everyday life. The church was an enduring force in people's lives. Ancient church spires punctuated the skyline. People identified with their parish and neighborhood church. They wandered past monasteries and convents, chapels, and church buildings. Church bells chimed the tempo of daily life. Religious festivals and sacred processions defined the annual seasons. Towns, or what in Italian was called "La Città," were often still surrounded by the walls and old city gates that marked the boundary of urbanity. The role of this border was still paramount, even if it was becoming fluid and outdated by the early nineteenth century. Old walls were often punctured with scars from cannon ball fire and were difficult to keep in repair. People, carriages, and carts trundled through a succession of ramparts, walls, and bastions, across earthworks and old moats, then through elaborate gates where they were stopped and searched. Everyone paid a toll. The walls help explain the compactness of European cities. Cities were enclosed places, forced to fill in every inch of space.

Yet this picturesque imagery of the early modern town can be deceptive. These were not sleepy, claustrophobic enclaves. Even if historic influences prevailed, Europe's cities were dynamic places where changes were absorbed into the patterns of everyday life. Newcomers regularly squeezed in as the population rolls stretched longer. Capital cities such as London, Paris, and Vienna always drew people into their urban whirl. From the mid-eighteenth century, towns and cities across the spectrum grew substantially, and this was particularly the case for smaller urban places at the grass roots of Europe's urban system. The expansion of agricultural production and arrival of new industries made small towns and even quasi-urban villages into vibrant trading centers with far-flung networks of exchange.[1] Despite their formidable presence, city walls were porous and urban boundaries endlessly elastic. Towns and cities expanded outward. Old walls were pulled down and new neighborhoods constructed, many of them elegant and fashionable, that were then encircled by new walls in the tree-ring pattern characteristic of European urban growth. Settlements even further out were often the domain of the poor and excluded ethnic groups such as the Catholic Irish in Belfast or Jewish shtetls outside eastern European towns. There was an ongoing ebb and flow between town and countryside. Landless poor and seasonal laborers moving between rural villages and towns to find work, skilled craftsmen, clerics and officials, roving peddlers and tradesmen, soldiers and seamen, political refugees, all made towns and cities mobile, restless places, open to the hurly-burly exchange of people. They were a world of opportunity and widened horizons. Rich and poor, esteemed citizens, and humble newcomers bumped elbows on the streets. They slogged through mud and around carriages and horse-drawn wagons. Scores of wide-eyed migrants passed through the city gates and traveled to-and-fro between provincial towns and large trading centers. Migration was the linchpin of urban growth. For centuries, the term "urbanization" was a synonym for this mass of humanity and their movement from the countryside to towns, and from towns to big cities.[2] Cities owed their fortunes to these waves of people who brought skills, money, and connections and the far-flung networks of trade and knowledge that went with them.

Together these elements corresponded to the traditional concept of an urban municipality that was familiar across Europe. It was the administrative functions that determined a place's legal statute as a "city," often as a royal city or the residence of a noble, or as the center for local administrative services such as courts and tax offices, or even as an independent sovereign entity. Formal acknowledgement as a city also brought with it rights of citizenship and collective privileges. The maintenance of order, the implementation of justice, the supervision of the grain halls, the bread supply, wine, oil, and other staples fell to the town hall and its officials. They initiated public works programs with new public squares and fountains, bridges, market halls and commercial exchanges, pillories and prisons. Inevitably, a prestigious coterie of noble and patrician families stood at the apex of power and wealth. As "men of property," their political rights were based on family position and wealth. They enjoyed the privileges of city offices and controlled the city's economic life through restrictive guild corporations. In larger cities, these municipal elites were joined by the intellectual milieu of universities and local scientific institutions. On the opposite end of the social spectrum, criminals faced the gallows on the town square before crowds of righteous onlookers. Egregious misdeeds, riots, and fearsome crowd violence kept jail cells packed.

Labor disputes could easily spill out into the street as artisans and tradespeople jockeyed for advantage within the guilds. Small and medium-size manufactories produced porcelain and glassware, tapestries and luxury items, the tools and equipment used daily. The sounds and smells of artisan work took place on streets long-named after their labors—cobbler street, glass street, butcher street. Wool, linen, and cotton textile producers and craftsmen toiling in leather and metallurgy were dispersed across a web of local villages along with pottery, wood carving, and papermaking. They were interconnected in a tight commercial and trading network that was region wide. These commercial transactions were the basis of the urban economy. The wheeling and-dealing in local markets defined urban life. It was controlled by merchants and the guilds and business associations that formed the town's burgher elites. They managed the city's affairs from the town hall and marched proudly in ceremonial public parades with their costumes and insignia.

The market square was a city's public arena and the heart of its commercial trade. Crowds gathered on market days in the main square or on time-honored streets to scrutinize goods produced by local artisans and farmers, the food and everyday merchandise, the luxury items. They exchanged wares and money, haggled at weigh houses, and grudgingly paid up taxes and duties. Country folks arrived on market days leading their farm animals through the streets to waiting buyers. Resplendent in traditional dress, they sold everything from embroidered lace to farm produce and dairy products. In 1827, an Englishman traveling on the Danube arrived in the Austrian town of Linz, where he came upon "the square filled with market-people and purchasers. The ground was covered with their large flat baskets, containing all kinds of provisions. By the side of each stood the vendor, in his or her provincial costume; and amongst the motley crowd moved the mistresses and maidens of Linz dressed 'à la Française....'"

In larger towns the market split into specialties that spread through the streets. Used clothing and books, kitchen wares, and household goods were on display along with exotic dyes, spices and sugar, haberdashery, and luxury items imported from across Europe and its colonies. Beggars pleaded for caste-offs. Street entertainers and streetwalkers worked the crowds. Onlookers sipped drinks in adjacent coffee houses and shops. Local officials waged an ongoing struggle to protect citizens from fraud and unscrupulous traders. The big commercial fairs took place on an annual cycle, turning towns into spectacles of deals and dickering. English author Elizabeth Rigby wandered through the Jahrmarkt, or annual fair, in Tallinn (also known as Revel) in the Baltic province of Estonia. Held in front of St. Nicholas Church, "the low wide-roofed booths surmounted with their different insignia, with wares of all colours floating around them, and merchants of all complexions swarming before them.... Here were Russians with their Siberian furs, and Bulgarians with their Turkish clothes, and Tula merchants with their cutlery."[3]

What distinguished Europe was the density of this urban archipelago—the thick concentration of urban places lodged along the rivers and roads. The overall population of Europe was around 200 million just after 1800 and a remarkable percentage of people were congregated in compact settlements. It was a well-peopled landscape of villages, towns, and cities. England, the Netherlands, Belgium, and Italy had the longest tradition and the densest network of urban places. Historically the "south" of Europe, which largely meant the Italian peninsula with its rich classical antiquity and artistic tradition, was considered more civilized than the crude "barbarian" north. This idea was losing timber by the late eighteenth and early nineteenth century. The vast geography of eastern Europe was less urbanized. The idea of "Eastern Europe" was a fairly new concept. There was no physical fault line, no great mountain range, that divided the continent into "west" and "east." These were cultural imaginaries whose boundaries remained vague. The idea of "Eastern Europe" was invented in the late eighteenth and early nineteenth century as a backward region between a "civilized" Western Europe and "barbarian" Asia.[4] It was also associated with Oriental despotism and the divide between the Catholic-Protestant churches in the west and an east anchored by the Eastern Orthodox church. The Scandinavian countries were the most rural.

Yet population measures do not capture the full complexity of Europe's urban patterns. In some areas, larger towns and cities predominated. They were prestigious places that enjoyed general admiration for their lively urban scene and influence. In other areas of Europe, the settlement systems depended on small towns and villages. Some towns remained closed tightly within their walls while others spread out across their hinterlands. Urban patterns were deeply historic and dependent on natural geographic features that did not necessarily conform to the boundaries of modern nations. Even more, the majority of Europe's urban places were harbor towns hugging the coastlines or carved by rivers and their tributaries. Historians of Europe have long been fixated on tracking the kinds and degrees of urbanization across the continent as a measure of development. Yet, for all the idiosyncrasies of the urban processes from the shores of the

Atlantic across to the Ukraine and beyond, what most characterized the European urban landscape was its stability. Despite rapid urbanization in the modern period, the network of urban places was the same in the late twentieth century as it had been in 1800.

Despite their traditional appearance and the wistful nostalgia that often accompanies it, Europe's cities and towns experienced a continuous stream of innovations from the late eighteenth century onward inspired by Enlightenment ideals. There was an explosion of published works of literature, science, history, and philosophy as well as in the public social settings where ideas could be hotly debated. The intellectual circles huddled around tables in the coffee houses of Europe's capitals sent a steady stream of broadsheets and newspapers out to the reading public. Literary and scientific societies abounded. It was this tension between tradition and modernity and the myriad outcomes it produced that made the urban realm so dynamic. The imminent historian Fernand Braudel called these cities "electric transformers," places that accelerated the rhythm of exchange and the transformation of urban life.[5] Larger towns enjoyed the print shops and bookstores, the coffee houses and theaters, that made them beacons of Enlightenment ideas. The introduction of something new, of improvements, was proof of a town's sense of progressive urbanity and its connection to mainstream European thinking. Beyond the provincial networks that rubbed off on local intellectual life lay international commerce. This became the vital medium for the transmission of new ideas and knowledge, and contemporary urban values, and it was maritime in character. The groundbreaking philosophies and reforms of the Enlightenment circulated around Europe's great capital cities and through towns and villages via the coastal shores and rivers that carried commercial trade.

Europe's biggest cities were port cities. The continent and the British Isles were shaped by their long, sinuous coastlines. The bays and rivers flowing around and through these landmasses molded urban geography. The majority of Europeans lived near the water. In a historic sense, to be truly urban was to be connected to water communication and commerce. The great seaports were at the pinnacle of Europe's urban pyramid, and they dominated the movement of people, products, capital, and information. Seamen and their mercantile backers were kingpins. Ports like London, Amsterdam, and Hamburg were global powerhouses—the urban hubs in the world capitalist system. Their ships sailed the high seas loaded with exotic cargo from the Atlantic and Asian routes. The Baltic and Mediterranean ports, the towns along the Black Sea at Europe's eastern edge were still robust maritime competitors. They operated within centuries-old trading networks with links to coastal and river towns across the continent. Port towns were spewed along Europe's inland waterways. They served the incessant demand for grains as well as salt, timber, pitch and tar, and metals. Smaller river towns specialized in short-haul shipping in a trading procession that sent cargo to the major port cities that controlled the delta estuaries. The great rivers of Europe—the Thames River in England, the Rhine and the Ruhr, the Elbe River in Germany along with the Seine and the Rhone rivers and the Garonne in France, the Vistula in Poland, and the Danube River in Europe's southeast— were the stuff of legend. A rich array of rituals, myths, and stories grew up around them. They carried the goods, the information and ideas, and the people that were essential to urban life. Whole regions lived on and by their broad sluggish rivers. Particularly in the early nineteenth century—before the railroad, the automobile, and airplane transformed travel—a journey along Europe's major rivers provides the most instructive perspective on European city life.

The product that dominated trade across Europe was grain. It was the key feature of the European urban economy in the early nineteenth century. There was an endless cry for the wheat, rye, barley, corn that were the basic staples of people's diet, especially for the laboring classes. The growing numbers of people packed into the cities of western Europe only intensified the already insatiable demand. Bread was the staple of every meal. The grain supply was the primary responsibility of municipal authorities. Water-powered grist mills were an urban fixture. They were everywhere. Cities were strewn with mills along creeks and rivers, churning out flour and then made into bread by local bakeries. Flour milling and bread making were big business. Stock markets ran on grain prices. Wholesale merchants traveled the continent searching out the highest quality grains for the best price. Cities built elaborate granaries and market halls, known as corn exchanges and *halle aux blés*, dedicated to the trade. They were public monuments to the commodity that was fundamental to urban life. Such was the symbolic meaning of the grain silo, it became an inspiration for modern architecture. Grain halls were often magnificent rotundas that evolved into the city's stock market. Shortages and spoilage of the precious supplies occurred all too frequently, especially with crop failures, and caused instant calamity. The cities in the north and west were especially dependent on the imported cereals arriving with the harvest from the plains of eastern Europe. In times of need, they were often distributed to the poor at rock-bottom prices. Bread riots were

Figure 2 View of the Grain Market and the Astronomical Column, Paris, eighteenth to nineteenth century, engraved by Mattheaus Deisch.

all too common. It is worth remembering that when the price of bread shot up in 1788 and 1789, Parisians finally lost patience and stormed the Bastille (Figure 2).

Bulk agricultural products like cereal grains traveled on rivers and along the coasts. The economy of eastern Europe in particular was dependent on this river hauling system. Poland's major export was the grain farmed by serfs on vast aristocratic estates and then sent out on the watery highways. The Vistula River with its tributaries and canals was Poland's largest, widest thoroughfare and its lifeblood. It wound its way through the fertile plains of the east, its banks dotted with river ports, towns large and small, and major cities from Kraków to Warsaw. Each had its warehouses, boatyards, and merchant quarters hugging the riverbank. Tall granaries decorated with gabled roofs were the town insignia. Grain traveled the Vistula's length all the way to Danzig (Gdańsk) on the Baltic Sea. The annual voyage was a mainstay of Polish life.[6] It was the opportunity for grain magnates and their retinue to travel and receive news from abroad. Jewish traders purchased grain from growers and resold it to merchants along the route. Wide flat-bottom rafts made of fir were stacked high with the golden cereal and floated along the muddy waterways. The towns of Sandomierz in southern Poland and Płock in central Poland grew as grain trading centers on the Vistula. The port of Toruń in northern Poland was known as the "Queen of the Vistula," its pitched-roof brick granaries stacked high along the riverfront. The market square buzzed with traders haggling over the wheat shipments coming from the hinterland and then sent on to Danzig. Often the local nobility introduced urban innovations in Poland by reinvesting grain profits in small-scale manufacturing of glassware, local luxury items, and textiles to expand river trade. Once at Danzig, the grain was stored in immense warehouses that lined the wharves and was then sent out on ocean-going vessels to Amsterdam and London.

The Baltic Sea ports were among the more important and wealthiest cities in Europe. They were the legacy of the Hanseatic League—the powerful urban network that for hundreds of years dominated trade in the Baltic and North seas. Situated at the mouth of the Vistula as it flowed into a wide bay on the Baltic, Danzig commanded the outlet to the sea. It was the great marketplace, the grain depot, and the largest city in Poland until Warsaw and Kraków caught up. Danzig was built for business. Fluctuations in its grain prices were pegged to the stock exchanges in Amsterdam and London. Even in 1804, when the glory years of Danzig's grain trade were behind it, the British traveler John Carr was mesmerized by the grain boats docked along the waterfront, with their single sail to catch the winds off the Vistula. "Heaven protect the being who visits this city without a commercial commission!" he barked. "The Danzigers keep a cash account of civilities, and never indulge in festivity without resorting to calculation."[7] Danzig's merchants were king and zealously guarded their privileges and their tax base. The corn exchange at Artus Court controlled the city's trade and the swapping of news and information. Bargaining between wholesalers, speculators, and shippers took place directly on the rafts or along the waterfront and Long Street (*Langgasse*). The wharves on the Motława River and Ołowianka Island were lined with granaries, the Great Mill, and the city's giant port crane that hung precipitously over the waterfront. Danzig's shipyards churned out grain boats, merchant vessels, and warships. The point of all this activity was to make the city richer.

In truth, Danzig looked as it had been for hundreds of years. It shared a Baltic brick-and-clinker appearance found in cities along the northern coast of Europe and identifiable as Hanseatic at its root. The Gothic Town Hall and Great Armory dominated the cityscape and provided a seamless historical continuity. Merchants coming from the landside made their way through the city outskirts and then stared up at the fortification walls. They entered Danzig through the Upland Gate, then crossed the drawbridge to the sumptuous Golden Gate. Once inside the city, they traveled down the *Langgasse* to the Long Market and Artus Court. There, they leaped into the haggling and banter on grain prices, the seaward weather, revolutions, and wars. Then they continued out through the Green Gate to the wharves. Danzig was a melting pot of ethnic identities from the local Kashubs of the surrounding Pomerania region to English, Scottish, Poles, Finns, Swedes, Danes, Russians, and Ukrainians. The city's harbor area was the magnet for a mélange of peoples occupied with production and trade. Salt and olive oil arrived from Spain and Portugal; herring from Scandinavia. Raw materials and industrial products were piled up and warehoused. English merchants hawked textiles and exotic colonial products such as sugar, coffee, and cotton. Tobacco came from the newly opened American market, while the French traded wine.[8]

Port cities like Danzig dominated Europe and were privileged sites for the emergence of cosmopolitan life. They were hubs in a rich commercial and cultural exchange that was complex and tenacious. It outlasted the vagaries of political crisis and the interminable territorial battles that swirled around. Like all ports, Danzig was a pluralistic crossroads filled with foreign merchants, bankers, and bookkeepers, especially Dutch and German. Danzig entrepreneurs traveled Baltic waters and Atlantic coasts, attended the great fairs at Leipzig and Frankfurt, and did business in cities across the Mediterranean. The city's patricians spoke German. They sported the latest British and French fashions and displayed all the trappings of social sophistication. Their palatial homes lined the *Langgasse*. They were built in a flamboyant Flemish-Italianate style, crowned with gables and lavishly festooned with "lions, angels, suns, griffins," Carr reported in his travel journal. "Nothing can exceed the fantastic appearance of the houses."[9] The *Langgasse* and its lavish patrician mansions were the symbol of merchant wealth and power.

Nonetheless, the battle for dominance in the Baltic Sea trade was fierce. It was a complex interconnected commercial system that stretched from Hamburg in northern Germany to Copenhagen and Stockholm, to Danzig and Riga, and across to St. Petersburg. Like all the imagined mesoregions of Europe—the Balkans, the Mediterranean, Central Europe, Eastern Europe, and so on—the idea of a Baltic region was constantly reinvented. But there was no doubt it was an incessant space of commerce and exchange. All of the Baltic ports were laden with merchandise and capturing even more of the lucrative east-west trade was everyone's ambition. Western Europe was eager not only for grain but also for flax, hemp, tallow, tar and timber, and iron and copper. Traders were willing to pay in precious metals for these high-demand commodities. Large or small, Baltic towns built up a store of industries tied to these commercial transactions. Trade generated flour milling, saw milling, brickworks, shipbuilding and maritime equipment, wagon-making, breweries, forges, leather, and textile production. Businesses flourished. The multiethnic, hybrid public sphere in cities on the Baltic coast was constructed from this to and fro of regional production and exchange and the transfer of information and ideas that went with it. A multitude of languages were spoken in the city streets and alleyways. It was a privileged cultural and economic mosaic—so bountiful that these cities retained their privileges and independence regardless of the political tides shifting around them. They were open gateways into eastern Europe, which remained, at least in the minds of westerners, a vague, unknown world.

Danzig faced powerful competitors as well as political adversaries. Cycles of economic warfare, wild speculation, boom-and-bust were a reality of life. In the first division of Poland in 1772, Frederick II of Prussia laid siege to the city and then set heavy tolls on the Vistula, cutting Danzig off from central Poland and strangling its grain trade. The Prussians constructed the Bromberg Canal that diverted commerce to the Oder River and to the German port of Stettin (Szczecin) on the Baltic coast. It was a clever engineering strategy that cut off Danzig's commercial lifeline. As travel by both sail and steamships increased, Königsberg and Hamburg became the favored ports of call for merchant ships and developed into the leading emporiums on the Baltic. To the east, Riga, Tallinn, and Helsinki captured the booming Russian market, especially in timber, flax, and hemp. Ships dropped anchor in St. Petersburg as well. Danzig's decline dramatized the oscillations in a city's fortunes, and the rivals willing to divide the spoils.

By 1800, the Baltic cities had all been annexed by the Russian Empire. The picturesque vistas captured by artists around this time highlight their busy waterfronts laden with goods and lined with ships. In the background hovers the traditional city skyline dominated by stately churches and town halls, and the massive ramparts that defended the western limits of the tsar's domain. Russians moved into the Baltic cities: not only military staff but also merchants, shopkeepers, skilled craftsmen, and workers. The town building promoted by the Russian Empire was based on Enlightenment ideals. It made the Baltic cities into small versions of St. Petersburg, a series of "windows on the West" graced with the classical form favored by the Russian court and local elites. Tiny Helsinki was christened the capital of the Grand Duchy of Finland (1812), given a new city plan and made into a neoclassical showpiece in imitation of St. Petersburg. In Tallinn, streets were straightened and paved. Public buildings were constructed with brick and masonry and given a classical patina. The baroque palace and gardens in the Tallinn suburb of Kadriorg commissioned by Peter the Great were a magnet for Russian gentry seeking the sun and sea. Russian, Tartars, Belarusians, and Jewish artisans built traditional Russian village districts, or *sloboda*, of wooden cottages.

Russian influences were grafted on to the German language and culture that had long dominated Baltic urban life. It was the edgy juncture between Russian and German customs, and local culture, that epitomized the Baltic world. German "Balts," as they were known, acted as intermediaries between Russian officialdom and the local population. The German character of the Baltic provinces was anathema to Slavophile purists, who urged strict policies of Russification. But the Russians conveniently allowed the Balts to manage the cities and make places like Riga and Tallinn into thriving port cities. Local elites were educated in Germany and learning in the Baltic was led by German masters. Cities in northern Germany and the Baltic had some of the highest levels of literacy in Europe in the early nineteenth century and were the image of enlightened sociability. A profusion of regional dailies and weeklies, broadsheets, and journals were inspired by Enlightenment ideals. Newspapers appeared early in the Baltic. Riga had a robust German-language press in papers such as the *Rigasche Rundschau* and *Rigasche Zeitung* as well as the Russian newspaper *Rigas Vestnesis*.[10] German merchants, intelligentsia, and civic officials, "men of letters" as they were known, fashioned a vibrant cultural life with theaters, universities and scientific societies, gymnasium, libraries, and reading and music clubs. The most progressive of these German-educated elites promoted a common Baltic identity that would break down class boundaries and lead to equality between the nobility, the burghers, and the intellectual literati. Riga's "Society for the Study of History and Antiquities of the Russian Baltic Provinces," founded in 1834, was a meeting place for local intellectuals anxious to preserve Baltic history and cultural heritage. These were the settings for elite sociability. Freemason lodges acted as a commercial and correspondence network, connecting them to a broad European fraternity and to the Enlightenment cosmopolitanism they aspired to.

Both militarily and perhaps more importantly symbolically, fortifications still marked the urban sphere in the Baltic. Inside the walls in places like Riga—in what was considered the city proper—new buildings were constructed in brick and masonry in the panorama of western architectural styles favored by Russian as well as local German elites. Outside the walls, buildings were constructed of wood and embroidered with local decorative patterns. The outskirts of Riga were the domain of the local Latvian population, which was considered by uppity Germans as a people without culture or nationality. Not everyone aspired to a hybrid Baltic identity, especially when it crossed ethnic lines. Although Riga achieved remarkable prosperity, its good fortune evaded the city's native inhabitants, exiled in their own separate world from the German Balts and Russian nobility ensconced in the city center. Each went along different paths. Russian workers settled along the roads east, in the districts dubbed the Moscow Suburb and St. Petersburg Suburb. The wooden settlements on the city fringes repeatedly suffered from the ravages of fire. They could also be put to the torch in case of enemy invasion along Russia's western frontier. It was a scorched earth policy that knew no bounds and was tested when Napoleon and his armies reached the Baltic provinces. Riga's wooden settlements along the road to Moscow were burned to the ground in preparation for the assault. Thousands were left homeless.

The same doom awaited Helsinki. The fishing port and garrison town on the shores of the Baltic Sea was a ramshackle collection of red wooden houses. It went up in flames in 1808 and the entire town was destroyed. Once it came under Russian rule a year later, Helsinki was transformed into a capital city for the new province of Finland. Berlin architect Carl Ludwig Engel was commissioned by the Tsar to reshape Helsinki's layout into a showcase city and design a neoclassical ensemble at its center. Senate

Square together with Helsinki Cathedral and the university gave the rebuilt city a new imperial grandeur, set off even further by an elegant tree-lined esplanade. French and English architecture flourished in the residences of merchant and bureaucratic peers. Hospitals, churches, and a new theater graced the streets. It was through Baltic ports such as Helsinki, Tallinn, and Riga with their mélange of German-Russian influences that Enlightenment urban reforms along with intellectual ideas reached eastern Europe. Cities were a medium for cultural exchange. News traveled not by road—the roads were terrible as every visitor attested—but by the watery system of rivers, tributaries, and canals connected to the Baltic Sea. Modern cultural values and a continuous stream of technical innovations were opening up even the most remote places. Cities and towns grafted these influences onto local cultural traditions. The result was multifaceted urban textures and identities among which was an impassioned ethnic nationalism. It was beginning to fracture the cultural hybridity that had long typified Baltic urban life.

Initially the Baltic ports fared well enough during the Napoleonic Wars. Their importance as commercial magnets initially gave them neutral status under French rule. Even when Napoleon's Continental System banned British shipping, the port cities of Hamburg, Stettin, Danzig, and Königsberg all became havens for notorious smuggling operations that undermined French control. Fed up with the impudence, Napoleon annexed the entire Baltic coast and saddled the ports with billeting troops, heavy taxation, military conscription, and waves of refugees. The brutality and destruction of the Napoleonic Wars ended the old ways of life across Europe. As the hostilities and military campaigns wore on, cities along the Baltic coast were ruined. Popular uprisings against the invaders and then the fierce reprisals, malnutrition, and disease brought untold suffering. The Baltic town of Lübeck was devastated by house-to-house urban warfare. Its port was occupied by the French navy and its commercial shipping collapsed. Napoleon's Grand Army besieged and bombarded Danzig for ten weeks. Grain boats were destroyed. The port stood empty. The grain trade that had sustained Polish towns along the Vistula River for generations slowed to a trickle. The town of Toruń, the "Queen of the Vistula," was occupied by Napoleon's army in 1806 and its granaries ravaged while it served as his military garrison. The grain traffic on the Vistula was finished off first by the Continental Blockade, and then by the British Corn Laws that saddled grain imports with punishing taxes. Even after they mobilized against the French, the towns along the Vistula struggled to regain their influence and watched their illustrious grain trade ebb away. In their campaign to defeat Napoleon, the Russian army then laid siege to Danzig in another devastating blow to the city. Death, famine, and typhus followed. What had been the jewel of the Baltic with over eighty thousand inhabitants collapsed. Only sixteen thousand forlorn stalwarts remained by 1812.

The year 1815 was terrible. The Napoleonic Wars finally ended, but many of Europe's cities and towns lay in ruins. Trade and economic production had disintegrated. There were food shortages everywhere. Then the massive eruption of the Mount Tambora volcano in the Dutch East Indies led to the "year without summer" in 1816. A dense cloud of ash slithered across the skies over Europe. Temperatures plummeted. Storms and toxic black rain resulted in failed grain harvests. The worst famine of the nineteenth century sent thousands begging for food in the streets. People demonstrated in front of grain markets and bakeries. Looting and riots took place in many cities. Thousands died from hunger and typhus. In his celebrated history on the wheels of commerce, the historian Fernand Braudel reminds us of the perils that accompanied the grain trade in these early years of the nineteenth century: "When it comes to grain, no regularity can be taken for granted; one never knows where the demand will come from, who will be able to meet it, or whether one will arrive too late when someone else has already delivered the goods." Only the most powerful merchants could take such risks,[11] especially amid the vagaries of war and climate disaster.

The opening of the great plains of southern Russia for grain cultivation provided a new source of food for Europe's hungry cities, especially once the Ottoman Empire lost its monopoly on the Black Sea. In the nineteenth century, the Black Sea region was described as the "pivot of history" where an entire constellation of powerful political forces converged.[12] The port towns along its northern coastline were highly productive commercial gateways and sieves of cultural exchange, with tentacles deep into the Russian hinterland. Once the Ottomans lost their grip on the region, Russia systematically ejected the ethnic Muslim populations. It then showered privileges on colonists willing to settle in the southern provinces—the New Russia as it was called—and gave away enormous estates to landlords willing to cultivate wheat, rye, barley, and oats for the cities across Europe that were choked by incessant wars. The port of Odessa on the northwestern shore of the Black Sea boomed in the early nineteenth century. It quickly grew into one of the Russian Empire's largest cities. Wheat from southern Poland, the Ukraine, and Bessarabia was barged down the Dnieper, Dniester, and Bug rivers to its harbor. Some nine hundred ships lay waiting on the quayside in 1803. Another 1,500 ships sailed into its harbor in 1815. Wines and silks, exotic cargo were offloaded on to the Odessa docks, to be replaced in the ship holds by wheat and other commodities that sailed the Mediterranean to western Europe and Great Britain. By the mid-1820s, most European powers had signed commercial agreements with the Ottoman Empire allowing them access through the Dardanelles and Bosphorus Straits to the flourishing Black Sea trade. Then the 1829 Treaty of Adrianople allowed complete freedom of navigation. Once the British Corn Laws were repealed from 1846 to 1849, the Black Sea trade became a veritable frenzy. Some 200,000 tons of mainly grains were exported annually from Odessa. Herds of oxen tramped through the streets each harvest season, dragging carts weighed down with huge sacks of grain to storage facilities. Over five hundred grain warehouses were jammed along the streets. Some fifty thousand peasants arrived each season to work on the docks.[13] They made up the fluid, flexible labor force on which port towns depended. Greek and Italian middlemen squabbled over payment on the wharves (Figure 3).

There were at least ten Italian firms exporting grain in Odessa. Greek merchants and shippers handled over half the trade.[14] Odessa's commercial bank and insurance dealers were quick to offer their services to the maritime entrepreneurs. The grain trade on the Black Sea and down the Mediterranean was controlled by a vast network of merchants—Greeks, Italians, and eventually Jewish—with contacts throughout the towns along Europe's southern coastline. They were the great merchant families whose common

Figure 3 Jewish merchants of Odessa.

kinship, fraternal organizations, and commercial holdings forged the commanding heights of the maritime economy and facilitated cultural exchange between east and west. It was a fascinating and contradictory brew—a hodgepodge of economic elites fused around ethnicity, religion, and culture. They dealt with the towns and cities along the Mediterranean as points on a time-honored commercial itinerary. It was a conveyor belt of goods, people, information, and ideas. Their ships stopped at Constantinople, and then plied onward in legendary travels to Trieste, Genoa, Marseille, and Toulon in France, and then all the way to London. It was a remarkable network of social and cultural transaction that tied Odessa more to Europe than to the Russian capitals at St. Petersburg and Moscow.

Odessa became one of Europe's most cosmopolitan cities. The city grew around a popular myth as open to the world, a special place springing up from nowhere, dedicated to trade and inhabited by the flux and flow of humanity. The Duc de Richelieu, appointed governor general by Tsar Alexander I, laid out a neoclassical city in the early 1800s. Acacia trees and lofty butter-colored houses lined the wide streets and public gardens. Odessa went from a miserable fishing village to an elegant city of 30,000 inhabitants almost overnight and the third-largest city in the Russian Empire by the 1820s. But it was the diversity of its population that marked it as distinct and claimed the city's roots in the ethnic mosaic of the Ottoman world. Traditionally, the Ottoman Empire was not ethnically based, nor was there a notion of nationality.[15] Religion determined identity, and even here, the faithful carrying out Jewish, Christian, and Muslim practices were basically accepted. Eastern Mediterranean cities were thus a potpourri of peoples who found some level of coexistence. Although their beliefs could be decidedly at odds, basic tolerance at the level of the everyday whirl was a valuable asset. Greeks, Galicians, Albanians, and Turks from the Ottoman Empire, Ukrainians, and Tartars, Jews from Belorussia, British, Germans, Italians, and French could all be found doing business in Odessa. This mix was fundamental to Ottoman urban tradition. Armenian Catholics were barbers while Bulgarians were gardeners. Russians were carpenters, plasterers, and coach drivers.[16] Craftsmen sat outside their shops or did business in the courtyards threaded through multiethnic settlements. Odessa was a safe haven for scholars and intellectuals, for the displaced and the avaricious. All this required a convenient measure of cultural and religious cohabitation along with the hand-waving babel of words and idioms used to communicate. Visiting in 1852, British traveler Laurence Oliphant was struck by the liberty and "unwonted freedom of smoking and conversation which prevailed among those with whom I mixed."[17]

But the myth of Odessa was also based on its legendary European charms. As an urban place, it was paradoxically Europe, but not Europe. The promontory overlooking the sea was turned into a grand esplanade between the Stock Exchange and the Governor's Palace. On the city side, Primorsky Boulevard was lined with hotels in imposing italianate style. Italian shipping magnates ran the city's chic Hotel du Nord and the Hotel du Club. It was here the beau monde of Odessa society ambled in the evenings under the trees, watching the sea glisten in the moonlight. Sitting in a hotel café "furnished and fitted up in a style superior to most in Paris," American explorer John Lloyd Stephens looked "upon the crowd still thronging the boulevards, I could hardly believe that I was really on the borders of the Black Sea."[18] Italian and Greek were the city's lingua franca and street signs were posted in Italian and Russian. Everyone attended Italian opera in the city's municipal theater. Odessa was the great mercantile emporium with sophisticated shops offering a profusion of extravagances and fashions. Its university, printing houses, the availability of books and pamphlets put Odessa at the forefront of intellectual exchange.

For all the cosmopolitan pageantry, Odessa was also distinctly local in character. The extravagant costumes and polyglot chatter, the ethnic and religious mingling marveled European visitors. The city's famed medley of bazaars and markets drew on Muslim tradition and were a riot of goods. It spilled out to a transient peddler trade that served the poor. Nonetheless, Odessa suffered the perils of any port town. Trade ebbed and flowed with the vagaries of the harvests. The city could suffer economic depression just as quickly as it enjoyed boom times. More than exotic goods arrived on the ships. The city was hit with a series of plague outbreaks: the epidemic in 1812 by far the worst. Normal life in the city ceased for nearly two years until the contagion finally ran its course. Typhus and cholera were a continual scourge. Drinkable water was a scarce commodity. Roads were unpaved, choked with dust in summer and waist-deep in mud in winter. Ethnic tensions cut into the myth of cultural and religious coexistence. Toleration had its limits and tempers were short. A multitude of ethnic rivalries and ill-treatment were part of daily life. The grain trade attracted ruthless greed and profiteering by crooks. Bribery and smuggling abounded. The city's underworld was renowned. The portside taverns and bars were a haven for organized crime and sex workers. Jobs on the docks drew a whirlpool of the marginal from runaway serfs to shysters, refugees, and vagrants. Yet the continuous streams of humanity helped knit the city's commercial culture together and reinforced its freewheeling, open-to-all reputation.

With its delta mouth in the Black Sea, the Danube River next became the grain and communication highway. The course of the wide Danube was a geopolitical fault line and the most significant element in urbanization from the Black Sea into the interior of eastern Europe. Under Turkish control for hundreds of years, the towns of Galați and Brăila (Brălia) built on bluffs on the left bank of the Danube were heavily damaged during the Russo-Turkish War that ended with the Treaty of Adrianople in 1829. The Russians annexed the mouth of the Danube River and under Russian protection, both cities quickly developed into thriving gateways. The cereals of the great eastern European plains were sent by ship from Galați and Brăila, past the Danube estuary, to the Black Sea and Constantinople, Trieste, and the Mediterranean. They were boom towns relishing the fortunes made from the insatiable demand for grain in western Europe and Great Britain. Grain framed global contact even in the smallest towns. With the abolition of the Corn Laws in Britain and the Great Famine in Ireland, a bevy of Danubian ports began exporting directly to the British market and importing industrial goods and coal. Ships from Liverpool, Marseille, and Antwerp appeared along the quays. The inauguration of the Danube Steam Navigation Company in 1829 was a milestone in making the Danube a transportation artery. Steam revolutionized travel and forged a new chapter in the grain trade and the linkages between the eastern reaches of the continent and the west. The Danube steamships were financed by the Hapsburg Monarchy and run by two enterprising British shipbuilders. They secured a quick river voyage between Vienna, Pest, and Constantinople with Galați and Brăila acting as the relay points for cargo, mail, and passengers. Already in 1842 over 200,000 travelers made the trip "in spite of crowded cabins, suffocation, mosquitoes, and fevers."[19]

By the 1840s the Danube grain trade was already competing with Odessa. Some 300 vessels were reported at the docks in Brăila in 1840, and its population had already reached 25,000.[20] The Danube steamers were competing with Russian and Ottoman companies and the British and French commercial interests all plying between Odessa, the Danube ports, and Constantinople. It was a competitive trading system reliant on the towns and cities along the waterway. Arriving at Brăila later, in 1890, the American traveler Francis Davis Millet reported that the

> stream was crowded with vessels of every description, from the native lotkas to the great English freight propellers, whose ugly iron hulls towered high over all local craft . . . miles of loaded lighters were anchored along the channel, and great steamers were moored to the quay several ranks deep, all receiving their loads of grain. Thousands of men of every nationality and in motley dress were swarming like bees all over the cargo boats, carrying sacks of grain from the army of carts on the shore and pouring it into the open hatches.[21]

The Black Sea straits and Danube delta were a haven for exiles, freebooters, and fugitives skirting the oscillating geopolitical boundaries between the Russian and Ottoman worlds. Galați and Brăila were places of refuge for ethnic groups fleeing armed conflict and persecution. The forced migration caused by Russia's conquest of the Caucasus and the Russian-Turkish wars, the flight of refugees during the interminable Balkan Wars created a fluid landscape of peoples. The hazards of hepatitis and cholera, the mandatory quarantine stations, and the mosquitoes that plagued the cities did little to stop the streams of humanity looking for asylum, quick riches, a new life. The multi-confessional, polyglot worlds of places like Galați and Brăila mesmerized western voyagers intent on experiencing the exotic east. Millet described the crowded marketplaces at Galați as "perfect museums of types and costumes. Albanians in fustinellas like ballet-dancers' skirts jostle Slovac raftsmen in their skin-tight woolen trousers; smart marines from the naval station . . . haggle with peddlers of Turkish tobacco; and florid-faced cooks of English steamers shoulder their way to the meat-shops, regardless of Roumanian, Bulgarian, Russian, Greek, or Jew."[22] For westerners, these were ethnographic curiosities. Eastern cities were an aesthetic construct filled with dramatic sights and smells, with mixtures of colors and peoples. Powerful polarities emerged between the civilized West and the barbarous East. Nevertheless, these picturesque scenes were evidence of the trade networks, the constant transfers of people, cultures, ideas that linked cities together and made for the shared cosmopolitan practices associated with city life. The gravitational pull of the west formed part of this emerging urban consciousness.

The slightest whiff of the Orient at Brăila and Galați were quickly extinguished by the Russians once they took control. The Turkish fortress, the twisted narrow streets with their low-lying buildings and courtyards, and the intricate patterns of Ottoman daily life were either destroyed in the Russo-Turkish War or summarily demolished. It was the erasure of an Oriental world deemed corrupt and outmoded. The Romanian well-to-do embraced Europe. French cultural influences began to replace the traditional sway of Greece and the Ottoman world. Their homes were built in neoclassical style and their libraries filled with French philosophy and the literature of the Enlightenment. French became the language of polite society. Eastern dress was forsaken for western styles. In place of the old Byzantine laws, the rising commercial classes pushed through the Organic Statues in 1831 that set out the first urban reforms in planning and municipal administration. Brăila was reinvented as a western neoclassical outpost with straight streets radiating out from the harbor. Its main commercial thoroughfare, Regală Street (Store Street), filled up with shops. Greek traders settled in with new houses, schools, and a theater. Jews began arriving from Prussia and Galicia to take up jobs as tavern keepers and craftsmen. Hotels and casinos quickly appeared. The local mosque was converted to an Orthodox church and the bulbous cupolas and spires of Russian Orthodoxy appeared along the skyline. Old believer Russians worked as coachman while Turks traveled in great red and gilt carriages drawn by water oxen.[23] Grain silos and warehouses lined the waterfront. By 1860 Brăila had a population of 26,000 inhabitants while Galați had grown to 36,000 population. The Danube was their lifeline. The Blessing of the Danube at Epiphany in Galați was described in folkloric flare by English traveler Mary Walker:

streams of costumed townspeople singing and carrying illuminated paper stars paraded through the streets. The procession ended on the frozen Danube where an enormous cross of ice was raised around which priests from the city's churches chanted and said prayers. "Two coarse wooden barrels . . . contain the water of the Danube that has been blessed. The devotees drink of this, and take away as much as they can carry; a provision of the water has already been made by the churches for use in baptisms."[24]

Some sixty kilometers north of the Danube, the city of Bucharest was turned as well toward the surrounding grain fields. Aristocratic *boyers* brought their harvests to Bucharest to be sent down river to Galați and Brăila, while news of the Enlightenment and French Revolution returned up river on the boats. By the 1830s, Bucharest already had a hundred small manufactories and a multitude of shops, coffeehouses, and inns. Its population reached 80,000 and the city was embellished with paved streets and numbered houses, new market areas and public squares, impressive churches, and private residences in the favored neoclassical style. An earthquake, floods, and then the Great Fire of 1847 provided the opportunity to clear away rubble and start over with modern construction. But it was the contrasts that most startled Western visitors. For British traveler Patrick O'Brien, the time-honored skyline was filled with "the thousand domes, spires, and turrets sparkling with almost dazzling brightness in the sun." Covered in tin, "They crowned the city like a silver diadem."[25] The city "is not the East, still less the West" intoned Florence Berger. The *nouveau riche* elites were crazy for everything French, yet it was a pastiche that ill-fit the realities of the city. Buildings along the main boulevard, the Calea Victoriei, oozed lavish filigree, decorative wreaths and rosettes, in imitation of Paris. The construction had the "appearance of hurried superficial work,"[26] and attracted a fluid, seasonal labor force who lived in the poor *mahala* districts on the outskirts. The European luster quickly faded on the city's periphery where Turkish influences remained. "And the picture of sordid wretchedness, the peasant himself shuffles along in the gutter, narrowly escaping being overturned as the elegant patrician, in his Paris-built Victoria and costly pelisse of Siberian elk, whirls rapidly by, showering down a plentiful cascade of mud from his carriage-wheels."[27]

The muddy villages along the Danube, places like Turnu Măgurele and Giurgiu, were modernized in anticipation of trade. Freight steamers puffed past on the river in a continuous parade. The riverbanks along the Danube were dotted with mills and granaries with their owner's names plastered on the walls in glaring white. The names marked the ethnic and linguistic heterogeneity and the polyglot cultures that dominated eastern Europe, even in villages and small towns. They were laid out with the marketplace at the center, encircled by layers of political and cultural hegemony—the remains of fortresses, old Turkish quarters with their cafés, mosques turned into churches, cookshops and bathhouses, French-Italianate structures, government buildings, with people in European dress, in Turkish dress, in local costumes. They were places of cultural encounter and widened horizons. On his travels on the Danube in 1841, French economist Adolphe Blanqui came upon Semendria (Smederevo), "a real Turkish town," while American artist Francis Millet described Semendria's narrow streets "blocked by hundreds of laden ox-carts, all patiently waiting their turn at the public scales, where the weight of the grain is guaranteed by the town officers before it is delivered to the lighters."²⁸ Westerners marveled at the gardens and greenery in towns along the Danube. There were no walls to mark the boundary of Ottoman town life. Instead, the transition to the rural world was imperceptible. Towns were marketplaces dependent on agricultural production and the all-important grain harvests.

Despite the coexistence that making money demanded, ethnic tolerance tragically broke down too frequently along this Danube borderland between Europe and the Ottoman world. In the early years of the nineteenth century the town of Belgrade was torn apart by clashes between the Hapsburg and Ottoman empires. Perched above the confluence of the Sava and Danube rivers in Serbia, Belgrade straddled the strained border between east and west. Fires and plague outbreaks finished the damage. Its fortifications were in shambles. Gloomy, unlit streets were nearly impassable. Only some 5,000 people remained after the violence, with the residual Serbs and Muslims fleeing or staying depending on the political winds. Coming upon Belgrade in 1841, Adolphe Blanqui was shocked by "the air of desolation and its solitude," though some new houses, "a caserne, hospital, a prison, modeled on ours, announced the presence of a nascent civilization."²⁹ Blanqui looked with the eyes of a westerner and found markers of urbanity he would see in a French city. The painted wooden houses, the mosques and white minarets, the domed palaces that were its Ottoman legacy alluded his gaze. On the other hand, in 1875, Czech Slavic writer Konstantin Jireček observed only the city's eastern quality:

> The foreigner stepping onto the Belgrade streets for the first time gapes with astonishment left and right, before and behind. Here already the Orient begins: your eyes, ears, nose and feet inform you of this. Everywhere along the streets are low, irregular little houses, roofed with curved tiles; here and there rises the tin-plated roof of a slender minaret; at every step singular costumes, unheard languages, unfamiliar goods.³⁰

Even in the river towns profiting from trade, local burghers distrusted the Greek and Jewish grain merchants with their fast money and lack of local roots. Facing discrimination and looking to avoid guild restrictions, traders shifted to the grain exchanges in the larger cities of Turkish Sofia, Bucharest, and especially Pest. There, the concentration of production, knowledge, and labor played a vital role in transforming urban economies, particularly when merchants reinvested commercial capital in new industrial enterprises.

Further up the Danube, flour milling became the leading industrial sector in Pest with the town's newly minted entrepreneurial class accruing vast profits from the mills and export of flour from Hungary's breadbasket. Pest was a newcomer along the Danube and a productive powerhouse. The older settlement of Buda perched on the hills on the west bank of the river was the official capital of Hungary. The fortress and palace were an imposing testament to the political power radiating from Castle Hill. It was the domain of the Hapsburg bureaucracy and the Hungarian nobility that occupied the heights of administration and governed Hungarian affairs. Pest was the upstart commercial hub on the opposite side of the Danube with a population of around 44,000. The Great flood of 1838 wreaked enormous damage to the two-pronged settlement straddling the river. Some two-thirds of the brick and timber buildings in Pest were consumed by the icy waters and reduced to rubble. Thousands were left homeless. But the result was breakneck rebuilding that gave Pest a modern metropolitan feel. The town center was connected by broad boulevards to four outlying districts named after Hapsburg monarchs. Street-naming and monuments to Hapsburg rulers was a deployment of cultural symbols in what was an increasingly fractious relationship between the Austrian Empire and Hungarian liberal elites. By the late 1840s, the population of commercially minded Pest had already jumped to 100,000 inhabitants. Pest's renowned market fair attracted upward of 30,000 people each August. It spread out along the Danube quay, in the Jewish quarter, in the market squares, and in the Jozsef district. "On the morning of the fair," wrote Johann Georg Kohl, "it was filled with thousands of busy traders, and the river was crowded with vessels of all kinds, including steamers." The largest riverboats were laden with wheat. Abandoning himself to the crowds, "The great stream of human animation was . . . flowing out of the town towards a large open space, covered with men and animals of all nations and races."[31]

Pest merchants formed a tight-knit entrepreneurial circle. As in many towns and cities in the Hapsburg Empire, the city's business elites were largely German and Jewish. Hapsburg edicts had removed many of the restrictions on Jewish life and opened commerce, artisan crafts, and government service to Jews and in return required their German-language education. The Pest merchants congregated in the city's coffeehouses where the latest news could be exchanged. They maximized the economic opportunities available to them by investing heavily in the mill industry. The urban networks around the grain trade steered a steady course to modern socioeconomic relations and industrialization. Steam power was first applied to milling operations at the Jozsef mill in Pest in 1841. Like Manchester's textile factories (see Chapter 2), they worked nonstop and introduced a bevy of technological innovations. The district of Ferencvaros on the low-lying east bank of the Danube was the milling industry's hub of operations. Mills and warehouses lined the wharves and were connected to a web of rail lines and roads. By mid-century, the Budapest milling industry was one of the largest in the world and Hungary was exporting more flour than all the countries of Europe combined. It was second only to the United States on the international market.

The grain trade along the rivers and coastal byways of Europe was among the primary mechanisms for the exchange of people, cultures, and ideas in the early nineteenth century. It linked towns and their hinterlands together in continental-wide and international systems that encouraged the cosmopolitanism associated with modern urban life. Sparked by the Enlightenment, new urban values were filtered through merchant networks, through German and French cultural influences, and through the Russian and Hapsburg empires. But by the mid-nineteenth century Europe's grain trade was undergoing a radical transformation and the dogma of agricultural exports as the motor of urban growth had been abandoned. In eastern Europe, the emancipation of the serfs spelled the end of the grain economy on which the great latifundia were dependent. Feeding the cities pushed the countries of western Europe into intensifying their grain production. France became the leading European wheat producer and the Seine River the new grain highway. Grain was exported from some twenty-seven different French port towns. New crops such as potatoes and rice were introduced to satisfy demand. Most importantly however, the market was flooded with wheat from the prairies of the American Midwest and from India, which crowded out the European suppliers. The arrival of the telegraph and railroad, and along with them new forms of banking, shifted markets and dispersed the trade networks that had long supported European urban development.

CHAPTER 2
TRAVELS THROUGH INDUSTRIAL LANDSCAPES

The grain trade was the essential feature of the European urban economy in the early part of the nineteenth century. Towns and cities acted as commercial gateways for their surrounding regions. They were tied together principally by rivers as well as by somewhat impassable roads in an urban system that had changed little since the eighteenth century. Small and medium-size towns were the norm. Large towns were rare. The coastal seaports enjoyed an international sphere of influence. The Baltic and Mediterranean ports still retained their predominance on the European urban landscape. Yet the grain trade as the mainstay of the European urban economy was being rapidly replaced by industrial production. Historians have moved away from the traditional idea of an industrial "revolution" and instead now emphasize the longer, diffuse changes in capital and labor, production and manufacturing. But there is little doubt that industrialization impacted cities in revolutionary ways. The appearance of belching factories, steam-powered railroads, and industrial slums both shocked and awed contemporary observers. In a very short period of time industrialization dramatically transformed European urban society. Cities were connected in a network of industrial exchange—labor, imports and exports, technologies, and energy resources—that spread across the continent and the globe. Free trade, a unified monetary system, and the gold standard were inseparable parts of this worldwide system, as were new forms of transportation and communication.

Manufacturing in Europe traditionally took place on a small-scale in a dense arrangement of villages and towns that depended on artisan trades and the putting-out system. Merchants subcontracted production to men and women working in their homes and workshops with simple tools and machinery powered by their own labor, by waterwheels, and by windmills. Infrastructure and operating expenses were minimal in a production network dispersed throughout the countryside. Skilled artisans and laborers often worked according to the seasons, supplementing farm work. Middlemen arrived with materials and supplies for piecework, and then picked up finished goods—garments, shoes and leather goods, lace, hand tools and metalwork, ropes, buckets, furniture —in a regular local circuit. The putting-out system was widespread in poorer agricultural areas and along creeks and rivers to take advantage of water power and easy transportation. It created a robust landscape of production. In some places, this was done by skilled independent artisans. But more usually the work was low-paid and took advantage of the poor and marginal who were at the mercy of unscrupulous brokers. Population growth in many agricultural areas made finding employment difficult.

In these circumstances, piecework in rural homes was a vital source of income. Although predominantly rural, small-scale manufacturing was dependent on the local town that acted as the commercial clearing house and gateway out to wider markets. Skilled craftsmen in towns finished rural products; merchants sold them and sent them on their way to waiting buyers. Towns such as Lille and Lyon in France, Leeds in England, Ghent in Belgium, and Barcelona in Catalonia long enjoyed robust economies acting as the principal pivot for this putting-out system.

The fortunes of this traditional production differed radically from region to region across Europe. In some places, rural production quickly died out under the pressure of industrialization and the expansion of the railroad network. The innumerable small manufactories carried on in rural areas and small villages simply ran their course. Nailmaking, tanning and charcoal burning, wood carving, pewter and pottery making, plain homespun linen cloth slowly disappeared.[1] In other areas of Europe however, the putting-out system matured into a proto-industry connected to export and colonial markets, especially for high-demand commodities such as light woolen and cotton textiles. Domestic industries were surprisingly flexible to market changes and adaptable to new technologies, and continued far longer than historians have traditionally thought. They spurred building construction, provided jobs for local workers, and offered merchants the chance to invest their capital and entrepreneurial acumen, and take part in the burgeoning commodity markets. Local expertise, personal and business networks, investment capital, and robust credit opportunities were essential to this adjustment to new economic conditions. In the best of circumstances, rural and urban production reinforced each other in a well-integrated regional economic system.[2] This was the case in regions such as the Lower Rhine Valley in western Germany. The Lower Rhine textile towns of Gladbach and neighboring Rheydt (now both the city of Möchengladbach) were centers for the German linen and cotton textile industry with the majority of the fabric produced by the putting-out system. In 1853, local entrepreneurs invested their capital in the first spinning mill along the new railroad line between the two towns. The Gladbach Spinning & Weaving Mill began operation with new mechanical looms. They then began investing directly in the production of textile machinery and opened an entirely new manufacturing sector. Proto-industries such as these laid out the contours of industrialization and urbanization, its regional dimension, and its capacity for malleability and change. A mid-century lithograph of Gladbach captured this moment of transition. The panorama featured the time-honored European cityscape with church steeples and recognizable local building styles interwoven with greenery. A traditional pastoral farming scene outside the city walls graces the foreground. It is a portrait of self-confidence and stability. Yet the fields are cut diagonally by the railroad and the steam train puffing its way to Rheydt. Textile mills line the city wall, their sinuous smokestacks reaching for the sky.

Industrialization did not necessarily replace small-scale workshops as the next stage in a rational sequence. The shift into the industrial age was not a "big-bang" universal event. There were a diversity of paths, transitional and overlapping stages, and cumulative processes. Rather than in textiles as in Manchester, for example, steam-driven machine production took place around flour milling in Budapest. In other places, the shift to machines was patchy and continued alongside traditional manufacturing. In a number of areas of Europe—silk weaving in the Lyon region of France, wool weaving in northern Italy and in Catalonia, and textiles and glass in Moravia and Silesia—dispersed cottage production churned along in parallel with factories well into the nineteenth century. Large-scale manufacturing was not the only path to urban modernity. Towns incorporated a myriad of local activities from manufacturing, to finance and trade, to market supervision and governance. This helps explain the vitality and density of the European urban system. It was the rich array of connections between cities, towns, and their surrounding areas that made regional economies so dynamic. Nonetheless, proto-industry could not keep pace with the incessant demand for goods and the new patterns of consumption. Merchants could only expand cottage production by adding more rural households and workers. A radical jump in the scale of manufacturing would require new sources of power, new technologies, and the centralization of labor in towns and cities.

Power was found in the fossil fuels and rich mineral veins beneath the soil. Industrial production was tied to the land and its coal, iron ore, its zinc, lead, and copper deposits. These were the natural resources that could be put to work in manufacturing, and they made industrialization a decidedly regional phenomenon. The most important mineral-rich areas of Europe are well known because they became the arenas of industry: the Black Country of Lanarkshire in Scotland, the North West and Midlands in England, the coalfields of south Wales, the coal deposits that stretched from northern France and Belgium to Dortmund in Germany, the mineral-rich Saar region, the coal, iron ore and zinc deposits of Silesia, and the coal reserves of the Donets Basin in the Ukraine. Town building took a decidedly different turn in this new mineral geography. What had been traditional market towns and rural backwaters were suddenly transformed by the precious resources that lay underground. Worker camps and informal settlements sprawled around the mines. They were spread out amid villages and towns that were overwhelmed by extraction and refining operations. Entire industrial regions took shape that were pockmarked by pits and slag heaps, derricks and furnaces, canals and railroads, and a web of settlements that belied any historical precedent. They acted together as a regional energy system, dependent on the minerals in the surrounding countryside that were dug up and carried by river and canal, by wagons, and eventually by railroad to factories, to be returned as waste by-products dumped into the water and soil. This industrial ecology was behind the patterns of urbanization and the experience of the industrial city.

In England, it was the industrial towns of the north and northwest—Manchester, Liverpool, Leeds, Birmingham, and Newcastle—that grew fastest. The city of Manchester and the surrounding Lancashire region have long been regarded as the birthplace of industrialization. What factors led to the jump into large-scale factory production at Manchester is thoroughly familiar to European scholars. Its trailblazing cotton textile factories were the brainchild of a local entrepreneurial culture alert to newfangled technologies that could whirr with the plentiful supply of local coal. It was not just the spinning mules and weaving looms that jump-started factory production. It was these together with cheap coal that were key to the region's success. It was the fuel of choice to run steam-powered machinery in the cotton mills and gave them an edge over foreign competition. Coal was a god. It was the main source of industrial energy even when the steam engine was gradually replaced by the electric motor in the late nineteenth century. Coal became one of Britain's chief exports. And its impact on urbanization was immediate. It shifted textile production from the putting-out system in rural areas to towns and into large-scale factories. Despite the legendary imagery of Manchester's mills, textile production did not stop at the city gates. It involved a multitude of villages and towns meshed together in a thick regional symbiosis. Manchester was at the head of some 280 towns and villages in the counties of Lancashire and Cheshire that churned coal and steam power into cotton textiles and dominated the British industrial economy. They acted together as an industrial system chained to the mines, the rivers and canals, and the railways. But their sweep was even grandeur. The British Empire was an entire world system of trade dependent on the global flows of cotton and manufactured goods, on the coaling stations that kept the Royal Navy and commercial steamships operating, on the vast pools of manual labor in Britain and throughout its colonies (Figure 4).[3]

Lancashire "is dotted over with little Manchesters, and these in turn each possess satellites," botanist Leo Grindon wrote on his travels through the region. Although the towns had once been pleasing enough, they "seemed to vie with one another which should best deserve the character of cold, hard, dreary, and utterly unprepossessing."[4] By the 1840s there were some fifty-three collieries and hundreds of mine shafts dug around the "coaly" town of Wigan to the west of Manchester. To the east were the towns of Oldham with twenty-seven collieries, Rochdale with twenty-four, while Bolton had some fifteen collieries. Pit work was considered the lowest form of labor and those stuck with it faced the constant dangers of flooding and mine explosions. Laced between them were hundreds of woolen and cotton mills, their chimneys belching acrid smoke into the sky. Alongside them were weaving sheds, bleaching and dying facilities, and chemical works, the iron foundries that produced the textile and mining machinery. It was an entire industrial

Figure 4 An engraving depicting Manchester as viewed from the London and North Western Railway. Dated nineteenth century.

eco-network created around the region's water resources and rich coal deposits. There was an intense jockeying for mill sites along rivers and canals. The waterways transported coal, cotton goods, and merchandise. The water was used for boilers, for preparing and dying cotton threads and cloth. The mills, dye-works, tanneries, and gasworks used the channels as a convenient dumping ground and heaved their waste back into the water. The pollution seeped into the soil and clung to the air. The atmosphere in the industrial towns turned a stinking, dirty gray. Buildings disintegrated from the insidious sulfur dioxide emissions and acid rain. Deaths from lung diseases soared.

The towns specialized in specific yarns and cloth types: Rochdale in woolens, Bolton in fustians, Wigan in linen. There were calico towns, those for cords, flannels, and velveteen. Clustering created skilled labor pools and economies of scale. Oldham became one of the largest cotton spinning centers in the world, with 120 mills by 1866, some 3 million spindles, 9,000 looms, and 28,000 "hands."[5] The mill girls at Oldham were recognizable by their silk bandanna headscarves. Smokestacks towered over the towns: "a dark pennon usually undulating from every summit—perhaps not pretty pictorially, but in any case a gladsome sight, since it means work, wages, food, for those below." Small entrepreneurs who had risen from the ranks of weavers rented portions of the factories in Oldham for their own profit. The factory fronts presented "tier upon tier of monotonous square windows . . . after dark, when the innumerable windows are lighted up, the spectacle changes and becomes unique."[6] The two great products of Lancashire—coal and cotton textiles—were then barged down the canals and sent by railway to Manchester and then on to the great port of Liverpool.

Thousands of rural workers left behind the domestic putting-out system and moved into the cotton towns for jobs in the factories. They were the pioneering foot soldiers of industrialization. Rochdale grew from 23,000 in 1821 to 68,000 in the space of twenty years. Bolton's population exploded to over 60,000. Some 10,000 people worked in the cotton trades in Bolton and thousands more in coal mining, engineering, and machine making. Fires and explosions were frequent and conditions in the mills and mines were unhealthy and dangerous. The workers lived in dreary rows of back-to-back redbrick and stone cottages built on speculation. They quickly turned into squalid slums with communal ash privies, open sewers, and primitive water pumps. A haze of brown smoke and coal dust, foul air and the smell of sulfur, slag mounds, fires from the furnaces permeated the atmosphere. Outbreaks of cholera, smallpox, and typhoid swept through poor neighborhoods with infants and children dying in frightful numbers. Wigan had some of the worst overcrowding and housing conditions in the country.[7] Laborers were vulnerable to unscrupulous landlords and merchants. Fluctuations in the cotton trade, alternating booms and slumps, brought the risk of desperate poverty, especially during the great "cotton famine" of the early 1860s. The suffering made labor unrest, strikes and riots regular events. Wigan and Bolton were the scenes of Chartist riots in 1838. Rochdale was an early center of working-class politics. Its weavers took part in the Chartist movement to obtain the working-class vote and organized one of the first consumer societies in the 1830s. The Wigan Workingman's Association lobbied for the Public Health Act of 1848.

Yet the cotton towns were more than just dreary factories and scenes of oppression. They were gradually outfitted with amenities and functioned as commercial gateways. Along with everyday goods and services, exotic and fashionable items from around the world brought new consumption patterns to Lancashire. A lavish cast iron and glass roofed market hall was opened in 1855 in the town center of Bolton. Its streets were lit by gaslight, and a newly built reservoir provided clean water. Fire, police, and library services were organized in the 1850s. The merchants and industrialists of Oldham sponsored a municipal park to ward off workers "from the allurements of the pernicious beer-house, and the bright lights and fiery spirits of the gin-shop."[8] Thousands attended the opening of Oldham's new park in 1865 as well as its new School of Science and Art. Promenades and gardens, and small theaters that drew local acting troupes appeared in Rochdale, Wigan, and Bolton. Sporting competitions, gambling, singing, and entertainment at local pubs shaped neighborhood social life. The pubs in Rochdale were a vital men's working-class institution, while for women church activities and social visits were a respite from work. Young men and women paraded in the municipal park in Rochdale in the "chicken run" to meet members of the opposite sex. Cultural and leisure activities such as these in the midst of what was often imagined simply as squalor created distinctive patterns of working-class identity and practice.

"To all these towns and villages," Leo Grindon went on, "Manchester stands in the relation of a Royal Exchange. It is the reservoir, at the same, into which they pour their various produce." Located on the confluence of the Ir, Irkwell, and Medlock rivers, Manchester was the commercial powerhouse for the entire Lancashire region and the greatest emporium for textile commerce in the world. "Manchester goods" was a synonym for textiles in general. Before 1850, Manchester had the largest concentration of steam-powered cotton mills in England with a workforce of some ten thousand. They were the great factories described by Charles Dickens in his novel *Hard Times* as illuminated fairy palaces where "the piston of the steam-engine worked monotonously up and down, like the head of an elephant in a state of melancholy madness."[9] The mills were connected by the rivers, the network of five major canals and six railways that cut through the city. Not only was Manchester a leading cotton factory town but it also exploited production in textile finishing and chemicals. Its engineering works produced the machinery and steam engines for the mills as well as the locomotives, the iron bridges, and viaducts of the industrial revolution. Thousands found their way to Manchester in search of jobs. The city's population exploded, growing nearly 50 percent in the space of just one decade in the 1820s. It was a landscape of frenzied construction.

The neighborhood of Ancoats was synonymous with Manchester's industrial revolution. It epitomized the best and the worst features of industrial urban life.[10] The district was crisscrossed by the River Medlock and the Ashton and Rochdale canals. Early on, it was the site of water-powered textile mills and small manufactories interspersed with weavers' cottages, machine-makers, and flour dealers. But by the early nineteenth century, its canals were lined with colossal eight-story cotton mills, machine and chemical works, and flint glass factories. Thirteen mills lined the Rochdale canal, fourteen along the Ashton canal. Over 1,500 men, women, and children tramped through the gates each morning at the huge Murrays' Mill and at the McConnel & Kennedy Mill. Coal yards, saw mills and stone yards, iron foundries, and gas tanks bunched around them. The factory chimneys spewed out a toxic brownish haze. The canals were inky black with pollution. The atmosphere in Ancoats was dark, colorless, evil-smelling. Grainy black-and-white photographs deepened the gloom in a testament to the noxious conditions. They reinforced negative public perceptions about industrial cities to the exclusion of any urban qualities.[11] With over 56,000 people packed into its confines in 1861, Ancoats was the most crowded area of Manchester. Dreary back-to-back tenement blocks were wedged between the mills. Whole families were squeezed into single rooms in buildings without water or plumbing. Half the children in Ancoats were street urchins without schooling or work. The worst slum was Angel Meadow where destitute Irish workers found shelter in squalid cellars beneath lodging houses.

The prejudice and hostility against the Irish were palpable. Migration was a normal part of life for Europe's working classes. But the Irish were a particularly conspicuous exodus. Millions of young men and women fled Ireland's calamitous potato famine. Some 1.7 million left in the 1840s, another 1.6 million in the 1850s, and then 2 million more in the 1860s.[12] They crossed the Atlantic to make new lives in America. They left for Scotland. And they streamed into the towns and cities of Lancashire where they found jobs as unskilled laborers in the mills and warehouses, the coal mines, and along the docks, and as domestic servants. By the 1850s, there were over 52,000 people in Manchester who were born in Ireland, or around 15 percent of the city's population. They often did seasonal work and sent money back home. But increasingly, they established their own families with both men and women working. Half the population of Ancoats was born in Ireland, a majority of them living in the district's "Little Ireland" and Angel Meadow. In the public mind the Irish were drunkards, feckless and violent, and the cause of the abject poverty and disease of the slums. Typhus was dubbed "Irish fever." Lancashire's mill towns were hit by riots against the Irish in 1868. Mobs of workers attacked the Catholic chapels in Oldham, smashing windows and battling with local police.[13]

Condemnation rained down on Ancoats and its Irish population. For James Phillips Kay, who worked for the Ancoats Dispensary and eventually became poor law commissioner, the Irish had taught the laboring classes of Manchester a pernicious lesson—how to live in ignorance and pauperism like savages. Kay's best-selling exposé was largely responsible for the notoriety of Ancoats. Descending into Angel Meadow, he found the loathsome cellar garrets, "frequently flooded to the depth of several inches." Angel Meadow was the haunt of prostitutes, "thieves and desperadoes."[14] During his stay in Manchester working for his father's textile firm, Friedrich Engels and his partner Mary Burns followed Kay's trail to Angel Meadow. Engels described the squalor in 1844 in his hugely influential book *The Condition of the Working Class in England* and then made it the basis for the class struggle in *The Communist Manifesto*. The two walked along a curve in the Medlock River crowded with colossal factories where about two hundred cottages housed four thousand human beings, "most of them Irish. The cottages are old, dirty, and of the smallest sort, the streets uneven, fallen into ruts . . . without drains or pavement. . . . A horde of ragged women and children swarm about here, as filthy as the swine that thrive upon the garbage heaps and in the puddles." It was assumed that the Irish were immoral and violent, and a threat to society. Gang violence by scuttlers in Angel Meadow kept Manchester gripped with fear. London-based investigative journalist Angus Reach visited Angel Meadow in 1849 to report on conditions for the *Morning Chronicle* newspaper.

> The lowest, most filthy, most unhealthy and most wicked locality in Manchester is called, singularly enough, "Angel-meadow." It is full of cellars and inhabited by prostitutes, their bullies, thieves, cadgers, vagrants, tramps and, in the very worst sties of filth and darkness, by those unhappy wretches the "low Irish."[15]

As reformers recycled each other's material and embroidered the hyperbole, popular perceptions assumed the Irish were clustered in every city in "Little Irelands" or "Angel Meadows" living in drunken, degrading poverty and perpetrating disease.[16] But immigration did not stop with the Irish. They were followed by Poles and Italians, who arrived in Ancoats for seasonal work. Italians worked in construction and street vending, then set up businesses and sent for families. Blossom and Jersey streets was a tight-knit "Little Italy." For all these immigrants, the local Catholic parish knitted together community bonds through mutual aid and social clubs for mill-hands and laborers.

The number of Manchester's cotton mills peaked in 1853. More than just a factory town, the city became the commercial and warehousing capital for the entire cotton textile industry. Here was the pride and wealth of industrial capitalism. Manchester cotton entrepreneurs were self-made men with no aristocratic heritage, no handed-down estates. "A genuine Lancashire man," Leo Grindon remarked, "would rather you praised his mill or warehouse than his mansion."[17] The cotton industry created a new urban elite of businessmen who were moving toward political power not only in the city but in Britain as a whole. Sharebrokers, accountants, insurance agents, and attorneys gathered in the area south of Market Street and east of Deansgate. It was close to the Royal Exchange, the Chamber of Commerce, and the Free Trade Hall. These were the institutions that made Manchester the spearhead for liberalism and free trade. The Exchange was the economic hub of the city, the "parliament house of the lords of cotton."[18] A new Exchange building was opened in 1809 at the bottom of Market Street and then expanded twice to become the largest trading floor in the world and the headquarters for a vast global market in cotton. It controlled the export business, especially after the entry of Manchester merchants into direct trade with India from 1814, with the Levant, or Middle East, from 1826, and with China after 1834. It was a nerve center of information with its own post office and newsroom. On "High Change" Tuesdays, merchants from around the world struck bargains with Lancashire spinners and manufacturers "together in one vast mass, each man intent on buying and selling, and helping to fill the room with a deep hum of voices like a gigantic beehive."[19] It was a visual spectacle of business, governed by the laws of supply and demand as well as by a strict code of conduct. A community of Greek and German merchants as well as Jewish businessmen worked the cotton business in Manchester along with their English counterparts. By 1870, there were 420 foreign firms in the city owned by fourteen different nationalities. The cotton goods were then sent by rail to the port of Liverpool, where it was sold by brokers (Figure 5).

Travels through Industrial Landscapes

Figure 5 The interior of the Royal Exchange, Manchester, England, in the nineteenth century.

The Exchange was close to the banks and railroad stations, to the businessmen's Athenaeum Club, and to the city's commercial library. Manchester had seven weekly newspapers by the 1820s. The Exchange was also the pivot for the surrounding warehouse district. The warehouses were marvels of organizational efficiency, "as much working machines as the cotton mills."[20] Many were designed in a sumptuous Italian palazzo style that emblazoned the fortunes of the merchants and manufacturers who owned them. Hundreds were built, especially in the district between Piccadilly and Princess Street. Drapers, shopkeepers, and tourists flocked to visit them. Close by were the luxury shopping districts of "dazzling splendor" in the words of Friedrich Engels, with the latest in fashions and exotic foreign goods, along with a show-off cultural scene that made Manchester into a cosmopolitan world.

Lancashire and the textile mills of Manchester were the stars in a galaxy of industrial towns clustered around the coal deposits in Great Britain—in the North West and Midlands in England and the Black Country of Lanarkshire in Scotland. In Scotland, the urban population was concentrated in a narrow belt of land in the Lowlands of the country. Edinburgh, Glasgow, Aberdeen, and Dundee were the four major cities. Some 60 percent of Scottish urban dwellers lived in Edinburgh and Glasgow. Glasgow was a city of about 32,000 people in 1750. Its transformation from a provincial town to an international center of commerce was initially due to the import of tobacco from the American colonies. Glasgow's famous tobacco lords were some of the great early capitalists and their vast sums of money poured through the city's banks. The warehouses along the Clyde River were stuffed with tobacco that was then reexported to Holland, France, Scandinavia, and Germany for top prices. After the Americans declared independence in 1776 the main commodity became cotton. Raw cotton for the city's flourishing textile industry was imported by Glasgow's wily merchants, who helped finance production and sold finished goods on the world market. In 1807, 6 million kilos of cotton were imported into Glasgow, and its processing and manufacture governed the city's economy and the whole west of Scotland until the 1860s. Cotton textiles transformed Glasgow's landscape into a scene of mills and warehouses, bleachfields and chemical works, foundries, and machine shops. By the 1830s some fifty cotton mills were already in operation and nearly one-third of the city's workforce daily toiled making cotton cloth. The population jumped from 77,000 to 275,000 in the first half of the century. Its industries made Glasgow into one of the richest cities in Europe. Industrial barons arrayed in burnished horse-drawn carriages cantered by grand public buildings, museums, galleries, and libraries. Little wonder that Nathaniel Hawthorne wrote in 1857: "I am inclined to think that Glasgow is the stateliest city I ever beheld."

Behind the gleaming veneer were the city's multitudes suffering in poverty. Glasgow's working classes were from the Scottish Highlands and from Ireland, Italy, and eastern Europe. Social reformers estimated that a full one-quarter of the city's population were Irish immigrants, the majority of whom were paupers living in squalid conditions in St. Mary's and Tron parishes.[21] The city's infamous slums were photographed by Thomas Annan in the 1870s. An early pioneer in urban photography, he was hired by the Glasgow City Improvement Trust to document the congested districts just before they were condemned and demolished. Annan's images were a visual spectacle of desolation and proof for slum clearance. Although they were praised for capturing the soul of Glasgow's back alleys, the places and people captured in his lens were pure visual theater. The narrow passages are dejected and hollowed-out. The dwellers in these shadowy places stare glumly into the camera. It is an inert world without the normal flow of life or the everyday relations that sustained the working classes and poor. Instead they are made specimens in a sensationalized visual discourse about morality and the dangerous classes (Figure 6).

Nonetheless, Annan's photographs became artifacts of memory, a stereotypical account of Glasgow's hidden world of misery. It was not just the wretched living conditions of Glasgow's slum districts that shocked Victorian sensibilities. The surrounding "Black Country" of Lanarkshire was dotted with canals and miserable colliery towns lost in the dark haze that covered the moorlands, the "curtains of vapor . . . the mists and films of smoke . . . the livid glare of fire" portrayed by a traveler passing through. The Black Country was a world of ebb and flow around the Clyde River tributaries and the rich coal and iron ore deposits. Draught horses hauled boats along the canals and dragged coal carts along the roads, miners shifted from one colliery to another, skirting the flooding and deadly mine blasts. It was a hard, dangerous life, reiterated across the industrial regions of Europe. Yet the Irish kept coming to Glasgow and the Black Country, as

Figure 6 Slums of Glasgow, Thomas Annan, 1861.

did Silesian and Italian workers, for jobs in the mines, the rolling mills, and shipyards. Despite the dismal conditions, they invented richly honed informal neighborhoods of their own. They married and relied on kin and social networks to sustain daily life. Stable homes and family support systems were fragile. The frequency of pregnancies outside of marriage soared. High birth rates meant legions of abandoned children left on the streets or on church doorsteps.

By the late nineteenth century, textile production had fallen off in Glasgow. Instead, marine engineering and shipbuilding employed thousands and kept ironwork and the coal mines running at full capacity. Glasgow's entrepreneurs moved into the manufacture of railway locomotives, factory machinery, bridges, and cranes. Whole districts of the city along the Clyde River were dedicated to heavy industry and the daily specter of blast furnaces at work:

> The Clyde was a veritable highway. All manner of vessels used its waters . . . great passenger ships maintained regular services to the United States and Canada . . . Cargo steamers of all sizes brought in raw materials for the industries of Glasgow and Central Scotland and food for the growing population. They returned

downriver with every variety of goods from the mundane coal and pig iron to the most complicated machinery and manufactures, bound for every corner of the world.[22]

Every inch of the city was crowded with densely packed warrens of tenement housing, factories, teaming commercial and residential buildings.

Once savvy entrepreneurs and skilled textile workers crossed the English Channel looking for opportunities, a whole series of textile towns and "little Manchesters" dotted the European continent. Energy consumption, overwhelmingly the use of coal in manufacturing, rose to unprecedented levels. The new regime took place unevenly. The patterns of industrial development were regionally distinct. Industrialization did not necessarily follow the British pattern. In many cases, dispersed, small-scale production adapted to market changes and continued right alongside the factories. Those towns with local access to coal and iron ore were at a clear advantage. In northern France, the steam-driven spinning mills around the towns of Lille, Roubaix, and Tourcoing turned out mountains of cotton and woolen materials while handloom weaving continued in small workshops. In Spain, the cotton textile industry was concentrated around Barcelona. In the first years of the nineteenth century, some 80,000 mostly women toiled in spinning and weaving workshops throughout the city and its hinterland. The introduction of steam-powered machinery in the 1830s began a new phase of calico production with workshops located near local energy sources; first rivers, then coal and iron ore mines. The industrial colonies and satellite towns around Barcelona—El Berguedà, Sants de Santa Maria, Sant Martí de Provençals, and Sant Andreu de Palomar—hummed with production and made Catalonia one of the largest textile centers in Europe. It became known as the "Catalan Manchester" and "The Factory of Spain." Hemmed in by its walls, Barcelona was flooded with rural workers looking for jobs in the factories. The population grew from 83,000 inhabitants in 1821 to 187,000 by 1850, when the population squeezed into the city was among the densest in Europe. Although Barcelona had become an industrial city, there was still some 30,000 small traders and clerks and another 20,000 domestic servants at work in the early 1900s.[23] It was an indication of a diverse economic culture reliant on a myriad of activities. There was no end of factories and assorted plants and workshops, tiny commercial establishments. Forced to import coal, companies turned to electricity as a new source of energy, especially once the first hydroelectric power stations in the Pyrenees Mountains opened. Barcelona's port encouraged the shipping industry, machine and chemical production, the making of paper and glass. It became a center of automobile manufacturing. The Hispano-Suiza Company was known for its luxury cars and aviation engines prior to the First World War. By that time, Barcelona had the largest industrial economy and the largest workforce in Spain. It was the exception in what was a vastly agricultural country.

The uneven industrial development in Germany was particularly marked. The expansion of cities in the western areas of Prussia, especially the centers for heavy industry in the Ruhr and Westphalia, made it quite different from the rural countryside in the east. Town clusters for cotton spinning developed in western Germany along the

Rhine, in Württemberg and Baden, in eastern Germany around Berlin and in Saxony. The region of Saxony was one of the most industrialized areas of Germany even in the 1830s and well on its way to becoming one of the most urbanized regions of Europe. The towns of Dresden, Leipzig, and Chemnitz formed a thriving textile belt based on traditional small-scale manufacturing. The first machine-powered cotton mills in Chemnitz were set up on the English model by two brothers who had honed their skills in Manchester. Once the railroad reached Chemnitz and the surrounding textile towns in the 1850s, they quickly became a hub for jacquard cotton production in intricate patterns. Chemnitz became the "Saxon Manchester" and built an entirely new industry based on the manufacture of the looms, presses, machinery, and boilers operated in the mills. It illustrated how textile towns were able to diversify their economies by moving into machine building and dye manufacturing. Manchester and Łódź (see further in this chapter) also followed this pattern.

In 1815, the Ruhr Valley was a pastoral landscape of low hills and broad valleys with a smattering of market towns and villages. The Baltic Sea ports were still more important and far wealthier. There was nothing to suggest that the Ruhr would become one of the most industrialized and urbanized areas of Europe. It was a compact agricultural world endowed with abundant waterways, especially the wide and easily navigable Rhine River that functioned as its main highway. Duisburg, Essen, Bochum, and Dortmund were traditional market towns on the well-trodden trade corridor of the Hellweg, dependent on small-scale manufacturing and food processing. As was typical throughout urban Europe, the Ruhr towns experienced an increase in population in the late eighteenth century. But they were still nestled within their old medieval walls with inhabitants well under ten thousand. The German urban system was traditionally polycentric with a network of vibrant small and medium size towns such as these. Once large deposits of bituminous coal were discovered, deep mine shafts were bored into the hills and fields, and the first steam engines appeared. This underground bounty was in the hands of Prussia, which was given control of the entire Ruhr-Rhine region by the 1815 Congress of Vienna. Entrepreneurs with ready cash poured into the Ruhr towns. The mining operations were run by private capitalists such as Friedrich Grillo, Mathias Stinnes, and the Irishman Thomas Mulvany. Foreigners plunked down investments in the mines and newfangled machinery while the German banks dangled easy loans. By 1850, there were already three hundred coal mines in operation in the Ruhr area around the towns of Duisburg, Essen, Bochum, and Dortmund. The coal was exported, processed into coke, or used in the production of iron and steel. The scale and speed of industrialization was astonishing, all of it concentrated around the open slashes in the landscape that led down into the mines.

By the 1880s, huge coal mining operations, goliath iron and steel conglomerates, textile mills, chemical works, and breweries employed thousands of workers. They transformed the Ruhr region into an industrial leviathan. The Ruhr casted more than half the world's high-grade steel. Railroad lines and canals crisscrossed the countryside and then joined the Ruhr and Rhine rivers. The giant coal mining company Gelsenkirchner Bergwerke AG overshadowed the town of Gelsenkirchen. The mining and machine builder Gutehoffnungshütte was in Oberhausen. Essen was the center for smelting and steelmaking with the mammoth Krupp steel conglomerate. The Krupp family achieved remarkable fame and fortune, especially under the leadership of Alfred Krupp, who became a legend in the Ruhr. The Krupp operations alone employed 30,000 workers producing cast steel for railway locomotives, heavy guns, and armor-plate. Krupp sold his ordinance to the Russians and Turks, to the Germans and Chinese, regardless of political enmities. Bochum's giant enterprises included the Bochumer Verein, the Bochumer Eisenhütte, the Gesellschaft für Stahlindustrie. On one side of Dortmund were the blast furnaces and steel works of the Dortmunder Union and of Carl von Born. On the opposite side of the city was the Hoesch steel works. Duisburg was at the confluence of the Ruhr and Rhine rivers and the location of the colossal Thyssen Iron Works along with a sulfuric acid factory, copper works, and steamship dockyards. The Thyssen family amalgamated every aspect of steel production under their roof. By 1900, they employed 24,000 people. Together, the Krupp and Thyssen families stood at the summit of Ruhr production. Their celebrated coal and steel empires mass-produced German armaments for the First and Second World Wars. The whirr-and-whine of machinery in engineering, tobacco processing, brewing, sugar refining, and textiles took place day in and out in the Ruhr. A hive of small businesses hung out their shingles in what became a sprawling multi-nucleated conurbation (Figure 7).

Industry formed a symbiosis with the Ruhr's natural environment. Coal and iron ore were dug out of the ground at dizzying speed. Water was an essential ingredient. The coal,

Figure 7 Inside of the Krupp factories, Essen (Germany), circa 1905.

iron, and steel industries all consumed hundreds of millions of gallons of water siphoned from the rivers. Water was pumped from underground to prevent mine flooding. All of the thick sewage and wastewater were then dumped back into the rivers, which became open sewers. The rivers were connected together with a web of crisscrossing canals. The Ruhr's waterways bustled with coal and iron ore traffic. Blast furnaces, warehouses, and coal-cranes lined the riverbanks. Mathias Stinnes opened a coal-tug service to Rotterdam, where the black bounty was offloaded and then refilled with textiles, grain, and colonial goods for the trip back up the Ruhr. Traveling on the Rhine in 1848, Englishman T. C. Banfield remarked that "the long rows of wretched horses that dragged the clumsy but picturesque boats . . . at a snail's pace up the noble river, are gradually diminishing, and powerful tugs are substituted, which smoke away with six or seven barges of 200 or 300 tons behind them."[24] Smoke-filled skies, polluted soil, and air savaged the Ruhr Basin and made urban living a dismal affair. But there was splendor in the industrial scene, which some observers saw as a thrilling tableau. A construction engineer standing on the Rhine Bridge at Duisburg in the evening saw the skyline "bathed in flames, white, red, blue, green, sometimes belching powerfully out of black craters, sometimes gushing in fiery streams like lava, sometimes flickering and dancing. . . . Rising out of the sea of fire, enormous, bulky colossi and slender obelisk-forms reach into the sky: clattering, clanking, and rattling creatures seem to snake their way about. . . . All of this reflects and refracts in the dark waves of the broad river."[25]

The Ruhr experienced the fastest population increase of any province in Germany. The growth was so explosive that the area was known as "Prussia's Wild West."[26] From 1850 to 1900, the population shot up from 300,000 to over 2 million and it became the largest industrial region in Europe. The demand for labor was enormous. The industrial combines squeezed in every hour of work possible to increase efficiency and stay ahead of foreign competition. Streams of workers arrived from the nearby Rhine Valley, from Holland and Belgium, and from East Prussia and Silesia farther east. The vast majority were young men. The endless calls for more manual labor and skilled hands meant high wages. But the vagaries of production meant workers lived with constant insecurity and were forced to shift in and out of the Ruhr towns in search of work. They adapted to a mobile way of life that depended on who they knew among the foremen signing up men for pitwork and the mills. Villages and mining camps became sprawling industrial settlements. Factory smokestacks towered above church steeples. Old city walls were pulled down, and makeshift commercial and residential districts sprawled outward. The population of Dortmund and Essen increased some eleven times in the second half of the nineteenth century. Duisburg's population shot up 700 percent.[27] Like Lancashire in the Midlands, or Lanarkshire around Glasgow, the Ruhr developed into a coherent industrial and urban system with far-reaching consequences. Development took place without any focused hub or capital city. Instead, the Ruhr became an industrialized polymorphous urban mass. The newer towns of Gelsenkirchen, Oberhaussen, Wanne-Eickel (Herne), and Wattenscheid (now part of Bochum) were every inch industrial sites. Oberhausen, for example, took shape as an ad hoc mix of mines and factories, migrant worker camps, and rural townships spread out over four different local political districts. It finally received designation as a town in 1874 and was only incorporated as an independent municipality in 1901.[28]

The sheer momentum of the urbanizing process carried it forward without any coordination. Traditional burgher elites took a hands-off approach to growth and did little to interfere in what were astounding moneymaking opportunities. They profited handsomely from their new industrial neighbors. The result was a riotous mix of new construction. Essen's population reached 400,000 by 1900 and spread out amoeba-like to absorb the surrounding villages and farmsteads. The old heart of Duisburg still carried on, but was encircled by the outlying districts of Neudorf and Hochfeld that became commercial centers in their own right. Not only were the Ruhr towns much larger, they were also more congested and their populations more socially diverse. As the industrial workforce expanded, Catholics outnumbered the traditionally Protestant inhabitants. Factory and mine workers outnumbered artisans. In 1845, about 20 percent of Essen's population worked in industry and mining. By 1859, it was 60 percent and they were all men.[29] The Ruhr's industrial barons remained aloof from all this hullabaloo. They were an exclusive cast that kept their distance from local life. Except for a few exceptions, especially the Krupp family, they were not native to the Ruhr area. They remained detached outsiders whose relationship with the local community was determined entirely by the needs of production.

The lack of housing was a constant predicament. Old houses in the city centers were cut up and rented out at premium prices. Private property owners cashed in on the demand and built housing complexes with three and four-story rental units. Worker housing on speculation was shoddy and unregulated. Laborers vegetated in cramped tenement rooms and grim hovels. Shelter was found in the shadow of the industrial facilities in claptrap buildings without basic services. Noise, soot, a brown polluted haze choked the atmosphere. Segeroth was Essen's working-class district, known for its Krupp workers, its mix of immigrants, and its tricksters, thieves, and prostitutes. It had the highest density in the city and the lowest quality of life. Drinkable water remained a precious substance. As mining operations siphoned off more and more water, the city's few water pumps and fountains dried up. The mines polluted and drained the local springs. Dozens of complaints were lodged against the mines for polluting the rivers and depleting water supplies. Protests erupted in Segeroth against drilling in the Mathias and Gustav mines that caused severe water shortages.[30] The poor sanitary conditions in working-class districts such as Segeroth caused frequent outbreaks of cholera, typhus, and diphtheria. Some 10 percent of Duisburg's population fell victim to smallpox in 1871.[31]

The harrowing conditions and fears of social unrest alarmed coal and steel companies that were perpetually in need of labor. There was intense competition for skilled laborers. Unlike the textile towns where the mills hired women and children, the Ruhr towns offered few employment options for women. It meant that working-class families were heavily dependent on one salary and steady employment in the gigantic iron and steel combines. Thousands of miners lived with their families in colonies near the coal pits, where they relied on social ties for survival. The lucky among them lived in company housing such as the numerous settlements constructed by the Krupp steel conglomerate.

Although they remained steadfastly hostile to any labor organization or trade unionism, the Ruhr's industrial aristocracy offered their workers paternalistic lodging and welfare schemes. By the turn of the century, some 20 percent of Krupp workers were living in company-built settlements. The Krupp initiatives totaled some 10,000 units before the First World War and were hailed as a far-sighted model of social benevolence. The estates were separate, closed communities within the city. They generally consisted of one to two-story brick buildings with four apartments, built in vernacular styles with attached garden. Most of the estates included schools and church, a grocery, and beer hall and offered the stability and services families craved. Larger housing complexes were built in the late nineteenth and early twentieth centuries, many of them influenced by the garden city movement. The most advanced was Margarethenhöhe, which was laid out in 1906 as a model garden suburb for Krupp workers in Essen. Situated away from the noise and smoke of the main Krupp factory and protected by a green belt, Margarethenhöhe contained a variety of amenities including bathing facilities and a library.[32] The high quality and low rents bound workers to the company and provided the opportunity for paternalistic social control. The estates were carefully watched over by guardians to ensure moral standards and commitment to the enterprise. Company anniversary celebrations assembled employees around the themes of "affection, loyalty, obedience."[33] It was a Faustian trade-off, but one working class families were willing to make for a decent life.

Europe's industrial regions followed the logic of natural resources and rarely adhered to political borders. They acted as magnets for thousands of men and women from the countryside in search of work. With their massive shipyards, the Baltic ports of Königsberg, Stettin (Szczecin), and Danzig (Gdańsk) formed a new industrial cluster churning out steamships and locomotives. The town of Stettin on the Oder River not far from the Baltic coast became the region's most important industrial port. Its Vulcan shipyard employed some 3,600 workers in the 1880s. The city's machine industry processed Swedish iron ore. Copperworks, coking plants, and tar factories grew up around it. Stettin's companies expanded into the manufacture of motorcycles and automobiles, trucks and buses, and airplane motors. Industrial clusters developed in the regions of Saxony, Bohemia, and Moravia with their rich deposits of coal, iron ore, zinc, lead, and silver. Some 15,000 people worked in the mechanized wool textile mills in the town of Brno (Brünn), based on the local coal deposits in the Moravian countryside. An industrial arc in the west of Poland took shape from Silesia through the town of Łódź, up to Warsaw.[34] The Kingdom of Poland (or Congress Poland) set up by the Congress of Vienna, dangled lucrative industrial incentives to German spinners and weavers willing to resettle eastward, especially to the Łódź region. The outcome was that Poland gained some 100,000 skilled textile workers. The emancipation of Polish peasants in 1864 created an entirely new pool of willing labor headed for the mills. New towns were established as centers for the textile industry including the Nowe Miasto just south of the town of Łódź in the province of Mazowsze.[35]

Łódź became a whirring hub of cotton and wool textiles serving the expanding Russian market, especially once customs barriers were abolished in 1850. The first steam-powered cotton spinning and weaving mill was Ludwig Geyer's four-story stone-walled building that went into operation in 1837. It was followed by the Grohmann and Von Lande's mills. Karl Scheibler, the scion of a German family of textile manufacturers, set up a spinning enterprise on the banks of the Jasień River that included one-room flats for the mill hands. With some 5,000 workers, the Scheibler complex was one of the largest in the world by the end of the nineteenth century and included cotton plantations in the Caucasian Mountains. Rather than strictly utilitarian construction, the mill buildings in Łódź showed off neoclassical and neogothic decorative flourishes. Each morning, workers poured through ornamental factory gates that celebrated the textile magnates. The massive Poznański factory complex, owned by Jewish entrepreneur Izrael Poznański, had its own power station and huge iron and glas roofed sheds that housed the weaving machinery.[36] Both Scheibler and Poznański prided themselves on their "Lodzermensch" shrewdness akin to the self-made "Manchester Man" of fame. Foreign capital poured into the city including French textile companies such as Leon Allart of Roubaix.

Łódź went from a sleepy rural town of 800 in the 1830s to over 300,000 people at century's end, far faster than any other industrial town in Europe. About 50 percent of the population was Polish, mainly textile workers, while 30 percent were Jewish and 20 percent German, mainly merchants and industrialists. By 1913, it was the second largest city in Poland after Warsaw, with 500,000 inhabitants and some 1.5 million cotton spindles and 12,000 looms operating at lightning speed.[37] The city's main street, Piotrkowska, was lined with factories and lavish buildings. Every empty site in the city was grabbed and old neighborhoods torn down to make way for redbrick tenements. The surrounding villages of Zgierz, Pabianice, Tomaszów Mazowiecki fused with Łódź to make up a huge industrial agglomeration. The Vienna-Warsaw railroad arrived in 1865 and another branch line snaked across Poland to Białystok and the voracious Russian market for cotton textiles.

Łódź played an outsized role in the Polish cultural imagination. It was an alien force in an overwhelmingly rural country. The musician Arthur Rubinstein, one of the city's most famous citizens, recalled in his biography *My Young Years*, that Łódź "appeared to be a foreign town right in the middle of Poland." The workers lived in a dense industrial agglomeration made up of roaring factories surrounded by blocks of speculative housing and sparse one-room worker flats. Lithographs of industrial Łódź from the late nineteenth century were almost indistinguishable from those of Manchester. They share the same urban density, the chaotic development typical of the industrial landscape, the same gray, dirty streets with hundreds of chimneys reaching into a sky invisible behind a screen of smoke and soot. The Łódź slum of Bałuty rivaled that of Manchester's Ancoats. Rubinstein recalled,

> Lodz was the most unhealthy and unhygienic city imaginable. . . . The air was so infected with gas from the chemical plants, and the black smoke from the chimneys which hid the sky was so thick, that our daily walks were, from a health standpoint, nothing but a ritual. At night Lodz was still worse. Lacking a modern

system of sewage, the city had to remove its excrement in small iron tanks, driven by horses, which filled the streets with an unbearable odor.[38]

Yet the city was known for its hustle-and-bustle, its ethnic diversity, and mix of languages and cultures. Visitors were astonished at the exotic atmosphere of everyday life. The Lodzermensch erected sumptuous white mansions alongside their factories. The "Jewish district" in the old city of Łódź grew up around its synagogues, including the Great Synagogue, one of the largest in Europe. On the other hand, Catholic journalist Władysław Reymont voiced Polish trepidations about the treacheries of the textile giant. In his 1899 novel *The Promised Land*, the Lodzermensch are ruthless Jews and the city a social evil: "Lodz is a forest, a jungle—in which, if you have good strong claws, you may fearlessly go ahead and do away with your neighbors; else they will fall upon you, suck you dry, and then toss your carcass away."[39]

At the turn of the nineteenth century, Upper Silesia was the most important industrial area in central Europe. It is worthwhile lingering there. Intersected by the Oder and Vistula rivers and by two major land routes eastward, it was one of the continent's great crossroads. The territory was largely under the control of Prussia and was historically a backwater of landed estates and the occasional town lauded over by the local land baron. Sleepy hamlets were still girded by their walls and gates, with only the main streets paved. Industry barely existed. On his travel through Silesia, English author Charles Marvin jotted down a typical western reaction to the town of Mysłowice: "As dull and wretched a place as any in Silesia. It is a strictly agricultural center, of 2,000 inhabitants, with half-a-dozen indifferent shops in its ill-paved thoroughfares, and two or three inns." In the surrounding area, "one would rapidly tire of toiling along a dusty or muddy road, full of ruts, with nothing to see except everlasting patches of wheat, barley, oats, millet, and buckwheat."[40] Once coal, iron ore, silver, and zinc were discovered, this age-old environment abruptly changed. The Prussian monarchy moved aggressively to experiment with British mining techniques and begin extracting the rich mineral veins. In 1794, the Royal Iron and Steel Works were opened in the town of Gliwice (Gleiwitz) by English engineer John Baildon. Its coke furnaces were the first on the continent for smelting iron. Pioneering production of pig iron and zinc from raw ore and the continent's first iron rolling mills were set up. By 1800, heavy industry in Upper Silesia was more developed than in the Ruhr. It was the ironworks of Silesia that produced the Prussian artillery used against Napoleon's Grand Army.

Nonetheless, the chaos of the Napoleonic Wars and Continental Blockade wreaked havoc on Silesia. It was only in the 1830s that Silesia's wealthy landowners began investing in mining operations. The tariff and currency reforms introduced by the newly created German Customs Union (Zollverein) in 1834 and the building of the railroad opened the potential for industry. Then the release of the coal mines from Prussian state management in 1851 inaugurated a boom era of private development. The Henckel von Donnersmarck family founded the great Laura Works in Siemianowice. The Hochberg von Pless and the Von Stechow-Ballestrem families built industrial empires from their mines and mills. The Winckler family obtained exclusive rights of extraction and mining in the heart of Upper Silesia's coal country, at Mysłowice and Katowice. They amassed over thirty mines and steelworks along with rights over local villages and towns. The mines were owned and managed entirely by Prussians. Even the Silesian nobility were of Prussian extraction. They continued as feudal landowners, made vast fortunes, and exerted tight-fisted control over the workers and peasants who labored in their fields, their mines and mills. Increasingly Upper Silesia's "smoke-stack barons" abandoned their local domains to overseers and took up residence in Berlin. Some of them, such as Prince Henckel von Donnersmarck, were among the wealthiest men in the German Empire.

Straddling the boundaries between Prussia, the Russian and Hapsburg empires, and Poland, the transformation of Upper Silesia often escapes notice. Although the Ruhr eventually became more productive, Upper Silesia's heavy industry skyrocketed in the late nineteenth and early twentieth century. In 1860, eighty-one mines were in operation. Just over ten years later, 120 pits were hauling out the black diamonds. The brew of coal mining, ironwork, lead and zinc smelting operations was the most productive in Europe. As just one measure, Upper Silesia produced 40 percent of the world's zinc.[41] Pit heads and coal yards, slag heaps spread across the landscape bringing with them a soot-filled fog and the acrid odor of burning coal cinders. The most distinctive symbol of the collieries was the headframe towers with their trusses, winding engines, and pulleys. Made of wood or wrought iron, each colliery had their own distinctive tower shape and insignia. Headframe towers and chimneys dominated the skyline in every town in Upper Silesia. They were urban monuments that signified the supremacy of heavy industry. The population of Upper Silesia doubled from 1.1 million in 1861 to 2.2 million in 1910, while the number of workers went from around 18,000 in 1852 to nearly 200,000 by 1913.[42] The three towns of Katowice, Gliwice, and Bytom formed a triangle of thick urban development at the heart of the region. The industrial sites of Zabrze and Huta Królewska with their worker camps filled in the urbanized space.[43] Urbanization then spread out to encompass nearly all of Upper Silesia. It went from a byword for the rural backwaters of central Europe to one of the most densely developed areas on the continent.

Katowice emerged as the largest town in the polynucleated pattern typical of Europe's industrial regions. It was the colonial outpost of Prussian administration in Upper Silesia. Prussian engineers, technicians, and administrators descended on the town and quickly set up the rudiments of German public life. The Winckler family's German architect gave Katowice an early master plan with attractive squares and avenues at the city's heart. Streets were named after Prussian heroes and public monuments dedicated to Prussian emperors. A German Protestant church and two modern hotels appeared along with beer halls and local shops filled with European and colonial goods. German theater productions, German newspapers, a school, and library gave Katowice a contemporary flair. German civilization was imagined as transforming a backward, unmanageable region devoid of any spirit of enterprise or modern aptitude. With only 5,000 residents in the 1860s, Katowice had, according to a traveler, "the colors of a big city." By 1905, the population reached 35,000. It was also an industrial powerhouse. Upper Silesia's industrial magnates made Katowice their headquarters. In its vicinity were six iron and eleven zinc works along with fourteen coal mines.[44] Headframe towers and chimneys jutted into the air alongside the emblems of German culture. It was a cityscape steeped in incongruous symbols.

Upper Silesia was a restive world. Despite the overarching Prussian presence, it resisted "Germanization" and remained staunchly local in character at the same time as it rapidly transformed into a formidable urban region. The industrial working classes were Slavic and Catholic, many of them from the local Szolnzok ethnic group. Poles considered them poor and indolent. The German elites showed them little else but disdain. Chief Prussian official Hugo Solger judged them "wholly without discipline, brutal, dissolute, often criminal." Most of them "lived in small huts . . . all are overcrowded. . . . Many of the lowest class have not even a roof, spending the summer in backyards and cornfields—you can count them by the thousands. In winter those that do not go back to their home villages sleep at the zinc works or the lime kilns. Anywhere to get a refuge from the cold. Though driven away ten times they always come back." Worker camps and shantytowns surrounded the mines and spread out through the haze. Adapted to the rhythm of work, they were zones for a distinctively Silesian working-class culture. It was a kaleidoscope of tight-knit micro-ethnic communities and immigrants from as far away as Russian Poland and Galitia. Everyday jargon was a blend of Slavic, Polish, Bohemian, and German.[45] It was impossible to assign nationality in a largely hidden world of such complexity.

Packed into their settlements, suffering abject poverty, the conditions for Upper Silesia's working class were miserable. Wages were a trifling. Corporal punishment for recalcitrant miners was the norm. Scurvy and infectious diseases were rampant. Workers in the zinc and lead mines suffered from severe neurological disorders. Solger judged the conditions "a model of European slavery."[46] The conditions sparked early protests. The first large-scale strike in Upper Silesia took place in 1871 at the Royal Mines. The Catholic church exerted tremendous influence over the Silesian working classes. It was the launch of the Catholic press in Polish that sparked organized political activism. The strike of 1889 involved some 15,000 men and provoked the founding of the Christian Worker's Mutual Aid Society of Upper Silesia. General strikes were called between 1905 and 1907 and then again in 1913 when some 55 percent of miners walked off the job, many of them taking the opportunity to quit Silesia altogether.[47] Anger and resentment persuaded thousands of workers to flee, especially to the Ruhr and Rhineland, where the pay was higher and living conditions far better. From 1871 to 1910, some 600,000 people abandoned Silesia. Far from the horrors of Silesia's mines, there was a Polish-speaking minority of 500,000 living and working in the industrial dynamo of the Ruhr.

King coal dominated the economic life of nineteenth-century industrial cities. Coal, coke, iron ore drove economic and ultimately urban development. But new sources of energy were sparking investment and moving into mass production. Oil extraction and refining still only represented a fraction of resource consumption in the nineteenth century. The hefty infrastructure and transport of crude oil made the transition long and incremental. Oil extraction in the foothills of the Carpathian Mountains dated from the mid-nineteenth century. The Carpathians curved through southern Poland, a corner of the Ukraine, and Romania. Although they are often relegated to the murky unfamiliar world of "Eastern Europe," the search for oil deposits in these mountains played a vital role in Europe's energy history. Early production took place at Bóbrka in the region of Galicia in southeast Poland. In Romania, oil pits were in operation from 1857 at Câmpina City, north of Ploiești. The pace of oil production in Romania steadily picked up after it became independent from the Ottoman Empire in 1877. Twelve oil distilleries and three refineries quickly launched operations. The Mines Law of 1895 opened the way to foreign capital. By 1900 most of the Romanian refineries were in the hands of German, Dutch, English, and French oil companies. The sprawling Steaua Romana Refinery at Câmpina comprised oilfields and wells, refineries, and a fleet of tankers on the Danube. By the turn of the century, it was the largest oil refinery in Europe. The American Standard Oil Company opened an affiliate in the Romanian oil fields, the French Columbia Company followed, and then Royal Dutch Shell opened the Astra Română petroleum company in 1910. On the eve of the First World War, oil production accounted for close to 90 percent of Romanian national output.[48]

The petroleum industry altered the urban landscape of Europe and moved it eastward. The population in the region of Bucharest, Ploiești, and Câmpina skyrocketed. What had been rural boondocks suddenly became urban. Peasants were turned into oil workers. Floods of men hoping for jobs followed the boom-and-bust cycles of resource extraction. Training and research centers for oil drilling and refining appeared in Ploiești and Câmpina. Dreary main streets where only the weekly market broke the boredom were suddenly alive with bustling crowds, banks, and swanky hotels. Bucharest and Ploiești were illuminated with a thousand oil-based kerosene street lamps. Kerosene dealers worked the streets along with water vendors. Romania's rail network used oil residue as fuel in place of coal. The rail lines converged at Bucharest, which became the central hub of an industrializing region that spread from the oil boom towns of Câmpina City and Ploiești in the north to the Danube River in the south with its port of Giurgiu. Once a rail link was opened to the port of Constanța in 1895, oil flowed directly out to ocean-going tankers on the Black Sea and then on to Turkey and Europe. The ports and rail lines on the Black Sea coast and along the Danube created an entirely new transport system for the raw materials and products of an energy revolution.[49]

Much of old Bucharest with its low-rise wooden buildings and Ottoman heritage had been destroyed in the great fire of 1847. The conflagration decimated the historic core and commercial heart of Lipscani on the left bank of the Dâmbovița River. Floods then ruined a third of the city in 1864 and 1865. Rebuilding took place as Bucharest became the capital of the petroleum industry as well as a newly independent Romania. For Romanian elites, it was the opportunity for the systematic removal of what remained of the city's Ottoman legacy and an open-armed embrace of westernization. The Russo-Turkish war of the late 1870s and the upsurge of Romanian nationalism were accompanied by ethnic cleansing that forced out the Turkish Muslim population under harrowing conditions. Yet despite its newfound status as a capital city and the brutal strangulation of its Ottoman past, on first appearance Bucharest looked more like a collection of villages. In the view of travelers, it was vaguely somewhere between the Occident and the Orient.

Ironically it was precisely this borderland amalgam of influences that made it the land of opportunity in the late nineteenth century.

With a population of 280,000, Bucharest was a melting pot across a wide swath of ethnic and cultural persuasions. It offered jobs and the opportunity for a new way of life. Merchants from Moldavia arrived in the new capital. Italians worked in construction, building the city's modern infrastructure. Textile mills and the food industry employed a budding working class, many of them Jews from Galicia and the Ukraine. The German colony in Bucharest made their mark in business. Heavy industry in Romania was dependent on German and Austro-Hungarian capital and technological know-how. Hungarians, Greeks, and Balkan immigrants of every ethnicity arrived hoping to make their fortunes. Newly freed from rural slave status in 1856, the Roma arrived in the capital in search of work. Foundries, metallurgical, and engineering workshops in Bucharest and the manufacture of oil equipment in Ploiești supported the oil industry and the military arsenal in the capital. They clustered along with heavy industry in the suburbs and around the new Filaret train station that linked the city to the port of Giurgiu on the Danube. Fleets of oil tankers plied upstream on the Danube and down to the port of Constanța.

There was an atmosphere of reconstruction, of shedding the past and joining the pantheon of European capitals, of imagining Bucharest as a modern, cosmopolitan city.[50] The socially privileged cultivated a quasi-official image of Bucharest as "Little Paris." Although the city center was meticulously planned according to French standards, it was a landscape of social complexity. An anarchy of tentacular development spread out along the roads and rail lines into the surrounding region, subsuming villages in its path. Bucharest remained polycentric; its *malhalla* neighborhoods, old villages, and industrial zones covered a vast territory interspersed with open area and noble estates. The Calea Victoriei was the city's most elegant boulevard with sumptuous homes and public buildings. Romanian boyars, Russian army officers, western consul-generals and foreign agents, and the well-to-do glitterati frequented the tree-lined promenade. There were "parades of peoples of all nationalities, smoking and chatting carelessly, with a female audience displaying 'European' and Oriental dressing alike," according to a Polish traveler. It was a rich social panorama. By the second generation in the city, many families were of mixed ethnic origin. But the foreigners were also seen as profiteers, who would talk "about their mission to convey standards of civilization in the area, being in reality concerned in amassing fortunes."[51] Brassy western oilmen flaunting their money, drooling over Romania's fossil fuel bonanza easily fit this caricature. They were anathema to nationalists who advocated "Romania for Romanians." On the other hand, westerners accused Bucharest of being a pit of urban dissolution and "the most corrupt city from Europe."[52] But the liquid gold was hard to resist. Bucharest hosted the 900 delegates of the International Petroleum Conference in 1907. By the outbreak of the First World War, Romania was Europe's leading producer of oil, fourth behind the United States, Russia, and Mexico in world production.

CHAPTER 3
ENTERTAINMENTS AND ROMANTIC DREAMSCAPES (1815–48)

The industrial boom towns and great European capitals of the nineteenth century have received the greatest share of attention by historians, in good part because they accentuate the spectacle of modern transformation. The nineteenth century was the great era of urbanization. In 1800, around 12 percent of Europeans lived in towns. By 1900, some 40 percent were urbanites. The lion's share of historical research has looked at this sweeping change through the lens of the big city, especially London, Paris, and Vienna. Yet there were other types of cities, especially commercial and administrative towns, provincial capitals, that tell us much about urbanizing processes in Europe. These were dynamic urban places and adapted to modernity in a host of ways. Their population growth was less dramatic. But a town's functions and spheres of influence could make it far more significant than the number of people might indicate. It was in these more-or-less provincial urban places that custom and novelty joined to create rich cultural practices and complex social structures. Their economies diversified. They were full of contrasts, equally rich in rustic localisms and cosmopolitan postures. The mixture of peoples, beliefs, ethnicities, and languages were the stew from which modern identities were formed and then inscribed in the urban landscape.

This was not a seamless process. In 1815, vast areas of Europe were recovering from the ferocity of the Napoleonic Wars and beginning to rebuild. Displaced refugees, political exiles and expatriate intellectuals, and seasonal laborers and itinerant populations formed a stream of humanity moving across states and between cities. The European continent was split up into a mix of nations, autonomous states, miniature principalities, separate regions, and multiethnic empires. The idea of the nation and national identity were only just coming into being. Regional and municipal loyalties were just as powerful as the broader currents of nationalism. The city was the fulcrum for all these allegiances that both conflicted with and reinforced each other. Belonging and inclusion, or exclusion, was played out in a city's public culture and everyday life. It was a divisive, contested terrain. Especially across Europe's borderlands, the mingling of cultures was a long-lasting, cantankerous affair that produced divided loyalties and dramatized the particularities of Europe's regional customs and traditions. Despite the repressive regime installed by the Congress of Vienna, cities were hotbeds of political turmoil, wracked by revolution and counterrevolution. Armed uprisings took place in the 1820s across the Mediterranean—in Turin, Naples, Athens, in Spanish and Portuguese cities. Cities across the continent were the theaters of revolutionary turmoil in the 1830s and the

1840s. The worst fighting took place in Paris and Vienna, Prague and Berlin. Political tensions broke down into violence not just in capital cities but also in provincial centers and small towns. Riots broke out, barricades went up, tax stations were ransacked, and food markets raided. In central and eastern Europe, towns were caught in the web of new boundaries drawn up by the Congress of Vienna that challenged political affiliations and the very nature of identity.

All these complications were easy to ignore in the jubilance over the end of the Napoleonic Wars. The arrival of peace in 1815 was the starting bell for an explosion of travel across Europe. Anxious to enjoy the fruits of victory and money in hand, the British in particular crossed the channel and headed for the continental experience. Unlike the lengthy Grand Tour of the eighteenth century that was accessible only to the privileged few, tourism in the early nineteenth century was becoming far more democratic and modern in character. The first guidebooks were published and tours organized. Rather than antiquated stagecoaches jolting along rut-infested roads, voyagers could now travel in relative comfort from place to place. Roads improved. Steamships plied Europe's rivers and coastlines. Railroad lines crisscrossed the continent in ever greater numbers. The new technologies of transportation collapsed time and space. The traditional route of the earlier Grand Tour had traversed France and Italy, and mainly stopped at Paris and Rome. But now even out-of-the-way places were made reachable and consumable as visual theater.

Capital cities and regional towns, coastal cities, and even the most remote settlements were becoming locations of culture and heritage. Voyages of historical discovery, of curiosity, and of culture were fueled by Romantic sensibilities. Armed with the first travel guides, visitors reveled in sublime landscapes and ruins of the past, the splendors of churches and palaces, the spectacle of exotic unknown regions. Folkloric festivals enthralled spectators. Wistful travelers contemplated landscapes and encountered historic art as a way to acquire cultural taste. Southern Europe along the Mediterranean, the far reaches of eastern Europe and the Balkans were newly discovered by more fearless adventurers. Napoleon's mapmakers had depicted the geography of his conquests in Poland, the Adriatic provinces, and in Italy. Now explorers followed suit, ignoring popular claims of the Mediterranean and Adriatic coasts as too dangerous. The ghastly tales of brigands, disreputable Jews, primitive Slavs and Greeks, mosquitoes and diseases did little to deter them. They went farther afield in search of exotic localities and encounters with local people. The wild reaches of the east beckoned, as did Turkish Europe, and the unknown lands along the Mediterranean with their towns splashed by the sea. Infatuation with travel led to an outpouring of travelogues and memoirs overflowing with lavish descriptions of what was seen.

Yet the tourist viewpoint was shifting. The nature of belonging, of traditional identity, and of *place* were changing. More than just wandering through landscapes and history, travel in Europe was a self-conscious confrontation with modernity, with what had changed since the Napoleonic Wars, especially in cities. The journey itself had been transformed by the railroad and steamship. Visitors were enthralled by miraculous train stations, by the great iron structures that housed city markets. Modern cities were a landscape of experience and adventure. Tourists were part of the new atmosphere of the urban crowd. They were agents of cultural transmission. But they could also find themselves unwelcome and scorned as obtrusive strangers. The public spaces of cities were heavily politicized in the first half of the nineteenth century. Eager pilgrims trooping around ancient churches could easily find themselves confronting barricades and revolutionary turmoil in the streets. The sites of uprisings were themselves added to the tourist itinerary. Visiting Madrid in 1822, Irish journalist Michael Quin walked into a mob of hundreds of protesters parading through the streets. In 1860, an English tourist found Naples "officially in a *state of siege*; practically, there is no Government at all."[1]

The redrawn map of Europe at the Congress of Vienna shifted urban identities and loyalties. In central and eastern Europe, what had been capitals of independent principalities or sovereign free cities found themselves incorporated into the Kingdom of Prussia, the Hapsburg lands, or the Russian Empire. A German Confederation of thirty-eight states was carved out of the jumble of lands in the old Holy Roman Empire. Poland was partitioned among the Great Powers. Austria extended its reach into the Balkans and Adriatic. Political boundaries on the Italian peninsula were redrawn. Amid this territorial unpredictability, cities played key roles in politics and in constructing a sense of place and identity. Yet how cities would be governed and by what citizenry was unclear. There was no uniformity, no coherency to legal rights and privileges, nor any agreement on how far democracy should extend. For people across Europe, the battles against Napoleon's armies were "wars of liberation" that released a wave of impassioned nationalist feeling and resistance. The forces of Liberalism battled for hearts and minds against the conservative regime installed by the Hapsburg emperor and his foreign minister, Klemens von Metternich. Cities were the stages for the talk of a united Germany or a reconstituted Poland, or a newly independent Greece that now meant much more than it had before. The concept of patriotism slid back and forth between the local and national scales. Under these pressures, the idea of locality, home and place, and who controlled them was the object of intense social negotiation.

These questions played out most clearly in the provincial cities, the traditional seats of governance, and commercial towns strewn across the landscape. These local central places are often described as stagnant or falling behind in influence during the nineteenth century. The accent has been on great capital cities as the crucibles of modernity, along with the new industrial regions. Their stories are well known, with the assumption that modern modalities flowed down through the urban hierarchy. Other towns were "recipients" of the modernity emanating from the great cities. Yet the full range of Europe's urban system flourished and adapted to modernity in a blend of ways. The overall population of Europe was increasing. More and more people were moving into towns and cities. The dynamics of modern life impacted places across the entire European urban spectrum. There were commercial capitals and market towns, provincial administrative centers, seats of royal and ecclesiastical power, military outposts, and sovereign cities. Other towns were banking or educational centers. The economies of agglomeration worked in favor of this traditional urban system.

Towns that functioned as railroad junctions experienced immediate growth. Britain was crisscrossed by railroads by the 1840s. Four thousand miles of tracks were laid across the German territories by 1850, and France was establishing its rail network. The clank and rattle of trains was transforming towns in southern and eastern Europe. Local artisan and commercial trades adapted to new markets, small-scale family businesses opened, and industrial districts sprang up even in small towns. In central Europe, places such as Munich, Leipzig, Bonn, Frankfurt am Main, Cologne, and Hamburg were vital trade and transportation hubs with expanding economies and commercial functions. In eastern Europe, the cities of Vilnius, Lemberg (L'viv/Lwów), and Kraków (Cracow) pulled in migrants and expanded their territory at the same rate as large capital cities. As culture and leisure became forces in their own right, the influence of these cities and towns actually intensified. Museums, libraries and academies, parks and promenades were established by urban elites across Europe. A host of towns situated along rail lines and main roads functioned in this urban system as cultural way stations. These places were the cultural capitals of their regions. They flaunted the public atmosphere and enlightened society associated with Europe's great capitals.

The form of the city, its material culture, architecture and landscape, and its rituals and celebrations became expressions of this tension between local belonging and modern identity. The old city walls and fortifications were coming down across Europe by mid-century. The outmoded privileges of urban life were replaced by Liberal ideals and by recognition of the urban expansion that was already well underway. Pulling down city walls was a symbolic act of immeasurable proportions, and one that travelers commented on frequently. American writer James Fenimore Cooper arrived in Frankfurt in the 1830s and immediately pointed to the demolition of the walls and the new gardens and promenades being created. It was something he saw in every large German city where he traveled. Düsseldorf, Bremen, Lübeck, and Hamburg were all leveling the old fortifications and moats and converting them into tree-lined alleys with gardens and ponds. Breslau (Wrocław) turned its bulwarks into wide streets lined with trees and stately mansions. Further east, Brno (Brünn) razed its fortifications and created the Franzensberg promenade, where "well-dressed citizens with their wives and children, drinking coffee under the trees, and wandering among the shady paths, enjoy the beauty of the evening."[2] At Frankfurt, Cooper noted that it took place alongside "political disturbances" that "proceeds from a desire in the traditional, banking, and manufacturing classes, the *nouveaux riches*, in short, to reduce the power and influence of the old feudal and territorial nobility. Money is changing hands, and power must go with it."

The forces of modernity were transforming urban space and culture. It was creating what was perceived as a shared European and decidedly bourgeois urban identity. Coming upon Stuttgart and noting its old-fashioned features, Cooper remarked that, still, it "is evidently becoming more European, as they say on this side of the Atlantic, every day; or, in other words, it is becoming less peculiar."[3] These same homogenizing influences were taking place in eastern Europe. In Riga, travel writer and geographer Johann Georg Kohl pointed to the stark differences between the German old town "with its narrow streets and alleys" and the Russian suburbs "with straight streets of immense length and width, coloured white or yellow, mostly wooden houses, with green or red painted roofs of iron or wood, and plenty of pillars." Increasing in population, power and riches, the suburbs "knocked incessantly at the gates of the privileged old German capital, demanding freedom and equality of rights." Old Riga "was like a besieged city" and the social frictions were deep.[4] The area outside the old fortifications had already been developed with an esplanade, wide avenues, and gardens. From 1857, the walls were razed altogether and a new city plan was in place.

At the same time, local identities persisted and even flourished and were laced with new meanings. The city moved to the center of concerns about how modern society should take place and be governed. Especially in central Europe, city life took on increasing significance as a bourgeois counterbalance to aristocratic influence. Although seemingly at odds, identification with state interests even empowered local bourgeois elites to improve their local civic life.[5] After 1815, non-noble professional classes began to serve regularly as local public officers, in bureaucracies and courts of law. It was assumed they were more loyal to state officialdom and to the city than the local nobility with their ingrained privileges. The seats on city councils and chambers of commerce were filled by merchants and bankers, by industrialists, and even by wealthy craftsmen. Guild corporations took up civic duties. Their elaborate guildhalls were among the most important institutions in the city. Municipal improvement committees and parish offices were filled with the civic-minded. Although they were excluded from politics, women organized their own voluntary associations, usually around charity work. Self-governance and a local community of interest corresponded to the belief in Liberal principles. Liberalism was the creed of the new business and industrial elites that made public life in their own image. Being bourgeois or a burgher was integral to local patriotism. The rhetoric stressed caring for the city and looking out for its prosperity. This was the ideal. These local loyalties and new spheres of influence were expressed in an explosion of voluntary associations, in public festivals and ceremonies, and in citizen meetings and civic institutions. They appeared not only in the great capital cities but also in provincial towns, commercial hubs, and local seats of government.

The thicket of associations and civic rituals that mushroomed after 1815 provided bourgeois elites the opportunity to organize urban life on their own terms. They became the gatekeepers of urban culture. This was what distinguished these new "cultivated" classes, that is, the educated and well-to-do, from the lower social echelons. Bourgeois identity was attached to art and education and to etiquette and appearance. They fashioned a vibrant cultural world of music and learned societies, reading circles, and sporting and social clubs. Public visibility was an essential feature of bourgeois identity.[6] The beau monde took their leisure at theaters and concerts and displayed their refinement in public promenades and civic processions. Large and small towns alike had lavish theaters. At the beginning of the nineteenth century, for example, there were already eighty theaters spread out across towns in Germany. The port city of Kiel in the duchies of Schleswig-Holstein built its City Theater in 1841 with financing from the city's wealthy businessmen. In the Czech lands theatrical and music performances took place in over a hundred towns.⁷ As they became bourgeois institutions, theaters changed from ribald entertainment to places of moral uplift and social improvement. Yet this civic realm also promoted social mingling across class divisions. Prominent bourgeois families socialized with local nobles and took on aristocratic pretensions. They hobnobed with newly minted industrialists and the upper echelons of the working world. Wealthy skilled craftsmen took up bourgeois airs. They organized self-improvement clubs and joined mechanics and craft institutes. The ranks of the privileged extended deep into urban society. The arena of public affairs broadened and worked to alleviate social tensions and political turmoil.

Supporting the arts and entertainment became municipal policy. Traditional ceremonies and festivals promoted pride in collective life. Along with amenities such as pleasure gardens and dance halls, parks and promenades, these public entertainments defined the experience of local culture for most people. They were the haunts of the rich and the poor alike and helped create a specifically urban form of sociability. Vauxhall was London's most lavish pleasure garden. Revelers at Cremona Gardens along the Thames River enjoyed dancing and balloon rides. In the process they rubbed shoulders with people from all walks of life. The bazaar and pantomime theater at Tivoli Gardens in Copenhagen made it among Europe's most popular venues. Vienna's Prater pleasure gardens were alive with music and refreshment booths, equestrian shows, and circus performers. On summer evenings, crowds gathered to enjoy fireworks over the Danube. It was precisely these amenities that attracted travelers and tourists anxious to fulfill their fantasies about Europe's cities. English traveler George Francklin Atkinson waxed eloquent on an evening at Hamburg's Alster Square, newly rebuilt after the Great Fire, where "the thousand lamps are reflected in the smooth mirror of the water, and the sounds of music float upon its tranquil surface." He admired the picturesque costumes of the flower girls in "their short coloured petticoats, their tightly-fitting bodices, and pink stockings." The city's ramparts had been transformed into a promenade and pleasure garden "where the honest Hamburghers luxuriate in shady nooks and pleasantly secluded spots."⁸

Churches, cultural institutions such as museums, universities, and academies played vital roles in local urban society. Churches, convents, and monasteries were long-standing urban enclaves and their influence over urban life is not to be underestimated, especially in the conservative resurgence after 1815. Local clergymen made pronounced efforts at religious revivalism. Both Catholic and Protestant elites undertook a spate of church building in urban areas to reinforce religious values. Magnificent churches were marks of urban identity while religious activism was fundamental to public discourse. The higher echelons of both the church and university were peers of the urban realm and regularly influenced city politics and daily life. University institutions with their "Latin Quarters" were the jewels of Europe's cities. Universities reemerged or were newly founded in the years after the Napoleonic Wars as part of a flourishing interest in intellectual life and scientific research. There was an explosion of published works on science, history, and philosophy. Local notables dabbling in scientific marvels founded museums of natural history and endowed libraries open to the public. Literacy increased. There was a dizzying array of newspapers and periodicals available in a variety of languages. Readers poured through "city stories" that created a common narrative about urban life. Great cities and provincial capitals, even mid-size towns enjoyed this cultural flowering.

The town of Uppsala in northern Sweden, for example, had a prestigious heritage of scholarly life. Its university, Royal Scientific Academy, and Botanical Gardens were a beehive of research led by early geneticist Carl Linnaeus. Astronomers and mathematicians sallied along with the city's well-heeled elites. As a measure of its prominence, the university inaugurated a new Institute of Botany in a splendid neoclassical building. It built a state-of-the-art astronomical observatory and a surgical clinic for the Faculty of Medicine. Uppsala's learned gentlemen put together idiosyncratic collections of scientific instruments, rare specimens, natural oddities, and technological curios that were proudly displayed as marks of intellectual virtuosity. Impassioned by Romantic idealism in the 1830s–40s, students at Uppsala's university staged political meetings and filled university halls with fiery patriotic songs and speeches. The number of clergymen at the university declined, while students came increasingly from the ranks of the middle-class and common families. Poorer students lived a bohemian life in shared garrets while a coterie of wealthier students sauntered the streets carrying riding whips and showing off in dandified tailcoats, white gloves, and student cap. They organized into "nations" that indulged in raucous celebrations of Walpurgis Night on Uppsala's Castle Hill and May Day in the city's taverns and coffee shops.[9] They were an enthusiastic youth, drinking and singing at noisy suppers and engaging in rhetorical jousts about the meaning of university education in an age of Liberal ideas.

The vogue for Romanticism released an outpouring of interest in local history and culture. It was in good part a response to urban transformation and to the shifting loyalties involved in the new political geography. Urban self-awareness became a complicated terrain of localisms combined with nationalistic patriotism. Even regional perceptions played a role. The concept of *Mitteleuropa* appeared frequently in geographical literature and political discourse as a broadly Germanic space. There was a wide spectrum in how these imaginaries were carried out in cities. Local patriotic societies, folkloric languages, customs and dress were all the rage. Performing rustic rituals and dances was imagined as a rediscovery of authentic local identity and a form of moral uplift for the city's lower classes. For tourists, watching these events were a way to consume "folk culture" as a new kind of public theater. Traveler Johann Georg Kohl witnessed Riga's traditional Flower Festival that took place on St. John's Day in June each year. The city was festooned with flowers, while "old and young, rich and poor, the whole city of Riga dance, play, and sing." Confectionary and fruit shops opened, flower-decked gondolas floated on the Dwina River, and the city was lit up at night for the festivities. Traveling in Turin in 1846, French social reformer Frédéric Le Play viewed the annual Eucharistic Procession with a thousand women in white marching through the streets with candles and religious banners. Following behind them were priests and women in habits and bare feet carrying the cross. "It was a magnificent spectacle that we can't see in France." Kohl came upon the Feast of the Assumption in the town of Posen (Poznań), when townspeople and peasants from the surrounding countryside paraded in holiday costume to church. Women dressed in voluminous petticoats with ribbons streaming behind carried bundles of flowers and vegetables to be sprinkled with holy water. "The fashion is immemorial to them, and not by any means borrowed from Paris."[10]

New forms of sociability blossomed and blended into the fabric of everyday life. Strolls along the new promenades, enjoying the gossip and newspapers in coffee houses, attending quasi-scientific societies were signs of civic engagement. Ladies' circles sprang up. Masonic lodges and charitable societies, drinking and shooting clubs, gymnastic clubs, concert and choral societies flourished in the new civil society. The passion for local associations was enormous. Bourgeois culture became common currency even in small towns.[11] Especially in central and eastern Europe, music operated as a medium of self-expression for a city's cultural elite and became central to the emerging public sphere. Learning music and playing an instrument were among the most important signs of bourgeois education and urbanity. Opera and musical concerts had been a mainstay of cities since the eighteenth century, much of it based on highbrow Italian and French influences. But this traditional repertoire changed in the early nineteenth century, when musical theater and music activities entered a golden age. More than just a form of elite sociability, songs and singing appealed to a broad public as a form of cultural communication and associative life. Local burghers established singing clubs and concert societies. They financed musical theaters and concert halls and arranged visits by Europe's legendary musical superstars. Churches were the scenes of religious music performances. Musical societies were founded by Catholics, Protestants, and Jews alike. For the Romantic, music was the language of feeling. In central Europe, it assumed almost mystical qualities.[12] Amateur theater and music groups and dance halls reached down even to country towns. The fun of dancing to wild tunes in the local pleasure garden attracted couples from all walks of life. Spectacular public balls were a fashion whirligig, especially during the Carnival season. Cities burst into song and rapturous musical performances. The overtones were local and patriotic, a means to rediscover language and heritage, and demonstrated the passionate ties to place.

The men's choral society, or music club, was initially founded in Berlin in 1808. Almost immediately, the idea was taken up in Hamburg, Leipzig, Dessau, and Göttingen. Stuttgart's music club inspired initiatives in Ulm, Munich, and Frankfurt em Main. The towns of Koblenz, Bremen, Nuremberg, Mannheim, and Cologne established their own music societies, all in the 1820s and 1830s. These kinds of boisterous choral societies and amateur bands, along with paramilitary gymnastic clubs, and drinking and sharpshooting clubs, were a modern form of masculine sociability. They were also forums for political rabble-rousing and easily morphed into direct action. Members were drawn from across the social spectrum, from merchants and bankers, industrial entrepreneurs, to officials in public administration, writers and journalists, master artisans, and the better-off working classes.[13] At a minimum, they were just regular gatherings in the local beer hall and the opportunity to belt out patriotic songs. But the wealthiest among them produced local concerts and operated mammoth public performances. Participants in these music festivals numbered in the thousands. The size and scope of the events signified the collective coming together of both the city and the German people, or *Volk*.

It was a new type of democratic public engagement and marked the transition to mass politics. The German model sparked amateur music clubs and song festivals in the Baltic provinces, in the cities of Königsberg, Danzig, Riga, and Tallinn. They were flamboyant celebrations of local culture and language, and the opportunity for an emotional outpouring of patriotism.

The choir movement was especially powerful in the Rhineland, where over one hundred clubs were established as platforms for regional and nationalistic loyalties. The Rhineland was one of the richest provinces in Europe. Its capitals of Cologne and Hamburg had long histories as independent cities with their own institutions and traditions: Cologne as a self-governing Imperial City and Hamburg as an independent commercial port. They were among the leading centers for private banking in central Europe. This distinguished past was undermined by the Napoleonic Wars, when both places were occupied by the French. Then after 1815 they were grafted on to the Kingdom of Prussia. The two cities had little in common with rural Prussia east of the Elbe and the polemics around this ambiguous territorial arrangement went on for years. Cologne had an especially cantankerous anti-Prussian reputation. It was displayed in repeated attempts by Cologne's city council to weasel back its long-standing independent powers. The Prussians would have none of it. In retaliation, they snubbed Cologne and appointed Düsseldorf as the new regional capital and Bonn as the seat of the new university. With some 80,000 inhabitants, Cologne was demoted to a defensive city along Prussia's western edge with a ring of eleven fortresses and a sizable Prussian garrison to keep the strained peace.[14] It did little to assuage local suspicions of Prussia's intent. Street brawls regularly took place between civilians and Prussian soldiers. In 1846, a parish fair ended in riots after the Prussian police attacked civilians with clubs and bayonets. The city's Catholics looked warily on their new Protestant masters. Anti-Prussian feeling encouraged local bonds and a self-conscious Catholic regional identity. Riots broke out when the archbishop of Cologne was arrested by the Prussians. For their part, Cologne's bankers worried about new taxes. The old banking patricians—the Schaaffhausen, the von Groote, and von Wittgenstein families—controlled the city's economy and its municipal government. Newcomers such as the Oppenheim family were major investors in the Rhineland's railways and pinpointed Cologne as its hub. They funded the Ruhr's iron and coal industries with a scheme to make Cologne a center for metalwork and machine building. It was a powerful, wealthy oligarchy deeply rooted in the Rhineland with few sympathies toward Prussia (Figure 8).

It was in this atmosphere that Romantic sensibilities and a fierce defense of urban heritage took hold in Cologne. Cruising the Rhine River was fast becoming a favorite of cultivated tourists. The first published Baedeker travel guide was dedicated to the picturesque tableau of castles and chocolate-box villages along the river bluffs. Reproductions of paintings by Romantic landscape virtuoso J. M. W. Turner accompanied starry-eyed descriptions of the Rhineland's past. Cologne was a must on the itinerary. The city was also among the most popular religious pilgrimage sites in northern Europe. Its tourist economy boomed. Reaching Cologne in 1814, English traveler Richard Boyle Bernard thought few cities had a more imposing appearance with its "vast extent of

Figure 8 View of Cologne, about 1840, steel engraving created in the nineteenth century, North Rhine-Westphalia.

buildings, a profusion of steeples, and a forest of masts" along the riverfront. In 1846, publisher Otto Elben set out for the German-Flemish song festival in Cologne. He traveled by steamship down the Rhine on what he described as a poetic journey. On board, he met members of the choral clubs headed for the city. Arriving in Cologne, Elben joined in the singing festivities and then went on local tours and excursions.[15]

Nestled inside its fortifications, the town on the left bank of the Rhine became a stage set for the city's past glories. Historic churches, monasteries and convents, chapels and abbeys lined the sinuous streets and cobble-stone alleyways. The vogue for historicism and the tourist itinerary was undifferentiated from patriotic posturing. The medieval tangle around Cologne Cathedral became a "beautification district" to make it more attractive for sightseers.[16] Led by church dignities and the city's burgers, a veritable treasure trove of local art and artifacts was put on public display, in good part in retaliation against Prussian rule. Religious pilgrimages and processions abounded, some of them, such as the procession of the Three Kings, drawing hundreds of thousands of worshippers. The Niederrheinische (Lower Rhine) Music Festival was a collaboration between Cologne and the towns of Düsseldorf and Aix-le-Chapelle that brought choirs of thousands to the city for a monumental public performance of the Handel and Haydn oratorios.[17] In 1823, representatives of the city's patrician families rekindled Cologne's traditional Carnival. It was the largest of the Carnival festivities that had a long pedigree in the Rhineland towns and reemerged as a form of political resistance against the Prussians. Carnival organizing clubs were a platform for raucous political debate. In Cologne, banquets and elaborate parades and a mammoth public ball capped an entire Carnival season. Patriotic songbooks and festival programs were passed out to everyone in the city. On Rose Monday, a fabulous musical procession paraded down the Hohe Strasse and around the "Four Winds" road junction with joyful revelers in historic costume and floats bedecked in regalia. It was among the most expressive moments in the city's cultural firmament and an unabashed promotion of Cologne's splendors. The Carnival committees wore their militia uniforms as a badge of their patriotic fervor and independence. Thousands of Prussian soldiers were stationed in the streets, where they endured the taunts of the crowds.

Above all, Cologne Cathedral was the defiant symbol of Cologne as a great city and the distinctiveness of its culture and urban life. The unfinished medieval cathedral along with a massive wooden crane perched on the south tower dominated the skyline. It was monumental, a "colossus" remarked French traveler Paul Baudry.[18] The rediscovery of the original plans for the cathedral in 1814 was the impetus behind a painstaking project to finally finish the iconic building. It unleashed a passionate campaign to use only the most historically authentic techniques and materials possible. Spectacular festivals took place to celebrate the cathedral in 1842 and again in 1848 amid political rallies and revolutionary protest. The entire city and some 30,000 visitors took part. Military marches and torchlight parades welcomed the Archduke of Austria, who attended the celebrations. Houses were illuminated for the festivities. The city transfigured into a fairyland for the thousands of admirers who saw Cologne as a Romantic dreamscape.[19] These urban spectacles were deeply Catholic. They were political demonstrations riddled with the tensions between homegrown patriotism and the role Cologne would play in the German nation. Modernity was interpreted through the lens of these powerful local practices and histories. They determined the ways in which memory, culture, and social structure were inscribed in the urban landscape.

Touristic sensibilities also found expression in cities such as Munich, which became the capital of the Kingdom of Bavaria in 1806, then one of the largest independent states in central Europe. Initially a modest town on the Isar River with a population around 65,000, Munich flourished in the years after the Napoleonic Wars. Crown prince Ludwig of Bavaria shaped the city into an intellectual and cultural showpiece that enchanted travelers. Visiting in the 1840s, John Barrow gushed that "Munich has risen, within the last thirty years, from a small crowded city . . . to an eminence that may fairly vie with the most celebrated cities of Europe, magnitude only accepted."[20] The fortification walls were torn down. A new extension to the north was laid out in a stately axial pattern in stark contrast to the gaggle of medieval alleyways and churches in the old city. Stylish new boulevards and squares gave the city a regal ambiance. The imposing Ludwigstrasse was lined with splendid palaces and government buildings. The royal coach and parade of splendid carriages glided down the boulevard in full regalia. The grandeur was a visual expression of Bavarian patriotism and its turn toward enlightened reform.

Munich was a Liberal stronghold in a deeply Catholic region. Around half of the city's inhabitants worked for the government, the military, or a religious or cultural institution. The Protestant middle classes filled the upper ranks of Ludwig's administration. They served in Munich's city council and launched an era of cultural enlightenment. Bavaria's leading university was moved to Munich with a majestic building on the Ludwigstrasse filled with Protestant theologians. Munich's Academy of Fine Arts and *Kunstverein* art association were among the most important in central Europe. The Pinakothek art museum and the Greek-inspired Glyptothek sculpture museum along with the national theater, library, and science academies graced the town's newly built extension. They were set off by neoclassical elegance and the triumphal gateway of the Propyläen. The Walhalla monument was dedicated to the Bavarian soldiers who had fought in the Napoleonic Wars. This cultural spectacle radiated Munich's new civic spirit.[21] The classical world was a cultural foil against the power of the Catholic church. Ludwig's admiration for all things Greek and Roman knew no bounds. He visited Rome fifty times and Munich's museums burst with his collection of ancient antiquities. By the 1840s they were already on the most anticipated tourist itineraries in Germany, as were the city's pleasure gardens, casinos, and beer halls.

Beer was big business in Munich. The first Oktoberfest celebrations made the city into a major attraction. The festivities featured rounds of musical entertainment with the city's residents decked out in Bavarian costume. The cultural pageants cemented Munich's reputation as a free-spirited city and "modern Athens." Development continued under Ludwig's son Maximilian II. Munich became the largest industrial center in southern Germany. A new grain hall symbolized the city's commercial resurgence, as did the Glaspalast, a soaring iron and glass exhibition hall, inaugurated in 1854. It was the second in Europe, after London's Crystal Palace. Urban hygienist Max Joseph von Pettenkofer was at the forefront of wiping out cholera in Munich and campaigning for clean air and water, and modern sewage disposal. The city was a beacon of urban innovation—a distinct mélange of science, art, and industry admired throughout Europe and one of the best examples of the fertile ground of regional capitals in the first half of the nineteenth century. By the 1850s, its population reached over 100,000.

Cities across Europe were caught up in the political crises that followed the Napoleonic Wars. The conservative backlash instituted by the Great Powers and then the revolutionary waves that followed kept city streets in constant uproar. Situated on the Vistula River in east central Poland, the city of Kraków was one of the most turbulent of Europe's urban places. The Royal Castle and Wawel Cathedral overlooking the city were testament to a distinguished past as the capital and intellectual heart of the former Kingdom of Poland. With the disappearance of Poland at the end of the Napoleonic Wars, possession of Kraków became one of the most divisive issues among the Great Powers. Unable to resolve the rivalries, the Congress of Vienna made Kraków a nominally Free City under the watchful eyes of Russia, Prussia, and Austria. It remained a fragile independent republic sandwiched between its avaricious neighbors from 1815 to 1846. Although it lost its role as Polish capital, it was master of its own destiny and enjoyed a period of economic prosperity and urban growth.

Kraków held a special place in the Polish imagination. With a population of 140,000 souls, it was a preeminent Catholic stronghold and living symbol of a nation robbed of its independence. Arriving there in the mid-1840s, Józef Mączyński was struck by the numbers of towers and church steeples that jutted into the sky. The traveler quickly

Entertainments and Romantic Dreamscapes (1815–48)

appreciates, he said, that "every step taken, every brick, every stone is marked by a thousand historic memories."[22] Governed by a Senate, the vote was restricted to noble landowners and wealthy townsmen, clergy and teachers, intellectuals and artists. The cathedral and university held key positions on the governing board and fought for control over the city's future. Beyond local politics, the Great Powers planned to turn Kraków into a commercial junction between western Europe and the Black Sea. It was designated a free trade zone and became a freewheeling entrepôt of commerce and smuggling. Spices and eastern commodities made their way west through the city to Warsaw and Danzig, as did Hungarian wine, while Silesian manufactures traveled through Kraków eastward.

Despite ongoing political turmoil and Kraków's precarious independence, the Senate embarked enthusiastically on an urban facelift. The defunct fortifications and nearly all forty-six bastions that encircled the city were torn down. In their place, Planty Park was laid out. It was open to all citizens and dotted with patriotic flourishes. Strolling the tree-lined promenade, stopping to enjoy the entertainment pavilions, the concerts, and dancing,[23] was a respite from the unsettling protests and dangers that marked the city streets. Foreign visitors were struck by its success. Enjoying the atmosphere in 1840, American traveler John Stephens noted that "on Sundays and fête days the whole population gathers in gay dresses, seeking pleasure where their fathers stood glad in armour and arrayed for battle."[24] Ambling through picturesque scenery was a display of gentility, etiquette, and appearance. Like many towns, Kraków had an assortment of gardens and green spaces open to the public, where elegant society promenaded and enjoyed their leisure. Meandering along the banks of the Vistula on a summer evening was a popular pastime, especially for social butterflies engaging in light conversation. The town's first pleasure garden, the *Kremer*, offered music under twinkling lamps, games, and balloon rides. The gardens were spaces where the norms of society could be subverted enough to allow for play, for flirtation and innuendo. The parks became the basis for the 1836 General Plan of Kraków. It incorporated numerous surrounding villages, provided new avenues and a bridge over the Vistula, and gave the city its modern appearance. Emotional reverence for historic monuments was wildly popular. Led by the university, the city's Wawel Castle was restored. The remembrance of the Polish nationalist leader Tadeusz Kościuszko took form in the massive Kościuszko Mound, constructed by the people of Kraków themselves. The city was a tableau to Polish patriotism.

Jagiellonian University emerged as a crucible of intellectual life and local identity. Scientific and cultural institutions flourished in the Free State of Kraków, including the newly organized Kraków Learned Society. It was attached to the university in the old town's Latin Quarter around St. Anne's Street and the Collegium Maius, which was renovated in local gothic style. The Collegium Minus, the Collegium Iuridicum, and the Collegium Phisicum completed the four faculties. The botanical garden and astronomical observatory, the applied mathematics institute, and the university's hospital clinics made Kraków the Polish educational trailblazer. A formidable cadre of professors, lawyers, and thousands of students gave the city its intellectual flare. Their radical politics filtered through everyday life and percolated down to the trade and artisan classes. Through incessant political turmoil in these years, the university acted as an independent institution. Its intelligentsia was the backbone of insurgency and counterweight to the forces of conservatism. The university held a special position in welcoming students from throughout the Polish territories. In central Europe, universities had been citadels of German language and culture. Jagiellonian University gave instruction in Polish. It carried the torch of Polish culture against the barrage of tenacious outside influences.

Kraków became a refuge for Polish nationalists, political outcasts, and conspirators, especially those returning from exile in France. It became a notorious lair of nationalist resistance and intrigue. The surrounding region of Galicia was one of the most ethnically diverse in eastern Europe. A distinguished Jewish community of some 30,000 lived in Kraków and the adjacent districts of Kazimierz and Podgórze. The bustling crowds in Kraków's main square could be a mixture of travelers and Catholic pilgrims, Jews, students and gentry from around Poland, traders and merchants from the east, and a mix of unruly dissidents followed by the Russian soldiers hunting them down. A Polish nationalist underground took shape among students and refugees, the wanted men and army deserters who poured into the city. Forbidden books and pamphlets were smuggled in. The tsar's spy was murdered in the street.[25] In retaliation, Russia and Austria set up security posts at the entrances to Kraków, attempted to deport foreigners and forbade the city's residents from harboring illegal aliens. But to no avail. The city went on protecting foreign insurgents, and Kraków's unruly independence became an international cause célèbre that only gained some measure of protection from England and France.

Emboldened by Romanticist dreams of utopian socialism, in 1846 agitators called for revolution and declared Kraków the seat of a new Polish government. They were led by a young university physicist, a literary critic, and a professor of Polish literature. Their *Manifesto* of social reforms caught the attention of Karl Marx and Friedrich Engels as a model for the future. It included universal suffrage and the abolition of all distinctions between Jews and other citizens. The ringing declaration caught widespread enthusiasm in the Jewish community. Demonstrations and riots quickly led to barricades in the streets. Eventually, the "hornet's nest" of Kraków and its "communist conspiracy," in the words of Metternich, were repressed and the city was annexed to the Austrian Empire. Widespread reprisals followed. A stern regime of Germanization was instituted. Kraków was to follow in step with Vienna. Merchants were ordered to pay new taxes on all their merchandise. As an act of defiance on the last day of independence, they dumped their stocks in the streets. Although it had lost its free status, Kraków continued its reputation for revolutionary turmoil. In 1848, riots broke out again and a Polish National Committee was formed. Pitched street battles were fought with Austrian troops who finally bombarded the city to bring it under control.

The mood in Kraków was somber at mid-century. The Hapsburg Monarchy imprisoned the city in a new ring of military ramparts. It was demoted to a fortress town on Austria's frontier. A black decade of repression followed, made worse by cholera outbreaks and finally the Great Fire of 1850 that gutted much of the timbered old town. The young Hapsburg emperor Franz Joseph entered Kraków in grand procession in 1851.

The imperial party mounted their horses and rode through Kazimierz, where the Jewish community lined the street and greeted the emperor with raised Torahs. The parade continued through streets strewn with flowers to the central square decorated with triumphal arches. A huge crowd waited to watch the troop parade.[26] It was a momentous occasion. But during his stay, English scholar W. G. Clark found the hotels filled with refugees and conspirators. He met "all sorts of odd waifs and strays flung together by the storm of revolution" ready to aid the insurgents in their fight for Polish freedom.[27]

Nowhere held a higher place on tourist itineraries than Italy and Greece. Their aesthetic splendors had long captured the cultured imagination and were obligatory stops in the education of Europe's elites. High society went to Greece and Italy in search of the ancient world. British sightseers were especially inspired by Bryon's poetry and the profusion of travel illustrations of Greece produced in the 1830s. They went in search of emotional drama and Byron's quest for liberty. The independence movements in Greece and Italy riveted the reading public as much as they flummoxed European diplomacy. Byron's defense of Greek independence from the Ottoman Empire and the death of Shelly and Keats in Italy made pilgrimages to these places a noble cause. Scholar Jean-Charles Sismondi wrote in 1832 that "Italy is crushed; but her heart still beats with the love of liberty, virtue, and glory: she is chained and covered with blood; but she still know her strength and her future destiny."[28] The territorial shifts in the Italian peninsula and the rise of nationalism made the "Italian Question" among the most talked about in Europe, although what actually constituted Italy remained blurred.

In the early nineteenth century, Italy's most important cities—Rome, Milan, Genoa, Naples, and Palermo—all had over 100,000 population. Italy was one of the most urbanized countries in Europe. But there was no denying the destruction wrought by the Napoleonic Wars. The occupation of Italy by Napoleon's armies was accompanied by an orgy of violence and ruin. Whole towns were razed and their inhabitants massacred. Rebuilding amid the repressive occupation by first French, and then Austrian troops was what fanned the flames of Italian nationalism. Travelers intent on rediscovering Italy could well be shocked by shattered cityscapes and violent street protests. Plus, travel overland in the south of Europe was still dependent on horse and carriage. Railroads were just coming into service. It also meant crisscrossing a host of territorial frontiers and enduring the suspicious eyes of security forces that could demand identity papers at a moment's notice. The tribulations of finding themselves confronted by police formed no small part of tourist accounts.

But came they did, and Milan's music and theater were one of the most exciting draws. The entry of the Austrians into Milan in 1814 marked the end of the city's brief role as capital of the Napoleonic Kingdom of Italy. Instead, the Congress of Vienna replaced Napoleon's Italian puppet-state with the new Kingdom of Lombardy-Venetia and handed it over to the Austrian Empire. It was a demotion for a city steeped in the heritage of Lombardy's independent republics. The region of Lombardy was long a crossroads, open to "goods, ideas, men, open for business but exposed to continual invasion."[29] France, Austria, and Spain perennially fought over its riches. The dense city life along the fertile Po River valley was the region's historic legacy. The towns went from

Montoue (18,000 inhabitants) to Pavia (21,000), Ancona (23,000), Modena (26,000), Padua (30,000), Brescia (34,000), and Bologna (65,000) with Milan as the region's capital. Recognizing Lombardy's thick urban constellation, even Napoleon had spread out his French administrative and cultural institutions among the cities.

Napoleon had been welcomed as an Enlightenment liberator and crowned king in Milan Cathedral. His plans for Milan were enticing. An Embellishment Committee was given vast powers to transform the city into a neoclassical vision. Wide avenues were laid out along with the triumphal gateway of the Simplon, the grand plaza of the Foro Buonaparte and an amphitheater built for military parades and imperial spectacles. The vast polygonal fortifications that surrounded the city and its ten gates were partially demolished and the ramparts replaced with a splendid tree-lined esplanade. It was graced with a whimsical great hall for festivals and concerts. Visitors remarked that the "inns, restaurants and bistros see a continual ebb and flow of people" and "there isn't a street without wine shops and two or three cafés with billiards, loto, etc."[30] Throngs of people strolled the city's new avenues on Sunday evenings, stopping to enjoy games of chance, puppet theaters, and street entertainers. These were the local sights that foreign explorers delightedly scribbled about in their notebooks.[31]

The Milanese had no love for their Austrian overseers. Yet even under the Hapsburg Empire, the city of 150,000 inhabitants thrived. Schools and hospitals were opened; literary societies, libraries, and colleges led the city's flourishing intellectual and cultural life. Milan's many theaters were a social whirl. The Scala Opera House reigned supreme as a grand musical institution with the most innovative operatic forms in Europe. The city was a powerhouse of Romantic music and music publishing. Milan's music was the patriotic symbol of a united and free Italy. The city leaped past Naples and Venice as the new Italian cultural capital.[32] French tour guides gushed over the city's Corso, the public concerts and music, and the cafés and theaters.[33] Twenty-five omnibuses ran on the city's streets. Wealthy merchants crowded into the Bourse to mastermind deals in the lucrative silk industry, the city's artisanal glass and fine toolmaking, and printing industries. Shipping houses ran express wagon convoys of merchandise to Venice, Vienna, and Lyon, as well as to Poland and Russia. By the 1840s, trains made these trips even faster.[34] Milan became Italy's main business headquarters. It was a measure of its early knowledge economy that it was also a magnet for mathematical and astronomical instrument making, the fabrication of globes, and the development of cartography. Scientific activities were the sign of Milan's capacity to lead the Italian nation.

And there was no doubting the hostilities toward the Austrians bubbling just beneath the surface. Visiting Milan's churches and libraries, and then strolling the Corso in 1846, British traveler J. S. Buckingham remarked that "even in the gayest promenades, whenever the Austrians appear, there is a sullen silence among the Italians, as if they hated their very presence and disliked to breathe the same atmosphere with them."[35] The Austrian reign was endured for thirty-four years. Milan's Liberal elites covertly organized secret societies and conspiracies. Although they tended to mimic the local nobility, they were cosmopolitan in spirit and aspired to the Liberal reforms espoused throughout Europe. The Milanese bourgeoisie ignored Vienna and drew their alliances with Turin, with London and Paris. They were backed by Milan's Catholic church and by the Lombard gentry. The funeral of a Milanese noble and patriot who died in an Austrian prison drew thousands into the streets. The arrival of a new bishop in 1847 was the occasion for celebration, the lighting by gas-light of the piazza Fontana, followed by the gusty public singing of patriotic ballads. The Austrian police broke up the festivities. Strikes and riots broke out. Angry crowds directed their wrath at the occupying troops. Bands of civilians regularly jumped soldiers at night. From the early days of 1848, the campaign against Austria broke into boycotts, protests, barricades and bloody street battles and culminated in the "Five Days" of guerrilla warfare between the nationalists and Austrian troops. Church bells rang across the city in a call for revolution. The uprising forced some 20,000 Austrian troops to retreat. But they quickly regrouped and laid siege to the city until 1853.

Visits to Italy had long been a mainstay for Europe's elites, even under the harrowing conditions of revolutionary turmoil. But traveling down the Balkan peninsula was another thing altogether. It was a territory of the Ottoman Empire, the "Slavic world," with few signs of what even the most hardened travelers considered "European" life. It suffered an unsavory reputation as a world of suspicion, predation, and violence. The roads were abysmal, the rivers unpassable, the mountains dizzying, the attacks by brigands too dangerous. Daring explorers could easily run into guerilla combat between warring factions, skirmishes led by local chieftains, and insurrections against Ottoman rule. The port towns along the Mediterranean such as Spalato (Split) and Dubrovnik (Ragusa) were picturesque, but only small affairs.

Putting aside biased western opinions of the Balkans, the region had genuinely deep-rooted Ottoman qualities. It was a borderland of rural wooden villages interspersed with the Sublime Porte's administrative and trade centers, principally Dubrovnik, Bosna, Sarajevo, Skopje, and Salonica (Thessaloniki). Their populations were a mélange of Turk, Greek, Christian foreign traders, and local shopkeepers. Balkan towns were Islamic outposts where both Christians and Jews were ostensibly tolerated. Acceptance of religious minorities was prescribed by Islamic law and ran across class lines. Towns along the Adriatic coast imported Italian wares and exported timber, wools, oils, and farming produce. Visiting the thriving town of Jannina (Ioannina) in 1809, intrepid Englishman John Hobhouse remarked on the city's surprising refinement, with elaborate marriage processions through the streets, puppet shows and entertainments, the presence of learned scholars and libraries.[36] With a covey of mosques, churches, and synagogues, and its Greek schools, the town was among the most important in the region. Jannina's local bazaar was the envy of the Balkans. To crush the power of its famed governor Ali Pacha, the Turks besieged the city and burned it to the ground in 1820.

Once bourgeois elites packed their backs and headed out to explore the continent, their intellectual tastes fixated on the Greek classical past. The route of the Grand Tour shifted away from the Italian peninsula to Greece and ultimately to Athens. With a population of 12,000 inhabitants in the early years of the nineteenth century, Athens was among the most important towns in the Balkan provinces of the Ottoman Empire. Its population of mainly Greeks, Turks, Jews, and Albanians lived in a maze of alleyways and ethnic neighborhoods, or *mahallas*. Their low flat-roofed houses were intermixed among lofty minarets and domed mosques, churches and ancient ruins. The city was crammed full with layers of its legendary history, all encircled by a hopelessly feeble perimeter wall. The bazaar, located on the remains of the Roman Agora, was the city's most important public place. Spreading out across three separate trading areas, it offered a profusion of goods and was also the civic and governing heart of the Ottoman town.

Europeans making their way to Athens inevitably gazed on the city from afar, spellbound by their infatuation with the ancient capital and the beauty of the Mediterranean. On first seeing Athens in 1812, English diplomat Walther Turner gushed "the city whose history had interested me from childhood, now stood before me adorned by nature with all its beauty." Yet it was typical of the western viewpoint that he could say nothing of the bazaars chock-full of culinary delights other than "Athens—glorious, delightful Athens! would still be a most enchanting residence—if one were not in danger of being starved to death in it."[37] Travelers routinely looked for familiar signs of European life: anything outside it was judged barbarism. After the war of liberation, Turner would have been rudely shocked at the devastation. During the Ottoman siege of Athens in 1826–27, much of the city was destroyed, its citizens fled, and the legendary monuments on the Acropolis shelled and left in ruins. When Athens was chosen as the capital city of the newly founded Greek State in 1833, only 6,000 brave inhabitants remained. Salonica and Smyrna were far larger. But Athens symbolized Europe's classical heritage. Ludwig I's son Otto of Bavaria left Munich and traveled down to Greece as its new king. The young nation began its life as a Bavarian outpost. Greece was eyeballed as a new German sphere of influence.

The rebuilding of Athens was considered one of the most important projects of the early nineteenth century. It was a lesson in the vagaries of war and the ways Liberal urban ideals determined urban experience on the borderlands of Europe. Rationalizing and regulating the city's physical environment was considered the basis for a modern metropolis. The venerable Ottoman fabric of Athens was immediately expunged. Greek elites were heavily influenced by the Enlightenment and French Revolution. This vanguard of European ideals acted as a foil against the hated Ottoman regime. Support for the rebuilding of Athens came from the Greek diaspora of wealthy merchants and commercial magnets who made their fortunes on the Black Sea and Mediterranean. They were a powerful privileged caste that controlled the import and export trades, the money markets, and shipping. Their hands were in every aspect of trade in the Ottoman territories, in Odessa, and in the river ports along the Danube. Indeed, the movement for Greek independence was sparked by clandestine societies gathered in the backrooms of Odessa. Cosmopolitan in outlook, the Greek merchant families remained expatriates outside their homeland. Yet they retained a highly romanticized ideal of Greek identity and place. Their loyalty to Greece drew deeply on its classical legacy and the influence of the Eastern Orthodox church. Athens was to recover its European birthright and be acknowledged as the capital of a sovereign state and independent Greek people. It would reemerge in all its glory as a European city.[38]

Architects from all over Europe submitted plans for the rebuilding of Athens, but the Bavarian urban ideal held the greatest sway. For the most part, the imaginary of a "Mediterranean region" was the work of German geographers, and it was imbued with ideals about ancient rationalism and aesthetic purity.[39] The same architects who had refashioned Munich laid out their fantasy for Athens as a coherent neoclassical ensemble. Ignoring the entrenched maze of roadways that had grown up over time, the city was reworked into a crescent-shape encircling the Acropolis and then extended with a rectangular grid.[40] Although the remaining inhabitants were desperate for basic services, the first buildings constructed were the university and theater. A library, museum, and exposition hall quickly followed. They were built in the neoclassical style then in vogue throughout Europe. In the minds of the Bavarian overlords and Greek elites pouring over the plans, it was a perfect architecture for modern Athens. It looked beyond the Ottoman past and instead harkened directly back to ancient Greece. Wealthy Greeks from abroad rushed to invest in real estate and built their mansions along Academias (Academy) and Panepistimiou (University) avenues close to Syntagma Square. These were the emblems of the European metropolis and the Liberal belief in education as the framework of democratic citizenship. Eminent Greek families founded schools and financed book printing. An urban intelligentsia sparked renewed interest in Greek learning and language.

Yet this grandiose refashioning of Athens into a European city floundered on the reefs of ceaseless modifications, the penury of resources, and the vagaries of politics and land speculation. Greece was a tentative, impoverished new nation. Although rich in monuments, mansions and palaces, what mainly typified nineteenth-century Athens was unplanned development, innumerable small measures, the informality and patchwork nature of construction that characterized Mediterranean settlement patterns. It was built modestly, bit by bit. Western hopes for a modern Athens faded. Regretting the changes to the classical vision of Athens already apparent in the late 1830s, American John Stevens found it had

> become a heterogeneous anomaly; the Greeks in their wild costume are jostled in the streets by Englishmen, Frenchmen, Italians, Dutchmen, Spaniards, and Bavarians, Russians, Danes, and sometimes Americans. But it was enough to attract a cacophony of visitors and risk-takers. European shops invite purchasers by the side of Eastern bazaars; coffee-houses, and billiard-rooms, and French and German restaurants are opened all over the city. Sir Pultney Malcolm has erected a house for hire near the site of Plato's Academy. Lady Franklin bought land near the foot of Mount Hymettus for a country-seat.[41]

Foreign capital was converted into real estate. Even public buildings depended on private investors, money jingling in their pockets, who forced modification of the original plans for their own designs.

Northern Europeans descended on the sunny Mediterranean with their cultural baggage in tow, busily searching for antiquity or bent on the discovery of exotic peoples and cultures. Guidebooks and travelogues enticed travelers with picturesque sketches of the Mediterranean coast with its churches and ancient ruins set in the landscape. In the meantime, daily life in the cities of southern Europe was oriented toward the Mediterranean Sea and its jumble of cultural and commercial bonds. The ports along the Mediterranean were some of Europe's largest cities in the early to mid-nineteenth century. With a population of some 430,000 in 1800, Naples was the most densely packed city on the continent. Lisbon's population reached 200,000 while some 180,000 people were crammed into Barcelona. The cities on the Mediterranean were also among the most cosmopolitan with a mélange of people passing through or starting new lives. They were crowded multiethnic, multi-confessional enclaves. Amid the political unpredictability and territorial swapping that marked these years, Mediterranean cities provided refuge and sanctuary. A brew of traders, expatriates, refugees, and local militants made these places crucibles for all shades of political activity, nationalist movements, for revolutionary insurrections. Rebel army officers and free masons in Lisbon plotted independence and set off insurgencies throughout Portugal in 1820. Radical factions in Barcelona and Valencia led uprisings in Spain in the 1840s and 1860s. The wave of uprisings in 1848 engulfed Marseille on the coast of France along with Rome, Naples, and Palermo on the Italian peninsula. In the eastern Mediterranean, Trieste and Dubrovnik boiled over with agitation by dissident political clubs and masonic lodges. Salonica was the launching pad for Bulgarian and Macedonian nationalism and for the Young Turk movement. Mediterranean cities shared an autonomy and freewheeling atmosphere that belied the oppressive strictures of states and empires. Cultural and social boundaries were more porous. Ideas, information, money, and resources flooded through a host of formal and informal networks.

There was no single model of urbanization along the European shores of the Mediterranean. The patterns of city development were complex and heterogeneous, with a myriad of divergent trajectories influenced by local culture. Yet the cityscape of places like Barcelona, Marseille, and Salonika shared the typical features of maritime trade. The best way to reach them was from the sea. Warehouses and open-air markets lined the wharves. Banks, custom houses, shipping agencies and insurance companies regulated the flow of merchandise and kept the quaysides bustling with activity. Inns and hostels provided lodging for traders and travelers. The seamen's dives were notorious for the sex trade, the dickering over drugs and illicit contraband, and the criminal pursuits that arrived with the ships. Maritime commerce drew an array of economic activities. Cities in the western Mediterranean began industrializing earlier than historians have traditionally reported. Once peace was established in 1815, British artisans and entrepreneurs made their way to Marseille, Barcelona, and Naples, bringing with them the latest industrial machinery and techniques. They were adapted to local manufacturing in leathermaking and textiles, to chemical production, and to the seafaring industries.

The taking of Algiers by French forces in 1830 made Marseille into a thriving colonial gateway with 130,000 inhabitants. Located on a hilly seafront on the Rhone River delta, it was the largest port on the Mediterranean. Visiting in 1838, Stendhal (one of France's most illustrious writers) noted that "in Marseille, everyone works at making their money."[42] Merchant elites from across the Mediterranean were on the lookout for investment opportunities that coordinated with their commercial enterprises. The city had large populations of Greek, Jewish, North African, Arab, and Indian traders. They were not always welcomed with open arms, but the scrabble of peoples was tolerated because they were essential to the city's maritime economy. The same networks, the social clubs, and newspapers that supported Mediterranean trade spread information on the latest innovations in industry and nautical transport. Not only French but also Greek, Russian, and German money fueled industrialization. Banks and credit operations opened. Entrepreneurs took advantage of the flow of migrants as cheap labor in local manufacturing. Marseille's port was lined with foundries and machine shops serving merchant and passenger ships. The volume of transshipment and goods flowing through the port increased exponentially, especially to the French colonies in Africa and Asia. Grain and goods were sent by barge up the Rhone River to Lyon, Paris, and the rest of western Europe. New wharves were opened along with railroad lines and canals. The result was that Marseille and cities like it in southern Europe functioned as productive pivots between the vast currents of industrialization and the Mediterranean (Figure 9).[43]

The population of Marseille shot up to 500,000 by the end of the nineteenth century. A monumental new Chamber of Commerce was built on the city's main thoroughfare, the Cannebière. Gaslighting graced the streets and a monumental triumphal arch dignified

Figure 9 Early autotype of Marseille, Bouches-du-Rhone, France, historical photo, 1884.

the entrance into the city. Stendhal found a crowded café "that would do Paris proud" where brokers were conducting their business. He attended the opera and boisterous vaudeville shows.[44] Southeast of the port lay the affluent districts. The grand promenade of the Prado was laid out. Spacious, lined with trees and stylish villas, it stretched from the place de Castellane down to the sea. But the city's growth was determined less by urban planning than by speculation and the tastes of private investors. The old walls encircling the city were demolished at the beginning of the century and construction stretched outward. Omnibuses clanged along the streets and out into the surrounding villages. Modest buildings with their distinctive "three windows" gave Marseille a native architectural appeal. Even the most sought-after neighborhoods had some sense of social mixing. But there were limits to the broad-mindedness born of maritime existence. The segregated North African neighborhood of Noailles grew up around the port. It was a lively entrepôt of informality where Arabic held sway. The working-class districts to the north at Le Panier and Belsunce were a warren of ancient buildings and narrow streets. Corsicans, Italians, Armenians, and Spaniards toiled in the workshops and roamed the quaysides looking for work. Marseille was a babel of ethnic communities. French was still treated as something of a foreign language. It was this kind of "foreignness" that attracted spirited travelers to the Mediterranean looking to experience the exotic sights and sounds.

Not everyone traveling through Europe was intent on a circuit of cultural gratification. An entire network of spa and thermal towns enticed the weary and those in need of respite. Others went in search of the uplifting benefits of coastal dunes and the sea, or simply to bask in the sun. Spas and seaside resorts were a category of urban Europe on the cutting edge of modernity and cultural exchange. They responded to the new forms of production and consumption and to the spread of rising living standards and aspirations.[45] Although the elites of society benefited most, even office workers, shop assistants, and skilled workers could afford to spend a few days on vacation. These new holiday venues shifted the gist of tourism and added to the continent's dense urban fabric. One by one, a web of fashionable and more mundane watering holes morphed into tourist meccas. Their populations doubled and tripled as they were connected by steamship and railroad to Europe's major cities. Every summer, spa towns and seaside resorts welcomed the rich and famous, the aristocratic and the well-heeled, the upright middle and working classes in search of the curative powers of water. They were escapes from work, from pollution and ill health, from the rat-race of city life.

The craze began with the spa towns of Bath, Malvern, and Cheltenham in England. In France, Trouville, Vichy, Evian, Biarritz, and Aix-les-Bains beckoned those in search of healing and a dose of well-being. Visiting the sulfur baths at Luchon in the Pyreenes Mountains in 1859, American journalist William Cullen Bryant noted it was "one of the gayest spectacles I ever saw." Although Luchon itself was "a shabby village," the area around the spa was well appointed for tourists. Visitors arrived early on the "noble street—broad, planted with a fourfold row of elms and lindens" on their way to the springs where "troops of servant-women in head-dresses of bright-colored handkerchiefs, red and yellow, run after them and crowd around them, offering travelers apartments. Companies of people, men and women, are departing on horseback—each with a guide . . . setting out for the meadows."[46] The healthy benefits of nature combined with the therapeutic powers of mineral waters and hot springs were the anecdote to all ills. When Vichy was first marketed for its thermal waters in the early 1830s, it welcomed fewer than a thousand patrons. Only thirty years later, their numbers reached 16,000 and grew to 70,000 by the end of the century. The cure-towns of central Europe became all the rage. A stay in Baden-Baden, Wiesbaden, Bad Ems, Karlsbad, and Marienbad was miraculous therapy in the public imagination. Seaside resorts sprang up along the North Sea and Baltic coasts. Picturesque fishing ports such as Scheveningen on the Dutch coast began branding themselves as beach getaways. Russian families headed for the coastal towns in Finland and the Baltic provinces. With their warm seawater and curative mud, Kadriorg and Haapsalu on the Estonian coast were stylish resorts. Yacht clubs with their colorful regattas typified the summer scene along the Baltic. These were cosmopolitan worlds that functioned within the standards of modern behavior and social practices accepted by Europe's elites.

Visiting the Mediterranean took off in the early nineteenth century. In the aftermath of the Napoleonic Wars, French and German geographers laid out the characteristics of the Mediterranean region as a distinct geographic unit based on its climate and physical morphology, and its ancient heritage. The first guidebooks were already swept off the shelves in the 1830s with itineraries to ancient Roman ruins and hidden-away medieval churches in the coastal villages. Sightseers braved the mosquitoes and marshes for ecstatic views of the sea. But it was only after Nice was transferred from the Kingdom of Piedmont-Savoy to France in 1860 and then the rail lines opened from Paris that the Côte d'Azur became a favored destination for vacationing glitterati escaping the chilly north. By 1880, some 25,000 tourists a year were spending the winter in Nice, the majority French, British, and Russian. The visit by Queen Victoria was a high point, with the crowds lined up to catch up a glimpse of Her Majesty. Nice was described as an earthly paradise, an elegant mix of French and Italian culture. Wealthy patrons constructed monumental palace-villas in a bevy of historic styles.[47] Luxurious hotels and casinos lined the waterfront. Each afternoon, fashionable vacationers strolled on the new Promenade des Anglais with its luxurious palm trees and gazed out on the azure sea.

Led by savvy entrepreneurs and local doctors, the resorts offered their clients a profusion of recreational and medicinal doings. Theaters and concerts, exhibitions, casinos and gambling, dancing and art lessons packed the daily schedule. Street and beach entertainment captivated vacationers. Local municipalities organized summer festivals and sporting competitions. The spa towns were fantasy places outside the constraints of conventional urban life. Yet they were model cities functioning within the European urban system. They were pristine, carefully maintained environments that responded to the increasingly sophisticated tastes of their visitors. Spas had the most modern water and sewage systems in Europe. They were decorated in a whimsical architecture with picturesque gardens and coastal landscaping. They were idyllically designed with railroad station, axial avenues, seaside hotels, and inns. Daily life took place around the promenade. It was the social highlight, the place to see and be seen, for gossip and news,

Figure 10 The Beach, Blackpool, Lancashire, 1894–1910.

for displaying spa manners and style. Public performance and voyeurism were essential to the entertainment. The fashionable whirl of artists and writers, journalists, the illustrious and the notorious were essential to the spa's reputation. There was a constant social jockeying, scenes of affluence and aspiration, of snobbism and flirtation. The spa town was high urban theater in the same category as the pleasure garden, the boulevard, and the international exhibition (Figure 10).

Europe's aristocracy was at the pinnacle of the spa social order and indulged in long sojourns in full splendor. Industrialists and bankers, and politicians and lawyers could all be found enjoying the summer ambiance with their families. As the wealth of the bourgeoisie increased over the nineteenth century, the watering holes increasingly catered to their needs. Each environment was said to have its unique medicinal qualities. Promenades along the beach or cliffs with sublime views of the sea was its own form of therapy. Even for those beyond the charmed circle of wealth and power in the great spas, Europe's coastlines were dotted with ports and fishing towns that accentuated their traditional maritime ambiance with holiday revelries. They catered to middle-class and lower-middle-class families in the local region. Early on, Liverpool outfitted its beaches with long lines of bathing machines and a floating pool for summer pleasure seekers, who could enjoy the added spectacle of ships coming into port. Once special excursion trains ran to the seaside town of Blackpool on the Irish Sea, it became an instant favorite for the workers and employees from Manchester and the surrounding cotton towns. The boardwalk was mobbed with noisy, exuberant weekend holidaymakers. The Winter Garden offered highbrow entertainment. On Blackpool's South Shore, the Pleasure

Beach amusement park was all the rage for thrill-seekers. A circus and a zoo, a roller-skating rink, a naval spectatorium, a casino, and a picture theater trussed up as an Indian palace, all kept visitors enthralled.[48] The Blackpool Tower and the gigantic Ferris Wheel were beacons for fun and entertainment, drinking and dancing. It was the largest entertainment venue in Europe. Nearly 3 million people visited Pleasure Beach each year by the turn of the century. Tourism and holidaymaking had filtered down to the working classes. Capital cities and regional towns, spas and coastal watering holes, even the most remote settlements became touristic spectacle. Visitors boarded trains and steamships and dashed across Europe, reveling in the sense of freedom and inquisitiveness. Armed with their travel guides, they inspected cultural heritage, aesthetic wonders, and exotic peoples. These were voyages of discovery that pictured the interplay between "then" and "now," between the past and the tangle of changes shaping the urban world.

CHAPTER 4
ROAMING THE MARKETS

By the late nineteenth century, cities had become the experimental field of the modern age. The floods of people, the unprecedented scale of commerce and industry, the advances in transportation and communication boggled the imagination of contemporaries. Cities were less a point on a map than a crossroads for people, goods, cultures, and ideas. Mobility was the key to modern urban life. Circulation and exchange made the largest impacts on its form. There was a general spread of urban bourgeois culture and practices and a new kind of public sphere that went along with them. Bourgeois sensibilities emphasized culture and refinement, the comforts of material wealth. Big cities in particular spread new habits and material desires. The growth of the *Großstadt*, *grande ville*, or *wielkie miasto* was relentless and an endless source of fascination for urban observers. Social elites and tourists were drawn to Europe's capitals to enjoy the range of entertainments they offered, from theaters and museums, to the bounty of goods spilling from the markets and trade fairs, and shopping in the newest department stores. The scale and complexity of commercial exchange was astonishing. It embellished the products of industrialization and created a new order of consumerism. Along with it, a new aesthetic became the face of the modern city. With liberating bravado, architects combined cast iron and glass into modern splendor. Enormous new railroad stations, industrial exhibitions, and basilicas of commerce were audacious markers of the modern urban scene.

After 1830, urbanization in Europe took off at an unprecedented rate. But tracking urban growth requires an immediate caveat. The traditional criterion for examining urbanization is population figures. But statistics about population growth were only coming into their own as systematic evidence and were at best uneven. They were also typically limited to the traditional municipal boundaries of a city. They tell us little about the expanse of metropolitan areas. An even more important caution is that most of the statistical evidence about urban development comes from western European countries. Given these forewarnings, we can say that in 1800, about 12 percent of western Europeans lived in cities, and that number was not dramatically different than it had been in 1700. Cities played an even lesser role in central and eastern Europe. In general, up to around 1800, the level of urbanization remained about the same relative to overall population growth. There were twenty-three major cities in Europe with populations over 100,000, and about 5.5 million people lived in them. This long-standing portrait of urbanization was upended in the nineteenth century when Europe entered a pivotal period in the transformation of cities. Demographer Paul Bairoch used the population figure of 5,000 as the starting point for a settlement to be considered urban. Using this definition, by

1850, about 20 percent of western Europeans were living in towns and cities. On the eve of the First World War, roughly 42 percent were urban dwellers. The number of people living in cities increased sevenfold between 1800 and 1910, rising from 19 million to 127 million. Towns grew into small cities, small cities into regional urban centers. Nearly fifty cities in Europe numbered over 250,000 inhabitants. By the end of the nineteenth century, there were 135 major cities in Europe with a total population of 46 million.[1]

In general, this headlong urbanization took place in those areas of Europe that were already relatively citified and densely populated. The European urban landscape reproduced itself. Great Britain was the most urbanized country in Europe. Sometime in the late 1830s, the level of urbanization in England passed 40 percent, and by 1880 nearly 70 percent of the country lived in cities. By that time, London had become a leviathan metropolis. It was a "World City" in the truest sense of the word. The area under the control of the London County Council (Greater London) had a population of just under 1 million in 1800, when the first census was taken. It then grew to over 2.6 million by 1851, more than doubling in size. It doubled again to 4.5 million by 1900. Towns and villages in the counties surrounding London were engulfed by the first waves of suburban expansion. Some 20 percent of the population of England was living in London. But more than just population, the "great city" came to mean the modern metropolis. London, Paris, Berlin, and Vienna were the exemplars. They were the exalted capital cities of wealthy, powerful nations and their empires. Three million made Paris their home. Two million people resided in Berlin and the same number in Vienna.

Based purely on population, these heights of the urban hierarchy do not account for the global reach of many urban places or their impact on European urban culture and society. Once these influences are taken into account, the mark of the "great city" was spread much wider across the continent. Just below the magic triad of London, Paris, and Vienna in the urban hierarchy were St. Petersburg, Budapest, and Warsaw in eastern Europe and Amsterdam and Brussels in western Europe. Manchester, Liverpool, and Glasgow in Great Britain reached the million mark at the century's end. In the Netherlands, 40 percent of the population lived in cities over 20,000 and the rest in small towns in a polynucleated pattern that urbanized a good portion of the country. France was less urbanized, with only 35 percent of people living in towns.[2] Paris dominated the French urban system. German urbanization took off after unification in 1871. The cities of Hamburg, Munich, Cologne, Frankfurt, Stuttgart, Dresden, Königsberg, Leipzig, and Breslau all crossed the threshold of 100,000 population. By 1910, Prussia had twenty-three cities with populations over 100,000, and 22.5 percent of the total Prussian population lived in them. The number of city dwellers was increasing everywhere. Even smaller cities experienced unprecedented population growth. Between 1890 and 1910, towns in the Hapsburg domains such as Lemberg (L'viv), Zagreb, Trieste, Debreczen, and Timişoara saw their inhabitants shoot up 50–60 percent.[3]

The causes behind this jump in scale, especially to "big city" status, were straightforward. Cities spread out geographically and absorbed surrounding towns and villages in their wake. In Germany, for example, Cologne, Leipzig, Magdeburg, Munich, Darmstadt, Dortmund, and Frankfurt all incorporated their inner suburbs. In 1846, Glasgow annexed a wide swath of surrounding territory, and then in 1891 embarked on further extension that immediately added 90,000 people to its population. As urban expansion swallowed up surrounding villages, it became impossible to tell where one community ended and another began. It was a complete break with the old town-country border that had traditionally been marked by city walls. This gobbling up of urban territory was taking place throughout Europe. In some places, the natural increase in the population was also an important contributing factor. Cities were becoming places where families thrived. In Greater London, for example, some 85 percent of population gain between 1850 and 1890 was due to natural growth. The excess of births over deaths rose as the century progressed, even though mortality—especially infant mortality—still remained high. Industrial cities in particular had high birth rates. They were filled with young workers who married and set up households filled with children. In general, service cities and administrative capitals had lower birth rates. White collar and civil service workers, skilled professionals, tended to have smaller families. On the other hand, life expectancy in cities was lower than in rural areas. Mortality rates in industrial cities remained high throughout the nineteenth century with dangerous factory and mine work, and diseases caused by severe overcrowding and unsanitary conditions, being the primary culprits.

The most important factor in the population boom was migration. Newcomers fueled the unprecedented urban growth of the nineteenth century. War, revolution, and ethnic hostilities should not be underestimated as causes for these multitudes. The nineteenth century saw the emergence of the "exile," the "refugee," and the "outcast" as a significant itinerant figure in a sequence of forced and voluntary migrations.[4] The refugee inhabited the outer edge of citizenship and relied on informal networks of sociability and aide. The French Revolution and Napoleonic Wars triggered tremendous dislocation, with refugees fleeing the violence and destruction. The territorial changes instigated by the 1815 Congress of Vienna, especially in eastern Europe, upended lives and caused a further rush into towns and cities. The conservative clampdown of protests and revolution caused yet another spike in refugees. For example, after the failure of the November Uprising of 1830 against the partition of Poland, perhaps as many as 8,000 Polish elites fled death sentences in the "Great Migration." Many found their way to exile in Paris and London. After the Greek war of independence, Cypriots took refuge in Marseille, Venice, and Trieste. The Russian-Ottoman conflicts in the Balkans was accompanied by waves of exiled and displaced. In the early years of the century, an estimated 250,000 Bulgarians left Ottoman territories in the Balkans for the provinces north of the Danube and southern Russia, the majority settling in towns, especially Galați and Brăila. The systematic, violent expulsion of the Muslim population of the Ottoman Balkans began in the early nineteenth century as the Imperial Porte receded. Muslims fled south of the Danube and continued their exodus into what territory remained of the Ottoman world. The litany of diasporas continued with Jewish families, especially those from poor areas of Galicia, who moved to Warsaw, Vienna, Budapest, Łódź, Odessa, and Berlin. Another wave of refugees followed the revolutions of 1848–49. Italian revolutionaries went to Madrid, Lisbon, and London, and then returned to Italy to fight again.[5] In 1885, foreign Poles were expelled from Prussia's eastern borderlands and forced to return to their homelands. It was an unending stream of outcasts. Largely without legal status or rights, refugees and exiles faced discrimination and the risk of crackdowns. The best way to protect themselves was by merging into the flotsam and jetsam of urban life. The mutability of urban populations was in some good part explained less by rural crisis and industrialization than this reality of political instability, ethnic violence, and war.

Some historians have estimated that more than one-third of the population of Europe was on the move in the nineteenth century. Cities were gateways to safety, to dreams and ambitions, to money and influence. Often less than half of the population living in Europe's great capital cities were actually born there. By mid-century, foreigners were a common sight in towns and cities everywhere. Migration had become a mass phenomenon. The increase in the general population was another crucial factor. By 1900, the overall population of Europe had doubled to 400 million. Between 1800 and 1850, the population of Britain doubled to close to 21 million people. By 1914, it was around 46 million—that of Germany also more than doubled (from 24.5 to 58.5 million), while that of France increased by 43 percent (from 29 to 41.5 million). Although population figures in eastern Europe are notoriously inaccurate, Hungary's figures jumped from around 11 million in 1850 to 18 million just before the First World War, while in Austria the population doubled from around 3.8 million to over 6 million. This put pressure on the countryside, where the demise of rural industries and repeated crop failures took a tremendous toll. Poverty meant peasants and landless laborers had little choice but to pack their belongings and leave—either to Europe's cities or to the new world.

The result was the largest out-migration in history, with some 46 million Europeans leaving the continent between 1846 and 1914. It was a huge rearrangement of European demography. Around 3.5 million people departed the Hapsburg Empire alone between 1876 and 1910, or about 8 percent of the population.[6] Droves of emigrants with families in tow crowded the railway stations, the hotels, and boarding houses in Europe's port cities. They shuffled through identity papers and bore the ordeal of emotional goodbyes on the piers in London and Liverpool, in Le Havre and Hamburg, in Rotterdam and Antwerp, in Marseille and Naples. They boarded jam-packed passenger ships and sailed away. The unprecedented spread of European people across the global—to the United States and to European colonial empires—had world-spanning significance. As the other option, the rural exodus resulted in a vast movement into Europe's cities where laborers could find work in factories or in domestic service and join the vast informal economy that allowed them to survive. Most often they were young men and women. Moving around was a way of life for them. They often formed a sub-proletariat, categorized as "aliens," who worked for the lowest wages. Hundreds of thousands of Irish escaping the potato famine moved to Glasgow, Liverpool, and London. Italians found work in the British factory towns and in the industrial areas of northern France and along the Rhone River from Marseille to Lyon. Floods of Polish peasants and workers found jobs in the Ruhr's industrial towns. There was a vast migration of rural peasants from the eastern areas of the German Empire to the west, especially to Berlin, to the Rhineland and Westphalia regions, and to the Ruhr coal and steel region. They formed their own ethnic communities in the towns where they settled, which allowed others to follow and gain a touchstone. Russians, especially Jewish workers and families living in the Pale of Settlement, moved westward to escape poverty and the brutality of frequent pogroms. People within the vast Hapsburg domains traveled long distances in search of work. The majority of foreigners in Vienna were from the Hapsburg Monarchy's Bohemian crown lands as well as from distant parts of the empire.

These migratory flows were always in a state of flux. People moved many times, to and from cities, in the search for a secure livelihood. They moved with greater frequency over longer distances than historians have previously imagined. The shift to an internationalized labor market meant that workers were traveling farther and across national borders. While total population figures provide important indications about the scale of urbanization, they tell us less about these turbulent streams of people between towns, and between towns and countryside. Seasonal and chain migration from villages and small towns to cities were vital to thousands of young and eager workers looking to improve their circumstance. This understanding of migration parallels rethinking about industrialization as a longer, diffuse process rather than a technology-driven revolution. The modern city was a dynamic, fluctuating environment tied to Europe's broader urban network and to the currents of migration and exchange. It is worth remembering that small settlements of 2,000 inhabitants, up to towns of 20,000 to 30,000 inhabitants formed a thick expanse across Europe. They were essential to these migratory flows. In 1871, two-thirds of the urban population of Germany—nearly ten million people—lived in towns with under 20,000 population.[7] Most urban dwellers still lived in small- and medium-size towns. They were nodes in a dynamic migratory web that was intensified by the arrival of the railroad, and indeed railroad construction itself created a pattern of temporary migration as workers found jobs laying track and rail sidings. The railroad collapsed time and space. What had taken workers and migrants weeks of travel to go from place to place now took no more than a few days. The boundaries between the urban and rural worlds melted away (Figure 11).

The railway became both the means and the symbol for this stunning flow of people and goods. Railway stations were glorious affairs—vast, sweeping sheds that embraced the possibilities of modern architecture. Cast-iron girders and iron joists were fitted together into colossal roof spans. The floors beneath were lined with train platforms and steaming locomotives, their iron tracks extending like octopus legs out into the city. Architecture and engineering together produced a modern technological aesthetic. The exterior facades of the stations were dressed in historicist styles that ennobled their function. When it was completed, the single-span arching roof of St. Pancras Station in London was the largest in the world. Its station front was adorned with the red brick Midlands Hotel in neogothic style. The Gare du Nord in Paris, opened in 1864, was a monumental structure in cast iron. Its grand facade featured allegorical statues of the train destinations. Keleti railway station in Budapest was among the most modern in Europe, with a majestic Beaux-Arts façade and triumphal arch.

The train station functioned as extraordinary architectural showpiece and grand public space. More than 22 million people left the British Isles for overseas between 1815 and 1914. In 1869, *Lloyd's Weekly Newspaper* reported the scene at St. Pancras, where

Figure 11 London Paddington station, antique photography-derived dot print illustration, 1895.

some 300 poor families from the slums of Whitechapel and Bethnal Green assembled on the platform to begin their voyage to Liverpool and then by steamship to Canada, where they would find new lives. "Grace was sung . . . and the walls resounded with the many voices now and then drowned by the shrill shriek of the railway engines. Hearty embraces, with 'God bless you,' preluded deep sobs and floods of tears, and then, suddenly, the train moved with a jerk from the station, as if to end a painful scene."[8] Traveling in Germany in 1886, Swiss journalist Victor Tissot arrived at the Cologne railway station "with its monumental atmosphere: the dining halls, the waiting areas, the ticket halls and baggage areas. There are scenes of immense gluttony to amuse an observer when several trains arrive at the same time . . . disgorging crowds of hungry voyagers who attack the buffets with their empty stomachs. . . . The English and the Russians are the most ardent at this feeding frenzy." For Tissot, "Cologne looks like a very prosperous city through which flows all the riches of the Rhine province, where production, factories, manufactures work without interruption, where the big cities, one would say, are strung together."[9]

The modern city was a perpetually shifting assemblage of peoples, traffic, and goods. The article "Passing Faces" in Charles Dickens's weekly magazine *Household Words* commented, "A walk through the streets of London will show us specimens of every human variety known. . . . Life, and all its boundless power of joy and suffering—this is the great picture book to be read in London streets." The Italian novelist Edmondo De Amicis arrived in Paris in 1878 at the Place de la Bastille with its "deafening clamor." The great square of the Bastille was "full of light, these thousand colors, the grand column of July, the trees, the rapid motion of the carriages and the crowd." Arriving on the Boulevard Beaumarchais, De Amicis is stunned by the "constant passing and repassing of carriages, great carts and wagons drawn by engines and high omnibuses, laden with people, bounding up and down on the unequal pavement, with a deafening noise."[10] The crowds and the accelerated rhythms of the city provoked a sharpened inquisitiveness. Wandering through the streets, merging into the crowds and observing people, movement, and behavior became a way of uncovering the modern condition. French poet Charles Baudelaire was the ultimate wanderer and urban observer, or *flâneur*. He gave voice to the world of bohemian Paris—young rebels and writers, living seemingly idle, free-spirited lives along the margins, yet capturing the modern condition with sharp insight. Baudelaire's prose poems captured the essence of the "huge city." He found the crowds "intoxicating. . . . The man who loves to lose himself in the crowd enjoys feverish delights."[11] But the sensations were enveloped in both bliss and despair. Sitting in a dazzling café, Baudelaire surveys "the blinding whiteness of its walls, the expanse of mirrors, the gold cornices and moldings." Yet the grim reality just below the glittering surface was reason for disquiet. Outside the window, he sees "a family of eyes," a ragged father with small boys, fascinated by the beauty of a place "where only people not like us can go." Baudelaire is touched and "even a little ashamed of our glasses and decanters, too big for our thirst."[12]

Baudelaire's vignettes revealed that the modern city was only knowable as a series of fragments, and even these were often contradictory and incoherent. There was deep ambivalence about an atmosphere in which an individual was tossed about like a leaf in the wind, drifting through a kaleidoscope of sensations and images. Even in the 1830s, French novelist Honoré de Balzac insisted that in Paris "you have to plunge into this mass of people like a cannonball." In Paris "everything smokes, everything glows, everything burns, everything boils, everything ignites, evaporates, dims, rekindles, sparkles, crackles, and is consumed."[13] It was a description that also fit London and any big European city of the nineteenth century. German sociologist Georg Simmel was the first to observe the city as a psychic as well physical experience. From his vantage point in Berlin, it was the tempo and complexity of the big city that affected mentality and distinguished it from small town life. The big city offered personal freedom. But the stimuli and intensity of its environment shaped a blasé attitude as a mechanism of defense. Simmel understood modernity as a cultural system based on an advanced capitalist economy that created a false consciousness of stability and order. For Simmel, its most damaging impact was this illusion that crippled the spirit. Behind it lay a "relentless matter-of-factness, and its rationally calculated economic egoism." It reduced the individual to "a single cog as over against the vast overwhelming organization of things and forces which gradually take out of his hands everything connected with progress, spirituality and value." For Simmel money and exchange took the place of everything. The metropolis as the seat of commerce was the surest sign of this truth. Wealth, rather than privilege, was the key to social and political power. Affluence was a testament to individual merit and talent. There were a host of opportunities for enrichment and a growing bourgeois class with lots of money to spend.

New models of the marketplace and a new material culture defined social relations. The good life was centered around commodities and the infinite desires of the prosperous middle classes. The ships dropping anchor at the wharves, their holds laden with stuff from around the world, made the possibilities of material well-being into an extravaganza, and it was linked inextricably to imperialism. Foreign trade grew exponentially, with Britain leading the way. Cities became the foremost spectacle of global consumption. Loaded on to railway cars that dramatically cut the cost of transport, the merchandise chugged out from Europe's great ports to towns across the continent. The flood of consumer goods and the possibility of owning everyday luxuries swelled as the price plummeted. Entirely new habits and comforts were shaped around devouring the global marketplace in commodities. It depended on the exercise of economic and military power in distant parts of the globe. All sorts of things, gadgets, and novelties played an increasingly prominent role in everyday urban lives—enameled porcelains, musical instruments, mirrors and clocks, books and jewelry, furniture, silverware and linens, mechanical toys, clothing, exotic collectables, and memorabilia. They became "necessary" signs of status. The canons of taste were dictated by buying, collecting, and displaying objects. Even the middling and working classes could claim some refinement and social footing by proudly displaying their possessions. Exotic goods filtered down through the urban system, from large cities to towns and villages.

Consumerism was carved into the city's topography. Much like the reorganization of production in the factory setting, the daring sites of shopping tied cities to wage labor and to an expanding global economy. Old commercial forms were surprising resilient and adapted to the new market dynamics. Alongside them were wondrous new public markets, trade fairs and international expositions, shopping galleries, and department stores. They were virtuoso performances of commodity culture where citizens learned to be consumers. The displays of abundance, the mesmerizing architecture and scale transfixed shoppers and bystanders alike. They were dream machines that made it possible to imagine a society of plentiful and cheap goods, an ever-changing universe of marvels and merchandise. London and Paris stood at the pinnacle of this new realm of material glitz. They were charismatic and glamorous, the great shopping meccas, and the largest centers of consumption in mid-nineteenth century Europe. The starstruck descriptions of both places were countless. Social reformer Flora Tristin visited the "monster city" of London in the 1840s and was enraptured: "London is superb! Its broad streets stretch to infinity; its shops are resplendent with every masterpiece that human ingenuity can devise; its multitudes of men and women pass ceaselessly to and fro. To see all this for the first time is an intoxicating experience."[14] Paris was the City of Light. The gas lamps of its boulevards made the city an intoxicating fairyland and "distributive centre of all the flitting fancies of France." On the boulevards, "one can say everything, hear everything, and imagine everything." The Paris department stores were a glamorous theater of abundance. In French literary great Emile Zola's 1883 novel *The Ladies Paradise*, the young Denise is seduced by the glow of the gas burners at the department store: "In the great metropolis, dark and silent under the rain, in this Paris of which she knew nothing, it [department store] was burning like a beacon, it alone seemed to be the light and life of the city."[15]

The surface of the city was commercialized. The pleasure of "just looking" was heightened by the fantasy architecture of glass and iron used to fashion the market halls, the arcades, and department stores. By mid-century, the availability of cheap plate glass along with gas lighting made possible the modern shop-front, and added window-shopping to pedestrian pleasures, especially on Regent and Oxford Streets in London, the Boulevard des Italiens in Paris, along the Leipzigerstrassse in Berlin and the Kartner Ring in Vienna. Strollers on the boulevards gaped at the bounty of things shimmering inside the shop windows. Cities came to be viewed as a stage set for commercial theater. The walls of buildings were plastered with advertisements and billboards. So were the inside and outside of omnibuses. The new commercial signage used common national languages rather than local dialects. Pedestrians sidestepped advertising carts and sandwich boards on the sidewalks. By the end of the century, "magic lanterns" projected dreamlike advertising images onto building walls. Nelson's Column in Trafalger Square, the National Gallery in London, eventually the Eiffel Tower were all used for advertising.

London was the primate city of the nineteenth century and the epicenter for the whole elaborate structure of global trade. London was gigantic. Its scale far outdistanced any other place in Europe, and the extravagant spectacle of London life was driven by empire down to its core. It was the "the clearing-house of the world" and the capital of an empire that stretched from Canada across to Hong Kong. The public buildings and monuments of The City and Westminster were a tableau of British world power. Towering over the Thames Embankment was Cleopatra's Needle with two large sphinxes. A new Foreign Office was control center for London's vast commercial and territorial realm. It included the India Office with its storehouse of information acquired over a century of British rule. London's great imperial institutions sent out explorers on colonial expeditions. The Royal Geographic Society supported the research of Charles Darwin. The British Museum was amassing such a collection (including the Rosetta Stone and Assyrian cuneiform tablets as well as the decorative frieze from the Parthenon) that it moved to an entirely new building. Most imposing was Trafalgar Square, which was opened in 1844 and presented a lineup of marble military heroes, especially Admiral Horatio Nelson. The pomp and circumstance of empire was celebrated in military parades and pageants. It was the subject of innumerable music hall revues. Missionaries of various denominations boarded ships in London for their colonial duties, as did merchants and traders searching for profits, and engineers to oversee the construction of roads, railways, and bridges throughout the empire. Retinues of Indian seamen, government officials, businessmen, and students traveled through or settled in London, as did contingents of Chinese. Arthur Conan Doyle called London the "great cesspool into which all the loungers and idlers of the Empire are irresistibly drained" (Figure 12).

The City (or as it was known the "Square Mile") morphed into the locus of dominion for the British Empire. The fortress complex of the Bank of England and the Royal Stock Exchange dwarfed the maze of lanes and alleyways around Threadneedle Street. They

Figure 12 Traffic outside the Bank of England and the Royal Exchange in the City of London, 1896.

were the commercial pivot, the governing bodies for the monetary system and financial flows that greased British hegemony and free-market capitalism. The nineteenth century worshiped at the altar of free trade. It was the secret of British prosperity. Whatever qualms were raised about the effect of capitalist market forces on society, they did little to bend loyalty to free exchange and economic progress. The entire imperial apparatus rested on the stability of the Bank of England, which was dependent on its gold reserves. In 1849, a fortune in California gold and Mexican dollars arrived by train and was paraded in overflowing wagons through the streets of The City to the waiting vaults of the Bank.[16] Bills of exchange and credit notes, securities and bonds, insurance underwriting, contracts created a mountain of paper that linked The City to the factories of London, Manchester, Glasgow, Birmingham, and then to a vast global dominion. Money from The City flowed into overseas investments, railways everywhere in Europe, and into ships and mines. Credit was easy. Speculation on the stock market became a new avenue to wealth. Everyone with spare cash invested. Their money flowed like water through The City's coffers.

While there were still people living in The City in the early nineteenth century, it quickly converted into a strapping business precinct. A tidal flow of men hurried to their jobs every morning, and then commuted home at the end of the workday. Platoons of clerks hunched at their desks carried out the daily chore of managing the London money market, from brokers and insurers to contractors and remitters. The square in front of the Royal Exchange was a scene of endless congestion with carriages, wagons, and staffs scrambling to their schedules. Warehouses of every size were squeezed into the City. They were stuffed with commodities and where haggling over every imaginable global product took place, from tea and coffee to textiles and furs. Banking dynasties, such as the Rothchilds and Barings, provincial, joint-stock, and overseas banks, well over a hundred insurance companies all set up lavish headquarters in the City.[17] Their fortunes were mind-boggling. Shipbrokers, businessmen, merchants, and financiers circled like vultures around them, all with the goal of making money. The feverish ambitions, the cycles of speculative boom-and-bust, the frenetic pace on the streets, in taverns and shops, made Britain's global marketplace into a daily urban pageant. The whole tempo of the city's life rushed at breakneck speed.

Although London's cityscape was packed with imperial monuments, the greatest testament to the British Empire was the Docklands. It was one of the sites that English people and foreign visitors most wanted to see. It contained more wealth and more stuff vital to Britain and its empire than any other place. The imagery of the Docklands was relentlessly upbeat. According to the Baedeker Guide, "Nothing will convey to the stranger a better idea of the vast activity and stupendous wealth of London than a visit to the warehouses, filled to overflowing with interminable stores of every kind of foreign and colonial product." Over the course of the nineteenth century, the docks devoured the riversides of the East End. The West India Docks opened in 1802 on the Isle of Dogs, followed quickly by the Surrey Docks, and the London and East India Docks. Then the St. Katharine and Millwall docks filled in what was left along the Thames. The insatiable demand for more docks, more wharves, more warehouses moved activity further east with the Royal Victoria and Royal Albert docks. Every available bend in the river was put to use. Thousands of ships, boats, and wherries plied the Thames River from Woolwich all the way to the "Pool" at London Bridge. In 1860 alone, some 30,000 vessels of every size and kind entered the port with over 7 million tons of cargo.[18] The river traffic was as dense as that along London's streets.

Britain followed an open-door, consumer-friendly imperial policy. Imports rose exponentially over the course of the nineteenth century. The value of the silks and tea from China was enormous. Raw cotton, indigo, linseed, and flax seed topped imports from India. Exotic spices from Southeast Asia and coffee from British Ceylon were disgorged onto the wharves. Tallow, flax, hemp, timber, and corn came from Russia, wine from France. Soap, candles, bread, margarine, marmalade, rubber, rain jackets, leather shoes, inks, dyes, paints, fertilizers, and wooden furniture were hauled into warehouses. Once emptied, the ships were loaded up again with British goods—cotton and woolen cloth, iron and lead, copper and steel, manufactures, glass and cutlery—to be sent out to the world. On this flow of commodities, a million or more workers depended for their livelihood.

At the capital of the far-flung British Empire, London's economy was largely centered around service industries, which employed nearly 60 percent of the city's workforce by the end of the nineteenth century. But the Docklands were the city's industrial heartland. The wharves were jammed with warehouses, finishing and manufacturing businesses, and trade offices. Around them clustered iron foundries, machinery workshops, coopers' yards, shipbuilding yards and collieries, coke, coal and gasworks, distilling operations, and chemical industries. The Isle of Dogs was a hodgepodge of steam factories, chemicals, soaps, rubber, dye, rope-making, sack-making, tin-canister making workshops. Sandwiched between the workshops and warehouses lay the notorious "rookeries," from which gorged each day the cheap labor on which London and its empire depended. The notorious slums of the East End existed in tandem with London's imperial institutions. Both were tightly intertwined with the processes of globalization and the capital accumulation by some sectors of society, and the dispossession of others. The Docklands were crawling with petty dealers fencing contraband swiped from the wharves and warehouses. Police made the rounds searching for thieves and smugglers. It was at the Docklands that Londoners could experience their global supremacy and their anxieties about its impact on the city. Socialist writer Margaret Harkness captured the foreignness in her 1889 novel *In Darkest London:*

> Whitechapel Road is "the most cosmopolitan place in London . . . a grinning Hottentot elbows his way through a crowd of long-eyed Jewesses. An Algerian merchant walks arm-in-arm with a native of Calcutta. A little Italian plays pitch-and-toss with a small Russian. A Polish Jew enjoys sauerkraut with a German Gentile. And among the foreigner lounges the East End loafer, monarch of all he surveys . . . it is amusing to see his British air of superiority. He is looked upon as scum by his own nation . . . he has a mind, although he does his best to destroy it by narcotics and stimulants."[19]

London's Docklands were at the pinnacle of the global supply chain. Alongside it, a string of ports along Europe's coastlines served as gateways to the whirligig of global trade. Steam packet ships and the opening of the Suez Canal (1869) helped diversify trade in luxury merchandise and perishable foodstuffs. The city of Liverpool as well as Birmingham imported goods well beyond the raw cotton headed for the textile factories. Liverpool's role in the import of cotton from India was pivotal. But the city's commodity traders and financiers also carried on trade with the United States, Asia, Argentina, Africa, and Australia, and with the Mediterranean ports. By the end of the nineteenth century, Liverpool's "gentlemanly capitalists" had diversified the import trade and made the city into a world entrepôt. It was overtaking London's Docklands in cargo. Imported tea and spices became major commodities. Import processing, especially in glass, chemicals, and sugar refining, became important industries. The city's extensive overseas connections were evident in the number of people from across the British Empire that drifted through the city, especially sailors. Liverpool's global claims were celebrated at the International Exhibition of Navigation, Travelling, Commerce and Manufacture in 1886. Opened by Queen Victoria, it commemorated the merchant fleets that "are living links which bind Britain to her Indian empire and to her colonies."[20] Queen Victoria's Diamond Jubilee in 1897 was celebrated in Liverpool with a four-mile long maritime display of ships and a procession of some 15,000 people to St. George's Hall, where jubilant crowds awaited the ceremonies.[21]

The opening of the Suez Canal also gave the Dutch ports of Amsterdam and Rotterdam a faster route to the Dutch Indies. Both cities had long served as key European entrepôts. Ships steamed into Amsterdam where warehouses were packed with goods from the Dutch colonies in Southeast Asia, while Rotterdam concentrated in trade with the Americas and Africa. Hamburg and Antwerp were central Europe's main gateways for global freight. Their ports boomed, especially trade with German colonies in East Africa and with South America. Hamburg's trade was estimated to be more than 50 million pounds sterling annually and ran the gamut from seal skins to musical instruments. The city's Speicherstadt district, built from 1883, was jammed with coffee and teas, cocoa and spices. The exotic smells wafted over the brick warehouses jutting up on timber piles. Lighters throttled along a maze of canals and dispatched the booty directly from their holds. The opening of the Kaiser Wilhelm (Kiel) Canal in 1895 connected the Baltic and North seas and became a major shipping lane. The ports of Königsberg and Stettin on the Baltic coast were connected by rail to Berlin and to Silesia and Galicia. Their docks were weighed down with imported iron ore, chemicals, petroleum, and coal. Marseille was the home port of France's largest shipping company, the Messageries Maritime, that carried goods and passengers across the French Empire. Like port cities across Europe, much of its workforce were foreigners. They were a transitory floating population packed into slum areas and connected in the public mind with the pilfering and petty crime that typified harbor life.[22] The construction of new port facilities at La Joliette assured Marseille's role as the biggest port on the Mediterranean.

The "Imperial Free City" of Trieste on the Adriatic coast was developed as the Hapsburg Empire's commercial port. Already by 1800, a full one-third of the empire's exports passed through Trieste. Then from the 1850s, the arrival of the railway and the opening of the Suez Canal made Trieste into a major gateway to the Middle East and Asia. By the end of the century, it was second only to Marseille in Mediterranean trade. With around 200,000 inhabitants, the city's pastel buildings hugged the harbor and looked out over the blue waters of the gulf. It was the fourth largest city in the Hapsburg Empire, after Vienna, Budapest, and Prague, yet suffered from an appalling lack of clean water or a proper sewage system.[23] Nonetheless, it was a polyglot world and the scene of linguistic scrabble typical of port cities. Clustering together at taverns and cafés, listening to news and gossip, pooling information were the taproots of its booming commerce. The city's Jewish, Greek Orthodox, and Serbian merchants enjoyed civil and economic rights akin to their Catholic counterparts. The extension of these privileges was a testament to their commercial skills. Religious tolerance and making money were the mantras of Trieste.

Together, the city's elites controlled the stock exchange, banking houses, and insurance companies that connected central Europe to a global trade network. Trieste was the port of entry for Egyptian cotton and for raw materials, which were then transported to the textile mills in Vienna, Łódź, and the Bohemian industrial centers. The city's insurance carriers had agencies throughout Europe as well as in Bombay, Shanghai, and Hong Kong. The Austrian Lloyd Shipping Company, which was the largest shipping company in the Hapsburg Empire, was first formed in the coffee houses of Trieste. On its own, the Lloyd Company made the city one of the ten largest ports in the world.[24] Its steamships shuttled goods, passengers, and information between Trieste and Marseille, Salonica and the ports of Constantinople, Port Said, and the Far East. This kind of global connectivity gave Trieste a singular character and made it the center for an emerging Adriatic regional identity as well as Italian irredentism. Local loyalties were overlapping. It was the untidiness, the refusal to tie oneself to a single identity, the opportunistic openness of Trieste that gave it such cosmopolitan appeal. The inhabitants were as much attached to the city as they were to any explicit Hapsburg, Italian, or south Slavic interests.

The crown lands of the Hapsburg Empire were dotted with provincial capitals, commercial centers, and garrison towns woven along a thick network of roads and railway lines. The Hapsburg Empire had among the largest and best-used railway systems in Europe. Thousands of kilometers of new roads and bridges were constructed by the Hapsburg state and by local governments. This connective tissue opened even local towns to global influences. They were in every way a part of the world. Tons of goods and thousands of passengers regularly trekked by rail and road through the Hapsburg territories. This traffic could be witnessed in Breslau (Wrocław) in Upper Silesia, where colonial wares such as ivory, tea, sugar, and chocolate tempted consumers ambling through the city's shops. In another indication of how widespread global commodities were, traveler Johann Georg Kohl visited the town of Stanislavov (Stanislau/Stanisławów) in eastern Galicia, on "the borders of civilized Europe" in 1859. He found the fancy shops "plentifully fitted out with the pretty toys of Vienna. . . . The apothecaries' shops were orderly and good, and the coffee-houses splendid."[25] Kiev (Kyiv) in the Ukraine drew a mix of venture capitalists investing in the city's sugar refining industry. The city acquired a reputation as the Russian Empire's capitalist Wild West. Its Jewish sugar barons depended on the banks, commodity exchanges, the regional fairs, and markets[26] that made Kiev into a thriving entrepôt.

The world expositions were born simultaneously with this global cornucopia and were its greatest showcase. They were spellbinding theater without precedence in the city. The idea of a large-scale exposition evolved slowly as a cultural phenomenon for almost a century before the first event identifiable as an international "world's fair" actually took place—Britain's legendary 1851 Exhibition in the Crystal Palace. In tandem with the industrial revolution, institutions formed in Britain and France with the specific aim of promoting the tantalizing new machine-made goods. The exhibition was a device for boosting trade, for publicizing the new technologies, and for educating the public about the benefits of consumerism. Ten French national exhibitions of industry were held in Paris between 1797 and 1849, each one increasing in size and scope. The Parisian successes encouraged other French cities to stage their own trade expositions in the 1830s and 1840s. The most impressive were held in Nantes, Lille, Bordeaux, Toulouse, and Dijon. They became a regular feature of the commercial calendar and participation in them quickly became essential to business. The British also held a series of early "exhibitions of art and industry." The Mechanics Institutes in Manchester and in London launched small-scale exhibits of industry from the 1830s. The Anti-Corn Law

League held a massive bazaar in London's Covent Garden Theater in 1845 that featured a spectacular display of goods. The theater's iron and glass structure was decorated in gothic regalia that the *Illustrated London News* dubbed the "cathedral of modern commerce."[27] There were similar industrial and trade exhibitions in the 1820s and 1830s in the cities of Brussels, Munich, Ghent, Stockholm, Haarlem, Dublin, Madrid, Moscow, and St. Petersburg. An All-German Exhibition was held in Berlin in 1844. The geographic extent and frequency of these shows marked them as fundamental to industrialization and the modern material age (Figure 13).

By far the largest and most spectacular of the events was the Great Exhibition of the Works of Industry of all Nations held from May to October 1851 in the Crystal Palace in London's Hyde Park. Some 14,000 exhibitors laid out a profusion of marvelous technologies and goods. After solemnly inaugurating the exhibition, Queen Victoria summed up the buoyant mood: "We are capable of doing anything." The exhibits were a pantheon to the astonishing scale and diversity of British manufacturing and its colonial possessions. The sentiments it aroused, from the Queen herself all the way down to the over 6 million people who visited it, were deeply religious, feelings of awe that God could inspire mankind to make such extraordinary things. Fully one-fifth of the British population visited London during the exhibition, many of them availing themselves of the travel packages offered by new travel agencies and taking the train for the first time. Train excursions brought at least 750,000 people from the north of England just to see the pageant of human genius. Inside was a phantasmagoria of objects. Textile

Figure 13 Great Exhibition of 1851 held in Hyde Park.

machines, steam engines and printing presses, early auto-carriages, and bicycles excited fairgoers' curiosity. Manufactured goods of every kind were laid out for inspection. The exhibit was presented as a tribute to global commerce and the world order of free trade. Spectators ogled over exotic luxuries and jewels from India, and sumptuous porcelains and enamels, sculptures and art works from around the globe. They huddled around the famous Koh-i-Noor diamond. Embroidered work in gold and silver, cashmere scarves, silks and dyed cottons, musical instruments and mechanical toys, cutlery and tools, decorative furniture, perfumes, and native products from across the British Empire tempted would-be consumers. It was a gigantic commodity market.

The exhibition was billed as a "palace for the people" and offered a chance for all classes of British society to intermingle. Reduced fee one-shilling days were set up so the working classes could attend. They were dubbed "shilling people." Although the organizers argued there was nothing to fear from the solid British working classes, many were anxious about the potential danger of the large crowds and the specter of workers and farmers stumbling through the glittering exhibits. Extra constables were at the ready on shilling days in case of bad behavior. The British media had a field day with the Great Exhibition and recounted the scene in a flood of magazines and newspaper articles. If the exhibition showed the British they were the most ingenious and richest people in the world, the *Illustrated London News* and *Punch Magazine* still depicted working-class families eyeing the displays as either "vulgar and ignorant" or "well-behaved and admiring." Along with the fantastic riches from Britain's colonies came native "specimens" in exotic costumes. Thomas Onwhyn's famously entertaining *Mr. and Mrs. Brown's Visit to See the Grand Exhibition of All Nations* illustrated a hapless British family "frightened out of their wits" by exotic Hottentots and Russian Cossacks.[28] Despite the exhibition's mantra of good will, the spectacles of social division, racism, and fear of foreigners were as much on display as the exhibits themselves.

The Great Exhibition of 1851 had an extraordinary influence on the development of London and on cities in general. The building itself was dubbed "The Crystal Palace" by *Punch Magazine*. Joseph Paxton (the head gardener to the Duke of Devonshire and active in railroad station design) conjured up the exhibition hall as a giant glass house framed by cast-iron columns. Piecing together the 300,000 individual panes of plate glass and iron girders to create a building structure of this scale was an entirely new venture. The building included newly designed rain gutters, a new kind of ventilation system, window screens to temper light, and an anti-slip wooden plank floor. It was built in seventeen weeks and covered nineteen acres of ground. The scale was so grand that it defied the imagination. The building was acclaimed enthusiastically as a dream world, a magical place. It seemed spectral and infinite—an immediate point of orientation for what it meant to be modern. Illustrations and early photographs of the building swept through Europe. The Crystal Palace became an instant icon and the site tourists to London wanted to see first. It was the city's most cosmopolitan zone, filled with people from all over the world. They adopted it immediately as a symbol of England's world vision and leadership, even if England's own ruling classes haughtily spurned it.

The Crystal Palace unleashed a frenzy of industrial exhibitions in cities throughout Europe. Any place wagering their importance on the European and world stage outdid themselves with multiple exhibitions in an ongoing extravaganza of local ingenuity and material wealth. Hundreds of exhibitions took place. Millions of people went to see them. Already in 1852, Breslau hosted its first exhibition of Silesian Industry. Rising on slopes above the Danube River, the city of Breslau was the capital of Silesia and one of central Europe's most important commercial cities. It was located at the junction of two historic trade routes, the north-south Amber Road and the east-west Via Regia (or Royal highway). Most of its 42,000 residents were German. But Breslau was symptomatic of east central Europe's cosmopolitan whirlwind. Most of the population were practicing polyglots and bantered back-and-forth between Hungarian in imperial communication, German for commerce, and Slovak for everyday conversation. By the 1840s, it already had three railway stations with connections to Berlin, Budapest, Dresden, Vienna, and Kraków. Goods poured into the city. Dealers bartered over goods and machinery at four annual blockbuster commercial fairs. Convoys arrived from the east as far as Russia, while merchandise flowed in from the west and from the Baltic ports. The 1852 Breslau Exhibition flaunted civic pride and local patriotism. It was held in an iron and glass gallery in imitation of the Crystal Palace, with a fountain of perfumed water at its center and the flags of Silesia waving from the girders. Visitors strolled through displays of Silesia's manufactures—ironwork, linens, and wool products—and luxury goods from porcelain and jewelry to perfumes.[29]

In 1854, it was Munich's turn, with an exhibition of the First General German Industrial Exhibition held in the massive Glaspalast. The iron and glass structure was one of the largest in Europe. Some 100,000 people attended its inauguration. But exposition fatigue was already setting in. By 1876, a jaded English journalist sent to report on yet another Munich event at the Glaspalast arrived, "Bored by monster shows, and more than skeptical as to the good to be got out of them."[30] But that did not stop the parade. The years between 1875 and 1914 were a golden age of exhibitions, many of them major events. Glasgow, for example, had a particular penchant for this kind of extravaganza with major exhibitions in 1847, 1865, 1886–87, and 1890–91, all of them showcasing the "imperial city." Vienna decked out Prater Park in 1873 in a gargantuan exhibition on trade and industry, while Antwerp and Brussels held theirs in the 1880s. Paris held three blockbuster industrial exhibitions by 1900. Some type of "exhibition of industry and the arts" took place every year as cities across Europe indulged in a competitive orgy for trade and tourism. Signature cast iron and glass exhibition halls appeared in cities all the way to Odessa and St. Petersburg. Winning the hearts and minds of the crowds meant spectacular displays and feats of scientific and technological wizardry.

If the exhibition circuit was any suggestion, material life improved profoundly over the course of the nineteenth century. Powerful bankers and financiers had a huge stake in promoting consumer tastes and the demand for products reliant on overseas possessions. This included the food that city dwellers ate and the quality of their nutrition and daily diets. They could increasingly depend on global markets and far-flung distribution networks to satisfy their insatiable demand for food: not just daily foodstuffs such as cereals and vegetables but commodities that had once been considered luxuries only the rich could afford. Railways and steamships outfitted with "cool chambers" brought products from across the globe. Railroad stations added "freight stations" to their infrastructure. The transportation revolution meant imported food was now comparatively cheap. The variety was staggering. Meat, fish, seasonal fruits and vegetables of every kind, dairy products, coffee and tea were enjoyed at regular meals. Even the working classes were spending less of their incomes on food and eating better. Fewer and fewer people relied on allotment gardens and instead purchased food with their weekly wages. Urban residents became taste consumers and food provisioning big business. The local market farms surrounding cities scaled up in response to mass demand. Paris had some 1,800 market gardens employing 9,000 gardeners, much of it within the city walls. London was the biggest demand center in the world and the largest food importer. Food processing was one of its biggest industries. Corn and flour mills, sugar refineries, distilling and breweries, food processing plants, all run by steam, employed thousands.

With the loosening of guild privileges and the advent of free trade, shopkeepers selling foodstuffs and colonial products in corner groceries and specialty shops became a regular part of the street scene. This was not just the case in major cities, but in smaller commercial and industrial towns as well. Cookshops and taverns where meals could be bought cheaply sprung up even in poor districts. For new arrivals from the countryside and craftsmen in declining trades, for the unemployed, setting up shop selling foods for fixed prices, or stands at weekly street markets, peddling and hawking food on the streets were ways to make money.[31] Street traders and peddlers were among the most recognizable fixtures of the urban scene. Their corners and spots, their pitches, the goods and services they offered were integral to daily life in laboring communities. Flora Tristin found her way to London's St. Giles neighborhood "full of shops displaying worn-out shoes, old clothes and rags; tinsmiths and dealers of bric-à-bric . . . nearly all the decrepit old hovels in this quarter serve as shops." In the Jewish quarter on Petticoat Lane

> the crowd is so dense that you can hardly move . . . everybody is constantly on the move—men, women and children. . . . They all speak at once, one to vaunt the goods he wants to sell, the other to denigrate the goods he wants to buy, so what with all the shouting, arguments and coarse insults, you cannot hear yourself speak.

Then on Field Lane, "there is absolutely nothing to be seen but dealers in second-hand silk handkerchiefs . . . prostitutes, children, and rogues of every age and condition come to sell their handkerchiefs."[32] The informal market around Whitecross Street on the periphery of London grew to between 150 and 200 stalls and was open late into the night on Saturdays when working-class families did their buying. Crowds of people haggled over heaps of fruits and vegetables, meats, and fish. They perused household goods and listened skeptically as vendors extolled their value. The social and material dealings carried on by this unofficial street trading remained outside the emerging rhythms of capitalist transactions.[33] It represented a populist sociability grounded in neighborhood and quotidian public territory. Street mongers were considered troublemakers and a vulgar nuisance by the authorities. Despite harsh restrictions on street selling and attempts to eradicate illegal street markets, thousands of costermongers worked the streets in an informal economy essential to the working classes and poor.

Even the authorized open-air markets were overwhelmed, unable to keep up with demand. Large cities increased the number of markets and market days. Hundreds of horse-drawn wagons from surrounding villages rumbled into town at night and wound their way to the wholesale terminals in big cities. In London, wagons packed with fruit and vegetables were offloaded at the wholesale market at Covent Garden, fish at the market at Billingsgate. Squawking poultry went to Leadenhall Market while herds of bellowing cattle and sheep wound their way to Copenhagen Fields and Smithfield market. The commotion went on into the wee hours. Thousands of animals were driven by screeching handlers through the streets to waiting slaughterhouses. Covent Garden was crammed with carts and wagons, and rickety stalls. Mounds of vegetables were heaped up in barrels and baskets. Vendors and peddlers battled for space, hawking their goods, out-shouting competitors. There were frequent brawls. The crowds jostled through the confusion cheek by jowl, followed by the shrill cries of costermongers. Prostitutes wandered through the throngs, soliciting customers. At night, the square transfigured into London's theater and sex trade district (Figure 14).

The sheer size of London's food provisioning system made these scenes spectacular. At different scales, they were repeated across Europe. Lithographs and early photographs capture the crush of men and women amid butchers hauling carcasses, the crates and heaps of produce, sidestepping cattle and horses, and the poor rifling through leftovers. The streets of all the major cities rang with a quasi-nomadic, informal economy. Thousands of street merchants sold everything imaginable, offered every imaginable service. If all else failed, the poor hunted the streets for caste-offs and dredged river edges for garbage—all of which they sold one way or another. Tumultuous crowds from every walk of life wound their way through the labyrinth of selling. The markets were a bonanza for thieves. Criminal elements operated openly. Young boys wandered through unsuspecting crowds, grabbing what they could. Gangs extorted market vendors, demanded squeeze, and purloined prized goods to be sold at outrageous prices on the black market.

Ironically, in an age when free-market capitalism was the order of the day, consumerism became one of the most systematized and regulated of urban activities. The wild atmosphere in street markets and places like London's Covent Garden and Les Halles in Paris made them frightening and offensive and an immediate target for reformers. For moral crusaders, the markets were filled with unscrupulous traders and chaotic mobs of people. The congestion made the streets impassable. The markets were spaces of transgression and immorality, and breeding grounds for disease. A London medical reformer described the "bladder blowers" and "horse slaughterers" of Smithfield market as depraved. He angrily pointed his finger at one yard that was "the receptacle of the offal of the neighborhood; while under the shadow of its mountainous heaps, may at night be discovered half-savage men and women, carousing and blaspheming around

Figure 14 Covent Garden Market, London.

cauldrons teeming with unblessed food."[34] Women merchants were perennially accused of prostitution. The carnivalesque feel of the open-air markets and the rough language and behavior were rebuked as shocking and barbaric.

Despite these harrowing descriptions, open-air markets were a commonplace site for cultural interaction and exchange. People from all backgrounds and social classes bought, sold, and ate food. All levels of society from bourgeois to artisans and laborers frequented, worked, and lived around the markets. They were an integral part of the urban fabric. Business went on day and night and took on its own idiosyncratic habits and mores. This vast network did not disappear, despite the crusades against it. It adapted to the rhythms of modernity and continued to provide jobs and essential goods at the level of everyday life. If anything, the influence of open-air markets expanded. Peddlers and hawkers, petty merchants spread out to the working-class neighborhoods on the urban peripheries. They broadened the range of cheap domestic goods available outside the city limits and beyond the scrutiny of police and do-gooders.

Nevertheless, urban reformers insisted that improved, regulated market facilities would increase the food supply, improve hygiene, and lead to higher morals and proper public behavior. Where they could, they demanded an enclosed, rationalized market space. The market hall itself was not an innovative concept. Elaborate grain and cloth halls were long-established urban institutions. By the eighteenth century, covered food halls graced many a European city. What was new was their scale and the organizational and administrative monitoring that went with it. The covered, enclosed market hall provided a clean, meticulously ordered environment for food provisioning. It was accompanied by municipal regulations on opening hours, stalls and vendor licenses, prices, weights and measures. Lighting and ventilation were improved. Police and market guards strolled through the crowds with an eye out for crooks. In the minds of reformers, this kind of monitoring protected respectable women as well as buyers and sellers from the offensive behavior of the lower classes and the unruliness of the street. It minimized the risks of violence and popular unrest. The market hall taught people new rules of acceptable behavior and correct "taste" in purchases.

By mid-century the palatial market hall had become one of the most important public buildings in the city.[35] They were unveiled across Europe, often with elaborate public ceremonies. The new market halls were spectacular spaces, resplendent in iron and glass. Along with the innovations in selling went an entirely new scale. Many of them were soaring structures with architectural flourishes in eclectic historicist styles. Glasgow was among the first to create an enclosed walled space, known as the bazaar, that was completely severed from the street. The cities of Liverpool and Birmingham, Leeds, Newcastle and Aberdeen all built immense market halls. Liverpool's iron and glass St. John's Market on Saint Charlotte's Street was gas-lite and divided into "shopping avenues" according to food types. It, along with Birkenhead's gigantic market hall, inaugurated an entirely new shopping experience. In London, the Smithfield Meat Market, Billingsgate Fish Market, and Leadenhall Market were all rebuilt and connected to the railway.

In Paris, local markets and food shops popped up everywhere as the city's population exploded. Covered food halls already existed on the city's Right Bank at the place d'Aligre and on the Left Bank in the Saint Germain district. The construction of the city's central food market, or Les Halles Centrales, began in 1853 as part of Baron Haussmann's modernization of Paris (see Chapter 5). It was designed by Victor Baltard and vastly expanded the wholesale food trade. Located on the Right Bank close to the Seine River, Les Halles consisted of ten iron-strutted market halls aligned in two rows. They were connected by glass-paneled passageways and organized according to food groups. The pavilion complex was the largest covered market in the world when it was built and a model imitated throughout Europe (Figure 15). By 1885, Berlin had twenty markets, the largest one with 1,300 stalls. The city council in Budapest established a network of six market halls throughout the city. The Great Market Hall along the Danube River in Budapest was a monumental structure. Designed by noted Hungarian architect Samu Pecz, its filigreed iron-trussed interior was set off with an exterior skin of brick and tile in flamboyant neogothic style.

Figure 15 Les Halles, the Central Market of Paris.

The great food markets of London and Paris, and those of big cities elsewhere in Europe such as Berlin and Budapest, were eagerly described by contemporary observers. The spectacle of Les Halles was portrayed by Emile Zola in his 1873 *Le Ventre de Paris* (The Belly of Paris), which takes place in Baltard's pavilions and the surrounding streets. It is these stereotypic images of the *charcutiers*, the *poissonnières*, the *marchands de volailles*, the muscular *forts* unloading the wagons, the human tumult of Les Halles, its materiality and quotidian rhetoric that were knitted into the fabric of urban memory. But the markets were more than just the visual phantasmagoria of laborers at their posts. Saturday night at the markets was a lively scene of shopping and free entertainment. Families marched up and down the aisles with their children, young couples and single people strolled the market in a flirtatious parade. They were introduced to a wide range of new products and gadgets. It was a place to shop and search for bargains, to haggle with traders and share gossip, to see and be seen. The market was one of the city's principal promenades, one shared by a cross section of urban dwellers from bourgeois couples to working-class folk and the inevitable tourists, all out to experience the urban parade. The gas lanterns, gilded girders and glass, the fountains and decorative stalls, the cornucopia of foods and household goods made the market hall among the most lavish and festive places in the city.[36]

London and Paris were the great retail meccas, with shoppers and tourists bedazzled by their glitz and glamour. They were the theaters of an increasingly commercialized urban society. Elegant districts such as the West End and Mayfair in London, the Palais Royale and Boulevard des Italiens in Paris offered every conceivable luxury under the sun. Shopping as a leisure activity was well established by the early nineteenth century. City shops sold domestic and imported "fancy goods" for fixed prices and created showy displays with mirrors and lights to seduce customers. Business boomed for clothiers, perfume merchants, milliners and haberdashers, gold and silversmiths, and furniture sellers. With increased prosperity, consumer demand flourished for household items such as porcelain, kitchen equipment, rugs and furniture, and watches and clocks. The urban middle classes were eager to enjoy the indulgences born of empire. Some shops in London were extravaganzas. Opened in 1796, Harding & Howell's Grand Fashionable Magazine on Pall Mall had four departments and sold fabrics and furs, hats, jewelry, and perfume. It was devoted to stylish women who were free to browse and shop in a safe, decorous environment. Regent Street was the epitome of fashion and elegance, an "avenue of superfluities,"[37] with modish shops selling imported and exotic luxuries. There were some fifteen bazaars in London with a dizzying array of fashionable merchandise, many of them offering entertainment for their customers such as music, panorama paintings, and a peak into a camera obscura.[38]

Paris was the epicenter of elegance and fashion, and its cache made it a draw for Europe's privileged elites. "We are the whipped cream of Europe," Voltaire had already mused in 1735. Revolution and war did little to dent this reputation. French fashions and luxury items were featured in *magasins de nouveautés* (specialty boutiques) that advertised their wares with showy frontages. The area around the Palais Royale on the Right Bank was famed for its shops, cafés, and restaurants, along with the racketeers and courtesans that were a regular part of its street life. The hedonism was scintillating. But it was the commercial venues developed in Paris over the course of the nineteenth century that struck the loudest chord and became the model for the rest of Europe. The arcade, an enclosed passageway of luxury shops, was a Parisian specialty. There were some twenty-five arcades that boasted the newest novelties and fashions, and mouth-watering gastronomic delights. Many of them were on the *grands boulevards* that were magnets for consumption and entertainment. In his *Arcades Project*, renowned urban critic Walter Benjamin described the arcades as magical "fairy grottos," and the uber-form of commodity fetishism. They were streets "of lascivious commerce . . . wholly adapted to arousing desires." The arcade was "a city, a world in miniature . . . from which the image of 'modernity' was caste."[39] The filtered light from their glazed glass roofs, the decorative pillars, and inlaid marble floors made these spaces intoxicating. The first public space in Paris to be illuminated by gaslight, in 1816, was the Passage des Panoramas on the Boulevard Montmartre. It sat between two panorama exhibits that were all the rage. The musical variety shows at the Théâtre des Variétés were just next door and along with it the Café des Variétés. Fashionable society swept through the elegant Passage du Grand Cerf and the Galerie Vivienne on the rue des Petits-Champs (Figure 16).

The arcades enjoyed tremendous popularity in the 1820s and caught on like wildfire across the major cities of Europe. The city of Leeds in West Yorkshire, England was a leading industrial and commercial center with its own stock exchange, numerous banks, and a chamber of commerce packed with savvy businessmen. The neoclassical Town Hall with its majestic tower was a tremendous source of civic pride. Its inauguration

Figure 16 The Subalpina Gallery in Turin, Italy, engraving by Ernesto Mancastropa from a drawing by Rodolfo Griffi, from *L'Illustrazione Italiana*, No 1, January 5, 1890.

was attended by Queen Victoria and the occasion for a music festival and exhibition of local industry. The city's wealthy middle class of merchants and manufacturers actively promoted the revamping of local amenities.[40] Ramshackle property on the city's east end was swept up for a new commercial district of luxurious arcade galleries. The Thornton Arcade, the Queen's Arcade, the Grand Arcade, the Victoria Arcade, and the sumptuous County Arcade were all erected by entrepreneurs and real estate speculators profiting from the city's redevelopment schemes. The arcades were graced with flamboyant entrances in brick and sandstone and decorated in italianate style. Three-storeys high with soaring glass roofs, chandeliers, and arched windows, marble columns and floors, they were the ultimate shopping experience. Their unveiling was the occasion for local pomp and celebration. Opening day of the Queen's Arcade took place during the Shah of Iran's visit to Leeds and greeted him with a music concert held in the lavishly decorated promenade.[41]

The department store, then, had a long lineage and a variety of ancestors. Many of its features were already in use in sophisticated shopping emporia. The department store did not spell the demise of these older commercial forms. Rather than describing urban retail as an unfolding evolution from these earlier commercial forms to the department store, the commercial spectacle diversified and offered an excess of opportunities. Even in 1914, department stores controlled less than 3 percent of retail trade in western Europe. The number of small shops, arcades and bazaars, and discount houses kept well apace as did the profusion of goods they offered.[42] Nonetheless, contemporary shoppers certainly saw department stores as striking symbols of modernity. They were "big city" phenomenon and self-consciously global institutions. They worked in coordination with international trade and the demand for exotic luxury goods. Department stores attracted customers by their bounty, the fixed prices and special sales, and their lavish displays. Their economies of scale and scope produced a thrilling commercial culture. The imposing mass of the department store buildings, the opulent facades, and their flashy locations along the boulevards made them instant symbols of modernity. The sheer numbers of customers and the vast range of merchandise on display were a sign of an urban society that increasingly saw its reflection in the variety of goods it consumed. Urban life was commercialized at an entirely new scale. The early advent of catalog sales meant that the new consumerism reached avid shoppers in provincial towns and cities across the continent. They became accustomed to modern "big city" tastes and to merchandise from around the globe.

Numerous bazaars already lined the *grands boulevards* in Paris. The Bazar de l'Industrie (1827–29) on the Boulevard Poissonnière and the Bazar de Boufflers on the Boulevard des Italiens (1829) were among the largest. They were constructed in cast iron and rose up two or three-stories with galleries grouped around a central nave. They housed hundreds of stalls, many of them run by women. In the 1830s, the Bazar Bonne-Nouvelle was the grandest commercial palace of its time, with three hundred shops on five levels, a restaurant, café, theater, and exposition hall. These were the close forerunners for the Bon Marché, the first Parisian department store. Opened on the Left Bank in 1869, its scale was immense. The iron and glass building designed by architects Louis-Auguste Boileau and Gustave Eiffel was as innovative as the merchandising. Customers in the Bon Marché wandered among lavish displays and counters draped with floral bouquets and seasonal decorations. They mounted the grand staircase in a stunning visual theater. The effect was breathtaking. Music drifted through the air. Customers could relax from their shopping labors in the Bon Marché's reading room and art gallery. Selling was a matter of showmanship. Urban spectacle, entertainment, and consumerism were indistinguishable (Figure 17).

The success of the Bon Marché inspired a bevy of competitors, in some cases founded by former employees. The Grands Magasins du Louvre opened in 1875. The Printemps department store and the Galaries Lafayette made the Boulevard Haussmann into one of Paris's great shopping districts. The Samaritaine overlooked the Pont Neuf in one of the premier locations in the center of the city. The department stores enriched the reputation of Paris as opulent commercial theater. The goods and decor blended into a fantasy land

Figure 17 Interior of Au Bon Marché department store, Paris, illustration from *L'Illustration, Journal Universel*, No 1518, Volume LIX, March 30, 1872.

of colors and sensations. Shoppers ogled at the exotic luxuries, the richly decorated rotundas, and shopping courts framed in tracery ironwork. They glided from floor to floor on newfangled "moving staircases" and lifts. Pneumatic tubes dispatched orders. The clink of the cash registers meant gleeful purchases. Contemporary estimates for the numbers of customers were astonishing: in the 1880s, 10,000 people were thought to have visited the Bon Marché on good days; between 15,000 and 18,000 a day may have entered in the 1890s. Observing the Grands Magasins du Louvre around 1882, French writer Emila Zola thought that 70,000 flooded through the doors on sale day.

By the turn of the century, an entire flock of department stores opened in Europe's big cities.[43] They mushroomed into large-scale businesses with mail-order catalogs and branch stores in towns and cities across the continent. London's first department store was Whiteley's in Westbourne Grove, which opened in 1864 next to a stop on London's railway. The customers came in droves, from the aristocracy down to working-class families looking for bargains in what was proclaimed the "universal provider." Whiteley's had tea rooms, a theater, and a golf course on the roof. It was the height of luxury entertainment. Harrod's opened in Knightsbridge across from the grounds of the Crystal Palace and thrived under a former manager of Whiteley's. Buchanan Street in Glasgow became an elegant shopping street with stores such as Stewart & McDonald's and Wylie & Lockhead. The latter boasted an iron-framed, glass-roofed building with four floors of shopping galleries and opened branches in London and Manchester.[44]

Small shopkeepers cried foul and tried to derail the new competition through political lobbying, but to little avail. For cities, department stores meant money and jobs. The sales clerks working in department stores were usually young, unmarried, and from working-class and lower-middle-class backgrounds. For a long time, the majority were men. Managers instructed them how to dress and speak correctly and how to deal with customers, especially well-to-do women. A store's success depended on the propriety and respectability essential to middle-class conduct. These were solidly bourgeois institutions. For the smiling young men and women standing behind the counters, the store was a form of cultural education and social mobility. It offered the possibility of a stable existence and a chance for advancement through faithful service to the firm. By 1890, over 6,000 people were employed by the Whiteley Company, while Harrods' employed 4,000. Many of the staff lived in company-owned, carefully supervised male and female dormitories and worked from seven in the morning to eleven o'clock at night, six days a week. It was long hours on best behavior in a deeply controlled environment, but worth it to many a young person with ambition. The paternalistic owners offered employees canteens, medical services and pensions, and leisure clubs.

The first department store in Italy, Alle Città d'Italia (originally called Aux Villes d'Italie), was opened in Milan in 1877, which then expanded with additional stores in other large Italian cities over the subsequent decade. Stockmann's department store opened in Helsinki in 1880 and slowly developed a network of branch stores in capital cities throughout the Baltic region. The origin of German department stores was in provincial towns. Georg Wertheim opened his department store in the town of Stralsund. Hermann and Oscar Tietz opened their first shop in Ger in east central Germany. Karstadt began his stores in the towns of Lübeck and Neumünster. With these first initiatives under their belt, department store magnates began chain operations that brought department stores to towns throughout Germany. Big cities such as Munich, Hamburg, Cologne, and Berlin had throngs of customers ready to part with their money. The Tietz department store on Alexanderplatz in Berlin changed the proletarian district into a bustling shopping venue in the heart of the capital. The hypermodern Tietz building was ablaze nightly with interior electric lights and a floodlit globe spinning on its roof. Enormous plate glass windows festooned with mannequins and merchandise enticed passersby on the street. The Wertheim department store on Leipziger Platz included eighty-three elevators, massive chandeliers, a barrel-vaulted atrium with electric and skylights. It was a dazzling stage set for goods from all over the world. Berlin observer Franz Hessel was enraptured by the experience: "Our gaze rests on marble and mirrors, drifts across glittering parquet floors. In atria and winter gardens we sit on garden benches, our packages in our laps. Art exhibits, which merge into refreshment rooms, interrupt stocks of toys and accouterments for the bath. Between decorative baldachins of silk and satin we wander to the soaps and toothbrushes."[45] The luxury retail palace Kaufhaus des Westens in west Berlin transformed the Kurfürstendamm boulevard: "Light streams toward us. To the right and to the left, one shop window after the next, laden with masculine and feminine elegance. A smartly turned-out throng of people moves along the street, laughing and flirting, enjoying life, with time to spend."[46]

The first Viennese flagship department stores were Herzmansky (1897) and Gerngross (1904). Herzmansky was one the largest textile houses in Austria-Hungary. The store offered velvet and silk fabrics, woolens, laces, and fancy goods in a sumptuous setting replete with plate glass facade. In Breslau, the modern department stores of Barasch, and later Wertheim and Petersdorff lured shoppers with their treats and indulgences. The Barasch department store was resplendent with an art nouveau facade and illuminated glass globe on its main tower that became one of the town's insignia. Russians on shopping expeditions in Moscow and St. Petersburg could wander through the Popov arcade with its florid decoration, the Solodovnikov arcade, the glass-enclosed Aleksandrovskii arcade, the Postnikovskii arcade, and the giant Muir & Merrielees department store. Across Europe, cities became commercial extravaganzas nurtured by industry and the global circuits of trade and colonialism. These productive forces dramatically shifted the scale and abundance of retail outlets. The markets and small shops that had long graced the cityscape were joined by a profusion of arcades and bazaars, emporia, and department stores. The meaning of modernity was attached to the joys of buying and to enthralling commercial displays. They made the built environment and public spaces of the European city into a hallucinating spectacle of consumerism.

CHAPTER 5
URBAN REFORM AND THE PLANNED CITY

The industrial production that made possible such a gigantic shift in the manufacturing and selling of goods had extraordinary consequences for urban life. Historians have described the metamorphosis of the cityscape in the nineteenth century as the creation of the modern metropolis. It is a seductive narrative that embraces the breathtaking transformations made by industrial capitalism, or as it is often referred to, the age of high modernism. The terms "modernism," "modernization," and "modernity" were all associated with a specifically European urban experience and with the particular look and feel the European metropolis attained. The European city became a global benchmark[1] as the cradle of modern life. This was most evident in the public projects that reshaped the built form of the iconic central districts. Certainly, there were major public projects and urban embellishment programs well before the nineteenth century. What, then, made the urban planning schemes of this period so different that they symbolize this paradigmatic shift into modernity? In the simplest sense, it was the grandiose scale of operations that distinguished them from the past. The creed of modernity vowed to wash away the debris of bygone years and replace it with a headlong lurch into the future. As preparation for this radical undertaking, the historic city was disparaged as decayed, obsolete, and a calamitous threat to civilization. The indignation was sulfurous. There was little sympathy for the urban fabric built up over centuries. The infrastructure projects of the mid- to late nineteenth century tore up the built environment and kept cities in a state of uproar for years. This ongoing process of creative destruction and reconstruction was in good measure what urban modernity was all about. New boulevards were hacked out of existing neighborhoods to free up the movement of people and goods. Acres of housing were demolished to construct railroad tracks and rail stations. Whole areas of the city were plowed under to lay water and sewer pipes, and subways. Daily living went on amid mountains of rubble and debris, and the continuous disruption of noisy, filthy construction zones.

More importantly, the urban reforms of the later nineteenth century were among the most successful testaments to the creative powers of the Liberal middle classes. Liberalism was the creed of the business, industrial, and bureaucratic elites that made public life in their own image. Their instruments were the modern institutions of the state and capitalist enterprise. The objective was to govern the city and to rationalize and regulate its physical environment. Urban renewal and infrastructure projects were the laboratory for creating an orderly and efficient urban realm. The chaotic, impenetrable strata that had built up over centuries were to be replaced with logical organization. In the minds of urban reformers, the spaces of the city could be torn up, reimagined, and made coherent and legible. At the most basic level, these were capitalist operations of property speculation and rent seeking. This vision of modern urban life was based around a utilitarian philosophy and the cult of progress. These values shaped perceptions about how the modern city should work and what it should look like. It was extended across the globe as the infrastructure of empire. One after another, "European cities" were constructed in colonial capitals as a model of modern life. They were recognizable by their boulevards and public spaces, the elegant buildings in the latest European architectural styles, and by state-of-the art cultural institutions.

Nonetheless, the narrative of modern transformation rested on shaky ground. There was nothing particularly original about these renewal strategies. There was a long European tradition of urban planning to draw on. The dramatization of urban form, royal avenues and the grand boulevard or *allée*, and gardens and open space were all motifs taken from renaissance and baroque urban design. This legacy was a treasured part of the urban fabric in many of Europe's cities. The eighteenth century saw a slate of urban projects based on Enlightenment principles for a rational city. In the years after the Napoleonic Wars even more urban embellishment projects were initiated. The architect John Nash gave London the triumphal boulevard of Regent Street, completed in 1825, that ended in the graceful curve of Piccadilly Circus. It was a theater of shopping and opulence for the well-to-do and one of the first examples of modern town planning. In the 1820s and 1830s, Ludwig I emblazoned Munich with the royal boulevard of the Ludwigstrasse adorned with monuments and cultural landmarks. A wave of urban beautification projects took place in Paris from the 1820s to the 1840s. New roads were laid out and gas lighting installed. The city's water supply and drainage were improved. Even the towering figure of Baron Georges-Eugène Haussmann in Paris, who has been credited by historians with the "transformation of Paris" and the advent of modern urban planning, has undergone a fall in stature. His infrastructure projects were well within the tradition of French planning. Even further, while they were busy tearing up the streetscape in the name of progress, the same urban elites were enthralled by historicist architectural motifs. The buildings installed along the boulevards were a relentless parade of pompous neoclassical, neogothic, and neorenaissance architecture. It was a search for modern meaning rooted in the past. Rather than representing a radical hegemonic break, architecture and planning took place along a continuum of traditions that served as resources.

Even if the modernist dynamic is taken as the touchstone, what exactly changed about European cities requires closer observation. The meaning of modern was fluid. It was embedded in both time and place, shaped by cultural heritage and myriad socioeconomic conditions.[2] Despite all the outrage against the historic city, modern planning was partial and uneven. Projects were hurriedly put into operation after fires, floods, or the catastrophe of war. Old patterns and particularities of place persisted. Modern forms were locally appropriated in ingenious ways and filled with contradictions. They were as much based on perceptions of the past as visions of the future. This viewpoint is particularly valuable because nineteenth-century urban reforms seemed to standardize Europe's cities around Liberal ideals formulated in London and

Paris. Urban infrastructure such as sewers, water mains, and boulevards looked the same everywhere. As sewer pipes were installed underground and roadways widened in cities across Europe, historians often interpreted them simply as mimicry. They were modeled after London and Paris. When exactly these improvements took place was an indicator of the "lateness" or "incompleteness" of modern development. But the realities behind these transformations were far more complex, and certainly more thought-provoking. Everywhere in Europe, modernity fluctuated, was contested, and reformulated to fit local circumstances.

What was modern about these master plans was the unifying logic. What broke the mold was the holistic, integrated approach to the city—in terms of circulation, uniformity, and governance. It was a deliberate and consciously thought-out effort to create a bourgeois city based on progress and capitalist relations. It was a form of cultural self-determination and tribute to their economic dominance. In eastern Europe, this quest to make the city modern was sharpened by nationalism and the emergence of new capital cities. The language of architecture and planning became central components in the formation of national identities. It had a unique ability to communicate all these social and ultimately political messages. The rallying cry of modernity was a means for the middle classes to claim the city as their own around the principles of a reasonable community of citizens and civic values. It seemed all the more necessary because a good half the people living in European cities were born somewhere else. How bourgeois elites responded to the gaggle of languages and ethnicities, to the working classes, and to the persistence of localisms was a critical part of the story. Once nationalism intervened, overlapping identities were barely tolerated. Everyone seemingly had to make a choice. But even if the forces of nationalism urged a radical rupture with former dispositions, much of this remained unresolved. Multiculturalism did not simply vanish. People got along in many roles over the course of their daily life, even if some identities were more salient than others.

Urban planning was also a sign of modern administration and the expansion of powers both at the municipal and state levels. Traditionally, city governance was done by local dignitaries with little qualification other than social status. Often incompetent and corrupt, they were averse to using what powers they had to resolve the nagging urban problems they preferred to ignore. In the mid-nineteenth century, modern city governments began to take shape with mayors and city councils, and offices filled by educated middle-class professionals. The extension of the suffrage brought a public voice to policy making. Government jurisdictions broadened as cities incorporated surrounding towns and villages. However, local government practices differed radically across Europe. Patronage and clientism forced concessions in municipal administration. As the vote was extended and made more democratic, politics could usurp urban policy and professional management. Municipal services often developed in a slow, hodgepodge way with private companies competing for contracts, lobbying by vested interests, and the thrashing out of new techniques by engineers and reformers. Each could defend their own turf to the detriment of the public good.[3] Whether municipal government could claim any real authority over a city's development also depended on the oversight of state institutions. Cities could be stymied by financial dependence on the State. Especially in capital cities, state governments wrested away control over urban improvements from local authorities. The quest to create places as national symbols overrode other priorities.

Urban life became an object of scientific study. Public health authorities and municipal statistical offices were set up. The first generation of social scientists set off on investigative missions to study social conditions and explain the process of urban growth. Statistical surveys and census-taking provided information about how the city functioned. Data on population, births and deaths, disease and mental illness, and crime backed up the belief that big cities threatened the moral order and social stability. This new urban science had moral value and carried with it the prospect of improving the urban environment. Wiping out the scourge of epidemics and improving public health could be tackled. Mapping and street-naming, dividing the city into administrative districts would order urban topography and make it governable.[4] The tools of civil engineering could be used to determine the cityscape and how it functioned. New technologies, communication, and circulation were the key elements in this imaginary about urban reform. It imposed a very bourgeois ethos on the city. In the minds of urban reformers, improvements to physical infrastructure would produce a cohesive well-run city. It was assumed that everyone's life would improve.

Perhaps no other enhancement symbolized this basket of beliefs than the wide, tree-lined boulevards that materialized in so many of Europe's cities in the late nineteenth century. In Europe as well as around the globe, the elegance and beauty of this infrastructure stood for the fresh possibilities of modernity. It was an atmosphere enthusiastically captured by artists and photographers. They locked their studios and flew outdoors to record the extraordinary transformations taking place. But there were both gains and losses in this remarkable vision. The repetition of ring boulevards from Paris to Bucharest made center cities more homogeneous in form and standardized their function. Public space and the street became a form of bourgeois theater. Yet they dramatically stiffened the contours of the city. For all the discourse about clearing out and making the urban fabric more scrupulous, the planning projects of the nineteenth century redoubled congestion in the core districts. Traffic jumped to unprecedented levels. The streams of vehicles in central Paris rose 300 to 400 percent once Haussmann's boulevards were put in place. The spreading social gradient of European cities—with social elites dominating the center and the less advantaged on the outskirts—was reinforced. Historically, middle-class, artisan, and working-class families coexisted to some extent in socially mixed housing and neighborhoods. Those with meager incomes were lodged in small flats higher up in buildings. This now became a rarity. Industrialization had already begun to break down this social terrain. Urban planning further accelerated the spatial division of the classes. The boulevards were as much of a social barrier as the old city walls had been.

The stylish buildings along the boulevards and squares were meant for bourgeois occupants. Their households enjoyed the luxury of a private domestic world in spacious apartments. Here was stuffed all the self-indulgent goods, the collections of curiosities and souvenirs, the creature comforts that were a signature of bourgeois culture. The construction industry continually produced a surplus of these luxury dwellings. Ownership of land in the city center became the domain of wealthy entrepreneurs and building societies. It became nearly impossible for small merchants and businessmen, or even middle-class investors with limited means, to own property in the inner city. The slum clearance for these new luxury districts also worsened the housing crisis for most urban residents. The demolition of whole neighborhoods increased crowding in the buildings that were left. Proprietors typically broke up old apartments into smaller units, with the result that the working classes and poor were squeezed into smaller spaces. Attic and basements without access to light and air were turned into rented hovels. As an alternative, the working classes were forced to outlying districts to find lodging. The public work programs did little to alleviate conditions in these peripheral areas, which reproduced the grim conditions of slums.

Although these transformations had long-term consequences, most on the minds of urban reformers dealing with everyday problems was public health and the blight of cholera that prowled the cities of nineteenth-century Europe. Like an evil vector, the cholera bacillus journeyed from India in polluted drinking water and the guts of travelers through central Asia and up into Russia, then across to Europe. It followed the path of rivers and railroads and settled into the warm pools of water in towns and cities across the continent. The first pandemic took place in 1830. A second wave hit in the 1840s, and then more outbreaks occurred in 1854, in 1863, and in 1881. Each time, it brought fear, utter misery, horrible suffering, and death. Half of all victims died from the disease. Cholera took thousands upon thousands of lives, particularly in larger cities such as Paris and London. In 1832, some 40,000 Parisians were afflicted. Twenty thousand of them died like flies. A second epidemic in 1849 claimed another 19,000 victims. The first cholera outbreak in Glasgow in 1832 killed 10,000 people. Outbreaks devastated Belfast, Dublin, Leeds, Sheffield, and Manchester. They ravaged cities across the continent and terrorized everyone. It had no respect for wealth or status. It struck the strong as well as the weak.

Doctors were initially at a loss to explain the terrible affliction and how it spread. Most believed it was a miasmatic disease brought about by direct exposure to filth and decay. "Filth" and "dirt" were code words for middle-class anxieties about the modern city. And so, public wrath fell directly on the slum districts. It was a common assumption that those who engaged in morally and physically intemperate behavior or who had inferior cultural practices were more likely to get cholera. The poor had only themselves to blame. Medical reformers pointed to an upsurge in personal depravity and the breakdown of social cohesion. The city had become "sick." The death rate in Liverpool was so high it was "The Most Unhealthy Town in England," while London was branded "The Big Smoke" and the "Venice of Drains" for its polluted air and overflowing sewers. And it was not just cholera. Typhus, which was spread by lice, ravaged Ireland between 1816 and 1819. An estimated 100,000 Irish perished. It broke out again in the late 1830s and between 1846 and 1849 during the Great Irish Famine. Known as "Irish fever," it spread through the industrial cities of England and to London, which suffered a terrible outbreak in 1837–38. There were serious typhus epidemics in Glasgow in 1837 and 1847. In Paris, 15,000 died each year from tuberculosis. Yellow fever killed hundreds of thousands of Europeans each year. Influenza epidemics occurred regularly. Smallpox and diarrhea ravaged infants and children. These contagions killed people of all social classes, but hit the lower or "unwashed" social strata the hardest as they eked out their lives in the slums. The working classes and poor suffered the ravages of disease far more than the wealthy. They also endured whooping cough and scarlet fever, measles, and smallpox. Disease was threatening social collapse.

Poverty and disease were indeed ugly bedfellows. What cholera and the contagions revealed was the existence of whole areas of miserable destitution—the teaming slums, the "fever," or "cholera districts" that otherwise remained out of mind and hidden from view. It was these stark extremes of wealth and poverty in London that always shocked city observers and travelers, and the seeming immunity to the injustice. Visiting London in the 1840s, American Henry Colman wrote of the tragedy: "In the midst of the most extraordinary abundance, here are men, women, and children dying of starvation; and running alongside of the splendid chariot, with its gilded equipages, its silken linings, and its liveried footmen, are poor, forlorn, friendless, almost naked wretches, looking like the mere fragments of humanity." The upper classes maintained their social distance and avoided dealing with the rabble. Well-off Londoners dined and visited with friends at their exclusive West End clubs. They were private institutions that encouraged a cult of egoism, seclusion, and detachment from the urban realm. Two palatial private clubs, the Athenaeum and the United Services Club, were ensconced on Regent Street, the West End's opulent avenue for the wealthy. It acted as a barrier against the encroaching rookeries and reinforced the extreme spatial divisions that characterized London's life. The upper classes did all they could to protect themselves from the unpleasantries and dangers on the streets.

The line between privilege and degradation was abundantly clear. These were cities of extreme social polarities. Surveying the condition of the working classes in Manchester in 1845, social reformer Friedrich Engels remarked that "the members of this money aristocracy can take the shortest road through the middle of all the laboring districts to their places of business without ever seeing that they are in the midst of the grimy misery that lurks to the right and the left." The elegant commercial and residential districts "conceal from the eyes of the wealthy men and women of strong stomachs and weak nerves the misery and grime which form the complement of their wealth." The same social divisions plagued Glasgow, which ranked as one of the finest and richest cities in Europe. Grand public buildings and a host of museums, galleries, and libraries were a tremendous source of local pride. Yet the city suffered from appalling destitution and disease. The splendid mansions in the West End were a world away from the alleyways of High Street, Saltmarket, and Gallowgate in the city's east.

The working classes and poor were generally pictured as unwashed, brutish, drunken, and immoral. Even worse, they were developing their own class consciousness, their own articulation of their plight and how to solve it. The real terror for the upper classes was insurrection. Big city conditions and poverty threatened to turn respectable workers into anarchists and lunatics. Labor troubles and protests broke out frequently. The barricades of the 1830 and 1848 revolutions were fresh in everyone's minds. Strikes, mass meetings, and riots took place during the fight for the Reform Bill to extend the suffrage to the working class. The mass rally crushed by cavalry in the Peterloo Massacre in Manchester (1819) and the Bristol riots of 1831 stoked fears of an uprising on the scale of the French Revolution. Disturbances took place in London in 1855, when threatening crowds showed up in Hyde Park to see how "the aristocracy kept the Sabbath." On a July Sunday, 150,000 people, mostly from the East End gathered to watch the beau monde drive in their carriages, saluting them with hisses and screams. The windows of fashionable houses in Belgravia were smashed. In February 1886, unemployed workers staged mass meetings in Trafalgar Square that included some of the roughest gang elements in the city. Six hundred police officers protected Buckingham Palace from attack. The mob went on a rampage past the gentlemen clubs of Pall Mall, through the streets of St. James and Mayfair, breaking windows and looting shops. In October the same year, huge crowds held demonstrations and invaded Westminster Abbey during a service. The crowd then moved to Trafalgar Square, where clashes with police ended with two people dead and hundreds injured.[5]

Like disease itself, the city's paupers could escape their miserable hovels in the East End and threaten the entire city. Disorder and disease were two sides of the same coin. Through doctor's reports during the cholera epidemics, the public was given a glimpse of the appalling conditions. It is hard to exaggerate the torrid descriptions of human misery and degradation that were built up around the Victorian slum. An entire genre of "slum literature" was dedicated to recounting the squalor in lurid detail. Muckraking journalists and social reformers alike wrote explosive exposés on the "rookeries" of East London. Hundreds of private charities and temperance societies descended on notorious slums such as Whitechapel and Seven Dials. The government built infirmaries, workhouses, and fever hospitals. Upper-class men and women and well-to-do philanthropists went on fashionable missions to investigate the poor, and others just went "slumming" as a titillating escapade. The perspective went from sober inquiry and service to do-goodism, prurient curiosity, and at worse, the slum as sensationalism and entertaining spectacle. Inevitably, these explorations focused on the flotsam left behind by industrial capitalism: the destitute and homeless, the sick, and the unskilled.

The East End of London became the tableau for the written and visual spectacle of social outcasts. Fictionalized depictions, such as those of Charles Dickens in novels like *Bleak House* and *Oliver Twist*, echoed the dire descriptions of urban reformers such as the intrepid Henry Mayhew. Mayhew's investigation of the London poor was published as the groundbreaking 1851 *London Labour and the London Poor*. Many of these accounts were serialized in popular newspapers. Readers were riveted by sensationalist descriptions of pestilence and horror. The "sunken sixth," as contemporaries called the poorest of the poor, lived in utter wretchedness. Their lot was made worse by extensive demolitions for railways, warehouses, and offices that squeezed the destitute into even meaner circumstances. Squatting, illegal tenancy, living on the street were strategies for survival. The widespread practice of homework such as rag-picking, sack-making, matchbox-making, rabbit-pulling made bad conditions even worse. Keeping small farm animals was common. Bathhouses were unknown in the poor districts and most households were reduced to using "privy-pails" as latrines. The sense of moral outrage and horror that characterized descriptions by evangelists is seen in Congregationalist Minister Andrew Mearns report in his 1883 exposé *The Bitter Cry of Outcast London*:

> Every room in these rotten and reeking tenement houses a family, often two. In one cellar a sanitary inspector reports finding a father, mother, three children, and four pigs! In another room a missionary found a man ill with small-pox, his wife just recovering from her eighth confinement, and the children running about half naked and covered with dirt. Here are seven people living in one underground kitchen, and a little dead child lying in the same room. Elsewhere is a poor widow, her three children, and a child who had been dead thirteen days. Her husband, who was a cabman, had shortly before committed suicide.[6]

This parade of grotesqueries was etched into the public psyche. It was an exercise in monstrous realism. The descriptions of the homeless and destitute on the streets of London captured the deep Victorian anxieties about the city's underbelly. It was also a strategy for excoriating the old city as the first step in its demise.

There was little nostalgia or aesthetic sentiment for the historic landscape among urban reformers, nor was there any real sense of the rookeries as lived environments worthy of respect. Malthusian economic theory argued that any surplus income given to the unfortunate would simply exacerbate over-population. Destitution, disease, and death had to be accepted as natural forms of population control. If anything, idleness and degeneracy were regarded as character defects. The poor should help themselves. Social reformers gave immense weight to middle-class concerns about outward respectability and worries about "moral corruption." They decried the gin-swilling, the debauchery, and violence outside pubs in the poor districts. Church leaders insisted that moral salvation was the first step, which would then improve social and physical conditions. Moral discipline was one of the thickest veins in the crusade to reform the big city and its "seething, pestilent, indiscriminate masses." Christian revivalist William Booth began preaching the gospel in a tent in Whitechapel, a London enclave of mainly Irish and Jewish immigrants. Eventually he founded the Salvation Army, so that "the poor could save the souls of the poor." Somehow reformers convinced themselves there was a redemptive value in misery. Both Protestant and Catholic churches led charitable campaigns to found refuges, asylums, and orphanages for needy children. They opened Sunday schools and educational classes for working-class children. As members of religious congregations, middle-class women volunteered to help poor women and extend aid to the indigent.

But no amount of Christian zeal could deal with the deep-seated poverty of the rookeries or the conditions that were a petri dish for epidemics. Part of the problem lay in the lack of public oversight. London had no central governing administration, which was also true of cities across Europe. It was divided between the squabbling cities of London and Westminster. Sixty parish-neighborhoods jealously guarded their turf. The elected vestries and some 300 public boards shared power in a moribund system riddled with corruption. There was no coherency to the city's breakneck growth nor possibility of dealing with the environmental crises. London was notorious for its polluted air. Smoke spewed from factory chimneys and then coagulated in the city's notorious fog to make a thick, acrid soup. Drinking water came from rivers and wells and was contaminated even to the naked eye. Public services for the removal of sewage and excrement were limited to cesspits. The accumulated morass was then dumped into the Thames River or sent to irrigation farms on the outskirts.

The catalyst for change was Edwin Chadwick's report on hygienic conditions in urban areas, published in 1842 as the *Report on the Sanitary Conditions of the Labouring Population of Great Britain*. Secretary to the Poor Law Commission, Chadwick was the standard bearer for the sanitation movement that campaigned to purify the urban environment as the best defense against deadly disease. The report was a hard-hitting factual exposé on environmental muck in the most squalid rookeries. The back streets and alleys where cholera and typhoid broke out were invariably near open sewers, stagnant ditches and ponds, gutters filled with putrefying waste, and cesspits. The remedy was to eliminate these sources of miasma and improve the circulatory flow through the city. In a series of reports, reform activists proposed an array of measures to improve water supplies, street cleaning, and sewage outflows. Clean spring water could be steam pumped through pipes into every tenement, which would be supplied with a water closet. A sewer system would flush out waste to sewerage farms for fertilizer. It was nothing less than an impassioned crusade for public health with the specific goal of removing filth and refuse. It was grounded in sanitation engineering. Yet the goal was a moralistic one. Cleanliness would defuse social conflict and make the "dangerous classes" sober, peaceful, and law-abiding. The sanitation movement was ultimately a moral battle for the political and social health of the city.

The rising tide of agitation finally spurred government into action. Cities in England extended the reach of municipal authorities to housing and public health. A wave of "sanitation acts" and "town improvement acts" were promulgated in the 1840s in Manchester, Nottingham, Liverpool, and Leeds. Public health inspectors fanned out to assess conditions. In 1848, Parliament passed the first Public Health Act that transformed sanitation in British cities. Municipal government could now assume responsibility for sewers and water supplies, and street cleanliness. A Central Board of Health was created. London anointed a General Board of Health, a Metropolitan Commission of Sewers, and a City Commission of Sewers. A Metropolitan Board of Works (1855) was made responsible for the construction of an integrated sewer and drainage system.[7] However, the Board deadlocked over the location of the sewer outlets during the sweltering summer of 1858. The stench from the industrial pollution and human waste flowing into the Thames was so intolerable that it was dubbed the "great stink." The heat cooked the effluent into a putrid stew that was literally sickening. The public panicked in fear of yet another contagion from inhaling the putrid air. The national scandal pushed the government into breaking the impasse. London's metropolitan sewer system, completed in 1865, was one of the greatest engineering feats of the nineteenth century. Under the watchful eye of chief engineer Joseph Bazelgette, sewer pipes eighty-two miles in length were tunneled beneath London and flushed away 420 million gallons of waste and rainwater daily almost entirely by gravity. It was dumped into the Thames downstream. The most noticeable addition was the Victoria Embankment along the Thames, built essentially as a lid over the main sewer conduit as well as the underground Metropolitan Railway. The ongoing excavations for Bazalgette's work disrupted the streets and traffic of London for years. It was a performance of modern governance and provided visible evidence of the radical transformation taking place underground.

The sanitation movement traveled from city to city in Britain as urban reformers began tackling the scourge of contagious diseases and shocking death rates. Chadwick's *Report on the Sanitary Conditions of the Labouring Population* covered cities in England, Scotland, and Wales. Publications such as medical expert Robert Cowan's *Vital Statistics of Glasgow* (1838) were a litany of horrifying conditions. Glasgow's first Medical Officer of Health, William Gairdner, carried out a detailed study of the public health crisis. The most groundbreaking solution was the Loch Katrine Scheme, opened by Queen Victoria in 1859, that provided fresh water to Glasgow's inhabitants via an aqueduct from the Trossachs lochs. The establishment of municipal washhouses and fever hospitals helped to reduce death rates, as did the "Cleansing Department" set up by the City Improvement Trust. The Improvement Acts passed in the wake of Glasgow's typhus outbreak in 1864–65 paved the way for clearance of the worst tenements. Wide boulevards were hacked through the ancient fabric of Argyle, Buchanan, and Sauchiehall streets to bring "light and air" into the city. By the 1890s Glasgow had more municipal services than any other place of its size. On the other hand, Manchester's progress came in fits and starts. The municipal government began tackling river and air pollution in the late 1870s. Fresh water was piped in from the Lake District by the 1890s. But even then, the distribution of drinkable water remained uneven. The activist Charles Rowley led an environmental justice campaign in Manchester's dismal Ancoats district that demanded access to bathhouses, clean water, and basic sanitation. But lack of political will and financing made urban reforms patchy at best. Muckraking journalism ended up the major catalyst for campaigns to clean up Manchester's slums. The city "was shamed and blackmailed"[8] into finally introducing proper sewage treatment in the early years of the twentieth century. Any real reduction in the ghastly rates of infant mortality did not occur until then.

The public health movement swept across cities on the continent. Early breakthroughs in Paris came with the investigations of medical doctors such as Claude Lachaise and his *Topographie médicale de Paris* (1822) and Louis-René Villermé and Alexandre Parent-Duchâtelet's 1829 *Annales d'hygiène publique de la medicine légale*, which became widely known throughout Europe. Health councils and surveys of housing conditions were established in the major French cities.[9] By the mid-nineteenth century sanitation engineering became one of the most significant topics of mutual exchange and knowledge transfer between urban activists. Countless study tours and conferences took place on public health. Reformers experimented with different techniques for water delivery and sewage drainage. Cities grappled with whether to rely on private companies to manage basic utilities, or whether to make them public and reap profits through utility charges. Despite all the impassioned debate about urban reform and public health, by and large, progress across Europe remained painfully slow. The improvements were incremental, trial-by-error, held back by the enormous expenditures and the aggravating disruptions and time-lags of construction. When they did undertake infrastructure projects, towns often shared the expense with business philanthropists and private charitable organizations. Typically, urban reform efforts and public utilities were limited to the city center. Water and sewage hookups in buildings and the installation of water closets took place only in better neighborhoods.

In many cities, hygiene reform was simply a knee-jerk reaction to the recurring cholera outbreaks that plagued cities well into the late nineteenth century. A deadly cholera outbreak in Vienna in 1873 kept away tourists and ruined the city's international exposition. Authorities in Budapest acted with meant-to-be indifference to outbreaks in 1866 and 1873. Only a few small wastewater projects had taken place in Germany by the time of the 1886 cholera epidemic. The outbreaks that hit Marseille and Milan in 1884 and killed thousands finally spurred these cities into reform. With their endless flows of people coming and going, Europe's ports were particularly at risk of contagion. In 1892 Hamburg was rocked by a major cholera epidemic. The authorities blamed Russian Jews on route to America for the outbreak. Door-to-door disinfectant campaigns exposed dreadful housing conditions. The working-class districts of many cities lacked vital sanitation services well into the twentieth century. In the worst-case scenario, the thousands of cholera-related deaths in 1884 and in 1911 in the poor neighborhoods of Naples was simply hushed up by corrupt local officials.

The sluggishness of hygiene improvements contrasts sharply with the showy urban planning schemes that took place from the 1850s and 1860s. While disease still haunted the back alleys, cities across Europe carried out sweeping projects for the "extension" and "embellishment" of the urban fabric and the construction of grand thoroughfares. They were undertaken in part as a response to the centuries of overbuilding and decrepit conditions in old cities, as well as to the public health crisis. But the hygiene narrative about "light and air" was most often used as a pretext for slum clearance and opening the city for development. The programs were also a response to the obsolescence of walls and fortifications as military strategy. They had largely fallen into various states of neglect. Their final demolition made available large tracks of land to create whole new districts with broad, tree-lined boulevards. The transportation revolution was also an impetus. It became possible to imagine surface infrastructure—streets, boulevards, and railroads—as a fluid circulatory system fusing the urban fabric. But these technical explanations belie the underlying Liberal ideological agenda behind the first great wave of modern urban planning. Circulation and communication had to be secured to permit free exchange. Cities had to be governed to "secure" society and promote economic progress. The city was "the arena of modernity."[10]

By the 1830s, the city of Hamburg had recuperated from the occupation by French troops during the Napoleonic Wars and its population reached about 120,000. It was a flourishing port on the Baltic Sea and a self-ruling autonomous Free City. If any city in early nineteenth-century Europe had the right to swagger, it was Hamburg. It was wealthy, powerful, worldly in outlook. Then in May 1842, a catastrophic fire devastated the heart of the city. For four days, the conflagration swept through the timber-framed buildings tangled in a maze of ancient alleyways. The city hall, stock exchange, the cherished medieval churches went up in flames. Some 2,000 residential buildings burned down. Pioneering photographer Hermann Biow captured the massive damage caused by the Great Fire on daguerreotypes, and in the process forged the earliest recordings of an urban disaster. In the general disorder and panic, some 70,000 people fled. Twenty thousand people, mainly the poor living in the old districts, were left homeless. Looters roamed the streets. A quarter of the city was left in ruins and its canals clogged with charred debris. While the city was still smoldering, disaster tourists arrived to gawk at the damage. Pillaged goods went on sale in the public market. The city churned out memorabilia and souvenirs—everything from commemorative coins to molten saucers.

Hamburg's Liberal reformers saw the catastrophe as a chance to wrest control from the old oligarchy that functioned as city government. The insular merchant patriciate had proved itself singularly incapable of managing the crisis and maintaining order. The bulk of municipal posts were traditionally voluntary, and public employees were barred from seats in city government. In response to the disaster, middle-class reformers organized citizen associations and demanded better government and the extension of citizenship. Reconstruction was the opportunity to modernize Hamburg and institute rational planning.[11] The English railway engineer William Lindley was put in charge of reconstruction. A disciple of Edwin Chadwick in England, Lindley stumped for sanitation reform in treks across Europe and was involved with the construction of sewer systems in over thirty cities. His vision for Hamburg was strictly utilitarian. He immediately distributed copies of Chadwick's *Report on the Sanitary Conditions of the Labouring Population* to Hamburg's trailblazers. The result of his campaign was that Hamburg was the first German city to provide a central water supply and had one of the most up-to-date sewer systems in Europe. The destroyed areas of the city were cleared away, and the land expropriated. In recognition of Hamburg's mercantile spirit, the stock exchange was made the central point of reference in Lindley's renovation plan for the civic center. Commerce was the driving force behind reconstruction. Around it, a rigid grid of straight thoroughfares was imposed that would open the city to light and air, facilitate circulation, and connect Hamburg to the highways to Hannover, Bremen, and Berlin. The river was damned to form Aster Lake as a source of water power. An elegant waterfront promenade was constructed to enjoy the calm vista over the reservoir. The reconstruction of Hamburg was a prophetic moment for Liberal reformers, although the reality of wrangling and disputes quickly woke them from the revelry.

Not everyone was pleased with the English influence. Resentment grew at the "Anglomania." Rather than experiments in modernity, the Great Fire spurred public interest in preservation and saving what was left of the old city. Counter proposals piled up, especially by the celebrated German architect Gottfried Semper. A native son, Semper was a flamboyant public figure. He believed that the built environment always told the story of urban society. His own alternative design for Hamburg was steeped in traditional artistic and cultural references. It imagined italianate porticos and loggias and richly appointed public spaces. Semper conceived the city's civic heart as a sequence of monumental squares—the City Hall square, the Stock Exchange square, the St. Nicholas Church square. Lindley's utilitarian plan offered little by way of this kind of opulent urban aesthetics. Semper's vision, on the other hand, luxuriated in textural and chromatic complexity with references to Venetian, baroque, and neoclassical styles.

The local political battles and chicanery over the redesign of Hamburg went on endlessly, as each of the city's factions fought for control. In the meantime, real estate speculation ran rampant. Brick and masonry replaced the old timber-frame buildings. Hamburg became a modern city of 500,000 through the idiosyncrasies of disagreements and contradictions, and the messy sorting out of public-private negotiation. Reconstruction forced many of the poor inhabitants out of the city. They relocated to peripheral areas beyond the interest or remit of Hamburg's burghers. In these blatantly overlooked outer areas, citizens' clubs took it upon themselves to rename streets and number houses. In an environmental justice movement akin to that in Manchester, they lobbied for proper sanitation, a decent water supply, and street lighting. Activists called for merging the outlying districts into the city in the hope of gaining desperately needed infrastructure. This glimpse of Hamburg after the Great Fire is instructive for a variety of reasons. Modern urban reform in Europe was often implemented in response to calamity. It occurred earlier in the century than scholars have suggested, in this case in the 1840s. The skirmishes over the design of Hamburg's central districts evidenced the assortment of contradictory ideas and experiences that went into urban modernization schemes. Despite the splendid plans, modern urban reform was more often randomly implemented than applied whole cloth and was continually disrupted by the vagaries of politics.

This provides a thought-provoking counterpoint to the image of Paris, which has traditionally received the most attention by historians as the herald of modernity. The urban projects of Baron Haussmann are extolled as the model reiterated across Europe. This narrative has been so dominant that infrastructure programs in the nineteenth century are perennially referred to as "haussmannization." The mastermind behind this vision was Louis Napoleon Bonaparte, who ruled France as president from 1848 to 1852 and then as emperor from 1852 to 1870. He spent much of his early life in England and was heavily influenced by British utilitarian thinking as well as by the sanitation movement. Napoleon III's and Haussmann's grand design for the modernization of Paris was a response to a variety of problems. But the main goal was to make the capital a showcase of imperial power. By 1850, the population of Paris had grown to over 1 million inhabitants. The city was congested, overbuilt, riven into a maze of twisting alleyways turned in on themselves. Substantial improvements were carried out from the 1820s through the 1840s, and some 150 new streets laid out. An inner ring of boulevards on the Right Bank formed a nearly three-mile-long thoroughfare that became the epicenter of Parisian society.[12] The sewage and water systems were improved. But the old medieval heart of Paris had barely changed. Most Parisians lived and worked within the few blocks of their neighborhood. They knew little about the city beyond these borders. There was a gross division between the wealthy districts to the west and the working-class neighborhoods of eastern Paris. The champions of urban reform reviled the eastern districts as the breeding grounds of pestilence. They were also hotbeds of political turmoil. The workers of the infamous St. Antoine district had raised barricades, launched rebellions, and fought off all efforts to repress them during the revolutions in 1789, 1830, and 1848. The maze of alleyways in the eastern neighborhoods was the strategic heartland of street fighting. Vast slum areas spread out on the Right Bank of the Seine. They extended down the Île de la Cité, the island in the Seine River presided over by Notre Dame Cathedral, which was one of the most poverty stricken, haunted areas of Paris.

Haussmann's solution was to drive a network of wide boulevards through the city, demolishing everything in their path. They were interspersed with splendid squares and prestigious monuments symbolic of Paris as an imperial capital. The blueprint was derived from Haussmann's admiration for the eighteenth-century design of Bordeaux. He came under the spell of its broad, tree-lined *allées* and encircling boulevard laid out by the visionary planner, the Marquis de Tourney. Applied to the capital of Paris, the ideal was a city of neoclassical monumentality, geometrical and axial spaces, and harmonious uniformity. If Haussmann looked to the past for inspiration, what was new was the emphasis on circulation and commerce. On the Right Bank, the rue de Rivoli was extended to create an east-west corridor through the city. Two new boulevards (Sebastopol and Strasbourg) jutted down from the north and eviscerated some of the worst "cholera districts." They connected with the Left Bank via two bridges across the Seine River. Together, they completed the *grande croiseé*, or great cross, with its axis at the Place du Châtelet. It cut through the maze of ancient streets and opened the cityscape to "light and air." People and traffic could circulate freely, the flow of business and commerce made easy (Figure 18).

Along the city's edge, the old customs barriers were taken down and the outlying districts annexed up to the city's fortification walls. The area was jammed with workshops, foundries and chemical works, mills and warehouses, railway yards, and the city's huge slaughter houses. Amid them was the Petit Pologne neighborhood, one of the most sordid areas of the industrial periphery and a hotbed of insurgency during the 1848 Revolution. Haussmann shaped an outer chain of boulevards that encircled the Right Bank along the path of the demolished customs barriers. The roadway was rammed through the Petit Pologne and any other pockets of working-class resistance. The cleared landscape was then redeveloped with roads and bridges, and with the Petit Ceinture rail line that formed a belt around the city. The state-owned Bois de Boulogne and the Bois de Vincennes, on either side of the city, were made into splendid public parks along with the Buttes Chaumont and the Parc Monceaux. An array of schools and hospitals were built. Victor Baltard's trailblazing market halls were constructed at Les Halles. Whole areas of the city were summarily dug up and new water and sewer systems laid out at enormous cost.

This was nothing less than an attempt to rearrange the entire city. It was a prodigious undertaking. The new Paris breathed an air of progress and modernity. The opening of

Urban Reform and the Planned City

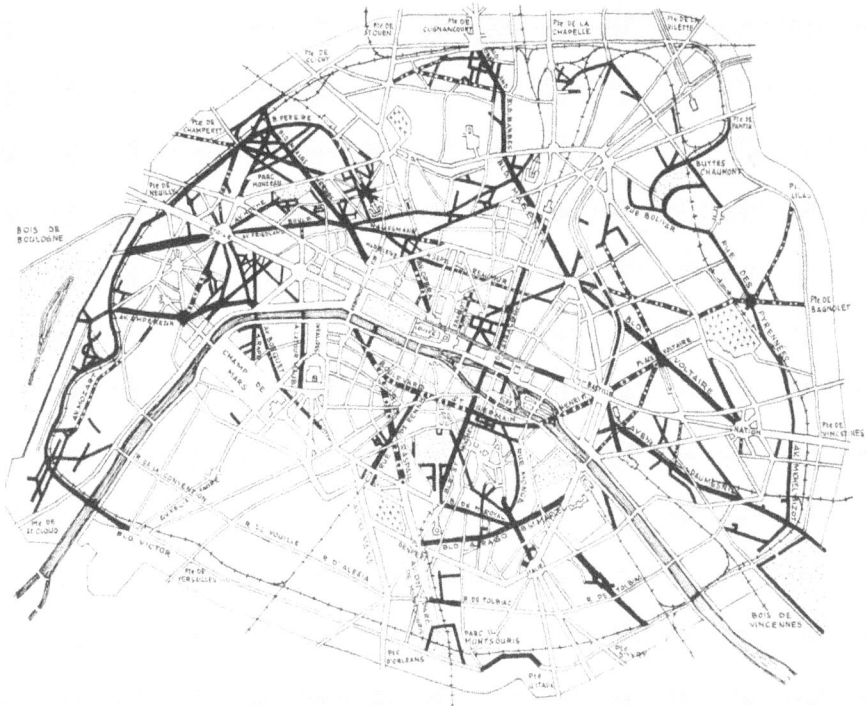

Figure 18 Plan of Paris, circa 1870, with Georges-Eugène Haussmann's boulevards superimposed in black.

every boulevard was celebrated with pomp and ceremony. Even the sewers were open for tours. Paris became a vast construction site that disrupted daily life for years. Some 350,000 people were displaced, especially in the eastern districts where the boulevards smashed through working-class neighborhoods. Haussmann's rebuilding of Paris was controversial from the start, not least of all because of the estimated 2.5 billion francs it cost. Critics laid into the aesthetic damages: the destruction of old buildings and streets of historic value; the ruthless insistence on broad, straight boulevards of monotonously uniform design; the imposition everywhere of a pompous, banal, official style of building. But there was little nostalgia for the urban fabric built up over centuries. Photographer Charles Marville was commissioned to visually document all the old neighborhoods and winding streets slated for Haussmann's wrecking ball. The ostensible reason was to create an historical record, but the underlying purpose was to provide proof of the miserable conditions in pre-Haussmann Paris and the positive good the redevelopment had done. They were "before" and "after" pictures[13] that rigged the contrast between the past and the future. Marville's lens focuses on the radical makeover of the built environment, but it is devoid of any normal flow of life. His street scenes are empty. Capturing the transformation of architecture and urban fabric became an end in itself. As Haussmann's campaign petered out under a barrage of criticism and he was eventually fired, many of the older parts of the city slated for demolition were actually saved. Historians have ratcheted back just how successful "haussmannization" actually was in transforming the Parisian cityscape. Vast areas of the city remained untouched. The urban order continued to reproduce itself. Nonetheless, the surface area of Paris more than doubled in size and the population increased by nearly 50 percent. The street area also doubled. Despite the squabbling and criticism, the new street system made traveling through the city by carriage and by horse-drawn omnibus effortless, especially to the new train stations. Spaces in the central city were secularized, ordered, and made domestic for the elites of Parisian society.

The haute-bourgeoisie were the main benefactors and financial backers of Haussmann's redevelopment schemes. They were "that new class of daring financiers, large-scale building contractors, big department store owners, hotel operators, and the rest of the 'nouveau riche' commercial breed." They purchased apartments along the boulevards and made the center of Paris their own. Standardized guidelines were established for the buildings. They were aligned, their heights fixed by decree and their facades carefully regulated to produce a unified streetscape. Lined with trees and glittering gas lamps, set off by luxurious apartment buildings with their wrought-iron balconies, the boulevards were immediately embraced for their glamorous ambiance. Here were concentrated the most fashionable shops and arcades, musical theaters and dance halls, and the deluxe cafés. That the atmosphere was breathtaking was made clear by the effusive descriptions by visitors to the "city of light." They were encouraged by a bevy of illustrated guidebooks in a media blitz to publicize Paris as the capital of luxury and entertainment. The gushing descriptions of fin-de-siècle Paris almost became clichés. The *Paris Guide* of 1867 prattled, "But what elegance, too, and what splendors! . . . All the world's seductiveness is here." An American guidebook enthused that the boulevards were "thronged with vehicles and pedestrians, and especially at night, present a brilliant spectacle. They are flooded with gaslight both from the street lamps, and from the windows of the shops, cafés and theatres, and the sidewalks are filled and often blockaded with thousands of pleasure seekers of both sexes and of all ages and conditions." The Boulevard des Italiens was "the gayest street in modern Paris . . . lined by hotels and cafés" where "lines of men are always seated in front of them in fine weather. You couldn't go far without meeting someone you knew . . . friend or enemy." Newspaper articles boasted "on the boulevard, one can say everything, hear everything and imagine everything."[14] The east end of the grand concourse of the Champs-Elysées was redesigned with a circus and panorama hall, restaurants and outdoor cafés with music and dancing (the famous café-concerts), ice-cream purveyors, and bandstands. The center of Paris became bourgeois public spectacle. Strolling the boulevard, window-shopping and leisurely spells at the cafés were indispensable signs of modern elegance and refinement. The virtuoso performance was the standard carved into Haussmann's reforms. The middle classes flocked outdoors to relish in the public recognition of their supremacy (Figure 19).

The enduring allure of Paris as open-air theater was codified by the impressionist art movement of the late nineteenth century. Our dreamy imagery of this world is

Figure 19 Boulevard Montmartre, spring, 1897. Artist Camille Pissarro.

still derived from their masterful work. The impressionists captured the modern city in a soft-focus treatment of its boulevards and public spaces. Paris became a blur of brilliant brushstrokes. It was immensely flattering of the capital's public whirl. Despite the gushing praise that has ever since accompanied impressionism as blockbuster art, the movement was also a grand purveyor of social messages. Exquisite tableaux depicted the excursions of urbane bourgeois families. Impressionist artists Claude Monet, Camille Pissarro, Gustave Caillebotte, Edgar Degas, and Auguste Renoir portrayed "la Parisienne" dressed in voguish fashion, enjoying outings in the parks, at the ballet and opera. Stylish crowds crisscross rainy streets and sidewalks, their umbrellas held high. Horse-drawn carriages glide under the gas lamps. The boulevards were rendered in rich colors to create an extraordinary visual narrative of modern life. Many of the impressionist artists themselves haunted the cafés and strolled the boulevards, imbibing the privileges of bourgeois public culture. The civic hero promenaded the public space from an "aesthetic" point of view, from that of taste and pleasure more than from real engagement with the city. Their gaze is detached, uninvolved, a spectator of the ebb and flow of modern urban life. The *flâneur* is capable of a multiplicity of perspectives, a certain relativism that comes from "understanding" and rationally accepting.

The mystique of Paris as "capital of the nineteenth century" stole the show. And it was easy to imagine that other places simply followed its lead, desperate to create a bourgeois public sphere of such sophistication. But once we turn our eyes elsewhere, the mixture of influences wrapped up in notions of modernity are perhaps more illuminating. The view from Barcelona provides insight into how urban reforms were refracted through local prisms. For reformers confronted with Catalonia's capital city, all the evils of industrial society were painfully evident. Although the population spilled out to the surrounding villages, the Old City of Barcelona was hemmed in by the peaks of Montjuïc and Tbidabo, by the Besòs and Llobregat rivers, and the sea. It was imprisoned inside its defensive walls, unable to expand because of military restrictions imposed by the Spanish government in Madrid—a circumstance that contributed to the seething animosity between the two places. Barcelona's dimensions had not changed since the fourteenth century. The result was some 187,000 people packed into ancient neighborhoods suffering from acute overcrowding and disease. Barcelona had among the highest population densities in Europe. Residents were packed into apartment blocks like sardines. Epidemics broke out regularly. Observers immediately blamed the cholera epidemic of 1854, which claimed 6,000 lives, on the ghastly overcrowding and unsanitary conditions. Suffocating heat, deadly illnesses, and riots were regular features of the long summer of 1854.

On lengthy visits to Paris between 1856 and 1858, the Catalan architect and civil engineer lldefons Cerdà (1815–75) examined Haussmann's work with the same professional precision he had already applied to diagnosing the social misery in Barcelona. He had wandered the city, measuring its streets and buildings, surveying the health and living conditions of the proletariat. His findings were published as *A Statistical Monograph on the Working Class of Barcelona in 1856*. Cerdà was among a growing number of progressives calling for the fortifications to be demolished and the city extended with a clear plan. This would guarantee a healthy balance between individual freedom and social cohesion in an egalitarian society. Cerdà believed that Haussmann's transformation of Paris was divorced from any help for the lower classes summarily evicted by his projects. It could never serve more than a narrow elite. Instead, Cerdà argued that expanding the city would keep land values and housing prices low enough for everyone to afford. Intimately involved in municipal politics in Barcelona and especially sensitive to the plight of the working classes, Cerdà pleaded for clean, affordable housing as the prerequisite for a better life (Figure 20).

Unlike Haussmann, who was an administrator, Cerdà was an urban theorist. His two-volume *General Theory of Urbanization* (1867) laid out his social philosophy and vision for a spacious, open city. His plan added nearly 5,000 acres to the cramped 500 acres in the Old City. It spread Barcelona out to the surrounding towns of Sants, les Corts, Sarrià, Sant Gervasi, Gràcia, Horta, Sant Andreu, and Sant Martí. The aim was to overcome social problems by using "street-blocks" of various sizes woven into a checkerboard pattern and intersected by three broad avenues. The orthogonal grid would ensure "light and air" as well as individual privacy, and most importantly to Cerdà, social equality. Beyond the spacious homes he envisioned, his diagrams for the Eixample (or the Enlargement) made room for schools, hospitals, markets, parks and passageways. Factories and workshops filled adjacent buildings. Traffic, sewer, and water systems were integrated directly into the design. The Eixample was a space of movement

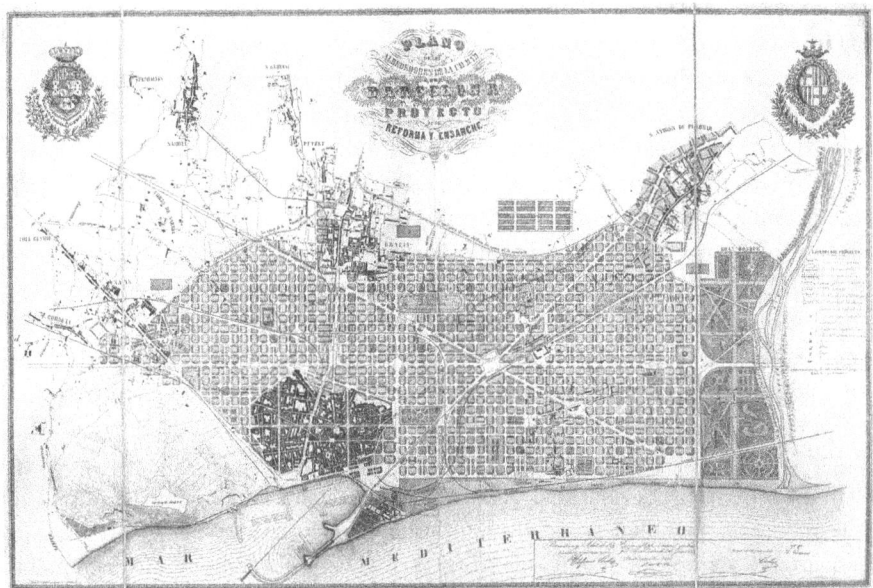

Figure 20 Plan of Barcelona by Ildefons Cerdà with his planned extension called the Eixample.

and circulation. An 1863 version of his plan included an extensive steam train network threaded through the blocks. Cerdà consciously aspired to create a "complete model of a broad-based industrial city" that would evolve gradually.[15] The elegance of his concepts and some sixty diagrams served as a guide for the expansion of Spanish cities such as Madrid, Bilbao, and San Sebastian.

The Eixample was a visionary strategy steeped in the optimism of the age. It was an uncompromisingly rational urbanism supported by the city's emerging capitalist bourgeoisie. The development scheme was formally inaugurated in 1860. For fifteen years, Cerdà oversaw construction and watched over the progress of the first 250 acres. Despite his oversight, the project was altered over time by Barcelona's municipal government and by private developers. The later regarded Cerdà's property restrictions as pointless interference in the highly lucrative real estate market. In 1897, the surrounding municipalities were incorporated into the city of Barcelona and by the early years of the twentieth century nearly all the original 1,000 blocks had been built. But they had wandered far from Cerdà's original ideal. The Eixample was far denser, higher, a more chaotic but certainly more profitable enterprise than Cerdà ever imagined.

Vienna suffered from the same thorny problems, the same tension between cohesive planning and riotous real estate speculation, although at a different scale. With a population of 426,000 in 1850, Vienna was the third largest city in Europe, after London and Paris. But in terms of surface area, it was confined to the three-square kilometers of the old city. This epicenter of the Hapsburg Empire was surrounded by the Danube Canal, the city walls, fortified bastions, and a 500-yard military glacis. It served as the capital of the far-flung Hapsburg domains in fossilized form. Further out, a wide masonry wall, the Linienwall, provided another layer of insularity and defense. The walls and glacis were a symbol of imperial power, but by the nineteenth century they were obsolete as military strategy. The glacis had already been turned into a tree-lined promenade with footpaths, fountains, and lanterns for an evening stroll. The Linienwall still functioned as a toll barrier. It was a favorite site for weekend excursions and popular entertainment, with inns and restaurants serving holidaymakers.

But the walls did have a leftover symbolic value. They sheltered the rank and pomp of the inner city and allowed it to retain its princely character well into the nineteenth century. The Hapsburg dynasty and its sumptuous court at the imperial palace was the pinnacle of Viennese society. The city's bourgeoisie were assimilated into this privileged aristocratic milieu. Their elevated standing was founded on a series of Liberal reforms in the 1850s that opened what had once been tightly guarded entrée to the upper echelons of Viennese life: freedom of property ownership and of profession, a unified legal system for all citizens, a reformed bureaucracy, the liberalization and modernization of the economy. New banks and insurance companies that served the empire were headquartered in pretentious buildings along the main arteries of the old city, especially in the Mariahilf district alongside the department stores on Mariahilferstrasse. Vienna was a world of conspicuous consumption. Couples promenaded the tree-lined Praterstrasse with its noble townhouses and its theater and café scene. It was an elegant society at the pinnacle of nineteenth-century Europe.

Beyond the imperial splendor of the old inner city lay Vienna's outskirts. This sprawling disregarded terrain suffered from a shocking lack of services and housing for its growing population. Traditionally, much of Vienna's population was German. But rapid industrialization meant a flood of newcomers from throughout the empire in search of work, especially after everyone in the Hapsburg Empire was legally granted the right to move freely in 1867. Streams of migrants arrived in Vienna, many of them farmhands and semiskilled workers from Bohemia, Moravia, and Galicia. They formed an overwhelming majority of the working classes and were resigned to living in the outskirts in multistory tenement barracks called *zinskaserne*, or found rented rooms or beds in claptrap buildings. They worked in the clothing trades and furniture-making. The first large-scale machine industries, electrical and engineering works gathered along the railroad lines that skirted the Linienwall and the Danube. The areas of Gumpendorf and Neubau evolved into manufacturing districts. Especially after the 1848 Revolution, anxiety about these threatening industrial suburbs were widespread among the city's elite sheltered in the regal cocoon of the old city.

It was only with the emperor's memorandum of 1857 that ordered the destruction of the walls that urban reforms went forward. The surrounding suburbs were incorporated into the city, and the cleared area of the fortifications and glacis were opened for speculative development. A lengthy new water conduit was constructed. Bridges were built across the Danube Canal and the flood-prone Danube River buttressed. These projects, along with the installation of a new urban rail system, or *Stadtbahn*, were in the hands of Vienna's famed architect Otto Wagner. A grandiose plan took shape for a ring of boulevards sixty-foot-wide and two-and-a-half-miles long with monumental public squares, parks, and resplendent public buildings. It would wrap around the old city like a luxurious necklace. An architectural competition for the design looked to the projects taking place in Paris, Munich, Berlin, Hamburg, and Geneva. More than just superficial splendor, the Ringstrasse represented the Emperor Franz Josef's ambitions to transform Vienna into a modern imperial capital. Much like Louis Napoleon in Paris, the emperor found willing administrators for the scheme—the Interior Minister Alexander von Bach and his chief of staff Franz Matzinger. Also like Paris, the project was controlled by the imperial government. Only later did Vienna's municipal leadership gain some influence over the project. The Ringstrasse opened on the first of May 1865. The construction continued until the First World War and the collapse of the Hapsburg regime. But by the time it was complete, the Ringstrasse was already out of date, excoriated for its puffery and heaviness. It no longer fit the image of modernity. Like the Hapsburg Empire itself, the Ringstrasse had become an anachronism. But during its long gestation, it was the stage for some of the most important and controversial intellectual and artistic achievements of the nineteenth century (Figure 21).

The Ringstrasse revealed the city's social complexities. If it symbolized Hapsburg imperial hegemony, it also celebrated the political and cultural emergence of Vienna's upper crust of wealthy bourgeoisie. It framed an era of emerging Liberalism. The public buildings stressed secular culture and constitutional government. The Parliament building, the city hall, the university, and the city theater were dramatically staged with

Figure 21 Panorama of the Franzring on the Ringstrasse, Vienna.

pompous historicist facades. Although they represented the currents of modern civic life, their grandeur was a triumph of Hapsburg absolutism. The magnetism of imperial culture continued to hold the middle classes in its grasp. Vienna exuded an aristocratic aura that neither Paris nor London shared. In 1879, the silver wedding jubilee of Emperor Franz Joseph and Empress Elizabeth (the popularly adored "Sisi") was celebrated with a glittering procession along the Ringstrasse with some 14,000 people dressed in historic costumes, gilded carriages escorted by cavalry, and the city resplendent in a sea of Hapsburg flags. It was a glittering urban pageant. On the other hand, most of the area around the Ringstrasse was earmarked for development by private real estate speculators. The Rathaus Quarter, around the new city hall, was the most sought-after neighborhood for luxurious apartment buildings in neobaroque and neorenaissance design. The lavish buildings and monuments worked harmoniously with the spacious boulevard itself. The urban bustle was drawn into the pageantry of the Ringstrasse. It provided a dramatic public stage for the city's elites.

Appearance on the boulevard, to see and be seen, was considered a social duty. For the stylish summit of Viennese society, decorum and genteel behavior had to prevail. Austrian artists Theodore Zasche and Carl Moll portrayed the fashionable crowds on the Ringstrasse, chatting and mingling while on showy display. Pioneering Austrian photographers such as Moritz Nähr, Wilhelm Burger, and August Stauda leaped to the occasion, aiming their bulky cameras at the Ringstrasse construction sites, then the ebb and flow along the boulevards, witnessing the city's modern emergence. Stauda visually captured Vienna's buildings, streets, and alleyways in thousands of photographs around 1900. He visually chronicled a big city on the cusp of modernity. The Ringstrasse materialized in these images as a sweeping modernist tableau set off by lines of trees and wide sidewalks, enveloped by stately six-story buildings that were the skyscrapers of the age. Trams and carriages slither along the avenue. Shot from overhead, the photographs create a panoramic view of an elegant city of avenues and open spaces, and monumental architecture. Surveying the photographic studios of Europe in 1882, English photographer Henry Baden Pritchard mused that Viennese life had much of the élan of Paris, while being particular to itself. The café life was more brilliant, music and theater a customary part of life. "The Graben, Kohlenmarkt, and Kärtner Strasse are always bustling and lively. . . . The handsome Opera Ring . . . forms a magnificent promenade, and so does the Volksgarten. Verily, there is but one Kaiserstadt and only one Ringstrasse." The sense of pleasure and enjoyment, the obsession with appearances, was also visible in the haunting memories of the great Austrian writer Stefan Zweig. Looking back on a world that had tragically collapsed in the First World War, Zweig called Vienna an "epicurean city" fanatical about art and the theater.

> Everyone met in the theater and at the great festivities such as the Flower Parade in the Prater, where three hundred thousand people enthusiastically proclaimed the "upper ten thousand" in their beautifully decorated carriages. In Vienna everything—religious processions such as the one on the feast of Corpus Christi,

the military parades, the "Burg" music—was made the occasion for celebration. . . . In this receptivity for all that was colorful, festive and resounding, in this pleasure in the theatrical, whether it was on the stage or in reality, both as theater and as a mirror of life, the whole city was at one.[16]

The imperial capital of Vienna became the model for cities and towns throughout the Hapsburg territories. As part of its Liberal reforms, the state granted municipal home rule and set out ambitious plans for its profusion of urban properties—royal cities, free cities, provincial towns. Under the aegis of imperial policy, ring boulevards, theaters and concert halls, city museums, and universities appeared in towns across the Empire. It was a blueprint for modernization and a new civic realm, and a sign that a place was becoming European. The projects were formally approved by the imperial government and carried out by official architects trained in Vienna and hired by the imperial ministries. Famed Viennese architects such as Camillo Sitte, Otto Wagner and his students worked with municipalities to fashion townscapes as ersatz versions of Vienna. Viennese architects Ferdinand Fellner and Hermann Helmer designed hotels, theaters, and opera houses that became landmarks in crownland capitals and provincial towns throughout the empire.[17] The favored architectural style for public buildings was neobaroque, often painted in the distinctive imperial yellow of the Hapsburg regime. Even street lamps, kiosks, and tram shelters were designed by Austrian firms and shipped out to cities. Modernization attempted to knit together the multiethnic empire into a homogeneous realm imprinted from the capital. Its form was distinctively urban and, for much of the nineteenth century, distinctively German in language and culture.

Even more then in the west, cities were mechanisms of self-representation in central and eastern Europe. Urban spaces and built form were an amalgam of historic heritage, the cultural ciphers emanating from Vienna and St. Petersburg, and the quest for a modern nationalist identity. This was no simple desire to emulate western European models. Instead, there was an openness to a myriad of inspirations, especially those from the past that could be translated by bourgeois elites through the prism of modernity. Budapest was a singular expression of this search for an indigenous form of the modern metropolis. The thwarted Hungarian nationalist revolution and war for independence against Austria in 1848–49 left Budapest vanquished. Fierce battles and the Austrian bombardment of Buda and Pest were followed by the destructive siege of Castle Hill overlooking the city. In the years after, the city was occupied by Austrian forces and subjected to martial law. It was ruled directly from Vienna. If anything, this fueled the fires of Hungarian patriotism. Popular demonstrations in support of Hungarian nationalism were a common sight. It was only after the Compromise of 1867 that gave Hungary autonomy in the Dual Monarchy of Austria-Hungary that Budapest took on the trappings of a capital. The city had already undergone substantial reconstruction after the devastating floods of 1838 (see Chapter 1). The old wall and gates around Pest had been replaced by a ring boulevard, or Kiskorut. Pontoon bridges were the only crossings over the Danube River until the construction of the iron Chain Bridge. It's inauguration in 1849 triggered an outburst of civic pride and inspired the merging of Buda (the center of royal power), Pest (the commercial town), and Obuda (the old market town) as one unified city in 1873. With 280,000 inhabitants, Budapest quickly became an east European powerhouse. It grew at a feverish pace in the late nineteenth century to reach well over 700,000 inhabitants by 1900 and then over 1 million by 1910. Outside of Berlin, it was the fastest growing city in Europe.

Buda was largely German-speaking, conservative, Catholic, and loyal to Hapsburg rule. Austrian Germans still controlled the purse strings in Budapest, and they dominated government from the ministries and Hapsburg royal palace on the heights of Castle Hill. But nationalist tensions and the search for a Hungarian path to modernity seethed below the surface. Pest was the epicenter of Hungarian nationalism and political radicalism. Most of Budapest's population lived on the Pest side of the Danube. Pest was the city's brash commercial and financial heart. Traveling in 1839, English poet Julia Pardoe noted that "Pesth, though now regarded as a garish intruder on the metropolitan pretensions of time-hallowed Buda, will one day become the capital of a country which is even now like a giant slowly awakening from a deep death-sleep."[18] Its flour mills, machine workshops, and factories hummed with an exuberant commercial spirit. The Ganz Works produced tram cars, railway equipment, and iron machinery for flour milling. Budapest's factories churned out iron bolts, sewing machines, and bicycles. Few of the city's buildings dated before 1800. It was a jumble of streets spreading out from the inner core along the river to a series of new districts, each named after a Hapsburg ruler. The city's elites lived in the fashionable neighborhoods close to the Danube, while the working classes settled further out as Budapest spread amoeba-like to accommodate its breakneck population growth.

At the same time, Budapest shifted from a multilingual and multinational city to a decidedly Hungarian one. Cities across east central Europe faced the dilemma that sprang from the political necessity of national unity and the reality of social and cultural diversity. Paradoxically, nationalism had both liberating and eliminating potential. The issue of who exactly would be included in the national fold and who would be excluded was pivotal. Nationhood was increasingly based on the linguistic and ethnic concepts that were widespread in the late nineteenth century. The city attracted a stream of Hungarian peasants and laborers from the surrounding region. The authorities deliberately manipulated emigration policies to engineer a homogeneous Hungarian population. Hungarian as the language of daily use was a sign of commitment to the nation. The majority of emigrants leaving Hungary were not native Hungarian speakers.[19]

The Hungarian nobility merged easily with Magyar financiers and commercial magnates. The city's wealthy bourgeois elites had little bond with the Hapsburg bureaucracy and state. Most of them were assimilated Germans, Jews, and a combination of Magyar and ethnic nationalities from around eastern Europe. Their cosmopolitan mindset merged with a modern European identity. This was especially the case with Jewish elites. By 1900, Budapest had a Jewish population of around 23 percent. Every third person in the capital was a newcomer. For many, entering the liberal professions in Budapest as doctors, lawyers, journalists, engineers was a jump in social status. For the *nouveau riche* especially, the city's property and real estate markets were favorite investments. Through buying property, through education and economic opportunity, assimilation became part of the urban experience. Budapest's fortunate formed a rising class of intellectuals and professionals, noble and non-noble, entrepreneurs and civil servants who all represented a modern cosmopolitan culture. They identified themselves with the Hungarian independence movement and with Liberal reform. Hungary would escape backwardness and step into a modern, progressive future.

The vision of Budapest as a European capital was promoted by Gyula Andrássy, Hungary's first prime minister after the Compromise of 1867. He had lived in exile in London and Paris and was determined to make a modern city equal to the western capitals and to Vienna. There was a movement for the Magyarization of place and street names. Public architecture in Budapest swung toward the monumental and grandiloquent. The most dramatic symbol was the grandiose neogothic Parliament building, inaugurated on the 1000th anniversary of Hungary in 1896. Set along the Danube River, its size and majesty left little doubt it was chest-thumping nationalism. The largest stock exchange in Europe was built in 1895 in Beaux-Arts style by Hungarian architect Ignác Alpár. Yet there was a Hungarian ambivalence about modernization. The search for Magyar consciousness led to the past and to popular folk traditions, to eastern and Ottoman influences.[20] Architect Ödön Lechner, one of the most important figures in the Hungarian renaissance, was inspired by Indian and Persian motifs. He combined them with vernacular Magyar ornamentation to create a unique architectural aesthetic. Lechner's buildings, most importantly the Museum of Applied Art, were richly decorated with majolica tiles made in the famed Zsolnay manufactory in Pécs, whose ceramics were perennial prize winners at international exhibitions. Majolica panels and tiles were the traditional facing material for Hungarian buildings. Used in Lechner's designs, they translated into a modern architecture that expressed national loyalties. The soaring Central Market Hall was designed by Hungarian architect Samu Pecz with a roof adorned with glazed tiling from the Zsolnay factory. The Royal Castle in Buda was rebuilt and enlarged. The Coronation (Matthias) Church was renovated with magnificent mosaics in the polychromatic glazed tiles of Magyar tradition. Making the city modern was a form of political iconography and an expression of Hungarian cultural identity. Both the Hungarian state and the Budapest municipal government supported these experiments as the soul of the new Hungary.

A Municipal Public Works Commission, modeled after London's Metropolitan Board of Works, was set up in 1870 to finance and manage the city's development. Engineer Ferenc Reitter was appointed as head of the technical department. He had traveled to London, Paris, Berlin, Vienna, and Munich to study urban planning. After methodical surveys of the settled areas of Budapest, he laid out an ambitious plan for a semicircular canal in Pest crossed by twelve bridges. It would be intersected by radial roads extending from the center to the city's outskirts. Reitter's vision did not come to pass. Instead, an international design competition for the city's master plan was won by Lajos Lechner, chief engineer for the Hungarian Ministry of Public Works. He replaced Reitter's canals with an outer-ring boulevard encircling the built-up area of Pest. The Nagykörút, or

Grand Boulevard, was built in sequence from 1871 to its official opening in 1896, with each section bearing the name of a Hapsburg ruler. Its completion coincided with the Millennial Exhibition. Yet unlike the Paris boulevards or Vienna's Ringstrasse, the Nagykörút was not constructed for social pageantry. It was essentially a traffic artery crammed with road junctions and intersections, and the traffic around the Western railway station. Rather than acting as a barrier, it integrated the inner city with the rapidly spreading outer districts. The radial streets crossing it continued to the outer neighborhoods.[21]

Instead, Budapest's social spectacle took place on the Sugárút, or Andrássy Avenue. It was a broad radial promenade expressive of Budapest's aspirations as a great city. Andrássy Avenue was in the tradition of Munich's Maximilianstrasse or even Berlin's Unter den Linden, intersected by open squares and ending in a large park. Along it, the city's social elites promenaded past the Opera House, the Academy of Music and museums, the city's elegant hotels, shops and department stores. Lined with gas lamps, kiosks, and fountains, it was dramatic public theater. The avenue was developed through private speculation by the city's commercial bourgeoisie and lined with luxury neoclassical apartment buildings. Underneath it ran Europe's first electric subway line, completed in 1896 and opened with great ceremony by the Emperor Franz Joseph. Andrássy Avenue crossed the Grand Boulevard at the new Oktogon (Octagon) Square, where an array of elegant coffee houses jutted out onto the sidewalks. It then continued to the Körönd (or Circus) and the arcade of colossal monuments commemorating Hungary's tribal chiefs and kings. Budapest's modernity lurched back-and-forth between new possibilities and a celebration of past glories.

The completion of the master plan was celebrated at the 1896 Millennial Exhibition. The fairground was staged in the new city park with its monumental entrance at the Körönd. The event promoted Budapest as a modern western capital on a par with Vienna and Paris and introduced it as an exciting tourist destination. Thousands flocked to the city to ogle at the buildings glorifying Hungarian identity. A ceremonial parade featured the city's leaders dressed in historical Hungarian costume. Visitors wandered along the new boulevards, rode the trams and the new electric subway line, stared awe-struck at the stupendous Parliament building. Over a thousand factories hummed with production. Traveling in Europe in the last years of the nineteenth century, American artist Walter Crane remarked that Budapest "is the most up-to-date city I have ever seen." The city as the surprising embodiment of modernity was shared by travelers. "We rolled into a big, bustling modern station . . . and came to a standstill beneath a mammoth steel shed with a glass roof, under which breathed the engines of a score of trains," reported American writer Frank Berkeley Smith in 1903. Outside his carriage was a city "with streets broader than Parisian boulevards, splendidly paved, with buildings erected with an extravagant expenditure. . . . With electric surface trams installed with the most modern system, with a modern underground railroad." The list of Budapest's wonders went on.[22]

But there was no real center in Budapest, no distinctive coherence. If Andrássy Avenue functioned as the city's promenade, so did the Corso that ran along the Danube embankment above the wharves. It was jammed with coffee houses, restaurants, and luxury hotels. Close by, Váci Street was the city's main shopping promenade. What characterized modernity in Budapest was its unfinished quality. It was marked less by the unifying composition found in Paris or Vienna, than the feverish speed of construction. Planning could not keep up with the city's growth. It became a modern city almost overnight. The upheaval was captured by urban observer Adolf Agai in his *Journey from Pest to Budapest 1843-1907*, first published in 1908 to immense popularity. Agai described the scenes on the city's squares with their "crowds of scoundrels and idiots," the marketplace for Jewish and Gentile traders, the pretty Gypsy violinists, the English princes and dandies. There were portraits of the prototypical Hungarian bohemian, the Slav assistants from villages, dervishes from Sudan, store detectives, boot-blacks, newspaper boys, magicians, and con men. Agai's sketches added up to a metropolis that was indisputably Hungarian in its color, eccentricity, and diversity.[23] It was the meeting point between east and west (Figure 22).

Legendary Hungarian photographer György Klösz captured Budapest in his lens at the turn of the century. As much as impressionism had been, the new medium of photography was enraptured by the vision of the modern city. The buildings, the streetscape and intersections, the urban spaces of modern Budapest were the subject of Klösz's camera. Many of the shots are panoramic, taken from above and panning out over the urban scene, relishing in the modern cityscape. These viewpoints were true from the very beginning of photography. The first image taken by Louis Daguerre in

Figure 22 Budapest, Andrássy Avenue.

1839 was the still-celebrated *View of a Parisian Boulevard*. It depicts the wide tree-lined Boulevard du Temple sweeping into the distance alongside the buildings of the French capital. Early photographers captured the beauty of modern surroundings, the opulence of the buildings, the grandeur, and openness of the boulevards and squares. These were celebrations of the urban subject and a powerful tool in witnessing the transformation of the urban fabric. The new photographic medium transformed the everyday world of cities into an idealized vision of modernity. The technical perfection of the images was itself a thing of beauty. Photography was a seductive medium capable of powerful rhetorical messages. Photographs forced the observer to *see* the process of urban transformation. It both portrayed and created the modern world as an extraordinary visual performance. It reinforced a city's identity as a powerful interlocutor on the world stage. But it hid the simmering social and cultural tensions behind these scenes.

CHAPTER 6
WANDERING CITY STREETS

In the late nineteenth century new sources of energy, new materials, and products reshaped the industrial landscape of Europe's cities. These changes took place across a vast range of manufactures from textiles and tools to umbrella making. Petroleum and hydroelectricity joined coal as power sources. This vastly increased the scale of production. Mechanical and electrical engineering, steel, and chemicals became the sunrise industries. Capital was concentrated in medium and large companies where mechanization could be revved up and rationalized for mass markets. Small-scale enterprises found it difficult to compete except through subcontracting. No one company, no matter how large, could handle all the processes required of this scale of production. Instead, Europe's industrial powerhouses tied together metropolitan areas in a tight web of in-house and outsourced fabrication. Centrifugal forces continued to push industries away from city centers and outward in a broad regional geography. The working classes followed the siren call of industrial jobs in an expanding metropolitan expanse. As the scale of manufacturing increased so did its environmental impact. Urban activists condemned toxic industrial pollution as one of the root causes of disease. The public health movement was bent on cleaning up the city and opening it to fresh air and light. Land-hungry industrial plants and noxious activities such as slaughterhouses were banished to the urban fringe where tracts of open land were cheap. They formed dense industrial belts along the margins of the city, pushing up against ancient boundaries and spreading into vacant areas on the outskirts where basic services and municipal regulations were nonexistent.

The city of Lyon and its environs along the Rhone River in southern France exemplified these changes to the industrial landscape of the late nineteenth century. With a population of 460,000 in 1900, Lyon was the second largest city in the nation after Paris. Coal and iron ore, metallurgy, and silk drove the economy of the Lyon region. Some sixty kilometers from Lyon, the St. Etienne coal and iron ore fields kept Lyonnais industries humming, including the manufacture of weaponry for the French army. Lyon was also an early center for the development of the automobile. Companies tinkered with their gasoline-powered vehicles on the streets of the city and on new roads gliding up the foothills of the Alpes. An automobile industry cropped up that gave daring drivers a choice of brands such as Berliet, Audibert et Lavirotte, Cottin-Desgouttes, and Rochet-Schneider. Automobile-parts manufacturers supplied everything from motors to car lights and tires. The workshops began in the center city and then moved to the outskirts as production expanded. The Rochet-Schneider company was already manufacturing 120 vehicles a year in 1898, when it opened a state-of-the-art plant on the rue Feuillat that was a model of efficiency and rational production. Inside the iron and glass sheds, skilled workers built and exported cars to Europe and the United States.[1] The Lumière Brothers opened their first small factory in Lyon and patented an early motion-picture camera and projector called the *Cinématographe*. The first demonstration in 1895 featured "workers leaving the Lumière factory in Lyon." A few years later they were commercially marketing the autochrome process for color photography.

Lyon's silk industry had a long and storied history. Over 300 silk factories with 210,000 workers were distributed across the metropolitan area. They varied in size from family-run shops to large-scale enterprises. But like many industries, by the late nineteenth century, silk production was reshaped by new techniques and materials. Synthetic fibers that could be made into rayon and silk blends democratized what had been a luxury. Lyon's sumptuous silken fabrics were sold in Europe, the Middle East, and Asia. The suburban town of Villeurbanne on the left bank of the Rhone became a silk textile citadel. Although Lyon's local government had annexed the nearby faubourgs as part of municipal reform, Villeurbanne stood fast as a separate entity on the outskirts. French workers and Italian immigrants streamed into Villeurbanne for jobs in the mechanized silk factories, especially in the Gillet & Sons silk dying plant. It alone employed 1,500 workers and was one of the leaders in the production of synthetic dyes. Gillet's black-dyed silks were all the rage in Paris department stores. The company further diversified its chemical production with skilled labor working in pharmaceuticals, photography, and artificial fibers. Large-scale factories dedicated to fabric dyes and chemical production popped up along Villeurbanne's riverbank. By 1913, they employed over 3,000 people.

Most of the Italian immigrants originated from Piedmont, and more specifically from around Turin, where the web of small towns had long supported seasonal work in the local silk industry. The two regions were economically joined. Laborers regularly traveled back and forth between them in search of work. But the switch to large-scale factory production meant that Italian families settled permanently in Lyon and Villeurbanne. By 1911, their numbers reached 12,630. The larger companies slapped up rudimentary dormitories for their workforce. The Villard company went further and laid out a *cité ouvrière* with side-by-side flats, while Gillet constructed low-cost housing. But this barely satisfied the growing demand for a place to live. Italian workers jerry-rigged their own self-help cottages or found lodging in the mix of ancient rural buildings that surrounded the factories. Villeurbanne exemplified the hodgepodge of built forms and pursuits as metropolitan regions spread out into the rural hinterland.[2] Factory workers lived side-by-side with farmers, artisans working in small trades, and with families still fabricating silk domestically. By 1881, Villeurbanne's population reached 11,000, and by 1900 it had more than doubled to 29,000 inhabitants. With the construction of the nineteen-kilometer Jonage canal and dam on a tributary of the Rhone River, hydroelectric power provided an even greater incentive to innovate. The silk factories hitched their fortunes to electric power, and Villeurbanne's industries further diversified into the production of hydroelectric energy. At the turn of the century, the Cusset hydroelectric plant was the most powerful in France. Chemical and mechanical engineering companies moved to Villeurbanne to take advantage of the unbounded new energy source. The town had transformed into a cutting-edge industrial enclave and a socialist stronghold.

These developments had far-reaching social and cultural consequences. The new industries of the late nineteenth century demanded a literate workforce with advanced skills and training. The migrants pouring into the city in the first phases of industrialization had largely been from rural areas and were reliant on only a rudimentary education. Often impoverished, with little hope of social mobility, they lived hardscrabble lives in the vast slum districts of the central city that so shocked contemporaries. By the late nineteenth century, working-class social structure had become more complex. Poverty continued, especially for those with little know-how or stranded in declining industries. There were many who hovered unnervingly close to indigence. Economic downturns and the loss of employment could spell disaster. But hardship ceased to be a foregone conclusion. The proletariat ranged from the unskilled and itinerant, to semiskilled and highly skilled wage earners with a better standard of living. For these last, floating from town-to-town for seasonal jobs became less frequent. They settled into urban neighborhoods with people from the same regions. Their home life was more stable. Higher wages and a few days off from work allowed working-class families to escape the grim facts of life. Even new waves of immigrants were often already citified and well versed in the rhythms of urban life. They boarded trains to take advantage of job opportunities across a network of towns and cities with a fluidity and speed unheard of a few decades earlier.

Better-off workers were self-aware and politically active through union and cooperative movements, working men's clubs, and political parties. Mass working-class demonstrations calling for extension of the suffrage and the legalization of trade unions eventually forced labor reform. The right to vote for men was granted in France in 1848 and in Germany in 1871. It was gradually extended in Britain to all men paying rent or owning property. In November 1905 thousands of people in cities and towns across the Hapsburg Empire rallied for a general franchise for men, which was finally granted in 1907. The broadening of voting rights brought the mass of wage earners into politics. A wave of socialist and leftist parties were founded across Europe and eagerly campaigned in elections. As they steadily gained political muscle, city after city in Europe went "red." Labor and socialist party newspapers flashed out bulletins and called workers into the streets. The strike became a powerful political weapon. In 1885, some 12,000 masons walked out in Berlin and succeeded in winning a ten-hour work day and raise. Women weavers in the industrial city of Bradford in the English Midlands went on strike in 1890 rather than grudgingly accept pay cuts. They organized a trade union and held demonstrations in the city's parks that led to the founding of the Independent Labor Party.[3] Strike waves and street protests became regular features of the public realm. The terrible conditions for dockworkers in the London Docklands made it a target of industrial unrest churned up by union organizers and socialist agitators. The famous 1889 walkout brought thousands of dockworkers into the streets carrying banners emblazoned with slogans and stakes crowned with stinking fish heads and rotting onions. The strike brought the Port of London to a standstill for six weeks before employers capitulated to worker demands. Membership in the trade unions soared. Marches for women's suffrage were on ongoing public spectacle. A long parade of British suffragettes brandishing red

Figure 23 Dockers Strike, September 7, 1889. From *The London Graphic*—"Dockers' Strike in the East End of London," published 1889.

and white banners slogged through rainy slush from Hyde Park to the Strand in the "Mud March" of 1907 and then rallied for voting rights at Trafalgar Square (Figure 23).

Newly legalized trade unions and socialist parties promoted an everyday political culture that was genuinely working class and neighborhood in tone. The union and the party organized marches and went door-to-door in canvassing campaigns. They provided relief funds when they were needed and fought for better housing conditions and tenant rights. They brought a new cohesion to urban working-class culture with a bevy of neighborhood celebrations of working-class solidarity. International worker tributes such as May Day became moments for local festivities and work stoppages. Working-class political activism meant educational programs and sports clubs, a chance to grow up in a social milieu of young people with shared backgrounds. In 1892, the industrial town of St. Denis north of Paris had twenty-five working men's cultural clubs offering everything from gymnastics to photography, music, and reading.[4] Hungarian writer Ferenc Molnár captured working class "coming of age" in Budapest in the immensely popular novel *The Paul Street Boys* (1907). Readers were riveted by the tale of bravery and honor as two gangs of teenage boys battled over an old saw mill amid the busy streets of the city.

In western and central Europe, governments also took steps to alleviate the plight of the working classes, largely as a tactic to curb social tensions. Germany was the leader in providing social insurance as well as primary education. In 1881, Chancellor Otto von

Bismarck introduced the first accident insurance and social security measures. Although great inequalities still persisted, working-class children in German cities were attending *völksschulen* and vocational training schools. Literacy rates soared. Following Germany's example, in 1888 Austria-Hungary created a comprehensive health and accident insurance program for all industrial workers. In France, most cities made primary education a priority by the late nineteenth century and made schools obligatory and free. In Britain, local school boards campaigned successfully for the expansion of education. By the 1880s the number of schools and students in British cities had doubled.[5] The British Liberal reforms of 1906–14 introduced national insurance, unemployment payments, and old-age pensions. Rising real wages for men in many industries allowed wives to forego outside employment and instead focus on domestic labor and consumption in the home. Families could afford better food and clothing. Purchasing furniture was a sign of real status and independence. The increasing availability of consumer goods changed working-class habits. Families joined the crowds at weekend markets and popular bazaars and bargained over the newest gadgets and novelties. Once a day off from work became standard, there was time for family leisure and special outings to the country or seaside. Although conditions varied across urban Europe, a distinct working-class identity and way of life took shape. With more time and money at their disposal, skilled workers and their families could gain a certain social respectability.[6] A genuinely working-class world was created in the spaces of the city.

Where to find shelter remained the quandary. The demand for affordable housing far outpaced availability across Europe. The hunt for lodging was a predicament even for better-off working-class families as well as for artisans, shopkeepers, and petty-bourgeois. The health reforms and public infrastructure programs of the mid- to late nineteenth century had improved the quality of urban life. But housing staggered calamitously behind these modernizing enhancements. The building industry unfailingly slavered to bourgeois demands for expensive multi-room apartments. By 1900, new buildings in middle-class areas of the city were generally equipped with running water, sewer pipes, and gas. About half of apartment buildings in Lyon and Manchester had running water. Two-thirds of buildings in Warsaw and Budapest were connected to water mains, which reflected new construction in these booming cities.[7] But older districts and urban peripheries rarely met these standards. Working-class families crowded into the ancient stock of buildings and boarding houses. Usually two- and three-stories high, they were a chaotic mishmash in the industrial districts and offered sparse rooms for rent with rudimentary furniture. This was the landscape in the northeast working-class areas of Paris, which remained untouched by Haussmann's public works projects.[8] Cities in the Rhine-Ruhr area were generally of this scale. Larger multistory tenement buildings were more common in central and eastern Europe as well as in the cities of Scotland. There, housing density in the working-class districts was far higher.

In general, dwelling space for families was shrinking in the late nineteenth and early twentieth century and rents rising sharply. Proprietors hacked up their buildings into smaller units and gouged rent payments. Squeezing into one- and two-room flats became the norm. Overcrowding was a way of life; privacy a luxury only the upper classes could afford. There were various policies to end packing people into miniscule spaces in old buildings. Glasgow introduced a ticketing system in the 1860s that affixed a metal plate on front doors specifying the building's capacity. There were midnight raids by police and public health watchdogs. German cities introduced police inspections. Building regulations and density zoning were adopted by municipal authorities. Although these hard-fought reform measures were significant improvements, they paled in comparison to need. The extent of the housing shortage was huge and made worse by the slum clearance programs that demolished buildings and banished the working poor to leftover districts. As city centers became open and elegant, the working-class world became more congested and overbuilt.

Laboring families and the poor were increasingly forced out of the central city to the peripheries, with the result that social and spatial segregation intensified. Newcomers found the cheapest housing at the margins. In cities such as Paris, half the population on the outskirts were immigrants.[9] Those of modest means could afford to rent a small bungalow with garden, or build their own on poorly serviced speculative lots. A cottage outside the city with clean air and greenery remained the dream of working-class families. Cottages and one- or two-story row houses and "back-to-back" dwellings were constructed by real estate speculators wherever cheap land on the outskirts could be found. Cottage estates were also built by cooperative societies and factory owners. The most destitute pieced together camps on open land left by demolished city walls and glacis. Families constructed flimsy huts from metal, wood, and tar paper, lived in covered wagons or abandoned buildings. The infamous *zone* in Paris was a shantytown on the northern edge of the city. Photographer Eugène Atget stomped out to the periphery and trained his wooden camera on the ragtag camps with their shacks and shadowy caravans and their ragpickers and scrap dealers. Egged on by sensationalist articles in the press, in the minds of Parisians, *la zone* became a violent underworld of vagrants and petty criminals. Fearful outsiders failed to see the covert bistros and garden plots, the warren of alleyways, the games of *boules*, and the gossip and news shared at laundry spots. The camps were loose, lively places that navigated the indignities of everyday life in poverty. Social solidarity was found among family and friends. They were highly successful as survival landscapes. So much so that informal settlements exploded as immigrants poured into the city and the housing crisis worsened (Figure 24).

The differences between the central districts, arrayed in elegant masonry buildings and monumental boulevards, and the formless outskirts, where wooden and slap-trap construction often reigned, became more and more dramatic. In an "underground guide to Paris" published in 1869, a visit to the "Villa des Chiffoniers" (rag-dealers) on the city's outskirts near the Place d'Italie was considered a must. It contained hundreds of tiny tin-roofed hovels, a "city within a city . . . the capital of poverty lost in the midst of the country of luxury." French social reformer Henri Sellier, who was appointed first director of the Société Française des Habitations à Bon Marché (Affordable Housing Office) in 1915, decried the living conditions on the outskirts of Paris: "Old villages, scattered here and there have become in a few years large centers of population, which in an uninterrupted chain meet to form a disorderly mass like a single city spreading continuously from the

Figure 24 Ragpickers, Porte d'Ivry, Paris, 1910–12. Eugène Atget.

center." The boundary between rural and urban was imperceptible. French poet Jules Romains recalled the banality of the Paris outskirts at the end of the nineteenth century, where thousands of people lived while working in a city beyond their means. The fringes of Paris were a mélange of houses, "a line of market gardens, a homeless camp, a city hall with its rubbish bins, a church, the offices of a tram company, a wax factory only recognizable by a few architectural details."[10]

New construction was determined by and large by the private real estate market. But the magnitude of the housing crisis and skyrocketing rents forced intense public debate, if for no other reason than the dread of social protest and insurrection. Progressive muckrakers and social militants pounded on the squalid housing conditions. Legions of activists and crusaders gathered at impassioned meetings. A myriad of experimental housing projects were hurriedly initiated. Models of working-class housing were presented at the Paris international expositions of 1867 and 1889. In Britain, the Royal Commission on Working Class Housing laid out the Housing Acts of 1885 and 1890 that gave some hope of rebuilding slum areas, as did the setting up of the directly elected London County Council (LCC). The LCC began the Boundary Street scheme in 1890 that demolished the infamous slums of Old Nichol in the East End and replaced them with the first social housing estate. Philanthropic housing blossomed into a full-blown crusade among reformers and industrialists anxious to stabilize working-class families and sooth over the threat of strikes. In the UK, the Port Sunlight project outside Liverpool was financed by the Lever Brothers for workers at their local soap factory. Chocolate manufacturer George Cadbury built worker housing outside Birmingham. Collective housing schemes with experimental "central kitchens" were built in Copenhagen, Berlin, Zurich, and Vienna. Reform-minded patrons in Vienna built the Jubilee Houses in 1898 to improve living conditions for highly skilled workers and assimilate them into society. Each spacious flat featured its own kitchen and bathroom, with access to gardens and playground. The housing complex was replete with laundries, shops, library, and health center. The Jubilee Houses became a remarkable model for Viennese social housing.[11] In France, the Société Française des Habitations à Bon Marché campaigned for low-cost housing. But by and large, for the *hauteur* world of housing activism, the prototype remained the romanticized family cottage arrayed in greenery. It was imagined as a place of moral uplift where families could live in dignity. In both France and Germany, the *cité ouvrière* with single-family dwellings built by private enterprise held sway. But these were little cure-alls for the magnitude of the housing crisis.

Eventually, reformers grudgingly acknowledged that the scale of construction had to increase and that tenement housing was the only viable solution to the emergency. Tenement buildings became iconic structures in cities across Europe. For the most part, they were built by real estate speculators who took advantage of exploding demand and filled the streets with rows of substandard edifices. The multistory tenement house or tenement barrack was ubiquitous in Berlin, Vienna, and Budapest. Most were built around interior courtyards with a single staircase to the upper floors. The flats were accessed through dim interior corridors or open galleries. Although the courtyards were meant for ventilation, they were quickly converted to commercial and workshop space. The one or two-room flat with basic cooking facilities became the standard. Families sublet a bed to night-lodgers to make ends meet. For example, typical construction in Budapest was the multistory apartment block with people packed into miniscule flats to keep the rents cheap. This was the case in Glasgow and Edinburgh as well. Hamburg's version was "slotted" construction with narrow flats aligned along a small atrium for ventilation. In Vienna, six to eight persons living in a one-room flat was frequent. The toilets and water-outlets (or *bassena*) were shared collectively in what were known in Vienna as *bassena*-houses (Figure 25).

Working-class neighborhoods both fascinated and terrified the bourgeoisie. The industrial outskirts were a strange netherworld. The lack of any social interaction with the working classes left plenty of room for stereotypes. They were labeled rowdy and repugnant. The phantasms of the urban periphery were of disorder, volatility, of a menacing void. It was a place of crime, drugs, and prostitution. As the bourgeois city preened itself on sophistication, the working-class world became more savage in the public mind. The respectable citizens of Liverpool screeched that they were terrorized by scoundrels from the slums. The notorious High Rip Gang went on a wild rampage through the streets, indiscriminately attacking people with knives and slingshots.[12] The authorities in Berlin and Hamburg agonized over urban *habstarke*, the degenerate young proletariat hanging out in the streets and markets. Police in Budapest targeted the "meeting place of hooligan elements" in the working-class outskirts. Three of the five largest industrial zones in Hungary were found on the fringes of the capital. They spread out to the north and south, where the working classes found shelter and eked out

Figure 25 Coburg Street, Glasgow Tenements.

a living amid the factories and workyards. The military was called out to quell rioting in one suburban town outside Budapest after the mysterious death of a local butcher. Local newspapers published accounts of horrifying crimes committed in the industrial borderlands far from Andrássy Avenue.[13] In Paris, the working neighborhoods to the northeast and south—Ménilmontant, Belleville, Bercy, and Butte-aux-Cailles—were the most frequently disparaged as places of criminality and violence. The worst dread however was saved for the industrial "red belt" around Paris. Here was to be found "a country dripping red in blood and death" according to writer Delphi-Fabrice, who ventured out beyond the "fortifs."[14]

The sheer numbers of people in the city was cause for anxiety, as was the din and disruption of the public works programs. The big city crowds were seductive but also alarming. Large numbers of people were out and about in the city. They relished the pubs and cafés, and the boisterous delights of amusement parks and music halls. They crowded the world's fairs and sporting events, and wandered thunderstruck through luxurious department stores. Mass culture seemed to shift control of the city precisely to these faceless throngs whose behavior was difficult to predict. By virtue of their number, their anonymity, and their explicit political convictions, the masses of the city threatened the hegemony that had only just been established by bourgeois urban elites. The middle classes succumbed to paralyzing fears of hold-ups or assaults on the streets, especially at night. The Vienna *Illustrierte Österreichische Kriminal-Zeitung* (Illustrated Austrian Criminal Newspaper) saw its duty to inform the public about the "uncontrolled trollops" and "pederasts" lurking in the midst of respectable people.[15] The anonymity of urban life allowed predator and prey to coexist. Police forces were beefed up. They reported mounting numbers of attacks on the streets—if only because their record-keeping had become more efficient. Police reports piled up on shoplifting and thefts in the department stores. Promenading the boulevards was not without risk. Middle-class women out alone risked being mistaken for prostitutes plying their trade in the fashionable districts. Modernity had its sinister underbelly, and the public spaces of the city were, in public sentiment, where it could be found.

These observations on urban society were particularly strident among the defenders of political conservatism and traditional values. English writer Matthew Arnold, known for his scathing social criticism, summed up his opinion of the working class that "raw and half-developed, has long lain half-hidden amidst its poverty and squalor, and is now issuing from its hiding-place . . . and is beginning to perplex us by marching where it likes, meeting where it likes, breaking what it likes—in this vast residuum we may with great propriety give the name of *Populace*."[16] For conservatives, urban crowds were easily perverted by evil elements. Public space could be overrun at any moment by loathsome mobs. They were a menace to society, driven only by cravings and desires. Social theorists argued that urban crowds had a particular psychology that did not conform to common sense. The "masses" were an unpredictable, pathological force. Most evocative to this way of thinking was French psychologist Gustave Le Bon's volume entitled *The Crowds* (1895). Le Bon was an extreme conservative who propagated racism, defended aristocratic elitism, and was vehemently hostile to popular democracy. He referred to the coming age as "the era of crowds" and saw them as a fickle source of disturbance. Crowds fell prey to a peculiar mentality that induced people to do things they would never do on their own. They simply reacted to the moment regardless of rules or discipline. For Le Bon, the crowds of the late nineteenth century (and by this he meant working-class people) sought nothing less than to destroy society. Civilization risked sinking into barbarism.

A steady stream of sensationalist slum novels and crime fiction stoked anxieties about the foul play and savagery lurking in the shadows. In 1842, French writer Eugène Sue began the serial novel *Les Mystères de Paris* in the French newspaper *Journal des débats*. It took willing readers on a journey into the back alleys and moral wasteland of the city's slums, where all manner of vice and crime happened. It was an instant success. Sue fashioned the city's poor classes into a caste of melodramatic characters. Unscrupulous criminals, wandering Jews, thieves, and prostitutes littered the pages. The novel triggered a wave of urban gothic thrillers from *The Mysteries of London* (1845) to the mysteries of Lisbon, Budapest, and St. Petersburg. In London, cheaply printed "penny dreadfuls" and "penny gaffs" proliferated. They were rip-roaring tales of unspeakable crimes in the shadowy margins of the city. The public could not get enough of the lurid reports about the savage underclasses. Attacks at night, bloodshed, and murders were embellished in the press in gory detail. Sexual fantasies abounded about the violent underworld of prostitution. The female prostitute came to represent all that was transgressive and corrupt about the modern city. Wicked, sensual, and unruly, the prostitute embodied all the dangers lurking in the public spaces of the city.[17] Newspapers were jam-packed with stories of innocent migrant women coerced into brothels by sex traffickers. The presumed sexual depravity of night-boarders in working-class households came under intense scrutiny. The general public became acquainted with homosexuality through this kind of sensationalist reporting. The murky borderline between crass sensationalism, pornography, and serious examination of the state of society all but disappeared. Articles proliferated in the popular press about police murder investigations and criminal gangs on the make. The sensationalized reporting of the Jack the Ripper serial murders in the slums of Whitechapel in 1888 kept London spellbound. Accounts of the mutilated bodies of his victims (five young prostitutes) were a voyeuristic tale about the evil waiting in the gloom.

Turn-of-the-century Berlin seemed to personify all the hopes and fears about the modern city rolled into one. It was the incarnation of modernity, of extravagance and extremes. The years between 1879 and 1914 were a period of spectacular growth for Berlin. In 1871, it was proclaimed the capital of the *Kaiserreich*, a newly united Germany. It became a metropolis, or *Weltstadt*, almost overnight. Located on the Spree River deep in Prussian territory, the city was surrounded by marshy woodlands and crisscrossed by canals, lakes, and streams. For much of its history, it was more a hopelessly provincial backwater than a major city. But by the end of the 1870s, its population suddenly reached 1 million, and only thirty years later, in 1900, it ballooned upward to 2 million. By 1914, the population stood at nearly 3 million. Berlin was the upstart, as art critic Karl Scheffler remarked in 1910. It had overtaken the older port cities of Hamburg and Bremen on the north coast. Its expansion was "reckless, violent, and established in a kind of no-man's land, far from the terrain of European culture." It was the speed of Berlin's rise, the exhilaration of its life that fascinated urban observers. Mark Twain visited Berlin in 1891 and remarked that "it is a new city: the newest I have seen. . . . The main mass of the city looks as if it had been built last week."[18] The famous "Berlin Tempo," the breakneck pace of its growth left little room for delicacy. For most observers it was rootless, an ugly jumble of a city, in a state of perpetual becoming.

The social divisions were stark. Berlin had long been a royal Prussian stronghold and military citadel. The Unter den Linden was the city's most prestigious boulevard and stretched from the Prussian Royal Palace to the Brandenburg Gate. Prussian *junkers* (aristocracy) and soldiers dominated its public life and the city's residents bowed to them in deference. Militarism and authoritarianism were the defining ethos. Frankfurt and Hamburg were traditionally the pecuniary powerhouses and claimed the leading stock exchanges in Germany. With the founding of the German Empire in 1871, Berlin pushed them aside and took over as Germany's financial center. The big German banks and joint-stock companies set up their headquarters in the new capital. The city's thriving economy created an atmosphere of wild speculation and materialistic flashiness encapsulated in the famous *Gründerjahre*, or boom years.[19] Large and small investors alike raced to plunk down money in real estate, railways, and new industries. Money was easy and the profits were mind-boggling. The *nouveau riche* spent lavishly on grand apartments in neighborhoods to the west in Charlottenburg, Rixdorf, Schöneberg, and Wilmersdorf, and even further out in leafy suburbs with street after street of opulent villas. The Prussian aristocracy and Berlin's *Bürgertum* mingled together as privileged, fabulously wealthy elites. On the opposite side of the city, the working classes lived and toiled in a broad industrial belt stretching north and east out to the urban fringes. It was shunned as a wild no-man's-land crammed with the tenements and factories that were the city's productive force.

Machine and electrical engineering, precision mechanics, and chemistry were Berlin's specialties and catapulted the city into a European economic powerhouse. It churned out everything from locomotives to trucks, engines, boilers, and sewing machines. The city's economic muscle was showcased at the Berlin Industrial Exhibition of 1896, a grandiose display of some 4,000 exhibits on the banks of the Spree River. At first, industries congregated north of the city. These traditional factory districts around the Oranienburg and Hamburg Gates were called the "Feuerland" for the iron factories belching out smoke and flames. Then the Ringbahn, or belt railway, around Berlin was completed in 1877 and gave industry access to cheap land further out on the city's periphery. Some 5,000 workers fabricated railroad equipment and locomotives in the Borsig workshops to the north in Moabit. Borsig attracted a cabal of heavy machinery and weapons manufacturers. Then it moved even further out to a huge site at Tegel, where it built Borsigwalde, an entire new settlement for its workforce. The Siemens plant northwest of the city, called Siemensstadt from 1914, churned out electric dynamos, telegraph cables, and communication devices. When Werner von Siemens and Emil Rathenau secured the German rights to exploit Thomas Edison's patents, Berlin became the headquarters for the nascent electrical industry. By 1907, the Allgemeine Elektricitäts Gesellschaft (AEG) already employed 70,000 people making every kind of electrical equipment. Companies manufacturing automobiles and aircraft, and industrial machinery congregated in Berlin's outskirts along with the chemical giant Actien-Gesellschaft für Anilin-Fabrication (AGFA). They were knitted together by a web of railroad tracks and junctions, electric tram lines, and waterways. The working classes followed. By the turn of the century, the population on the outskirts of Berlin was growing faster than in the center city.

The question was, how could functional buildings be designed for these new industries? The gloomy brick factories of the earlier industrial era were impractical for the new scale and technical range of production. In 1907, architects Peter Behrens and Joseph Maria Olbrich founded the Deutscher Werkbund, an association of architects and industrialists anxious to improve mass production techniques and Germany's clout on the world market. Their mission was to create a machine aesthetic based on standardization and modern product design for mass society.[20] More important than the material itself was the spirit that it represented: good, practical form as industrial philosophy. An entire generation of avant-garde artists and architects were first introduced to the idea of modern design through the Werkbund. Peter Behrens was hired by AEG and tasked with the appearance of everything from the design of the company's factory to its advertising. The result was the immense turbine hall for the AEG electrical plant in Berlin's Moabit district. It was a revolutionary steel-framed building with towering glass walls. The glazed facade was emblazoned with the company's logo. It represented the Werkbund dream of a high-quality production facility that was clean, luminous, and would dignify the worker as a human being (Figure 26).

Figure 26 AEG Turbine Hall, Huttenstrasse, Berlin Moabit district, 1950s. Peter Behrens.

Factory architecture was becoming corporate branding in the hands of avant-garde architects. The first Werkbund Exhibition in 1914, held in Cologne, featured a cavalcade of building prototypes linking architecture to the productive forces of industry. Architect Bruno Taut designed the wildly original Glass Pavilion as a showcase for the products of the German glass industry association. Its crystalline glass dome was framed in steel. The interior was a kaleidoscopic wonderland of colored glass changing every twenty seconds. It was an entirely new architectural aesthetic merged with commercial advertising. Werkbund influence was evident in the Fagus Shoe Factory in the town of Alfeld in Saxony. Designed by architects Walter Gropius and Adolf Meyer, the trailblazing structure in concrete and brick was a new kind of work space—open, functional, with a transparent glass facade. Its design signified modern shoe manufacturing articulated in three-dimensional form. Gropius and Meyer designed the production machinery, the corporate offices, and created the Fagus logo, business cards, and stationary around a modern industrial aesthetic.

While exceptional structures such as these would lead the way to modern architecture, the working classes in Berlin toiled in sweltering factories and workshops. It was the banal reality of heavy industry that most marked Berlin's outer districts. To a certain extent, the Hobrecht Plan of 1858–62 had prepared for the expansion of Berlin and laid out broad boulevards and squares beyond the municipal boundary of the custom walls. But Hobrecht had certainly not anticipated the teeming slums woven through the industrial outskirts. Floods of newcomers arrived with dreams of freedom and opportunity. They

Figure 27 View into the parlor of a Berlin worker family in the apartment house Liegnitzer Strasse 9, 1910.

were from Brandenburg, East Prussia, and Silesia. Thousands were Russian Jews escaping pogroms and poverty. They found an exasperating housing shortage. Thousands were homeless. Shanty towns sprang up along the edges of the city (Figure 27).

The majority of the new immigrants were crammed into the *miethausen* or *mietskasernen* (rental barracks) as they were pejoratively called.[21] They were slapped up by real estate speculators in the outlying districts of Wedding, Moabit, Neukölln, and Kreuzberg. The massive five-story structures stretched over an entire block and became the dreary symbol of Berlin as an industrial city. The facades were often decorated in neoclassical or ornate italianate style. But the showy street front hid the reality inside. The *mietskasernen* were divided into miniscule one and two-room flats designed to extract the maximum in exploitative rental profits. Over 40 percent of Berlin's households lived in one room and another 28 percent lived in two-room flats. The corridors were dark and unventilated. Households in the *mietskaserne* shared communal water spigots and privies. The flats surrounded an internal courtyard that filled up with claptrap structures, innumerable small trades, many of them spewing out noxious odors and pollution. Disease was rampant. The largest buildings, such as the Meyers Hof complex in Wedding, housed thousands around a succession of courtyards in a gloomy and oppressive maze.

The depiction of this foreign, frontier world of working-class Berlin engrossed urban observers. Riding the electric streetcar to the northern outskirts of Moabit, a fearless explorer looked out

> over a different Berlin than the one that can be seen from the windows of the Café Bauer, Unter den Linden, or on the Kurfürstendamm. . . . The north is the reverse side of the coin . . . rental barracks with deep courtyards and narrow side and diagonal buildings, depressed faces on the streets, many children, shopkeepers, many bars, hospitals, and so on. The air is thicker than in the Friedrichstadt, and a veil seems to float over the whole area.[22]

Artists Franz Skarbina and Hans Baluschek rendered Berlin's gritty industrial world and proletarian life with the frankness of critical realism. Their paintings captured the soullessness of the industrial districts. Bent and weary workers arrive for their shifts against a backdrop of factories, railroad spurs, and the brick overpasses of the thundering Stadtbahn. The drudgery of life is expressed in their sour faces. Shanty shacks litter the snow below a railroad trestle, as better-off Berliners walk by impassively. Artists such as Skarbina and Baluschek recreated the locales—the streets, the railroad viaducts, the factories, the tenements—of proletariat Berlin. On the other hand, the quintessential "gutter artist" Heinrich Zille pushed the dingy underbelly of the city into a different light. His drawings and photographs chronicled working lives with startling dignity. The humorous sketches lifted them up out of misery. Zille excelled at photographic "doorstep portraits" that revealed the capacity of working men and women to make their own lives. Zille switched the typically abysmal angle on the working-class districts and turned Berlin's ugliness into beauty. He portrayed the *mietskaserne* as an intimate world. The courtyards bustle with activity: "Residents and boarders came and went; vendors and street artists, such as organ grinders, conducted business; coal and wood piles catered to various customers; trash boxes and privies were visited regularly; and children danced and played"[23] (Figure 28).

These artistic caricatures were a spectacle of Otherness, akin to Charles Dickens's portrayals of London's East End and Emile Zola's descriptions of the slums of Paris. Nevertheless, Zille highlighted the complexity of working-class social space. Street life was essential to the everyday experience of the working classes. Despite social exclusion and brutal hardship, the street was a lived environment where daily life took place. Wandering the streets meant interacting with flower sellers, costermongers and hawkers, barbers, vagrants and vagabonds, pimps and their ladies. Workers often changed lodging, but they remained in the same neighborhood and relied on these close social networks. Ethnic groups banded together, provided casual resources, and formed tight-knit communities around their tenement buildings and local markets, and their places of worship. Shopkeepers and market-sellers shared gossip and information and

Figure 28 "In front of the milk shop," 1924/25, Heinrich Zille.

kept informal credit tabs. The most marginal and disenfranchised found support in the obscurity of these ordinary spaces. Neighborhood was key to the quotidian solidarity found within the cosmopolitan melting pot of the big city.

Neighborhood was also a highly politicized space. Here lay an intimate topography of resistance. There were widespread fears among the middle classes that conditions in industrial neighborhoods could eventually explode into insurrection. Marginal figures such as Jews and immigrants came under intense scrutiny. In public opinion, they were aliens without legal residence, paid no taxes, and voted socialist. Conditions at home as well as at work did indeed radicalize the proletariat. Protests and skirmishes in the street were frequent. Lodgers in the tenement houses boycotted rising rents and went on strike against landlords. In 1910, raucous rent-strikes were organized in over 200 tenement houses in Budapest.[24] The everyday familiarity of working-class neighborhoods easily merged into surreptitious political activities. Gathering in likeminded taverns and cafés, local firebrands hashed out complaints and whispered the latest political rumors. They plotted their next forays into the streets. Local shopkeepers and families joined up with workers as they trudged in protest, carrying placards and shouting their grievances. At open-air gatherings, motley crowds of people sang and danced, passed political leaflets, and listened to speeches. Anniversaries of revolutionary struggle, even funeral processions became political rallies that reinforced community identity. Traditional folk pageants slipped into rowdy demonstrations. The *Vachalcade*, a carnivalesque street celebration of life and liberty, took place regularly in the working-class outskirts of Paris, under the watchful eyes of the police on the good chance that disturbances would end the day.

The belief that the urban masses constituted a potentially volcanic force and that their pent-up grievances might boil into mutiny manifested itself in virtually every city. Strike waves rolled through Europe's cities between the 1870s and 1914. The decade began with the bloody Paris Commune. The Franco-Prussian War and the defeat of Napoleon III at the Battle of Sedan provoked an extraordinary crisis in the capital. The city's population refused to give up the fight as the German Army proceeded to ring the city and starve it into submission. Led by the working classes, Parisians proclaimed themselves independent and heroically defended their turf for ten weeks. Workers streamed into Haussmann's newly embellished central districts and began to institute radical social reforms. They took control of factories, rents were frozen, schools were opened to everyone, and aid given to the poor. The government saw the insurgents as cutthroats and criminals. The French army was ordered into a beleaguered Paris and brutally crushed the rebellion street by street. The enraged rebels filled the Tuileries Palace (next to the Louvre) with gunpowder, smeared it with tar and gasoline, and set it ablaze. Among the buildings destroyed in the battles were the City Hall, the Law Courts, the Police Headquarters, the Ministry of Finance, and sections of Haussmann's cherished rue de Rivoli. Some 20,000 people were slaughtered. Mass executions left the Seine River marbled with blood. Those among the working-class leadership who survived were sent off to prison on Devil's Island.

Violent strikes took place in French and Italian cities throughout the 1880s, with a massive strike in Rome at the end of the decade. There were bloody riots in Frankfurt. In 1889, a massive work stoppage took place among coal miners in the Ruhr. Brutal clashes between workers and police roiled Berlin in 1890. Strikes and lockouts were a constant feature of London life. The construction projects that dramatically transformed London into a modern world city were the target of continual labor unrest, often plunging into battles with police. One of the fiercest industrial disputes of the nineteenth century was the builders' strikes of 1859–61 that marshaled the city's master builders and construction workers in a prolonged campaign of walkouts and public protests. Anarchist riots in 1891–92 in Paris led to a hellish explosion in a restaurant that wounded scores of people. A bomb went off in the Chamber of Deputies. Small terrorist cells staged indiscriminate attacks against cafés, railroad stations, and on the city's famed boulevards. Hamburg endured a bitter labor conflict and harbor strike in 1896–97.

The strike movements in the first decade of the twentieth century reached record proportions. These were moments of extraordinary tumult, transgression, and social leveling. Italy experienced its first general strike in 1904 with episodes of unchecked violence in the industrial cities of the north. There were insurrectionary movements in a rash of French cities including Marseille. The ferocity of the revolutionary waves of 1905, especially in the Russian Empire, was unprecedented. Columns of some 50,000 to 100,000 workers marched through St. Petersburg and converged on the Winter Palace on January 22, 1905, and were gunned down by the tsar's troops. Around 200 were massacred and another 500–800 injured. Bloody Sunday set off a groundswell of strikes, protests, and troop mutinies. Marshall law was declared and troops stationed at strategic points in St. Petersburg where they battled with insurgents. In Odessa, the mutiny by sailors on the battleship Potemkin was followed by riots and bloodshed. By October a paralyzing general strike forced Tsar Nicholas II to capitulate and issue the October Manifesto that granted civil rights and established a popularly elected Duma Parliament.

There was a whole range of grievances that sparked the revolutionary groundswells in 1905 throughout the Russian Empire. Among them were resentment at Russification and conscription in the Russo-Japanese War, the long hours in the factory for paltry pay, the foreign control of the factories, the high rents, and wretched conditions in the slums. In Poland, clashes broke out between Russian troops and organized bands of workers and students in Warsaw, Vilnius, and Łódź. The weavers and spinners in the Łódź textile mills had already staged protests in 1892 that ended in street battles. In 1905, thousands of workers took part in general strikes and occupied the Scheibler textile mills. The murder of a worker by the Russian cavalry in June sparked bitter demonstrations. Local militias erected barricades in the working-class districts and launched attacks against the police and military patrols. The city came to a standstill as fires raged and clashes left the streets littered with the dead and wounded. Around 200 men, women, and children perished. The rebellion ended tragically for the insurgents. The turmoil was brutally crushed by Russian troops and then followed by marshal law.

The aftershocks of the 1905 revolution can be viewed as well in Riga. In the late nineteenth century, Riga was a thriving industrial port and the fifth largest city in the Russian Empire. It was situated on the wide Daugava River that flowed from Belarus down through the forests and marshlands of the province of Livonia to the Baltic Sea. A web of railroad lines linked Riga to Warsaw and St. Petersburg, and to towns and cities throughout central Europe and the Balkans. The railroad was a powerful stimulus to economic development that took place from two sides—Riga was traditionally German and then rapidly Russified by official Imperial policy. The entrepreneurs behind the city's industrial boom were mainly Baltic Germans and Reich Germans. Much of Riga's state-of-the-art industrial technology and capital arrived from Germany. The wealthy commercial and industrial magnates established themselves in fashionable new districts west of the old historic center (see Chapter 7). Riga had long been an eastern enclave of German business and yet it was also a crucial outpost of the Russian Empire. Grain from southern Russia was exported through its port. Massive grain elevators, beer and tobacco processing facilities lined the quays along the Daugava. Some 50 percent of Russian industrial production actually took place in Riga. Its industries manufactured everything from textiles to machinery, electrical equipment, chemicals and rubber, and railroad cars. Twenty-seven major businesses were chartered in the city in 1894–99 alone. The huge railroad car manufacturer Russo-Baltic Wagon produced the first automobile in the Russian Empire and pioneered airplane construction. The Provodnik Corporation was one of the world's largest producers of automobile tires. Its Riga plant employed 14,000 workers.[25]

From just over 100,000 inhabitants in 1867, Riga's population shot up 500 percent to 500,000 by 1914. Only Moscow, St. Petersburg, and Łódź had larger working classes. Thousands flocked to Riga for jobs in the factories. The new arrivals were Latvians, Poles, Belarusians, and Lithuanian Jews. Many were highly skilled, literate, and assimilated rapidly into a radicalized working class. The Riga Polytechnic Institute produced highly qualified Latvian engineers and technicians and played a vital role in the Russian Empire's industrial research. Others toiled in rudimentary jobs and lived in abject poverty. Together, they dramatically shifted the ethnic makeup of the city. Latvians began to supplant Germans as the largest ethnic group. Some 40 percent of Riga's Latvians worked in manufacturing, 30 percent of the city's Russians, and some 50 percent of the Jewish population were employed in industry. By the late nineteenth century, the new working classes represented well over half the city's population. They moved into the port district and eastern Moscow suburbs with its jumble of old wooden cottages, brick factories, and warehouses. Dreary tenements rose five and six-stories around a maze of bleak internal courtyards. The social segregation was profound, and became more so as the population swelled. Class and ethnic divisions were a constant source of bitter strife.

Riga's leftist New Current movement and the Latvian Social Democratic Workers' Party thrived on the grievances of factory workers and unrest in the streets. The revolutionary turmoil of 1905 sparked a wave of protests in the Moscow suburbs. Mass meetings were held. Large crowds marched along Moscow Street to the city center, carrying banners and singing revolutionary songs. This claiming of the streets was treated as an immediate threat by the Russian authorities. As they approached the iron bridge over the Daugava River, soldiers opened fire and killed more than seventy people. Incensed by the murders, labor leaders called for a general strike and barricades went up. Armed workers descended on the city's jail and police headquarters and attacked the Provodnik rubber factory. Jubilant crowds gathered in Riga's park to celebrate after Nicholas II issued the October Manifesto granting freedom of speech and an elected Duma in response to the insurrectionary waves. But it did little to quell the insurgency. More than 20,000 workers went on strike on May Day 1908 followed by another wave of walkouts in 1910–12. In 1910 amid the turmoil, Nicholas II and his family visited Riga in a spectacle of pomp and reconciliation. Early film footage captured their arrival on the Daugava, the military parades on boulevards festooned with flags. A regal procession wound in aloof elegance to the unveiling of the statue of Peter the Great at Riga's central square. Despite the pageantry, there was little hope for social peace.

This kind of urban warfare became all too frequent as working-class injustices boiled over into insurrection. "Bloody week" in Barcelona raged from July 26 to 31 in

1909 and hit a new level of savagery. Thousands marched seething through the streets. Roving bands of rioters overturned streetcars, cut telephone and telegraph wires, tore up cobblestones, and manned barricades. Other thousands watched the gory spectacle from windows in the surrounding buildings. Pitched battles between insurgents and military troops turned the city into a scene of carnage. Catholic churches and schools were set ablaze. Some 100 buildings were reduced to ashes. In Berlin workers went out on strike in the industrial district of Moabit in 1910 and fought police and soldiers in the streets. Strikes and street combat hit the Ruhr in 1912. Some 200 people were wounded in the Liverpool riots of 1911. Miners, dockers, and railwaymen rampaged through the towns of Liverpool, Southampton, Hull, and Cardiff into 1912. Buildings were set ablaze and looters grabbed what they could. Some 50,000 police and troops were used to quell the disturbances.[26] The outbreak of the First World War in August 1914 spelled the end of working-class agitation and political violence. Millions of men donned uniforms and were sent to the fighting fronts. For a brief moment, the treacherous crowds on the street were transformed into patriotic citizens waving flags and cheering the troops as they marched off to war. The public spaces of the city changed into a tableau of nationalistic fervor.

It is somewhat uncanny that amid this mayhem, the working classes and poor somehow survived and found pleasure in a variety of everyday diversions. They insisted on living well, regardless of the limits of life circumscribed for them or the outcomes of their rebelliousness. The tenement house itself was a space of intense social solidarity with ample opportunity for sharing daily life. Leisure and entertainment took place in the courtyards, alleyways, and streets. Some pursuits were derived from older-style enjoyments; others were more modern in scope. They existed side-by-side. Religious festivals and traditional celebrations such as Carnival happened in the collective space of neighborhood. The anonymity and overturning of social norms during Carnival or at masquerade balls were instances of ribald reverie and subversive play. The city pleasure gardens were open to all. Although those of modest means kept their own space, commentators remarked on the mix of social classes promenading and enjoying the entertainments in the pleasure gardens. Market and livestock fairs and folk festivals had their traditional quotient of jugglers and puppet shows. Acrobatic troops and organ-players with trained monkeys or bears were a ubiquitous feature at outdoor markets and seasonal fairs. The arrival of a traveling circus was signaled by a boisterous procession through the streets. These pastimes offered moments of spontaneity and merriment, of sociability and courtship. They were also free entertainment, which made them popular for working-class families with few coins to spare.

The modernist avant-garde eventually dipped down into this potpourri of pastimes for creative ideas. Generally, however, these older forms of play were slowly disappearing in the face of newer kinds of amusement. In British cities, early pub-based music entertainment and "free and easies" popped up in working-class districts with their entertainment geared to local patrons. There was no charge for admission. Both men and women enjoyed the merriment, especially after payday on Fridays. The music and performances were drawn from immigrant culture, particularly Irish traditions. Local performers sang comic songs and sentimental ballads with the audience joining in. The atmosphere was boisterous and convivial. The Green Gate Tavern and the Eagle Tavern in London's East End did a roaring business. In Berlin the suburban beer-gardens offered military concerts, or *Sängerfest*, with the audience belting out songs. Despite the patriotic overtones, they could descend into chaos with brawls breaking out between performers and spectators.[27] The working-class café played the same role in cities and towns across France. The overwhelming majority of cafés in the capital of Paris catered to the working classes and lower-middle class. After Haussmann's renovations, there were around 22,000 of these drink shops. By 1900, their numbers had grown to as many as 27,000 establishments.[28] They formed a dense fabric in the working-class strongholds in the northeastern districts, especially along the old custom walls and peripheral faubourgs (Figure 29).

These social rituals had fault lines and pockets of isolation, especially for the poorest and indigent. But the proletarian café and pub, the local bistro and beer joint, served a wide variety of functions from living room to political haunt, from labor exchange to factory annex. It was a democratic space and oasis of geniality, especially for immigrants and new arrivals to the city. The camaraderie was dominated by men. Women were not excluded, but the drink shop's atmosphere of flirtation and the temptations of prostitution made them risky. Late-night revelries and gambling, drinking, and the sex trade were the shadow side of modernity. These were places of resistance, where protests and walkouts could be plotted. The collective drinking and singing stirred up political emotions, with the flinging of insults and mockery, the sneaky ridicule in smutty lyrics and vernacular slang. Radical weeklies and newspapers were read and political agitators found an eager audience. The drink shop festivities were breeding grounds of radicalism and quickly jumped into strike action and political protest.

Figure 29 Hofbräuhaus in Munich, circa 1886.

The defiant quality of these entertainments made them hugely popular as well as highly creative spaces for shaping modern music and dance. Sailors and fishermen in the taverns and brothels of Lisbon's port districts sang melancholic *fado* music to the strains of the guitar. The lyrics were charismatic and politically militant. In Seville and the cities of Andalusia, and then in Madrid, the *café cantante* was the birthplace of Flamingo. Berlin's Tingeltangel joints offered skits lampooning the greedy upper classes and plenty of naughty entertainment that pioneered burlesque theater. The plebian dance halls of Paris attracted street gangs called *les Apaches* that concocted dance pantomimes of a lovers' fight. Often enacted to Tango music, it was laced with sexual violence. Dances such as the Tango, Cakewalk, and Ragtime were foot-worked by working-class hoofers and then filtered up to a broad urban public. The *bals musettes* on the outskirts of Paris and the dancing-saloons popular in the eastern suburbs of Berlin were filled on weekends with local workmen and their families, with prostitutes and petty criminals sprinkled through the merriment. English press correspondent Henry Vizetelly described the scene at the Villa Colonna outside Berlin, where the dancing and music were frenetic with "girls striving to outdo each other in wild and passionate movement. As the evening wears on loud laughter and shouting from carousing groups . . . mingle with the lively music, while clouds of dust and tobacco-smoke float above the heads of the flushed and frenzied dancers."[29] Although the popular culture of the working classes was pillared by social elites, descending into these other-worlds was a mischievous adventure for pleasure seekers. Slumming became a favorite excursion into the city's proletarian underbelly, so much so that the bistro and dance hall owners routinely advertised performances. The myth of the city as Modern Babylon created a seductive, risqué fantasy that swelled profits.

Budapest was the Hapsburg Empire's unofficial capital of nightlife and popular entertainment. It was famous for its music halls, cabarets, and coffee houses. The strains of gypsy music were omnipresent in the train stations and pleasure gardens as well as in cafés and restaurants. Music streamed out of the city's Terézváros neighborhood, where most of the city's Jewish working and lower-middle classes lived. By the turn of the century, the population reached over 100,000 in Terézváros and the surrounding districts. Jósef Kiss, the great chronicler of Budapest life, captured the atmosphere on the main thoroughfare of Király Street in his 1874 potboiler *Mysteries of Budapest*. "One experiences the genuine rhythm of a world city, with its hustle and bustle, its comings and goings, its effervescence and hurried way of life. This is the throbbing heart of the capital, which never sleeps, never rests, and is full of noisy life."[30] It was a teeming spectacle, jammed with people, with street markets, second-hand clothing stores, kosher restaurants, shops and warehouses. Cafés and beer halls lined the sidewalks. The cabarets and Orpheum theaters were a nonstop cavalcade of music shows and stand-up comedy. Their biting, hilarious commentary on Budapest life packed the houses. Turning out for the acts was a titillating escapade. Revelers rubbed shoulders with pimps and prostitutes and petty crooks. The Yiddish music halls were poo-pooed as entertainment for poor people and a threat to Hungarian assimilation. But they were booming businesses and reached an ever-broader public.

The demand for escapist pleasures was immense. Savvy impresarios and municipal authorities capitalized on the public's appetite for amusement and conjured up a torrent of exciting prospects. Entertainment became more commercialized and more spectacular. Traveling variety theaters and illusionist shows were immensely popular. The *Théâtre Gallici-Rancy* was an elaborate performance of magic and acrobatics that traveled through France at the turn of the century from Toulouse to Marseille, from Nantes to Bordeaux, from Amiens to Rouen.[31] Music halls were fabulously popular and boasted sold-out performances. The costs were kept low to attract large audiences and volume business. Everyone from slumming aristocrats and snooty bourgeois couples to working-class fans packed the seats along with the inevitable tourists and gawking sightseers. They offered a repertoire of song and dance, farces and comedy routines, acrobats and animal acts. The older raucous working-class song culture was channeled into profitable businesses with professional performers. The commercial venues did not replace the neighborhood leisure subculture. They existed side-by-side. The fluid transmission of styles from the populist pub and café to the music hall stage was obvious in the provocative material and acts. The songs and skits played out big city life with biting satire and hysterical comic relief (Figure 30).

In 1851, the Canterbury opened in London with its "Sing-Song" and "Free and Easy" nights. It became the prototype for the commercial music hall. Just a few years later, London had thirty-three large music halls and several hundred smaller ones. France adopted the British music hall concept in 1862, and the Folies Bergère, the Alhambra, the Moulin Rouge, and the Olympia opened their doors soon after. Most of these music halls and cabarets followed a seasonal cycle of performances. Sexual innuendos and erotic routines added to the excitement. Berlin had its Walhalla, the Bellevue, the Amerikanisches Theater, the Orpheum, and the fabulous Wintergarten. At the Walhalla, audiences swooned at a fountain on stage that spouted illuminated water and half-naked women in sequence. The music halls enticed men with a menu of sensual pleasures with many of the performers working as prostitutes. Odessa's swank Severnaya music hall featured upward of fifty acts and was the scene of nightly scandals and drunken incidents. Although the snobbish belittled the music hall as vulgar amusement, they opened in cities everywhere. They were uproariously entertaining and openly seditious, which made them quintessential modern art forms.

Provincial cities might have been slower paced than London or Paris, but people still boarded trains and headed for their local capital to relish the entertainment. Liverpool and Birmingham each had six music halls. The People's Palace and Empire Theatre of Varieties in Bristol could seat upward of 3,000 people and offered family entertainment.[32] For a small fee, families could enjoy versions of the Folies Bergère in Lyon, in Le Havre and Rouen. Impresarios hired actors for a season, rented theaters, and stayed for a few weeks or months in cities and towns across Europe. By 1900, steamboats and railroads cut travel times between western and eastern Europe to a fraction of what they had been just a few years before. Climbing aboard with costumes and props in tow, theater troupes played a major role in transferring modern cultural forms from London and Paris to towns from Tbilisi to Kiev. Through the press, readers

Figure 30 The Royal Victoria Coffee Palace and Music Hall, London, Illustration from *The Graphic*, vol. XXIV, no 612, August 20, 1881.

could keep up with performances and music hall gossip beyond their local worlds. The immense popularity of the music hall and vaudeville entertainment was part of the visual phantasmagoria of the modern city. Increasingly, urban culture was infused with extravagant spectacles and thrilling entertainment. The rhythms of modern life were captured in the boisterous performances on the music hall stage and its raucous mockery of norms and conventions.

Spectators could gulp in traveling circuses and monkey-theaters, wax museums, and panoramas. Ever popular "Zulu Shows" and "People Shows" (*Völkerschauen*) toured regularly through Europe. African and Island people arrayed in native costume were put on display in specially built backdrops and dioramas. The much-anticipated appearance of a "People Show" was considered the sign of a first-rate European city and colonial power. Season after season, the central European city of Breslau welcomed an exhibition of Nubian tribes from Sudan, Australian Aboriginals, Ashantis from the Gold Coast, and the Futa people of Guinea. "Believe-it-or-not" exhibits mesmerized multitudes every year. Süring's Universum and Umlauff's World-Museum in Frankfurt, the Gabrieles Panopticon in Munich, and the Hanseatic Panopticum in Hamburg offered a blend of amazing sideshows with dioramas and wax displays.[33] Whole entertainment districts took shape around the flashy world of show business. Leicester Square was London's first great entertainment zone. Over the course of its repeated metamorphosis, gadabouts could take in the exhibits at the Royal Panopticon of Science and Art and climb into the interior of Wyld's massive Great Globe, sixty feet in diameter. Robert Barker's brick rotunda building presented two-levels of panorama exhibits. The Alhambra Theater in its splendorous Moorish building was a pageant of circus and musical hall performances. This kind of foreign pastiche, from Hindoo to Moorish and Egyptania, was taken as Britain's talent for enjoying the fruits of empire. The parade of modern urban entertainments shared the visual optic of wondrous scenes from the colonies. The Empire Theater rivaled the Alhambra with its French *café-chantant*, panoramas and variety shows, with its prostitutes roaming the upper balconies. Close by was the Cavour restaurant with its bawdy dancing, burlesque entertainment, and "midnight orgies after the Alhambra had finished."[34] Leicester Square was a place of extravaganzas, illusions, and nine-day wonders designed to tickle the fancy of the common man.

In Paris, the *grands boulevards* on the Right Bank were a riot of music theaters and cafés, with the Musée Grévin wax museum topping the attractions. The great hill of Montmartre overlooking the city and the neighborhoods of Clichy and Pigalle at its foot became the hedonistic nerve centers for the city's well-known cabarets and dance halls. The Chat Noir cabaret and the frolics at the Moulin de la Galette achieved international fame. The Elysée-Montmartre and the Moulin Rouge outdid themselves in spectacular performances of the can-can. Promoted by impresario Charles Zidler, the Moulin Rouge became the toast of Paris.[35] Entertainers such as La Goulue and Jane Avril enjoyed celebrity status with their risqué gyrations and music. Although the can-can originated in working-class dance halls, it was the women of the Moulin Rouge with their swishing skirts, high kicks, and cartwheels that made it famous. Nightlife in Paris was sexually charged. By the turn of the century, the area around the Boulevard de Clichy and Montmartre was notorious for its prostitution and rough criminality. The Théâtre du Grand Guignol at the foot of Montmartre specialized in lurid sexual scenes with lifelike special effects. The profusion of erotic entertainment and libidinous excess gave the city its reputation as the pleasure capital of Europe. Partygoers and tourists ready for a good time were hypnotized by the city's blend of sensual gaiety and extravagance. But for some people, Paris was no longer Paris. Conservative Edmond de Goncourt morosely complained that it had become a "kind of free city in which all the thieves of the earth who have made their fortunes in business come to eat badly and sleep with the flesh of someone who calls herself a Parisienne"[36] (Figure 31).

The programs in the music halls and theaters inevitably featured clever gadgetry. The "big three" music halls in Munich—the Kolosseum, the Blumensäle, and the Deutsche Theater—competed for customers with evermore thrilling shows, including a simulated guillotine execution. The Apollo Theater in Düsseldorf, which was built around 1900, included a panorama exhibit, an American bar, and slot machine hall. By the early twentieth century, theaters began unveiling kinescope devices and flickering motion pictures. The Folies Bergère in Paris showed moving pictures between song and dance and acrobatic numbers.[37] Even moderate-size towns throughout Europe could boast

Figure 31 The exit of the Moulin Rouge, circa 1900.

three and four theaters that offered a mixture of live routines, panorama exhibits, and grainy film shorts. Showman Arthur Duncan Thomas created ciné-variety extravaganzas shown in music halls throughout towns in England, from Brighton's Alhambra, the Argyle Theatre in Birkenhead, to the Winter Gardens in Morecambe. The Rekord Theater in the town of Tallinn (deep in the Baltic region of eastern Europe) tempted patrons with a wisecracking comedian and a xylophonist as the warm-up to the main feature—a silent movie starring a wily detective.[38]

Panoramas were one of the most wildly popular attractions of the nineteenth century. Millions of people were caught up in "Panoramania" and flocked to see the shows. Virtually all large cities in Europe had at least one if not several panorama productions. They were huge 360-degree translucent cloth panels painted with fabulous scenes, backlit with lights, and then projected in specially built rotunda buildings. Spectators were taken into a magic circle and transported in time and place to cities, historical events, and scenic landscapes. The public was enraptured by the visual illusion. Viewing the fantasy scenes through the gauzy filter of silk and colored backlights was a touristic excursion, a virtual grand tour. The most famous early panorama was Robert Barker's show at Leicester Square. Without leaving their seats, audiences were transported skyward for a bird's eye view of London in realistic detail. Charles Dickens, among others, poked fun at the panorama phenomenon, creating a character named Mr. Booley, who traversed most of the known globe—following the Overland Mail to India, ascending the Mississippi River by steamboat—all without leaving the confines of Leicester Square. Well over a hundred panoramas were exhibited between 1793 and 1863 in London alone, with Leicester Square, the Strand, and the Colosseum shows the most popular.

The American Robert Fulton, better known as the inventor of the steamboat, opened two panorama rotundas in Paris and dazzled audiences with bird's eye views of Paris. They gasped as they recognized familiar buildings resplendent in the light and pointed excitedly to places undulating on the gossamer screen. Viewing the city on high captured the imagination of the public in good part because it rendered the entirety of the urban realm comprehensible. People delighted in the sight of the city. They reveled in the aerial vantage point at a time when hot-air balloon rides were also all the rage. Fulton's partner James Thayer built two rotundas framing the city's first shopping arcade, the Passage des Panoramas. Thayer captivated audiences with silken "sound-and-light" views of Lyon and Amsterdam. The enchanted scenography transported spectators to Naples, Antwerp, and London. Reflecting on Paris in the nineteenth century, urban critic Walter Benjamin pointed to the parallel between the panorama spectacles and the new commercial arcades such as the Passage des Panoramas. They made up a dream world, a phantasmagoria summoned up by technological wizardry and the new consuming vision. They were sites of *flânerie*—one virtual, the other real—and an expression of modern life. In 1823, Louis Daguerre, known for his experiments with light shows and invention of the daguerreotype (early camera) went further and created a 3-D effect with an illusionist diorama show. The first one was opened on the rue Sanson in Paris, just off the place de la République.

The panoramas were passed from one proprietor to another, went on tour from one city to another, until they were finally reduced to tatters. Along with music hall and vaudeville performers, the circuses and exotic "People Shows," they were part of Europe's entertainment circuit. As each amusement set up tent, the shows were publicized with street parades and noisy barkers, and posters plastered around town. The Leicester Square panorama went on tour to Hamburg, Leipzig, and Vienna. German architect Karl Friedrich Schinkel's *Panorama of Palermo* was a triumph and journeyed through Germany and across Europe. To welcome the panorama displays and their clever props, Frankfurt, Cologne, Leipzig, and Munich all built sumptuous baroque-style panorama rotundas. The showman Carl Gabriel opened the *Internationale Handels-Panoptikum* in Munich. It was a five-story extravaganza of sideshows and pseudo-science with an "anatomical museum" and traveling panorama displays.[39] In Berlin, the Hohenzollern Gallery was a massive sixteen-sided polygonal panorama building. Its shows transported audiences by steamship to New York with sound-and-light effects and undulating images imitating a rolling sea. There were over 250 Kaiser Panoramas, a type of camera obscura, in operation in towns throughout Germany, and Austria.[40] In Budapest, the first panorama opened in the city's park in 1885. But the largest exhibit took place during the Millennium celebrations in 1896, when an enormous rotunda was erected for a show entitled "The Arrival of the Hungarians." The screen was shipped to London for exhibition, and then returned to Budapest where it was installed near one of the city's famous thermal baths. Nine other panorama exhibits appeared in the city in the years following the Millennium celebrations.

The older-style pleasure garden gave way to the modern amusement park. The appeal of the amusement or "Luna Parks," as they were called, transcended age, gender, and class boundaries. Millions of people visited them each year. They were phenomena of mass culture and temple to modernity that drew on the city as spectacle. Luna Park was fun city. The mix of garish lights and carnivalesque architecture, the high-speed roller coasters, whips and water chutes, the thrill of the fairground was a liberating experience. It was a release from the routine of working life and satisfied the voracious demand for novelty. Luna Park shared the sense of wonder and excitement with the panorama, with the department store and international exhibitions. For the hordes of people enjoying these places, modern life meant a huge dollop of entertainment and amusement, and the captivating experience of novelty and technological sorcery. In the first years of the twentieth century, some thirty major parks operated in towns across Britain. Hungarian-British showman Imre Kiralfy was a central figure in the craze for public amusements. His "White City" in the west London borough of Hammersmith became one of the city's great exposition sites with pavilions in flamboyant orientalist style, an open-air theater, and funfair rides including the Flip-Flap machine that projected thrill-seekers sixty meters into the air. Millions of people visited White City. Luna Park in Paris at the Porte Maillol featured a roller coaster, water chute and ghost train, and nightly dancing under twinkling electric stars. In 1895, Austrian impresario Gabor Steiner opened the theme park "Venedig in Wien" (Venice in Vienna) in Vienna's Prater Park. It was a techno-dreamland with glittering electric illumination, electric boat rides on the canals, and chances to see newfangled phonographs and picture shows. Berlin's Luna Park on the west end of the Kurfürstendamm opened in 1910 and attracted a million visitors in its first year of operation. Amusement parks were omnipresent in big cities across Europe. They were a moment of kaleidoscopic enchantment, worlds away from the reality of everyday life.

For many in the upper classes, music halls and amusement parks, the panoramas and sideshow amusements were dens of inequity that broke down the traditional social fabric. The mixing in these places was hard to control. Class distinctions based on appearance and how one spoke, on the proper norms of behavior were clear to everyone. Yet the boundary between the respectable and the rabble was becoming hard to maintain. If the working classes could finally enjoy some joyful respite from their misery, bourgeois anxieties and insecurities bristled. Nonetheless, it was impossible to stop the flood of mass cultural entertainments that were dramatically transforming urban life. Added to the marvels was moving pictures. Audiences were first introduced to grainy black-and-white film, often only a few moments long, in traveling shows set up in amusement parks and fairgrounds, or even at town halls, railway stations, and factories. Showmen arrived with their ornately decorated "palace on wheels" fitted out with dazzling lights and mirrors and kinetoscope machines inside for viewing the films through a peephole. They were an instant hit. The traveling picture shows toured from big cities to medium-sized and small towns and were viewed by thousands. In Germany alone by 1907, some 500 traveling cinema shows were visiting 700 locations each year.[41] Like panoramas, the magic of movies were part of an urban entertainment circuit that swept across Europe and spread the new mediums of mass culture with amazing speed.

By the early years of the twentieth century, most cities, large and small, had a fixed movie house. The growth in movie theaters was phenomenal. By 1914, London had nearly 500 while Paris had some 260 movie theaters. Most of the movie houses were neighborhood affairs in converted music halls or cabarets. But the big cities were known for their fabulous movie palaces. Two old Paris hippodromes were converted into spectacular movie palaces—the Cinéma Pathé on the Boulevard du Temple and the Gaumont Palace in Montmartre. With their grand corner entrances and flamboyant interiors, they were the height of cinematic luxury. On the other side of the continent, St. Petersburg had over a hundred movie houses, the most popular being its Pikkadilli electric theater, which drew 915 customers a day. Moscow had seventy-one movie theaters and Kiev, a city of around 250,000, had a few dozen.[42] Thousands went to the movies every day and viewed a repertoire of mainstream serials, amateur film shorts, and international blockbusters. In an indication of how far mass cultural entertainments spread, film buffs in Kiev enjoyed American comedies and westerns in the years before the First World War.[43]

The universal language of film represented all the excitement and trepidation of mass entertainment. It was an industry catering to rising expectations and capable of producing a continuous stream of fantasies. The tempo of urban life was broken up into work-time and leisure-time, the drudgery of six-day workweeks and the day off for enjoyment, days of boredom, and days of fun and excitement. Demand continuously rose for the next high-wire experience. Sites across the city were dedicated to consuming visual sensations, to play and pleasure. Scholars have argued that the commercialization of entertainment made people into passive spectators mesmerized by advertising and technological wizardry, by the flashy performances. The onslaught flatlined any possibility of creativity at the level of everyday popular culture. There was some point to this. But popular, working class, and marginal expressive forms were endlessly dynamic and continued to bubble to the surface. They were co-opted and appropriated by commercial enterprises, and at the same time street culture seized upon commercial forms, transmuting and manipulating them in the process. This ongoing cultural grinding and blending produced new kinds of cultural practices and urban spaces that were tuned to the rhythms of modern life.

CHAPTER 7
SIGHTSEEING IN THE BIG CITY (FIN-DE-SIÈCLE)

The restless motion of the metropolis, the pace of its life seemed to accelerate. Newcomers arrived in droves. People were out and about, merging into the crowds and encountering strangers, rushing around, jumping into carriages and on to streetcars. Trolley tracks and telephone wires crisscrossed the streets. Throngs of shoppers whipped through department stores and rushed in and out of shops and markets. Newsstands, advertising boards, vendors, and hawkers clogged the sidewalks. The city's topography was constantly fluctuating as new buildings and factories sprang up. New streetcar and rail lines suddenly appeared. There was an unremitting process of creative destruction and rebuilding. Movement and speed were the modus operandi. It was a chaotic, mesmerizing spectacle. The hectic pace of the metropolis was exhilarating. But it was difficult to get any fixed point of orientation amid all the sights and sounds. Any sense of a cohesive world evaporated. Bombarded by stimuli and the unexpected, urban chroniclers warned that the individual confronted with all this risked falling into catatonic shock. The big city was incoherent, impossible to fully comprehend.

Novel communication and transportation technologies were shifting the ground of everyday life. The telegraph and telephone made communication instantaneous. London and Manchester, Glasgow, Liverpool, Edinburgh, Birmingham, and Bristol were all connected by telephone trunk lines by the late 1870s. Telephone companies were one of the first services to employ women. They operated the switchboards, helped customers make calls, and provided on-the-spot information. Women literally became the voices of connectivity. The first telephone exchanges opened in Brussels, and by 1886, seven cities in Belgium including Antwerp, Ghent, and Liège offered telephone service. In the Netherlands, people in Amsterdam, Rotterdam, The Hague, Groningen, Haarlem, and Arnhem were all speaking through the new marvel. The Siemens Company opened the first public telephone exchange in Berlin. Italy had over 8,000 subscribers in twelve cities. In the 1880s, the American Bell Telephone Company began installation of telephone networks in St. Petersburg, Moscow, Warsaw, Odessa, Riga, and Łódź. By 1893, a telephone news service in Budapest went to the homes of 6,000 subscribers. The speed at which the telephone took hold was extraordinary. By 1914, 3.5 million telephone lines already existed in Europe.[1] Even small villages had access to a telephone switchboard run by a local operator who chatted with customers and hooked lines into a local network. Distances were collapsed, space and time compressed.

Thousands of miles of railroad track crisscrossed Europe and linked cities and towns together in a transportation system that cut travel time by ninety percent. Britain and

Belgium were the first to develop a rail network. France, Germany, and Italy quickly caught up. The vast territories of the Hapsburg and Russian empires followed suite. Rail travel became commonplace for millions of people. Suddenly, any town or city with a rail connection had outsized influence. Any town without one immediately slumped. Flamboyant railroad stations became ceremonial gateways in and out of the urban realm with passengers rushing to catch trains. Hotels, cafés, and shops clustered around the stations. A web of iron tracks slashed through city spaces. Along with the railroad, streetcars became the symbol of the modern city. The period from 1870 to 1914 was the great age of the streetcar. Horse-drawn trolleys glided along iron tracks down the boulevards with passengers stepping on and off and pedestrians darting around them. Although horse-drawn vehicles and streetcars dominated the cityscape, they were already becoming antiquated. Electric and gasoline-driven vehicles whizzed by them. Their speed was intoxicating. Werner von Siemens demonstrated the first electric streetcar in Berlin in 1881. They were coasting down the streets of Prague by the 1890s. In 1901 in Kraków, crowds of curious onlookers gathered to inaugurate the new electric streetcar festooned with flowers and flags.[2] Motor buses lumbered up alongside the trolleys. With horns blaring, automobiles maneuvered around them in the last years of the nineteenth century. Taxi cabs were already clogging the streets in Paris, Berlin, and London. The noise and traffic congestion were ear-splitting. There were no traffic regulations, nor were any real measures taken against motorists zipping through narrow alleyways and speeding down the thoroughfares. Promenading on the Friedrichstrasse in Berlin triggered an explosion of senses:

> Cacophonous blowing of horns in the traffic, melodies of organ grinders, cries of newspaper vendors, bells of Bolle's milkmen, voices of fruit and vegetable sellers, hoarse pleas of beggars, whispers of easy women, the low roar of streetcars and their screech against the old iron tracks, and millions of steps dragging, tripping, pounding.[3]

Crossing the road became a perilous contest between fearless pedestrians and vehicles. Newspapers were filled with reports of mishaps and accidents. Subways zoomed underground. New electric subway cars were replacing the old steam models. London's Underground was the world's first subway with the inauguration in 1863 of the line from Paddington to Smithfield in the City. The Prince of Wales opened London's first electric subway line in 1890. The subway under Andrássy Avenue in Budapest was opened in 1896. The first line of the Paris Métro that stretched across the city between Porte de Vincennes and Porte Maillot began operation three years later during the 1900 International Exhibition. The four main lines of Berlin's S-Bahn were already in construction. Steams of commuters vaulted up the steps of subway stations in the morning and burst onto the street, and just as rapidly disappeared underground on their way back home in the evening.

Sporting events from bicycle and automobile races to football (soccer) were a mass phenomenon with thousands of spectators cheering in the stands and along the stadium perimeters. Town-to-town automobile races were mega-events that drew throngs of people into the streets. Automobile makers Louis and Marcel Renault regularly tested their prototype cars in races, and won the Paris-Toulouse, Paris-Berlin, and Paris-Vienna runs. These *Courses des Capitales* that crossed national borders were immense media events. Thousands mobbed the finish of the Paris-Berlin race to adorn the winners with wreaths. The Peking-to-Paris race in 1907 ended with throngs bursting past police barriers, cheering the winners as they drove through Paris to the offices of the *Le Matin* newspaper, which sponsored the race. Italian journalist Luigi Barzini accompanied the winning driver and recorded their arrival. The Republican Guard attempted to clear their path, but the crowd grazed the wheels of the car: "The pavements are black with people. . . . The cheering becomes clamorous, intense, continuous."[4] Above all, the airplane captured the popular imagination. Airplane rallies held in the skies over cities brought masses of people onto the streets, their heads craning to see the pilot-heroes in their flimsy biplanes. In 1908 the Zeppelin flew down the Rhine River and over Basel, Strasbourg, Mainz, and back to Stuttgart to the amazement of the hordes gathered to witness it. A crowd of 300,000 spectators assembled in the early morning at the Paris airfield to watch French heroes Jules Védrine and Roland Garros take off for the start of the Paris-Madrid air race in 1911. Some forty different types of aircraft were built in Kiev's factories between 1909 and 1912, where thousands turned out on Sundays to see test flights over the city: the "whole public is enraptured" reported the local newspaper (Figure 32).[5]

Mass culture created a new scenography of modernity with the city as backdrop. Military parades drew throngs of people along the route. Berlin was the scene of

Figure 32 The Diamond Jubilee: Queen Victoria's carriage passing the National Gallery, London, 1897.

countless military processions by the elite regiments guarding the Hohenzollern Palace. Their colorful uniforms and high-stepping maneuvers were a crowd favorite. Military bands paraded through the Hapsburg Empire's towns and cities each year on the Emperor Franz Joseph's birthday. Queen Victoria's Diamond Jubilee in 1897 was a spectacular urban event. London became dramatic theater for the celebration of Britain's imperial might. Three million people visited London for the celebrations. The streets were festooned with garlands of flowers and flags. Some 25,000 soldiers from across the British Empire camped in tents in Hyde Park. More than a million people jostled for places along the parade route the week before the parade. In full imperial regalia, the procession wound six miles through the streets to thunderous applause. The ostentatious 1898 and 1908 processions down the Ringstrasse in Vienna to commemorate the fifty- and sixty-year jubilees of Emperor Franz Joseph assembled thousands of costumed participants strutting down the boulevard. Millions of Hapsburg subjects attended local festivities and packed churches and city halls for ceremonies to mark the grand occasion. Town centers were draped in jubilee decorations.[6]

Open-air pageants were an immensely popular form of entertainment, especially in England. These productions went beyond mere visual theater. Their appeal was based on scale and spectacle with extravagant costumes and elaborate scenery, whole castes of choirs and dancers, and masses of ordinary people taking part. It was the opportunity for performers to make their own entertainment that made the pageant so successful. The Pageant of London during the Festival of Empire Exhibition in 1911 was one of the most elaborate. It was staged over three days by 15,000 volunteers drawn from London's boroughs. Forty magnificent scenes dramatized London's history as an imperial city and heart of the British Empire. Even small towns across England staged historical pageants. The town of Sherborne (population 6,000) hosted a 1905 pageant attended by 30,000 people. Local places rediscovered their heritage and staged elaborate costume dramas drawn from the past. Cultural clubs in the city of Strasbourg dug out authentic Alsatian folk dress and trimmed members out for historic pageant-fairs.[7] This kind of mass performance knew no bounds. The Baltic song festivals of the late nineteenth and early twentieth centuries were staged outdoors in Riga and Tallinn as mass choir performances. Thousands of participants clutched their songbooks and belted out patriotic hymns as part of their "cultural awakening."

The modern city was interpreted in good part as a vast arena for public spectacles, the foremost of which were the international expositions and "decorative and applied arts" exhibitions of the turn of the century. They evolved from the earlier Crystal Palace and trade shows into modernity's most opulent metaphor. The number of these affairs was staggering. They were the first true mega-events and played an outsized role in creating a European image of modernity. Major events took place in Paris, Vienna, Berlin, Prague, Barcelona, Budapest, Brussels, Dublin, Amsterdam, Düsseldorf, Turin, Milan, Liège, Antwerp, Leipzig, Glasgow, Kraków, Lemberg, Bucharest, and the list goes on. They were the ultimate tourist destination. The expositions were jaw-dropping displays of national prestige and imperial power. The fairgrounds were chock-full of new fangled technologies and the latest amusements. They showed off the most innovative ideas in urban planning and design. Staging an exhibition was the occasion for major public investments in new infrastructure, streetcar and subway lines. Every aspect of the event was meant to put the modern European city "on view." The exhibitions structured the spatial and temporal dimensions of modernity at the local level where they took place. At the same time, they were among the first venues where a European ethos was experienced culturally by millions of people.

All told, streets and public thoroughfares, stadiums and parks, and exposition grounds were powerful entertainment and performance spaces that electrified the citizenry from the privileged down to the working-class families lining the parade routes. All of these jumbo events took money and labor to mount and helped to stimulate the local economy.[8] Extravagant scale, monumental perspectives, technological wizardry were the characteristics of modern urban imagery. It brought in tourists and branded the city as an object of fascination. The metropolis was transformed into an enchanted dream world. The crowd was enveloped in a theatrical aesthetics of extraordinary magnetism. Public museums added to the urban pageantry. The mania for commemoration, collection, and display turned the city into a showcase of artifacts. City history museums and those dedicated to arts and crafts, natural history and ethnography, and ancient civilization proliferated, not only in capital cities but also in regional centers, where local culture was represented in remarkable new ways. The flamboyance of the modern city, all the goings-on, the flow of traffic and crowds merged into an intoxicating spectacle.

Electricity was perhaps the most emblematic of urban technological enchantment. Famed French science-fiction writer Albert Robida penned the novels *The Electric Life* (1892) and *The Twentieth Century* (1882) in which he imagined a future where all passenger traffic took place in the air and the deafening racket of earthbound vehicles was replaced by the melodious humming of electrical currents. "Electricity circulates everywhere, facilitating all social interactions with its motive force or light. Thousands of musical chimes and bell sounds coming from the sky, from homes, and even from the ground, merge into one vibrant, metallic melody . . . named the great symphony of electricity!"[9] Electricity was a life force. It was imagined as a sort of technological sublime, a magic fluid that turned night into day. The turn of the century saw a cascade of exhibitions dedicated to electricity as Aladdin's lamp. Vast sums were spent on dazzling electrical illumination that turned the city into a glistening fairyland and enraptured the public. The blockbuster event was the 1900 Universal Exposition in Paris. It was dedicated entirely to an electrical world and was visited by 50 million people. Fairgoers rode electric trains and tried out traveling sidewalks and electric escalators. Every evening tens of thousands of visitors crowded together on the exhibition stairs and terraces to see the show at the Palace of Electricity. Five thousand multicolored incandescent bulbs were lit at the flick of a switch. Combined with the water display of the Chateau d'Eau with jets of water illuminated in changing colors, the effect was breathtaking. The exhibition's monumental entranceway, the Porte Monumentale, was a silhouette of gleaming jewels in the colors of the rainbow. The banks of the Seine River and its bridges were decked out in electric lights. Electricity at the fair was described as a morphine (Figure 33).

Figure 33 The Chateau d'eau and Palace of Electricity at the 1900 Paris Exposition.

The breakthrough for electricity transmission over long distances came with the 1891 Electrotechnical Exhibition in the town of Frankfurt am Main in western Germany. Some ten German manufacturers of electrical equipment set up shop in the city including the German Edison Company, which later became the Allgemeine Electricitäts Gesellschaft or AEG. The German Siemens company pioneered electric lighting in the streets of Berlin and installed lighting in St. Petersburg's Nevsky Prospect and the Winter Palace. The Ganz company in Budapest generated electricity and lit up the cities of Luzern, Rome, and Vienna. The humble electric light bulb was among the most transformative commodities in people's everyday lives. Lighting at the pull of a lamp string was one of the most sought-after benefits of city living. Gerard Philips established his light bulb and lamp factory in Eindhoven, in the Netherlands. By 1914, the United Incandescent Lamp Company in Budapest churned out tens of thousands of light bulbs daily with its workforce of 3,000 employees. City theaters, spectacular grand hotels, department stores, elegant restaurants, and banks were adorned with electric chandeliers and electric elevators.

Urban modernity claimed a universal applicability and shaping of reality. Speeding trains and streetcars, automobiles and motorcycles, airplanes overhead, the telephone, electric lights—these new technologies were the signature of the modern experience. City people across Europe were consciously aware of the metamorphic urban culture to which they belonged. The city person, the "big city type" became an acknowledged character. They expected gas and even electric lighting, water and sewage services, paved roads, modern infrastructure. They rode the streetcar and train as a matter of course and dealt with strangers every day. They read big city newspapers and kept up on the latest news. They shopped in department stores and wore the same style of modern clothing, so much so that traditional ethnic dress disappeared from the city streets. They reveled in the same music hall shows and watched the same films. They enjoyed the excitement at Luna Parks and sports events, airplane and automobile rallies, and international expositions. There was a fundamental commonality of experience that was increasingly "European," modern, and cosmopolitan. European-ness was a product of the culture of circulation and a way of being in the world. Traveling through Europe in 1906, Slovenian writer Josip Lavtižar complained about modern "Europeanization":

> If you have seen one big city, you have seen them all. Everywhere wonderful buildings and magnificent shop windows, trams and the new technological creations of the human mind. However, when you keep seeing the same thing over and over again, you get fed up. . . . It is the same with the inhabitants. Their clothes follow the same fashions. . . . People also talk about the same subjects . . . Why? Because their knowledge comes from the same books and because they read precisely the same newspapers.[10]

The city represented a freedom from constraints. It offered opportunity and an opening up of world view. Residents mixed daily with people of different origins, languages, and habits and practiced a basic everyday leniency toward other people. Cities were powerful brews of social and cultural experience. Among German scholars surveying the impact of the *Großstadt* at a 1903 conference in Dresden, Heinrich Waentig argued that city people were characterized by "extreme alertness . . . and intensity at work and at play." The city is the great leveler; it easily forgets. "How lucky for those who want to start a new life."[11] Surveying Berlin, art critic August Endell admitted that "despite all the ugly buildings, despite the noise, despite everything in it that one can criticize," the big city "is a marvel of beauty and poetry to anyone who is willing to look." Endell viewed the straight street as aesthetically valued above all others because "the straight line gives the feeling of speed."[12] Otto Wagner, who was the most celebrated architect working in Vienna, saw the modern city as a place of unconstrained freedom, and greater intellectual and material opportunities. He thrived on its energy. "The number of city dwellers who today prefer to vanish in the mass as mere numbers on apartment doors is considerably greater than those who care to hear the daily 'good morning, how are you?' from their gossipy neighbors." The modern metropolis reversed the parochialism of the past. In his "The Development of the Great City" (1911), Wagner argued that anonymity was one of the basic attributes of mass society. Lifestyles had changed, and the cityscape had to adapt to contemporary life.[13] It was the tempo of the metropolis and the acceleration of interactions and transactions that counted for Wagner.

In contrast to the fast-paced spectacle on the boulevards that Wagner found so arresting, many voiced their outrage at the *reality* of the city around them. If one left the charmed world of Regent's Street or the Ringstrasse, suddenly there "were no public buildings of any importance, no municipality, no gentry, no carriages, no soldiers, no picture-galleries, no theaters, no opera." In British novelist Walter Besant's 1882 novel *All Sorts and Conditions of Men*, a visit to the East End of London revealed a dull utilitarian world. Instead of these diversions, there were

> mile upon mile of streets with houses—small, mean, and monotonous houses; the people living the same mean and monotonous lives. . . . Here, in the East End, there are no strollers. All day long the place is full of passengers hasting to and fro, pushing each other aside, with set and anxious faces, each driven by the invisible scourge of necessity which makes slaves of all mankind.[14]

From this point of view, cosmopolitanism was born out of cultural privilege. It projected a moral and political hierarchy grounded in social relations. The strike waves and protests that traumatized cities and towns, the persistent ethnic violence, suggested that cosmopolitanism could simply be a veneer enjoyed by the upper classes.

Regardless of how cosmopolitan they may or may not have been, cities absorbed modern changes and at the same time shifted their meaning. Modernity sidled in from the wings and grafted on to European identity in a host of different urban places. Conservative tastes and traditions continued their hold on local cultures despite the encroaching patterns of modernity or could indeed be enhanced by its magic spell. The result was hybrid urban environments that took shape around encounters between a modern cosmopolitan sensibility and local or even national ties. Allegiances and loyalties overlapped. The city of Lemberg (L'viv/Lwów) in Hapsburg Galicia was a thriving provincial capital with an array of modern public institutions. But it celebrated the Sobieski Festival in honor of heroic Polish kings with a procession to the cathedral and religious service attended by thousands dressed in traditional local costume.[15] Religion continued to play a vital role in the everyday lives of urban dwellers. For the middle and upper classes, church attendance and active involvement in parish activities was a social duty. Houses of worship were hubs of charitable work and volunteerism on behalf of the needy, especially for upstanding women. But even the working classes looked to baptism, marriage, and Christian burial as rites of passage. City people—the rich and the poor alike—participated in church processions through the streets with all their regalia. They joined religious pilgrimages and mass gatherings to sacred sites across Europe. These were as well phenomena of mass culture. The lived experience of cities was complex and paradoxical, with layers of cultural meaning and identity.

Once more, numerous cities and towns underwent modern urbanizing processes without large-scale industrialization. They remained commercial and administrative capitals, or local transportation hubs. Even small and medium sized towns made themselves modern with an array of public infrastructure projects. Electric streetlights, new school buildings, libraries and theaters, new railway stations, and streetcar lines graced townscapes across Europe. For many of these places, modernization sharpened the tensions between local culture and the forces impinging from outside. Values and loyalties seemed more contentious. Commemorating and celebrating traditional customs and history became even more meaningful. Architecture and urban design were loaded with symbolic significance, especially in central and eastern Europe where modernization was official Hapsburg imperial policy. The influence of Vienna was often viewed with resentment or rejected outright. Austrian urban theorist Camillo Sitte, whose impact in central and eastern Europe was profound, argued for the historical experience of cities as the basis for progress rather than the cookie-cutter projects impinging on urban life. The experience of the city was influenced by history and ethnology, by religion, and by local institutions. Places should be embellished, according to Sitte, by projecting past examples into the future. The emotional attachment to place should be the basis of planning. In this way, the townscape would bestow happiness and delight.[16]

Early sociologists and urban theorists focused on the psychological impact of the modern city. Especially important was the medical research on the human nervous system that found a direct correlation between external stimuli and both physical and emotional reactions. In France, the public lectures of French neurologist Jean-Martin Charcot in the 1880s gave credence to the idea of individual nervous disorders and even national ill health. The sensory overload of the modern metropolis was a widely discussed factor in national degeneration and the feeling of general malaise. Sociologist Emile Durkheim argued that modern progress was inseparable from anomie and alienation, made worse by consumerism and unregulated capitalism. Nonetheless, he argued that cities were liberating and that new forms of solidarity and mutual interdependency would be forged. German sociologist Georg Simmel's famous study *The Metropolis and Mental Life* (1903) detailed the powerful pressures exerted on the individual: "The rapid and continual shift of external and internal stimuli . . . with every crossing of the street, with the tempo and multiplicity of economic, occupational and social life, the metropolis impinges on the mental state of the individual." To adjust to this sensory overload, the metropolitan type acts intellectually from their head, rather than emotionally, and takes on a "blasé attitude" that gives them a measure of personal freedom.[17]

Urban consumer culture was ripping up the moral ideals of the past. There was a new openness. Youth and sex appeal were blatantly on display. For the first time in a century, trim bodies became fashionable. Women's public roles expanded. A French etiquette manual warning that a respectable young man would never sit on the same couch with a young woman, seemed by 1913 to be absurd. Dandies, bohemians, and city types strutted their public style. Homosexuality gained greater public visibility. Berlin had about forty gay bars, and the police estimated there were some 1,000–2,000 male prostitutes roaming the streets, especially along the Friedrichstrasse. The general easing of censorship produced a flood of pornography and smutty pulp literature. Sexuality was openly flaunted in the booming retail sector, in advertising, and in the bawdy cabaret and music hall performances. The popular press fueled the fascination with celebrity and cranked out racy articles on the exploits of public personalities in the world of entertainment and high society. The reaction was a sense of moral panic about deviance and decadence. The opening of Diaghilev's Ballets Russes and the performance of *The Rite of Spring* in Paris in May 1913 with Nijinsky dancing the lead role, music by Igor Stravinsky, and sets by Jean Cocteau provoked outrage. Garbed in wild costumes and makeup, the dancers indulged in jerky staccato movements and vertical hops, as if they were marionettes. They acted out a primitive pagan ritual. The celebration of primal emotions, sexuality, and eroticism horrified the audience. Fistfights broke out during the performance. The ruckus in the audience drowned out the music, and the dancers reacted by synchronizing their steps to the noise. For the avant-garde, anything was preferable to stultifying conformism, even moral disorder and confusion. Shock and provocation became instruments of art.

Conservative thinkers argued that big cities were "active instruments of demoralization." German historian Oswald Spengler disparaged big city living in his classic *The Decline of the West* (1918), fuming that "in place of a world, there is a *city, a point*, in which the whole life of broad regions is collecting while the rest dries up. In place of a type-true people . . . there is a new sort of nomad, cohering unstably in fluid masses, the parasitical city dweller, traditionless, utterly matter-of-fact, religionless, clever, unfruitful."[18] Pulp books, newspapers, and mass entertainment stimulated subversive ideas and gross passions. German sociologist Ferdinand Tönnies lamented the loss in urban societies of close social bonds and a strong sense of community. He feared the sense of rootlessness in cities. These influences seemed to spiral into a "crisis of modernity," degeneration and decline. German sociologist Max Weber was even more strongly convinced than Tönnies that the world was undergoing a process of disenchantment, and that modern man was locked in an iron cage of his own making. A "polar night of icy darkness" was his prediction for the future.[19] A sense of nostalgia and melancholy for a lost world took hold and with it, pessimism about the future.

The modern city was also endless fascination for artists and illustrators, journalists of the popular press, and pioneers working in the new mediums of photography and early film. Each had their say on the urban experience. The crowds of people and ceaseless activity were spellbinding. Capturing the hyperactive, perpetually changing city scene became central to public discourse and to the modern cultural imagination. The mass media was a powerful social and political force in the first decades of the twentieth century. Cheap daily newspapers, tabloids, and illustrated weeklies churned out a million copies per issue. People came to rely on them for information and for interpreting the bewildering urban spectacle. The press depicted typical "city people" and humorous stories about the foibles of daily life. They featured the streets and places that readers themselves were familiar with as well as exotic, unknown locales. There were sketches of public life along the boulevards, everyday scenes on the streets, vicarious expeditions into proletarian neighborhoods. They featured a cast of characters from the shyster to the country "rhub" who arrives bewildered in the big city. Writer Peter Altenberg was a familiar figure in Vienna. He wandered the streets of the capital and then found refuge in the Café Central on the Herrengasse, where he scribbled down his impressions on scraps of paper. The episodes and fragments of the city's life were then published in the illustrated news: "You've got troubles of one kind of another—get thee to the coffeehouse! / Your boots are torn—to the coffeehouse! / You make four hundred Crowns and spend five hundred—coffeehouse!"[20] Like the panoramic bird's-eye urban views that spectators flocked to see, these vignettes were self-conscious portrayals of the urban realm, as much entertaining fiction as they were real.

Early photography and amateur film captured the new geography of modernity from the Strand in London across the continent to Nevsky Prospect in St. Petersburg. In a real sense, visual media helped to produce the modern cityscape. Boulevards with their streetcars, railway stations, department stores and shop windows, and music halls were the subjects captured in the camera's lense. Photographer John Thompson recorded street life in London and the myriad of social types in the cosmopolitan capital. The Fleet Street news agencies produced countless photos of the traffic and crowds on London's streets. Photography studios such as Neurdein and Maurice-Louis Branger covered social and political life in Paris, the streetscape of markets and café terraces, the crowds on streetcars and in metro stations. They documented events from the 1910 flood in Paris to automobile races and the universal expositions. Moving cameras were often mounted on carriages and streetcars to capture the thrill of speeding through the city, taking in the sights in a new form of *flânerie*. Like the city itself, the scenes and impressions are fleeting. Pedestrians rush along, dashing in every direction. Streetcars and horse-drawn and gasoline-powered vehicles of all sizes and shapes zigzag across the boulevards. Everyone, everything is in motion. The cacophony of traffic is framed by the modern buildings jutting up along paved sidewalks, whizzing by the camera's view. Crowds at street markets bobble back-and-forth in front of the camera. Film documented sightseers at the Paris Universal Exposition in 1900 taking in the sights and jumping on to the moving sidewalk with glee. They goof-around in front of the camera, performing their antics with complete self-awareness at being chronicled. The films are portraits of modern European cities and modern people at the turn of the century, nearly ubiquitous in their appearance. They are scenes of urban progress and the dynamic forces of urban life.

The crowded city center was matched by the unrelenting spread of the metropolis out to the surrounding territory. The railways and omnibuses, and the steamboats on the Thames that ran every half-hour in winter and every fifteen minutes in summer, created a new pattern of daily life in London. Residents scattered daily to the peripheral districts, while The City was where Londoners worked. Cheap workingmen's fares on the railroads pushed urban development to the outlying districts adjacent to industry, where working-class families could find cheap rent and a better quality of life. The East End of London stretched outward with rows of mean and airless back-to-back terraces and unpretentious laborer's cottages. In the 1880s, workers using the special fares to commute to London numbered around 25,000. Just twenty years later, some 325,000 people, most of them taking the Great Eastern from their homes in the northeastern outer districts, were buying cheap tickets to travel into London. The appearance of these working-class suburbs raised the ire of urban observers. English journalist Thomas Crosland scoffed at the "ha'penny newspapers, cheap music halls, police and county courts, billiard-matches, minor race-meetings, third-class railway-carriages . . . whatever, in short strikes the superior mind as being deficient in completeness, excellence and distinction may with absolute safety be called suburban."[21]

For the upper classes, the outskirts had traditionally been a bucolic respite from the noise, smells, and coarse crowds of the city. Carriage rides out amid the rustic scenery and rural villages, strolling along country lanes, was a favorite weekend pastime. The first waves of suburbanization in the mid-nineteenth century had mainly involved wealthy mercantile and industrial elites. They deserted their stately mansions in the central districts for the respite of prestigious villas on the outskirts. The middle classes soon followed suit, fleeing the city for cottages in the suburbs.[22] The word "suburb" had not originally meant social superiority and was just as often used to delineate artisans and workers seeking cheap lodging on the urban periphery. But as the nineteenth century wore on, the term was increasingly associated with flight from the teaming masses and the worst aspects of city living. These trends took place earliest in Britain, in cities such as Glasgow, Manchester, Liverpool, Birmingham, and London. The suburban residents of Acock's Green and Olton outside Birmingham "kept to themselves," according to a local journalist. Despite "an unseen tide of bricks" that flowed through the area, "A railway service suited to the few rather than the many, kept them select . . . and enabled both places to set at defiance the advancing tide from a great town."[23]

Old rural villages became epicenters for the new arrivals. Housing estates by speculative builders sprang up everywhere on the urban fringe, especially along streetcar and railroad lines. Roads were laid out and plots advertised for sale. Real estate was a secure form of private investment. Options ranged from elegant bourgeois villas to modest cottages for the less affluent. Clerks and shop owners, teachers, and civil servants boarded the trains in search of their suburban dream. In Great Britain, terraced houses and Victorian cottages in redbrick with manicured front lawns became the middle-class ideal and symbol of social status. In 1899, English author William Pett Ridge described the south London suburb of The Crescent that "has been built for something like twelve years" whose streets "are one day blank spaces, next day a row of thirty-five-pound villas; the day after inhabited by joyful young married people, taking the brightest views of everything." Every week-day morning, the domestic haven of The Crescent "dispatches its grown-up male inhabitants in search of gold. . . . Some of these pioneers leave home with a good-natured wife who is at the window urging a baby to make gestures of adieu."[24]

By the end of the century, it was difficult to tell where cities ended. The highest population growth was often taking place in outlying districts. From 1901 to 1911, the population of inner London slightly decreased to around 4.5 million, while that of the London metropolitan area nearly doubled to over 5 million. The city was surrounded by a gigantic halo of jumbled development. Earlier inner suburbs were eclipsed by new neighborhoods spreading further afield. Powerful centrifugal forces were spinning the movement of people and activities outward into far-flung urban regions. Even museums and expositions left behind the constraints of the central districts for roomier sites on the outskirts. The district of South Kensington outside London was developed as a museum complex adjacent to the popular exhibition arenas of Earl's Court and Olympia that offered circuses and exotic entertainment. The relentless growth of the metropolis spurred vigorous debate among reformers. The mass suburb was imagined as a new kind of society. The older ideal of city beautification as the anecdote for urban ills, represented, for example, by German architect Gottfried Semper and Austrian Camillo Sitte, battled against growing demands for rational and pragmatic planning for the entire metropolis.

Empirical data collection reached a new level of intensity. Liverpool shipowner turned socialist Charles Booth organized a small army of assistants to survey conditions throughout London. Published as *Life and Labor of the People in London* (1889, 1891), it classified each segment of the population, describing their condition in detail. Booth spent years interviewing families and gathering information from schoolboards and then rendered the data in color-coated "Poverty Maps."[25] They illustrated the state of things for the entirety of the inner districts and suburbs from Hammersmith in the west to Greenwich in the east. The investigators were accompanied by policemen, whose impressions of their beats were recorded in notebooks as part of the study. The detailed diagrams were a pioneering social science technique and provided a mirror of London's metropolitan social form. Booth's objective was to provide concrete evidence as a foundation for state intervention to alleviate poverty. Pioneering Scottish town planner Patrick Geddes argued that the city was a living environment with *élan vital*, capable of metamorphizing in complex ways. The growth of the metropolis could be directed through comprehensive surveys and regional planning that took into account geography and ecology, the economy and social structure, culture and history as the basic units of analysis. These were the motive forces of urban life and the seeds of transformation. Town and regional planning were forms of civic education that would control the spread of amoeba-like urban conurbations and open the door to a democratic awakening.

Progressive crusaders championed a rationally organized and equitable settlement system. Although he wrote only one slim book, Ebenezer Howard was among the most important urban philosophers calling for reform. In *Garden Cities of To-Morrow* (1902), Howard envisioned a radical transformation of the social and physical environments. His garden city would be formed by a population of 32,000 people living on 1,000 acres of land. It would be self-contained and locally managed as a joint-stock company that attracted light industry and services. In the pioneering spirit of homesteading, people would build their own homes and start their own small-scale businesses. For Howard, the garden city offered the benefits of urban living together with the advantages of country life. Once the garden city reached its planned limit, another would be started a short distance away, all of them connected by a rapid transit system. These communities would eventually fashion a network within a vast, planned agglomeration dubbed the Social City. Howard laid out his dream at the first garden city of Letchworth (1903) 30 miles north of London, followed by Hampstead Garden Suburb (1906).

The garden city ideal had profound influence on urban reformers throughout Europe. The reaction to Howard's sophisticated fusing of urban design with social reform was unrestrained enthusiasm. Soon after its publication, *Garden Cities of To-Morrow* was translated into a host of languages. Garden city and garden suburb experiments popped up across Europe. Two of the early efforts were Berlin's garden suburb of Falkenberg and the garden suburb of Hellerau near Dresden. The garden village of Margarethenhöhe was developed by the industrial Krupp family on the outskirts of Essen in the Ruhr from 1912 (see Chapter 2). Reformers envisioned tranquil towns and villages nestled amid a leafy landscape. These sylvan hollows would temper the forces of modern life. Living in nature was associated with healthiness and purity of the soul, with getting "back to the land." Many of these projects became middle-class enclaves. They were often associated with quirky alternative communities of privileged middle-class reformers who espoused everything from vegetarianism to utopian communitarianism. Some projects were developed by railway companies eager to provide suburban housing for middle-class commuters.[26] Milanówek in the outskirts of Warsaw was developed along the Warsaw-Vienna railway line as a summer resort for the city's wealthy residents. The Moscow-Kazan Railway Company began construction of the first model garden city in Russia at the Prozorovskaia Station, twenty-five miles east of Moscow.

The early twentieth century was rife with planning competitions and meetings where vigorous debates on metropolitan expansion took place. Hundreds of delegates gathered at these summits, which were the first of their kind. They were a modern form of urbanistic colloquy and a catalyst for the town planning movement. A broad spectrum of proposals was hashed out for the master plan for greater Vienna, the general plans for the expansion of Stuttgart and Düsseldorf, the plan for Greater Berlin, and the expansion of Amsterdam. The German Cities' Exhibition of 1903 held in Dresden gathered 128 city governments, 400 manufacturers, and drew 400,000 visitors. They poured over a vast compilation of data and displays on the city as a social organism.[27] Leading urbanist Werner Hegemann was the mastermind behind the town planning movement in Germany and guided the Universal City Planning Exposition held in Berlin in 1910. It was visited by some 65,000 people and then traveled to Düsseldorf. The British Royal Institute of Architects held a town planning gathering in London the same year. Pioneering French urbanist Marcel Poëte and the social scientists gathered around the Museé Social in Paris grappled with controlling the *ville tentaculaire* and lobbied for a regional vision of "Grand Paris." Patrick Geddes created the widely acclaimed "Cities and Town Planning Exhibition" that traveled to Edinburgh, London, Dublin, Belfast, and Ghent. At the Ghent International Exhibition of 1913, Geddes organized a survey of cities with a plethora of historical, geographical, economic, demographic, and public health data. Spectators wandered through galleries on "Modern Civic Administration" and "Civic Improvements." Geddes and Belgian urban reformer Paul Otlet organized an exhibit comparing cities worldwide. The International Congress of Cities that took place during the event was attended by a host of urban reform luminaries. Squabbling local governments were one of the thorniest difficulties in this quest for comprehensive metropolitan planning. Exhibitions and congresses such as these were opportunities for activists to develop professional expertise that offered a way forward through the infernal political bickering. This regime of expertise was among the most important sources of urban modernity and cosmopolitanism. They were an urbanistic frontline and put ambitious proposals to the test. At Ghent, the assembly of urban notables promoted the idea of a "World City" that like a universal exposition would bring together all the leading institutions of the world and would be dedicated to peace.

The scale of the metropolis had radically changed. By the early years of the twentieth century, the charmed world of the Vienna Ringstrasse and the Paris boulevards already seemed out of date and at odds with modern life. No sooner had the *grands boulevards* been built than the vanguard began to rebel against them. This was particularly true in the arena of art and architecture. The impulse behind experimentation in the arts at the turn of the century was a quest for liberation, a break, in both artistic and moral terms from central authority, from bourgeois conformity, and in short from a European tradition that had largely been dictated from the great capitals of Paris and Vienna. The whole notion of a cultural "avant-garde," that is trailblazers who seem to be out in front, defining modernity, came from their rebellion against the bourgeois world of the boulevards in Europe's great cities. The avant-garde responded to the rapid transformations taking place around them and attempted to depict its consequences— which for them meant the disintegration of a moribund nineteenth-century society. The middle classes needed to be shocked into the realization that their values were simply passé veneer. This radical edginess was a decidedly urban phenomenon. Young rebels pledged themselves to artistic innovation in the Rūķis circle in Riga, the Manes group in Prague, the Sztuka circle in Kraków, and Young Finland in Helsinki.[28] The European-wide cult of youthful innovation was labeled Jugendstil (youth style) in Germany, the Secession in the capitals of central Europe. It went by the phrase Art Nouveau in France and Belgium, and Stile Liberty in Italy. The Russian avant-garde assembled under the banner of Style Moderne.[29] All these urban movements embraced modernity with gusto and defined the spirit of the age.

Rather than relying on officially sanctioned artistic salons, the avant-garde huddled together in coffee houses and cabarets. These haunts became the sites of an urban bohemia operating along the edges of bourgeois society. The turn-of-the-century cabaret was a fusion of popular and high culture. Like the music hall, from which it often took material, song and spoken-word were its principle creative mediums. They were a rapier weapon for lampooning contemporary life and mocking authority. The cabaret was a laboratory for artistic invention, often rooted in the native languages, the folk theater and plebian festivities the avant-garde saw as natural cultural forms. Unlike the music hall, which entertained large audiences, the cabaret was more intellectual and self-consciously artistic. The performances were held in the back rooms of bistros and cellars. The intimacy of the cabaret allowed for a back-and-forth between actor and audience that lent itself to radical experimental performance, to cheeky social and political satire, and to clever monologues and sketches. Anxious city authorities saw this as amoral hedonism, and it was precisely shock and provocation that the avant-garde was looking for.[30] They appeared in Europe's cultural centers from Paris to Kraków, from St. Petersburg to Odessa.

The cabaret was born in 1881 when Rudolphe Salis opened his *Chat Noir* on Martyr's Mount, or Montmartre, in the northern outskirts of Paris. Far from the city's elegant boulevards, Montmartre retained its rustic character with winding dirt roads and windmills, working men's bistros, antiquated buildings and cottages. The gleaming white cathedral of Sacré Coeur had recently been dedicated atop the hill to commemorate the last bloody battle of the Commune of 1871. The rebels had retreated up the slopes as the French army closed in. Originally, the *Chat Noir* was a modest gathering of writers, poets, and painters who performed their work among friends. When it opened to the public, audiences reveled in its biting ridicule of middle-brow culture and its shabby notoriety. A critical success, the cabaret moved to the rue Victor Massé where it was all the rage among the free-spirited habitués of Parisian nightlife. Numerous other cabarets sprang up around it and Montmartre's reputation drew the rich and famous, nosy tourists, and youthful disciples of bohemia. The most successful cabarets were those in which showman Aristide Bruant performed his songs and spoken-word in colorful street argot about the lives of the city's social outcasts.

The Paris cabaret became the model for much of bohemian nightlife across Europe. Railroads gave avant-garde rebels the chance to travel around the European cultural capitals absorbing the latest artistic trends and then refracting them through a local lens. With a more relaxed attitude toward censorship than elsewhere in Germany, Munich attracted the avant-garde from near and far. The district of Schwabing on the city's outskirts was a haven for misfits, outcasts, and the culturally restless. It was a notorious literary and artistic scene that tested the boundaries of social and sexual protocols. Its cafés and cabarets and its carnival balls were a magic theater of bohemian goings-on. "The sidewalks are packed with a half-crazed throng," wrote an American music student on the last day of the carnival season, "some in vari-colored costumes, others in street dress, but all pelting one another with confetti, while the street itself is crowded with slow-moving lines of carriages whose occupants join no less wildly in the fun." Diving into a coffee house, her companions jump onto the stage and perform an impromptu mockery of a pompous orchestra conductor.[31] Schwabing's cafés—the *Stefanie*, the *Luitpold*, the *Mégalomania*, and above all the *Simplicissimus* (where Germany's most outrageous satirical magazine was born) became inspired platforms. The avant-garde theater *Die Elf Scharfrichter* (The Eleven Executioners) set up in the backroom of a local inn on the Türkenstrasse in 1901. The performances and verse were often jarring, sexually explicit, bent on acerbic embarrassment of bourgeois society. The homoerotically charged Cosmic Circle around poet Stefan George cultivated a mystical paganism as the touchstone for their creative arts.[32] Schwabing absorbed the exceptional from around Europe, from Thomas Mann and Wassily Kandinsky to Vladimir Lenin.

When Schwabing became passé, many of its devotees decamped to Vienna and set up the *Nachtlicht* (Nightlight) cabaret on the Ballgasse. It transformed into the more sophisticated *Cabaret Fledermaus* (The Bat) in a cellar beneath the Kärntnerstrasse, its décor designed by architect Josef Hoffmann and the Wiener Werkstätte. Peter Altenberg attended the performance of a "young Moroccan dancer" at the Fledermaus. "The altogether new," he remarked of the atmosphere, "is preferable to the habitual. . . . It's an energizing stimulant like tea, coffee, cigarettes. However skeptical and reserved you might be, something or other of the inertly traditional is rattled and disturbed. . . . It spawns a change in you, a change for the better."[33] Vienna had its own version of the *Simplicissimus*. But the real center of Vienna's intellectual and cultural life was its coffee houses. By the turn of the century, puffed up estimates gave their numbers at 600 establishments that served everyone from the literati to journalists and politicians. Customers spent hours at their regular spot indulging in intellectual banter and chatty gossip. The café was a capacious arena for artist's circles and discussion of the latest creative trends. Patrons devoured the assortment of newspapers, especially the *Neue Freie Presse*, the bastion of the liberal press and pulse of contemporary urban life. The most elegant cafés were the Café Griensteidl, the Central, the Herrenhof, the Café Museum, the Imperial, and the Sperl.[34]

The cabaret traveled eastward. The *Zielony Balonik* (Green Balloon) opened in Kraków's *Jama Michalikowa* (Michael's Den) café, which was decorated with unflattering caricatures of the city's politicians and elites. It reveled in contempt for religion and the city's moribund veneration of the past. *The Stray Dog* and *Crooked Mirror* in St. Petersburg and *The Bat* in Moscow spoofed bourgeois cultural pretensions.[35] In Odessa, the Russian avant-garde opened the satarical *Bi-ba-bo*. In Budapest the cabaret became a locus for disrupting the cultural influence of German-speaking Vienna. The quest for a modern Hungarian identity led to an extraordinary flowering of intellectual and cultural life in Budapest. The goal of the "Young Ones" was to rescue Hungarian culture from its "backwardness" and give it a modern form. It was a national ideal that rested on the people. The Hungarian avant-garde of poets, painters, and architects rejected western cultural idioms, especially those coming from Vienna. In 1907, the *Bonbonnière* cabaret became an instant success with witty spoofs from celebrity journalist Endre Nagy and performances in Hungarian. The next year the elegant *Modern Theatre Cabaret* opened on Andrássy Avenue. When Nagy took over and transformed it into the *Modern Stage Cabaret*, Budapest entered a golden age of cabaret culture. Nagy's biting political monologues and theatrical journalism made their way into the press and halls of political power.[36]

Where it was a new institution in cities such as Vienna or Paris, in Budapest the coffee house had a long tradition associated with the Ottoman Empire. They were folksy neighborhood meeting places, open seven days a week. Contemporary estimates put their numbers at 500–600. The coffee house was a larger-than-life cultural symbol where everyone caught up on news and hashed out the topics of the day.[37] The most elaborate were along Andrássy Avenue. The *New York*, the *Abbázia*, the *Múzeum*, the *Japán*, and the *Centrál* were sumptuous environments decked out with marble walls, gilded mirrors, and velvet drapes. Whatever their size and opulence, Budapest's coffee houses were an intellectual whirl where literary and artistic mavericks mingled with liberal-minded bourgeois elites. The main attraction was their inexhaustible selection of newspapers. There were twenty-two daily newspapers printed in Budapest—more than in Vienna. As in Vienna and Prague, a large portion of the culturally privileged were assimilated Jews. They were wealthy, cosmopolitan, and eager to demonstrate their modernity. Through their travels, businessmen and industrialists were acquainted with the newest artistic trends in the capitals of Europe. At the same time, they were driven by nationalism and led the struggle for its open recognition within an increasingly moribund Hapsburg Empire. It was the confidence in their cultural identities that allowed them to embrace

Figure 34 Café Central in Budapest about 1910.

a new urban vision and stake out their own interpretation of modern living. They acted as patrons for a generation of artists and channeled the defiance of the avant-garde into innovative projects that made the city into a testing ground of modernism. Their goal was to reshape urban life from domestic interiors to the public spheres of art and architecture (Figure 34).

These were the precepts behind the art nouveau movement. There was a firm belief that modern creative arts could enhance social goals and contribute to national or regional identity. It was a new aesthetic language and a sign of the robust self-assurance of the turn-of-the-century bourgeoisie. The wealth of the *nouveau riche* was openly on display in the city. It was not just about designing buildings but a search for a modern style of living that included fashion and personal accessories, furniture and decorative luxury items. It was an absorption with the new material world and a product of plutocratic privilege. Opulent, style-conscious, and radical, art nouveau reigned supreme. The Paris 1900 International Exposition was considered the highpoint of art nouveau with its pavilion prepared by art dealer Samuel Bing, who owned an art gallery in Paris called the Salon de l'Art Nouveau. But the zenith of this avant-garde movement was not in the great European capitals of London or Paris. Its greatest flowering was in cities where modernism exposed the quest for regional or national identity—in Glasgow with Mackintosh style, in Turin with the work of Raimondo d'Aronco, in Brussels, Munich, Vienna, Barcelona, in Kraków, Prague, and Brno, in Riga and Lemberg, and in Helsinki. They have rarely loomed large enough in chronicles of urban modernism. The network of 200 technical and craft schools, and museums and applied art schools, set up in towns across the Hapsburg Empire was a hotbed of imaginative fervor. These new institutions and local artistic societies nurtured the flow of creative ideas. Artists and architects took to the railway and traveled around towns and cities, bringing with them the latest trends and innovations. Even in St. Petersburg, Style Moderne was common currency by the early years of the new century.

The decorative ostentation of art nouveau has often relegated it to architectural frippery, a detour on the road to modernism. But its flamboyance had much to do with its standpoint on the margins and borderlands of Europe, where the new art represented revolutionary ideas. Rather than a cohesive movement, the evolution of modern urban form was a prism that fractured into an assortment of aesthetic, cultural, and localized expressions. Regional styles displayed themselves in all their originality and distinctiveness. The strength of the modern movement came from this ventriloquism and diversity. Everything about art nouveau exuded quirky invention, the sense of being custom-made, the adaptation of patterns from vernacular or folk culture, from nature with organic motifs and botanical flourishes, and a rebellious anti-rationalism. Modernist impulses such as this encompassed a variety of local lineages. For some, it meant forging a national or regional style, while for others modernism expressed a democratic spirit, or some combination of both. It embodied universal truths and an international perspective. Art nouveau was simultaneously cosmopolitan and local in orientation. It epitomized a modern secular, bourgeois culture. It was a quest for liberation, a break, in both artistic and moral terms from the historicist conventions that weighed down architecture like a stone. Yet it often found its roots deep within a romanticized folkloric past.

With these infinite variations, any definition of art nouveau can be confoundedly imprecise. But unspooling its short period of extraordinary success tells us much about urban life at the turn of the century. It was a mirror of bourgeois society that was both cosmopolitan and open to cultural exchange, and at the same time steadfastly nationalist and regionalist in orientation. The earliest origins of art nouveau were found in Brussels, where it was treated as national imperative. Brussels enjoyed an unrivaled prosperity at the turn of the century. It was the capital of the newly independent country of Belgium founded in 1830. It was an industrial powerhouse with a liberalized capitalist economy. The wealth of material resources that lay beneath the soil—coal, iron, zinc, lead, manganese, pyrite—were mined for the city's heavy industries. The commerce in Belgian steam and diesel engines, railroad equipment, machinery and tools, and weaponry was global.[38] These industries were dispersed across a system of towns clustered around the capital of Brussels. They were also connected to Belgium's colonial economy. Brussels grew rich on the genocidal plunder of Belgium's vast colony of the Congo Free State. With Machiavellian ingenuity, shiploads of precious goods and resources poured into the capital from the Congo. The bourgeoisie had expensive tastes. Brussels became a global trade hub with access to a commodity culture of unprecedented proportions. The city was cluttered with foreign exotica and prized objects from across the globe. Architecture and urban design are never neutral. In auguring a new way of life, art nouveau exhibited

Belgian imperial pretensions and the vicious exploitation of its colony. All of it was readable in the city's beautification and architectural ostentation.

The Belgian king Leopold II was eager to embellish his capital in the style of Napoleon III's rebuilding of Paris. With around 800,000 inhabitants, the old center city of Brussels was grossly overcrowded and antiquated. Residents endured dusty, deafening urban renewal projects that cleared away working-class slums and displaced thousands. They were replaced with wide thoroughfares and ring boulevards interspersed with formal gardens and squares. Grandiloquent public buildings, triumphal arches, and imperial monuments celebrated Belgium's colonial achievements. New railroad stations and streetcar lines, commercial arcades, and an ostentatious Palais de Justice in the "upper town" made Brussels the epitome of the modern city. New districts were laid out in the city's outskirts, especially in Ixelles and Saint-Gilles, and Schaerbeek, and then linked to the center by electric streetcar. These areas were claimed by Brussels' Liberal bourgeoisie anxious to abandon the cramped city center. They enthusiastically supported avant-garde architectural bravura. Art nouveau became the style most representative of the city's modernization. Over 14,000 buildings were constructed between 1880 and 1905.[39]

Hundreds of new residences, schools, cafés, and shops competed for artistic originality in the new districts. There was an unconventional avant-garde culture in Brussels that was unencumbered by the historicist pastiche that dominated much of nineteenth-century architecture. Orbits such as *Le Circle des XX* and *La Libre Esthétique* were salons of free-thinking Belgian artists who saw themselves as creating the material conditions for a new society. Their work matched the social reformist views of Brussels' powerful bourgeois elites and their proclivities for modern style. It was a distinctly Belgian modernism wrought in good part from colonial designs and the ruthless extraction of resources from the Congo.[40] In this case, art nouveau was an expression of western supremacy and deeply embroiled in the violent practices of empire. It was given free rein at the 1897 Colonial Exposition in Brussels dedicated to the display of Congolese colonial plunder, and at the new Royal Congo Museum.[41] Gallery upon gallery displayed colonial raw materials fashioned into *objects d'art* by the modernist alchemists of art nouveau.

It was the idiosyncratic traits of the Belgian avant-garde that they were designing shrines to brutal colonialism while simultaneously supporting the working classes. It was slippery terrain. Among the first commissions of Victor Horta, who became the leading architect in Brussels, was the design of the new Maison du Peuple for the Belgian Workers' Party in the working-class Marolles district. Its experimental use of brick, glass, and white cast iron made it one of the most influential art nouveau buildings in Brussels. Horta and members of *Les XX* and *La Libre Esthéthique* allied closely with the socialist party and applauded the advent of universal manhood suffrage and the entry of socialists into Parliament. Improving the lives of the working classes was the ambition behind much of their creative work. The competition to design model workers' homes for the Liège Exhibition in 1905 also demonstrated the social ambitions of architectural experimentation. The joy and energy of art nouveau design were seen as an antidote to social misery. Colorful decoration and a new modern style would replace the drab housing tracts of the working-class outskirts.

Horta's Tassel House, built for engineer Emile Tassel and one of the first masterpieces of art nouveau, was based on the traditional building style in Brussels. It was reinterpreted in modern guise through the use of cast iron, stone and plate glass, with sensuous arabesque and organic motifs. The interior's twisting, whiplash decorative details and luxurious materials made it a revolutionary style of living. The building was immediately celebrated as the first modern building free from historical constraints. It expressed *élan vital* and the free rein of imagination. Horta built sumptuous houses in art nouveau style for the industrialist Armand Solvay, the son of the chemical magnate Ernest Solvay, for wealthy financier George Deprez, and for Edmond Van Eetvelde, secretary general of the Belgian colony of the Congo Free State and the mastermind behind the king's imperial ventures. Eetvelde's mansion featured stylized patterns based on the Congo's flora and fauna. Horta's art nouveau experimentation appeared in the Congo Pavilion for the 1897 Exposition along with Brussels' L'Innovation department store with its wide display windows open to the street, and the Grand Bazar Anspach (Figure 35).

Figure 35 A L'Innovation department store, Brussels, Victor Horta, 1901.

Brussels indicated the Gordian knot behind the unprecedented housing boom and opportunity for architectural innovation at the turn of the century. The Latvian capital of Riga did as well. We have already encountered Riga as a heterogeneous melting pot of communities from Baltic German traders to Russian workers, and an affluent bourgeoisie that was both cosmopolitan and nationalist in orientation. For these last, the city was a rite of passage into modern nationhood. The older hopes for a Baltic identity fell out of fashion for its too-close association with German culture. Instead, an ethnic Latvian identity was crafted on to nationalist pretentions. It generated one of the most creative periods in Latvian culture and the arts. The city's new western districts were a bourgeois enclave filled with coffee houses, theaters, the new Polytechnic Institute, Riga Art Academy, and the Riga City Art Museum. The trappings of a modern European city were essential to nationalist identity. Elegant residential buildings were outfitted with steam radiators and elevators, and with extravagantly decorative facades. Around 800 art nouveau buildings were constructed in Riga's western districts. The architects were local graduates of the Polytechnic Institute and their designs an eccentric version of the new style. Amblers strolling along the streets were treated to a dazzling ornamental display. The facades were decorated with fanciful floral motifs, human faces and figures, animals, sphinxes, dragons, and geometric forms.[42] The frontages of the buildings along Albert Street were flamboyant visual theater, so exaggerated they veered into wild abandon. The movement continued in the city's northern outskirts with the development of one of Europe's first garden suburbs at Kaiserwald (Mežaparks). Over 100 fanciful art nouveau villas for Riga's upper-class elites were constructed in a hamlet nestled amid the pine forests on the shores of Lake Ķīšezers. The scheme included a zoological garden, amusement park and sports grounds (Figure 36).

Riga's lavish art nouveau embodied a national romantic style—a kind of aesthetic rage against both Germanic influences and Russification. It was deliberately demonstrative of a Latvian National Awakening. The city's wealthy elites founded the Latvian Association in 1868 and organized the first Latvian Song Festival in 1873. The air thundered with Latvian folk ballads sung by a thousand-member chorus and thirty orchestras. By 1910, the Riga song festival had become a patriotic gathering with upwards of 5,000 singers and 25,000 spectators joining in the rousing music-making. The municipality organized an exhibition on the cultural history of Riga that received rave reviews from a wide public. The Latvian Ethnographic Exhibition in 1896 showcased Latvian history and cultural achievements. These events marked the emergence of Riga as the ostensible capital of Latvia in opposition to both the German establishment and the repressive policies carried out by the Russian Empire in the Baltic provinces. The city's wealthy middle-class elites emerged as leaders of a cultural renaissance at a moment when the Latvian language and culture were still officially censored. Like art nouveau itself, the Ethnographic Exhibition was a form of resistance against foreign domination and a frontline in debates about the city's multiethnic identity. Modern Riga was again put on display at the 700th Jubilee of Industry and Craft in 1901. Postcards issued for the festivities illustrated block-after-block of spectacular art nouveau buildings and gas-lite boulevards lined with trams and busy sidewalks.

Figure 36 Art Nouveau building designed by Mikhail Eisenstein on 4A Strelnieku Street, Riga.

Modernist impulses encompassed a variety of local lineages that were by turn fascinating and bemusing. A stop on the art nouveau itinerary in the city of Turin gives full play to the particularity of place and the forging of a distinctive Italian style. At the turn of the century, the region of Piedmont in northwest Italy and its golden triangle around Milan-Turin-Genoa were becoming an industrial powerhouse and commercial transit point at the core of the Italian economy. Some 40 percent of Italy's rail network was located in Piedmont. With the abundant water and geothermal heat of the Alpes, the region was at the forefront of hydroelectric power. Europe's largest hydroelectric plant was constructed on Piedmont's Adda River. The Alpine tunnels gave the region direct access to Europe while the port of Genoa was modernized for transatlantic shipping. Milan became a major banking center. The city of Turin experienced the fastest economic growth rate in Italy and emerged as the newly unified country's industrial capital. Its fiercely ambitious entrepreneurial class aimed to shape Italy's *Risorgimento* around its own progressive agenda.

Eclectic and cosmopolitan, the urban culture of Turin would be a catalyst for nation-building. The Royal Polytechnic of Turin provided the best engineering education in Italy and spearheaded the development of electric engineering. The city's Industrial Museum linked Turin to the most important European technological innovations and disseminated the findings to a broad reading public. The local metallurgical and engineering, chemical and textile industries flourished. Over a hundred small companies manufactured bicycles and assorted vehicles. But the focal point of Turin's industrial development was the automotive industry. In 1899, Giovanni Agnelli established his Fabbrica Italiana de Automobili Torino, or Fiat, with fifty workers. By 1914, Fiat employed 4,000 workers and produced 4,000 cars a year. Turin became a Fiat city. It employed one-third of the industrial population of the city. Turin's skilled workers were a privileged elite and a vanguard of working-class politics. The automobile industry led to a spin-off of supply and service companies in the city and entirely new industrial sectors.[43] Along with industry, the population boomed. The 1880 population of 250,000 nearly doubled to 415,000 by 1911.

As in Brussels and Riga, art nouveau was enthusiastically promoted by Liberal bourgeois elites searching for a new urban identity. Modernism was bent to their own ends. Turin's socialist party was dominated by humanistic middle-class intellectuals who believed in the moral elevation of the working classes. Together with the city's industrialists, they formed an "industrializing bloc" in local politics dedicated to economic progress, social reform, and patronage of the new arts. According to the local *La Stampa* newspaper, they were "a new bourgeois class endowed with energy and talent, open to all questions."[44] Edmondo De Amicis's *Turin 1880* was an elegant travel guide to what was imagined as an ideal Italian metropolis. It was a panoramic portrait of Turin that took readers on a stroll through the "wonder and pleasure" of its neighborhoods, boulevards, and piazzas. In De Amicis's vision, the city was well-run and logically organized as a sort of permanent exposition.[45] This image was portrayed in a series of spectacular events that celebrated the city's arrival as an industrial dynamo. Turin's 1902 Esposizione Internazionale d'Arte Decorativa Moderna promoted a self-consciously Italian modern style in production and consumption. Italian architect Raimondo d'Aronco was selected to design the exposition buildings. The pavilions were exuberantly decorated, brilliantly colored, with a wild combination of motifs helped along by d'Aronco's years as chief architect to the Ottoman Sultan in Constantinople. They introduced art nouveau to the public as an expression of an authentic Italian identity. The Automobile Hall, filled with the latest Fiat models, was draped in flamboyant electric illumination. The exposition was a unique mixture of Turin's distinctive industrial culture and the grander hopes of Italian nationalism.

Vienna's version of this avant-garde flowering also sprouted from the city's coffee houses. It was places such as the Café Sperl and the Café Zum Blauen Freihaus that provided a meeting place outside the stifling chokehold of the Academy of Fine Arts that controlled official art and architecture in Viennese Ringstrasse society. In 1897, a young generation of artists and architects founded the "Vienna Secession" artistic salon and the Wiener Werkstätte (Viennese Workshops). Consisting mainly of graduates from Vienna's Applied Arts School, they railed against nineteenth-century architectural pomposity as tasteless and barbaric, and against the shackles of appearance in Viennese society. The Secession House was built as the movement's headquarters and exhibition space. Emblazoned on the building was their motto: "Der Zeit ihre Kunst. Der Kunst ihre Freiheit" (To every age its art, to art its freedom). Rather than the extravagant curvilinear designs found in French and Belgian art nouveau, the Viennese variety featured simple geometric shapes, evident in the cubic forms and flat surfaces of the Secession House. The secession artistic rebellion was heretical, yet it was supported by Vienna's industrial bourgeoisie. Financing for the construction of Secession House was partly supplied by patrons such as the steel tycoon Karl Wittgenstein, one of the wealthiest men in Europe. Motivated by utopian and socialist ideals, the Wiener Werkstätte achieved a revolution in twentieth-century design and branding. It was financed by the textile magnate Fritz Wärndorfer, who was also behind the Mackintosh design style and a crucial go-between for the avant-garde movements in Vienna and Glasgow.

By 1910, with a population of 2 million inhabitants, Vienna was the fourth largest city in the world after New York, London, and Paris. It had annexed the working-class suburbs outside the Ringstrasse, a realignment that required a coherent plan for the sprawling metropolitan area. Otto Wagner won the competition for the master plan for greater Vienna (1893), which became his manifesto for a modern metropolis. It was a fundamental break in the city's design. Wagner was a bold, uncompromising architect and urban planner, and nearly a cult figure among Vienna's cultural elite. He insisted on the necessity for public rail transportation as well as for straight streets and traffic arteries. They meshed the city and outlying districts together. Vienna would spread out uniformly with its railways and radial streets acting like a giant spider web. All the districts would be rationally arranged with simple, multistory apartment buildings. It was a complete rupture from the mental world of the Ringstrasse. For Wagner, practicality and uniformity expressed the democratic nature of modern society. He was assigned development of Vienna's Stadtbahn, or Metropolitan Railway, and the upgrading of the Danube Canal that flowed through the city. This required construction of locks and sluice gates, viaducts, bridges and tunnels, and thirty-six rail stations. These became demonstration pieces for Wagner's ideas. He found common ground with the Vienna Succession and rebelled against the historicism that too long held sway over the Ringstrasse. Instead Wagner crafted an architecture that responded to the rhythms of modern life. The railway stations were designed in a sinuous art nouveau style. His Postal Savings Bank on the Ringstrasse was a revolutionary modernist fusion of marble, aluminum, and glass, and filled with glistening light.

The view from Barcelona also provides insight into the particularistic features of urban culture in these years. Its avant-garde launched the rebirth of Catalan culture from the *Els Quatre Gats* (The Four Cats) cabaret at the entrance to the commercial arcade known as the Passage del Patriarca. The cabaret combined Parisian-inspired artistic performances with the popular traditions of shadow theater and puppet shows. It was a seedbed for Catalan modernism. By the 1870s, Barcelona's *modernismo* movement had spread to all fields of linguistic, literary, and artistic expression. The city's wealthy bourgeoisie fully embraced it as a lifestyle equivalent to what they witnessed in other European cities and yet was specifically Catalan in tone. *Modernismo* meant freedom from Spanish domination. It meant the revival of Catalan language, music and festivals, and traditional arts and crafts.

The 1888 Barcelona Universal Exposition was the platform for an outpouring of Catalan creativity. Some 2 million visitors toured the pavilions and attended the revival of the Jocs Florals (Floral Games) poetry competition with its roots deep in local culture. The exposition was the catalyst for the renewal of the city's ancient Ribera district and construction of the iron and glass El Born public market with materials manufactured in Catalonia in *modernista* style. A model hospital and prison were laid out and electric street lighting installed along the boulevards of Las Ramblas and Gran Viá de la Corts Catalanes. Antoni Gaudi (1852–1926) was the great genius of the Catalan artistic idiom. Many of his commissions were for homes for the city's powerful bourgeois elite in the Eixample. The textile magnates Eusebio Güell and Josep Batlló were his most important patrons and hailed the modern movement as a Catalan renaissance. Gaudi was profoundly nationalistic and deeply religious. His aesthetics were embedded in the natural landscape, history, and religious culture of Catalonia. The colors and curvaceous shapes found in marine life were his inspiration for the Casa Batlló (House of Bones). The facade and entire building seemed to ripple like water. The building indulged in a decorative flamboyance that was uniquely Catalan.

These scenes of aesthetic and architectural originality played out across Europe's cities, inspired by a search for modern identity rooted in local culture and place. They were supported by self-assured wealthy elites who imagined urban culture as an amalgam of shared cosmopolitan values with nationalistic overtones. The cityscape became an idiosyncratic palette for imagining this new urbanity. The experiments saw their most flamboyant expression in the peripheral borderlands of Europe, where cities contended with expanding populations made up of multiple ethnicities and the crying need to modernize. The result was a cornucopia of stylistic interpretations that were often described as national romanticism.

The city of Lemberg (L'viv/Lwów) captures this cultural and aesthetic complexity. It was at the heart of the Hapsburg Empire's oil producing region and was a manufacturing and financial center as well as the capital of the newly designated Kingdom of Galicia. Galicia was the territorial unit invented by the Hapsburg Monarchy from their slice of Poland after it was carved up by the imperial powers at the end of the eighteenth century. Located in the Polish southeast in what is now the Ukraine, Galicia was one of the most poverty-stricken areas of Europe. Its southern frontier was shaped by the Carpathian Mountains. Once oil was discovered on the slopes of the Carpathians, adventurers from around Europe descended on the area in search of black gold. The vast stretches of countryside in Galicia were remote and poor, sprinkled with rural villages. But oil wealth was one reason Lemberg was a center of economic development and a booming construction site. Lemberg financiers bankrolled the oil barons.[46] It was among the first cities to switch to petroleum-based public lighting. By the turn of the twentieth century, the population reached 160,000 and quickly grew to 200,000. It was the fifth largest city in the Hapsburg domains.

Although the Hapsburg Empire promoted the city's modernization as part of its civilizing mission, German "Lemberg" was shaped by Polish elites and by Polish cultural influences, as well as by its Yiddish and Ukrainian worlds. Hence the variety in its names. In 1925, German novelist and traveler Alfred Döblin strolled along Legionow Street "with its profusion of light, the brightness of day. . . . The wide pavement teems with swarms of people in front of the radiant and fashionable shops. These are tall slender Poles, with dark faces, wearing coats in modern style, pointed shoes. . . . Confusion, shoving on Legionow Street. Two lines of people, a drive belt . . . . The profusion of light gathers the people, and the wide rows float straight ahead." About half the city's residents were Polish Catholic. The rest were Jews and Ukrainians/Ruthenians, and all increasingly saw themselves in modern national terms. "Thus three nations live together, side by side, in Lwów" Döblin remarked, "Poles, dominating the city . . . Jews, disunited, preoccupied, and aloof . . . Ukranians, invisible soundless here and there . . . dangerous, grieving, surrounded by the tension of conspirators and insurgents." On Legionow Street, Döblin passed, "Jews in groups and troops, in black and brown velvet hats. . . . Polish priests on the street: blurred faces, coarse and rustic, good-natured. Aristocrats and patricians . . . . Green soldiers keep marching by. Steel helmets, their rifles slanting across their shoulder. Lots of rain; the trees are bare."[47]

As the hub of a railway network with nine separate lines, the city was graced with a Hapsburg-style Ringstrasse lined with a galaxy of hotels, theaters, and opera house. They complimented the city's heritage of baroque churches and monasteries. Lemberg was an elegant up-to-date outpost in an antiquated Galicia. The local press and movie theaters thrived. Jugendstil garnishing graced the facades of its new buildings. Supported by local elites and the Polytechnic and Applied Art schools, local architects leavened their work with Viennese secessionist motifs and blended it with folk ornamentation. Sumptuous murals and stained-glass windows, ornate architecture traced a "Hutzul style," named after the ethnic group that inhabited the western Ukraine. It was also branded as a Ukrainian-Ruthenian secession. This Galician twist on Lemberg modernism was evident in the Mikolasz shopping arcade with its iron and glass ceiling and festive painted murals, and the city's new Central Station with its soaring copulas. On the occasion of the Galician General Provincial Exhibition in 1894, the first electric tram system began operation from the Central Station to the city center and out to the fairgrounds in Stryiskyi Park. The exhibition celebrated progress and modernity in Galicia with a powerful emphasis on the traditional features of the province. A narrow-gauged railway puffed visitors around pavilions designed in a profusion of whimsical styles. They delighted in ethnographic displays and a fairytale Galician village replete with folk cottages and costumes. Galician Byzantine-inspired religious art was among the highlights of the exposition.[48] A gleaming white rotunda was built to display the Racławice panorama depicting the famous battle for Polish independence. Special discounted trains arrived with fairgoers from Warsaw, Kraków, Vienna, Bern, and Prague.

The First World War was the gravedigger of what had been a century of extraordinary urban advance. The years just before the war represented a zenith of Europe's urban culture and influence. City living was infused with an atmosphere of progress, confidence, and gaiety. Yet there was a subliminal uneasiness that it wouldn't last, almost a sentimental melancholy about a modern world about to disappear. It was easy to ignore the military build-up along the Baltic coast and in the Ruhr, where workers in cities such as Kiel, Stettin, Königsberg, and Essen were churning out warships and heavy artillery. Machine guns and flamethrowers came off the assembly lines at Britain's Royal Arsenal at Woolwich, and in factories in Paris and Lyon. The crowds cheering the soldiers departing for the front in August 1914 remained blind to the imminent catastrophe. A sea of humanity gathered on the Unter den Linden in Berlin to greet the Kaiser, sing patriotic songs, and celebrate the outbreak of war. It was a scene repeated in Paris, London, Vienna, St. Petersburg. The railway stations in every city were crowded with chaotic multitudes.

The First World War was not known for urban warfare, at least not on the Western Front nor in central Europe. On the surface, city life went on as before. The theaters were crowded with musicals glorifying the deeds of the army. The cafés were still packed. Women ran city services and public transportation while the men were away at the front. Yet it is worth peering into the abyss of war to realize its impact on urban life. Behind the gay scenes were the daily bulletins from the war zones and the awful letters delivered on doorsteps that a son or husband or brother had died in battle. People crowded into cities to work in munitions factories and war industries. The leading metallurgical and engineering companies in Europe swung into war production, which proved a bonanza. Some 75,000 people were working at London's Woolwich Arsenal in 1917. In Paris, the Citroën and Renault factories switched to building military vehicles and tanks. In Turin, Fiat was flooded with military orders for truck and airplane engines. Its workforce climbed to 40,000 during the war years. German factories in the densely industrialized areas of the Ruhr and Upper Silesia were relocated for safety to the center of the country around the towns of Hanover, Magdeburg, and Halle. New munitions and aircraft plants were established in Rostock on the Baltic coast. Petrograd (St. Petersburg) was the Russian center for military production.

Food shortages, spiraling prices, imitation products and substitutes, and the inevitable black market spread from one city to the next as the war dragged on. Luxury items, soap, wool, and cotton all disappeared. Step-by-step, meat, sugar, potatoes, eggs, and milk were all rationed. The food shortages exaggerated social tensions. Women from the East End of London marched to Harrods in Knightsbridge to demand sugar. Some 3,000 people waited in line for margarine in London, until their exasperation finally broke down into mêlée. In Berlin, street protests in the working-class districts of Wedding and Lichtenberg spread to Neukolln, Charlottenburg, and elsewhere. Food riots led by angry women took place in Vienna and Prague. During the terrible winter of 1916–17, malnutrition stalked cities in central and eastern Europe. Berlin bakeries and butcher shops were looted. Over 300 businesses and 300,000 workers went out on strike and the protest spread to Leipzig, Halle, and Magdeburg. In February 1917 thousands of Russian women factory workers instigated a bread riot that turned into a massive demonstration in Petrograd. More than 100,000 people flooded the streets demanding the end to food shortages. By the war's end, starvation and freezing cold overwhelmed daily life. Millions of civilians lost their lives due to malnutrition and epidemics. The concentration of troops and multitudes of people packed into cities were fertile ground for disease, especially the influenza pandemic of 1918.

The deprivation and suffering caused by the First World War was astounding. About 6.6 million soldiers died on the continent. There were 5 million civilian victims. Approximately 300,000 men from London, Paris, and Berlin died during the war. A significant percentage of urban casualties were clerks, teachers, and in general the middle and lower-middle classes who served as officers. But in terms of absolute numbers, the majority of urban casualties across Europe came from the working classes. Funeral corteges wound through the streets from hospitals to cemeteries. Street shrines appeared. Fighting on both the Western and Eastern Fronts cut a swath of destruction. Civilians and refugees fled the advancing armies. Towns became military encampments, food and accommodations were requisitioned, and civilians brutalized by occupying armies. As the war years wore on, refugees wandered from town to town in search of sustenance. Many were herded into temporary camps. On the Western Front, the main theater of war was the trenches that snaked from the Channel Coast through Belgium and France. Urban battles were limited. But the once prosperous towns of Ypres and Louvain in Belgium stood in the way of the German Army's advance and were turned into rubble. The towns of Rheim, Arras, Saint Quentin, and Bethune in northern France shared the same fate. Verdun was pounded by shelling and left in ruins.

On the Eastern Front towns and cities were on the front lines of colossal battles and were occupied and destroyed. Already in 1914, Lemburg was the scene of a major battle and fell to Russian forces. The Turkish fleet attacked Odessa. Belgrade was bombarded in 1915 with a devastating loss of life and material damage. Once the German Army crossed the Danube and entered Belgrade, there was vicious street fighting as the Serbs attempted to defend the city. Split between the Hapsburg Empire, the German Empire, and the Russian Empire, Polish territory was the scene of the fiercest fighting and sustained tremendous human and material losses. Its cities were on the frontlines. As the German Army advanced, some 1 million Polish refugees fled eastward behind Russian lines. By the end of 1914, Warsaw was already flooded with 100,000 refugees. Marshall law was declared. Then the city was occupied by German forces in August 1915 and came under direct military control. The economy was in shambles. Inflation spiraled out of control. Unemployment stood at 75 percent and some 50,000 workers were evacuated. The city's population declined by nearly 20 percent, and then ballooned again at the war's end.[49] Polish towns and villages were left in ruins, their factories dismantled and shipped to Germany. They were looted and abandoned by the retreating Russian armies. Crowded with refugees, cities on the Eastern Front were besieged by contagious diseases. Malaria, dysentery, typhoid accounted for four times the number of deaths caused by direct combat. Utter misery, death, and despair were the legacy of the war. In every sense of the word, it was a debacle of extraordinary measure.

CHAPTER 8
ELECTRIC CITIES AND AVANT-GARDE ITINERARIES (1920s–30s)

When the representatives at the 1919 Paris Peace Conference finalized negotiations and emerged triumphantly with a new map of Europe, many of the continent's cities had been in a state of crisis for years. Despite the high hopes, very little went right in the early postwar years. The streets of St. Petersburg and Moscow were reeling from the Bolshevik Revolution. Cities in the defunct Russian and Hapsburg empires had been occupied and pillaged repeatedly by German and Russian armies. Ironically, some of them were grandly anointed capital cities by the Paris Peace Conference at a moment of unprecedented turmoil and political crisis. There were scenes of desperation and dire poverty, of the greedy speculation and looting that always accompany war. Street clashes and protests of every sort, even outright rebellion, sapped any sense of security or normal everyday life.

Workers in Katowice and Upper Silesia staged an armed uprising, as did the sailors and soldiers in the Baltic city of Kiel. The jolt of the Bolshevik Revolution electrified Europe's desperate soldiers and workers. A wave of workers' soviets was set up in towns and cities across the collapsing geography of Europe's great empires. In 1918, three massive industrial strike waves upended hopes for rapid economic recovery in Austria and Hungary. By 1919, Budapest momentarily became the capital of the Hungarian Soviet Republic amid huge public demonstrations. There was an aborted left-wing revolution in Vienna. Berlin had seen violent coup attempts, strikes, assassinations, vicious pogroms against the city's Jews, and then the collapse of the mark in a devastating inflationary spiral. The defeated capital of Prussian Germany was a "laboratory of the apocalypse"[1] and stumbled from one economic and political crisis to another during the early 1920s. It was a magnet of vice and careerism and a cesspool of the unwanted and displaced. Even the wartime victors France, Great Britain, and Italy—had little to celebrate. Everything was in short supply. Weakened and malnourished, untold numbers fell victim to the devastating influenza pandemic of 1918. To add further horror to the war's carnage, influenza attacked young adults with particular ferocity.

Despite the instability, or perhaps because of it, the 1920s were years of unprecedented cultural experimentation and genuine hopefulness for the future. There was a brassy extroversion about the "twenties." People were jubilant about the modern age and the potential of revolutionary change. They abandoned themselves to the razzle-dazzle of new technologies and the entertainment industries. The cultural and intellectual scenes in Europe's cities exploded in a kaleidoscope of new horizons. This cultural production was fueled in part by émigré communities. The war and ongoing political turmoil brought more foreigners into the big cities. A good number in this migratory vortex were demobilized colonial soldiers who had fought at the front as well as colonial students and political dissidents, many of whom were under police surveillance. The ties of empire were everywhere in London and Paris. London hosted the massive Wembley Imperial Exposition in 1925 with "human zoos" at colonial pavilions and thousands participating in the spectacular "Pageant of Empire" performance. The Paris International Colonial Exposition held at the Bois de Vincennes in 1931 was a stunning imperial fantasyland. Some 33 million visitors roamed exhibitions of colonial products and exotic trappings. They gaped at the sumptuous *colonial moderne* buildings staged with brilliant lighting, including an extravagant replica of Cambodia's Angor Wat.

Beyond this official imagery of imperialism, both London and Paris became the intellectual nerve centers for anti-imperial activism. Students from India, Asia, and Africa flocked to London and Paris during these years. West African and Afro-Caribbean intellectuals worked out their anti-colonialism and pan-African political aspirations from the hostels, black clubs, and mutual aid societies hidden in London's Soho and Camden districts. A student from Trinidad recalled that the racism meant "an almost complete withdrawal—intellectual and emotional—from the English . . . he joins all the 'International Clubs' and 'Commonwealth Clubs' and 'Overseas Students' Clubs,' he makes friends with coloured people from other countries. . . . He discovers an affinity with them. . . . He has become a black man, taking his side in the array of black versus white."[2] Soho in London's West End had a long-standing reputation for raffish nonconformity. It was a polyglot sanctuary for exiles and wayfarers. Soho's nightlife vibrated with the jazz music of dance halls and nightclubs. Its gritty streets were the haunts of London's streetwalkers and brothels and a zone of homosexual notoriety.[3] Bloomsbury was another intellectual scene and terrain of foreigners, especially Indian and West Indians fermenting their nationalist partialities and independence movements.

France had the largest contingents of refugees and migrants. A mishmash of peoples found themselves setting up lives in Paris. Working in the kitchen of a hotel near the Place de la Concorde, writer George Orwell witnessed, "Different jobs were done by different races. The office employees and the cooks and sewing-women were French, the waiters Italians and Germans . . . the *plongeurs* of every race in Europe, beside Arabs and negroes."[4] There were already a reported 100,000 Italians and 70,000 North Africans in the Paris region by 1930. East European intellectuals and artists from cities such as Budapest and Zagreb were hanging out in Paris with Surrealists and the avant-garde. The political upheavals in Latin American drew some 15,000 mainly upper crust and intellectual expatriates. The number of students from Vietnam and China soared. They made student hostels and cheap bistros of the Latin Quarter into a bohemian hotbed of anti-imperialist doctrine and communist activity.[5] Some of them, such as Zhou Enlai and Deng Ziaoping, would emerge as political leaders. The tiny Vietnamese and Chinese restaurants that popped up across Paris became meeting places for political activism and mutual aide. There was a diaspora of entertainers from the United States who congregated in the nightclubs of Montmartre and the dives of Montparnasse. The cheap watering holes and hotels on the Left Bank were the haunts of American expatriate literati. The Place Pigalle at the foot of Montmartre was a crazy scene of bars and nightclubs, drugs and sex, a combustible mixture of decadence and originality. African American jazz musicians mixed with White Russian exiles, leering tourists, and a whirlwind of refugees from the war years.[6]

The displacement and forced migration caused by the seismic territorial reconfigurations in Europe were sweeping and violent. Some 700,000 Germans left the new state of Poland and over 100,000 Germans left Alsace-Lorraine, which became part of France. Between 1 and 2 million Poles fled the revolution and civil war that tore apart Russia. Many were Jewish families fleeing persecution. Those left along the border with the new Soviet Union were caught in violent border clashes and the bloody civil war. Another 1 million Russians who sympathized with the whites in the civil war left for Europe or the Far East. The new Baltic states of Latvia, Lithuania, and Estonia were flooded with tens of thousands of Russian refugees. Some 500,000 Hungarian deportees were driven out of the territories lost in the peacetime settlements and stumbled into Budapest, homeless and with little hope. In Yugoslavia, migration policies drove the exodus of Germans, Bulgarians, Hungarians, and Muslim Turks. The death march and massacre of Armenians in the Syrian Desert by the Turkish military provoked a wave of desperate survivors. Some 1.35 million Greeks were forced out of Turkey, while half a million Turks and other Muslims were expelled from Greece. Sweeping population exchanges took place between Greece and Bulgaria.[7] Between 50,000 and 100,000 Slavs fled Italy as Mussolini's fascist regime revved up its hyper-nationalism.

Europe's big capital cities were the main destination for all these castaways compelled to make new lives under harrowing circumstances, many of them following a vertiginous course from one place to another. They arrived with their haunting tales of survival. Many were well-educated, prodigiously talented members of the intelligentsia. They embodied the creative lives somehow carried on in a crumbling world. Novelist Joseph Roth was an example of the displacement and wandering that characterized many intellectuals after the First World War. Born to a Jewish family in the town of Brody in eastern Galicia, Roth moved first to Lemberg and then to Vienna for his studies. He was a product of the ethnic melting pot of the Hapsburg Empire and experienced profound loss at its collapse in the First World War. After 1920, he became a journalist in Berlin reporting on modern urban life. Riding on Berlin's S-Bahn, Roth looked out as "evening comes, an overhead light goes on. Its illumination is oily and greasy; it burns in a haze like a star in a sea of fog. We ride past lit-up advertisements, past a world without burdens, where commercial hymns to laundry soap, cigars, shoe polish, and bootlaces suddenly shine forth against the darkened sky."[8] By 1925, he was in Paris and settled there once Hitler came to power in Germany. The Russian Revolution and Civil War drove masses of Russians westward to Europe's great capitals. Writer Vladimir Nabokov fled his native St. Petersburg, first to Crimea, then to England, and then settled in Berlin for a time where he found himself penniless living off relatives and the occasional language and tennis lessons. Some 200,000 Russians lived in Berlin's western districts of Charlottenburg, Schöneberg, and Wilmersdorf, while another 200,000 took up residence in the western districts of Paris. Intent on preserving Russian language and culture, they formed a tight-knit émigré community with their own schools, Orthodox churches, tiny restaurants and theaters, shoe-string publications and newspapers.

Powerful migratory forces continued to shift Europe's population into cities. The majority of the 93.5 million people added to the population roles in Europe during the interwar years were urban dwellers, some 80 million. The city acquired a clear dominance over rural life. Europe had some 265 towns with over 100,000 population. In western and central Europe, towns absorbed almost all of the population growth. In southern and eastern Europe, which were predominantly rural, the greatest population increase also took place in towns and cities. The urban growth rates in the east, especially in the Balkans and the Soviet Union, were the highest in Europe. Cities sucked in refugees and the displaced, and immigrants from the countryside in search of employment. The largest metropolises were absorbing a growing share of Europe's population, and that was especially true of the great capital cities. In 1920 there were eight European cities with over a million inhabitants. By the end of the interwar period, this number had doubled.[9] The greatest population increase took place in the newly designated capital cities in eastern Europe, which were undoubtedly the least able to manage the influx. Although the giant metropolises of the nineteenth century were still growing, their center districts were losing population to the peripheries. London, Paris, and Vienna were spreading out into vast amoeba-like urban agglomerations.

Mass culture and democracy, mass production, and mass communication were the symbols of the age. "Americanism" in the 1920s was a European term for anything connected to materialism, mechanization and standardization, and entertainment. All the influences making up mass culture were somehow related to the colossus across the Atlantic. Hollywood films, glossy advertisements, and the skyscraper imagery of New York City mesmerized European city dwellers. They were rapt listeners of Black American ragtime and especially jazz, the improvisational avant-garde music coming from Harlem and Chicago nightclubs. Jazz was modern, exhilarating, and exotic. Patrons of the great Paris jazz clubs, like Mitchell's or Zelli's, risked bumping into criminals from Montmartre. But they could hear the sound of the modern age by both American artists and French jazz musicians who were learning from the American black community in Paris. Jazzman Sydney Bechet and "The Most Famous American Southern Syncopated Orchestra" performed in Paris in May 1921 and toured through Europe, reaching Moscow in 1926. American performers such as Josephine Baker and Louis Armstrong took Paris and Berlin by storm. Baker and dance partner Joe Alex captivated audiences with their exotic *Danse Sauvage*. They were an overnight sensation. Her *La Revue Nègre* toured Europe's major cities as far as Bucharest in the 1920s. Variety shows featuring eroticized black performers were part of the broader trend of "Negrophilia" that was also unmistakable in the primitivist "People Shows" and human zoos at the colonial expositions that were all the rage. Many also condemned jazz as a menace to Europe and warned of the evil influence of both black Africans and American gutter music.

The seductive power of both American capitalism and the Soviet communist experiment to the east was laid out as tempting visions of the future. Both exuded a hyper-optimism about the possibilities of twentieth-century mass society that was genuinely infectious as well as apprehensive. The Soviet Union was a beacon of hope for those who espoused an egalitarian society and social harmony. While industrialists and entertainers exalted American panache, left-wing artists, architects, and social reformers embraced the communist ideal and the notion of devoting their expertise to the service of the state. Nonetheless, European practices were more than a matter of following the all-encompassing cultural logics of *Americanismus und Bolshevismus*. Europe developed its own mass cultural styles that were made even more distinctive by the strength of national customs and political economies. These influences were absorbed into the urban fabric and transmuted by the depth of local circumstance.

Although the years after the First World War were beset by political and economic crises, they were also a moment of stunning industrial breakthroughs. There was a mythical view of American capitalism as the embodiment of economic productivity. Capital accumulation, assembly-line production and scientific management (known as Fordism and Taylorism) were quickly adopted by large European manufacturers. The electrical engineering and chemical industries matured in the 1920s and 1930s and created entirely new skilled workforces. Large cities throughout Europe were festooned with electrical cables, telephone poles, and a spaghetti-mix of wires that crisscrossed the sky. Making electric equipment provided employment for thousands of workers across Europe. The French Compagnie Générale d'Electricité, with headquarters in Paris, employed 20,000 people by 1930 and controlled fifty companies manufacturing electrical apparatus. In Budapest, Duna Electric mass-produced electric cables, wires, and telephones while the United Incandescent Lamp Company employed 5,000 workers by the 1930s. With branches in Vienna and Warsaw, the later made and boxed up light bulbs for export to fifty-three countries. Basic household electric appliances were coming within reach of the average consumer. Sweden's Electrolux Company manufactured refrigerators and vacuum cleaners in plants outside Stockholm, Berlin, and Paris. Telephones, radios, and phonographs were displayed in department store windows for rubbernecking shoppers. The Philips Company produced electric shavers, radios, light bulbs, and vacuum tubes in its factories in Eindhoven. The demand for these consumer products was enormous.

The chemical and materials industries were churning out new products, especially aluminum and rubber alloys, pharmaceuticals, agricultural fertilizers, and photographic equipment. The largest industrial companies in Britain were the chemical giants Imperial Chemical and Lever Brothers. The Rhône Poulenc company developed industrial and specialty chemicals at its factories at Saint Fons near Lyon and pharmaceuticals at Vitry-sur-Seine in the Paris region with a workforce of 10,000. The Saint Gobain and Kuhlmann conglomerates, each with 15,000 employees, concentrated on chemical fertilizers, glues, and pastes at a web of plants in the Paris suburbs as well as in Bordeaux, Marseille, and towns throughout France. In Germany, the firms of BASF and IG Farben founded research laboratories in dyes and pharmaceuticals, synthetic fertilizers, rubber, and plastics. The Leuna-Buna-Bitterfeld "Chemical Triangle" began to take shape in northern Germany around the towns of Merseburg and Bitterfeld and the local coal and potash deposits. AEG constructed the biggest electric power plant in the world to supply the triangle's chemical giants such as BASF and AGFA. Some 20,000 people produced synthetic products at the BASF (Badische Anilin und Soda Fabrik) plant at Leuna. The AGFA conglomerate hired 10,000 workers in the production of synthetic fibers and photographic film, including the first color film.[10] Formed in 1925 from a series of mergers and headquartered in Frankfurt, IG Farben was the largest corporation in Europe. Its 100,000 strong workforce manufactured everything from dyes and pharmaceutical drugs to synthetic oils and rubber, explosives and poison gas. The ultramodern IG Farben headquarters in Frankfurt was the largest office building in Europe.

And this is to say nothing, of course, about the growing impact of the automobile on urban life. Automobile ownership was still largely the domain of the wealthy and growing middle class. Enthusiasts could wander through the posh automobile showrooms on the Champs-Elysées in Paris and in London's West End. But as more and more people moved out to peripheral suburban areas, the automobile became an essential part of daily life. For example, in 1931, nearly half a million people were already commuting daily between the suburbs surrounding Paris and the center city.[11] Motorists began to demand the right of way and roads built for speed. Mass motorization was on the agenda. The numerous pioneering car producers were winnowed down to those able to leap into assembly-line mass production. Initially France was just behind the United States in automobile production. André Citroën is credited with the first mass-produced automobile in Europe. The Paris plant on the Quai de Javel was entirely rebuilt to manufacture the revolutionary front-wheel drive "Traction Avant" that was the sleekest car on the roads. Citroën established another plant in Paris's northern industrial district of Saint-Ouen. The assembly line was not the only American practice Citroën embraced. In 1925, he created an uproar by adorning the Eiffel Tower with the Citroën logo in 250,000 electric lights. Renault's massive plant on the Ile Seguin southwest of Paris was hailed as the "factory of tomorrow" and was a bastion of labor militancy. At its peak in the 1930s, some 37,000 people passed through its gates each morning and clocked in for work.

Britain overtook France to become Europe's largest car producer. The tiny Morris Minor automobile along with the Austin Seven and Ford Eight became instant triumphs. The Ford Motor Company plants were initially in Cork, Ireland, and in Manchester. In 1931, Ford opened the Dagenham complex in the Docklands of East London. It became known as the "Detroit of Europe." Many of the auto factories were concentrated in the West Midlands around Coventry and Birmingham, where car part suppliers encircled them. In the 1920s, Austin's massive Longbridge facility in Birmingham dominated the UK market for cars. The imposing "Fort Dunlop" north of Birmingham churned out thousands of tires each year. It was one of the largest factory complexes in England. By the early 1930s, the Morris plant in the town of Cowley was turning out more than 60,000 cars a year.[12] Fiat was synonymous with the automobile market in Italy. It moved to mass production with its sprawling Mirafiori and Lingotto plants in Turin and began production of the tiny Topolino and Balilla models. The Lingotto factory complex was the largest in the world in the 1920s with five floors and a spiral roadway that vertically moved finished cars up to the rooftop test track. In the 1930s, Fiat executives toured Ford's River Rouge plant in Dearborn Michigan and returned to Turin to design the new Mirafiori plant as a model of American-style production with 40,000 employees. In Sweden, Volvo started production of passenger cars and light trucks in the town of Gothenburg. The German city of Zwickau in Saxony was an automotive capital with Horsh and Audi factories. Ferdinand Porsche designed Hitler's "people's car," the "KdF-car" or Volkswagen, that was launched in 1936 from the automotive plant in Wolfsburg. The American Ford Motor Company and General Motors also opened assembly plants on the continent as far as the Soviet Union. Moscow became an "auto city" with the help of Ford and Fiat management at the massive Zil automobile complex (Figure 37).

Mass production and consumption became the driving forces in a city's economy. The new nation of Czechoslovakia came into possession of a large share of the Hapsburg Monarchy's industrial legacy. Some 70 percent of the entire industrial capacity of the Hapsburg's warhorse region of Cisleithania was concentrated in Czechoslovakia. With 13.6 million inhabitants—hardly more than a quarter of the defunct Hapsburg Monarchy—Czechoslovakia possessed an economy on a par with western Europe. Bohemia and Moravia were the most urbanized regions of the country, with the capital of Prague (676,657 population) and the industrial cluster of Pilsen, Hradec, Králové, Pardurbice, Liberec, and Ostrava. They formed one of the major manufacturing areas of Europe with textile and machine tool factories, and chemical and glass works. Czechoslovakia also inherited an arms industry dominated by the Skoda Works in

Figure 37 Fiat Lingotto Factory, Turin, 1921–23.

Pilsen. The Moravian capital of Brno and the nearby town of Zlín became industrial powerhouses in their own right.

The Baťa Shoe Company in Zlín morphed from a small shoemaker's business to a modern industrial enterprise. After visiting industrial regions in Germany and Ford's River Rouge plant in Michigan, Thomáš Baťa overhauled and "Fordized" his Zlín factory. By the early 1930s, the company's thirty-building production facility employed a staff of 18,700 people making 144,000 shoes daily—a sign of the new power of mass-produced fashion. Baťa established some 1,800 retail outlets in towns throughout Czechoslovakia, some of which eventually expanded into department stores. The Baťa store in Prague on Wenceslas Square was a vision of modernism fused with marketing. The only ornament on the facade was the company's logo resplendent in neon lights. Anxious to extend his reach, Baťa built his own film studio in Zlín that became a center of Czech filmmaking.[13] Not only did the Baťa company employ and house most of Zlín's inhabitants but it also supplied the town's power and communication services. The city's housing, schools, the department store, hotel, and cinema were all based on standardized modules. Working with architects and factory managers, Baťa laid out a local garden city with an industrial aesthetic. Prefabricated flat-roofed family homes were constructed of reinforced concrete combined with brick and glass facades. The company headquarters was ensconced in a sixteen-story glass and steel skyscraper—one of the first high-rise buildings in Europe. By the 1930s, Baťa was one of the world's largest shoe manufacturers. It built factories and worker housing on the Zlín model in a host of European cities as the company expanded operations.

Thousands worked as salaried employees in sales and in managerial positions and administration. Banking and insurance, retail commerce, entertainment and media, and transport became the new industries. They generated a new middle class, a recognizable mass of young workers "whose existence—especially in Berlin and other big cities," German cultural critic Siegfried Kracauer opined, "increasingly assumes a standard character." They were young, educated, risen above proletarian existence, and addicted to commerce, fashion, and entertainment. The independent "New Woman" sashayed with panache along the streets. Their hair was short, their dresses shorter. They smoked, drank, and drove motorcars. Their airs were wildly sophisticated. Franz Hessel, a well-known observer of Berlin, commented that "a new type of woman is emerging . . . the young avant-gardiste, the post-war Berlin woman. . . . Their healthy smiles and the confidence with which they force their way in pairs through the afternoon melee on Tauentzienstraβe and Kurfürstendamm are refreshing. . . . Sharp and smooth, they steer up to the window displays."[14] The new generation embraced mass culture, city life, and for Kracauer, they indulged in a "cult of distraction." They were addicted to the spell of entertainment, glamour and fads, and the allure of blockbuster films meant to appease the masses.[15] Sumptuous movie palaces sold out every day (Figure 38).

The advertising industry depicted buying as bliss and spurred cravings for automobiles, radios, as well as cigarettes, cosmetics, and the newest fashions. The democratization of taste and consumption set the tone for urban society. Advertising was everywhere—on buildings, on streetcars, on display boxes, and advertising columns on the sidewalks. It lit

Figure 38 Crossing the Kurfürstendamm, Berlin, 1926.

up the city in an explosion of neon lights. It was the current of urban life. Berlin's electric braggadocio hit a new level in October 1928 when the city's retail association staged the "Berlin in Light" week. It featured four nights of full electric illumination of the city's monuments and commercial buildings.[16] The Kurfürstendamm became the premier shopping boulevard in Berlin. Developed during the 1910s, it overtook the old center city and made the western districts into a symbol of the new society. The avenue was a byword for the changing face of Berlin, its transience, speed, the drama of its modern life. Its Café des Westens was the hangout for bohemians and the city's intellectuals. For Joseph Roth, the only permanent characteristic of the Kurfürstendamm was its unrelenting capacity for change. "And so the Kurfürstendamm stretches out endlessly day and night. . . . For a long time I've tried to guess its secret, the quality that enables it to remain itself through all of the sudden changes in its physiognomy—yes, to become still more Kurfürstendamm. It is immutable in its mutability. Its impatience is heroic. Its inconsistency is insistent."[17] It was a dazzling theater of neon illumination and extravagant electric advertising, department stores, and luxury boutiques. Interlaced among them were variety shows, restaurants and dinner clubs, and spectacular movie palaces. The Kurfürstendamm was the dream of the new middle classes and their devotion to mass culture and entertainment as integral to their identity.

Capturing the feverish pace and exuberance of Berlin became a fixation for the city's artists and intellectuals. Their penetrating gaze is the foremost record of the city's creative ferment of these years. In Walter Ruttmann's 1927 experimental film *Berlin, Symphony of a Great City*, the camera follows the city's frenetic pace, the hectic street scene, the nights blazing with neon. Pedestrians rush in pandemonium, typewriters click, newspapers roll out from presses and are jumbled together for sale by street hawkers. Just to the east of Berlin's historic districts, Alexanderplatz was a zone of department stores and cinemas, new office buildings, chaotic traffic, and ear-splitting construction for a vast underground subway station. "What is Alexanderplatz in Berlin?" Walter Benjamin queried. "It is the site where for the last two years the most violent transformations have been taking place, where excavators and jackhammers have been continuously at work, where the ground trembles under the impact of their blows and under the columns of buses and subways, where the innards of the metropolis have been laid bare deeper than anywhere else." Alfred Döblin was the city's most incisive chronicler. Benjamin quipped that Döblin "spoke from within Berlin. It is his megaphone."[18] Döblin depicted the phantasmagoria of Alexanderplatz in his 1929 literary masterpiece *Berlin Alexanderplatz*, in his newspaper stories, his radio programs, and in the 1931 film adaptation of his novel. Through the eyes of a small-time criminal attempting to redeem himself, Döblin captured the fearsome pace and seedy underbelly of the big city. It is a grimy, bitter place, with nobodies lost in the daily grind. The novel revels in the Berlin slang of popular culture, of movies, and advertising (Figure 39).[19]

Tabloid newspapers, radio, and film became the media for the masses. In each major city, two or three large dailies owned by press empires churned out sensationalist news and flashy advertising. Reporters kept up a frenzied pace running in and out of

Figure 39 Alexanderplatz with the train station, Wertheim department store, and the tower of the Red City Hall, Berlin.

newspaper offices on the main boulevards, while workers manned the machines making newsprint into daily reading. The Parisian *Le Figaro* newspaper unrolled a giant-size version of its advertising pages down the facade of its headquarters on the Champs-Elysées.[20] In London, Fleet Street vibrated with the clatter of typewriters in the nerve centers of the *Daily Mail*, the *Daily Telegraph*, the *Daily Mirror*, and the *Daily Express*. Mass-market magazines and comic books sold in the millions. Broadcasting was a new connective medium that joined up Europe's cities and towns in a continental-wide system of transmission towers. It homogenized and unified the urban experience in entirely new ways. The "miracle" of radio was a staple of European domestic life while early television sets with cathode ray tubes were going into commercial production. When the British Broadcasting Corporation (BBC) became a public entity in 1926, there were over 2 million radio receivers in the UK. At the end of the 1930s, the number of tuned-in wireless sets jumped to 9 million. Nearly three out of four British households owned one. The BBC Broadcasting House on Portland Place, London, was a modernist art deco headquarters in keeping with on-air media as the future. It was designed for radio transmission and outfitted with special recording studios. France had more than 4 million radio receivers, Russia had 4.5 million. Czechoslovakia, Sweden, and the Netherlands had more than 1 million radio sets each. The demand for wireless radio broadcasting soared. New radio stations grew so quickly the mid-range radio frequency bands were unable to keep up. While in 1926, there were 123 stations transmitting throughout Europe, by 1939, some 463 stations were on air.[21] Poland had the most developed radio service in eastern Europe. Polskie Radio had stations in Warsaw, Kraków, Katowice, Wilno (Vilnius), Poznań, Toruń, Lwów (Lemberg/L'viv), and Łódź. In nearly every middle-class and many working-class homes, families gathered in front of an imposing radio set listening to broadcasts. There were over 4 million radio sets in Germany in the 1930s. With over 1,500 employees and some 40,000 freelancers, the German radio industry was big business.[22] Weimar Republic radio buffs tuned into the music and news programs offered by Deutsche Welle from Berlin's modernist Broadcast House in the city's west end.

At the end of the First World War, the artist George Grosz returned to Berlin. "These were wild years. I threw myself madly into life and teamed up with people who were searching for a way out from this absolute nothingness."[23] For a brief moment the German revolution of 1918 had raised hopes for a radical new world. Artists and intellectuals joined the Communist Party and Workers and Soldiers Councils. They staged Dadaist shock performances and art happenings in Berlin's streets and public spaces. In the 1920s, the city's forty theaters staged brilliant productions. Playwright Bertold Brecht was one of the leading lights of political art and spoke for a modern generation captivated by American jazz and cinema, spectator sports, and detective stories from across the Atlantic. Yet at the same time, he was a steadfast member of Germany's Communist Party. Brecht's production of *The Three Penny Opera* dramatized the meanness of capitalist society with the tricksters and thugs of Berlin's underworld. His experimental cabaret-style dramas *In the Jungle of Cities* and *The Rise and Fall of the City of Mahagonny* laid out the degeneracy of the modern metropolis. George Grosz

Figure 40 Tiller Girls in the Haller Revue, 1927.

painted fashionable pedestrians along the Kurfürstendamm as a venal bourgeois class, immune to the realities of human suffering. His caricatures were of Berlin's prostitutes and profiteers. Berlin was a great gasping city, gulping everyone into its heartless tumult. Uncaring, ugly, his portrait of Berlin was meant to shock and offend (Figure 40).

This sense of decadence was most explicit in the overt sexuality that pervaded public culture. The city was famous for its revues—extravagant stage productions featuring music and dance, elaborate sets and costumes, and kick-lines of smiling beauties in seductive stages of undress. They were monster spectacles that drew eager audiences to the theater district around the Friedrichstrasse. It was a scandal-ridden, publicity-hungry cosmos. A night on the town meant cruising the cabarets and nightclubs with their nude shows. Dancer Anita Berber, one of the most scandalous stars of the era, flaunted her bisexuality and danced radiantly naked at the Berlin Apollo and the Winter Garden. The Eldorado nightclub featured rows of dazzling drag-queens. Secret dance parlors and strip clubs became the rage. Berlin's eroticism, its uninhibited sexuality, its red-light districts, and the open secret of its homosexual subcultures drew scores of devotees and curiosity seekers. Sex tourism was a booming industry. The city's "sexual depravity" and the titillating atmosphere of its nightlife were the subject of pornographic literature, untold numbers of health reports, raids by vice squads, and attacks by reformers, especially those willing to point fingers at the city's Jews. But it did little to stem the tumultuous abandon and exuberance.

With the war's end and the collapse of the great empires, once provincial cities in the old imperial domains suddenly emerged as the capitals of newly established nations. The terms of the various treaties that ended the First World War sketched out an entirely new political geography for central and eastern Europe. Finland emerged as an independent country with its capital at Helsinki. The new Baltic capital cities of Tallinn in Estonia, Riga in Latvia, and Vilnius in Lithuania were grandly proclaimed. Poland was reconstituted as the Second Polish Republic with its capital city of Warsaw. Prague was decreed the capital of independent Czechoslovakia. Vienna continued as capital of a shockingly shrunken Austria. The Ukraine declared its independence with its first city of Kiev. The term "Balkans" to designate the region of southeastern Europe and the popular expressions "Balkanism" and "Balkanization" came into vogue as Ottoman influences receded and the Hapsburg and Russian empires disintegrated.[24] In an entirely remade regional geography, Belgrade was declared capital of a united Yugoslavia. Sofia was the capital of Bulgaria. In 1920, Tirana was christened the capital of independent Albania. In some cases, such as Tirana, the new capital was neither the largest nor the most important city. It was instead the result of geopolitical haggling. Regardless of the reasons, these cities emerged as vibrant hubs of modernist culture during the 1920s. Creating a capital city was tantamount to joining the family of European nations. It was a singular act of symbolic importance.

Despite the jubilation over independence, the line of new states forged from the war's rubble faced tremendous challenges—social and economic exhaustion being the first. Especially along the contested borders with the new Soviet Union, violence and civil strife continued into the 1920s. The economic toll taken by the new territorial frontiers was immediate. The traditional distribution and transportation networks woven through the Hapsburg, German, and Russian domains crumbled. Riga's industries suffered wholesale sabotage and destruction during the war. Its Russo-Baltic automobile factory was carted off to Russia in 1915. There was little left but shells of the city's once-powerful industrial companies. The loss of the Russian market made it nearly impossible for them to regain prewar levels of production, even by the 1930s. Romania was ransacked during the German occupation and oil production fell to one-third of its prewar levels. The Hungarian film industry in Budapest was suddenly cut off from Kolozsvar Studios in Transylvania and lost its extensive market in the Balkans. The Balkans were plagued by mutual enmity and insecurity. Blinded by nationalist passions, the successor states each attempted a clean break and walled themselves in with foolhardy policies of economic self-sufficiency. Although local industry did develop with the help of western European capital, the strategy did nothing but impair their development. Despite the weight of geographic proximity and historic practices, trade between the new states of central and eastern Europe, and with the new Soviet Union, shriveled to a minimum.[25]

The First World War devastated Poland and the first order of business for the newly independent Polish Republic was reconstruction. About 40 percent of the country's urban fabric was ruined, mainly small towns and villages. In the east, Galicia especially was overcome by the war's savagery. Whole towns were set to the torch by Russian soldiers. Vicious pogroms forced thousands of Jews from their homes. Towns in the western areas of Poland with brick construction and modern infrastructure fared somewhat better. Those in the less developed eastern areas, often overgrown villages of wooden construction, were unable to recover and were often simply abandoned.[26] Instead, people flooded into cities in search of jobs. But in 1918, only half the factories in Warsaw were still functioning. A quarter of a million workers in Łódź were unemployed. Without its primary market of Russia, the textile mills stood still. Łódź changed from textile boom town to perpetual torpor. Poland's metallurgical industry was immobilized. Mines were flooded and abandoned. Further development of the upper Silesian coal fields was impractical. The region was first occupied by British, French, and Italian armies and then sliced up by Poland and Czechoslovakia. The mandated Silesian plebiscite to determine the region's fate ended with a ferocious rebellion from 1919 through 1921. Beyond the political calamity, the competition from the Ruhr basin was too great for any expansion of Silesian industrial output. The coal pits around Katowice in Upper Silesia stagnated as rail connections were broken up by the twisted territorial borders and trade plummeted.

Knitting together the uneven geography between its industrial west and the rural east proved a daunting challenge for the new Polish government. Regional differences in ethnicity, language, and customs were still politically charged. The first step was purging the Russian legacy of the eastern borderland settlements and Jewish shtetls by swapping street names and sign posts from Russian to Polish. Modern infrastructure became a strategy to cure the east's "backwardness" and merge it into the Polish nation.[27] The new government ministries conjured up extravagant reconstruction projects to jumpstart the country's economy. Workers laid out track for a railway from the Katowice industrial area to the Baltic Sea. A new Central Industrial Region covering a vast area at the center of the country was staked out. The towns of Lublin, Rzeszów, and Sandomierz all jealously vied for designation as its pivot. The construction of modern shipyards and a seaport at Gdynia on the coast became the largest project in the Baltic Sea area. The big Polish cities—Warsaw, Łódź, Lwów, Poznań, Kraków, Katowice, and Toruń—set out extensive urban plans and began modernizing their market halls, hospitals and schools, tramways and rail lines. These early achievements were acclaimed at the great National Exhibition in Poznań in 1929. A full 280 acres in the city's heart were turned over to an opulent display of Poland's "native pluck and tenacity."[28] Some 4.5 million people toured the exhibits to witness the future. The pavilions were designed in a modernist classicism as a Polish national style. It was extended to Poznań's new railroad station, hotel, and residential buildings in a conscious endeavor to "re-Polonize" the city's spaces (Figure 41).[29]

Figure 41 View of Warsaw with the Alexandrovski Bridge across the Vistula, 1925.

Nowhere was this determination to forge a modern Polish identity stronger than in the capital of Warsaw. Under the Russian Empire, the city had been a fortified military outpost. Some 40,000 Russian troops were stationed in the city and daily patrolled the streets. A ring of fortifications squeezed the population into the teeming central districts. With nearly 900,000 inhabitants, the city was massively overcrowded. It had one of the densest populations of any city in Europe on the eve of the First World War. The dilapidated medieval Old Town of Warsaw was becoming fashionable among city elites, its houses restored, and square beautified. To the south, the new neighborhoods around Krakoskie Przedmieście and Ujazdowskie boulevards were filled with monumental public buildings and wealthy residences. Here were the scenes of elegant society. Electric lighting graced the streets. Streetcars and automobiles whizzed by horse-drawn carriages and carts on the main avenues, especially Marszałkowska Street, the city's main shopping and entertainment boulevard.

The population declined precipitously during the First World War as people fled and deaths climbed from disease and hunger. With the end of hostilities in 1918, Warsaw once again became a magnet. An endless flow of immigrants meant the population shot up by 70 percent over the next twenty years. Half the population was born outside the city. Some were Jews coming from what was left of the eastern shtetls. Contemporary observers noted their increasing presence in the city and warned against the "Jewish danger." Warsaw was deeply split along ethnic lines. The Jewish quarter around Nalewki Street was a jumble of trade and industry, with abject poverty alongside the city's Jewish middle and upper classes. Jewish residents represented some 40 percent of the city's population in 1917, and then declined to around 30 percent by 1938. Still, Warsaw had the largest Jewish community of any city in Europe.

In the hopeless search for cheap lodging, some portion of the newcomers faded into the primitive villages encircling the city and slipped away from public view. They crammed into ancient wooden hovels devoid of basic services. Cut off from the central city by the fortifications, the fringes of Warsaw were a chaotic brew of factories and squatter settlements. Old rural byways were deluged with settlers, many of them illiterate, floating between work and penury.[30] Prostitution and the city's underworld thrived. The industrial periphery of Wolna was known, according to a journalist for *Ekonomista*, "only for its cutthroats, audacious murders, bold robberies, and daily crimes." To rectify the lawlessness, the city limits were expanded to the tenements and factories in Wolna and the southwestern districts, and to Praga on the east bank of the Vistula, which grew faster than any other area of the city. With its factories and three major railway stations, Praga was the hub of Warsaw's trade and industry. The hue and cry for housing and public services in these districts was crushing. The city's territory tripled again in the "great incorporation" of 1916, when one journalist for the daily *Praca Polska* described the peripheries as "neglected in every respect; largely deprived of sewers, pavement, and suitable lighting, they are in deplorable sanitary condition."[31]

Despite all these tribulations, the atmosphere was buoyant with the advent of independence. Warsaw was predicted to become the next London or Paris. Geographically, it was at the intersection of Europe's premier commercial markets. It was a transport hub with a new airport ready to welcome passengers on the tarmacs. The first skyscraper, the eighteen-story Prudential Insurance Building, appeared on the skyline. Factories were rebuilt using up-to-date machinery and industrial production shot up. Electrical and metallurgical plants hummed. Automobiles, processed foods, and pharmaceuticals flew off the assembly lines. Warsaw emerged as one of the country's major industrial complexes, just behind Łódź and Upper Silesia. The predictions for the capital's renaissance seemed accurate as the population exploded to nearly 2 million inhabitants. It grew faster than any city in central Europe. With the help of modernist architects, a "Functional Warsaw" plan was envisioned for the entire region[32] replete with seven well-appointed super districts. A series of exhibitions—"Warsaw of the future" (1936), "Old Warsaw" (1937), and "Warsaw yesterday, today and tomorrow" (1938)— predicted brilliant fortunes ahead. This last, held at the new National Museum, attracted half a million visitors. Plans were hatched for a universal exposition to be held in 1943.

Warsaw emerged as a dazzling model for Poland's reemergence. Streets and squares were renamed after Polish heroes. Polish cultural and intellectual life shifted from Kraków northward as the city blossomed into an acknowledged European capital. Warsaw University and the Polytechnic reopened. Publishing, film, and entertainment blossomed into major industries. Splashy headquarters for the *Zycie Warszawski* (*Warsaw Life*) newspaper went up on Marszałkowska Boulevard. By 1936, the first television broadcasts took place from the Prudential Insurance Building. Sphinx Film Studio produced mainstream movies, with their glamorous premiers in Warsaw's cinemas. With the advent of talkies, musicals featuring stars from the city's cabarets and music theaters conquered the silver screen. Moviegoers flocked to glamour comedies to see their favorite cinematic idols and heartthrobs. The theater marquees along Marszałowska boulevard lit up the night alongside trendy clubs and cafés. The city's cultural renaissance was remarkable, much of it led by the Jewish community. Warsaw was the scene of myriad cabarets and musical reviews that showcased performers from every ethnic background and indulged in scathing political satire. The Qui Pro Quo was the pinnacle of the cabarets, with seating for an audience of 500 and attracting the cream of Warsaw society.[33] It was located beneath the glamorous Luxemburg Gallery's glass-roofed arcade lined with cafés and cake shops, fashion boutiques, and a sumptuous movie theater. The Polish jazz bands Karasiński & Kataszek Jazz-Tango Orchestra and the Petersburski & Gold Orchestra became sensations. They brought down the house in fashionable hotspots such as the Adria Café and the Morskie Oko, and recorded with the city's lucrative Syrena-Electro record company.

Warsaw was indicative of the creative momentum that stretched across European capital cities in the interwar years. In January 1918, the Bolshevik government returned the Russian capital to Moscow. It was a symbolic gesture and not an easy fit for the victorious revolutionaries. The Kremlin citadel stood guard over a city that was the embodiment of old Russia—the crown, the church, and the bureaucracy. The skyline was dotted with church spires. Monasteries and convents intermingled with noble mansions. Making it into the "Red" capital for the new Soviet Union would entail an entire remaking. The circumstances were catastrophic. The city was ravaged by years of war, strikes and street violence, looting, and famine. The Bolshevik secret police indulged in an orgy of terror with indiscriminate violence and killing. Thousands fled to their native villages or were conscripted into the Red Army. Many others died of starvation or disease. By the end of the civil war, the city's population was down by half. The economy was at a standstill. This accretion of misery was piled on to the harrowing conditions inherited from the late tsarist years. Moscow's poverty, the desperate living conditions in the slums, the lack of housing and basic infrastructure had long been decried as a moral scandal.

Moscow was also the epicenter of the oldest industrial area of the Russian Empire, the so-called Central Industrial District. The blackened smokestacks of the Morozov textile mills, the Prokhorov mills, the Bogorodsk mills jutted up on the skyline. They were owned by the city's homegrown millionaire industrialists and churned out the cloth that gave the city the moniker "Calico Moscow." Railroad construction, machine and metal work, paper and printing, and food production employed thousands. The industrial sector cascaded down to a myriad of small-scale workshops and yards. The entire region around Moscow was a sprawling mosaic of industrial plants, tenements, and ancient hamlets with their wooden houses and muddy streets. The proletariat were crowded into jerry-built dwellings and appalling flophouse barracks that mushroomed in the outlying fringes around the city. Many of the seasonal workers had no residence at all and instead found night-lodging where they could. The lack of adequate sanitation services and clean water was a long-standing disgrace. Shockingly high mortality rates set both Moscow and St. Petersburg apart from other European capitals. The inhabitants lived with the constant threat of epidemics in what amounted to pathological urban environments.[34]

Yet there was another side to Moscow, one that exuded the atmosphere of a modern western metropolis. A 1903 guidebook remarked that the city had transformed "completely from a big village with an aristocratic tint to a huge, crowded commercial and industrial city."[35] Streetcars and automobiles wove perilously around horse-drawn wagons and pedestrians. The British department store Muir & Merrilees welcomed savvy shoppers. Multistoried bourgeois apartment buildings equipped with electricity, elevators, and telephones appeared in the fashionable districts. In 1912 young English diplomat Bruce Lockhart arrived in Moscow and took a room in the Metropole Hotel:

> As I walked through the hall to the restaurant, my first impressions were of steaming furs, fat women and big sleek men; of attractive servility in the underlings and of good-natured ostentation on the part of the clients; of great wealth and crude coarseness, and yet a coarseness sufficiently exotic to dispel repulsion. I had entered into a kingdom where money was the only God.[36]

Moscow was dynamic, multifaceted, a mishmash of Russian tradition and modernity.

The brave new communist world taking shape on this shaky foundation was a fascinating spectacle. The 1917 revolution was imagined as a blinding light that opened the possibility of an entirely new society. Every arena of urban life was open to transformation. There was a surge of speculation about the future, much of it captured in science fiction. Over 200 science-fiction works appeared in the 1920s, all of them imagining a totally urbanized, industrialized world. Typical of this genre, Yakov

Okunev's *The Coming World* depicted the entire land mass of the earth covered in a sprawling megalopolis in 2123. There were no social classes. Instead, egalitarianism was daily practice. Welfare, peace, and harmony reigned.[37] Constructivist architects dreamed up mammoth schemes for the new socialist city, or *sotsgorod*. Much of the art and architecture of this period had a mystical, cosmic quality that expressed the dream of a communist utopia. Aviation and flight became a metaphor for personal and political liberation. New models of urban living were imagined by Konstantin Yuon in *A New Planet* (1921), Georgii Krutikov in his *Flying City* (1924), and Anton Lavinskii's *City on Springs* (1923).[38] Escaping the confines of earth, colonizing distant galaxies evinced the buoyant optimism about the communist future.

The Bolshevik State worked to translate these idyllic visions into reality. The luxurious dwellings of bourgeois and aristocratic elites were handed over to the workers as communal dwellings. So acute was the housing shortage in Moscow and St. Petersburg that no one, even the most well-connected, had a separate apartment. Once the civil war was won, Lenin introduced the New Economic Policy (NEP, 1921–25) that slowed down radical reform and allowed private businesses on a limited scale. It jump-started the urban economies in both St. Petersburg and Moscow. By 1926, the population of both cities was back to pre-revolutionary levels and the motors of industry once again purred. Despised "Nepmen" inhabited a demimonde of petty vice and swindlers. Food rationing and bread lines were an everyday struggle. The black market thrived. Visiting Moscow in December 1926, urban critic Walter Benjamin navigated the sheets of ice on the street to find "cordons in front of the state stores: one stands in line for butter and other important staples. There are countless shops and even more merchants whose entire inventory consists of little more than a washbasket of apples, tangerines or peanuts." Cabarets and jazz clubs reopened. Cinemas showed the latest films. Department store window displays teased the weary. Benjamin was shocked at the "luxury that has lodged itself in this ailing, run-down city like tartar in a diseased mouth."[39]

The government launched a campaign to create the new Soviet Person ready to build socialism. In the quest to eradicate disease, personal hygiene received special attention in Soviet propaganda with detailed instructions on cleanliness and clothing. Towels, soap, toothbrushes became the stuff of socialism. Schools, factories, and houses were checked regularly by health inspectors. Public drinking was condemned. Traditional working-class pastimes such as billiards and dancing were denounced as uncultured. Instead, the Soviet authorities opened workers' clubs that promoted a new regime of health and sports and self-improvement. They were constructivist blasts into the socialist future. The Rusakov Workers' Club in the Sokolniki district of northern Moscow and the Zuyev Workers' Club on Lesnaya Street were dramatic architectural statements with cantilevered concrete and glass cylinders. Inside were theaters and cinemas, libraries, and night classes to build the Soviet citizen. The Narkomfin Communal House in Moscow's Presnensky district was a social laboratory. Its shared kitchen, laundry, nursery, and gymnasium were meant to emancipate women from the drudgery of housework.[40] Grandiose plans appeared for Workers' Palaces, Proletarian Houses, Palaces of Culture. It was a communist urban typology with a robust aesthetic dimension (Figure 42).

Figure 42 Zuyev Workers Club by Ilya Golosov, Moscow, 1928.

The NEP was a period of intense artistic and intellectual creativity on all fronts. Avant-garde artists enrolled in the service of the new communist government with the goal of democratizing artistic production. This was especially true of the movement known as constructivism that took shape in Moscow and St. Petersburg. Constructivism was heroic, exhilarating, spirited, filled with the possibilities of the Revolution and a new era in world history. It was wholly endorsed by Lenin's government as revolutionary culture. Artists and architects descended into the streets. A monumental agitation-propaganda (agit-prop) campaign was launched to cover the entire surface of the city with slogans and evocative iconography. Political posters, murals, and street decorations celebrated the Revolution in a media blitz of creative energy. Great shrines were erected in Moscow and St. Petersburg with names such as "Fire of Revolution" and "A Glimpse of the 21st Century." Architect Vladimir Tatlin designed a model for a Monument to the Third International as an openwork spiraling steel beam housing the latest media technologies from telephones and radios to giant film screens. Although it never went past the planning stages, the model was paraded through the streets of St. Petersburg in November 1920 during the mass theatrical performance of *The Storming of the Winter Palace*. The production took place in the public spaces of the city with 10,000 citizens and performers. Spectacles such as these were not merely designed to commemorate Bolshevik power. They were meant to usher in a new kind of urban theater. The working masses were heroes. Street festivals, or *prazdniki*, were a central element in Russian

Figure 43 A procession through Moscow's Red Square to celebrate the annual May Day holiday, 1929.

cultural heritage and the new regime appropriated them in pioneering ways. Parades and demonstrations, flags and uniforms were revered as emblems of revolutionary loyalty (Figure 43).

The entire city was a stage. During the two most important Soviet holidays, May Day and the November 7 anniversary of the Revolution, huge models of steam engines and rolling mills, a sea of red banners, painted panels of colossal dimensions went up in the capital. The decorations for the 1920 May Day festivities in Moscow were meant to "imagine the Communist city of the future."[41] Massive crowds of people streamed into the center of the city. This drama of urban life was captured in the 1929 experimental film *Man with a Movie Camera*, directed by filmmaker Dziga Vertov. His ambition was to film the cities of Kiev, Moscow, and Odessa as hypermodern, with the new scale and excitement of communist urban life. The street scenes are jam-packed, fast-paced, driven by the speed of electric trams and automobiles. Vertov filmed the sequences from atop a speeding automobile, capturing the breakneck tempo of the city. Technology and machinery are the textures of modern life. The camera points to elevators, typewriters, telephones, cash registers, whirring machinery, trains, and airplanes. There was little about this film that differentiated it from the modernist exposés of Walter Ruttmann's *Berlin, Symphony of a Great City*. But it was filmed as a montage of Soviet urban ideals.

Moscow was envisaged as the largest city in the world with verdant green belts and satellite settlements, with linear strips of industry and residences jutting out from the old center. The "General Plan for the Reconstruction of Moscow" was the dazzling model for socialist societies around the world. Elaborate plans spilled off the drawing boards. Massive new factories were constructed and old ones refurbished. By the late 1930s, the city was producing half of the country's machine tools, some 50 percent of its automobiles and 40 percent of its electrical equipment.[42] Slum areas were cleared away as residues of barbaric Russian capitalism. The city's churches, monasteries, and nunneries came under ruthless assault and were demolished along with a multitude of historic landmarks. Thousands of workers dug the colossal Moscow-Volga canal. The construction of the first lines of the Moscow Metro with its lavish underground stations was one of the country's proudest achievements. A splendid athletic stadium made football all the rage. The 1,200-room Moscow Hotel near Red Square was a palace. Lenin's granite mausoleum appeared on Red Square, which became the focus of state pageantry. Museums to Lenin, to the Revolution, and to the Soviet Army popped up everywhere. One of the most ambitious projects was a towering Palace of Soviets that would be higher than the Empire State Building just constructed in New York.[43] Soviet filmmaker Alexsandr Medvedkin showcased the *New Moscow*[44] in a 1939 film extolling the construction sites and the futuristic city arising from the dust: "Like in fairytales, new buildings spring forth." Despite the extravagance of this veneer, Moscow's deficiencies were just as glaring. It was a vastly overcrowded city. Industrialization and collectivization under Stalin's Five-Year Plans brought a flood of peasants into Russia's cities. The Moscow region absorbed some 2 million of them. By the end of the 1930s, its population had risen to over 4 million inhabitants.

As in Berlin and Moscow, urban elites in the new capital cities across Europe embraced the modern age and the exhilarating cultural currents that came with it. Especially in southeastern Europe and the Balkans, the modern city played a striking symbolic role. It represented "progress and civilization" for what was generally belittled as an unruly backward territory. Modern towns and cities would weave together each new realm taking its place among the nations of Europe. The creation of new capital cities, the reconstruction of cities damaged by war, the remodeling and expansion of existing settlements were opportunities to showcase the future. Interestingly, this same commentary could be found among reform-minded Ottoman elites who saw themselves as guardians of the Porte's territories in the Balkans. The Ottoman Empire had initiated significant urban and infrastructure reforms from the mid-nineteenth and early twentieth centuries. But with the joy of independence, the new nations associated progress with "westernization" and "de-Ottomanization."[45]

Over the course of the nineteenth century, the European territories of the Ottoman Empire were step-by-step relinquished through wars, uprisings, and dynastic clashes. Yet the Ottoman legacy left a lasting imprint. The entire Balkan region was itself an Ottoman legacy.[46] In 1900, the Balkans and southeastern Europe was considerably less populated than central or western Europe and their societies were predominantly rural. Often less than 15 percent of the population lived in towns, and most lived in small settlements and rural villages. Town dwellers were small-time merchants, craftsmen, and government bureaucrats. The connective tissue of railroad lines played a fundamental role in shaping the urban system of the Balkans. As in western and central Europe, it triggered the decline of some flourishing cities (such as Adrianople), and the development of others. By 1900, a web of railroad tracks linked Ljubljana, Zagreb, Sarajevo, Belgrade, Sofia, Skopje, and Bucharest to Istanbul, as well as to central Europe.[47] Textile production, iron and steel, metal and machinery, and chemical manufacturing took root in the 1920s and 1930s. But the economy of the Balkans remained heavily reliant on food processing and on the export of cereals and forest products, livestock, and tobacco and in the case of Romania, on petroleum.

Romania was the fourth largest oil producer in the world. With its capital city of Bucharest, its busy ports on the Black Sea and a constellation of small towns, the country possessed an active urban life. Serbia was also a mosaic of small towns numbering between 5,000 and 10,000 souls. Other than the capital of Belgrade, the larger Serbian settlements such as Požarevac, Leskovac, Kragujevac, and Niš still had under 20,000 inhabitants. Bulgaria was the most urbanized of the Balkan countries with a thick web of small and medium sized towns evenly distributed across the territory, a number of which had 20,000 to 40,000 inhabitants. Most of this urban system was tied to the agrarian sector and to small-scale production. Although westerners imagined this landscape as a rural backwater of derangement and suspicion, entrepreneurs traveled to markets around the region and to the ports along the Danube to hawk their wares. It was a well-honed rural economy with towns acting as trade and communication hubs. The ports of Ruse on the Danube, Varna, and Burgas on the Black Sea, the inland towns of Plovdiv and Tarnovo as well as the Bulgarian capital of Sofia supported larger industrial production. Cities along the Mediterranean coast such as Salonica, Kavala, and Dedeagach (Alexandroupoli) were lively commercial centers tied to the shipping routes along the Adriatic.

Throughout the Balkans, the traditional town reflected the mix of ethnic identities. The Ottoman legacy typically shaped towns around an irregular pattern defined by the interior worlds of the *mahalla* villages. Their inhabitants confessed to various sects of Islam, Christianity, and Judaism. There was no deliberate division by ethnicity or social class. Even small townships were an ethnic mix. Low houses with their gardens were hidden behind stone walls and scattered along a tortuous maze of alleyways and cul-de-sacs. Each district had its public fountain, crossroads square, artisan street, and place of worship. These were the places of sociability. The loose urban fabric surrounded the town center, or *çarsis*, devoted to trade and the bazaar. Public life took place in mosques, churches, and synagogues, in the bustling coffee houses and reading rooms, and in the marketplace. These last were pools of news and information.[48] Church steeples and mosques with their spindly minarets stood out on the skyline. Lavish railway stations were among the most prominent symbols of modernity in the large cities. By 1914, Balkan towns with over 50,000 inhabitants and a good portion of smaller towns had electric lighting in the central districts. Electricity gave even those towns steeped in tradition a glittering quality (Figure 44).

With large Muslim populations, the towns of Tirana, Skopje, and Sarajevo still operated within this Ottoman legacy in the 1920s and 1930s. Tirana was the capital

Figure 44 The market in Sarajevo, 1930s.

of independent Albania. Its busy bazaar alongside the grand mosque was the age-old mix of Muslim traders and peasants with their animals and wares. Traveling across the mountains to Tirana in the 1930s, writer Joseph Roth remarked on, "The veiled women, the hundreds of ownerless dogs led on the wind's leash, the fezzes on fat heads and turbans on bearded faces, the colour-postcard vendetta-artists with revolvers for bellies, and rifles for umbrellas."[49] Located in Macedonia, Skopje became part of the new Kingdom of Serbs, Croats, and Slovenes at the war's end and was then incorporated into the new nation of Yugoslavia. But its Turkish roots were plainly evident. Slender minarets stretched upward over the cityscape. The city's mosques marked a vibrant Turkish quarter of small cottages and open-air shops. Sarajevo was the chief town in Bosnia, which also became part of Yugoslavia. The city suffered malign neglect under the fledgling Yugoslav government. It was a tradition-bound world on the Miljacka River, where the evening ritual of the *passeggiata*, the promenade of strollers dressed in finery, still held sway. Its Muslim population was blamed for its backwardness. They were distinguished, in the words of a Bosnian Serb official, "by laziness, hypocrisy . . . and a tendency towards homosexuality." Western travelers were fascinated by the city's oriental qualities. Films from the early twentieth century and even into the 1920s and 1930s[50] captured Sarajevo's exotic "oriental" quality with scenes of the *mahalla* neighborhoods, their mosques and busy bazaars. In the Ben Bacha quarter, cameras focused on white-washed buildings, the men with their fezzes and women veiled in hijab. Traveling to Sarajevo in 1938, British journalist Rebecca West looked out "on the mosques, on the domes of the old caravanserai among the tiled roofs of the bazaar, on the poplars standing over the city like the golden ghosts of giant Janizaries." The Turkish costumes "makes Sarajevo look like a fancy-dress ball. There is also an air of immense luxury about the town, of unwavering dedication to pleasure. . . . This air is, strictly speaking, a deception, since Sarajevo is stuffed with poverty of a most denuded kind." Europeans harped on the features of Islamic society they found most backward. It was why Serbian officials proposed "social de-Islamisation."[51]

Step-by-step, the model of the European city had engulfed the Ottoman urban world over the course of the late nineteenth and early twentieth centuries. The capitals of southeastern Europe were reshaped into vanguards of modernization with a new sense of belonging to Europe. Sofia was rebuilt as the capital of the new Principality of Bulgaria. The Turkish quarters were abandoned during the Russo-Turkish War of 1877–78, when Bulgaria gained independence from the Ottoman Empire. A poor town of only 18,000 inhabitants in the mountain foothills, Sofia suddenly ballooned into a capital of over 100,000 inhabitants and an emblem of Europeanization. Muslim public buildings and mosques were pruned away. The Jewish ghetto razed: Muslim and Jewish cemeteries vandalized. Streets were renamed. With the help of French architects and engineers, the aim was to erase Sofia's oriental qualities and refashion the old precincts into a modern European enclave. A sumptuous palace and cathedral were constructed as symbolic landmarks of the new regime. The National Assembly building overlooked the prestigious Tsar Liberator Boulevard along with mansions for the city's elite and the foreign diplomatic corps. A new Municipal Market Hall based on Les Halles in Paris nullified the old world of the Islamic bazaar. Telegraph and postal services were established. The first newspaper appeared.[52] "A quarter of a century ago it was a squalid Turkish town," Scottish travel writer John Foster Fraser remarked on his travel there in 1906. "The squalor has been swept away. The ramshackle, wheezy houses, bulging over narrow and ill-smelling passages, have disappeared as though swept by a fire. There are now big and broad thoroughfares, fine squares, impressive public buildings"[53] (Figure 45).

When Belgrade became capital of the independent Kingdom of Serbia in 1882, the Ottoman garrison dispersed and with them went much of the city's Turkish population. Coming upon the city, Fraser noted with typical western aplomb that already the Serbian capital

> is not at all Asiatic in appearance. It is bright and white, broad-streeted, and clean, wide-spreading. . . . Within easy memory Belgrade was a Turkish town. . . . But the Servians have rebuilt their capital. Evidence of the Turkish occupation is removed. Electric tramcars whiz along the streets; the electric light blinks at you as, in the dusk of a sultry day, you sit beneath the limes and sip Turkish coffee—the one legacy of the Turkish occupation the Servians accept.

With around 90,000 inhabitants, Belgrade was small in comparison to Bucharest or Athens. Most of the buildings were still timber-frame. Nonetheless, by the turn of the century wide avenues were lined with brick and masonry buildings in a blend of

Figure 45 Belgrade, Kingdom of Serbia, Croatia, and Slovenia.

historicist and secession styles. Terazije Square, Kralja Petra Street, and King Milan Street took on the trappings of any European city with hotels, restaurants, and shops. The Ministry of Justice, National Bank, and the Applied Arts Institute stood out as public buildings. The city's first newspaper began publication. The Beko Textile factory stood over the city's small industrial district along the river.

Elegant boulevards, train stations, banks, opera houses and theaters, museums and universities were the visible markers of western progress. They became a form of national iconography. The strict separation between the commercial and residential districts that was typical of the Ottoman town disappeared. Gone as well was the multiethnic and religious cohabitation that characterized Balkan cities under Ottoman rule. At least superficially, cities looked and felt "European." The new districts of Belgrade spilled out past the old Ottoman town on the slopes of the Danube and left it behind. Walking the city's streets in 1911, Croatian writer Franjo Ksaverski Horvat-Kiš satirized ethnic stereotypes and instead saw a cosmopolitan city: "I'm not seeing Belgrade in its everyday dress. There are too many foreigners, so that you don't know what is specific about the people of Belgrade at this moment. . . . I look at the faces, and try to find particularly Serbian features on them, but don't see anything." Lena Jovičić, daughter of a Scottish mother and Serbian father, noted the extremes of Belgrade: "Side by side with the peasant in homespun clothes and sandaled feet walk smartly dressed people of the wealthier classes. The creaking ox-cart has the right of way alongside the luxurious limousine car, and tall modern structures tower above dilapidated little houses in the strangest fashion."[54]

Balkan cities were paradoxical. Fragments of their Ottoman past percolated up through the western veneer. Serbian urban observer Pavle Zorić groused about

Belgrade's Turkish texture that "nowhere could one encounter such a worthless, anarchic arrangement."[55] Mosques and Turkish bathhouses were quirkily salvaged for other uses. Off the boulevards, the built environment reverted back to the time-honored mélange of miniscule houses and cottages, crooked alleyways and cobblestone streets, and the hodgepodge of neighborhoods. Food, music, coffee houses, and everyday practices kept up the Ottoman legacy. In rare film footage of the 1904 coronation of King Peter and his procession through the Belgrade streets,[56] cheering crowds are dressed in a mixture of stylish western clothing, Serbian peasant finery with embroidered aprons and scarves, and traditional Turkish garb. Despite heavy-handed westernization, the Ottoman world still lingered. As Belgrade's elites promoted Serbian identity, the ideological and cultural differences between Muslims and Christians deepened. In surveying Belgrade, Fraser noted the "few decrepit old men who sit in the cellars of the lower town [along the Danube], puff their narghilis, slither to the little mosque, as shaky as themselves, kneel on the ragged carpets and worship Allah."[57] Broiling hostility between the Europeanized capitals and the surrounding, often impoverished countryside lay just beneath the surface. The modernization of capital cities appeared to detractors as an unwarranted luxury and a threat to the rural heartland. "I would not wish Belgrade to be representative of Serbian culture," warned urban critic Miloš Cosić, "for whoever comes to Serbia in order to see her culture, will not find it in Belgrade: he is much more like to find a foreign culture in Belgrade, as Belgrade gladly accepts foreign culture."[58]

Thousands of refugees of all ethnic stripes poured into Yugoslavia's cities after the war. Given the wartime damage in Belgrade, the living conditions were shocking. Recounted by novelist Ivo Andrić,

> Life in Belgrade in the year 1920 was gaudy, lusty, unusually complex, and full of contrasts. Countless diverse vital forces flowed parallel with obscure weaknesses and failings.... Down the worn and partially destroyed streets came this foaming and swelling flood of people, for each day hundreds of newcomers dived into it head first, like pearl fishers into the deep sea.... There were many of those whom war had thrown up to the surface and made successful, as well as those it had rocked to their foundations and changed, who now groped for some balance and for something to lean on.

The new capital of Yugoslavia ballooned into a city of 100,000 inhabitants. The currents of urbanization intensified with independence. Belgrade, Sofia, and especially Bucharest emerged as impressive industrial centers, and their dominance grew as they consolidated their political positions as capital cities. Along with Athens and the port city of Salonica, these were the largest cities in southeastern Europe. Other key cities such as Plovdiv, Novi Sad, and Banja Luka and even Salonica itself fell into the shadows as the new capitals stole the limelight. Nonetheless, the choice of capital cities was not without disagreement, especially in the multiethnic patchwork of the new Yugoslavia and its six constitutive republics. The new nation was plagued by constant ethnic turmoil. Although it was the capital, Serbian Belgrade found itself in continuous battles with Slovenian Ljubljana and

Bosnian Sarajevo, and especially with Croatian Zagreb. They were each chief cities of powerful ethnic enclaves with their own awakening nationalistic ambitions.

Ljubljana was devastated by an earthquake in 1895. Rebuilding after the disaster was a labor of Slovene nationalistic fervor and its image changed drastically. The number of buildings tripled; wide streets were laid out. Theaters, museums, department stores, and hotels remade the city into a coherent vision of urban modernity. The fourteen-story art deco Nebotičnik tower, the tallest skyscraper in Yugoslavia, stood over the city's new commercial district. Yet rather than simply mimic western modernization, Ljubljana's elites probed their own imaginations. They were both national and cosmopolitan in outlook, and reconfigured progressive styles to accommodate homegrown identity. The most important architects responsible for the urban fabric of Ljubljana were Jože Plečnik and Ivan Vurnik. They espoused the civilizing virtues of Slovene culture and were instrumental in establishing the first Slovene university. Its faculty of architecture became one of the leading lights of innovation in eastern Europe. Plečnik designed Ljubljana's core around symbolic public squares and monuments glorifying the Slovene past. Historic memory was revived in his sumptuous National Library and the renovation plans for Ljubljana castle and the old districts ruined by the earthquake. A modern indigenous aesthetic took shape that drew on both the Ottoman legacy and on local folk traditions. Vurnik's design for the city's Cooperative Bank used traditional Slovenian zigzag folk motifs to embroider the building facade. The interlacing pattern was set off with a riot of primary colors. The richly ornamented interior was based on peasant decorative patterns and the colors of the Slovene flag.[59]

Ethnic fervor was even more evident in Croatia. Travelogue films from the 1920s and 1930s[60] flaunted the Croatian capital of Zagreb as a glamorous western city with wide tree-lined boulevards bustling with automobiles, buses and trams. On Yélatchitch Square, well-heeled pedestrians dressed in western fashion perused store windows dripping in the newest luxuries. The walls of buildings were covered with advertisements. The Bayer Company neon logo glimmered above Ban Jelačić Square as a symbol of the city's new economy. Zagreb boasted fifty large industrial companies. Over 56,000 people were salaried employees working in the new service and media industries and in the public sector. They spun through the revolving doors of seventy-five banks and insurance companies and some fifty publishing companies.[61] Newspapers and magazines flew off sidewalk kiosks. The influential weekly *Zvijet* (*The World*) promoted "modern" life while Radio Zagreb began broadcasting in 1926. The city was a hub for all the whizzbang novelties of the 1920s. Crowds lined up nightly at dozens of cinemas. Jugoslavija Film began operation in Zagreb and opened a cinematography school. Auto shows and expositions, as well as celebrity sporting events, gave the city an international flare. Josephine Baker brought her banana dance to Zagreb and immediately found captivated audiences.

The Yugoslav avant-garde was small, rife with ethnic rivalries and artistic contradictions on the path to an alternative modernity. A circuit of idiosyncratic cells filtered through bohemian districts, installing art exhibits and staging theater performances. In Zagreb, Ljubomir Mici´c's experimental Zenit movement and his *Zenit* magazine claimed an international audience. Mici´c hosted Zenit evenings in Zagreb, Lujbljana, and Belgrade and organized the First Zenit Exhibition of New Art in 1924 that included works from ten countries. It was a grab bag of influences from Russian constructivism and German expressionism to the worship of American films. Anxious to stake a claim among the European avant-garde, it espoused a nationalistic pan-Balkanism. For six years, Mici´c and his disciples championed a freewheeling creative locus around their native vision of modernity. Rather than simply copying European artistic currents or falling prey to the view of the Balkans as "backward," Zenit intended to rejuvenate Europe with the wild "barbaro-genius" of the region's cultural world.[62] It was a radical spin on the enthusiasm that greeted the remade Balkans in the interwar years.

In Zagreb, avant-garde circles met at the café in the luxurious Esplanade Hotel, built in 1925 and at the Theatre Café on Masaryk Street and Elite Café on Jurišić Street. They were the social pinnacles of the Europeanized Lower Town. Croatian literary figure Miroslav Krleža captured modern Zagreb at the Esplanade Hotel and the social disjuncture that riddled the city:

> Please come with me, if you would be so kind, to the terrace of Zagreb's Esplanade Hotel . . . Hot and cold water, French cuisine . . . the ebb and flow of passers-by in white linen outfits with tennis rackets, against the background of expensive English and Italian automobile models, a man would think he really was in "Europe."

This was the social milieu of the city's commercial and banking elites who were well connected to Vienna and Budapest. But the legacy of the past weighed heavily on the city and chastened any idealism. On the other side of the railway tracks in working-class districts such as Trnje, Krleža found "gas lamps, mud to the ankle, single-storey houses with provincial fences, shaggy dogs with no pedigree, animal sheds . . . open cesspits, stench. . . . All grey, all disgusting, all offensive. All—Balkan, a sorry province."[63] Nestled within the encircling Green Horseshoe of city squares and parks, the Upper and Lower towns of Zagreb exposed the ethnic and social tensions that made the Balkans a cauldron of violent instability.

CHAPTER 9
MODERNISM AND THE CITY

The problems facing municipal governments in the years after the First World War were daunting. In the immediate aftermath of the fighting, famine and disease prowled through towns and cities in much of Europe. An endless stream of desperate people, many of them refugees and displaced, scavenged for food and shelter. Millions of war veterans were readjusting to civilian life and searching for work and a place to live. Staggering monetary inflation shattered hopes for a peacetime recovery. As currencies lost value, once prosperous people were reduced to poverty. In cities caught on the frontlines, public health, transportation, education, and vital municipal services were at a standstill. The war years had put a halt to housing construction and drastically worsened the long-standing shortage of a decent place to live. The housing crisis alone was responsible for deep-seated bitterness. Families were packed into run-down overcrowded tenements. While environmental diseases such as cholera had been conquered, the deadly influenza epidemic and then pneumonia and tuberculosis were acute public health emergencies. The scourge of tuberculosis, or the "white plague," ravaged working-class neighborhoods. It was considered a sign of urban poverty and poor housing conditions, and the cause of more deaths than any other chronic disease. Even worse, metropolitan areas spread out amoeba-like far beyond the jurisdiction of any one municipal authority. Few municipal governments had the power or resources to deal with these adversities, although the calls for change were loud and fierce.

Undaunted by the political instability and social crises, buoyant about a future that often teetered on the edge of uncertainty, urban crusaders went to work. What was distinctive about their endeavors were the political agendas behind them. Europe's urban places became the experimental field for advocates across the political spectrum from municipal socialism to fascism. The interwar years have often been written off by scholars as devoid of any real urban progress, especially as measured by the arresting imagery of the grand boulevards of the nineteenth century. Only the glitz and glamour of central districts in Paris and Berlin catch the eye during the "Roaring Twenties". But the urban improvements of the 1920s and 1930s are found elsewhere—in much-needed public services, in public housing programs in working-class districts, in the vision of modernity laid out by architects of the modern movement. It was a visual theater of the imagination. It also produced real reform amid extraordinary political and social dislocation, as well as ethnic and nationalistic strife. Locating this history requires journeying to a diversity of places—from the great capitals to provincial towns, and to the Mediterranean urban world. It is a uniquely European heritage that fractured the prism of modernity into a variety of political as well as aesthetic hues, and had immense influence over the form of cities. It also laid the groundwork for the great programs of the post-Second World War welfare state.

Once the war was over, there was tremendous hope in the world-shattering possibilities of the future. The war's sacrifices demanded nothing less than a transformation of everyday life. Marches and rallies in the main squares of cities by organizations across the political spectrum demanded change. Public demonstrations could easily turn bloody. There were violent protests and strikes across Europe as political activists attempted to seize power in the vacuum left by the war. The Bolshevik Revolution in Russia paved the way. In 1919, riots broke out in Britain's major towns and cities. Public spaces became a subversive arena where breaking a few heads was the price of political power. Rival political factions occupied symbolic streets in a complex performance of chants, aggressive posturing, and confrontation.[1] The police clashed with hundreds of striking workers campaigning for a forty-hour week in Glasgow's George Square. Strike waves and the occupation of factories in French and Italian cities caused national alarm in 1919 and 1920. Berlin workers staged a general strike in 1920 to defend the feeble Weimar Republic against a right-wing coup attempt. Over 2.5 million workers walked out in the general strike across England in 1926. Vienna was hit by an attempted general strike in 1927 and the Palace of Justice burned down by a mob. Membership in the labor movement and working-class unions soared. Hundreds of thousands joined socialist parties and newly organized communist parties throughout Europe. The establishment of the Third Communist international, or Comintern, gave credence to the "Red Scare" and fears of a proletariat conspiracy to overthrow capitalism.

Workers were a heterogeneous lot and their urban lives multifaceted. The enduring legacies of class discrimination and the pecking order among workers themselves filtered down into everyday life and could be traced in the streets. Most advanced European countries had put in place basic social insurance measures and primary schooling. Skilled workers could depend on steady work and increasing benefits, especially from large companies that often worked with municipal housing offices to provide flats in better buildings. This elite among the working class commanded respect as union leaders and shop foremen. Better-off working-class families often supplemented their incomes with borders and bed-renters. They valued cleanliness, thrift, self-respect. Their children went to school and young people had the opportunity for occupational training. But this security was fragile. The introduction of new technologies and assembly-line production could make even the position of skilled workers tenuous, as did the Great Depression of the 1930s. Less qualified workers suffered chronic periods of unemployment and were paid paltry salaries that left many struggling to pay for food and rent. An endless stream of laborers packed their bags and moved frequently in hopes of finding a better life. Many of them grabbed a foothold as small traders, relied on unsteady informal work, or sank into poverty. This was especially the case once the Depression set in. It bitterly deepened the sense of exploitation and social injustice. The life of the unemployed was an exact hell, and there was little public relief. Unskilled ethnic minorities had even fewer opportunities and suffered daily smearing as dangerous social outcasts. Poor Czech bricklayers living in barracks in Vienna's notorious industrial slum of Kreta were labeled rogues and hoodlums. They were accused of drinking themselves to destitution.[2] It was a long-standing stereotype.

With few other options, rank-and-file members of socialist and communist parties and labor unions could depend on a thick web of support at the level of everyday life. It encompassed mutual aide, clubs and associations, sports and leisure activities. Everyday culture became the stuff of politics. Many working-class neighborhoods were veritable socialist fortresses. It was entirely possible for a union or party member to spend both their working and non-working lives within the orbit of left-wing political movements. They attended party functions, spent leisure time, and celebrated holidays with local comrades. Socialist and communist parties sponsored dances and social evenings at the local pub or tavern. Families joined in May Day marches and socialist and communist festivals. Party newspapers and weekly periodicals rolled off the press aimed at tenants, consumers, and women. Fellow travelers descended into the streets together when called to protest.[3] Not all workers participated, and some rejected or only partially accepted involvement in the movement's milieu. Yet this kind of solidarity sustained everyday life, especially during the Depression. Leftist pubs and meeting halls, local party and union networks and mutual aide, sympathetic neighbors and shopkeepers formed an intimate coded knowledge. It was an entire counter-cultural world at the level of neighborhood and community.

Family and ethnicity were the traditional bonds of working-class life. The ambitions of most people were modest and practical: a decent workday, a stable home, trips to the cinema or dance hall on a weekend, opportunities for their children. Families regularly went to the "talkies" and cheap nickelodeons, or to the local dance hall to shuffle through the turkey-trot and Charleston on Saturday night. They were an escape for the multitudes of factory workers and employees who could only afford to go out once a week. The Palais de Dance opened in London's working-class neighborhood of Hammersmith and hosted the Original Dixieland Jazz Band. By the early 1930s, there were twenty-three local dance palaces in London where for the price of a shilling, young people could indulge in the latest dance craze.[4] The seductions of mass culture were loosening traditional ties and shifting the sense of working-class consciousness. Mass-produced clothing and cosmetics gave even those of modest means the opportunity to display an assertive modernity. Young working-class women took part in the "flapper" craze. Bobbed hair and short skirts were a form of social and sexual rebellion. Thousands of working-class men played on local sports teams. Football and cycling clubs were manically popular, with thousands devoted to their favorite athletes. Families roamed the market bazaars and department stores for bargains. The newest novelties and consumer products filtered down to the working classes. Although it remained a symbol of affluence, radios were becoming a fixture in living rooms. Listening to music and sporting events were favorite pastimes. Brownie Box cameras were widely affordable in the 1920s and family photographs became a new hobby.

Despite these improvements in daily life at least for those better-off, the pent-up longing for a decent home remained endlessly frustrated. The debates over solutions were nearly as interminable. Providing a home for the urban multitudes stymied urban reformers. Thousands of families were still stuck in rudimentary shelter. Liverpool was actually the first city in Europe to provide public housing, as early as 1869. Over the years that followed other municipalities followed suit. But these groundbreaking programs were limited in scale under the assumption that the private market would provide the bulk of lodging needs. The war then brought housing construction to a standstill, just as demand skyrocketed with the peace. The crisis propelled housing reform forward with new resolve, if nothing else than as recognition that the working classes had borne the brunt of the war's hardship and sacrifices.

In the early years after the war, the garden city was still the rallying cry. Faced with the war's destruction in Belgium, the International Garden City Congress in Ghent in 1919 made an impassioned plea to clear away the ruins and build a better, peaceful world. There was a sense of urgency, a need for comprehensive town and regional planning that dealt with everything from transportation to food supply, and especially with housing. The garden city emerged as the most forward-looking ideal. It took the traditional small town as its model with rustic-like ensembles of picturesque housing, winding streets, and lush greenery. The aim was to improve the social and hygienic well-being of the working classes. The garden cities and garden suburbs that sprung up across the European landscape were copious in number. They were often small prototypes of future living laid out on the urban periphery as public housing programs or by private housing cooperatives. In France, the garden city ideal was implemented by Henri Sellier, longstanding urban reformer and mayor of the town of Suresnes, on the eastern periphery of Paris. A committed socialist, Sellier was deeply involved in the French trade union movement. The metropolitan area around the city of Paris was gaining almost 94,000 people a year between 1921 and 1931.[5] Under Sellier's influence, sixteen planned garden cities, or *cités-jardins*, were laid out between 1916 and 1939 in the suburbs of Paris as public housing projects. They favored picturesque cottage-style housing and row houses in the tradition of Ebenezer Howard's original vision at Letchworth (see Chapter 7). But it quickly became apparent that these would not solve the massive housing problems in the Paris suburbs or anywhere else for that matter. The ideal of the garden city as the future of urban settlement was no match for the scale of the housing shortage in Europe and the desperate need to solve the problems of urban growth.

The accumulation of urban problems brought left-wing socialist parties to power in a wide variety of cities in the 1920s and 1930s. In France, Britain, Belgium, and the Netherlands, the socialist Left emerged after the war as a commanding new political voice. It ascended on the political stage in Germany, Austria, and the Scandinavian countries as well. Their enthusiastic base was trade unions and organized worker's movements, especially among skilled and semiskilled workers. They gained support among left-leaning intellectuals, who provided an influential public voice for their agendas. A substantial middle class of technicians and engineers and civil servants joined their ranks. In solidly working-class towns, progressive pioneers had already taken the lead in the years before the war. Their influence paralleled the extension of the suffrage, the restructuring of municipal governance, and the growing trend to democratically elect mayors and city councils. Cities began operating gas, electricity, and water as public services rather than relying on private businesses. Britain had a long-established tradition of "gas and water" socialism in industrial cities such as Birmingham and Sheffield. Reformers honed their expertise in the years before the war at a galaxy of international expositions that shaped collective knowledge and ideas about civic improvement. At the level of the city, this kind of social reformism translated as a widespread movement. It was politically polyvalent and could be enacted with little controversy by centrist and left-leaning reformers as well as more radical activists. The term "socialism" was embraced as practical municipal improvement that would relieve the glaring social inequalities. Nonetheless, battles raged between agitators on the radical left plotting the demise of capitalism and reformers willing to work within its constraints. The quarrels left the socialist parties of the 1920s and 1930s unwilling to shed their Marxist dogma yet abandoning revolution for practical projects. Socialist strongholds were also often at odds with national governments, which tended to be far more conservative and saw in the urban masses the specter of revolutionary turmoil and communism.

Despite financial constraints and the vagaries of local politics, municipalities became laboratories of experimentation. In control of mayors' offices and city councils, they embarked on programs of municipal socialism to improve the quality of life for hundreds of thousands of working people. The goal was to fashion the socialist city and create an all-encompassing proletarian culture in which habitat would play a central organizing role. This became a near mythology. The way forward entailed not just decent housing but the rational provision of health services and schools, clean air, water and sanitation, quality of daily life, and a sense of social solidarity with the masses of people who had too long endured the miseries of run-down, miserable slums.[6] Social reformers railed against alcoholism and juvenile delinquency as the causes behind public disorder and riots. They charged what they saw as the rough drinking and gambling culture of the overcrowded tenements, the sexual promiscuity and macho horseplay as primitive escapes that robbed the working class of its humanity. All this would be shed once life improved. They stressed cleanliness, sobriety, cultivation, and learning. Although it was already ingrained in working-class culture, urban crusaders promoted a vision of working-class respectability grounded in family life. The physical and mental welfare of children and young people were at the center of this agenda. Sports and physical fitness were powerful symbolic affairs. They were considered a leisure revolution that offered not just health and fitness but also community and solidarity. Dreams of urban reform transmuted into a broad vision of municipal management and social welfare. The features of municipal socialism were almost identical across Europe. They were shared widely among socialist reformers as applicable internationally on behalf of the working classes. It was a prelude to the welfare regimes put in place after the Second World War.

Towns such as Sheffield in England were bastions of labor. Located in South Yorkshire, Sheffield was an industrial city of about 500,000 people with an economy based on large-scale steel production, engineering, and a tool and cutlery industry. Its East End was a landscape of steel plants and forges, but they fell on hard times for much of the interwar years. The economic slump and chronic unemployment provoked protests and demonstrations by thousands and propelled the Labor Party into power in the municipal elections of 1926. Sheffield was the first major English city to elect a Labor majority to the city council. They immediately embarked on a series of down-to-earth local projects as a new civic vision. Their goal was to "use the great municipal machines for the improvement of the city and bring the greatest health, educational and cultural benefits to the people."[7] Clearing out the old tenements and building "council housing" took pride of place in Labor's radical reforms. Between the two wars, some 28,000 public housing units were constructed. Schools and public health clinics, the provision of bathhouses, maternity and child care services appeared in working-class neighborhoods. New market halls and public slaughterhouses were built. Work exchanges and meeting houses figured prominently as symbols of the socialist city. A modern administrative structure and municipal boards were put in place to regulate city services. Noted urban planner Patrick Abercrombie was called in to create a city master plan as well as a regional strategy for Sheffield and the surrounding area. As a result, workers in English cities such as Sheffield could rely on steady employment and a shorter working day as well as decent housing and a battery of urban services.

Health, fresh air, and cleanliness were among the highest aims of reforming hygienists. Uncleanliness was not only associated with disease, especially the scourge of tuberculosis, but also with a fatalism that was holding down the working classes. Sports and physical fitness were a sign of moral and civic strength as well as a strategy for solidifying political support among the working classes. Thousands of people were involved in local sports activities made possible in part by shorter work weeks. Sports stadiums and public swimming pools emerged as distinct building types in the 1920s and 1930s. They were a new form of urban iconography and civic space, and more evocative of urban modernity than they have been given credit for. Hundreds of stadiums and pools were built in cities across Europe. They became symbolic of political ideologies as different as Soviet communism, Italian fascism, and homegrown municipal socialism. Swimming pools combined reformer anxieties about working-class health and hygiene with recreation, and expanded on the earlier ideal of the public bathhouse.[8] Many were designed in sumptuous art deco style. In general, art deco was the backyard of imagination for reformers searching for a style that epitomized municipal progress. The scale and design of the art deco indoor swimming pools were breathtaking. Soaring barrel-vault canopies hovered over expanses of sparkling water. They were aquatic palaces in striking modernist décor. Balconies and open walkways for viewing the watery frolics made them into visual spectacles. The pools were an enormous source of civic pride. They were hailed as cutting-edge architecture and were among the most popular of municipal improvements. Millions of ordinary people took to the water each year and relished the lively scene around public swimming pools (Figure 46).

The Piscine Molitor in Paris kickstarted the fad for art deco pool complexes. Abutting the Bois de Boulogne, the Molitor was inaugurated by Olympic swimming champion Johnny Weissmuller in 1929. The neobaroque Széchenyi bath complex in Budapest, opened in 1913, took advantage of the city's thermal springs and expanded in 1927 to three outdoor and fifteen indoor pools. The Palatinus thermal baths and indoor swimming pool were opened on the city's Margaret Island in the 1920s. The indoor pool

Figure 46 Piscine Molitor, Paris, 1930.

with its parabolic arches and cathedral-like spaces was designed by Hungarian architect and Olympic swimming sensation Alfréd Hajós. The stardust that rubbed off on projects such as these made them instant triumphs. Often built in working-class neighborhoods, public pools became community hubs on the spot, especially for young people. The pool was a new world of social informality and broke down public barriers between men and women.[9] The public pools in Berlin's working-class Neukölln and Mitte districts were glamorous stage sets, the former with elaborate neoclassical decoration and the latter with a modern industrial motif. In Paris, the public swimming pool in the working-class Butte-aux-Cailles district on the Left Bank was ensconced in a redbrick art nouveau building. The vaulted roof with it sinuous cement arches soared above a pool fed by natural spring water. Huge open-air aquatic complexes combined swimming pools with sports, gardens for sunbathing, and restaurants. The craze for swimming extended to seaside towns that promised sunshine, open-air pools and beaches, and family fun. The Saltdean Lido in Brighton was designed by architect Richard Jones in 1938 in a streamlined moderne style with its building's elegant curvilinear form imitating an ocean liner.

In France, universal voting rights for men ensured that the socialist movement had strong representation in city halls. In 1919, the socialist party was victorious in Marseille, Lille, Toulon, as well as Boulogne and Saint-Denis in the suburbs of Paris. By 1925, socialists controlled 532 towns in France including Strasbourg, Grenoble, Bordeaux, and Toulouse.[10] In the city of Toulouse in southwest France, the socialist party was elected in 1925 and then reelected in 1929 and 1935 with Mayor Etienne Billières at the helm. Straddling the Garonne River, Toulouse was the historic capital of the region of Languedoc with a population of around 155,000 in 1911. The city's industrial base expanded during the war with an armaments industry and then tobacco and agro-chemical production. The pioneering Aéropostale aircraft company established Toulouse as an early hub of French aviation as did the first regular flights between Toulouse and Casablanca and Dakar, and then to Rio de Janeiro. Legendary French pilots Jean Mermoz, Antoine de Saint-Exupéry, and Henri Guillaumet took off in their flimsy aircraft from the runways at the city's Montaudran Airport. By the mid-1930s, 4,000 people were working in aircraft construction. Thousands of metallurgists worked in armaments and manufactured railroad and agricultural machinery. Their numbers swelled with the arrival of Italian and Spanish immigrants. Within a short span of time, Toulouse had become a worker's city of 225,000 people.

Jean Montariol became the city's chief architect charged with designing a modern socialist city. A Toulouse native son who studied at the city's Ecole des Beaux-Arts, his vision merged vernacular aesthetics with socialist ideals. It was precisely this type of homegrown interpretation of modernism and its political meaning that represented the complex tangle of urban transformation across Europe. Montariol began with a series of public housing estates in the industrial neighborhoods and continued with garden suburbs along the periphery. Over the course of his tenure, eight schools, a sports complex on the Ile du Ramier in the Garonne River, an institute for physical education, public washhouses, swimming pools, and public dance hall were constructed. Many of these projects took form in working-class neighborhoods such as Bonnefoy, Saint-Cyprien, and Minimes. A municipal food program distributed 800,000 meals each year. Summer camps were organized for children. A new Bourse de Travail was constructed that provided municipal jobs during the Depression.[11] These improvements appealed not just to the rank-and-file socialist membership but to a middle class anxious for progressive reform. The sports park on the Ile du Ramier included three swimming pools surrounded by bleachers for 2,000 spectators and a grand art deco hall with indoor swimming pool, gymnasiums, and spaces for local festivities.

Montariol essentially designed a model socialist city down to the newspaper kiosks. Libraries played a triumphant role in this urban conception. The moral uplift and education of the working class was of prime importance. Creating a modern city meant constructing spaces of social progress. Montariol designed the Toulouse municipal library as a resplendent art deco structure in reinforced concrete, decorated with glass mosaics, forged iron, and bas-relief created by local artists. The resplendent reading room was open to natural light with expansive windows and a translucent dome towering above the cathedral-like space. It was dramatic theater, a "modern palace of thought."[12] The building's facade was decorated with the redbrick and stone of Toulouse's time-honored built environment. It was a bow to the local form of urban modernity.

Likewise, municipal reform in Lyon, France, was initially guided by the vision of Tony Garnier, one of France's leading architects whose political roots were in both socialism and anarchism. Garnier was born and lived in Lyon and was commissioned by the city's socialist mayor to build a public housing estate (the Quartier des États-Unis), a new slaughterhouse, hospital, textile training school, and a new sports park. He worked there from 1906 to 1920, extending his concepts for his *cité industrielle* and designing in the rationalist architectural style known as the *école lyonnaise*. The Gerland sports park was located on terrain along the Rhone River set aside for Lyon's 1914 International Exposition on the modern city. The war interrupted the plans and only the athletic stadium and swimming pool were built as a taste of the future. With its four massive ferro-concrete archways, the stadium was applauded as a key example of the modern movement.[13]

While Garnier's distinctive modernist buildings were emblematic of Lyon, they also rippled through the textile town of Villeurbanne in the suburbs. By the early 1920s, Villeurbanne had grown to nearly 100,000 inhabitants with little planning. Nearly 70 percent of the population was working class, and 16 percent were Italian and Spanish immigrants. They lived in an assortment of abodes, from crumbling cottages and low-cost flats to public housing projects. Mayor Lazare Goujon was the son of a steel worker and avowed socialist. Under the refrain "to change the city is to change life,"[14] Goujon embarked on a major redevelopment scheme with a new town hall and Palais du Travail as their centerpiece. The design was a bold modern statement with a grand avenue lined with high-rise apartment buildings leading to the central square. Some 1,500 housing units were constructed, each open to light and air and equipped with heat and hot water. A soaring art deco skyscraper set off the monumental ensemble with one wing containing the mayor's office and the other dedicated to public health and community services. The adjacent Palais du Travail on the main plaza was a veritable temple to the working class with an employment exchange, meeting rooms, theater, sports facilities, and swimming pool. The architectural panache of Villeurbanne symbolized a new urban civilization. It was a crusade to create a working-class collective culture. Villeurbanne was a barometer of urban socialist values—an awe-inspiring urban fabric and a new form of living.

It was the anticipatory nature of municipal socialism that differentiated it from public housing projects alone. Shelter was only one aspect of a broader vision for a future socialist society. Municipal reformers set out to supervise the family from conception to adulthood. The most impressive example of municipal socialism was Vienna, where the Sozial-demokratische Arbeiterpartei (SDAP) won the municipal election in 1919 and controlled an absolute majority on the city council. Vienna emerged from the First World War with only 1.8 million inhabitants in a diminutive Austria of 6.4 million people. It functioned both as a city and a state within the Austrian Federal Republic. Rather than the multiethnic capital of a far-flung empire, the city had only two significant ethnic minorities by the 1920s: a Czech population that represented about 6–8 percent of the city and about 200,000 Jews who made up around 10 percent of the citizenry.[15] With the socialist party and trade union membership in full support, mayors Jakob Reumann and Karl Seitz embarked on ambitious programs to reshape the physical and social landscape of Vienna into a new *Wohnkultur*, a new form of socialist living based on egalitarianism and collectivist values. The vote was extended to all men and women without condition. Paid vacations were established and factory councils set up. A comprehensive system of education was put in force including kindergartens and schools, summer camps, and after-school programs. Medical care was introduced in schools along with healthcare centers for mothers and babies, homes for invalids, orphaned children, and the old. These measures succeeded in immediately reducing the city's appalling rates of infant mortality.

Health and sport were at the top of the agenda. The International Workers' Olympiads were international sporting extravaganzas organized by the 2 million-member strong Socialist Workers' Sport International. Held between 1925 and 1937, they were a rival to the Olympic Games that were criticized by left-wing reformers as elitist. The Workers' Olympiads were held under the banners of social solidarity and peace, and unlike the Olympics, were open to women. In the summer of 1931, Vienna hosted the Workers' Summer Olympiad with nearly 100,000 athletes from twenty-six countries. The Danube was packed with steamers arriving with competitors from Hungary and the Balkans. Special trains were organized. The sports competitions were held in Prater Park in a new 60,000-seat stadium built alongside one of the largest swimming pools in Europe. The events included a run-and-swim biathlon that saw athletes sprinting through the streets of Vienna to the cheers of the crowds. Thousands stretched their muscles in a mass gymnastics event. As a finale, the Olympiad contestants marched in ranks with banners held high through the inner city, down the Ringstrasse, to the stadium. There, the playing field was transformed into an immense stage on which a cast of 4,000 performed a drama on the victory of socialism. The sea of red flags mesmerized the audience.[16] The symbolic power of these mass spectacles was spellbinding.

Vienna's socialist government declared decent housing the fundamental right of all citizens. The extent of the housing crisis was staggering. Only 50 percent of Viennese workers lived in a flat of their own, and those that did often lived together in one-room bedsits. Only 18 percent of these destitute hovels had water, gas, and electricity. The Social Democrats turned to large-scale multistory construction as the only practical solution. A massive public housing program was financed by a building tax and resulted in 64,000 new apartments housing 200,000 people in ten years. The construction was inserted into the urban fabric along the city's perimeter where the need was greatest, close to public transport, schools, and hospitals. The tenants were often young families drawn from the "respectable" working class and petit-bourgeoisie, who could be depended upon to vote socialist. It was a huge social achievement.

The famous Karl-Marx-Hof public housing complex alone contained 1,325 flats. It was a colossal red working-class fortress set along Vienna's outer ring road, the Heiligenstädterstrasse, in the neighborhood of Döbling. Like much of the SDAP's public housing, it was designed in a consciously Viennese concoction of architectural styles meant to crystallize the new socialist way of life. Sculptures, murals, and majolica tiles decorated the exterior. Socialist banners streamed from its towers. Grand archways led inside, where courtyards were a web of parks and playgrounds. There were schools, a library, and health clinic, and communal kitchens and laundry rooms. It was a complete working-class collective community set to the rhythm of everyday life. The Karl-Marx-Hof was epic in scale and symbolism.[17] It represented an ideal socialist city, a "people's palace" and vanguard of the urban future. Its heroic meaning made it an instant target for the forces of right-wing adversaries. The Karl-Marx-Hof became one of the main battlefields in the brief Austrian Civil War of 1934. Its bombardment, like its construction, became an emblem—this time not of municipal socialism but of a fascist radicalism bent on destroying the red menace they saw written into its design (Figure 47).

Figure 47 Karl-Marx-Hof, Vienna.

The contributions by European urban crusaders were numerous, from groundbreaking social housing projects such as the Karl-Marx-Hof to the modern architectural imaginaries of the Bauhaus and *Congrès internationaux d'architecture moderne* (CIAM). Implementing these visionary projects was a real possibility as cities struggled with the persistent housing crisis and the pent-up expectations of the politically emboldened working classes. Increasingly, the provision of large-scale social housing was accepted as the only solution to the dreary reality of tenement life. How it should be constructed received widespread public attention and engrossed politicians and architects alike. Modern functional architecture captured the imagination of urban reformers. There was a fearless, blazing idealism to early modernist projects. Openness and flexibility in building design, simple form, were associated with aesthetic honesty and social democratic principles. The virtuosity of inexpensive construction materials and prefabrication received tremendous publicity. Access to natural light and air was considered essential. But it was not simply a design preference. Tuberculosis was a massive scourge across Europe, and public health authorities were convinced that poor housing conditions were directly responsible for the spread of the disease.[18] Light and air were the only known preventative measures to this persistent threat to public health. Given this enthusiasm for "building" and health reform, modern architects were able to claim real public significance for their work. They devised a philosophy of architecture as socially transformative. Imagining built structure was an expression of modern mass society. This impulse to see in the physical fabric of the city the possibilities of a new world followed reformers throughout the twentieth century. It was pursued with its own kind of evangelical fervor.

In Germany, this was mainly the work of architects Walter Gropius and Bruno Taut, who did much of the conceptual heavy lifting for architecture as social revolution. Both were involved in various radical groups including a Working Council for the Arts in Berlin that called for artistic production "for and by the people." Taut was an outspoken social democrat and active union supporter. His avant-garde theories predicted the impending death of those "great spiders," the old cities. Taut's writings were filled with visions of crystalline architecture intended as symbols of hope for Europe. He believed the new socialist era would exude a higher life-force, a spirit that would emerge from the dust of the past.[19] There would be no state boundaries, no private property. Instead the new world would be defined by spiritual regeneration and harmonious social relations. For Taut, the revolution meant a new era of democracy and brotherhood. In sum, he endowed architecture with overpowering emotional force. The need for 750,000 new dwellings in Germany was not just a practical necessity; it was an entire program for the future.

After 1924, every major city in Germany attempted to supply the voracious demand for housing. The development and acceptance of modern architecture in Germany was made possible because of this demand. The architects devoted to the New Building (*Neues Bauen*) or New Objectivity (*Neue Sachlichkeit*), as it was called, wanted clients and work. They coordinated directly with the public building programs of the Weimar Republic to produce their functional aesthetics. The socialist party and trade unions also supported limited-liability building societies for construction. A total of 2.5 million flats were built in Germany from around 1924 through 1932. Some 9 million people set up their lives in the new abodes. They were social as well as political experiments. In the mid-1920s, Bruno Taut became chief designer for the GEHAG, the Berlin cooperative housing society. Under his supervision, the GEHAG constructed a startling number of housing projects ranging in size from 100 to 1,200 flats. Taut's innovations in modular design made them among the most important architectural work in Germany. This was especially true of the Hufeisensiedlung, or Horseshoe Estate, in Britz in the outskirts of Berlin. The central area was designed as a horseshoe-shaped crescent with four-story flat-roof apartments. The remainder of the 1,000-unit complex was laid out in efficient straight rows. Each standardized apartment was equipped with bathroom, kitchen, and open balcony. The architecture was simple, functional, and made ample use of color and gardens to create an intimate community atmosphere. It was a self-contained urban settlement. The Horseshoe Estate epitomized Taut's belief in creative building as the spark to social revolution.

This was also the ideological backbone of the Bauhaus despite the constant turnover of its faculty, location, its years mired in controversy and persecution. The school opened its doors in April 1919 in Weimar under the direction of architect Walter Gropius. For Gropius and the charismatic figures that gathered around him, the purpose of the Bauhaus was to erect the cathedral of socialism.[20] They called for a "new community," both spiritual and social in character, in which architecture would act as a commanding force for the citizens of the new democratic state. It was this vision of a new society that lay behind the school's feverish determination to create simple, genuine design available to everyone. Architecture was purged of bombast and decoration. For Gropius, "We want an architecture adapted to our world of machines, radios and fast motor cars, an architecture whose function is clearly recognizable in its form." Caught in the crossfire of brutal political debate, the Bauhaus was forced into a nomadic existence, finding respite finally in the town of Dessau. The school's iconic Dessau building, designed by Gropius as a functional steel and reinforced concrete structure with wide expanses of glass, was a model of Bauhaus ideals. It was a combination of utopian egalitarianism and functional utility.

In the early 1920s, the Bauhaus began displaying prototypes at Dessau for prefabricated, standardized, low-cost housing units. They were austere white-washed cubicles, and their radical design made them among the most talked-about buildings in Germany. Even more important for publicizing the functionalist style in housing was the Stuttgart Weissenhof Exhibition in 1927 organized by the German Werkbund. The city of Stuttgart was one of the most exciting epicenters of cutting-edge architecture in the "pure form" of the *Neues Bauen*. The exhibition was under the general direction of architect Mies van der Rohe. The most prominent architects in Europe (Le Corbusier, Walter Gropius, Bruno Taut, and others) were invited to present original designs for housing that would introduce the public to "the great struggle for a new way of life." On a hillside in Stuttgart, a model village took shape of daring modern designs for bungalows, terraced houses, and apartment buildings. The construction featured steel framing, concrete panels, and the pragmatic marvel of prefabrication. The interiors were bright and airy with functional furniture, kitchen equipment, and decorative trimmings. It was one of the most powerful architectural showcases of the twentieth century. Pilgrimages to exhibits such as these fashioned a generation of architectural trailblazers ready to transform urban life. As many as twenty thousand visitors a day came to see what the new dwelling looked like. The coverage in the press was unprecedented and the exhibition pronounced enthusiastically as an "inexpressibly beautiful paradise"[21] (Figure 48).

These interwar years of experimentation bore a variety of fruit. German architect Ernst May put his concepts to work most successfully in the "New Frankfurt" initiative. Like Stuttgart, Frankfurt am Main was a hotbed of reform initiatives in the 1920s and early 1930s. It was a city of 500,000 inhabitants that suffered record homelessness and a surge of refugees from the regions ceded to France after the First World War. The newly elected social democratic municipal government incorporated the surrounding suburbs into an enlarged metropolitan area and appointed May as chief architect. With May's help, Mayor Ludwig Landmann conceived of a Neue Frankfurt that would embody a new era of modernity and social reform.[22] Ten percent of the city's population would be resettled in twenty-four satellite towns. They were experiments in a new concept of living culture, or *wohnkultur*, one of the key utopian concepts used by modernists in their attempt to use architecture and planning as instruments for revolutionizing society. In Neue Frankfurt, housing was constructed using the latest prefabrication techniques and state-of-the-art materials. The buildings were minimalist flat-roofed bungalows. They assembled into coherent neighborhoods with schools and daycare facilities, community centers, shops, and workplaces. Neue Frankfurt won immediate international acclaim at

Figure 48 A block of flats by German architect Ludwig Mies van der Rohe in the Weissenhof Siedlung Housing Project at Stuttgart, 1927.

the second Congress of CIAM held in Frankfurt in 1929 and was widely praised by the Bauhaus for its modernist purism.

What is distinctive about these years was this outpouring of European architectural creativity and the degree to which it fashioned the modern urban environment around profound social ideals. Modernism was about a new way of living. CIAM was founded in La Sarraz, Switzerland, in 1928 by a group of twenty-eight European architects. They were initially led by Le Corbusier and Sigfried Giedion. CIAM was one of many manifestos in the 1920s meant to advance the cause of architecture as social art. But its influence was especially widespread. The CIAM meetings, or congresses, held in Frankfurt, Brussels, Athens, and Paris acted as rallying points for modernist architects determined to take on the challenge of housing, urban planning, and industrial design. Their purpose was to question the fundamental nature of architecture and its role as a social and political tool. They enthusiastically embraced the possibilities of the modern age. The fourth CIAM Congress in 1933 carried out an analysis of thirty-four different cities and proposed practical solutions to their long-standing urban problems. The conclusions were published as "The Athens Charter," which became one of the most influential documents on the city produced in the twentieth century. It espoused a functional built environment with citizens settled into modernist housing blocks and an orderly pattern of development promoted by rigid zoning. It was among the most braggadocio statements of modernist urban proclivities.

We see the same progressive agenda practiced in the capital of Stockholm in Sweden, a city of about 300,000 people. The social democratic party came to power in Sweden through close links with the labor, education, and temperance movements. Their shared vision of social welfare applied not just to the working class but to the whole of society. The idea was encapsulated in the Swedish concept of the "people's home" or *folkhemmit*.[23] Based on the ideals of community and social solidarity, it promoted the role of the state in creating the good society. Passionate about the possibilities of the future, reformers understood themselves as social engineers. Sociologist Alva Myrdal and modernist architect Sven Markelius were leaders in advocating communal housing as a way to emancipate working women from the burdens of housekeeping and childrearing. Their modernist Collective House apartments in the Arvik district of Stockholm included childcare facilities, shared kitchen, and social space. Its restaurant was a meeting place for radical socialists, many of whom lived in the complex. Communal living was part of a broad debate on the nature of urban society as reformers sought solutions to the dilapidated slums and social crisis of the metropolis.

The Swedish model of social democracy applied to the city was among the most important sources of inspiration for European urban reformers, especially in eastern Europe. It was given material form in the 1930 Stockholm Exhibition.[24] The chief organizer was Gregor Paulsson, author of the best-selling book *Better Things for Everyday Life*. Held on the island of Djurgården in central Stockholm, the exhibition was visited by over 4 million people. The model housing displays were a revelation in lifestyle for the working and middle classes. A galaxy of Swedish avant-garde architects set out their visions for functional cooperative housing, apartments, and bungalows. The interiors were light-filled and airy with simple, functional furniture in tubular steel and teak, and kitchenettes outfitted with the newest stoves and refrigerators. The exhibition paraded a universe of Swedish modernist design in applied arts and consumer products. Scandinavian design gained a cult following. The pavilions were arranged along the waterfront and interspersed with a festival square, illuminated concert stage and dance floor, planetarium, and the celebrated Paradise Restaurant—a thrilling modernist structure with exposed steel frame and glass facade. Towering advertising masts were decorated with the logos of participating companies. The Stockholm Exhibition showcased a utopian social democratic city that, far from just hallucinatory, actually seemed imminent. It was a vision shared across Europe despite ongoing political crises and the precipice of the Great Depression. Even the hodgepodge of local fiefdoms and infernal political wrangling that beset every city and brought reform to a standstill could somehow be overcome.

A tremendous optimism about the possibilities of urban life made the city into a playground of social invention and aesthetic ingenuity. It was an experimental field for partisans across the political spectrum. What was most distinctive about these endeavors was precisely the full-throated ideologies behind them. The fascist version highlights the complexity and moral ambiguities, if not downright perversion, of the outpouring of urban imaginaries produced in these years. There was a deep contradiction in the fascist attitude toward cities because fascism was fundamentally anti-urban. Fascist ideology fixated on the city as a place of decadence and chaos. It was the site of cultural and social decay and working-class bedlam. The city was the breeding ground for the red plagues of socialism and communism. It teemed with the pestilence of lower races, especially

Jews. There was a fiendish logic here, because cities were also to perform a psychological, quasi-religious, an even magical function as gathering points for fascist celebratory propaganda. Even though cities are always a messy mix of peoples, fascism was bent on cleansing away these depravities and reshaping the urban fabric into monumental political spectacle.

In 1870, Rome became the capital of the newly unified country of Italy. It was also the spiritual center of the Catholic church at the Vatican. The comings-and-goings of prelates stamped its public life. Despite its long and storied history and its prominent status, the once heart of European civilization was a diminished city of only 225,000 people. Rome suffered from centuries of indifference and had literally sunk into decay. The long-neglected ancient core around the Seven Hills on the left bank of the Tiber River was awash in historic artifacts and edifices, many submerged underground by the ravages of time. An 1899 American travel guide to Italy cautioned against heading for Rome first since "there is no continuity at all in Rome: it consists of scraps and odds and ends from everywhere."[25] There was no industry. The main source of wealth was still agriculture. The city had a pastoral, picturesque quality that enchanted visitors but was oddly out of sync with the modern urban improvements underway elsewhere in Europe. Rome was a shadow compared to the robust Italian industrial cities of Turin and Milan in the north, or even Naples and Palermo to the south.

Once it took on the mantel of national capital, its visual landscape began to resemble a modern secular metropolis. The city was to embody a cohesive Italian national identity, different from the Catholic Rome of the popes. New government ministries were built. The Piazza Venezia became the new center of the capital and the grandiose monument to King Vittorio Emanuele II completed. New thoroughfares were carved out of the dense maize of ancient neighborhoods. Archaeological excavations began to reclaim the city's heritage. Landmark buildings in the historic center were restored including the Colosseum and sections of the Roman Forum. The Tiber River embankments were shored up. Tenement blocks lined the streets. Along with a deluge of new civil servants, thousands of poor peasants flocked to the capital. These last survived on the streets or in makeshift shanty towns or *borghetti* along the city's eastern perimeter among the factories and rail yards. The population of 460,000 by the century's turn was jammed into an overbuilt, chaotic city. Despite the grandiose visions of Rome as a symbol of united Italy, the city's expansion actually took place without much planning or control. Visiting in 1929, French journalist Henri Béraud described the traffic jams on Rome's narrow streets as dreadful: "By some sort of concerted profanity, the drivers blast their horns—as if on Judgement Day—day and night in these revered old neighborhoods once made for dreaming and strolling . . . the roar is unimaginable."[26]

When Mussolini and his fascist squads swaggered through Rome in October 1922, they not only took control of the Italian government. They also conquered a city where historic heritage was scrawled into every street and edifice, above and below ground. Mussolini was obsessed with Rome. Its ancient imperial fabric was the birthright he shrewdly manipulated as the visual spectacle of fascist power. Although Mussolini had nothing but contempt for the "masses" who actually lived in the city, he believed the politician could shape the multitudes and forge the will of the people. They were a raw material that could be molded into obedience through his aesthetic vision of mass politics.[27] Fascist pageantry was chock-full of marching parades, flags and banners, lights and music. Rome was turned into an ongoing fascist performance. Surveying the city in 1929, Béraud remarked on "the multicolored profusion of public posters, the frenzied displays, that first strike the foreigner. Life is lit up in a fiery, anxious light. Everywhere the same exhilarating words are constantly repeated: war, heroes . . . victory, resurrection, the homeland . . . and the flags and flames."[28] The Birth of Rome was the first celebration instituted by the fascist government. Mussolini reveled in spectacles that put him center stage. Perched on a balcony above the Piazza Venezia, his rabble-rousing speeches to adoring crowds triggered roars of "Duce! Duce!"

The tenth anniversary of the March on Rome was the occasion for a lavish Exhibition of the Fascist Revolution (1932–34). It was a visual extravaganza dedicated to fascism's made-up heroic history. Mounted on horseback, Mussolini led a parade of 15,000 athletes through the streets. Train fares were reduced to a pittance to draw all of Italy to the capital for the events. Millions of Italians saw Rome for the first time. Open-air masses dedicated to fascist martyrs drew thousands. In 1938, Mussolini sponsored a blockbuster show entitled "The Rome of Augustus" at the Palazzo delle Esposizioni. It was a celebration of the city that included Adolf Hitler as guest of honor. An extravagant new railway station was built to welcome the Fuhrer. The city was festooned with flags and banners, and its ancient monuments floodlit. Thousands gathered to celebrate Italy's victory in the conquest of Ethiopia. They swooned at the war booty put on display. Columns of strapping youth arrayed in colorful uniforms paraded on the city's streets. Expositions were regularly held in the Circus Maximus. In 1938, the Dopolavoro organization turned the Circus Maximum into an extravagant festival of sports and leisure replete with flamboyant pavilions, swimming pools, lavish gardens, and spectacular water fountains. The city's workers and salaried employees by the thousands luxuriated in the fascist version of a "people's park." Rome was the showpiece, the mecca to see the Duce and admire the fascist spectacle.

The Duce envisaged a new "third Rome" vastly increased in size and population from the already 1 million inhabitants crammed into the city. "In five years," he told the city council, "Rome must appear wonderful to the whole world, immensely orderly and powerful as she was in the days of the first empire of Augustus." Archaeologists dug into the city's bowels in search of its imperial past. The forums of Caesar and Trajan were excavated, temples uncovered, and sections of the Capitoline Hill restored. With the help of Corrado Ricci, one of the most influential Italian senators and urbanists of this period, Mussolini plowed through a slew of renaissance and medieval buildings and archaeological ruins deemed irrelevant to fascist symbolism. The wholesale destruction of medieval Rome was the price to pay. Mussolini himself ceremoniously wielded the first pick in the high-profile demolition projects such as the "liberation" of the mausoleum of Augustus. Whole areas of medieval Rome were flattened to construct the Via Del Mare through the city center. The Via dell'Impero, a broad thoroughfare running from the Piazza Venezia, across the Roman Forum to the Colosseum was rammed through one of the most densely populated areas of the city. The two boulevards of the Via dell'Impero and the Via del Mare opened up the traditional chaos to traffic and circulation. The Via dell'Impero became the great fascist ceremonial avenue, a "spiritual path," where the forces of fascism pompously marched before the Roman crowds. For Hitler's 1938 visit, a parade of thirty thousand troops, three thousand men on horseback and four hundred artillery trucks wound their way down the Via dell'Impero to the Piazza Venezia. Featured continually in propaganda newsreels, the Via dell'Impero became the face of the entire nation (Figure 49).

The spectacularized ancient imperial fabric was merged with plans to transform Rome into a modern showpiece. The reveries of a future fascist city were extravagant. A Palace of Fascism was to tower above the Roman Forum. A Forum of Mussolini was planned for an immense area along the Tiber River. Despite the obsession with antiquity, Mussolini's "Third Rome" actually had little resemblance to the past. Instead, it absorbed

Figure 49 Inauguration of Via dell'Impero in Rome, October 28, 1932.

a grab bag of legacies and produced an idiosyncratic version of modern architecture and planning. Stadiums and sports fields were integral to this imaginary. Rome was conceived as a "sports city" in line with the regime's dedication to the health and physical fitness of Italian youth. Indoor and outdoor swimming pools, tennis courts, and football pitches were constructed for the Balilla, the fascist youth organization. Cinemas and theaters, sports and recreational facilities, and health clinics appeared in the districts of Trastevere, Ponte, and Parione and on the city's working-class peripheries. In this regard, fascist reforms had much in common with municipal socialism. Urban modernism across the political spectrum was rooted in desperately needed populist improvements. The annual "Campo Dux" gathered members of the fascist youth organizations by the thousands for a series of sport competitions along the Tiber River. The event's culmination was the parade of some 25,000 participants down the Via dell'Imperio to greet the Duce.[29] The Foro Italico was a vast sports complex north of the city inspired by the ancient Roman Imperium. On the southern outskirts along the Via del Mare the EUR (Espozitione Universale di Roma) complex took shape to celebrate the twentieth anniversary of the March on Rome with an international exposition in 1942. Its theme celebrating "The Olympics of Civilization" was also in preparation for the 1944 Olympic Games. Fatefully, the Second World War abruptly ended these grandiose schemes.

As a national capital, the state-led modernization of Rome, in this case under fascism, was unsurprising. But there were relatively few capital cities in the Mediterranean region, and certainly none of Rome's stature. In general, Mediterranean cities were overgrown places developed bit by bit through a murky blend of formal and informal land tenure and settlement patterns. The same complexity is true of their economies. Mediterranean cities developed with pockets of large-scale industrialization alongside micro-production and commercial businesses capable of shrewd adaptation to market conditions. An industrial labor force worked together with self-employed artisans and shopkeepers, family entrepreneurs and laborers, all of them tapping into a well-honed informal sector for resources. Kiosks and dwarf workshops were as important to the modern Mediterranean economy as factories. It was further evidence that industrialization took place within the context of local urban economic cultures. The Mediterranean was a messy, hybrid urban world. The commerce and trade routes linked to their ports were as essential to these workaday spheres as were major industries.

Naples was a characteristic example of this urban metamorphosis. Hugging the coastal bay in the southern region of Campania, it was by far the largest Italian city in the early twentieth century with the densest urban space in Europe—ten times the density of Victorian London. A "human anthill" was how one visitor described the jam-packed center districts around the Via Toledo, the city's main street.[30] Migrants from the surrounding countryside swarmed into the city. In the early years of the century, a steelworks and cotton factories were established in the outlying district of Bagnoli. But by the end of the First World War, demand collapsed and the labor force was cut back. The abject poverty and grim realities of life in Naples had long drawn urban critics such as Renato Fucini's 1878 journalistic investigation *Napoli ad occhio nudo* (Naples to the Bare Eye). The suffering was made worse by the devastating cholera epidemics of 1884 and 1910–11. But even by these unfortunate earlier standards, the 1920s and 1930s were particularly lean years. The city's working classes relied on their wits and hole-in-the-wall commercial and artisan stalls, many of them attached to the daily rhythms of the seaport and its storehouses. This was the so-called "mystery of Naples"—people survived without productive industry. Informal labor, vendor stands, and petty trading in the city's bazaars, semilegal bargaining took place alongside legitimate jobs. Or, in the words of political philosopher Antonio Gramsci, they joined the "retinues of servants and lackeys" catering to the bourgeois landowning families who ruled the city.[31] Illiteracy was the norm. Success was a matter of luck and chance. It was a poor, run-down city bedeviled by organized crime and political corruption.

With the conquest of Ethiopia, Mussolini's government promoted the city as the "port of Empire." Cities such as Naples survived on multi-layered networks from the local to the global ties of trade that were the secrets to their so-called economic "mysteries." A huge exhibition hall was built for the 1940 showcase "Italian Lands Overseas." In fascist imperial dreams, Naples was imagined as the hub of the Mediterranean and link between Europe and Africa. Trade and tourism would jump start the city's future. A new maritime terminal in art deco style welcomed ocean liners and ferries crammed with voyagers. It complemented the seafront promenade and aquarium. A new airport and subway system were built. Middle-class Neapolitans and tourists strolled the thoroughfares and enjoyed the city's cafés. An automobile assembly plant and machine shops began operation. But these projects were set against the grim realities that seemed impervious to modernization schemes.

Naples was one of the capitals of Italian cinema. Neapolitan realist cinema reveled in capturing the working-class underbelly of the city's life. Cameras in tow, film crews journeyed into the abyss and shaped a melodramatic scenography of the plebian worlds hidden in the city's back alleyways, the tenement blocks and staircases shoved into the hills, the charnel houses and caves. The films were often shown in the city's arcades, where they formed a populist cinema.[32] In her many documentaries, such as "Il ventre di Napoli (The guts of Naples)," Neapolitan director Elvira Notari attempted to capture the feelings and motivations permeating the city's shadowy spaces. They were places of raw emotion where family allegiances, guilt and punishment, and sheer cunning determined survival. Passion, revenge, domestic violence shaped daily life. It was a place of contrasts—between beauty and ugliness, paradise and hell. Neapolitan philosopher Benedetto Croce attributed this proverbial phantasm of Naples as a backward "paradise inhabited by devils"[33] to centuries of exploitation and misrule (Figure 50).

Imaginaries about Naples frothed into a mesmerizing visual drama framed by the blue waters of the bay and by Mount Vesuvius. They formed part of the long-standing myths and stereotypes about Mediterranean urban life that were entangled with reality. Northern travelers to Naples gushed over the city's striking atmosphere. Even the intellectual avant-garde succumbed to the exotic attractions of Naples and the cities of southern Europe. There was a sense of mystery and danger. Yet the chaotic spaces of Naples contained modes of sociability and creative practices outside the rigid chains of modern life. They allowed the disenfranchised a measure of openness, of inspired

Figure 50 Narrow street in Naples, 1937, Martin Hurlimann.

urbanity that was transformative in quality. Urban critic Walter Benjamin traveled to Naples in 1925 with Latvian revolutionary Asja Lacis. Their musings described the city's maze of buildings and alleyways as a theater of improvisation "which demands that space and opportunity be preserved at any price." On this populist stage, "even the most wretched pauper is sovereign in the dim, dual awareness of participating, in all his destitution, in one of the pictures of Neapolitan street life that will never return, and of enjoying in all his poverty the leisure to follow the great panorama."[34]

This sense of creative force resonated throughout the modernist architectural movements of the 1920s and 1930s when *mediterraneità* came into fashion, especially among the Italian avant-garde. *Mediterraneità* meant classical models in dialogue with the vernacular forms of everyday life. The Italian Futurists, for their part, were enthralled by the "primitive" qualities of ordinary settlement found in the south. Austrian architect Adolf Loos, whose work was vital to the modernist movement, admired the unassuming local architecture on his Italian voyages to Naples and Venice. Le Corbusier had undertaken his own Mediterranean odyssey early in his career and visited towns in the Balkans, Athens, Rome, and Naples. He waxed effusively on the built form of the Mediterranean with its luminous white cubic houses, lime-washed each spring.[35] In 1933, the members of CIAM boarded a ship in Marseille and cruised the Mediterranean coast on their way to Athens, with stops to explore Mediterranean vernacular architecture as a primal source for the modern movement.

All these chimeras were embroidered by the procession of people passing through Mediterranean cities. They were privileged meeting places between east and west, cities of strangers and transitions, where the displaced and dispossessed made their way in the flotsam and jetsam of urban life. They might have heartily disliked each other, but his flow of humanity acted as agents of a pragmatic tolerance and cosmopolitanism. Walter Benjamin and Asja Lacis described Naples as porous: "Porosity is the inexhaustible law of this city, appearing everywhere."[36] The city of Genoa, the capital of the Liguria region in northeastern Italy, shared this quality. Hemmed in between the mountains and the coast, the old city was a maze of steep alleys and stairways, with "streets so narrow that you may touch the houses on both sides as you pass, and across which stretches row after row of snow-white linen so that the view of the sky is almost shut out" according to a British traveler.[37] Genoa's archaic tangle of passageways lent the city an intoxicating air of secrecy and mystery. These were the familiar stereotypes about Mediterranean places. But Genoa, like many cities in southern Europe, was engulfed by a population that nearly doubled between 1900 and 1936 and changed the city's traditional social fabric. Thousands of nomads from across Italy swept into the city in the early twentieth century, many looking for jobs building ships and railcars, and in the city's mechanical engineering workshops.[38] They shared a kind of informal citizenship and engagement with the city at the level of daily life. The use of the local Genoese dialect declined as the newcomers conversed in Italian. Many more thousands of pilgrims from southern Italy, from central and eastern Europe gathered on the wharves with their belongings, waiting to embark across the Atlantic to the New World. Genoa and Naples, as well as Marseille, were the exit points for this diaspora. It was an unprecedented mass migration that only ended with the Great Depression and the Second World War.

This permeability, the population currents through Europe's cities, especially along the Mediterranean, was among the most significant features of the first half of the twentieth century. The European city evolved within a rich system of migration, connectivity, and sociocultural transmission. Marseille was the haven for North Africans, Russians fleeing the Bolshevik Revolution, Armenians escaping the holocaust in Turkey, Spanish running from the brutal civil war of the 1930s, and Italians and Corsicans seeking a better life. A "little Naples" took shape in Marseille around the Le Panier district of the old city, where Neapolitans settled or used it as a jumping off point for crossing the Atlantic. Armenians clustered along the Boulevard des Grands Pins. Himself a refugee from the tightening grip of fascism, German cultural critic Siegfried Kracauer found himself in Marseille in 1940 observing "the arrival and departure of ocean liners, aglow as they disappear over the horizon. . . . In the spongy depths of the harbor quarter the fauna of humanity is teeming. . . . The mass of humanity in which the peoples of different nations blend together is flushed through the avenues and bazaar streets. These define the borders of the districts into which the human tide disperses."[39]

While it is tempting to interpret it as one of the great strengths of the urban environment, the human cost of this diaspora was painful and profound. As always, war worsened the deluge of anguished castaways. In the case of Salonica, the Balkan Wars and then the breakup of the Hapsburg and Ottoman empires were devastating. The city hugged the coast of the Aegean Sea in Macedonia. It was touted as the "crossroads of the world," and the "most modern city in the Ottoman Empire." Salonika was one of the most eclectic, cosmopolitan places on the Mediterranean. In the years just before the First World War, travelers marveled at the "strange mélange of people, accoutrements, languages and costumes" and the crowds of "turbaned heads, befezzed heads, a 'Frenk' flaunting his Western felt."[40] Salonika's 157,889 inhabitants were a gordian knot of mainly Sephardic Jews, Turkish Muslims, and Greeks, along with Bulgarians, and a mix of Serbs, Armenians, Roma, and westerners. They were divided into their own ethnic precincts, but the city's public spaces were a mishmash of people. Traversing the streets meant a profusion of encounters. The stone buildings with their red-tile roofs gave the city its Middle Eastern air. Few streets had official names. It was the Turkish cafés and bazaars, the Turkish baths, the mosques with their tapering minarets, the domed synagogues, and Byzantine churches that marked the topography. The trade along the waterfront in opium, saffron, and luxurious fabrics were a mesmerizing spectacle.

While agog at the phantasmagoria, it was the modern face of the city's crowds that most struck French urban observer Léon Abastado:

> This whole world passes by indifferently, without looking at each other. At all the tram stops the motley crowd storms the already jam-packed cars. It is not a carnivalesque procession that we see constantly strolling the streets of Thessaloniki, it is the whole of humanity that passes before the eyes, with all their miseries, every member of this great family nourishing its ideals, its chimeras."[41]

The city absorbed them all. Salonika was one of the largest industrial centers in the Balkans. Its workers were increasingly militant and well-organized. Liberty Square along the waterfront radiated the growing influence of the west with its Olympus Palace Hotel, the fashionable Patisserie Floca and Stein department store, all housed in the latest art nouveau buildings. Viennese operettas and the cinema were all the rage. The city was the base of operations for the Young Turks, the political movement determined to replace the Ottoman Empire's decrepit monarchy with western-style reforms and a constitutional government. Plots and assassinations, political rallies, and processions upended daily life. Some 20,000 refugees from the Balkan Wars flooded into Salonika. Greeks and Bulgarians were sworn enemies and fought for control of the city. Then during the First World War, the city became a major military base for the Allied Expeditionary Force disembarking for battles on the Macedonian front. The harbor and waterfront teemed with some 200,000 soldiers and tons of military equipment.

It was in the midst of this turmoil that disaster hit. In 1917, an enormous inferno destroyed two-thirds of the city. The lower city to the waterfront collapsed in a wall of flames. With it went the Ottoman appearance of Salonica. Some 80,000 people were instantly made homeless, the majority the city's Jewish residents. Tent camps and barracks were slapped together on the outskirts. Traders selling rummaged materials lined the main roads. In the years after, the conflicts between Greeks and Turks were an accretion of thuggish bloodshed, ethnic atrocities, expulsions, and deportations. Some 45,000 Turks and 6,000 Bulgarians were driven from their homes and abandoned Salonika in the forced migrations at the end of the disastrous Greek-Turkish wars. Well over a hundred thousand Greeks fled Asia Minor and crossed the Aegean to find safety in Salonika. The refugee tides continued with the compulsory exchanges mandated by the Treaty of Lausanne in 1923. Over 1 million people classified as Greeks in Turkey were swapped for some 350,000 Muslims from Greece. The "population transfers" destroyed Salonica's heritage of multiculturalism and replaced it with a dogmatic Greek national identity. The new arrivals were set up in the deserted houses of the Muslim neighborhoods. Schools and churches and warehouses were requisitioned for shelter. A sea of tents and squatter colonies littered the city and its outskirts. By that time, evacuees and the displaced numbered nearly half the population.

When Salonica reemerged, it was transformed into the modern European city of Thessaloniki. French architect Ernest Hébrard and French military engineer Joseph Pleyber were called into design the lower town along the seafront according to the classical Beaux-Arts tradition. It was a strategic choice by a Greek government anxious to "Hellenize" the city. Mosques were turned into churches. Native son Leon Sciaky watched as "Arabic characters had vanished from shop fronts and from posters stuck on the walls of corner houses, and Greek ones had taken their place."[42] Hébrard worked with Aristotelis Zachos, a Greek architect from Macedonia appointed directly by the government who had spent years exiled in Germany and had no association with the Ottoman past. An orthogonal street plan was laid out with the city's Greek monuments as focal points in a network of public spaces and long vistas. Commercial activity would be the city's new driving force. The old-fashion bazaars were replaced by modern shops. Multistory office and residential buildings lined the streets. The Ottoman fabric disappeared, except for a few select Byzantine churches and Turkish baths that were carefully preserved as a nod to the city's past.

Despite this European remake, the design for Thessaloniki was actually carried out higgidy-piggidy amid the refugee crisis and ongoing political turmoil. The city ballooned outward with little oversight other than the desperate need for housing. There was a cognitive dissonance between the planned center and the surrounding peripheries. As was often the case along the Mediterranean, urban development took place less by planning fiat than by the contingencies of land ownership and speculative real estate. While the central districts took on the air of a modern European capital, the outskirts were a mélange of residential districts with buildings in a homegrown vernacular style. The built-up area doubled in size and the population rose to nearly 250,000 by 1928. The city had been radically transformed by war and its human calamity of castaways and evacuees, by fire and rebuilding. Many of the refugees became an impoverished underclass, while others among them revitalized the city's industry and commerce, and set up new businesses in the food, textile, carpet, and tobacco industries.[43] The Greek majority controlled the city. The Jewish population was a shadow of its former self. The migratory waves continued when thousands of Jews left for Paris, where a Jewish community from Thessaloniki numbered some 20,000 by 1930. During riots in 1931, Thessaloniki's Orthodox Christians attacked Jewish families and set the Jewish suburban neighborhood of Campbell aflame. Anti-Semitic attacks continued in the 1930s. In response, another 10,000–15,000 Jews fled to Palestine in the 1930s.[44] The modern Mediterranean world was an uneasy balance between cosmopolitanism and nationalistic chauvinism, ethnic tolerance, and outright bigotry. Salonica's multicultural heritage was exchanged for ethnic cleansing.

Sweeping across the Mediterranean brings us to Barcelona. By 1930, Barcelona had become a modern industrial and commercial city of 1 million inhabitants. Its population growth was vertiginous, with its new arrivals drawn from across Spain. Yet it was distinctively a city of the Mediterranean. Bolshevik leader Leon Trotsky was escorted under arrest through Barcelona and famously described it as "Big Spanish-French kind of city. Like Nice in a hell of factories. Smoke and flames on the one hand, flowers and fruit on the other." The Barcelona International Exposition of 1929–30 was held on Montjuïc Mountain overlooking the city. A grand promenade was constructed to connect the central districts with the exposition grounds. At the same time, the municipal government undertook a series of grand-scale infrastructure projects. The old fortification rings around Montjuïc were demolished and became new public spaces. The first metro lines were opened. Local palaces were turned into cultural institutions for concerts and the opera. Tennis courts, a municipal swimming pool, and an athletic stadium provided needed recreational venues for the city. The exposition left a powerful imprint on Barcelona and gave it the trappings of a dynamic European metropolis.

Yet it was its disreputable side that most engrossed travelers and urban observers. The city was known as the capital of anarchist terrorism, of vice and crime. Its back alleys were governed by raw instinct and passion. The dilapidated Barrio Chino near the harbor was a hidden maze of narrow streets and smoke-filled dives, Flamenco dance halls, prostitutes, spies and informers. Its infamy was heightened by a tabloid press on the hunt for scintillating material on the "turbulent and shadowy streets of this picturesque and depraved neighbor-hood." French writer Henry de Montherlant described its denizens as "these men, if you observe them, have a bounty of gestures, of looks, of words, of graffiti, of obscene blasphemies . . . always goaded by erotic obsession."[45] Cities along the Mediterranean straddled the line between urban modernity and the exotic world of the Orient. Visitors to Barcelona could submit to both, touring the flashy exposition pavilions and then descending into the steamy underworld of the Barrio Chino. Or they could stroll Paral-lel Street and imbibe the popular entertainment in its bars and dance halls, jazz clubs and cabarets. Barcelona was a place of otherness, of libertine pleasure punctuated by working-class protest and violence.

The new athletic stadium was to welcome the International Workers' Olympiad in 1936. But the onset of the Spanish Civil War dashed these hopes. The civil war sparked uprisings in Barcelona, Madrid, and throughout the towns of Spain. It revealed the social incongruities that plagued the urban realm, despite the appearance of modernity. On the one hand, municipal reforms and the massive public works projects undertaken for the exposition provided a sense of real optimism. Wealth was amassed by rich speculators and the city's powerful industrial elites. The stable working class and members of the lower-middle class lived well enough to indulge in the city's entertainments. Cinemas and dance halls, rolling skating, and football matches were immensely popular. They found decent lodgings along the fringes of the Eixample and joined local Catalan groups and cultural societies. Barcelona's working people saw themselves as urban and modern, and yet stuck within an archaic Spanish nation controlled by Madrid. The radical left-wing and anarchist movements drew their support precisely from these Catalan patriots.[46] On the other hand, the poorer working classes and immigrants seethed with accumulated grievances. Their labor constructed modern Barcelona, but they were stuck in the neglected spaces of the city where housing and services were a misery. For an increasingly angry working class, the skyrocketing cost of living outstripped paltry wages. The city's old neighborhoods of La Barceloneta and L'Hospitalet were a jumble of shanty towns inhabited by fishermen, factory and dockworkers, where only market gardens and informal street trading alleviated the grim poverty. It was only a short distance from the fashionable crowds promenading under the plane trees along Las Ramblas.

The anger boiled over into the city's streets. Strikes and demonstrations regularly broke into ferocious street fighting. Bombings and assassinations were the flip side of the rakish, fiery Mediterranean city, and disrupted the exposition's veneer of urban modernity. The jarring juxtaposition between violence and entertainment was an all too evident part of public life. Finally, in 1936 the city's workers came to the defense of the Spanish Republic threatened by Spain's right-wing armed coup. After days of bloody street fighting, the workers of Barcelona took over the factories and launched a radical experiment in collectivization.[47] Then in the May Days of 1937, Barcelona was torn apart by the vicious struggle between left-wing factions supporting the Republic. The entire city took up arms. The streets were littered with barricades. People dashed through the streets, dodging barrages of machine gun and rifle fire. Bodies littered the pavement. George Orwell reported the scenes in his 1938 account *Homage to Catalonia*:

> The whole huge town of a million people was locked in a sort of violent inertia, a nightmare of noise without movement. The sunlit streets were quite empty. Nothing was happening except the streaming of bullets from barricades and sand-bagged windows. Not a vehicle was stirring in the streets; here and there along the Ramblas the trams stood motionless where the drivers had jumped out of them when the fighting started. And all the while the devilish noise, echoing from thousands of stone buildings, went on and on and on, like a tropical rainstorm.[48]

Thousands were killed, thousands wounded during the Spanish Civil War in Barcelona. Finally, between 1937 and 1939, the city suffered nearly 400 bombing raids by the Italian Air Force of General Franco's ally, Benito Mussolini. The Metro tunnels were the only safe place from the shelling and explosions in the embattled city. The port and working-class areas along the harbor were obliterated. In the 1938 propaganda film "Catalunya Martir" (Martyred Catalonia)[49] cameramen descended into the streets to record the trauma, the shocking devastation, and deadly toll of the bombing attacks. In January 1939, Barcelona fell to Franco's nationalist forces. His armies marched triumphantly down Las Ramblas. It was a portent of things to come.

CHAPTER 10
SEARCHING THROUGH THE RUBBLE (1939–50s)

The Second World War was fought for and in cities, from the bombing of London across Europe to Stalingrad on the Volga. More civilians than soldiers lost their lives. The German historian Karl Schlögel refers to the war's devastation as "urbicide," the systematic annihilation of a city, its inhabitants, and its history.[1] Railways, seaports and airports, roads and bridges, heavy industry across Europe were systematically destroyed. London and Coventry were obliterated. In the Netherlands, Rotterdam was all but wiped off the map. In Italy, Naples, Milan, Turin, Pisa, Verona all grievously suffered. In France, Le Havre, Caen, Rouen, Brest, Lyons, Marseille were devastated. Allied attacks with high-explosive bombs reduced Dresden and Hamburg to a wall of flames. In eastern Europe, the wasteland of ruins was caused by German Luftwaffe air raids and Blitzkrieg warfare, Russian artillery bombardment, and by systematic destruction carried out by the Germans as they retreated. The Anglo-American air raids during the last year of the war added to the fiasco. Wreckage and rubble stretched across the continent. Leningrad, Kiev, Kraków, Berlin, and Warsaw were decimated. The toll from the Soviet siege and Allied bombardments in Budapest was staggering. Two waves of aerial bombardment rained down on Belgrade and nearly half the housing stock damaged or destroyed. The Allied bombing raids on Sofia in Bulgaria decimated thousands of buildings and killed or injured thousands of people (Figure 51).

Warsaw has come to embody the catastrophe the war wrecked on Europe's cities. On September 1, 1939, the German Luftwaffe pummeled Warsaw with Stuka dive bombers. In the weeks that followed, around 20,000 to 25,000 civilians were killed, 40 percent of the buildings were severely damaged and 10 percent completed destroyed. Initially, the Jewish population in Warsaw dramatically increased as thousands of refugees fled the military front. The Jewish districts of Muranów, Powązki, and Stara Praga were packed with people. The Nazi authorities expelled all ethnic Poles from these neighborhoods and ordered the transfer of thousands of Jews from the surrounding suburbs into the three districts. In October 1940, the Jewish ghetto, covering about 2.5 percent of the area of Warsaw, was walled off with ten-foot high walls and watchtowers. The ghetto's 500,000 prisoners lived under appalling conditions. Disease and starvation claimed thousands. The only real means of survival was smuggling and barter. In 1941, the German SS began the "resettlement" of Jews, the euphemism for annihilation, to the east. Some 300,000 men, women, and children were packed into cattle cars and sent to the Treblinka death camp. This left a Jewish population of some 60,000 people in Warsaw's Ghetto. When they were warned of final deportation, they prepared themselves with small arms and Molotov cocktails and faced off with the German SS units. The Jews held out against

Figure 51 A view of rubble and ruined buildings covering the streets after the German bombing of Warsaw, 1939.

overwhelming force for twenty-seven days before they were finally crushed. Those not killed in the uprising were deported to Treblinka. The ghetto was burned to the ground building by building and the entire area reduced to rubble. Warsaw's Great Synagogue was blown up in fiery celebration of the German victory.

The Nazis planned the complete liquidation of Polish Warsaw. Hitler envisioned the city as a provincial German town of 100,000 people in his quest for *lebensraum*, or living space for the German race. Planners drafted drawings and a miniature model of a picturesque German settlement with only the Polish Royal Castle left to serve as Hitler's residence. By 1944, when it became apparent that Warsaw would fall into the hands of the Allied forces, an unprecedented effort was made to destroy anything left of the city. Special destruction detachments demolished house after house, turned streets into rubble, and dynamited underground installations. In a blatant attack on Polish intellectual heritage, the city's national monuments, libraries, and archives were systematically obliterated. In response, the Polish Resistance, or Home Army, staged a second Warsaw Uprising to liberate the city from German occupation. The uprising was timed to coincide with the Soviet Union's Red Army approach in the eastern suburbs as the German forces retreated. But the Soviet advance was stopped short by Stalin, enabling the Germans to regroup and demolish the city while defeating the Polish resistance. Brutal street fighting took place under a barrage of German artillery and air power. A German officer wrote in his diary that "almost all Warsaw is a sea of flames." By January 1945, between 85 and 90 percent of Warsaw had been destroyed. The entire population had vanished. They either fled or were dead or were hiding in a ghostly scene of devastation.

Searching through the Rubble (1939–50s)

Minutes after the announcement that war had begun in September 1939, air-raid sirens screamed over London. Everyone expected the bombs to rain down. They knew what to expect from the blitzkrieg attack on Warsaw. Trainloads of children were evacuated and sent to the countryside or to the United States with their name pinned to their clothes. Windows in London buildings were crisscrossed with tape and walls reinforced. Street and directional signs were taken down. The blackout plunged London into a pitch-black gloom each night. Every Londoner received a gas mask. Air-raid shelters were set up. The Blitz began in September 1940 when German bombers destroyed the London Docklands in the East End. Warehouses, factories, and miles of docks were a surreal scene of towering flames and smoke. When the Luftwaffe launched a second massive raid, hundreds of British Spitfire and Hurricane aircraft battled the attackers. Daring residents ran outside to watch the dogfights in the skies over the city. For the next few months, London endured the constant pounding of German bombardments. St. Paul's Cathedral was set ablaze, lighting up the streets for miles around. The Houses of Parliament and Westminster Abby were wrecked. The Blitz reached its peak of terror on May 10, 1941, when the Luftwaffe flew more than 500 missions over London in one night. By the end of the Battle of Britain, virtually every historic landmark had been ripped by bombs or gutted by fire. Tens of thousands of stores, offices, factories had disappeared. Over a million homes were gone, whole neighborhoods demolished. Some 20,000 people died and well over 20,000 wounded.

On June 22, 1941, 3 million German soldiers attacked the Soviet Union. It was the last of Hitler's Blitzkrieg strikes and the greatest military campaign in history. Stalin drained Leningrad (St. Petersburg) of ammunition and supplies to protect Moscow from the invasion. The military commander in charge of Leningrad, General Andrey Zhdanov, worked feverishly to prepare the city for the onslaught. Hundreds of thousands of children were evacuated. Thousands of citizens were mobilized to construct a 200-mile defense barrier, the Luga Line, southwest of the city. Others cobbled together shelters and dug trenches. Tens of thousands of men, women, and teenagers joined the "People's Volunteers" and held off the German Wehrmacht for nearly three weeks. Finally, the Germans broke through and cut Leningrad off from the rest of the Soviet Union in a death grip. Hitler made a calculated decision to starve the city's 3.4 million people into submission. From 1941 to 1944, thousands of German bombs rained down on Leningrad each day. Over 3,000 buildings were destroyed. German bombers hit the city's warehouses. Starving people watched helplessly as the remaining food supplies went up in flames. A million people died of hunger and another 750,000 died in the attacks before food began to arrive by truck across the frozen mass of Lake Ladoga.

Even in those places that did not suffer this kind of horrendous destruction, life during the German occupation was calamitous. Cities were gray and empty. Nightly blackouts, curfews, and punitive public repression curtailed any and all suspicious activities. The Gestapo units were ever present. Street traffic was restricted. All public signage was switched to German; public clocks were set to Berlin time. Only Germans had access to gasoline and automobiles; everyone else resorted to walking or bikes. The German occupation forces confiscated food, goods, animals, machinery, and simply stole whatever they could. As the war dragged on, food shortages engulfed daily life. Rich or poor, everyone was given ration coupons for a weekly modicum of sustenance. Illicit trade and the black market were the only way to survive. People watched as Jewish men, women, and children were rounded up and marched off to detention centers, and then to the extermination camps. This took place in full view on the streets. The horrifying scenes were too numerous to recount. In 1942, the French police rounded up some 13,000 French Jews in Paris and herded them into the Velodrome d'hiver stadium north of the city. They were left without food, water, or sanitation before they were deported to Auschwitz. In 1943, the Germans launched the Factory Action in Berlin. Thousands of Jews were seized from their place of work and loaded onto wagons for Auschwitz.

The Allied bombing raids over Europe's cities added yet another layer of destruction. In March 1942, over 200 British Royal Air Force (RAF) bombers attacked the German Baltic port of Lübeck and destroyed the city's medieval heart with incendiary bombs. Raids against the Baltic ports of Rostock and Kiel followed. These attacks so enraged Hitler that he ordered Luftwaffe strikes on the historic English towns of Exeter, Bath, Norwich, York, and Canterbury. In May 1942, the British bomber offensive took a huge leap into the surreal with the first 1,000-plane raid against the German city of Cologne. The massive force devastated the city's center. By far the most horrific raids took place in 1943 in Operation Gomorrah against Hamburg, Germany's second largest city. In July 1943, 800 RAF bombers dropped high-explosive incendiary and phosphorus bombs on the city. The attack converged into a catastrophic firestorm. A one-and-half-mile-wide column of superheated air rose 8,000 feet in the sky, sucking out oxygen and suffocating thousands of people, uprooting trees, collapsing buildings, and hurling people into the flames. Another attack followed in late July and a final one in early August in what became one of the worst orgies of death and destruction perpetrated by military attack during the war. The raids wiped out nine square miles of the city and killed at least 60,000 people. Another 750,000 people were left homeless. British Bomber Command struck at many other German cities during 1943, culminating in a series of sixteen devastating raids on Berlin in the last ferocious battle of the war.

In 1942, during one of the worst years of the war, architect José Luis Sert and his CIAM colleagues penned a small volume entitled *Can Our Cities Survive?* When it was published, the question was not a rhetorical one. It was an apocalyptic moment, when the dystopic scenes of urbicide came to represent the end of the world. To walk around European cities at the end of the Second World War was to walk through acres of rubble and bomb craters and the deserted carcasses of once vibrant places. The American diplomat George Kennan passed through the Finnish city of Vyborg in September 1945, which had been fought over twice since 1939:

> The onetime modern Finnish town of Vyborg . . . was, so far as I could see, devoid of habitation. . . . I took refuge . . . in what had been the doorway of a fine modern department store, now gutted and wrecked. . . . Looking around, I discovered that I was sharing the shelter of the doorway with a goat. The two of us, it seemed, were for the moment the sole inhabitants of this once thriving modern city.

Searching through the Rubble (1939–50s)

Alfred Döblin, who had written so expressively about effervescent Berlin in the 1920s, visited the destroyed city and saw "images of terrible devastation, of immeasurable boundless destruction. . . . It almost no longer has the character of reality . . . an improbable nightmare in broad daylight."[2]

There was a perverse fascination with the eradication of centuries of urban development. Once the fighting stopped, the skeletal remains of cities were documented in a vast photographic and newsreel record by the victorious armies and a phalanx of journalists, their camera equipment in tow. The emotional power of these images was enormous. This was especially true of the scenes of obliteration in Warsaw and Berlin. The black-and-white film and photographs surveyed a sinister landscape of crumbling buildings with their guts exposed, piles of rubble, empty forlorn streets. The pictures did not capture the dead nor corpses scattered about, the few living amid the wreckage. Instead, they exaggerated the sense of nothingness, a suspension of life. The ghostly remains were a bizarre nightmare, or perhaps more like an aesthetic of ruins. They also stood as stark witness to the tragedy. The first film made in Poland after the war rendered the fate of Warsaw in heartbreaking detail. It was shown as part of the "Warsaw Accuses!" exhibition held at the National Museum of Warsaw in 1945. The exhibit spoke for the extraordinary cultural loss and toured Europe and the United States as testimony and propaganda for rebuilding. For the survivors of the city's destruction, viewing photographs and films of the "dead" city was an emotional experience that triggered an immediate search for the past, for memories. Memory books with pictures and recollections were eagerly published.[3] Collecting and viewing photographs of the urban fabric, its streets and landmarks as they had been before the catastrophe was a form of commemoration and mourning. Side-by-side comparisons of the historic city before, the pictures of ruin, and then the new face of the reconstructed city became extraordinary talismans. The sequence of photos told the story of the putting back together of home and identity.

With the war's end came a massive movement of brutalized and shell-shocked people. Thousands upon thousands were victims of postwar savagery as armies occupied and liberated cities. Rape and murder were the revenges of war. Millions were left homeless and gathered into barrack-shelters and displaced persons (DP) camps. This immense dislocation of people ended up remolding national demographics and facilitating the ruthless ethnic cleansing. Jewish survivors of the death and labor camps were ferried through emergency services and found their way home. Especially in eastern Europe, they were encouraged to leave permanently by emigration policies. Many migrated to the United States and to the new state of Israel. Some 11 million forced laborers and prisoners of war in German and Soviet territories returned to their homelands and sometimes migrated again. Millions of civilians who had been evacuated from the fighting zones set off back to see what was left in the wreckage. As territorial boundaries were redrawn in eastern Europe, millions more became refugees and exiles, forced to leave their homes behind and flee west. Around 1.5 million Poles were forced out of the Soviet Union and the western Ukraine. Hungarians fled Romania and Slovakia. Italians escaped Yugoslavia. Germans in eastern Europe were swept into concentration camps and awaited deportation. They were expelled en masse, especially from Poland and Bohemia. Before long, Germans were pushed out of the Soviet occupied zone of East Germany as well. Millions fled west to escape newly established communist rule. Altogether the population movements in eastern Europe involved 15 million to 20 million people. The most significant exodus was some 12 million people into West Germany before the border was closed by the Iron Curtain.[4]

The shadow of war was long in Europe. The winters of 1945 and 1946 were among the coldest on record. Europeans were still suffering food and fuel shortages. Access to heating fuel became a matter of life and death. Hunger haunted everyone and every place. Ration cards provided the bare minimum of food, supplemented by the swindles of the black market. The working classes and modest middle classes, the aged, widows, and single women suffered most. People in destroyed, or even intact, cities lacked clothes, shoes, domestic gear, tools. In those countries with functioning currencies, severe inflation robbed people of resources. Where the monetary system collapsed, people resorted to barter, often using cigarettes as money. Unsurprisingly, by 1947 a wave of strikes and unrest swept over the continent. In Paris, the 30,000 workers in the Renault factory walked out and French labor unions called for a general strike. In Łódź, the walkouts shook the city.

Although these scenes of destruction and chaos in the war's aftermath left a powerful legacy, what was most striking was how quickly cities actually returned to life. The city was celebrated as the ultimate expression of the will to live. People relished the end of suffering and exploded out on to the streets. Markets opened, orchestras played, and theaters staged performances. Boisterous parades and ceremonies commemorated wartime victories and celebrated heroes. Buildings and urban spaces were sanctified in the task of reconciliation and remembrance. Young people bolted out of hiding, mixed with occupying troops, danced and socialized in bistros and cabarets that opened seemingly out of nowhere. Parisian Colette Bouisson remembered that "after four years of immobility an explosion of dance shook the city. There had never been so many evenings of dance, places to dance . . . here the waltz, there the tango or even the charleston."[5] After so much misery, people just wanted some normalcy and the chance for some happiness.

The reconstruction of Europe's cities was nothing short of a miracle. The scale of rebuilding carried out by untold numbers of people made this one of the most prodigious moments in Europe's history. In city after city, men and especially women spontaneously cleared away mountains of rubble. Even in cities that were entirely ruined, there were buildings still standing that were cobbled together as temporary shelters. Building foundations, brick and stone were salvaged and reused. Volunteer brigades repaired roads and put water and sewage back in operation. Every restored government had to make the reconstruction of cities its main priority. Nevertheless, exactly how they should be rebuilt was a political quagmire and the subject of ferocious debate. The massive wartime devastation unleashed a passionate desire to restore what had been lost. The immediate sentiment was to restore cities as phoenix arising from the ashes (Figure 52).

Searching through the Rubble (1939–50s)

Figure 52 A group of volunteers working to rebuild Dresden.

Local builders and engineers went to work. The construction industry boomed. Jobs were there for the taking. European countries opened their doors to foreign workers. The line between displaced person and who constituted a "foreign worker" became murkier as refugees and DPs were tapped to help rebuild with promises of employment and a new life. Thousands of migrants from southern Europe and guest workers recruited from Turkey, North Africa, and the former European colonies made their way to devastated cities and took up hammer and nail. Restoring time-honored urban places symbolized a tenacious hold on national spirit. The city was understood as an artifact of identity. People wanted their city back—the historic buildings, the landmarks, and visual features that they recognized and made places distinctive before the war. Despite the desperate need for housing, historic monuments were often the first structures to be rebuilt as a sign of patriotic resilience. Thousands upon thousands of ordinary buildings across Europe were rehabilitated much as they had been before. The known patterns of streets and public spaces reemerged from the wreckage. These currents resulted in a pragmatic "reconstruction style" under the strained conditions of the early postwar years. Despite pleas from radical modernists, there was no clean sweep of the past. An idiosyncratic patina of regional and national stylistic traditions merged with modernism.[6] It took decades to rebuild and the layers of memory and meaning were blatantly clear in the renewed urban fabric.

Architects and urban reformers seized the opportunity of destruction to imagine ways to preserve the past. The Normandy coast of France was the scene of the famous Allied invasion of Europe in 1944. Allied planes blanket-bombed its cities in preparation for the amphibious landing. The port of Le Havre and the city of Caen were among the primary targets and both were bombed to smithereens. They were Normandy's largest towns. At the war's end the renowned French architect Auguste Perret was handed the job of rebuilding Le Havre. His design became one of Europe's most celebrated examples of reconstruction style. Perret envisioned Le Havre in the European classical tradition. The traditional street pattern and placement of public buildings was carefully preserved. Straight streets, linear axes and open coastal views, controlled building heights created a refined urban ensemble of reemergence. The buildings in reinforced concrete were simple with repeating window treatments, the exposed walls softened with a variety of textures. The modest flats were open and airy. They hovered over shops on the ground floors, many with open colonnades to carry out the classical motif. Perret's formal design gave the city an impressive order and elegance. It was assembled around a grand boulevard that extended from the rail station to the monumental place de l'Hôtel de Ville, and then to the beach and the sea beyond.

It took years for reconstruction to be completed. Although places like Le Havre enjoyed immediate acclaim, innumerable towns in Europe faced a long unnoticed road to recovery and utilitarian patching up typical of the late 1940s and 1950s. Money, building materials, volunteer and labor forces were channeled into countless rebuilding programs. The town of Giessen in Germany's Hesse region, just north of Frankfurt, suffered devastating bombardment in 1944 that destroyed over 75 percent of the town. After violent street battles, the city was captured by American armed forces. It then became an American army garrison and supply depot. Voluntary crews cleared away the rubble for years. The city was slowly rebuilt in the sparse reconstruction style typical of the 1950s. Only in 1955 did the economy recover enough to support a few thousand jobs.[7] The town of Zadar on the Mediterranean coast in Croatia was bombed over seventy times by the Allies and left in complete ruin. What had been a town of 24,000 people dwindled to 6,000 souls. Recovery lasted over a decade. Although no end of utopian schemes were laid out for rebuilding the city, reconstruction was a mixture of politics and aesthetic compromises.[8] Since Zadar had been under the tutelage of Italy and briefly occupied by German forces, any traces of the fascist past were immediately expunged. The city's venerable Italian population escaped revenge at the war's end and fled the city. Incorporated into Yugoslavia, Zadar was remade by its new communist overseers as a decidedly Croatian city. The ancient cobble-strewn street grid was carefully preserved and the center city deliberately restored as it had looked in earlier times. This historicist renewal took place alongside experiments in concrete slab apartment buildings along the outskirts. They were slapped up in the hurried effort to put roofs over the heads of desperate families. The public outcry for housing dominated urban policy in both western and eastern Europe—on both sides of the Iron Curtain—for years after the war.

The idea of "Eastern Europe" had always been a work of geographic imagination. But exactly where it was located became crystal clear in the division of the continent in the war's aftermath. The territory that became known as the Eastern Bloc was dramatically cut off from the West and its border hardened by the Iron Curtain. It stretched, in the words of Winston Churchill in his famous 1946 speech, "from Stettin in the Baltic to Trieste in the Adriatic." This new political geography overruled all previous categories of eastern Europe, southeastern Europe, the Balkans, or the Baltic. Cities were consigned by geography to the Soviet sphere of influence either by legal means or by force. The territorial boundary split Germany into eastern and western partitions. It slid southward carving the frontier between Austria and Hungary. The communist seizure of power set off another wave of refugees headed toward western Germany and Austria. Draconian policies were put in place to stop the leakage and prevent any further emigration from the Eastern Bloc. Labor and human capital were needed to rebuild war-devastated countries. The economies of eastern Europe were nationalized and planned along Soviet lines. On Moscow's instructions, each nation declined participation in the Marshall Plan for European economic recovery. Instead, the Cominform, or Communist Information Bureau, was set up as a countermeasure, first in Belgrade and then in Bucharest.

The reconstruction of cities in the Eastern Bloc proceeded under Soviet control. Unsurprisingly, the rebuilding of Warsaw was especially fraught with political tension. Poland suffered staggering losses during the war and postwar deportation schemes. Between 5.6 and 5.8 million people, some 16 percent of the country's total population, had perished, including 3 million Jews. Poland lost another 7 million Germans to expulsion. The trail of destruction across the country was immense. Although many Polish towns and cities suffered devastation, the reconstruction of Warsaw was the ultimate testimony to national resurrection. Proposals flew off the drawing boards, including abandoning the city altogether and preserving it as a war memorial. As was frequently the case in the war's aftermath, the residents of Warsaw instinctively returned to the shattered city and "voted with their feet" for rebuilding. Despite the appalling destruction, by 1946 Warsaw's population already reached 500,000. People found shelter where they could and squatted in ruined flats. In his 1953 exposé *The Captive Mind*, author Czesław Miłosz recounts

> his first stroll along a street littered with glass from bomb-shattered windows. . . . Further down the street, he stops before a house split in half by a bomb, the privacy of human homes—the family smells, the warmth of the beehive life, their furniture preserving the memory of loves and hatreds—cut open to public view. . . . Its formerly influential and respected owners, now destitute, walk the fields in search of stray potatoes.[9]

Relief agencies, the black market, and smugglers stitched together supplies of basic goods. Semi-tolerated street markets operated an illicit trade in everything from cosmetics to American military gear. The tempo of Warsaw's life returned with amazing speed.

Preservationists allied with the Polish resistance movement called for reconstructing the center of Warsaw in the monumental style of the historic capital. The landscape of ruins quickly became a revered shrine and provoked a patriotic desire to restore the city's heritage as a symbol of Polish identity. The proposal met with violent attacks from those who saw in the *tabula rasa* of devastation the possibility of an entirely new city. But the hue and cry for restoration was too loud to ignore. The communist leaders of the Polish People's Republic supported a loving rebuilding of Warsaw's Old Town on the embankment overlooking the Vistula River and the Royal Route. The core of the capital would be revived as a nostalgic vision of the Warsaw that had endured for centuries. Architects used eighteenth-century panoramic cityscapes by Venetian artist Bernardo Bellotto as a reference guide. The Stalinist policy of socialist realism in architecture corresponded to this Polish patriotic sentiment. This synthesis between nationalist and socialist agendas was a key component of reconstruction. "National in form, socialist in content" championed the expression of historic styles in rebuilding as a way to capture popular feeling in the cause of communism. At least in architecture, communism would march forward to the past. Warsaw's Old Town reappeared as a dreamy hallucination of the historic European city (Figure 53).

The remainder of Warsaw was transformed into a visionary socialist city on neoclassical lines. Constitution Square was a display of socialist realism and monumental site for parades and festivals. It was the people's assembly place and opened on to a transformed Marszałkowska Boulevard. The ensemble was inaugurated in 1952 with a spectacular celebration. The new buildings surrounding the square were draped in banners and sculptural bass-reliefs acclaiming the workers and engineers who had toiled in their construction. Pageants and parades rejoiced in the capital's miraculous resurrection.[10] In the Muranów district of the former Jewish ghetto, the rubble was left in place and the new building foundations built directly into the ruins as commemoration of the human catastrophe. Hundreds of rebuilding projects around Warsaw were featured in a series of public exhibitions in 1950–51. Public solidarity was enormous. Warsaw was

Figure 53 Plac Konstytucji, Marszalkowska Street, Warsaw, 1956.

the symbol of the entire nation. Thousands of people were involved in its reconstruction. Young people joined up in voluntary construction brigades. Stakhanovite workers were lionized as they rebuilt the capital brick-by-brick. They were celebrated in music and art. One of the best-known paintings in Poland was artist Aleksander Kobzdej's *Pass Me the Brick!* (1950) that portrayed three bricklayers as magnificent heroic figures working on a building site. Poland's first feature-length color film *Przygoda na Mariensztacie* (Adventure in Mariensztac) followed the budding romance between two young bricklayers. The opening of each restored section of the capital was hailed in July each year with festivals and parades of young people waving banners on high acclaiming the capital. "Heroic Warsaw" was fixed in communist mythology as a sign of the future.

Although Warsaw was an exceptional case, the drama of reconstruction took place across eastern Europe. Rebuilding cities played a vital role in jump-starting socialist society in the territories controlled by the Soviet Union. Cityscapes and architecture became political pageantry. The 1945 decree that declared all land as communal property made reconstruction more straightforward than was the case in western Europe. From the Baltic to the Black Sea, from capital cities to small towns, ostentation and monumentality paid tribute to the new socialist world order. Yet the future of cities initially looked to the past. City after city followed the path of socialist realism and stayed faithful to national architectural heritage as reconstruction form. What appeared to be contradictory perspectives coexisted. National building styles and ornamentation were charged with symbolic meaning. In communist East Germany (the German Democratic Republic or GDR) a National Reconstruction Program designated Berlin, Dresden, Leipzig, Magdeburg, and Rostock as priorities. What was left of the entire historic center of Berlin was incorporated into the Soviet sector of the city. The ruined Stadtschloss or City Castle, a foremost symbol of Prussian militarism, was ritualistically demolished. The few Prussian civic buildings allowed to reemerge were Humboldt University, the Opera House, and the State Library on the Unter den Linden. They were rebuilt in their original historic styles. The flagship socialist boulevard in Berlin was Stalinallee. It was the penultimate example of socialist realism. The boulevard was a theater of propaganda. It was widened for military parades and demonstrations, flanked by creamy white neoclassical apartment buildings, and decorated with socialist realist murals and sculptures.[11] In Dresden, rebuilding favored baroque along the main boulevard of the Thälmannstrasse. In Rostock, the Lange Strasse was reconstructed with buildings in gothic brick, a trademark of Hanseatic cities. The Hanseatic town of Lübeck as well reappeared in medieval gothic guise with its signature turreted gates and warehouses.

Despite looking backward for architectural heritage, socialist realism was ultimately about the creation of the New Socialist Man. The city was seen as the vanguard of modernity and an educational tableau meant to awaken society from the moribund torpor of capitalism. Infrastructure and rebuilding were a form of indoctrination as political repression descended on eastern Europe. "Palaces of Culture" soared over towns still reeling from war. They were lavish towers in the wedding-cake style of Stalinist architecture, their construction a propagandistic celebration of Soviet friendship, joy, and optimism. In Warsaw, the Palace of Culture and Science rose thirty stories high and spread over an entire neighborhood razed to the ground to make way for construction. Inside was a salute to socialist culture: a sumptuous congress hall and ballrooms, theaters and cinemas, club rooms, and swimming pool. Domestic life for the working classes was relegated to the spartan flats rising on the city peripheries. Instead, collective life and work were the focus of communism. Showy entrances into factories and steelworks signified the Five-Year Plans and communist commitment to economic recovery. City centers became a spectacle of monuments. Heroic stone and marble sculptures to the Soviet liberators adorned public squares. Soviet tanks were made into shrines. Colossal statues of Stalin surveyed the public domain as a viscous cult of personality descended over the Eastern Bloc. Ceremonial squares and *magistral* boulevards were saturated with patriotic insignia. Countless banners screeching communist slogans swung from building facades. Public festivals were revived to celebrate historic events and socialist anniversaries added to the annual calendar of festivities. Grandly orchestrated World Youth Festivals took place in Prague in 1947, followed by Budapest in 1949, East Berlin in 1951, Bucharest in 1953, and Warsaw in 1955. Over 30,000 people from over a hundred countries took part in Moscow's 1957 Youth Festival. They paraded through the city and ended with a mass spectacle of marching phalanxes and undulating banners in the newly opened Lenin Central Stadium. It was a phantasmagoria of color and music, and for many participants, a life-changing experience.

The Cold War counterpart to these communist dreams in the east was Western Europe, which reemerged as the capitalist bloc under the tutelage of the new American colossus. There, reconstructing cities meant modernization and a better way of life based around material consumption. Beginning in July 1945, the United States poured resources into Europe through the United Nations Relief & Rehabilitation Administration. Then the Marshall Plan facilitated a stream of aid, machinery and goods to countries desperately in need. The public was treated to a slew of expositions at the war's end meant to showcase the new ideals of abundance, mass consumption, and the living standards that went with them. Modernity was domesticated and made available to everyman. After years of deprivation, millions of people strolled through displays of visionary city plans and spanking-new infrastructure. The shows highlighted a cornucopia of household consumer goods in gleaming plastics and formica, electrical appliances, designs for houses and home interiors. Modern forms of living that had been revolutionary in the 1920s were now displayed as reconstruction style. The Marshall Plan and US officials unleashed an unprecedented propaganda campaign for the "American Way of Life" in which consumerism and material accumulation defined citizenship. A flood of American companies headed across the Atlantic to set up shop. Coca-Cola, Kellogg's, and Kraft Foods opened for business in Europe and hawked American-style soft drinks, cornflake cereal, and mayonnaise. They dangled these lures along with the satisfaction of every consumer desire at a generic place Americans ingenuously called "Europe," by which they meant "Western Europe." For some in "Europe," this American onslaught was an affront. The intellectual reaction was virulent. American mass culture was condemned as vulgar. But for millions of ordinary people desperate for a better life and decent home, the dreamland of American consumerism just seemed mesmerizing.

Notwithstanding the postwar economic miracle and the easy optimism of the Americans, the majority of people in Europe still lived frugally on tight budgets, many of them hand to mouth. Austerity was the watchword of the day. Rationing was not fully lifted until the mid-1950s. The housing shortage was a way of life. Flats were scarce and expensive. A decent apartment remained an elusive dream for many a young married couple. Food was the primary expenditure in household budgets. Governments tried to manage expectations with campaigns about making-do and the benefits of a spartan lifestyle. Against this backdrop of scarcity and the thorny ambivalence about flashy Americanism, the reconstruction expositions were an immense success. The 1946 Exposition of American Techniques in Building and Urban Design at the Grand Palais in Paris featured American tools and equipment such as bulldozers and scrapers for road work as well as housing prefabrication techniques that were adopted by the largest European construction firms. American model homes, with tags such as "the Arcadia," the "Woolaway house," and "the Jeep" were built in the suburbs of Paris, London, Berlin. The international exposition on Urbanism and Habitat took place at the Grand Palais the following year. Nine European countries participated in a sweeping showcase of visionary plans. The primordial significance of housing was demonstrated by the exposition's declaration that "the house . . . is the most essential of human necessities. It should satisfy the needs of the body, that of the spirit, those of the individual, the family, the nation, and those of society as a whole: it is the clearest sign of the level and quality of civilization." Attendance at the 1951 Salon des Arts Ménagers alone reached well over 1 million.[12] Parisians drooled over the displays of ideal kitchens equipped with the latest appliances, washing machines, and sleek furniture.

Other cities held their own glimpses of the future. In May 1940 Nazi bombers swept over Rotterdam and pounded the city with thousands of tons of high explosives. It turned into an inferno. The entire city was obliterated. With the war's end, an army of 20,000–30,000 people cleared away millions of cubic meters of rubble. What was left of the underground network of pipes and sewer lines was dug up. Then the city began to rebuild. A series of exhibitions celebrated the city's reemergence: "Rotterdam in the Near Future" (1947), "The City on the Maas Gets Back on its Feet" (1949), and "Rotterdam Ahoy!" (1950) pumped up public optimism. Many of these shows were sponsored by Marshall Plan administrators and idealized domestic life chock-full of the latest consumer appliances made in America. In 1949, the US Office of Military Government in West Germany sponsored a show in Frankfurt on "How America Lives." The West Berlin Marshall House Pavilion with its dream of domestic comfort bedazzled tens of thousands of Berliners each week. The GDR countered in 1953 with a show in East Berlin on "Living Better, Dwelling More Beautifully."[13] The VDNKh exhibitions in the 1950s in Moscow and the capital cities of the Soviet Republics celebrated the achievements of the communist economy with eye-popping displays and new products. The pioneering Eastern Bloc exhibit "Apartment for Our Circumstances" took place in Ljubljana in 1956. But communist influences crisscrossed with western imagery in exhibits such as the "This is America" exposition and the Museum of Modern Art's "Built in the USA" that toured eastern Europe's cities in the 1950s (Figure 54).

Figure 54 The Royal Festival Hall and other specially-erected buildings at the site of the Festival of Britain on the South Bank of the River Thames, London 1951.

The 1951 Festival of Britain was undoubtedly the most heroic of these reconstruction era extravaganzas. It was held in a bombed-out area on the South Bank in London that had been left rubble-strewn from the Blitz. Despite shortages of labor and material, the breathtaking Dome of Discovery and Skylon mast took shape as visions of the future. The festival was publicized as a "tonic for the nation" and a showcase for the achievements of Britain. It was the British public's first encounter with modern architecture, especially the Royal Festival Hall in brilliant white concrete with an expansive glass facade and suspended concert auditorium.[14] Thousands of visitors strolled through enticing prototypes of future homes, neighborhoods, and new towns. The Festival of Britain's "live architecture" exhibition was located on the Isle of Dogs in London's decimated East End, where over a million houses had been destroyed and thousands killed during the Nazi Blitz. The display simulated an English pastoral village meant to appeal to a broad British public optimistic about the future yet yearning for a romanticized past. The festival was opulent promotional machinery for reconstruction and British welfare reforms. Beyond the London site, festival exhibitions took place in towns and cities throughout Britain in a nation-wide celebration.

A generation of modernist architects was waiting for this moment to resurrect civilization. Experimental housing projects flew off the drawing boards and into the hands of construction companies. Giant cranes hung over the skyline in cities across Europe. The dust and debris of construction sites, the infernal din of bulldozers and building equipment became a way of life. Desperate families eking out existence in

Searching through the Rubble (1939–50s)

temporary camps and crumbling slums were evacuated to system-built housing units in the suburbs. The completion of each new building was celebrated with the fanfare once reserved for royalty. The Sarcelles housing estate, begun in 1954 in the open fields north of Paris, was one of the first prototypes. It became a byword for all the triumphs and failures of the grand endeavor to build a better future for Europe's young families. The first residents, luggage and children in hand, picked their way through freshly poured concrete slab apartment towers and linear bars. They stared in wonder at the drawings and diagrams of the finished estate and listened excitedly to the promises of pedestrian footpaths and parks, schools and shopping centers, and plenty of automobile parking. Six years after construction started, Sarcelles was already home to over 32,000 people. The massive apartment blocks of raw concrete at Park Hill outside Sheffield in England were built to rehouse 3,500 steel workers and their families stuck in antediluvian center city slums. It was the epitome of modernist thinking with elevated pedestrian "streets in the sky" connecting buildings that snaked around open plazas with every modern convenience. The Italian government's Ina-Casa public housing program churned out 500 new homes a week in the early 1950s, then 700 homes each week by the early 1960s.[15] The "satellite city" of La Falchera in the outskirts of Turin was a modernist experiment with three-story apartment blocks for 6,000 people intertwined with green spaces. The Varesino estate in Milan was a regimented series of modernist tower blocks that stood over the city. Across Europe, young families stepped into visionary modernist housing estates and into the future. The flats were minimalist, but they were light, airy, with ample heating, modern kitchens and bathrooms, and space for a coveted television set. For young families, the news they had qualified for keys to an apartment in one of the new housing estates was a miracle. The first arrivals at Sarcelles moved in before the paint was even dry and marveled at "the bathroom, the toilet, the kitchen. . . . We watched in delight as the children ran around the immense living room. It [the flat] was so big that for two years we didn't even use one of the rooms"[16] (Figure 55).

Despite the enthusiasm about modern housing and its utopian hopes, shortages were still one of the defining features of these projects of the late 1950s. Prefabrication, experimental lightweight materials, mechanization of work on the building sites were a response to scarcity. Although these construction techniques were pioneering, they were also untried. The residents of Sarcelles struggled mightily to deal with the immediate heating and electricity problems, the broken water and sewer lines, the lack of basic services. They organized a community association that could "bring a thousand people on to the streets" and relieve them of the banal, boring loneliness and isolation that French newspaper *France-Soir* dubbed "Sarcellite." It was the beginning of a nonstop press campaign that harped on every glitch, every shortcoming of modernist housing.[17] Glitzy magazines, especially aimed at women, cheerily encouraged the new tenants to adopt modern, largely Americanized, models of domestic life, replete with labor-saving domestic appliances. But it was a far cry from the daily experience of these early housing estates. French comedian and filmmaker Jacques Tati lampooned the pulverizing forces of modernization and the sterile existence in the housing estates. His wildly popular 1958 film *Mon Oncle*[18] depicted a clownish resistance against the concrete housing

Figure 55 The Housing Estate in Sarcelles, 1963.

blocks rising up in the Paris suburbs and sentimentalized the picturesque *petit quartier populaire* that traditionally enveloped working-class life. But the young pioneers living the dream of domestic bliss remained steadfast in their belief in the future. Life in these early housing estates was hard, but for one resident of Sarcelles "on the whole, we were happy to take part in this experience."[19]

In any case, despite the media campaigns and the romanticized images of American domestic life, modernization did not amount to a simple transmission of American culture and the arrival of the American "way of life" to Europe. There was a back and forth cultural transfer between the United States and Europe that shaped a consensus Westernization. The American cultural flood that reached European shores after the Second World War merged with European ideas and traditions and national cultural patterns. There were multiple east-west as well as north-south exchanges of everyday practices and commodities.[20] Even more, there was a well-honed internal logic to European urban development into which these cultural influences flowed and took different, nuanced forms. The industrial working-class urban milieu was at its height in Europe during the reconstruction years and early 1950s. Trade union influence and membership reached its peak. Massive parades and festivals to celebrate May Day and labor anniversaries, strikes and demonstrations were an ingrained part of urban life in the postwar world. Moreover, in eastern Europe, the working classes were celebrated in the victory of communism.

Once rationing ended and the economies of western Europe were deregulated, working men and women were more confident, more prosperous, more urbane than they had ever been before. The gross social inequalities of the prewar years were fading away. Those countries with the lowest income levels in both western and eastern Europe developed the fastest. By the 1960s, jobs and decent incomes were the norm virtually everywhere. There was more disposable wealth than ever before. It became commonplace for consumers to buy on credit. European social welfare regimes with free medical care and pensions, education, subsidized public housing and transportation helped create a degree of security and comfort for broad ranges of working people that had never before been achieved. These defined specifically European patterns of cultural consumption. A unique brand of European vacation culture appeared. These first steps toward the welfare state did not immediately transform social hierarchies. The 1950s were largely a period of restabilization. Social and cultural dynamics would only begin to change by the end of the decade. But the years of scarcity were left behind. Families rushed to fulfill material aspirations and pent-up dreams of a better life. For war weary Europeans tired of poverty and rations, consumption offered a new kind of social respectability and quality of life.

Families rushed to buy clothing, household appliances and furnishings. A survey conducted by the *Financial Times* found that from 1957 to 1959 alone, the number of British households owning a television set increased 32 percent, washing machines by 54 percent, and highly coveted refrigerators by 58 percent.[21] A slew of household consumer items beckoned on store shelves, the bulk of which were produced in factories in the cities of Europe. Unilever and Swiss Nestlé were the largest consumer goods companies and profited from the craze for frozen foods and home products from cleaning detergents to personal hygiene. Bayer, one of the successors of the IG Farben conglomerate, produced no fewer than 12,000 products, most of which were unknown before the war. Siemens manufactured an assortment of domestic appliances and electronics. Customers perused the inexpensive laminated furniture in the Hille showrooms in the UK. The newest Bang & Olufsen television sets and Braun kitchen blenders were snatched up as the signatures of modern lifestyle. The "art of living" well and comfortably became the shared aspiration of millions who followed the dream of trouble-free consumption.

The majority of Europeans in the 1950s still purchased food and everyday items from neighborhood corner stores, food halls, and weekly markets. Their reappearance after years of scarcity was the surest sign of everyday normality. Nonetheless, they suffered years of slow asphyxiation in the face of new commercial operators. The daily shopping routines that had defined urban life for centuries were step-by-step forsaken for weekly expeditions to self-service supermarkets. There, shoppers wandered through a dizzying array of food choices and examined price tags. Europeans spent more on food and clothing than did their American counterparts, and the selection of these goods was based around uniquely European tastes.[22] In the UK, Tesco opened its first self-service supermarket in 1954. By 1961, the largest store in Europe was the Tesco on the outskirts of the town of Leicester. It was perched over a parking lot for a thousand cars and offered "drive in and buy" services. Shoppers could find "everything from A to X" and plop their children in the seats of waiting shopping carts. "You cannot imagine the excitement in Leicester," one observer recalled. "The goods just flew out . . . queues of shopper waited to rush in the moment the doors were thrown open."[23] Founder Jack Cohen pursued an aggressive policy of expansion in the 1960s and opened hundreds of stores in suburban areas. French Carrefour (one of the largest supermarket-department store chains in the world by the twenty-first century) opened its first sales outlet in suburban Annecy in 1957. The Monoprix chain, which started as a grocery store in Rouen in 1932, switched to self-service in 1950. Just ten years later, there were already over 200 Monoprix supermarkets filled with customers in the suburbs of French cities. The Aldi supermarket began life as a self-service store in Essen and became one of the largest no-frills retailers in Germany with over 300 stores in 1960. The 1961 grand opening of the Supermarket Italiani in Florence was mobbed by 15,000 customers gawking at the sumptuously stocked shelves and American-style check-out rituals. The police had to be called in for crowd control.[24] These new distribution strategies moved consumerism downward socially and outward beyond Europe's big cities to towns across the continent. Fast-food restaurant chains followed suit. Nordsee Quick catered to fast-paced modern lifestyles and expanded to 300 outlets in West German and Austrian towns in the 1950s and 1960s. The first Wimpy Bar opened on Coventry Street in London in 1954 and spread to high streets across British cities selling the newest sensation of hamburgers and milkshakes to teenagers. Friedrich Jahn opened his first Wienerwald restaurant on Munich's Amalienstrasse and made a killing selling ready-made roast chicken as an everyday family meal. The Wienerwald franchise grew to be one Europe's most successful fast-food chains in the 1960s (Figure 56).

In Cold War discourse, Europe east of the Elbe River was the no-man's-land of the Eastern Bloc. Although the countries in the Soviet sphere never identified with the category "Eastern Bloc" or "Eastern Europe," they were seen in western eyes as a common

Figure 56 Monoprix store in Caen, Ouchacoff and Bataille architects, about 1960.

territory suffering from tyranny and socioeconomic backwardness. The catastrophic destruction of the Second World War only heightened this imagery. Housing construction lagged behind in eastern Europe, much of which lay in complete ruins. Thousands of families were still living in the same neglected working-class tenements that had defined proletarian life since the beginning of the century, or they lived in dilapidated lodgings in the forgotten urban peripheries. Although the collective urban spaces of socialist realism were heroic, the domestic world of the everyday was bleak. Dreadful living conditions stretched across the Soviet Union. In the vast expanses of the Urals and Siberia, families crowded into dormitories and barracks that were universally dismal.[25]

In 1957, thousands of people across Yugoslavia flocked to Zagreb to goggle at the Supermarket USA exhibit organized by the US government.[26] But its hallucination of abundance was stinging irony when many were still dealing with rationing and scarcity. Commodities were cheap but scant in eastern Europe. In East Germany, rationing of basic goods at the gloomy *Konsum* cooperative outlets continued until 1961. Anyone wanting something extra headed for the Handels Organisation (HO) shops that sold goods without ration coupons and enticed customers with fashion shows and trendy merchandise. The HO store on Alexanderplatz, the hub of East Berlin, was a showcase of proletarian panache. The HO shops and *Konsum* outlets planned along Stalinallee were to be a shopper's paradise. But the vision of opulence was thwarted by perpetual shortages. Until the Wall divided the city, Berliners freely traveled across sectors on shopping sprees to find the best prices. In Günter Grass's 1963 novel *Dog Years*, Matern's train stops at Zoological Station in West Berlin, "where he decides to stop for a minute, exchange his West marks for East marks at the profitable capitalist rate" before he heads to East Berlin. "Besides, he has to buy razor and blades, two pairs of socks, and a change of shirts; who knows whether these vital necessities are available over there at the moment?"[27]

There was still a bleak grayness to cities in the late 1950s and early 1960s in both east and west. They were difficult places to live. Bombed-out buildings and vacant lots of weeds and rubble, bullet-scarred buildings still blemished the cityscape alongside construction cranes and muddy building sites. There was little left of the big city excitement of the prewar years. It was both remarkable and poignant that young people surfaced in these dismal spaces with a defiant headlong energy of their own. The first generation of "teenagers" created a spectacular cosmopolitan youth culture. It was mashed together from everyday working-class experience, pickings and fantasies from a variety of places, and especially by coopting American popular culture. In Britain, a subculture of young people emerged in skiffle and beat clubs, jazz and rock 'n' roll basements hidden away in working-class districts and provincial towns, and the suburban housing estates around London. Obscure backwaters were a kind of gift that nurtured a taste for subversive music. They gathered on Scotland Road in Liverpool, a local hotspot for working-class teenagers out for a pub crawl. Underground music clubs opened in the city's seedy district near the waterfront with amateur groups experimenting with Merseybeat. Liverpool's melting pot of ethnicities, its "Cunard Yanks" bringing back sounds from across the Atlantic gave them plenty of material for improvisation.[28]

The Teddy Boys, dressed as Edwardian desperados and captivated by American films and music, excelled at conjuring up mayhem. They harassed anyone who caught their ire on the street, especially immigrants. Racial tensions spilled into violence in the race riots in Nottingham, when mobs of Teddy Boys attacked West Caribbean homes on Bramley Road. The rioting and attacks went on for days. The Mods dressed up in high-camp suits and raced around on Lambretta motor scooters. Rockers were working class, macho, and aggressive. Gangs of "Rocks" and "Mods" met for ritual rumbles on the streets. They terrorized South London in 1965 after the film opening of Bill Haley and the Comets' *Rock Around the Clock* when hundreds gathered to dance "Mambo Rock" on Tower Bridge, blocking traffic and setting up a cacophony of frustrated horn-blowing. In just a few years, hippies, punks, and skinheads would take their place as urban antiheroes (Figure 57).

This youthful dissidence was on display in cities across Europe, on both sides of the Iron Curtain. Sporting long hair, black leather jackets, and cowboy boots, France's *blousons noirs* rowdies and Italy's *vitelloni*, Dutch *nozem* and Germany's *halbstarken* were regarded as a dangerous species. They roamed the urban wastelands left by the war's ruins or the construction sites near their apartment blocks along the urban periphery. Disturbances by young gangs became standard fare after rock concerts and films. They were condemned by the authorities as juvenile provocateurs, immoral hooligans who threatened public respectability. It was hard for respectable opinion to shake these stereotypes and suspicions. But teenage rowdiness in the streets and clashes with police

Figure 57 Teddy Boys on a Sheffield Street.

were a new kind of public spectacle. Until the construction of the Berlin Wall in August 1961, teenagers streamed back-and-forth between East and West Berlin. The western sector of the city was a mecca of jazz and beat clubs, movie houses featuring American films, and shops with jeans, leather jackets, and vinyl records. East Berliners jived to western music on shortwave radio and watched West German television.

Although American pop culture often receives the most attention, teenagers in the east cobbled together a variety of insignia and totems. Macho young rebels wore Italian styles and sipped Italian expresso. Their music scene was influenced by Italian popular music, French *ye-ye* sounds, and German *schlager* pop melodies. The Zagreb Festival, one of the first popular music festivals in Europe, was modeled on the Italian Sanremo song contest that was broadcast live on the radio in 1951. Music festivals became powerful public venues for young people. The festival in the Croatian town of Opatija was a premier showcase for popular music, drew thousands, and was televised across Yugoslavia.[29] From the late 1950s, the Thaw brought a partial opening of eastern European societies. Thousands of youth-oriented clubs and cafés embraced western music and dancing. Bill Haley and the Comets were met by thousands of hysterical fans during their European concert tour in 1958. Their Leipzig concert was the official invasion of rock music into East Germany.[30] For "rebellious" youth in the Eastern Bloc, western music and clothing were awkwardly absorbed into life under socialism alongside communist youth leagues and joyful marches at Youth Day parades. In Warsaw, the *bikiniarze* (bikini boys) mimicked what they imagined to be the style of American youth. They arrayed themselves in jeans, smoked Camels and Lucky Strikes, and adopted English from American movies. In Budapest, *jampecs* rifled through the city's black markets looking for castoff clothing to match their bouffant hairdos.[31] Brooding rockers and Elvis Presley look-alikes strutted their stuff and made the city a scene of social rebellion. In the Soviet Union, the *stilyagi*, or style-obsessed, aped western fashion and created their own dance moves and slang. One of Moscow's best-known cafés, the Molodezhnoe, became a bohemian youth hangout with amateur cool jazz sets.[32] The blockbuster 1957 Youth Festival in Moscow featured official delegations from over a hundred countries and an embarrassment of musical styles. For the global phenomena of youth, the Iron Curtain was entirely permeable.

The pursuit of higher living standards drove eastern Europeans into the arms of the west. For intellectuals and artists stuck behind the Iron Curtain in the dreary years of the 1950s, Paris was the mythic destination. Artists, art exhibitions, and films traveled back and forth between Paris and east European capitals.[33] The *New Tendencies* Pop Art Biennial opened in Zagreb in 1961 and became a regular event. Underground production studios churned out black market recordings of western music. A flood of images from across the Iron Curtain seduced eager consumers. Exhibitions by foreign companies displaying western products took place regularly and communist entrepreneurs visited their counterparts in western Europe, especially in Paris. French fashion designers Yves Saint-Laurent and Christian Dior took part in fashion shows in Moscow in 1957 and 1958. The American National Exhibition in Moscow the summer of 1959 was an unprecedented event and the site of the famous "kitchen debates" between

American president Richard Nixon and Soviet Premier Nikita Khrushchev. Held inside a translucent geodesic dome, it introduced visitors to an intoxicating array of consumer goods and household appliances. The model of a typical American home included General Electric's "Miracle Kitchen." American consumer brands such as Levi jeans were status symbols. Objects with "Made in the USA" tags were collector's items.

It was in part the glaring differences in the quality of life between east and west that spurred a wave of local revolts and pushed the Soviet leadership into de-Stalinization and modernizing communist ideals. In 1953, thousands of Berliners poured into the streets to support striking construction workers including those at the Stalinallee building site. Marches formed in the industrial suburbs and wound their way to the Potsdamerplatz. Kiosks were set ablaze and shop windows smashed. Soviet tanks were met with a hail of cobblestones. Police cars were overturned and set on fire. The Communist Party headquarters were stormed and the red flag torn down from Brandenburg Gate. The massive crowds in Berlin sparked protests in Dresden, Halle, Leipzig, and cities across East Germany. Workers shut down the railways, the steelworks, the Leuna chemical plant, the machine plant at Magdeburg, and the Berlin electrical power plant. Police headquarters were stormed. Soviet tanks brutally dispersed the demonstrations and 300 people died in the melees. Tens of thousands of skilled workers left the GDR and fled West. Metal workers in Poznań went out on strike in 1956 and were crushed. Warsaw witnessed mass protests in 1956. Budapest spiraled into revolution as students and workers staged marches in support of democratic reforms. Violent clashes between police and demonstrators, lynching of Communist Party members, brutal street fights

Figure 58 Hungarian Uprising. Jubilant insurgents outside the Hungarian Parliament Building, Budapest, October 1956.

threw the city into a state of siege in October 1956. Lajos Kossuth Square in front of the Parliament building became a war zone. Soviet tanks rumbled through the streets, and the revolution was brutally crushed. Some 3,000 Hungarians died during the uprising and by death sentence. Thousands were sent to prison, lost their jobs or were expelled from universities. Some 200,000 people escaped Hungary immediately after the failed revolution. Although this mass unrest was crushed, it gave the green light to Khrushchev's de-Stalinization and a more independent road to socialism for its east European satellites (Figure 58).

With millions leaving the Soviet Bloc, the borders were finally sealed in 1961. The symbol of this tragic division of Europe was the building of the Berlin Wall. Symbolically, the first place to be sealed was Potsdamerplatz, once one of the most urbane, busiest urban arenas in Europe. The Wall dramatically divided the city. Huge concrete slabs topped with pipe and barbed wire separated the city into two halves—east and west. Watchtowers manned by border guards stood over a sandy no-man's-land loaded with trip wires. The insane landscape was illuminated by floodlights after dark. Windows and doors in buildings along the wall were bricked up. Underground, the subways were cut and sewers secured by electrified fences. Ironically, it was its outlier status as a sealed-off island in the communist world that made West Berlin into a showcase for Western democracy. It was a freewheeling "happening" that attracted hordes of young people just as the older generation was abandoning the city. West Berlin seemed to defy political geography. It was no longer the German capital. It was a Cold War island in the middle of a communist sea. The shop windows along the Kufürstendamm were filled with consumer bling. The newest films and music, the cafés and bars—even if dingy—were glimpses of the cosmopolitan, world-city status of the years before the war. Berlin was cheap, gritty, open.[34] It was a scene of youthful hedonism and left-wing activism in what was a rapidly changing European urban society.

CHAPTER 11
CAR TRIPS THROUGH THE CITY (1960s–70s)

Once the painful reconstruction years were left behind, Europeans moved to cities in record numbers. It was Europe's second colossal urban boom, akin to the urban groundswell in the nineteenth century. The causes were multiple. The rapid shift from agriculture to industry and later services pulled people from rural areas into cities. Prior to the war, rural exodus of this kind was partially siphoned off globally in the great emigration waves of the late nineteenth and early twentieth centuries. This subsided after the Second World War. Instead rural migrants remained in Europe, packed their bags and headed for cities. They arrived in their own local capitals or crossed into different countries to try their luck. Many were young people leaving behind the stultifying atmosphere of isolated villages and small towns. Big cities were youthful territories. Moving to the city meant opportunity and education, a better job, and the dream of a better life. They settled in, married, and raised gaggles of relatively pampered children. The baby boom added to the urban population rolls as did foreign workers, especially those coming from overseas looking for jobs.

By the end of the twentieth century, the overall population of Europe had risen to around 600 million. For the first time, over 50 percent of Europeans lived in cities and towns. Urbanization slowed down in the 1980s and 1990s. But by the end of the twentieth century, a full 75 percent of people in western Europe lived in urban areas. The most urbanized countries were predictably Great Britain, Belgium and the Netherlands, Germany, and Sweden. Eastern Europe was not far behind, where the speed of urbanization was especially dramatic. In the Eastern Bloc, stepped-up industrialization and the collectivization of agriculture catapulted the region into urban living. There was a massive redistribution of population toward towns and cities.[1] Urbanization reached close to 70 percent in the Czech Republic and Bulgaria, and 63 percent in Hungary. In Yugoslavia, which was historically one of the least urbanized areas of Europe, people migrated to cities in record numbers. Even remote rural areas in the Balkans became more urban. Historically, "urbanization" had also largely meant urban concentration. But from the 1960s, this trend was reversed. Cities across Europe exploded into vast polynucleated metropolitan regions. Urbanites did not just settle in Europe's great capitals. In what urban scholars identified as an "epoch-making turning point,"[2] they also moved into towns spread throughout vast metropolitan areas. Even small towns and medium sized cities in these amoeba-like urban geographies experienced high population growth.

Beyond population growth, there were other factors required for this scale of urbanization. After two devastating wars, Europe finally enjoyed a long period of political and social stability accompanied by robust economic investment. Despite the bitter oratory of the Cold War, the political situation in a divided Europe was more stable than it had been at any other time during the twentieth century. It created a new kind of normalcy in everyday life and underpinned a "golden age of prosperity" until the 1973 oil crisis. It was a thirty-year period of spectacular economic expansion without precedent. Both production and consumption soared. Even more, the benefits of the new wealth were widely diffused. The future appeared audacious. Rather than repeating the misery and class struggle that plagued earlier decades, these years were characterized by cooperation between management and labor. Full employment, a living income with moderate wage raises, social welfare benefits created a confident, prosperous working class. Jobs were plentiful, salaries and earnings increased.

The 1960s and early 1970s were the golden age of the welfare state, when entire populations could rely on a comfortable net of health and disability protection, unemployment, and old-age benefits. Free medical care, better education, and subsidized housing provided a new security. This took place in western Europe, where the classic welfare state reached its apogee, as well as in the collectivist east. Europeans enjoyed the highest standards of living they had ever known. With it came a new respectability. For people on both sides of the Iron Curtain, paradise was a comfortable home, a nice car parked in front, a new television. A consumer revolution swept through the continent that transformed everyday culture with a cascade of glittering commodities. What had once been luxuries for the lucky few were now available to almost everyone. This rising affluence was the unique feature of the golden age of prosperity. It made the postwar system a total way of life. The impact on cities was profound.

Governments on both sides of the Iron Curtain forged ahead with massive plans for modernization. Master planning was envisioned as a magic formula. It was applied to virtually every arena of human activity and wrapped in the moral cloth of progress. It would propel people into a future of happiness and abundance. Thousands of technocrats, technicians and engineers, architects and planners rolled out elaborate schemes to create a better world. Funding was poured into slum-clearance schemes, into housing construction, highways and airports, colossal sports stadiums, and shopping malls. Cities became the setting for ambitious state-sponsored mega-projects. These were the benchmarks of modernization. They were nodes in a vast geography of production and consumption—an entire system of vital resources, consumer goods, logistics and distribution, and transportation. Both the Common Market in the west and Soviet-led Comecon in the east were crucial to this geography. Yet despite this totalizing vision of a new world, either in its capitalist or socialist guises, it was rarely carried out to completion. The way long-established cities were built and lived in was mediated by a host of influences specific to place. European variations on both unbridled American-style capitalism and inflexible Soviet-style socialism reworked their effect and the ways they were embedded in cities. The same can be said about the architecture and urbanism that was the scaffold of modernization in both eastern and western Europe. The archetypes offered by modernism were carried out in different urban places with more-or-less power and resources. Yet at the same time, there were striking similarities in the urban transformations taking place across Europe. This interaction between the modernist regime and local circumstance marked the entire urban landscape of Europe in the 1960s.

Labor migration was also essential to these modernizing processes. The economic boom of the late 1950s and 1960s sparked a new exodus from Europe's periphery to its industrialized western European countries. The number of foreign workers in western Europe tripled. With jobs aplenty, many countries established open immigration policies with the appeal for workers initially aimed primarily at white Europeans. A stream of guest workers from rural areas in Ireland, Italy, Spain, and Greece, and later from the newly communized countries of eastern Europe journeyed to western Europe's cities in search of jobs on construction sites and in heavy industry. Poles continued their traditional passage westward. Thousands of Hungarians fled west after the failure of the 1956 Uprising. In 1968 two-thirds of the foreigners in France were still European, mostly from southern Europe and Poland.[3] By 1970 there were over 12 million foreign immigrants in western Europe.[4] Their willingness to put up with poor working conditions and low wages contributed to the general stability of the boom years. They were mainly young, single men in search of temporary work, with the intention of returning home to start families and businesses. Women from Spain, Greece, Turkey, and Yugoslavia were recruited in the clothing and textile, food and hospitality industries.

The disintegration of Europe's empires added a fractious side to this population migration. Programs such as the British Nationality Act of 1948 gave all Commonwealth citizens free entry into Britain. West Indians (African-Caribbean) along with citizens of India and the new country of Pakistan moved into the neighborhoods of Brixton and the East End in London. Migrants from Indonesia and the Dutch colony of Suriname settled into cheap housing in Rotterdam, Amsterdam, and The Hague. Turkish workers clustered in fleabag hotels and boarding houses in Kreuzberg and Mitte in Berlin. Immigrants from the French colonies of Algeria, Morocco, and Tunisia risked entry into France under the harrowing conditions of decolonization and the Algerian War of the late 1950s and early 1960s. In Paris, Algerians lived in run-down lodgings around the Gare de Nord or in desolate shantytowns on the northern and eastern fringes of the city. Belleville in the city's north was Chinese, while the 13th arrondissement in the south of Paris was a Vietnamese enclave. The political tensions around decolonization and the hostility against foreign migrants ran deep. Race riots and hate crimes against migrants broke out all too frequently. Mobs of white teenagers attacked black Caribbeans in the 1958 Notting Hill riots in London. Algerians in Paris were under constant surveillance. Riots and police raids in North African neighborhoods were savage. The animus culminated in the brutal massacre of some 200 Algerians in Paris by the French police in October 1961.

Modernization also required vast energy resources. Cities engaged in a tight symbiosis with environmental and material assets. In the years between 1870 and 2000, energy use in Europe increased sevenfold while at the same time the population doubled. It meant that at century's end, an average person in Europe had slightly more than three times the energy at their disposal than the same individual in 1870.[5] Oil, natural gas, and electricity were the great fuels of modernization. The breakthrough into an oil economy took place after the Second World War. Cheap oil flooded the European markets and continued until the price shocks of the early 1970s. It was imported from the vast reserves in Russia, the Persian Gulf, Sub-Saharan Africa, and the North Sea. Giant oil tanks and oil refineries hung over ports in Rotterdam, Southampton, and Hamburg, and at the Mediterranean ports of Marseille and Genoa. Oil pipelines stretched from distant oilfields and coastal ports to cities in the interior of the continent. The largest corporations in Europe were the oil and gas giants Royal Dutch Shell with its headquarters in The Hague and research laboratories in Amsterdam, British Petroleum in London, and French Total with its oil and gas refining and transportation arms. French Total's tower headquarters loomed over the skyline at the La Défense business district west of Paris. The Soviet Union supplied eastern Europe with petroleum through "Friendship Pipelines." The longest from Siberia wound its way to Warsaw and Rostock and down to Budapest and Zagreb. Eventually Russian Gazprom was founded in 1989 with its headquarters in Moscow. Massive electrical power companies such as Electricité de France (EDF) and GDF Suez, both headquartered in Paris, and ENEL, headquartered in Rome, generated the electricity that was the lifeblood of modern living. Modernization was dependent on these energy flows. Thousands of people worked for these companies as administrative staff, technicians, engineers and designers, and skilled labor.

The oil refineries and electric power plants surrounding every large-scale metropolitan area of Europe were perhaps the most emblematic and overlooked symbols of these flourishing "miracle years," or as the French dubbed them, the *trente glorieuses*. But there were others. Concrete was the material of modernization. It was an agent of change— and it was everywhere, in every town and city. It was shaped into apartment blocks, highways and parking structures, made into shopping malls and stadiums. It was used in hotels and churches. Schools, hospitals, cinemas, and office buildings were constructed of prefabricated ferro-concrete. The suburbs became a concrete world. Notwithstanding its jolting character, people identified and lived with concrete as representing the progress taking place around them. For architects and engineers, concrete was a catalytic medium and playground of experimentation. It offered the possibility of realizing utopian ambitions. It was celebrated for its sculptural malleability and richness of design. Combined with steel and glass, the forms were bold, passionate expressions of the modern age. Even the tint of the built environment changed. The distinctive gray-brown color and texture of concrete became omnipresent. It was left unabashedly exposed and unadorned to speak for itself. The architectural movement known as brutalism carried the salute to concrete craftsmanship to its monolithic and bitter end.

The automobile was yet another cipher of modernization. It was already a pervasive feature of cities with traffic hurtling down—or crawling—through the streets. But in the 1950s and 1960s, the automobile had a magnetism and celebrity that made it a cultural icon. French urban philosopher Roland Barthes dubbed the car the "equivalent of the great Gothic cathedrals: I mean the supreme creation of an era," consumed by the whole population "as a purely magical object."[6] Owning a private vehicle was a measure of affluence and independence. The craze for motorization extended to motorcycles and scooters. Between 1950 and 1964 the numbers of these last jumped from 700,000 to 4.3 million in Italy.[7] The Italian Vespa motor scooter was an unprecedented success and a head-turning item on city streets. The major automakers in Great Britain, France, Germany, and Italy increased their production by more than sevenfold and by 1970 outproduced the United States for the first time. Cars shrank in size to fit smaller budgets. A swarm of spunky vehicles chugged through the city streets from West Germany's VW Beetle and Goggomobile, Italy's Fiat 500 and 600, the French Renault 4CV to the British Morris Minor and Leyland Mini. They ruled supreme as pop icons and were the darlings of a young generation—easy to run, easy to fix, and fun to drive on narrow cobble roads. The Fiat 500 Topolino (little mouse) was treated as a fun, affectionate family member. Turin became "auto city" indelibly linked with the miniature Fiats rolling down the ramps of its storied factories. Annual car shows such as the Paris Salon d'automobiles and the Amsterdam AutoRAI drew thousands of aficionados. Car caravan tours and races were all the rage. By the late 1960s, there was one car for every six people in western Europe. Parked cars lined the streets and choked sidewalks. The Italian magazine *Epoca* reported, "In the piazzas, in front of offices, at the cinema, at the theatre, hundreds, no, thousands of cars are lined up."[8] Even the main squares in Italy's remote villages were jammed with Fiats (Figure 59).

The display of cars from the west cast a shadow of longing in eastern Europe. Socialist cars were far too expensive for most people and acquired only after a wait of years. The desire was immense. Soviet film comedies such as *A Driver by Accident* (1958) in which

Figure 59 Mods ride their scooters along the seafront at Hastings, East Sussex, 1964.

the main character finds himself gloriously behind the wheel of a car and the Cinderella story *Queen of the Gas Pump* (1963) found delighted audiences.[9] By the mid-1960s the automobile industry was given higher priority in the shift to a socialist consumer society on a par with the "economic miracle" taking place in the west. These were not just shabby knock-offs of shiny western vehicles. The Soviet authorities hired both Fiat and Renault to modernize their automobile factories for upscale production. The Moskvich "car for everyone" and the prestigious Volga for upper-class nomenklatura were soon cutting through city streets. By the 1970s, the mass production of the Lada model made it the first "people's car" in the Soviet Union.[10] East Germany (GDR) had the most highly developed automobile sector. The East German Trabant was the ultimate example of the Socialist Car. Made of Duroplast, it went into production in the factory at Zwickau in 1957 and continued for three decades. By the late 1960s and early 1970s, there were more cars on the road in socialist societies, a greater variety of models, and more ways of acquiring one.[11] And they were laden with political undertones. The capital cities of central and eastern Europe were infested with Moscow's agents and the secret police. In writer Anna Funder's portrait of *Stasiland*, former resident Julia recalled life in the GDR in the 1970s,

When we were teenagers the local lads would come by in summer time—my sisters and I would be on the balcony sunbaking. They'd hoon up and down on their motorbikes. . . . But there was also a car—for the GDR an expensive car, a Russian Lada—that would sometimes come and crawl slowly along the street in front of our house. . . . The Lada had two men in it. That was creepy.[12]

The infamous East German Stasi and their informants were on every street, in every building, every café.

Vehicles were deeply embedded in the image of the modern young European. It was a complicated love affair with deep implications for urban life. The image of cool was from behind the wheel of a slinky sports car. Exploring the city, the sense of speed and adventure, was now a matter of sitting in the driver's seat. The family car became an indelible part of everyday life. *Autowandern* in West Germany meant cruising the highway enjoying the sights. Automobiles were idolized in film and became the stuff of cinematic legend. In Federico Fellini's 1957 *Nights of Cabiria*, the Fiat 500 was the height of aspiration for the underworld of prostitutes and pimps. Moviegoers flocked to see Sean Connery use his Aston Martin as a lethal weapon in the 1964 James Bond classic *Goldfinger*. In the 1969 British comedy *The Italian Job*, Turin police pursue the slapstick gang of robbers through a paralyzing traffic jam. The crooks speed their three Mini Coopers through the shopping arcades, down stairways, jump between rooftops, and finally push the Minis off a mountainside. Youthful angst was worked out in Director Wim Winders's 1970 experimental film *Summer in the City*. Disgruntled protagonist Hans scrutinizes West Berlin through a car window. He pays a driver twenty marks to drive him around the city in a new form of *flânerie*. The car wanders aimlessly through the road traffic, while buildings, store windows, gas stations, the sidewalk parade of people pass by. The car provides an aloof detachment from the city. The freedom and mobility of the automobile trumped any attachment to place. There was a wildness, the ability to go wherever and whenever, that made automobiles endlessly seductive.

The famous Buchanan Report on the UK's automotive future, published as the popular book *Traffic in Towns* in 1963, warned that the car should not be allowed to monopolize cities the way it had in the United States. Nonetheless, traffic flow became the guiding principle of urban planning. Highway construction boomed in the 1960s and early 1970s. There were flyovers, roundabouts and spaghetti junctions, flashy directional signs, and no speed limits. Cities were encased in a ring of asphalt highways. The inauguration of every new project was a media extravaganza. In the minds of planners, urban regions congealed into an abstract matrix of traffic flows and dynamic connectivity between population nodes. Traffic pulsed through space in an imagined circulatory system. In 1990, French author François Maspero traveled on the highway to Charles de Gaulle Airport north of Paris, disoriented by the

> connecting roads cutting under and over artificial embankments . . . then there's all this asphalt running over your head, the railway line, and the motorways you keep cutting across, the bridges and tunnels, and all the vehicles pelting along, overtaking, overlapping and separating, watch your left, watch your right, and not a single pedestrian to give the whole thing a scale.

Just a few years later, British urban explorer Stephen Barber headed to the edge of eastern Paris to find "all around, motorway overpasses traverse the edges of the city in a fierce, relentless medium of noise. Once they have left the peripheral road behind, those highways divide and subdivide into a swirl of elevated channels, as though the logical fulfillment of their endless proliferation would be the transformation of the city's border zone into one great open highway."[13]

BP and Total gas stations became ubiquitous features on the streetscape. Road signage and traffic lights, car showrooms and repair shops, and highway service centers transformed cities and urban regions into an automobile landscape. It created a new kind of verticality. Multilevel concrete parking structures rose up in city centers while underground parking garages descended into the depths below. Automobility was designed and managed by huge construction and civil engineering companies that employed hundreds of thousands of people across the continent. The gargantuan French company SGE (Vinci SA) did everything from highway, airport, and building construction to parking structure management. By the end of the century it alone employed upward of 100,000 people. Bouygues Construction also worked in France. In Great Britain, Balfour Beatty built highways and power stations. The Austrian Strabag Company and Germany's Hochtief Group were instrumental to Europe's automotive labyrinth of highways, tunnels, and bridges (Figure 60).

The maze of highways shrank the time and distance between cities and bound together the continent. They were imagined as routes to the future and their alchemy rivaled that of the railroad in the nineteenth century. Soon after the Second World War, the United Nations designated a European-wide system of trunk roads, each artery

Figure 60 Traffic jams in Paris, 1968.

receiving a unique number from E1 through E30. They formed an international network across western Europe that was eventually extended to central and eastern Europe down through the Balkans as well as to the Nordic countries.[14] West Germany took the lead in highway construction with 2,100 kilometers of the *Autobahn*. Italy was not far behind with the *Autostrada del Sole* that slithered down the peninsula. Italian highways went from 1,300 kilometers in 1961 to 4,300 just ten years later.[15] The B1 artery through the Ruhr was widened to six lanes and extended with a tunnel through the town of Essen. Britain opened its first segments of the M1 and M6 highways in the late 1950s. They were the start of a highway network that linked London to the industrial north.

The new "motorways" caught the public's imagination. Speeding down the open highway was a thrilling experience. They were destinations in themselves, as much entertainment as liberation. When the M1 opened in 1959, thousands of motorists piled into their cars to try out the new road, creating an instant traffic jam.[16] Thousands of young volunteers joined construction crews to build the "Highway of Brotherhood and Unity" that joined Ljubljana, Zagreb, Belgrade, and Skopje in Yugoslavia. Canadian author Michael Ignatieff remembered the highway, when each summer of his youth, "we travelled, in a magnificent black Buick with lots of fins and chrome, to Lake Bled in Slovenia."[17] The Adriatic Highway joined towns along the coast. These instantly became the roads south for holidays. Highway service areas became pageants of automobilism and highway architecture. The Forton service center on the M6 featured a hexagonal concrete tower with an American-style restaurant floating overhead. Mario Pavesi's sleek Autogrill service stations were the jewels of Italy's *Autostrada del Sole*. Their self-service restaurants were wildly popular. From the late 1960s, some 600 industries were located along the *Autostrada del Sole*. Motor-hotels opened. Highways became ribbon extensions of urban life with seductive shopping malls and business parks planted at the exits.

The impact of these vast modernization and infrastructure schemes were most telling in the Netherlands. The Dutch *Wirtschaftswunder*, or miracle years, was a period of spectacular economic growth for the delta region crisscrossed by dikes and polders. The heart of its territory became known as the Randstad, or Rim City, an urbanized ring that connected the four cities of Amsterdam, The Hague, Rotterdam, and Utrecht.[18] Before the Second World War Amsterdam was still a city of short distances, despite a population of 800,000. Residential expansion had been carefully planned to retain the city's intimate appeal with most people traveling by bike or walking. While Amsterdam was the recognized national capital, The Hague was the historic royal court. Rotterdam was the industrial city on the Maas River. Once a deep waterway was dug to the sea, Rotterdam became the continent's premier port. Heavy industry sprang up along the waterfront that drew an endless stream of workers. Just before the war, Rotterdam's population shot up to 600,000 inhabitants. Tragically, all this curdled into disaster. The war devastated the Netherlands. The German onslaught either destroyed the coastal cities (in the case or Rotterdam the destruction was total) or turned them into a militarized "Atlantic Wall" that left thousands homeless. Some 60 percent of the country's productive capacity was obliterated.

Like Warsaw, Rotterdam was praised in the 1950s as a heroic labor of reconstruction. Rather than rebuild what had been considered an antiquated city, planners instead bid farewell to the past. The objective was to catapult Rotterdam into "one huge industrial and port complex"[19] and make it a city of the future. A Basic Scheme reimagined the city center as a diamond-shaped business and transportation hub. Traffic circulation was fundamental to the design, which sketched out wide streets and copious intersections. The automobile was seen as a virtue: planners quipped "better a row of shiny cars than a carriage full of old ladies."[20] The main avenue of the Coolsingle was widened into a Champs-Elysées with the Town Hall, Stock Exchange, banks and logistic companies, and the headquarters of KLM Airlines. Next to it, one of the first outdoor shopping centers in Europe took shape. Designed as a concrete grid with pedestrian concourse and procession of stylish boutiques, the Lijnbaan was a prototype of the new urban lifestyle. It was surrounded by apartment towers and new roads that linked Rotterdam to the country's highway system. Like much of the city's reconstruction, the creation of the Lijnbaan was mythologized in promotional films and in the press with shots of workers valiantly manning machinery and muscling construction of the futuristic emporium. American urban critic Lewis Mumford strolled through Rotterdam in 1957 and reported the Lijnbaan as "warm, lively, almost gay . . . the unity and harmony of all this delights the eye. . . . Here is a sound urban form that can be adopted anywhere."[21] Publicity shots depicted shoppers strolling the concourse, gazing at the shop windows and glittering signage. Rotterdam reemerged as a prototype for an endlessly appealing European modernism (Figure 61).

The Randstad remained an idealistic concept—a sprawling constellation of towns and cities connected by highways. The magic of traffic science would transform the

Figure 61 The Lijnbaan in Rotterdam, 1960.

Netherlands into a modern nation. It was a blueprint for social engineering. The car was imagined not just as mobility but as a "reality-changing force."[22] Between 1960 and 1980, the three cities of Amsterdam, The Hague, and Rotterdam together lost over half a million inhabitants, a quarter of their total population,[23] as people fanned out across the Randstad region. The Haarlemmermeer polder around Schiphol airport filled in with development and garden-style villages. Banking and finance and insurance companies moved to the southern districts of Amsterdam and the adjacent area of Amsteelveen. The Hague and the towns of Dordrecht and Breda extended the Randstad outward in the southern provinces. Utrecht, Haarlem, and Amersfoort fused the center of the country. To the north, the new towns of Almere and Lelystad were constructed in the reclaimed polder of Flevoland. Small towns and villages, shopping malls, and industry within sight of the highways merged into a modernist landscape punctuated by dikes and canals, and valiant strips of open space hanging on despite the development pressures. The Randstad was a product of engineering and tightly-regulated sprawl. By 2000, the region was home to 7 million people spanning out across one of the most densely populated metropolitan areas of Europe.

Automobile ownership skyrocketed, along with CO_2 emissions and air pollution. The Netherlands became a motorized country. In 1950 there were 139,000 cars, in 1960 more than 500,000, and by 1970 that number quadrupled.[24] Millions of cars were on the roads. Personal attachments were still with the quaint Dutch towns and their idiosyncratic personalities. But families faced a daily nightmare of traffic as they crisscrossed the Randstad region in their automobiles. The number of car journeys within the city of Amsterdam doubled between 1960 and 1974, while the number of journeys crossing the city's boundaries quadrupled. The number of bicycle journeys halved. Protests mounted against the traffic jams. Activists published the notorious "White Bicycle Plan" against the "Asphalt terror of the motorised bourgeoisie."[25] Despite the protests, a wide ring-road was constructed around Amsterdam that connected to six national highways covering 1,200 kilometers, and then grew to 2,000 kilometers by 1980. Heroic highway engineering included tunnels and bridges over-and-under canals, vast windscreens, and connective junctures. They were stunning examples of the sweeping infrastructure projects that opened vast areas for development. People dashed from one place to another, chasing housing and jobs. Fully one-third of the Netherland's working population was commuting.

There was little appreciation for historic city centers in this utopian regionalist vision of the 1960s and 1970s. Planners confidently predicted the demise of the traditional streetscape. Long-standing neighborhoods and shabby housing nestled along cobbled lanes fell to the wrecking ball. The old streetcar lines were removed. Space was cleared for parking structures, business and shopping districts. They were a 1960s urban renewal strategy associated with the rise of the service and consumer economy. With its peak population of 600,000, The Hague embarked on a car-centered redevelopment scheme for the inner city that set out massive prefab office blocks and a six-story parking garage. Families out for a night on the town could zoom into a parking space and then happily amble out into a glitzy entertainment and shopping district. The smaller city of Utrecht, with 250,000 inhabitants, took on the automobile age with the Hoog Catharijne scheme that converted the run-down district between the rail station and city center into a concrete business and shopping extravaganza. A 1970s promotional film for the project began with a flyover of Utrecht. It was the breathtaking aerial view of the city that captured the imagination of planners. The film captures wrecking balls pulverizing the old neighborhood and then revels at the crowning office towers that replaced it. An immense elevated pedestrian concourse spanned the main traffic artery and spread out to thousands of square meters of glittering commercial shops. Customers skyrocketed up escalators from the underground parking garages and instantly came upon flashy automobile showrooms. The camera lingers over the food courts and opulent window displays, and follows the crowd around the concrete maze.[26] The Hoog Catharijne shopping mall suited an affluent urban society that depended on consumerism, services, and the car. It was an immediate success.

Urban renewal schemes such as Hoog Catharijne took place in cities across western Europe. The blueprint for the future meant work and shopping in the city, while families lived happily in the suburbs in spanking-new housing complexes. The Stockholm city plan of 1962 advocated the wholesale demolition of historic districts and their replacement by broad thoroughfares, eighteen multilevel parking structures, and pedestrian concourses surrounded by commercial buildings. In 1968, Stockholm inaugurated *Skärholmen Centrum* ten minutes from the city center. It was a concrete behemoth dedicated to the automobile and consumerism. Shoppers could drive from three motorways directly into a multilevel parking garage, and then abandon themselves in the terraced maze of some eighty-six shops.[27] Especially in western capital cities such as Stockholm, high-rise office blocks and shopping precincts represented a competitive edge in the new economy. The European Common Market and the forces of international capitalism intensified the jockeying for economic position. Fashioned after the American shopping mall, the Europa Center opened its doors in 1965 in the Charlottenburg district of West Berlin. Shoppers strode along concrete pedestrian bridges to enter the complex. Filled with swanky shops, an ice-skating rink, and the world's largest film screen, the Europa Center was a propaganda piece for western capitalism. It was flanked by a steel-and-glass office tower, then the highest in Berlin, topped with a revolving Mercedes-Benz logo.

To catapult Paris into the future, sweeping plans were drawn up in the mid-1960s to demolish vast swaths of the notoriously scrappy districts of Les Halles and Saint-Merri on the Right Bank in the city's heart. Victor Baltard's iron market sheds were bulldozed. The area was slated to become a prestigious world trade complex with luxury apartments, office towers, anchored by a subterranean shopping mall and regional transit hub. Vast areas of the Left Bank around the Montparnasse rail station and in western Paris along the Seine were flattened. To the shock of Parisians, the spiny modernist Montparnasse Tower rose on the skyline. It soared above a multilevel shopping mall and gigantic apartment complex. To the west, the Front de Seine redevelopment project replaced a ragtag district with glass-walled office buildings and apartment towers perched on a multi-layered concrete slab, below which were pancake layers of parking. If that wasn't enough, Paris was encased in the multi-lane Boulevard Périphérique—the "ring of death" as it was known. Then the legendary beauty of the historic districts was defaced with a highway along the banks of the Seine River. Hundreds of thousands of cars sent up waves of ear-splitting noise and spewed out noxious pollution daily.

The reaction against these nightmarish modernist scenarios began in the late 1960s and gained momentum as activists put together savvy anti-urban-renewal campaigns. It was a populist resistance against the blitz of modernization, much of it organized by local firebrands, squatters, and students. In 1968, protests took place in West Berlin against the demolition of the famed Kurfürstendamm and the bombed-out Kaiser Wilhelm Memorial Church. In Amsterdam, the demolition of the eighteenth-century Nieuwmarkt district for the construction of a highway and office towers led to fierce battles with grassroot militants. They seized control of the neighborhood, occupied the buildings, and organized protests that ended in bloody scuffles with police. The brazen plan for the demolition of Les Halles and the Baltard pavilions in Paris met with a storm of resistance in 1968 that coincided with the student demonstrations. For days, protesters marched around the abandoned iron sheds and used them for theatrical happenings and art exhibits, rock concerts, and popup discotheques. Despite a struggle that captured the imagination of the 1960s counterculture movement, the pavilions were pulled to pieces in 1971 and the redevelopment of the district went forward. When run-down Tolmers Square in London's Camden district was eyed greedily by real estate speculators, squatters and community activists campaigned against the demolition of the buildings to make way for office towers. As counter measures, they began repairing the derelict Georgian-style houses themselves and organized street festivals to reclaim their neighborhood territory. It became fashionable for London's radical lawyers to join them at squatter parties and sing resistance songs.[28] Hemmed in by the Berlin Wall, the West Berlin district of Kreuzburg was a derelict cul-de-sac populated by immigrants, bohemians, and students. When planners zeroed in on the district's replacement by tower blocks and highway interchanges, student activists and tenant groups hunkered down in resistance. The protest reached its height in the 1970s, when thousands of squatters took control of buildings slated for demolition. Rabble-rousers staged marches, blockades, and confrontations with the police.[29]

The utopian dreams of planners were a far cry from the ghetto leftovers in the inner city and forgotten outskirts. The old tenements were allowed to deteriorate in preparation for the demolition squads. They were cheap housing for poor families who formed a new urban underclass in the city shadows. Low-wage workers of every stripe suffered severe hardship. Many of the derelict neighborhoods slated for slum clearance were precisely those filled with guest workers and foreign migrants who reached record numbers by the late 1960s and early 1970s. While the run-down housing in Kreuzburg awaited the wrecking ball, migrant workers from Turkey and Yugoslavia moved in. Tolmers Square in London was a diverse community of English and Irish working-class families living alongside newly arrived wayfarers and squatters. Activists there cleverly made their own documentary film to make the case for saving their neighborhood. The urban scenes in *Tolmers: Beginning or End?* were portrayed as a "living part of the city" with its mixture of kebab houses, a Hong Kong printing service, African craft stores, tandoori takeaways, and the local union headquarters.[30] In Copenhagen, the tenant's association and squatters in a poor working-class inner district formed block protection units and barricades, and battled police for two weeks when the city attempted to demolish their homegrown children's playground.

The shocking lack of decent housing made the squatters movement a deluge throughout urban Europe. In West Germany, the cities of Cologne, Hamburg, Frankfurt, and West Berlin all had fearsome squatter initiatives with students, the unemployed, radical left-wing militants, and anarchists setting up camp for their political work in abandoned buildings.[31] Thousands participated in the squatter crusades. Boarded-up social housing slated for demolition became the refuge for the homeless. The BBC television drama *Cathy Come Home*, which first aired in Britain in 1966, was a searing portrait of a young homeless family forced to find shelter in a squatter's camp and then the bombed-out remains of an inner city building in London.[32] The film triggered a watershed public outcry against homelessness. Islands of poverty existed across what appeared as a rising sea of urban affluence. The booming port in Rotterdam in the 1960s and early 1970s depended on guest workers from southern Europe, from Turkey and Morocco who gathered in poor districts south of the River Maas. Decolonization brought waves of immigrants from Cape Verde, Indonesia, Surinam, and the Dutch Antilles. Thousands of migrants found work and lodging in obscure, clandestine zones along the urban fringes. The *bidonville* at Nanterre, west of Paris, was infamous. North Africans lived in camps of claptrap sheds and blockhouses on rotting wastelands. With its foot in the Mediterranean, Marseille attracted thousands of North African repatriates and immigrants in the 1950s and 1960s. They roomed in the shoddy hotels of the city's northern districts or in makeshift hovels in the *bidonville* camps on the outskirts. The worst of the shantytowns were eventually razed in the mid-1970s and their occupants sent to bleak slab apartment towers and left in destitution.

The creative destruction of modernization knew no bounds. The sound of the wrecking ball, the booming din of collapsing buildings, the dust and debris became part of everyday urban life. Acres of old tenements in the central districts met their demise. Despite the protests by determined activists, year by year in the 1960s, residents packed up their belongings and resettled in spanking-new apartments in housing estates in the suburbs. Thousands of people, mainly young families, vacated the inner cities each year. Nations enacted "million homes" programs to provide every inhabitant with their own welcoming modern flat. Massive system-built housing estates in places as far flung as the fringes of Glasgow, Berlin, and Belgrade sprouted up with amazing speed. The open, flat fields on the urban periphery became a happy landscape of modern living. It was allied with the ideal of social welfare, which reached its zenith in the 1960s. Subsidized public housing was a mythic form of social equity. High-rise suburban living was associated with openness and living close to nature. Residents could rely on promises of local community centers and sports fields, schools, and health clinics as part of the ensemble.

These were a visible cipher of postwar political rhetoric on both sides of the Iron Curtain. Solving the appalling housing shortage once and for all was interpreted as the fruit of both a centrally planned socialist economy and a freewheeling capitalist one. The competition to build housing was part of Cold War rivalry and bombast. When people saw the cranes jutting up over the city, the apartment blocks rising up in the distance, they were confident that a paternalistic government was fulfilling the promises of social welfare. Scottish writer Andrew O'Hagan's reflections on his grandfather's fight for decent housing was captured in the memoir *Our Fathers*. Known as "Mr. Housing," his grandfather was elated at leaving behind the teaming slums of Glasgow. He championed a "city of modern dreaming" with "high-tech castles in the air. . . . Twenty-four high. Reinforced concrete. Cement cladding. Balconies on four corners. Top of the line in their day. Each built in a month and a half."[33] Modern architecture was the spirit of the age and a sign of social progress. Each project, each French *grand ensemble* and German *großsiedlungen*, was celebrated in newsreels, films, and television shows as a rhetoric of hope for the future.

The apartment towers and linear slab blocks that spread across metropolitan regions looked identical. They were a top-down, state-planned operation.[34] Architects provided diagrammatic layouts in intricate geometric patterns. The modular buildings were then assembled from concrete panels lifted into position by cranes and held together by mortar and leveling bolts. Concrete was everywhere. The buildings were often perched on vast concrete decks with shopping malls and layers of parking below. Avant-garde flying saucer, curvilinear, box-shaped building forms echoed across the continent. The buildings were hardcore modernism and exuded the ideology of raw concrete and prefabrication.[35] Often the same construction companies were assembling the system-built housing estates on both sides of the Iron Curtain. The French Camus prefabricated construction scheme, the British Airey and the Dutch Dura-Coignet systems, and

Figure 62 The Bijlmermeer Housing Estate outside Amsterdam, 1973. Hans Peters.

Belgrade's IMS-Žeželj became European standards. The prefabricated housing estates were so omnipresent that "prefab" itself became a symbol of the age. Their pervasiveness across space and culture took on a nearly mystical cast (Figure 62).

Two examples stand out as evocative of the utopian hopes captured in Europe's housing estates and the inevitable controversies that plagued them: the Bijlmermeer outside Amsterdam and the Märkisches Viertel outside West Berlin. When Amsterdam annexed the Bijlmer polder southeast of the city in 1966, plans were hatched to create a new housing district for 100,000 citizens who would pack up and move out of the old city center. The Bijlmermeer was envisioned as a suburb for the motorized age with over thirty colossal nine- to fifteen-story apartment buildings arranged as a honeycomb around greenery, elevated highways, multistory parking garages, bike and pedestrian pathways. Tubular walkways connected the apartments with the car stalls where each family had their personal space. Like all the prefab housing programs, the Bijlmer was acclaimed in films and newsreels. It was flaunted as a daring experiment in modern living. The buildings were graced with a bounty of community amenities from schools to theaters and bistros. The modernizing zeal and sheer magnitude of the project made it visionary. The first residents receiving the keys to their new homes were treated as pioneers of the future. "Moving in" was eagerly filmed by television cameras, even while the racket of construction equipment was still in the background.[36] The Märkisches Viertel housing estate on the northern fringe of West Berlin matched Bijlmermeer in bravado. It was the flagship project of an ambitious urban renewal program initiated by Mayor Willi Brandt in 1963. Some 56,000 dwellings in the hated *mietskasernen* rental barracks in Berlin's working-class districts were to be demolished. Then, 140,000 Berliners would find new life in the suburbs. Märkisches Viertel was a concrete city of soaring apartment towers divided into 17,000 flats. The architects took great pains to avoid the disgrace of a monotonous void. The towers were adorned with colorful facades and open balconies. They were interlaced with schools, playgrounds and sports facilities, and market squares to foster community life. Some 40,000 people toured the information exhibit on the construction site as excitement rose about the model city of the future.

The inventory of vast prefab housing estates in western Europe was astounding and the virulence of the reaction against them even more so. They became the *bête noir* of the media and intellectual pundits, scorned as demonic soul-killing environments. Sociologists wailed that the rich pattern of everyday working-class life was destroyed by forced exile to the concrete slabs of suburbia. In the bestselling book *The Murdered City* (1964), German journalist Wolf-Jobst Siedler likened the slum clearance and housing plans to the second destruction of Berlin after the wartime bombardments. It was turned into a screenplay and aired on West German television. A turbulent rally against the lack of community services at Märkisches Viertel in 1970 was stormed by police who evicted the protesters.[37] The vitriolic campaign against the housing estates wiped away any value in the modernist vision of the city. Some 15,000 people lived in the Cité des 4000 in the northern suburbs of Paris in what was despairingly described as "wartime Beirut." The massive concrete estate on the outskirts of Rome baptized Il Nuovo Corviale was a utopian micro-city turned squat for illegal immigrants. The gigantic Aylesbury Estate in south London was one of the largest housing complexes in Europe with dwellings for some 10,000 people. With its entrenched poverty and social problems, it epitomized the failure of modernism in the public mind. The Wyndford Estate in the outskirts of Glasgow, where the first residents felt they had "died and gone to heaven" became known as a bleak "Barracks." The reproduction of this miserable imagery across Europe was astonishing.

Ironically, the scale and radical standardization, the massive solidity of concrete made them fragile environments. Beyond suffering from architectural hubris, many of the housing complexes lacked basic maintenance and almost immediately went downhill. Although the outcries against the psychological evil of prefabs might be dubious, the real complaints about structural failures, malfunctioning elevators, and the lack of promised amenities were legion. The spectacular downfall of the Ronan Point system-built residential tower in East London bore out the denunciations. On May 16, 1968, a gas explosion in Flat 90 blew out sections of the outer wall. The floors collapsed like pancakes down to the ground. Bijlmer became the most stigmatized space in the Netherlands. It was branded a place to settle for one-parent families and singles, especially homosexuals, with few other choices. By the early 1970s, immigrants from Suriname and the Dutch Antilles moved in. Bijlmer was battered as a "Black neighborhood," a notorious no-go zone in the popular imagination, a marginalized and obscure place of vandalism and crime, sheathed in the xenophobic narrative of immigration. To add insult to injury, a Boeing 747 cargo plane from Schiphol airport crashed into two of the buildings in

1992, killing at least forty-three people, many of them illegal immigrants. Bijlmer joined the ranks of some of the most infamous housing estates in Europe, pilloried as the new ghettos—places such as Les Minguettes in France, Märkisches Viertel in Berlin, or Broadwater Farm in north London.

Yet paradoxically, despite the visual omnipresence of these modernist mega-schemes, their gargantuan failures, and condemnation, the urban fabric in these places could be quite distinctive. Modernization was uneven, and the problems did not lie in the architecture. The housing estates were subject to the vagaries of local politics and domesticated by local circumstance. The original projects were plagued by political infighting, construction delays, scarce resources, and budget shortfalls. Despite the extravagance of their appearance, the lifespan of mass-produced housing depended on the everyday banalities of maintenance and steady public support. Urban form changed in diverse ways in response to these forces. Overtime, their resident turnover made them multifaceted environments. Residents often waited years for promised services. But in the meantime, they added their own flavor. Balconies were enclosed and made into living room extensions. Green spaces and playgrounds were commandeered for parking lots. The buildings were decorated with television antennas and satellite dishes. They were surrounded by makeshift garages and worksheds. Ground floors were converted into mini-marts, video shops, and hair salons. As the population changed and immigrants moved in, informal social networks and bric-a-brac jobs flavored everyday social life. Ethnic cafés and mail-order companies were tucked into unused spaces. Services and local goings-on were carried out in the flats. There was a depth of complexity to these places that fashioned a multitude of quotidian idiosyncrasies.

The Cold War in Europe was in good part a battle over lifestyles in these places.[38] Most urban dwellers in the Soviet Union and eastern Europe still eked out existence in one or two rooms in crumbling apartment buildings. The housing crisis was catastrophic. In response, there was a radical shift in the late 1950s away from the grandiose socialist realist projects of the reconstruction years. Soviet Premier Nikita Khrushchev's "thaw" was a period of modernization meant to kick-start a progressive socialist society and improve material life. The Soviet Union launched an all-out drive for standardized mass-produced housing. Khrushchev commanded architects and planners to build "better, cheaper, and faster." Down-to-earth practicality and functional prefabricated construction would solve the acute housing shortage.[39] The Soviet Union would catch up with and overtake the West.

While peering at the mammoth housing estates on the western side of the Iron Curtain certainly inspired communist planners, modern housing followed its own logic in the Soviet Bloc. The scale of urban transformation was greater than in western Europe. Central planning and mechanization were so rationalized that identical buildings could be rubber-stamped across large swathes of territory.[40] Propagandistic films and photographs from the 1960s unshakably featured young families cheerily setting up life in their new flats, women promenading with their prams and chatting with neighbors, and children enjoying the playgrounds. The reality could of course be quite different. The serial construction of system-built high rises instantly opened them to criticism as dreary and monotonous. But the public wailing was more muted than in the west. Given the deplorable housing situation in eastern Europe, the housing estates that popped up in the fields around cities were genuinely successful at offering modern living for the first time. The communist regime delivered on its motto of "Light and air for all!" Thousands of thrilled working-class families in the 1960s stepped through the dust and debris of construction sites and received the keys to their own small apartment. Even in the 1980s, remembered Croatian writer Slavenka Drakulić,

> Apartments were for us mythical objects of worship. They were life prizes, and we still regard them as such. Once you get one, it is all you can expect for the rest of your life. We seldom changed it, as we didn't change our job or the city where we lived. We were stuck with it, it became a part of our destiny.[41]

The landscape of modernism in eastern Europe rivaled anything the west had to offer.

The view from the Baltic city of Rostock is instructive of this process. While the public buildings in Rostock were reconstructed after the war with the historic panache of socialist realism, housing was decidedly modern. Beginning in the 1960s, planners laid out a linear band of prefab apartments along the main highway between Rostock and Warnemünde on the coast. The area had been Rostock's industrial heart with aircraft factories and shipyards lining the Warnow River. German bombers were built at the Heinkel and Arado aircraft plants while the Neptune shipyards churned out warships. The armaments industries made Rostock an immediate target during the war, and it was heavily bombed by the British Royal Air Force. With reconstruction and the Iron Curtain division of Europe, Rostock became East Germany's only deep-water seaport. Thousands of Germans headed north to the city for jobs in shipping and the port industries. Housing was planned for some 60,000 people.

The car drive along Highway 103 from Rostock to Warnemünde was a journey through the centrifugal forces pushing the city outward and the currents of construction that shaped urban form. Horizontal bands of six-story prefabricated slab apartment buildings stood like dominos in the district of Lütten Klein. The standard two-room flats evoked the spartan construction of the early 1960s. Schools, a small shopping district, and hospital clinic completed the complex in the politically driven model of mass-produced socialist housing. Alongside, *plattenbauen* in the districts of Evershagen, Lichtenhagen, and Schmarl were added in the 1970s with larger, spruced-up apartments signifying the rising standard of living. The earlier monotonous design was exchanged for decorative elements with rooflines and facades echoing traditional Baltic architecture.[42] Farther north along the highway, the district of Groß Klein was constructed in the late 1970s at an entirely new scale. Some 8,200 flats for 20,000 people were designed as curving ribbons of contemporary apartment blocks and towers interspersed with green belts and pedestrian walkways. There was little sign of political ideology in Groß Klein. Instead, the atmosphere was personalized by inhabitants taking part in public art and landscape projects. From its socialist realist historic center of the early 1950s to the linear bands of mass-produced housing estates through the 1980s, Rostock was a microcosm of the socialist-built city (Figure 63).

Figure 63 The Lütten Klein Housing Estate, Rostock, 1969.

The momentum of urbanization doubled in eastern Europe during the communist era. The Moscow agglomeration grew from 2.9 to 4.9 million people, while St. Petersburg added 2 million inhabitants to its population rolls and also reached 4.9 million. The population of Bucharest climbed from 1.1 to 2 million, while Sofia grew from 0.6 million to 1.2 million people. The population of Belgrade, then capital of Yugoslavia, shot up from 0.4 to 1.7 million inhabitants.[43] Until 1948, Yugoslavia maintained a close relationship with the Soviet Union. But once Stalin demanded control over Yugoslavia's fortunes, charismatic leader Josip Tito broke with the Eastern Bloc and charted his own course outside the bifurcated world of the Cold War. The communist government of Yugoslavia was internationally open and operated with popular consent. Belgrade was acclaimed the capital "loved by all our peoples." Official public festivities were occasions for full-throated displays of patriotism. Liberation Day in October was celebrated with a grand military parade through the city streets. Memorial rites took place at the ancient fortress of Kalemegdan where the public could stroll through exhibitions on the construction of *Novi Beograd*. Youth Day in December, first celebrated on Tito's birthday in 1945 and continuing for forty-three years, was a gigantic festival involving thousands of young people in a baton relay through the towns of Yugoslavia, ending in the hand-off to Tito himself in Belgrade's stadium. Huge crowds greeted the participants as they sprinted through Belgrade's streets.[44] Yugoslavia opened to the West and adopted an independent, liberalized interpretation of socialism. It enabled a prosperity and consumer culture unlike any other in the Eastern Bloc. Yugoslav factories churned out automobiles and mopeds, and consumer goods from telephones to detergents. The period of liberalization lasted through the 1950s and 1960s, to be followed by a repressive crackdown.

Thousands of young people had joined labor battalions to rebuild Belgrade after the war. But in the mid-1960s, living conditions were still precarious and substandard apartments the norm. The housing shortage was interminable. For many, there was no choice but to share a flat with other families. Illegal constructions of every stripe proliferated.[45] For Tito's government, the solution was to build a new city of Belgrade as the seat of the federal government. The symbolic importance of *Novi Beograd* was immense. It was a showcase for Yugoslav "Third Way" socialism with a monumental Communist Party headquarters at its core. It also signaled a wave of urban expansionist policies across Yugoslavia including the construction of Novi Zagreb and the new town of Nov Gorica in Slovenia. New Belgrade grew out of the marshlands at the confluence of the Sava and Danube rivers, at what had long been the edgy frontier between the Hapsburg and Ottoman empires. It was a concrete utopian experiment with a monumental pedestrian axis lined with civic buildings and flanked by apartment towers. The housing blocks spread out across the new cityscape. Serbian political activist Borislav Pekić had little love for the apartments in the new township in his 1970 memoir *The Houses of Belgrade*. He saw them as "all identical, empty, hardly giving any sign of life; their flylike eyes, lit by the morning sun." Crossing King Alexander Bridge, Pekić scarcely paid attention to "the white carcasses of reinforced concrete which, like some dissected giant caterpillar, were scattered along the main road; or to the auto repair shops behind their wire fences; or to the abandoned building sites with heaps of ballast, pebbles, and sand; or to the billboards, traffic, passersby."[46] Nonetheless, New Belgrade represented a Yugoslav brand of communist architecture that looked less to Soviet proclivities and more to the modernist tenants of CIAM. It was an unfinished memorial to the mega-structural creed, bereft of the promised amenities, the commercial services, and cultural facilities that never arrived, and among the most ironic examples of a Yugoslavian national aesthetic.[47]

The prefab housing estates on the margins of Europe's cities were among the most photographed, filmed, and hotly debated of urban forms. The speed at which they were constructed and the scarcity of material supplies, especially in eastern Europe, made them victims of their time. Housing was one of the most intractable dilemmas of twentieth-century Europe, made all the more calamitous by the destruction of two world wars. It is well to remember how severe the housing crisis had become by the 1950s and 1960s and the terrible conditions in which people lived before receiving the keys to their new flats. The apartments in housing estates such as Bijlmermeer and the Märkisches Viertel, in Rostock's *plattenbauen* or even in New Belgrade, were bright and spacious, outfitted with modern kitchens and bathrooms, with generous space and sweeping views. Families lived out their lives; children grew up in apartment towers with astonishing comforts that are now simply taken for granted. For many of them, the denigration of prefab mass housing was the ravings of lunatics. The inhabitants invested their neighborhood with their own life force. They mobilized as communities to demand better services. Residents in Bijlmeer fought back when their estate was "crushed to smithereens by the written press, filmmakers and opinion makers."[48] The passionate belief in social welfare and the role of the state in bettering people's lives propelled these projects forward. Thousands of smaller-scale residential estates throughout Europe, both within city limits and outside them, avoided the trap of utopian hubris and laid claim to real success.

Moving into a modern flat was experienced as social transformation. It meant living a modern life. In the 1960s and early 1970s in both western and eastern Europe this ideal was framed around the culture of consumption. It was a lifestyle revolution associated with the shift to the spanking-new apartments in the suburban housing estates. There was an insatiable appetite for the stuff beamed daily on television, in magazines, and in advertising. What made this possible were rising wages and the ability to buy on credit. Real wages increased dramatically across Europe in the 1960s and 1970s. Although the bounty was still unevenly distributed, the possibility of affluence and domestic possessions reached enough of the urban population to sustain it as a mass cultural ideal. Even in what were belittled as remote towns and villages, people dressed in modern styles and were buying modern appliances and furniture. The home became the site of self-expression and domestic bliss. Families across Europe filled their flats with stuff. The French magazine *L'Express* investigated the new consumerism in 1968 and found that Pierre G., son of an agricultural worker who had risen to a position as a salaried executive, lived with his family in a four-room flat in the outer suburbs of Paris. "They have a refrigerator, a cooker (with four burners, the latest model), a washing machine, a rotisserie, a camera, a television, a three-band transistor radio, a record-player."[49] These objects of desire were shaped by American and European companies and then appropriated in the socialist east with its own hybrid flair. Prosperity remained lower in eastern Europe than in the west. There were fewer consumer options and towns were only lightly speckled with flashy stores. But worker wages grew in every socialist country. Families in Czechoslovakia, Hungary, Yugoslavia, and East Germany, where living standards dramatically improved, enjoyed the fruits of socialist consumerism.

Young people led the way in establishing the new standards of taste and patterns of consumption, and they dramatically transformed city life in the 1960s. Throngs of young people, especially women, flocked to cities for university studies and became a new urban constituency. Free public education became a powerful force for generational convergence. Enrollment in universities soared across the continent. It was a unique rite of passage that determined cultural and political values. The number of students quadrupled in university towns and capital cities. They founded bookshops, experimental theaters, New Left and socialist student associations, nightclubs, and underground rags in the local Latin Quarter. The "street" became the vital laboratory for the twists and turns of youth culture and activism. "Happenings" and "spontaneous actions" became widespread phenomena in Europe's cities. The Sixties generation gorged on the glitzy world of consumerism and then spit it out in disgust.

In the 1960s, swinging London replaced Paris as the pivot for cultural production. London was, in the recollection of one of its aficionados, "the most intoxicating city on the planet."[50] The narrow byway of Carnaby Street in a run-down area of Soho became a mecca of fun-loving hedonism and permissiveness. It was the hangout for the Mods who captured the youthful imagination. Mod was a matter of commodity selection. They indulged in a furious gambit of clothes and accessories as codes for the self. It became hip to drink cappuccino and zip around town in a Vespa or Fiat. The cool continental, puffing on Gauloise cigarettes, replaced the American imagery of youth.[51] Filmed at locations in London, Director Michelangelo Antonioni's steamy 1966 film *Blow Up* became a Mod masterpiece. Mary Quant introduced the miniskirt on King's Road in the Chelsea district as street-scene cool. Terence Conran's first Habitat store in Chelsea opened in 1964 and sold a Sixties pop aesthetic in everything from lamps to storage jars. Hip youngsters jammed on to Carnaby Street with its trendy fashion boutiques. It was a high-energy psychedelic precinct. Well-educated, employed, money jingling in their pockets, young Londoners strutted down the sidewalks like peacocks dressed in bright miniskirts and bell-bottom jeans. Unlike the bourgeois parades on the boulevards of the nineteenth century, this urban pageant took place in the city's sleazy backstreets that had ducked the wrecking ball. Carnaby Street and Chelsea were the haven of anti-establishment mods, skinheads, and bohemians.

Music was the ultimate binding force of this eternal youth. The arrival of the Beatles from what was considered the backwater of Liverpool dramatically transformed popular culture. They became the most recognized symbols of the "swinging sixties." Their fan culture cut across nationality, gender, and social class. From their start in the shabby districts of Hamburg and the underground clubs of Liverpool to the iconic Olympia Theater in Paris, Beatlemania surged across the continent. On their 1965 European tour, they performed in local stadiums in fifteen cities to accommodate the ecstatic crowds. Their arrival inevitably provoked pandemonium. Thousands of screaming teenage girls swamped airports and city streets to welcome the "Fab Four." The media joined in the frenzy. Phenomenally successful bands such as the Rolling Stones, The Who, and the Kinks emerged from Carnaby Street coffee bars and clubs, and the surrounding Soho nightspots. The 2i's Coffee Bar in Soho became a showcase for rock talent hoping for fame and fortune.

A distinctive socialist version of the Good Life surfaced in the most prosperous of east European cities by the late 1960s and 1970s.[52] Food, housing, education, and health care were cheap and taken for granted. Consumers could travel between countries in eastern Europe, purchase inexpensive exotic goods, and smuggle in purchases to sell on the black market. Small-scale dealing, the illicit trade between city and countryside were largely ignored by officialdom. Instead, the State responded to the subcultural exchange in sought-after goods by opening its own consumer meccas and kept the subsidized prices low. Stores were stocked with locally produced merchandise advertised on State television. Stylish young people dragging on cigarettes and listening to portable radios set the tone. Dreams of political freedom were traded for Kristall refrigerators, Praktica cameras, Schwalbe mopeds, and Trabant cars in the golden years of the Sixties. Commercial shops could be masterpieces of socialist modernism. In 1962, the "Supersam" self-service supermarket appeared on Mokotowski Square in Warsaw. It was a dramatic statement in reinforced concrete and ultramodern design, with a sloping roof held in place by exposed steel girders and cables. The shelves were piled with a profusion of products. In the GDR, throngs of shoppers rifled through the luxury goods in the state-controlled Exquisit and Delikat stores that appeared in the 1960s. The Centrum department store chain was most attuned to desires and helped shoppers navigate the dos and don'ts of acquiring things. It opened in Berlin on Alexanderplatz (Karl-Marx-Platz) in 1970 in a thrilling modern building.[53] The Centrum was a shopping paradise with branches in Leipzig, Erfurt, Dresden, Rostock, and the new town of Halle.

With the thaw, Budapest became a more prosperous city and favorite shopping destination. Shop-window displays in the Corvin Aruház and Allami Aruház department stores once again made the Hungarian capital a magnet for the fashionable. In 1963, the luxurious Luxus department store opened on Vörösmarty Square. It was an elegant area of the city with up-market shops and coffee houses. Shoppers rifled through high-priced German and Italian merchandise and jeans with British labels. The flagship Skála department store in Budapest had sixty branches throughout Hungary. By the late 1970s, Yugoslavia had 410 department stores, with the most located in Croatia, especially Zagreb. The city enjoyed a sophisticated retail culture. The NAMA chain (Narodni Magazin) opened a giant department store in the suburbs of Zagreb with ample parking as well as branches throughout Croatia's small towns. Shopping was an exhilarating experience on both sides of the Iron Curtain.

In eastern Europe, young people appropriated western rock music as their own cultural form. Rock was ubiquitous, yet infused with local meaning. Young music rebels shared tapes and records across cities in an extraordinary network of flea markets and underground barter. Even in remote Siberian towns, taped versions of the newest western albums were available almost immediately.[54] After the split between Tito and Stalin, Yugoslavia turned toward a west they imagined in their collective dreams. Yugoslavia had one of the highest economic growth rates in the world. The consumption of consumer goods rose faster there than any other socialist country. Yugoslavians could travel freely with their "red passport" and regularly zipped crossed the border into Italy for shopping expeditions in Trieste. They brought back Vespa motor scooters, spare parts for the family car, domestic appliances, and clothes.[55] Although Yugoslav popular culture became more westernized, these seductive trinkets were woven into life under communism. Teenagers twisted the night away in communist youth clubs. In 1964 the first *Gitarijada* rock music festival was held in Belgrade's Fair Hall with 5,000 enthusiastic fans. By the mid-1960s, there were already eighty-eight official rock bands in Belgrade. Beatles and Rolling Stones music streamed daily on Radio Luxemburg and Belgrade's radio show *Sastanak u9i5*. The musical *Hair* opened in Belgrade soon after its premier in New York, London, and Paris. The crew of the Apollo 11 moon mission arrived in Belgrade to acclaim. Yugoslav factories launched production of Pepsi and Coca-Cola.[56]

The pubs of Belgrade were the hangout for a mixed bag of bohemian circles opposed to the communist regime. But because censorship was more severe in Belgrade as the federal capital, the Yugoslav counterculture movement was wilder elsewhere, especially in Zagreb, Sarajevo, and Ljubljana. The avant-garde art groups *Exat51* and *Gorgona* in Zagreb were behind the *New Tendencies* Biennial that showcased Pop Art. Yugoslavia's premier record company, *Jugoton*, was located in Zagreb and modernized in 1963 in response to consumer demand. Public gestures of outright defiance took place around the heart-thumbing strains of rock music. The most popular and influential rock band in Yugoslavia was *Bijelo Dugme* (White Button), based in Sarajevo. After years on the margins in the 1960s performing at small venues and on television, the multiethnic band broke out at the BOOM Festival in Ljubljana clad in glam rock costumes. It let loose a wave of "Dugmemania" among devoted fans. Their nonconformism and ethno-rock synthesis (much of it based on Balkan folk music) got them into immediate trouble with the censors. When GDR officials disbanded rock bands in 1965, some 2,500 young fans rallied and fought with police in the town of Leipzig.[57] The Rolling Stones' Warsaw concert in 1967 at the Palace of Culture turned explosive when security forces were sent in to stem the rioting. Despite official communist efforts to stem the tide of western rock music, the 1968 World Youth Festival in Bulgaria's capital of Sofia turned into a jam fest with bands playing on open-air stages and hippies camped out in the parks. An abandoned monastery in the center of L'viv in Poland was converted into an indulgent hippie commune. In Budapest, young rebels hung out around the "Great Tree" at the foot of Buda Castle and paraded through the city in a disruptive public spectacle meant to aggravate any passersby.[58]

The rebellion of youth and the countercultural movements of the 1960s were inexhaustible in content and turned subversive by the late 1960s. Radical left-wing firebrands roiled against the capitalist regimes of production and consumption. They fused together an amalgam of revolutionary philosophies and repertoires of defiance, including squatting. It amounted to a radical urbanism, the search for an autonomous city freed from the entanglements of modern society.[59] The avant-garde Situationist International lambasted modern Paris as alienating and drifted through the city's streets in search of everyday life outside the spectacle of capitalism. They twisted the daily routines of forgotten urban places into zones of imagination freed from commodity culture. West Berlin became a magnet for tens of thousands of young people drawn to its freewheeling leftist atmosphere. They took part in demonstrations and sit-ins, teach-ins, and happenings in the streets. It was a flamboyant performative theater and rebellious political tactic. An urban geography of dissent took shape. The agit-prop artists of Subversive Aktion staged rebel performances in Berlin, Munich, and Stuttgart.

The Dutch Provo group used pranks in Amsterdam to awaken those numbed by glitzy consumer culture and the uproar of city traffic. They declared their own republic of the Orange Free State and called for Amsterdam to ban cars from the central city. They introduced a fleet of white bicycles for free use, which were immediately confiscated by the police. Beatniks, hippies, and students were bent on revolutionizing society from the bottom up. Amsterdam and Copenhagen were hippie havens especially once soft drugs were legalized. Young backpackers and low-budget tourists flocked to Amsterdam. They smoked dope on the Dam Square and tripped into the psychedelic Milky Way in an old dairy factory, the Paradiso in a converted church, and the Fantasio. Recalling the weekend market at the Milky Way, English travel writer Patrick Richardson described "an astounding scene, with hundreds of hippies wandering about the stalls, or queuing at the tea counter for 'space' (marijuana) cake .... The market was swarming with outlandish-looking characters"[60] (Figure 64).

Figure 64 Happening of the "Kommune I" on the Kurfürstendamm, Berlin.

Squatting was a mutiny against banishment to the concrete world on the city margins. Hippies formed a squat in an abandoned military barracks on the edge of Copenhagen and formed the "free city" of Christiania with handicrafts and organic food, a hashish market, and a psychedelic decor. Squats in Berlin and political communes such as Kommune I became a countercultural way of life. In 1966, Kommune I organized a "Christmas Happening" in front of a café on the Kurfürstendamm and lit a Christmas tree decorated with American flags on fire. The police broke it up and arrested sixty-three protesters. The next week, activists merged into the throngs of Christmas shoppers on the Kurfürstendamm and began spontaneous protests. The police rushed in welding batons.[61] Hippie communes infamous for drugs, drinking and "free love" settled into basements and abandoned buildings. Notting Hill and Piccadilly in London became hippie experiments loaded with squats and communes along with radical gay living experiments and Afro-Caribbean self-help groups. Rock band Pink Floyd played Notting Hill in 1966 in support of the London Free School. Radical groups peppered London with graffiti and staged "mob-ins" at Selfridges department store. Western consumerism was a hot point of contention. The volatile atmosphere burst into carnage when the famed L'Innovation department store in Brussels caught fire in May 1967 during an exhibit featuring American merchandise, killing hundreds of customers. The inferno was blamed on Maoists protesting American capitalist consumerism. Incendiary bombs left by radical leftists inside two department stores in Frankfurt exploded and set the buildings ablaze. In West Berlin, police shot a protester at point-blank range for demonstrating against the arrival of the Shah of Iran.

The Parisian *enragés* were perhaps the most politically idealistic and influential of the 1968 movements. Students occupied university buildings and plastered buildings across the Latin Quarter with posters and artwork proclaiming revolution. By May, they barricaded the streets and fought police in the bloody "Night of the Barricades." Workers at the giant Renault automobile plant and other large-scale manufactories joined them in the streets in a massive labor strike. Protests in Italian universities as well as in the cities of West Germany and Britain exposed the shared generational ethos. Marches and violent clashes hit Berlin and Frankfurt, spurred on by the killing of a student protester by police and the attempted assassination of student leader Rudi Dutschke. Students and young workers in West Berlin occupied an abandoned factory and the Bethanien Hospital in Kreuzberg. They rallied in the streets, took over parks and public squares, and battled with police.

The widespread student activism spliced a diagonal across the Cold War. In March 1968, waves of protests, student riots, and strikes broke out in Warsaw and cities across Poland. In July, students in Belgrade, Zagreb, Ljubljana, Sarajevo, and Novi Sad barricaded their universities and launched sit-ins, teach-ins, and samizdat publications against the corruption and hypocrisy of the Yugoslav regime. Belgrade's university was proclaimed the "Red University of Karl Marx" as students spilled into the streets. Borislav Pekić watched "all of them densely packed and growing denser as more arrived, were moving down toward Brankova Street and the concrete apron in front of the King Alexander Bridge, where a three-deep cordon of police were waiting for them."[62] In the spring of 1968, the frenetic rock scene in Prague was emblematic of the brief moment of public freedom. Czech-French writer Milan Kundera called the Prague Spring "a drunken carnival of hate" against Soviet despotism. "But no carnival can go on forever."[63] When Warsaw Pact troops invaded Czechoslovakia in August, it was long-haired hippies and rock hooligans who took to the streets in massive protest, slinging cobblestones at the tanks. But the crackdown could do little to stop the seething anger. The political tensions and violence continued into the early 1970s.

CHAPTER 12
CROSSING URBAN BOUNDARIES AFTER THE BERLIN WALL

By the end of the twentieth century, the map of Europe was to some extent reintegrated by the fall of communism. The symbolic apparatus of communist utopia had become little more than kitsch even by the 1980s. For Milan Kundera it was "idiotic tautology." People did their best to feign enthusiasm at May Day parades. Women wore red, white, and blue blouses. As the bands and marching troops passed by the reviewing stand "even the most blasé faces would beam with dazzling smiles, as if trying to prove they were properly joyful or, to be more precise, in proper *agreement*."[1] False pretense was just as evident in the communist structures strewn across the urban landscape. An unsubtle monumentalism accompanied the choleric last years of communism. Examples of the brutalist architecture in vogue in the late 1960s and 1970s were found throughout Europe. Opinion of the concrete monoliths veered wildly from appreciation for their artfulness to utter disdain for their ugliness. Generally, brutalism was lambasted as a vile specimen of architectural hubris. However, the style was especially associated with the communist Eastern Bloc. Even after they lost their sheen in the west, concrete brutalist monuments continued to be official architectural allegory in eastern Europe. It was profoundly emblematic of communist ideology and a pompous claim on the future that was both cosmic and downright menacing. The communist avant-garde was always good at marrying aspirations with architectural fantasy (Figure 65).

Yugoslavia under the popular dictatorship of Tito was a hotbed of brutalism. Cities and towns throughout the country were strewn with tectonic geometric monoliths in exposed concrete. They were radical, sharp-edged commemorations of the communist world and tactics of Yugoslavian national imagery.[2] The Macedonian capital city of Skopje was illustrative of how extreme the urbanistic discourse of brutalism became. The picturesque city of minarets, Byzantine churches, and Ottoman houses was devastated by a massive earthquake in 1963. The city was flattened, thousands buried in the rubble, and some 100,000 people left homeless. Skopje was then rebuilt from the ground up based on a plan by famed Japanese metabolist Kenzo Tange and a cavalcade of international architects. Communism was the best shot brutalist architects had of seeing their fare-flung imaginaries actually materialize on a cityscape. The plan for the rebuilding of Skopje elicited an intense public debate. Thousands flocked to see the designs put on display at a 1965 exhibition. The city center reemerged as a jumble of communist block housing and staggering brutalist structures. This aggressive posturing held sway in the massive concrete blocks stacked up to make Skopje's Saint Cyril and Methodius University, the white geometric planes of the Macedonian Opera and Ballet

Figure 65 Saint Cyril and Methodius University in Skopje, Marko Mušič, 1974.

complex, and the linear bays of concrete in the GTC shopping mall. They were futuristic monuments molded into fantastic ziggurat, cubic, and rectangular shapes—testaments to how far the use of poured concrete and steel could go in the espousal of modernism.

The television tower was also an unmistakable emblem of the late Soviet state apparatus. The TV tower soaring above the skyline of cities represented an all-seeing communism and its commitment to television and mass media as both technological wizardry and state propaganda. Television was also equated with the beneficence of communism and rising living standards for ordinary people. A transmission tower was a high-status logo. The Ostankino Television Tower in Moscow's northern suburbs was a tribute to the Soviet space age and the highest structure in the world when it was inaugurated in 1967. Built of steel and concrete, it was celebrated for its space needle design and became an instant Moscow landmark. Inside, state-of-the-art media technology beamed television signals throughout the Soviet Union. The glass floor at the observation deck and the revolving "Seventh Heaven" restaurant followed the time-honored tradition of vertiginous views of the city combined with the nighttime scenery of electric stars.[3] The Tallinn TV Tower in Estonia was built in the suburbs for the 1980 Moscow Summer Olympics sailing regatta. Constructed in the 1980s, the space-missile Zizkov Towers loomed over a working-class neighborhood in Prague. Bratislava's (Pressburg) Czechoslovak Radio Tower just off the main square was a brutalist inverted pyramid in steel and rust-colored concrete with garden terraces to somehow make it more civilized. Nicknamed the "iron fist of the regime," its recording studios blasted out government propaganda in the 1980s. It complemented the Kamzík TV Tower that stood over the city. In each case—in Berlin, Riga, Vilnius, Kiev, Tbilisi, Budapest—

Crossing Urban Boundaries after the Berlin Wall

Figure 66 The Ostankino television and radio tower nears completion in Moscow, July 26, 1967.

the reinforced concrete TV tower-minaret was the tallest structure in the country, dominating the landscape and providing a surreal panopticon view of the city and surrounding countryside (Figure 66).

If communist television transmission merged with the ideal of complete surveillance, it also provided everyday entertainment for millions of people. Popular TV shows were modeled on American series and sitcoms. The first Yugoslavian prime time series, *Pozorište u kući* (*Theater at Home*), first broadcast in 1972, depicted the life of an average Belgrade family with a stereotypical cast of characters. The Petrović home was the stand-in for an urban middle class secure within the state socialist system. It embodied the modern aspirations of young Yugoslavians and the tension between ethnic traditions and their desire for a western lifestyle. The popular series *Vruć vetar* (*A Hot Wind*) depicted the adventures of an ordinary family from the provinces in bustling, money-mad Belgrade. The opening shots feature the hero wandering through the streets, peering at the tantalizing consumer goods in shop windows. Country bumpkins flummoxed by Belgrade's cosmopolitan energy are depicted with good-natured humor. Overtime however, with hard work, the family prospers and moves into a comfortable apartment with a contented lifestyle. By the mid-1980s, television narratives about big city life changed. Belgrade families faced a decade of economic crisis, unemployment, and downward social mobility. Eastern Europe's exposure to the world economy through loans from Western creditors, which had propped up the consumer golden age, sent their economies into a tailspin just as the global recession hit. The prime time family series *Bolji život* (*Better Life*) broadcast in 1987–88 and 1990 portrayed an upper-middle class Belgrade family at this moment of transition. Living in the city center with their three children, the parents struggle to find a better life in a tumultuous city where economic security had disappeared.[4] The communist world was peering over the cliff.

The complexity of these meanings made the public spaces beneath the television towers as well as the towers themselves instant sites of political struggle as the Soviet Empire crumbled. The Fernsehturm Television Tower on Alexanderplatz in the heart of East Berlin was opened with great fanfare in 1969. With its observation deck and revolving restaurant, it was part of the prestigious ensemble of Stalinallee and Marx-Engels-Platz and immediately became one of the most recognizable emblems of the city. Journalist Peter Schneider looked up on an evening to see the moon "behind the spire of the television tower, changing it into a Turkish minaret for the rest of the night."[5] It was also a magnet for demonstrations and mass rallies. The sea of people on Alexanderplatz beneath the tower on November 4, 1989 (broadcast live on East German television), was the largest protest in the German Democratic Republic's (GDR) history and led to the fall of the Berlin Wall. In the Lithuanian fight for independence in 1991, Soviet tanks launched an assault on the television tower in the capital of Vilnius, which was held by militant nationalists. The massacre was televised worldwide and provoked global outrage. Fighting raged for control of the television tower in the Georgian capital of Tbilisi in 1992. Thousands of radical militants in the Soviet Union attempted an armed coup in 1992 by storming the Ostankino television studios below the TV tower in Moscow. The siege turned violent when riot police attempted to break through. In the short civil war in 1993 between President Boris Yeltsin and the Russian Parliament, thousands of pro-Parliament demonstrators clashed with troops and right-wing militants in the Ostankino Television Tower. It was seized by an armed mob and hit by rocket launchers and grenades—a battle that left a trail of dead and wounded.

The 1989 fall of the Berlin Wall and the political explosion that followed was immediately recognized as an historic turning point. There was a sense that the entire communist epoch had suddenly disappeared. It began an eradication of communist symbols across the cityscape. Street names were "de-communized," monuments torn down by vengeful mobs, the despised headquarters of the secret police and Communist Party sacked. Communist buildings were boarded up. A fractious public debate ensued over the politics of memory and what of the communist past should remain inscribed in public space. The choices were ambiguous and controversial. Some ideological symbols such as the Palace of the Republic in the center of Berlin were demolished. Others such as the grandiose Palace of Culture and Science in Warsaw remained, although what to do with the landmark elicited a storm of polemics. In the end it was grudgingly acknowledged as the symbol of Warsaw's city center. It was easy to smirk at a communist utopia that sat alongside the flashy Złote Tarasy (Golden Terraces) shopping mall with its jumbo-sized advertising billboards. Other brutalist structures were left to decay into the rust-colored ruins of retro-futurism. The Soviet regime had been chased out, but the residue of its autocratic gestures remained on a newly capitalist landscape. The communist years cast a long shadow.

With the spectacular collapse of the Soviet bloc, the metaphorical Iron Curtain split open to reveal eastern Europe once again. The imagined bipolar division of Europe into "East" and "West" disintegrated. The world watched in awe as Berliners hacked away at the hated Wall, destroying it bit by bit, standing atop the remains in a joyous ode to freedom. East Berliners streamed across no-man's land and drove their Trabants to the Kurfürstendamm to stare at the window displays. Hundreds of thousands poured down the boulevard, rushing in and out of stores. They plunged into the world of consumer capitalism. In Budapest, the official reburial of fallen leader Imre Nagy in June 1989 drew hundreds of thousands to Heroes' Square to mark the end of communism. In Prague, demonstrators marched to Wenceslas Square to declare the Velvet Revolution. The capital cities of eastern Europe became deeply political landscapes. Symbolic sites were revived and appropriated by demonstrators. The events and images, the witnessing on the streets of the city became momentous historic gestures. Despite the epoch-making quality of these moments, it is important to avoid the trap of imagining eastern Europe as an unknown world suddenly open to discovery. This western geographic perception had a long history. The veil across eastern Europe had a see-through quality even during the darkest days of communism. There was a surprising flow of travel, communication, and connectivity alongside the all too evident political oppression of Communist Party rule. Eastern Europeans themselves, especially those living in cities, always retained an outward view toward the west as well as to the wider world.

Nor was socialism or its collapse homogenous experiences. In 1991 the Socialist Federal Republic of Yugoslavia disintegrated as its regions retreated into a hostile ethnic nationalism. In the radical territorial surgery that followed, Slovenia and Croatia declared themselves independent followed by Bosnia-Herzegovina and Macedonia. Massacres and mass rapes were used to speed ethnic cleansing. Hundreds of thousands of refugees fled besieged towns and villages. The deliberate destruction of the Balkan's cultural legacies devastated the region. The Serbian siege of Bosnian Sarajevo tragically embodied the ferocity and insanity of ethnic conflict. The siege took place from 1992 to 1996 under the supervision of the United Nations blue-helmeted peacekeepers and was televised worldwide. Bosnian writer Semezdin Mehmedinović stuck it out in Sarajevo throughout the war and was active in the resistance movement. He passed "through the shrouded streets, hidden from the gaze of snipers endowed with infrared rays that can pick me out in pitch darkness. At night, the red laser beam strays over the facades. I walk by feeling helpless, aware of the next second in which maybe I'll be, and maybe I won't." Mehnedinović pondered the collapse of the public realm and its European boulevard life. Instead, the long and the short of pedestrian law was *"Don't put yourself on display."*[6]

The black market and smuggling, theft and looting were the only ways to survive. Sarajevo's airport and its underground tunnels were ground zero for the criminally-led clandestine transactions that kept the city functioning.

The irony was that although the breakup of the Soviet Empire was brought on by frustrated demands for a higher standard of living, the revolutionaries now had to submit to the rules of the market. Cities and regions were plunged into capitalism as a form of "shock therapy." The demise of socialism was accompanied by privatization and chaotic restructuring that added new layers to the urban fabric. Aspirations were immense. But the expectation of economic boom was just as quickly disappointed. The newfound wealth was unevenly distributed and grossly aggravated social divisions. The *nouveau riche* profited handsomely while most people struggled to make ends meet. Wandering the city broke down into scenes of grimy streets and the debris of socialism. State-owned industries were broken up and looted by vulture capitalists. Shady deals and gangsterism, unpaid wages, massive layoffs followed. Housing was subject to the whims of the speculative market. The communist welfare net of medical care, schools, and services disintegrated.[7] The response was a bricolage capitalism. People traded in bazaars and makeshift stalls, snack bars, and food stands. They sold out of their homes. Cities became collections of tents, stalls, and booths. Overnight, Warsaw's Plac Defilad around the Palace of Culture became the biggest bazaar in eastern Europe. In its heyday in the late 1990s, the Jarmark Europa bazaar in the 10th Anniversary sports stadium in Warsaw's Praga district included some 7,000 trading posts and employed over 20,000 people. It was a multiethnic encampment.[8] Moscow's Luschniki and Dynamo stadiums became huge marketplaces. The Józsefváros railway station in Budapest was taken over by small-time entrepreneurs in a vast souk. Residential areas were suddenly dotted with repair shops, corner groceries, hair salons, and a myriad of survival strategy trades. Every available space in the large housing estates from basements to staircases was commandeered for commercial exchange. The murky transactions along the edges of the informal economy involved everything from the sex trade to minerals and high-tech weaponry.

Multinational companies and investors on the make rushed in to capitalize on new markets. Banks and stock exchanges opened; international hotel chains and consumer conglomerates appeared. Billboards advertising the latest global brands adorned building facades and public spaces. Poster shops tore down their portraits of Marx and Lenin and replaced them with Madonna and Michael Jackson. New SUVs replaced old Fiats and Trabants. Fast food was the new cuisine. The first McDonald's in Warsaw swung open its doors to 45,000 patrons on opening day in June 1992.[9] Foreign chains swooped in like vultures to pick apart communist companies on their last legs. Dutch Ahold bought out the Czech Mana supermarket chain. Carrefour quickly moved into Poland, the Czech Republic, and Hungary. Tesco entered the Czech Republic and Slovakia in 1996 by buying the old Prior department stores. By 2002, Tesco had 144 stores across eastern Europe and employed a staff of forty thousand around the region.[10] Hundreds of new office and residential buildings were erected in the most prosperous inner districts. Monumental spaces such as Potsdamerplatz in Berlin became glitzy totems of the capitalist takeover with the towering headquarters of the Daimler-Benz and Sony corporations sporting their logos over the city.

Geographical concepts such as "Eastern Europe," the Eastern Bloc, or the Balkans disappeared as countries joining the European Union went through a process of "Europeanization." The Balkans reemerged as "southeastern Europe," a new symbolic landscape that played out most persuasively in towns and cities. The step by step entry of Poland, the Czech Republic, Slovakia, and Hungary into the European Union and NATO between 1999 and 2004 crystallized a new geographic imaginary of "east-central Europe." After the Iron Curtain crumbled, intellectuals challenged the idea of eastern Europe altogether and declared the return of "Central Europe." Writing in 1984, Milan Kundera understood Europe as a spiritual, cultural notion synonymous with the word "West." For Kundera, the great revolts against Soviet control that took place in Warsaw and Prague were "a drama of the West—a West that, kidnapped, displaced, and brainwashed, nevertheless insists on defending its identity."[11] Hungarian intellectual György Konrád argued that "if there is no Central Europe, then there is no Europe. Then Europe is only a nostalgic spectacle for tourists, a monument for preservation."[12] The idea of central Europe was rooted in an "in-between" geographical space and renewed interest in a common Hapsburg cultural and intellectual tradition. Italian scholar Claudio Magris constructed a mythical Hapsburg legacy around the lost world of the Danube River Basin. There was renewed interest in the urban culture of 1900 and "turn of the century" Vienna, Budapest, and Prague. The rediscovery of the great age of urban modernization was a counter to communist colonialism and to the idea of "backwardness" inherent in Cold War ideology.[13]

Anyone visiting Vienna, Budapest, or Prague in the year 2000 could easily distinguish the urban fabric of 1900, even if it was degraded by wear and neglect. Although cities had undergone profound modern transformation, the grand boulevards and sumptuous buildings of the "turn of the century" were all still there. The historic centers of cities were as identifiable as they had always been. What had changed was the scale of the metropolitan regions around them. The majority of the European population that reached well over 700 million by the beginning of the twenty-first century were urbanites living somewhere in metropolitan localities that stretched far beyond the central districts. From the 1970s to the 1990s, the size of Europe's legendary housing estates increased spectacularly. The Wohnpark Alt-Erlaa outside Vienna was a mammoth compound of ziggurat tower blocks made up of 3,000 apartments and a host of services from indoor pools to medical clinics and a shopping mall. It was its own enclosed urban realm. The Osiedle Ostrobramska on the outskirts of Warsaw was a dramatic panorama of massive high-rise apartment buildings. Mega-structures such as these for 20,000–30,000 people proliferated across the continent. The huge Marzahn housing estate on the northeast edge of Berlin was one of the largest in Europe. It was the showpiece of East Germany's housing program, the most advanced version of prefabrication meant to retort the legion of complaints against mass-produced housing. The apartments were larger, outfitted with every amenity including television antennas and cable hookups. The privileged of the GDR could live the modern socialist way of life. The original plans called for

13,800 units housing 175,000 people in ten-story apartment blocks and was later revised upward. These were breathtaking figures. By 1989, a half million people called it home. The buildings were interlaced with greenbelts, pedestrian and traffic arteries. A massive shopping mall catered to every conceivable desire. Marzahn represented upward social mobility and domestic paradise. On receiving the keys to their apartment, one family opened the door and "a giant empire appeared, with enough room for five family members. Central heating, warm water from the wall, and a six-meter-long balcony! This is what happiness looks like."[14] Everything from dance halls and schools to retirement homes were handily available. Community life took place around gardening, barbeques, and holiday festivities. But in the tragic irony of East Germany, the Stasi secret police were intimately involved with its design and execution. Marzahn was imagined as a new kind of city open to surveillance in every nook and cranny. The number of Stasi arrests in the complex skyrocketed.

These colossal settlements also became easy targets for the disgruntled with modern living. As laboratories of the urban future, we can sensibly conclude they fell on the reefs of excessive ambition. By the 1990s, the massive system-built housing estates in France had been obsessively photographed and filmed, and the images circulated in a veritable frenzy. Places such as Les Minguettes in the suburbs of Lyon, the Cité de la Muette in the Paris suburb of Drancy, and the Cité des 4000 housing complex in La Courneuve, northeast of Paris were bywords for "slab" living, excoriated for their psychological and social evils. The emotional impact of a lonely life pigeon-holed in a remote housing estate became the stuff of fiery investigation. The estates were blamed for mental depression, for social breakdown, for juvenile delinquency. Despite the utopian hopes for creating an urban ambiance, their scale and shape were condemned as a form of incarceration. In Mahdi Charef's 1983 novel *Tea in the Harem*, the young hero Majid, the son of Algerian immigrants, wanders hopelessly through the concrete jungle known as "Flower City": "Acres of concrete. The smell of piss. Cars, cars, and more cars. And dog turds. Row after row of tall, soulless apartment blocks. No joy, no laughter, just heartache and pain. A huge estate, sandwiched between motorways, ringed by factories and by police."[15]

The most infamous scenes of social horror were captured in Mathieu Kassovitz's 1995 film *La Haine*. Shot in the impoverished suburban housing project of Cité de la Noé outside Paris, it caused a sensation. The characters Vinz (who is Jewish), Hubert (Black), and Saïd (Arab) skyrocketed to fame on their alienation and entrapment in dead-end lives. These portrayals of ethnicity were themselves unsettling to a French public trying hard to ignore the social crisis of immigration. Waves of migrants from Europe's former colonies found the housing estates a foothold in a new land. But in the minds of many, the settlements were synonymous with foreign elements, crime, and violence. They were no-go zones of marginality. In this, they followed the long-established phantasm of the periphery as an urban void. The landscape of *La Haine* set the symbolic imagery of the notorious Paris *banlieue*. With few prospects, the three friends drift away their days in a concrete jungle. The housing blocks were cold, bleak, and cruel: the public spaces barren except for a few courageous weeds. By the last years of the century, horrified French watched suburban mayhem fill their television screens with cars ablaze in the night,

French riot police battling with young men in hoodies, smoke trails of tear gas and stink bombs.[16] By that time, the worst of the housing estates such as Cité de la Muette and the Cité des 4000 were solemnly demolished. The great cement hulks were emptied out, padded with explosives, and blown up.

From the 1970s, the nature of immigration changed. Europe's open-door labor policies of the reconstruction years came to an end with the 1973 oil shock and recession. The guest worker program reached its climax in 1973. Foreign laborers had been drawn mainly to Germany (2.5 million) and France (2.3 million) where they represented about 12 percent of the German labor force and 10 percent in France.[17] By then many migrants had sent for families and stayed on, becoming permanent ethnic minorities gathered in the poor neighborhoods and suburbs of Europe's cities. English playwright Hanif Kureishi lived with his English mother and Indian father in a "two-up-two-down semi-detached" in the South London suburb of Chislehurst. His father had been in London since 1950. But to his exasperated son, he was an exotic specimen practicing yoga in the living room and dressed in Indian pajamas. He still "stumbled around [South London] like an Indian just off the boat. . . . I sweated with embarrassment when he halted strangers on the street to ask directions to places that were a hundred yards away in an area where he'd lived for almost two decades."[18]

The end of colonialism in Africa and Asia created a long trail of migrants to the metropoles. This diaspora was less organized than the labor and guest worker relocation of the 1950s and 1960s. They were most often young men, but with their spouses and young families. Their passage to Europe was more spontaneous, with legal migration merging with the murky underworld of irregular and illegal arrivals. Indians in West London, Pakistani and Indian families in Birmingham and Bradford, Algerians in northern Paris, and Turks in the Kreuzberg and Mitte districts of Berlin added to the tradition of Europe's capitals as multiethnic global places. As European capital flowed south for urban development, cities such as Marseille, Madrid, Barcelona, Rome, and Athens absorbed the swelling numbers of arrivals. Migration was much more linguistically, ethnically, and culturally heterogeneous. As urbanites, the new settlers created their own ethnic communities with their own religious and cultural traditions. They found low-paying manual jobs in construction and industry, or as domestic workers and caregivers. Small-time entrepreneurs opened ethnic shops, neighborhood groceries, and restaurants. Not just those in precarious circumstances but also more affluent, better educated people made their way to Europe's cities in search of better lives. Hundreds of thousands of migrants traveled back-and-forth between Europe and their country of origin, spending months in their native villages and towns, maintaining family ties and contributing to local incomes. Cities and towns were connected in a global flow of people, money, information that reached far beyond officialdom into a world of informal familial and social ties.

There were few social protections for new immigrants, especially those arriving clandestinely, and the backlash against them was virulent, especially by local working people already threatened by globalization, job insecurity, and the devaluation of their skills.[19] The influx of new migrants from the Middle East and Africa shifted the religious plurality of cities and became a political flash point. By 1990, Islam had 20 million followers in Europe, of whom 8 million were from the Balkans and 12 million from Africa and the Middle East.[20] Makeshift mosques appeared in ethnic enclaves. Many of these ethnic groups were painted as little more than social plague. Left with few options amid the growing racism, young migrants took to the streets. Sporadic riots broke out in suburban housing estates around Paris, Marseille, and Lyon. In 1979, a slab project in a suburb of Lyon was the scene of mayhem with French police battling mainly North African teenagers. It was a scene repeated regularly as the *banlieue* around French cities became equated with primitive terrain inhabited by violent delinquents and immigrants from the Maghreb and North Africa. A 1983 "North African March" against racism from Marseille to Paris was greeted in the French capital by some 100,000 waiting protesters.

By the 1990s, a massive influx of political refugees and asylum seekers joined the ranks of the dispossessed. Without legal status, they were exploited by human traffickers and faced harrowing journeys and unknown futures. Initially these waves were associated with the crumbling Soviet Empire and the seduction of the prosperous west. Hundreds of thousands of ethnic Germans fled eastern Europe each year in the late 1980s and early 1990s and sought asylum in Germany. People fled the iron-fisted Ceausescu dictatorship in Romania and the violent breakup of Yugoslavia. The most dramatic flights were from Albania to Italy in 1991 and 1997. Roma and ethnic minorities from Romania and Bulgaria joined the exodus. Smuggling and trafficking from eastern Europe and the Balkans into western Europe became a flood. Many lived clandestine lives and dissolved into the forlorn concrete jungles on the edges of the city. Then the expansion of the European Union and the Schengen Agreements implemented in the early 2000s created an open border policy. People were free to move around European Union countries without border checks. Some 2 million Poles traveled west. The Baltic countries experienced a veritable brain drain.

They were followed by refugees from the brutal dictatorships and violence in Africa and the Middle East. By the turn of the twenty-first century, the numbers of people fleeing political violence skyrocketed. New arrivals, many of them illegal, settled into the poorest inner districts or in the housing estates left to ruin. Opportunities for jobs and social mobility were held back by the lack of language skills and social ties and by the ethnic discrimination that was a fact of life. Neglected and bereft of care, they faded into oblivion, only visible as shiftless young men on street corners, the homeless, or as street traders hawking trinkets and knockoff fashion brands. Bitterness and anger at their plight boiled over into violence and made them easy targets for political extremism. Iraqis and Afghan refugees isolated in remote suburbs outside Stockholm exploded in violent protests in 2013. North Africans (especially Moroccans) and Turks tended to settle in the Brussels neighborhood of Molenbeek. Poverty and searing social isolation scarred the once vibrant working-class community. Nearly half the population of Molenbeek was Muslim. Islamic terrorists used it as the jumping point for murderous attacks such as the 2004 commuter train bombings in Madrid. The suicide bombers in the 2015 Paris attacks were also traced to Molenbeek. Governments struggled with the balance between recognition of ethnic and religious diversity and the integration of Muslim communities into the national fold with its European values and culture.

The dream of domestic bliss in a single-family home in the suburbs rubbed out the nightmares about crumbling housing estates and terrorist attacks. Rising affluence and the boom in automobile ownership made "suburbia" an attractive lifestyle choice. It was supported by local governments that racked in tax revenues from land development schemes. Families traded off the daily grind of commuting for open space and the suburban ideal. Spanking-new cottages enclosed with their garden and barbecue, and guarded by the family car, spread out in patterns typical of urban peripheries—along highways and ring roads or clustered around ancient villages. The Midlands and London in the UK, the Netherlands and Belgium, western and southern Germany, and northern Italy were submerged in endless suburbs. The Rhone River corridor between Lyon and Marseille became a geography of urban sprawl. Coastal areas along the Mediterranean in France, Spain, and Italy were dotted with strips of detached houses and villas with automobiles parked outside. In eastern Europe as well, with the demise of communism, people abandoned center-city living for the suburbs. The number of cars in cities such as Sofia and Bucharest skyrocketed. Development around Warsaw and in Upper Silesia in Poland spread out to cover entire metropolitan areas.

Agricultural land and greenbelts were sold and cut up into subdivisions. Posh gated housing estates were laid out by real estate developers. These was not simply replicas of the legendary American "little boxes made of ticky-tack." Instead, European suburban construction often reflected local building traditions and the reemergence of historic patterns of settlement. Decorative elements were pasted on to building facades as a local aesthetic. Local materials such as stone and brick were added to reproduce a sense of distinctive heritage. A postmodern Mediterranean pastiche served a variety of purposes from tourism to local real estate interests. Homes on the Mediterranean coast of Portugal, for example, revived traditional terra cotta chimney crowns on the roofs of suburban villas. In Sofia, suburban homes surrounded by tall enclosures were reminiscent of Bulgaria's Ottoman-era gated family compounds.[21] The heritage and built environment of old villages were retained as suburban sprawl enveloped them. Nor did the legacy of the great housing estates, socialist or otherwise, disappear. The new suburban communities grew up alongside them and added to the potpourri of the built environment.

The explosion in suburban living was followed by the construction of millions of square meters of shopping malls surrounded by asphalt parking lots. The dinky mom-and-pop stores of an earlier era fell into oblivion. Local and regional styles of consumption were stripped away, as were the traditional material distinctions between bourgeois and working classes. Instead, choices were standardized on a European as well as a global scale. There is no doubt that the juggernaut of mass consumer culture made European urban living more uniform. The same cars, televisions and electronics, and the same household goods were on shelves and showrooms everywhere. As they bought up rivals, the Aldi and Tesco supermarket chains and the Carrefour and Auchan department stores became among the largest commercial conglomerates in the world. The bright-red Tesco logo was a ubiquitous presence in shopping centers across Europe, visible from the highways and beckoning customers to exit and abandon themselves to buying. Motorists whizzed by the giant blue big-box Ikea outlets. Shoppers in eastern Europe flocked in droves to the hypermarkets and malls. They were a symbol of the profound changes that took place with the end of socialism. Big-box retail malls popped up around Polish cities in unprecedented numbers. Duna Plaza and the Polus Center outside Budapest both opened in 1996 to rave reviews. The flashy Duna Plaza and its adjacent parking structure hugged the main boulevard north of the center city amid a mélange of housing estates and suburban cottages. The Polus Center sported a hundred stores and nineteen bars and restaurants. Over 100,000 people showed up for the mall's first weekend.[22] The extent of the shopping center landscape in eastern Europe quickly outstripped that in the west. Malls, home improvement centers, and factory outlets lined the highways, many of them promoted by foreign investors eager to cash in on the transition to capitalism. By the early 2000s, Latvia, Bulgaria, and Romania were building malls faster than any country in Europe. Not even economic recession stopped construction. The suburbanization of commercial activities was one of the most marked trends in eastern Europe after socialism and defined the evolution of urban form (Figure 67).[23]

Shopping malls were derived from the long lineage of covered marketplaces, arcades, and department stores that marked the modern city from the nineteenth century. Like these forerunners, the mall was a hub of social life and a lively scene of free entertainment. It was prime public space. Families and young people, bands of mothers with baby strollers promenaded the corridors and met friends at the food court, the Cinemax theaters and restaurants. Award-winning Scottish author Ewan Morrison trolled Glasgow's shopping

Figure 67 Shopping center, Bucharest, Romania.

mall and found "Father" taking the escalators to the fourth floor at two o'clock each afternoon for lunch at Burger King. "Over the months he has learned that there are other regulars in the food court. They are not there to shop, only to eat. They are old men. They never learned how to cook, perhaps, and have now lost their wives." In the meantime, would-be pick-up artists "Dave" and "Raj" hang out at Starbucks and see "at least a hundred girls" walk past "with their shopping bags and extremely intimidating push-up bras." They finally zero in on a group of teenage mothers with their baby buggies.[24] Leisure and recreation were merged in a light and muzak-filled spectacle of commodities and social encounters. The ordinary world of hairdressers, dry-clean laundries, and shoemakers joined global retailers in an extravaganza previously unknown on the urban margins. Malls were inseparable from daily life. Everywhere in Europe, they employed millions of people. They became suburban development nodes together with upscale office buildings and high-tech parks. Although it spread employment opportunities throughout metropolitan areas, it also meant increased reliance on the automobile along with rising pollution and traffic snarls. Even smaller towns throughout Europe were surrounded by commercial strip development along the highways. Auto dealerships, garden and furniture outlets, bottle shops and roadside hotels, McDonald's and Burger Kings hugged the exit ramps. They were a ubiquitous out-of-town landscape.

This first great wave of suburban commerce was quickly surpassed by whopping factory outlets, mega-malls, and leisure complexes with a cavalcade of entertainment. At the Puerto Venecia mega-mall in Zaragoza, Spain, customers paraded through a consumer paradise and took in wide-screen Cineplexes, sport and adventure activities. By the twenty-first century, the largest mega-malls were in England and Russia. At the Trafford Center outside Manchester, shoppers could abandon themselves at a Legoland, mini-golf course and arcade games, indoor football, and a skydiving center. Opened in 2016, Avia Park in the outskirts of Moscow was a shopping and entertainment extravaganza that followed a "destination" marketing strategy. Mega-malls became ersatz versions of Disneyland that upended the condemnations about the Disneyfication of historic city centers. Disneyland Paris was in fact Europe's number one tourist destination. Located east of Paris in the suburb of Marne-la-Vallée, its high-speed TGV train station was jammed with families sporting Mouseketeer ears. The park's 15,000 employees also made Euro-Disneyland one of the largest single employers in France. It became a new development hub for a carnival of hotels, restaurants, and entertainment zones as well as the themed new town of Val d'Europe with its mega-mall inspired by the Disney Company. Tourists reversed the time-honored pattern of basking in Parisian glories and then boarding the train for a day at Disneyland. Instead they lodged in the Disneyland entertainment district and took a day excursion into historic Paris, which became just another theme park.

Viewing these transformations from the Spanish capital of Madrid is enlightening, especially because of its location in southern Europe. With the Eurozone crisis that began in 2009, southern Europe was branded with the disparaging term "PIGS" (Portugal, Italy, Greece, and Spain), which economists classified as a backward region of endemic frailty. It was an age-old stereotype of the Mediterranean south. Despite this typecasting,

Madrid developed historically as a paradigmatic European city with a compact, densely built-up urban core. It retained these features through the mid-twentieth century while the surrounding region remained relatively rustic. Then between 1960 and 1990, the city's population doubled. Poor quality high-rise apartment blocks were slapped up along the urban periphery. The population in outlying areas exploded with rural settlements such as Chamartín de la Rosa and Vallecas jumping from a few thousand residents to 60,000–70,000 inhabitants, when they were then annexed by Madrid and folded into the city's topography. The municipal government of the 1970s and 1980s set about providing better housing and improved urban amenities, especially in working-class suburbs such as Palomeras, where teams of international architects designed vernacular red-brick council housing with pedestrian streets and public squares in the style of "Red Vienna."[25]

By the turn of the twenty-first century, Madrid had become a global city with a metropolitan area of nearly 6 million people. The boom was fueled in part by over one million immigrants, mainly from Latin America, eastern Europe, and Africa. Madrid's inhabitants spread across some fifty-two municipalities, with the entire urban region spewing out to cover 179 municipalities, nearly 12 percent of Spanish territory. It was the largest metropolitan area in Europe after London, Paris, and the Ruhr. A web of highways and high-speed trains fanned out across the expanse. The oldest historic districts lost population while development leapfrogged over vacant land to settle around the ancient web of outlying towns, especially to the east and to the south along the A-2 highway. Universities, hospitals, private corporations followed, relocating along with shopping centers and leisure parks. Madrid's Xanadú mega-mall south of the city was one of the largest in Europe. Aerospace companies clustered around outlying Barajas Airport. The capital's creative industries were concentrated in the historic center, but also in the suburban towns of Alarcón, Móstoles, and Leganés. Madrid's financial sector ranked just below London, Paris, and Frankfurt. Suburban corporate parks and high-tech campuses fed Madrid's global economy. The suburban town of Pozuelo de Alarcón with its regionalist-inspired redbrick Church of St. Mary of Caná was one of the richest in Spain and the favored location of corporate head offices. By the early years of the twenty-first century, Madrid was surrounded by a polynucleated urban region in which outlying towns reached populations of 100,000 to 200,000 inhabitants.[26]

Portuguese cities as well underwent this dispersion into spread-out metropolitan territories. Portugal was traditionally one of the least urbanized countries of Europe. Even in the 1970s, only around 40 percent of the population lived in compact towns and cities that were clear-cut from the surrounding countryside. Most urban dwellers lived in the capital of Lisbon in the country's south or Porto in the industrial north, both along the Atlantic coast. Urbanization finally took off from the 1960s and early 1970s. Initially it was triggered by rural to urban migration and the housing policies of the Salazar regime. Then the return of people from the Portuguese colonies and foreign migrants brought another wave of urbanites. While the populations in the stunning old cities of Lisbon and Porto grew moderately, those in the outlying towns around them skyrocketed. With the construction of a new radial highway system from the 1990s, speculative clusters of big-box malls, strip commercial malls, and knowledge-economy businesses spread out across the entire Lisbon region of 2.5 million people. The areas surrounding Porto and the city of Aveiro were gorged with development. Picturesque villages were girdled in a potpourri of housing estates, gated communities and vacation rentals, informal *bairros*, and squatter settlements. They swept across the Algarve landscape in the heterogeneous pattern typical of Mediterranean urban development. It was some of the most intense urban sprawl in Europe.[27] All along the Atlantic and Mediterranean coasts, wealthy foreigners, especially sun seekers from the north of Europe, scooped up vacation houses and villas with swimming pools. Governments brandished a no-restrictions development policy to entice residential development and the tourism industry. A startling, largely unregulated sprawl engulfed Europe's sun-drenched coastlines.

Increasingly, European cities relied on tourism such as that along the Mediterranean to keep businesses humming and people employed. Global tourism became one of the most dynamic economic sectors in Europe. The great capital cities had long been a magnet for cultured travelers embarking on the Grand Tour. Holidays and travel took off in the early nineteenth century as the middle classes joined in the cultural pilgrimages (see Chapter 3). The arrival of mass tourism with journeys by train and steamship, and especially the immense popularity of the international expositions, made travel into a thriving industry. Organized group holidays offered sightseers with lesser means the chance to enjoy adventures across the continent. The right to paid vacations achieved in many European countries during the 1930s made a summer holiday possible even for working-class families. But tourism in the late twentieth and early twenty-first century far outpaced these earlier touristic escapades. Rising affluence and urban lifestyles triggered an unparalleled boom in leisure expeditions. The rush to the beaches became an annual summer exodus for the dolce vita of the Mediterranean. High-speed trains and budget airlines were jammed with families; highways clogged with cars and campers headed south. The 1985 Schengen Agreement allowed Europeans to hip-hop through the European Union without needing a passport. On long weekends, throngs of sightseers paraded through the streets of prettified historic districts in cities across the continent.

Great capitals and historic towns became stage sets of urban heritage and welcomed millions of visitors each year. The Ramblas in Barcelona, the Kurfürstendamm in Berlin, the Champs-Elysées in Paris as well as time-honored promenades in places across Europe were packed with out-of-towners. The crumbling boulevards of once insulated capitals in eastern Europe were suddenly crowded with sightseers and lined with stylish bars and cafés. It was part of the growing backlash against wholesale modernization and a fixation on inner-city refurbishment. The first "historic preservation districts" were designated in the 1960s. "Walkable" cities and pedestrianized historic precincts became all the rage. Municipal authorities reinvented the urban past as touristic pilgrimage and displayed their golden ages as visual register. Monuments were landmarked and restored and surrounded by buffer zones that offered perfect camera angles. Meticulously restored buildings, cobbled streets, open-air terraces and bistros, shade trees and street trimmings evoked the charm and elegance of the past. The medieval and early modern contours with their town halls and churches, their sinuous passageways were resurrected as picturesque tourist districts. The Normandy town of Rouen in northern France revamped the cobbled rue du Gros Horloge into a pedestrian promenade with views of its splendid medieval astronomical clock. Rouen Cathedral became a favored tourist destination. The stunning half-timbered Norman buildings that lined the city streets was fastidiously repaired and put on display. A promenade around Rouen became a voyage into the past, often led by student guides from the local university. In the process, cultural memory and the meaning of urban place shifted. The value of the urban fabric was dependent on scenic aesthetics and consumption. Municipal governments slapped preservation labels on their Old Towns, organized heritage trails, and promoted the unique historic qualities of their city on the global marketplace. Eccentric museums assembled quirky local artifacts and displayed them for outsiders. By the late twentieth century, Europe's cities vied for designation as a UNESCO World Heritage Site. What constituted "authentic" local experience was bought and sold in the new heritage economy.

The historic districts of the Estonian capital of Tallinn were reinvented precisely on this touristic heritage model. Tallinn was devastated by Soviet bombing in the counteroffensive against Nazi forces during the Second World War. The Old Town suffered extensive damage. Then Estonia was summarily annexed by the Soviet Union. Under Khrushchev, the slow restoration of Tallinn's medieval Hanseatic heritage began. Facades were given a facelift, the city walls and towers repaired. In 1966, the first historic protection district in the Soviet Union was established for Tallinn's Old Town. A frenzy of refurbishment then took place around the 1980 Moscow Olympics, when Tallinn was selected for the sailing regatta. The Town Hall and St. Nicholas Church, the stone towers and gates made Tallinn's medieval grandeur into dramatic display. It looked and felt like Hanseatic history. The timber-framed houses with their gabled and mullioned windows, the red-tile roofs and church spires, the tangle of cobbled lanes were converted into a picturesque vision frozen in time. The visually arresting scenography begged tourists to aim cameras in every direction. Soviet guidebooks and travel films from the 1960s onward promoted Tallinn's Old Town as a premier tourist destination.[28] It was quickly co-opted as the setting for numerous cinematic costume dramas. The early twentieth-century wooden "Lender houses" and the "Tallinn houses" with their stone entrance halls had long been snubbed and slated for demolition. Especially after Estonia gained independence in 1991, they were lovingly restored as local birthright. Places became hyper-real, imbued with viewpoints and panoramas, with legends and stories, with heritage walks and guided itineraries. Sightseers and citizens alike became spectators in enchanting theaters to the past. The social and political ambiguities of urban space were pushed aside for idyllic spectacle (Figure 68).

By the later years of the twentieth century, the culture industry became a key driver of the post-industrial economy. Abandoned industrial wastelands and derelict waterfronts were revived as culture and entertainment zones. Gritty scrublands of forlorn warehouses, polluted docks and harbors in cities such as Liverpool and Glasgow were converted into memory districts and places of consumption. A decaying shipyard in Belfast where the ill-fated *Titanic* passenger ship was built was repurposed as the "Titanic Quarter" with upscale apartments, hotels, and interactive entertainment. The most spectacular case of waterfront revitalization was the Guggenheim Museum project in the city of

Figure 68 Tallinn's Old Town, Viru Street and the towers of the medieval Viru Gate.

Bilboa, the capital of the Basque region in Spain. The shine had long dulled on what had once been a vibrant industrial port on the northern edge of the Iberian Peninsula. Its obsolete machine industries and shipyards along the Nervion River were boarded up. Unemployment reached as high as 25 percent by the 1980s and the economy slipped into depression. Even more devastating was the Basque separatist movement that racked the city and left it with an unsavory reputation for terrorist bombings and murders. Bilbao was run down and worn out by years of neglect and violent struggle. People abandoned the city and left the polluted industrial wastelands along the river to decay. The scale of dereliction along Bilbao's winding waterfront was shocking.

From the early 1990s onward, Basque civic leaders jumped into action. The municipal authorities put the weary locale in the hands of internationally acclaimed architects who transformed it into a spectacle of sophisticated visual imagery. The stations for the new metro system were designed by British architect Norman Foster. Santiago Calatrava devised the new airport and the pedestrian bridge over the Nervion River. American architect Cesar Pelli sketched out a scheme for the derelict waterfront area of Abandoibarra that included Frank Gehry's Guggenheim Museum. Opened in 1997, the museum was immediately hailed as a masterpiece. Set amid reclaimed public space and a stylized river promenade, the building's international celebrity set off a frenzy of investment in the long-ignored city of 350,000 people. Although culture had not traditionally been Bilboa's strong suit, urban cultural aesthetics were carefully maneuvered by a municipal entrepreneurial campaign. It made Bilboa into an international sensation. The Guggenheim's shimmering titanium facade was endlessly reiterated in photos

317

across the globe as a sign of architecture's capacity for urban revitalization. Bilboa became a breathtaking scenography of elegant facades and esplanades along the river. The surrounding lush green hills added to the intensity of the visual imagery. Viewing it became the ultimate urban experience. Urban officials around the world dreamed of repeating the "Guggenheim effect" with their own Frank Gehry museum.

Increasingly, cities competed for recognition and money with sweeping redevelopment schemes, world-class stadiums and convention centers, and blockbuster museums.[29] Designation as an official "European Capital of Culture" meant an infusion of European Union funds for cultural and tourism initiatives and a promotional platform for local culture. Staging flagship buildings and the visual qualities of architecture and the streetscape became commonplace strategies of "city branding."[30] But there were prices to pay for these ambitions and reliance on the lucrative mass tourist industry. Mega-projects were often a catalyst for a transformation in urban governance. A city's future was determined less by democratic processes and more by wealthy elites and real estate development schemes. Elected mayors and municipal councils bowed to democracy. But the city came under the dominion of entrepreneurial decision-makers in tune with the global market.

Among the biggest of these projects in Europe in the early twenty-first century was Hamburg's Speicherstadt and HafenCity. The grungy warehouse district on the quayside was converted into a scrupulously designed urban canvas. Impeccably refurbished brick warehouses were interlaced with pedestrian bridges and cleaned-up canals, terraced cafés, and art galleries. The marquee projects were the Hamburg Maritime Museum and the landmark Elbphilharmonie concert hall. Hundreds of acres on the waterfront was opened for development as an "innovation zone" with high-tech office space and luxury flats. The Speicherstadt was immaculate and safe, heavily securitized to avoid any mayhem. As places such as these were seized for cultural regeneration, local inhabitants, many of them poor, were summarily displaced. Ambitious speculative ventures tuned to the global market, they quickly hijacked local history and indulged in the creative destruction of urban areas deemed superfluous. Scrappy worn-out riverfront and harbor areas were turned into a concoction of business and entertainment wonderlands for tourists, the talented, and the upwardly mobile. They were places most Europeans could only stare at.

Cities were choked with travelers and historic centers turned into no-go tourist zones jammed with hotels, overpriced restaurants and sidewalk cafés, and souvenir shops. Lines of gargantuan tour buses squeezed through narrow alleyways and surrounded historic monuments. The crush of guided walking tours overwhelmed public squares and sidewalks, as did the CCTV cameras peering down on the revelers. Flotillas of cruise ships disgorged thousands of travelers onto the city streets. Cities such as Venice were all but abandoned by its citizenry. In 2017, Venice was bursting at the seams with more than 20 million visitors wandering what had become an archipelago of ornamental islands. But the number of inhabitants had dwindled to only 55,000 hangers-on. One of its last remaining native residents decried a city "where all real life has vanished . . . and consists entirely of façades backed by hotel rooms and tourist apartments."[31] The early years of the twenty-first century saw a bevy of citizen anti-tourism campaigns challenge the open-door policy of municipalities eager to cash in on the holiday business. Bargain airlines and package tours brought throngs of weekend sightseers. The rise of sharing services such as Airbnb and Uber exacerbated tensions. Tourism was increasingly viewed by the disgruntled as a frontal attack on a city's social fabric. Led by Venice and Barcelona, and then spreading across Europe, local citizens marched against the hordes of visitors out for an escapade, the unchecked drinking and carousing, the traffic jams and environmental damage caused by tourism. What became a hot political issue forced mayors to institute regulations and crack down on illegal services and gross behavior.

Hallmark sports and entertainment events became an indelible part of city branding and a mark of civic self-confidence and pride. Staging spectacles such as the European Capital of Culture, the Olympic Games, and FIFA World Cup was the framework for reimagining the urban fabric and jump-starting redevelopment and infrastructure projects. European cities had a long tradition of extravagant events as a tool for urban revitalization—the international expositions chief among them. Their legacy was evident in spectacular icons such as the Eiffel Tower for the 1889 Universal Exposition, Brussels's quirky Atomium built for the 1958 International Exposition, and the London Dome for the Millennium 2000 Expo. The Olympics followed in this blockbuster legacy. It quickly became the pretext for massive investments in transportation, telecommunications, and housing. Grenoble's 1968 Winter Olympics, the Winter Olympics in Sarajevo in 1984, and Barcelona's 1992 Summer Olympics were all catalysts for transforming these cities. The extent of Barcelona's revitalization was remarkable and achieved international acclaim. Billions were poured into the redevelopment of the waterfront, a new airport, a futuristic communications tower, new museums, and sports venues. Host cities also took on the risks of mega-events as political platforms for activists and extremists. Munich's 1972 Summer Olympics was overshadowed by the tragic massacre of eleven Israeli athletes and coaches by Palestinian terrorists. On the other hand, the 1998 FIFA World Cup in Paris released a frenzy of national unity when star footballer Zinedine Zidane, from an Algerian working-class family, led the French to victory in the spanking-new Stade de France in the gritty working-class suburb of Saint-Denis. A million people poured onto the Champs-Elysées in a sea of tricolor flags. Zidane's image was projected on the Arc de Triomphe. In the 1990s, outdoor music festivals joined the ranks of urban mega-events. The Sziget Festival in Budapest and the Exit Festival in Novi Sad in Serbia grew into epoch venues with tens of thousands of music pilgrims descending on the cities. Vienna's Donauinselfest, held on an island in the Danube, was the largest music festival in the world with over 3 million visitors in 2014. Tomorrowland, an electronic music and dance extravaganza held in aptly named Boom, Belgium, stretched over two weekends with hundreds of thousands of fans ogling the spectacular stage designs and firework displays.

The largest metropolitan areas benefited most from the entertainment and culture industries as well as other fast-growing economic sectors such as financial services, information technologies, and medical research. By 2000, every European country was predominantly a service-oriented society, and an urban one. These trends were exaggerated by the juggernaut of globalization. Those capital cities with the strongest money industries gained the most as the global economy moved increasingly toward financialization. London, Amsterdam, Paris, and Frankfurt led the way. They were the nerve centers for the virtual currency flows and split-second financial transactions, the business deals, and information transfers that kept the global economy zooming at unheard of speeds. They networked financial capitals together across the globe in ways that far surpassed physical distances, and instead relied on the flashes of light on computer screens. The old central districts lost their economic weight to hi-tech business zones on the periphery. As historic cores were carefully preserved and given over to tourism, glass skyscrapers materialized on the borders of the city, attached to the center by six to eight lane ring highways and regional train lines. The La Défense area west of Paris was developed from the 1970s into France's premier business district. It was laid out across an immense platform esplanade that extended the line of sight from the Champs-Elysées past the Arc de Triomphe, westward across the Seine River to end at the lavish Grand Arch. The cubist structure in marble, granite and glass rose over an ensemble of gleaming glass towers as well as over the entire western skyline of the Paris region. Alongside it was the Quatre Temps mall, the largest shopping center in Europe at the time. The sweeping curved roof atop a vast convention center signaled the dealmaking going on among business elites. During the 1980s, the prestigious Zuidas World Trade Center district took shape south of Amsterdam. It sat next to a new entertainment zone with the Ajax football stadium, a multiplex movie theater, and Heineken concert hall. These outlying business districts had a ubiquitous look, identifiable by their modernist glass office towers and a signature architectural marvel identifiable on the city's skyline. They were the plaything of real estate moguls and world-famous architects who fashioned them into surrealistic landscapes of global capitalism.

London generated Europe's largest cluster of financial industry jobs. In the 1970s and 1980s, companies abandoned their command posts in The City for the wilds of Canary Wharf on the East End. The final days came suddenly for the old Docklands on London's East End. It was unable to accommodate the large vessels when the shipping industry containerized cargo. One by one, the famed docks along the Thames closed down. The market-driven London Docklands Development Corporation was created in 1981 to oversee the redevelopment of what had become a derelict scar on the city's landscape. The West India Docks and the Isle of Dogs—where the bounty of the British Empire had once spilled onto the wharves—were reinvented as the Canary Wharf business district. Angry local residents about to be displaced released a flock of sheep and thousands of bees into the audience during the groundbreaking ceremony. Despite the protests, the project went forward including the new Jubilee line for London's Underground. Canary Wharf quickly filled up with global banking institutions housed in some of the tallest buildings in Britain. By the early years of the new century around 100,000 people were employed at Canary Wharf. Not to be outdone, London's traditional financial hub in The City, or the Square Mile as it was known, seduced developers into constructing high-profile office towers by celebrity architects. A phalanx of hyper-designed iconic shapes appeared on London's skyline. The Gherkin Tower with its signature curved helix-shape and the concave glass Walkie-Talkie Tower continued the tradition of panoptic urban views with their observation decks and Babylonian "sky gardens" overlooking the city. The cloud-busting 95-story Shard by architect Renzo Piano soared over London Bridge and became London's newest celebrity building. They were a field day for architectural critics who either waxed eloquent on their majesty or grumbled at the egregious errors plonked onto the cityscape.

The emergence of the German city of Frankfurt as Europe's other financial citadel was not a certainty. There were other claimants for this title. Eight stock exchanges were opened in Germany after the Second World War: Hamburg, Bremen, Hanover, Düsseldorf, Munich, Stuttgart, Berlin, and Frankfurt. Even before the war, Hamburg's port activities made it Germany's second most important banking center after Berlin. At the center of the Ruhr industrial region, Düsseldorf controlled a huge portion of the credit market. Frankfurt actually had few people working in the money industry. It was traditionally known for its trade fairs and book printing as much as for banking. The city was also decimated by wartime bombing. But its central location in the Rhine-Main region of western Germany and its large airport, plus the presence of the American military headquarters, made Frankfurt the favorite of the Allied authorities. The entire Rhine-Main region benefited mightily from the division of Germany, with West German federal offices located to the town of Wiesbaden and media companies clustered around the new ZDF television broadcasting center in Mainz. Frankfurt was chosen as the location for the German Central Bank (Bank Deutscher Länder) and the Kreditanstalt für Wiederaufbau (KfW) in 1948. Private and state-owned banks followed the siren call to Frankfurt. The Bank for Reconstruction and Development that distributed Marshall Plan funding moved into the city's budding financial district. The Deutsche Bau—und Bodenbank AG that specialized in housing construction began operations there. The Dresdner and Deutsche banks stationed their headquarters in Frankfurt. When the German Mark was made fully convertible in 1958, foreign banks set themselves up in a city that had grown to 600,000 inhabitants.

By the mid-1960s, every bank in Germany had headquarters or offices in Frankfurt. Clustered around the stock exchange on the Börsenplatz, the *Bankenviertel* was a daily spectacle of moneymaking and financial deals. With the oil crisis of 1973 and the collapse of the Bretton Woods agreement, there was an unprecedented growth in the international money market. Transactions were done at lightning speed with the arrival of the internet and information technologies. The result was a massive expansion of financial trading. By 1987, some 50,000 people were working in banking and insurance in Frankfurt.[32] Sixty foreign banks opened their doors and by the early 1990s they accounted for 50 percent of Frankfurt's dual-platform stock exchange transactions. The conversion of the stock exchange into the Deutsche Börse AG with a full range of financial services was a quantum leap in Frankurt's monetary supremacy.[33] The city's global status pushed companies into claiming prestigious addresses in the host of skyscrapers appearing on the horizon. The halo of light in the nighttime skyline intensified with the Eurotheum, Silbertum, and Citibank towers. In a second wave of construction, the silhouettes turned more postmodern with the twin trapezoidal towers of the Deutsche Bank Headquarters, the Japan Center, and Commerzbank redoubt. The bravura of the Frankfurt skyline matched the city's global pretensions as the monetary polestar. The establishment of the European Central Bank (ECB) in 1998, which administers monetary policy for the entire Eurozone, dramatically shifted the complexity and scale of financial transactions. The selection of Frankfurt as its headquarters made the city into Europe's preeminent financial gateway, able to dictate policies across the continent. The striking profile of the ECB headquarters on the riverfront was a potent symbol of Frankfurt and of Europe. By the early 2000s, the Rhine-Main region around Frankfurt had the highest concentration of banks and credit institutions anywhere in Germany.[34] Vast money flows and international capital transfers blazed through computer and financial terminals lodged in offices stacked high above the city's streets (Figure 69).

Globalization and the transformation of the European economy toward finance and services was also accompanied by the painful disappearance of industrial production. The famed industrial regions of Europe that had been the indomitable engines of growth became flagging rust-belts. Factories and steel mills closed, their derelict remains cordoned off by chain-link fences. Unemployment prowled the once vibrant industrial towns of the Ruhr area, the industrial heartlands of Glasgow, Manchester and Birmingham, and Lille. Joblessness became the fixed reality of everyday life for those caught in the downward spiral. In eastern Europe, communist policy remained fixated on heavy industry, even as run-down factories and industrial machinery teetered into obsolescence. Full employment and smokestack technology carried the flag of communist ideology. The outdated iron mills and coal mines around Katowice in Upper Silesia chugged along, still operational. Each morning, some 17,000 men walked through

Figure 69 Frankfurt skyline at the business district.

the gates of the famed Gdansk shipyards in Poland. It was there, under the leadership of Solidarity and shipyard electrician Lech Wałęsa, that civil resistance pushed communism into collapse.

The result was an exaggeration of differences between declining regions and those that profited from the globalizing economy. The phenomena of "shrinking cities" across Europe had major social and political implications. Medium-size, small towns, and villages unable to compete on the global stage faded into backwaters while the major metropolitan centers vacuumed up young people looking for jobs in the new economy. Old textile towns such as Łódź in Poland emptied out of job opportunities and people. In some cases, this involved entire regions, especially in the former Eastern Bloc. Towns across eastern Europe experienced tragic population declines between 1995 and 2005. Socialist urbanization had already concentrated growth in large cities at the expense of smaller settlements. Then small towns and villages were hit by the transition to capitalism in the 1990s. The demise of state industries and the lack of public investment tragically eroded the quality of life. Young people fled and birth rates declined. Entry into the European Union made moving West too enticing for those stuck in dreary towns without prospects. In the early 1980s, the giant Lenin steel mill in the Hungarian city of Miskolc northeast of Budapest still employed 18,000 workers. It was a socialist bastion. The sprawling complex, once the pride of communism, was shuttered like an old relic amid the global economic crisis, and the town lost 100,000 people. Old working-class tenements were abandoned and communist-era housing estates left to deteriorate. The city's main boulevard soured into a forlorn scene of general neglect. Miskolc fell from grace as a model socialist city, forgotten in one of Hungary's poorest areas.[35]

Places such as Miskolc increasingly banked on culture and heritage for regeneration and to entice young residents to stay put. By the early years of the twenty-first century, new cafés and bistros appeared and musicians roamed the main boulevard in Miskolc as the town began to recover. Light opera performances were staged beneath its crumbling communist-era television tower. The town's university emerged as an education and research pole while a new industrial park was inaugurated, although both competed mightily with the same initiatives in the Hungarian towns of Pécs, Debrecen, and Szeged. Some declining towns were able to conjure new identities and take advantage of the culture industry. Łódź, for example, staked its future on filmmaking. Young people in the town of Debrecen in eastern Hungary flocked to jobs in call centers set up by global businesses. But the distinctions between dynamic and "backward" regions were grossly magnified by the currents of globalization.

On the other hand, thriving new regions emerged. Some east European cities reindustrialized with foreign investment. The International Monetary Fund and World Bank supported the transition to a market economy. The steel, machine tools, and food processing industries took off in the Donetsk region in the Ukraine. An automobile manufacturing hub appeared in a crescent from the Czech Republic through Upper Silesia, and into Slovakia. Like the Donetsk Basin, this was historically one of the industrial heartlands of Europe. Coal and steel, heavy industry were their heritage. The major European automobile giants poured investments into new plants and test tracks, along with equipment suppliers and subcontractors. Volkswagen purchased and refurbished the old Skoda plant. Renault, Citroën, and Opel and the Japanese carmakers set up plants and employed tens of thousands of workers. Car production in the region reached record levels in the early twenty-first century. With over 5 million inhabitants, the area of Upper Silesia around Wrocław (Breslau), Katowice, and Kraków became one of the densest and fastest growing urban regions in Europe. In Slovakia, carmakers congregated around the cities of Trnava, Martin-Žilina, and Bratislava.

Situated on the Danube River in the foothills between the Alps and Carpathian mountains, the Slovakian capital of Bratislava was historically at the crossroads of central Europe. Initially Bratislava prospered during the Second World War from the boom in its oil refining and armaments industries. Then the city's Jewish population vanished into the concentration camps, and both its German and Hungarian populations were expelled in the territorial machinations that followed the war's end. Nor did the city fare well under the repressive communist regime, particularly after its leading role in the failed political revolutions of 1968. Much of the inner city was left empty and in ruins. It was surrounded by a dreary landscape of prefab housing blocks. Mind-numbing functional zoning left little trace of Bratislava's traditional urban fabric. The imposing Kamzík TV Tower hovered threateningly over the skyline. Urban explorer Stefan Hertmans captured the atmosphere in 2001 as he walked down "the empty grey streets," to see

> building after desolate building, sooty black and decayed blocks of flats with dark stairwells covered in peeling Baroque motifs. . . . In the local McDonald's the progressive rabble assembles . . . the McDonald's here is the place to be: hip-hoppers, caps, heads shaking to thumping rhythms of music listened to on Walkmans and gyrating bottoms, Nikes have been scrimped and saved for and sometimes even the odd roller-blader.[36]

The reemergence of Bratislava just a few years afterward was indicative of the magic created by auto manufacturing, food processing, and chemical production alongside the new post-industrial economy. Some 17 percent of the workforce was employed in manufacturing, while 19 percent worked in trade and another 19 percent in public services.[37] Young people gravitated from around Slovakia in search of jobs in the capital. They found cheap rent in dispirited neighborhoods that became hip. Global service and high-tech firms set up outsourcing and service centers, especially in the Digital Park complex opposite the Aupark Shopping Center on the D1 highway. They advantageously squatted between the city center and the densely populated suburban borough of Petržalka. By the early years of the twenty-first century, the Bratislava metropolitan area and its 650,000 inhabitants rapidly emerged as one of the richest in the European Union. The entire metropolitan region between Vienna and Bratislava had historically been among the most dynamic on the continent. It was a sign that Europe was reknitting back together. What characterized Europe's urban geography was its continuity and longevity. Despite profound changes over the course of the twentieth century, the urban order had reproduced itself.

CONCLUSION

In 2016, the European continent remained one of the most urbanized areas in the world. Some 75 percent of the 742 million Europeans at that time lived in urban areas—the number has only grown over the last several years. The widest urban footprint is in the Dutch Randstad and Rhine-Ruhr area. In comparison to the world's leviathan mega-cities—the 37 million people living in the Tokyo metropolitan region, New Delhi with 29 million, or Shanghai with 26 million—the population of Europe's largest cities pales in comparison. As they have been historically, the largest metropolitan areas in Europe are London and Paris, with around 12–14 million people each. Moscow also has a population of around 12 million. They are followed by Madrid, Berlin and Barcelona, and Milan. With the same degree of urbanization found in Japan or the United States (where about 80 percent of the population live in urban areas), Europe is instead characterized by numerous large but not mega-sized capitals and regional cities, medium- and small-sized cities, and multi-city regions.[1] During the 1990s, the concept of the "Blue Banana" tried to capture these dense urban archipelagos with their powerhouse economies. It stretched from London, down through the Dutch Randstad and Brussels, across the Ruhr and Rhine areas, and then down to Milan. Other mega-regions of dense urban development have been identified, such as the European Sunbelt that stretches from Valencia in Spain across to Genoa in Italy, the arch of concentrated urbanization in east central Europe, and the band of development along Portugal's coast. As described in the earlier chapters, the impact of urbanization extends far beyond metropolitan borders. Even in small towns and villages, Europeans live urban lifestyles and expect typical urban amenities.

Given the forces of globalization and migration, is there still something that can be called a "European city"? Life in cities changed markedly over the two centuries discussed in this book. The urban experience in 1815 was vastly different than in 2015. These two centuries were the key period during which European cities emerged as the primary laboratory of modernity. It is of vital importance to understanding urban society. Yet modernity did not produce a generic European model. There is no one vision of urban Europe. This book highlights the highly complex, fluid nature of modernity and modernization as they took shape across geo-historical space, and the ways in which local urban cultures influenced modern transformation. Modernity was not monolithic. It was an uneven mixture of forces that interacted with everyday life in countless, often edgy and contradictory ways. The full range of Europe's urban system flourished and adapted to modernity idiosyncratically. It has always been exposed to global markets, to the vast movements of people, to information and communication flows. Cities were spaces of encounter. People concocted ways of interacting and negotiating between different social groups and ethnicities, different commercial, cultural and ideological interests. The result is that there are many European cities and a plurality of urban experiences. Yet there is no doubt about the fundamentally European character to all these urban places. The stability of the European urban topography was remarkable. It reflects the legacy of the past. Traveling through the urban landscape, looking for traces of this rich history, provides the framework for understanding the complexity of modern transformation. There is a deep structural unity in the European urban experience that gives it a specific disposition and praxis, a sense of European-ness. The city is an expression of this wild amalgam of forces and stimuli – local, regional, global. In this respect, my hope is that the book offers a provocative, often paradoxical look at the processes making up European urban life.

NOTES

Introduction

1. Peter Sloterdijk, *Falls Europa Erwacht* (Frankfurt: Suhrkamp, 1994), 50.
2. Max Weber, *The City*, trans. Don Martindale and Gertrud Neuwirth (Glencoe, IL: Free Press, 1958).
3. Hartmut Häussermann, "The End of the European City?" *European Review* 13, no. 2 (2005): 242–44.
4. Arnaldo Bagnasco and Patrick Le Galès, eds., *Cities in Contemporary Europe* (Cambridge: Cambridge University Press, 2000). Also chapter 2 of Patrick Le Galès, *European Cities: Social Conflicts and Governance* (Oxford: Oxford University Press, 2002).
5. Yaroslav Hrytsak, "The Borders of Europe—Seen from the Outside," https://www.eurozine.com/the-borders-of-europe-seen-from-the-outside/
6. Homi K. Bhabha, *The Location of Culture* (London; New York: Routledge, 1994). Dipesh Chakrabarty, *Provincializing Europe: Postcolonial Thought and Historical Difference* (Princeton, NJ: Princeton University Press, 2000).
7. See the excellent series of articles in "Urban Societies in Europe" including the introduction by Simon Gunn, "European Urbanities since 1945: A Commentary," *Contemporary European History* 24, no. 4 (2015): 617–22 as well as Moritz Föllmer and Mark B. Smith, "Urban Societies in Europe since 1945: Toward an Historical Interpretation," pp. 475–91.
8. Walter Benjamin, *The Arcades Project*, trans. Howard Eiland and Kevin McLaughlin (Cambridge, MA and London: Belknap Press of Harvard University Press, 2002). Siegfried Kracauer, *The Mass Ornament: Weimar Essays*, trans. Thomas Y. Levin (Cambridge, MA and London: Harvard University Press, 1995).

Chapter 1

1. Jan De Vries, *European Urbanization 1500-1800* (Cambridge, MA: Harvard University Press, 1984), 259.
2. See Giuseppe Dematteis, "Spatial Images of European Urbanization," in Bagnasco and Le Galès, eds., *Cities in Contemporary Europe*, 52.
3. J. R. Planche, *Descent of the Danube, from Ratisbon to Vienna During the Autumn of 1827* (London: James Duncan, 1828), 147. Elizabeth Rigby Eastlanke, *Letters from the Shores of the Baltic*, 2nd ed., vol. 2 (London: John Murray, 1842), 100–1.
4. On the idea of eastern Europe, see Larry Wolff, *Inventing Eastern Europe: The Map of Civilization on the Mind of the Enlightenment* (Stanford, CA: Stanford University Press, 1994).
5. Fernand Braudel, *The Structures of Everyday Life: The Limits of the Possible*, trans. Sian Reynolds (New York: Harper & Row, 1981), 479.

Notes

6. See the chapter on the Polish grain trade in Norman Davies, *God's Playground: A History of Poland*, vol. 2: *1795 to the Present* (New York: Oxford University Press, 2005), 198–215.

7. John Carr, *A Northern Summer; or Travels Round the Baltic, through Denmark, Sweden, Russia, Prussia, and Part of Germany, in the Year 1804* (Philadelphia, PA: Robert Gray, 1804), 285.

8. For the diversification of the Baltic trade in the late eighteenth century, see J. A. Faber, "Structural Changes in the European Economy during the Eighteenth Century as Reflected in the Baltic trade," in W. G. Heeres et al., eds., *From Dunkirk to Danzig: Shipping and Trade in the North Sea and the Baltic, 1350-1850* (Hilversum: Verloren Publishers and Amsterdamse Historische Reeks, 1988), 83–94.

9. Carr, *A Northern Summer*, 283.

10. For the Baltic trade and communication network, see Michael North, *The Baltic: A History*, trans. Kenneth Kronenberg (Cambridge, MA and London: Harvard University Press, 2015).

11. Fernand Braudel, *Civilization and Capitalism*, vol. II, *The Wheels of Commerce* (New York: Harper & Row, 1982), 457.

12. Halford J. Mackinder, "The Geographical Pivot of History," *Geographical Journal* 23 (1904): 421–37 quoted in Dan Diner, *Cataclysms: A History of the Twentieth Century from Europe's Edge*, trans. William Templer (Madison: University of Wisconsin Press, 2008), 7.

13. Lewis Siegelbaum, "The Odessa Grain Trade: A Case Study in Urban Growth and Development in Tsarist Russia," *Journal of European Economic History* 9, no. 1 (1980): 118.

14. Constantin Ardeleanu, "The Opening and Development of the Black Sea for International Trade and Shipping (1774-1853)," *Euxeinos* 14 (2014): 38–40. See also Gelina Harlaftis, "The Role of the Greeks in the Black Sea Trade, 1830-1900," in Lewis R. Fischer and Helge W. Nordvik, eds., *Shipping and Trade, 1750-1950: Essays in International Maritime Economic History* (West Yorkshire, England: Lofthouse Publications, 1990), 63–95.

15. On religious and ethnic coexistence under the Ottoman Empire, see the Introduction in Mark Mazower, *The Balkans from the End of Byzantium to the Present Day* (London: Weidenfeld & Nicolson, 2000).

16. Two excellent sources on Odessa in the first half of the nineteenth century are Patricia Herlihy, *Odessa: A History, 1794-1914* (Cambridge, MA: Distributed by Harvard University Press for the Harvard Ukrainian Research Institute, 1986), especially Chapter 6 and Charles King, *Odessa: Genius and Death in a City of Dreams*, 1st ed. (New York: W.W. Norton & Co., 2011), Part I.

17. Laurence Oliphant, *The Russian Shores of the Black Sea in the Autumn of 1852, with a Voyage Down the Volga, and a Tour through the Country of the Don Cossacks*, From the 3d. London ed. (New York: Redfield, 1854), 331.

18. John G. Stephens, *Incidents of Travel in Greece, Turkey, Russia and Poland* (Dublin: William Curry, Jun. and Company, 1839), 263.

19. Brother Peregrine, "The Danube," in *Fraser's Magazine for Town and Country*, 22 (November 1840) page 560 as quoted in Ardeleanu, "The Opening and Development of the Black Sea for International Trade and Shipping (1774-1853)," 1–2.

20. William Beattie and W. H. Bartlett, *The Danube, Illustrated in a Series of Views Taken Expressly for This Work*, 5 vols. (London: G. Virtue, 1842), 228–29.

21. Francis Davis Millet, *The Danube from the Black Forest to the Black Sea* (New York: Harper & Brothers, 1893), 273–74.

22. Ibid., 279.

Notes

23. See in particular the wonderful publication on Brăila's multiethnic community, Camelia Hristian et al., *Greeks, Jews, Lipovan Russians, Turks . . . Brăila* (Brăila: Museum of Brăila and Istros Publishing, 2014).

24. Mary Adelaide Walker, *Untrodden Paths in Roumania* (London: Chapman and Hall, Limited, 1888), 21–25.

25. Patrick O'Brien, *Journal of a Residence in the Danubian Principalities, in the Autumn and Winter of 1853* (London: Richard Bentley, 1854), 57.

26. Walker, *Untrodden Paths in Roumania*, 172.

27. Florence K. Berger, *A Winter in the City of Pleasure; or, Life on the Lower Danube* (London: R. Bentley & Son, 1877), Quotes from pages 35 and 45.

28. Adolphe Blanqui, *Voyage en Bulgarie pendant l'année 1841* (Paris: W. Coquebert, 1843), 111. Millet, *The Danube from the Black Forest to the Black Sea*, 187.

29. Blanqui, *Voyage en Bulgarie pendant l'année 1841*, 66–67.

30. "Srbsko, země a lik," Osvěta, 1875(V-VII) translated and quoted in Wendy Bracewell, ed. *Orientations: An Anthology of East European Travel Writing, Ca. 1550-2000* (Budapest and New York: Central European University Press, 2009), 225.

31. J. G. Kohl, *Austria, Vienna, Hungary, Bohemia and the Danube, Galicia, Styria, Moravia, Bukovina, and the Military Frontier* (London: Chapman and Hall, 1843), 208–9, 12.

Chapter 2

1. H. Matzerath, "The Influence of Industrialization on Urban Growth in Prussia 1815-1914," in H. Schmal, ed. *Patterns of European Urbanisation since 1500* (London: Croom Helm, 1981), 154–56.

2. Jon Stobart, *The First Industrial Revolution: North-West England, C. 1700-60* (Manchester and New York: Manchester University Press, 2004), 10.

3. See Sven Beckert, *Empire of Cotton: A Global History* (New York: Vintage, 2014) and Steven Gray, *Steam Power and Sea Power: Coal, the Royal Navy, and the British Empire, c. 1870-1914* (London: Palgrave MacMillan, 2018).

4. Leo H. Grindon, *Lancashire: Brief Historical and Descriptive Notes* (London: Seeley & Co., Ltd., 1892), 66, 70.

5. *Handbook for Shropshire, Cheshire, and Lancashire* (London: John Murray, 1870), 183–84.

6. Grindon, *Lancashire*, 73–74.

7. For a description of Wigan's housing conditions, see John T. Jackson, "Nineteenth-Century Housing in Wigan and St Helens," *Transactions of the Historic Society of Lancashire and Cheshire* 129 (1980): 125–43.

8. "Parks for Oldham. Public Meeting," *The Manchester Times and Gazette*, Issue 949, December 26, 1846.

9. Charles Dickens, *Hard Times* (London: Bradbury & Evans, 1854), 27.

10. For descriptions of Ancoats, see Michael E. Rose, Keith Falconer, and Julian Holder, *Ancoats: Cradle of Industrialisation* (Swindon: English Heritage, 2011).

11. Katy Layton-Jones, *Beyond the Metropolis: The Changing Image of Urban Britain, 1780-1880* (Manchester: Manchester University Press, 2016). 42.

Notes

12. These statistics from the 1876 *Report and Statistical Tables Relating to Emigration and Immigration* are given in John Darwin, *Unfinished Empire: The Global Expansion of Britain* (New York and London: Bloomsbury Press, 2012), 93.

13. "Murphy Riots at Oldham," *Manchester Times*, Issue 548, May 30, 1868.

14. James Phillip Kay, *The Moral and Physical Condition of the Working Classes Employed in the Cotton Manufacture in Manchester*, 2nd ed. (London: James Ridgway, 1832), 21, 34–36.

15. Quote from Engels from "The Great Towns," in *The Condition of the Working Class in England* (1845) Panther Edition, 1969 available online at https://www.marxists.org/archive/marx/works/download/pdf/condition-working-class-england.pdf. Angus Bethune Reach, *Manchester and the Textile Districts in 1849*, ed. C. Aspin (Rossendale: Helmshore Local History Society, 1972), 53.

16. For an excellent analysis of the popular influence of these reformers, see Mervyn Bustee, *The Irish in Manchester* (Manchester: Manchester University Press, 2016), 20–34.

17. Grindon, *Lancashire*, 126.

18. W. C. Taylor, *Notes of a Tour in the Manufacturing Districts of Lancashire* (London: Duncan and Malcolm, 1842), 9.

19. *Handbook for Shropshire, Cheshire, and Lancashire*, 166.

20. Terry Wyke, "Rise and Decline of Cottonopolis," in Alan Kidd and Terry Wyke, eds., *Manchester: Making the Modern City* (Liverpool: Liverpool University Press, 2016), 75.

21. *The Moral Statistics of Glasgow in 1863, Practically Applied by a Sabbath School Teacher* (Glasgow: Porteous & Hislop, 1864), 54.

22. Peter Reed, ed., *Glasgow: The Forming of the City* (Edinburgh: Edinburgh University Press: 1993) quoted in John F. Riddel, "Glasgow and the Clyde," in David Goodman, ed., *The European Cities and Technology Reader: Industrial to Post-Industrial City* (London and New York: Routledge, 1999), 69.

23. Angel Smith, "From Subordination to Contestation: The Rise of Labour in Barcelona, 1898-1918," in Angel Smith, ed., *Red Barcelona: Social Protest and Labour Mobilization in the Twentieth Century* (London and New York: Routledge, 2002).

24. T. C. Banfield, *Industry of the Rhine: Series II. Manufactures* (London: C. Cox, 1848), 24. See also Norman J. G. Pounds, *The Ruhr: A Study in Historical and Economic Geography* (London: Faber and Faber, 1952).

25. Quoted in Woerl, *Führer durch Duisburg*, 10, in James H. Jackson, Jr., *Migration and Urbanization in the Ruhr Valley, 1821-1914* (New Jersey: Humanities Press, 1997), 121.

26. Franz-Josef Brüggemeier, "A Nature Fit for Industry: The Environmental History of the Ruhr Basin, 1840-1990," *Environmental History Review* 18, no. 1 (1994): 36. See also Mark Cioc, *The Rhine: An Eco-Biography, 1815-2000* (Seattle: University of Washington Press, 2002).

27. Klaus J. Bade, *Migration in European History*, trans. Alison Brown (Malden, MA and Oxford: Blackwell, 2003), 41. Jackson, *Migration and Urbanization in the Ruhr Valley, 1821-1914*, 5.

28. Hinze Reif, *Die verspätete Stadt: Industrialisierung, Städtischer Raum und Politik im Oberhausen, 1846-1929* (Köln: Rheinland Verlag, 1993), quoted in Werner Abelshauser and Wolfgang Köllmann, *Das Ruhrgebiet im Industriezeitalter: Geschichte und Entwicklung*, 2 vols., vol. 2 (Düsseldorf: Schwann im Patmos Verlag, 1990), 75.

29. Hermann Burghard et al., *Essen: Geschichte einer Stadt* (Bottrop and Essen: Pomp, 2002), 310. See also David F. Crew, *Town in the Ruhr: A Social History of Bochum, 1860-1914* (New York: Columbia University Press, 1979), 110–11.

Notes

30. Burghard, *Essen*, 310.
31. Jackson, *Migration and Urbanization in the Ruhr Valley, 1821-1914*, 120.
32. Cedric Bolz, "From 'Garden City Precursors' to 'Cemeteries for the Living': Contemporary Discourse on Krupp Housing and *Besucherpolitik* in Wilhelmine Germany," *Urban History* 37, no. 1 (2010): 90–116. See also Chapter 5 in Erik de Gier, *Capitalist Workingman's Paradises Revisited: Corporate Welfare Work in Great Britain, the USA, Germany and France in the Golden Age of Capitalism, 1880-1930* (Amsterdam: Amsterdam University Press, 2016).
33. Crew, *Town in the Ruhr*, 154–56.
34. Piotr Franaszek, "Poland," in Lex Heerma Van Voss, Els Hiemstra-Kuperus, and Elise Van Nnederveen Meerkerk, eds., *The Ashgate Companion to the History of Textile Workers, 1650-2000*, First published in 2010 by Ashgate Publishing ed. (Abingdon, Oxon and New York: Routledge, 2016), 401–3. See also Norman J. G. Pounds, "The Industrial Geography of Modern Poland," *Economic Geography* 36, no. 3 (1960): 231–53.
35. The new textile towns were Babiak (1815/16), Ozorków (1816), Aleksandrów (1822), Kranosielsk (1822), Poddębice (1822), Zdunska Wola (1825), and Tomaszów Mazowiecki (1830).
36. On these details, see the excellent article by Irena Poplawska and Stefan Muthesius, "Poland's Manchester: 19th-Century Industrial and Domestic Architecture in Lodz," *Journal of the Society of Architectural Historians* 45, no. 2 (1986): 148–60. See also Marek Koter et al., *Wpływ Wielonarodowego Dziedzictwa Kulturowego Łodzi Na Współczesne Oblicize Miasta* (Łódź: Wydawnictwo Uniwersytetu Łódzkiego, 2005).
37. Ivan Berend, *Case Studies on Modern European Economy: Entrepreneurship, Invention, and Institutions* (London and New York: Routledge, 2013), 194.
38. Arthur Rubinstein, *My Young Years* (New York: A. A. Knopf, 1973), 8. See as well Andreas Kossert, "'Promised Land'? Urban Myths and the Shaping of Modernity in Industrial Cities: Manchester and Lodz," in Christian Emden, Catherine Keen, and David Midgley, eds., *Imagining the City, Volume 2. The Politics of Urban Space* (Bern, Switzerland: Peter Lang AG, 2006), 169–89. Also, Stanisław Liszewski, "The Role of the Jewish Community in the Organization of Urban Space in Łódź," in Antony Polonsky, ed., *Jews in Łódź, 1820-1939* (Oxford: Littman Library of Jewish Civilization, 2004), 27–36.
39. Ruth R. Wisse, *The Modern Jewish Canon: A Journey through Language and Culture* (Chicago: University of Chicago Press, 2000), 141.
40. Charles Marvin, *The Region of Eternal Fire: An Account of the Petroleum Region of the Caspian in 1883* (London: W.H. Allen and Co., 1884), 13–14.
41. William John Rose, *The Drama of Upper Silesia: A Regional Study* (Brattleboro, VT: Stephen Daye Press, 1935), 100–1.
42. The statistics on the number of workers in heavy industry in Upper Silesia differ substantially depending on the source. Tomasz Kamusella, *Silesia and Central European Nationalisms: The Emergence of National and Ethnic Groups in Prussian Silesia and Austrian Silesia, 1848-1918* (West Lafayette, IN: Purdue University Press), 200.
43. Frédéric Durand, "La Construction métropolitaine en Haute Silésie," *Espace, Populations, Sociétés* 2 (2011): 4.
44. Kamusella, *Silesia and Central European Nationalisms*, 200.
45. Ibid., 140.

Notes

46. Hugo Solger, *Der Kreis Beuthen in Oberschlesien* (Breslau, 1860) quoted in Rose, *The Drama of Upper Silesia*, 102. These conditions and quotes from Solger are also described in Emil Caspari, *The Working Classes of Upper-Silesia: An Historical Essay* (London and Edinburgh: Simpson Low, Marston & Co., 1921), 34–36.

47. See Lawrence Schofer, "Patterns of Worker Protest: Upper Silesia, 1865-1914," *Journal of Social History* 5, no. 4 (1972): 447–63.

48. D. Turnock, "The Industrial Development of Romania from the Unification of the Principalities to the Second World War," in Francis W. Carter, ed., *An Historical Geography of the Balkans* (London: Academic Press, 1977), 326. See also Maurice Pearton, *Oil and the Romanian State* (Oxford: Oxford University Press, 1971).

49. Charles King, *The Black Sea: A History* (Oxford and New York: Oxford University Press, 2004), 199.

50. On Bucharest's "perpetual becoming," see Samuel Rufat, "Bucarest, l'eternal retour," *Géographie et cultures* 65 (2008): 53–72.

51. See O'Brien, *Journal of a Residence in the Danubian Principalities*, 61. Quotes from Daniela Bușă, ed., *Călători străini despre Țările Române în secolul al XIX-lea* (2010) and T. T. Jeż, "Współczesna Rumunia," *Ateneum* 2 (1884) in Raluca Golesteanu, "Representations of Central and Eastern Europe in Travelogues of Romanian and Polish Public Figures," *Linguaculture* 2015, no. 2 (2015): 43–61.

52. Wilhelm Zerboni di Sposetti, 1865–66, quoted in Paul Cernovodeanu, *Foreign Travelers* in Adrian Majuru, "Bucharest: Between European Modernity and the Ottoman East," *CUPRINS Romanian Review of Eurasian Studies* 4 (2008): 84.

Chapter 3

1. Michael Joseph Quin, *A Visit to Spain; Detailing the Transactions Which Occurred During a Residence in That Country, in the Latter Part of 1822, and the First Four Months of 1823* (London: Hurst, Robinson and Co., 1823), 240–41. W. G. Clark, "Naples and Garibaldi," in Francis Galton, ed., *Vacation Tourists and Notes of Travel in 1860 [1861], [1862-3]*, vol. 2 (Cambridge: Macmillan, 1861–1964), 16.

2. Kohl, *Austria, Vienna, Hungary, Bohemia and the Danube*, 524.

3. James Fenimore Cooper, *A Residence in France, with an Excursion up the Rhine, and a Second Visit to Switzerland* (Paris: Baudru, 1836), 168 and 75.

4. J. G. Kohl, *St. Petersburg, Moscow, Kharkoff, Riga, Odessa, the German Provinces on the Baltic, the Steppes, the Crimea, and the Interior of the Empire* (London: Chapman and Hall, 1843), 327.

5. These points are made in chapter 1 of Celia Applegate, *A Nation of Provincials: The German Idea of Heimat* (Berkeley, CA: University of California Press, 1990). See also Madeleine Hurd, *Public Spheres, Public Mores, and Democracy: Hamburg and Stockholm, 1870-1914* (Ann Arbor: University of Michigan Press, 2000). And Gisela Mettele, "Burgher Cities on the Road to Civil Society: Germany 1780 to 1870," in Friedrich Lenger, ed., *Towards an Urban Nation: Germany since 1780* (Oxford and New York: Berg, 2002), 46–47.

6. Among the many excellent studies of bourgeois culture, see Simon Gunn, *The Public Culture of the Victorian Middle Class: Ritual and Authority and the English Industrial City, 1840-1914* (Manchester and New York: Manchester University Press, 2000).

Notes

7. Luďa Klusáková, "Cultural Institutions as Urban Innovations: The Czech Lands, Poland and the Eastern Baltic, 1750-1900," in Malcolm Gee, Tim Kirk, and Jill Steward, ed., *The City in Central Europe: Culture and Society from 1800 to the Present* (Aldershot; Brookfield, VT: Ashgate, 1999), 95.

8. George Francklin Atkinson, *Pictures from the North, in Pen and Pencil; Sketched During a Summer Ramble* (London: John Ollivier, 1848), 35-36.

9. Sten Lindroth, *A History of Uppsala University, 1477-1977*, trans. Neil Tomkinson (Uppsala: Almqvist & Wiksell, 1976), 181-82.

10. Kohl, *St. Petersburg, Moscow, Kharkoff, Riga, Odessa*, 334. Albert Le Play, ed., *Frédéric Le Play. Voyages en Europe 1829-1854. Extraits de sa correspondance* (Paris: E. Plon, Nourrit et Cie, 1899), 261.

11. See in particular Wolfgang Kaschuba, "German Bürgerlichkeit after 1800: Culture as Symbolic Practice," in Jürgen Kocka and Allen Mitchell, eds., *Bourgeois Society in Nineteenth Century Europe* (Oxford/Providence: Berg, 1993), 392-422.

12. Alexander Ringer makes this point in "The Rise of Urban Musical Life between the Revolutions, 1789-1848," in Alexander Ringer, ed., *The Early Romantic Era: Between Revolutions, 1789 and 1848* (Basingstoke: Granada Group and Macmillan Press, 1990), 7.

13. Joep Leerson, "The Nation and the City: Urban Festivals and Cultural Mobilisation," *Nations and Nationalism* 21, no. 1 (2015): 12.

14. On Cologne's history, see Adolf Klein, *Köln im 19. Jahrhundert: Von der Reichsstadt zur Großstadt* (Köln: Wienand, 1992).

15. The Bernard quote is found in Richard Boyle Bernard, *A Tour through Some Parts of France, Switzerland, Savoy, Germany and Belgium During the Summer and Autumn of 1814* (London: Longman, Hurst, Rees, Orme, and Brown, 1815), 286. The description of Elben's journey is cited in Kaschuba, "German Burgerlichkeit after 1800: Culture as Symbolic Practice," 419. See also Michael Rowe, "La redécouverte du Rhin par les princes prussiens au lendemain de 1815," in Nicolas Bourguinat and Sylain Venayre, eds., *Voyager en Europe de Humboldt à Stendahl. Constraints nationales et tentations cosmopolites, 1790-1840* (Paris: Nouveau Monde, 2007).

16. On Cologne's early tourist infrastructure, see Gabriele Knoll, "Historischer Tourisme- Köln," *Touristik & Verkehr* 1 (1987): 87-95.

17. Arnold Jacobshagen, "Cologne, un chantier musical au XIXe siècle," in Jean-François Candoni and Laure Gauthier, eds., *Les Grands centres musicaux du monde germanique (XVIIe-XIXe siècle)* (Paris: Presses de l'Université Paris-Sorbonne, 2014), 304. See also Laure Gauthier and Mélanie Traversier, eds., *Mélodies urbaines. La Musique dans les ville d'Europe (XVIe-XIXe siècles)* (Paris: Presses de l'Université Paris-Sorbonne, 2008).

18. Paul Baudry, *Trois semaines en voyage: France, bords du Rhin, Belgique* (Rouen: Mégard et Cie, 1855), 133.

19. James M. Brophy, "Carnival and Citizenship: The Politics of Carnival Culture in the Prussian Rhineland, 1823-1848," *Journal of Social History* 30, no. 4 (1997): 873-904. See also Jeremy DeWaal, "The Reinvention of Tradition: Form, Meaning, and Local Identity in Modern Cologne Carnival," *Central European History* 46 (2013): 495-532. Also Jonathan Sperber, *Rhineland Radicals: The Democratic Movement and the Revolution of 1848-1849* (Princeton, NJ: Princeton University Press, 1991), 311.

20. John Barrow, *Tour in Austrian Lombardy, the Northern Tyrol, and Bavaria in 1840* (London: John Murray, 1841), 314.

Notes

21. See Joshua Hagen, "Shaping Public Opinion through Architecture and Urban Design: Perspectives on Ludwig I and His Building Program for a 'New Munich,'" *Central European History* 48 (2015): 6. Also Chapter 1 in Peter Jelavich, *Munich and Theatrical Modernism: Politics, Playwriting, and Performance, 1890-1914* (Cambridge, MA: Harvard University Press, 1996).

22. Józef Mączyński, *Cracovie et ses environs. Description historique géographique et pittoresque de cette ville et de ses contrées* (Kraków: Joseph Czech, 1846), 77. On Kraków's history, see Tomasz Jeleński, "Tradition and Heritage in the Image of Kraków," in Tomasz Jelenski, Stanislaw Juchnowicz, and Ewelina Wozniak-Szpakiewicz, eds., *Tradition and Heritage in the Contemporary Image of the City*, vol. 1 (Kraków: PK, 2015), 95-124.

23. Géza Hajós, "Die Stadtparks der österreichischen Monarchie von 1765 bis 1867 im gesamteuropäischen Kontext," in Géza Hajós, ed., *Stadtparks in der österreichischen Monarchie, 1765-1918* (Vienna, Cologne, Weimar: Böhlau, 2007), 67-68. On pleasure gardens, see also Peter Borsay, "Pleasure Gardens and Urban Culture in the Long Eighteenth Century," in Jonathan Conlin, ed., *The Pleasure Garden, from Vauxhall to Coney Island* (Philadelphia: University of Pennsylvania Press, 2013), 49-77.

24. Stephens, *Incidents of Travel in Greece, Turkey, Russia and Poland*, 454.

25. On the Free State of Kraków and the 1846 Uprising, see Davies, *God's Playground* as well as Piotr S. Wandycz, *The Lands of Partitioned Poland, 1795-1918* (Seattle and London: University of Washington Press, 1974). For a detailed discussion, see Stefan Kieniewicz, "The Free State of Cracow 1815-1846," *The Slavonic and East European Review* 26, no. 66 (1947): 69-89.

26. Daniel Louis Unowsky, "The Pomp and Politics of Patriotism: Imperial Celebrations in Habsburg Austria, 1848-1916." Order No. 9970301, Columbia University, 2000. Ann Arbor: *ProQuest Dissertations*. Web. October 13, 2017, 78-79.

27. W. G. Clark, "Poland," in Galton, ed., *Vacation Tourists and Notes of Travel in 1860 [1861], [1862-3]*, vol. 2, 237.

28. J. C. L. de Sismondi, *A History of the Italian Republics, Being a View of the Origin, Progress, and Fall of Italian Freedom* (London: Longman, Brown, Green, & Longmans, 1832), 365.

29. Alain Pillepich, *Milan capitale napoléonienne, 1800-1814* (Paris: Lettrage Distribution, 2001), 53. See also Olivier Faron, *La Ville des destins croisés. Recherches sur la société Milanaise du XIXe siècle (1811-1860)* (Rome and Paris: Ecole Française de Rome, Boccard, 1997).

30. These quotes by Gioja (1802) and Mantovani (1805) are given in Pillepich, *Milan capitale napoléonienne*, 383.

31. Barrow, *Tour in Austrian Lombardy, the Northern Tyrol, and Bavaria in 1840*, 141-43.

32. Mélanie Traversier, "Venise, Naples, Milan. Trois capitales pour l'opéra italien, XVIIe-XVIIIe siècles," in Christophe Charle, ed., *Le Temps des capitales culturelles, XVIIIe-XXe siècles* (Seyssel: Champ Vallon, 2009), 235-36.

33. See Giovanni B. Carta, *Nouvelle description de la ville de Milan* (Milan: Jean Pierre Giegler Ferdinand Artaria: Frères Bettalli, 1819). And Anonymous, *Les Curiosités de la ville de Milan et des ses environs, une description de tous ses monuments* (Milan, Paris and London: Vallardi and Delaunay [Paris], 1822).

34. These details are recounted in Kent Roberts Greenfield, *Economics and Liberalism in the Risorgimento: A Study of Nationalism in Lombardy, 1814-1848* (Baltimore: John Hopkins University Press, 1934), 73-74.

35. J. S. Buckingham, *France, Piedmont, Italy, the Tyrol, and Bavaria: An Autumnal Tour*, vol. 1 (London: Peter Jackson, Late Fischer, Son & Co., 1847), 49.

36. John Cam Hobhouse, *A Journey through Albania and Other Provinces of Turkey in Europe and Asia, to Constantinople, During the Years 1809 and 1810* (Philadelphia: M. Carey and Son, 1817), 160–61.
37. William Turner, *Journal of a Tour in the Levant*, vol. 1 (London: John Murray, 1820), 320–21, 435.
38. Lila Leontidou, *The Mediterranean City in Transition: Social Change and Urban Development* (Cambridge and New York: Cambridge University Press, 1990), 49–51.
39. See Vaso Seirinidou, "The Mediterranean," in Diana Mishkova and Balázs Trencsényi, eds., *European Regions and Boundaries* (New York and Oxford: Berghahn, 2017), 85–86.
40. The most famous plans were those of Stamatis Kleanthis and Eduard Schaubert (who were students of Karl Friedrich Schinkel) and Otto's Bavarian court architect Leo von Klenze. Among many good analyses, see Vilma Hastaoglou-Martinidis, "City Form and National Identity: Urban Designs in Nineteenth-Century Greece," *Journal of Modern Greek Studies* 13, no. 1 (1995): 99–123 as well as Alexander Mirkovic, "Who Owns Athens? Urban Planning and the Struggle for Identity in Neo-Classical Athens (1832-1843)," *Cuadernos de Historia Contemporánea* 34 (2012): 147–58.
41. Stephens, *Incidents of Travel in Greece, Turkey, Russia and Poland*, 62.
42. Stendhal, *Voyage dans le Midi de la France* (Paris: Le Divan, 1930), 261.
43. See the excellent article by Gérard Chastagnaret and Olivier Raveux, "Espace et stratégies industrielles aux XVIIIe et XIXe siècles: exploiter le laboratoire méditerranéen," *Revue d'histoire moderne et contemporaine* 2, no. 48 (2001): 11–24.
44. Stendhal, *Voyage dans le Midi de la France*, 236.
45. See the Introduction in Peter Borsay and John K. Walton, eds., *Resorts and Ports: European Seaside Towns since 1700* (Bristol, Buffalo, NY, Toronto: Chanel View, 2011), 1–2.
46. William Cullen Bryant, *Letters of a Traveller* (New York: D. Appleton & Company, 1859), 35–36.
47. Claude Prelorenzo, *Une Histoire urbaine: Nice* (Paris: Hartmann, 1999), 55.
48. See chapter 2 in Josephine Kane, *The Architecture of Pleasure: British Amusement Parks 1900-1939* (New York: Routledge, 2013). See also Deborah Philips, *Fairground Attractions: A Genealogy of the Pleasure Ground* (London and New York: Bloomsbury Academic, 2012).

Chapter 4

1. These population figures are drawn from Paul Bairoch, *Cities and Economic Development: From the Dawn of History to the Present*, trans. Christopher Braider (Chicago: University of Chicago Press, 1988), 216–17 and Bade, *Migration in European History*, 41.
2. Bade, *Migration in European History*, 42.
3. Cited in Peter Judson, *The Hapsburg Empire, a New History* (Cambridge and London: Belknap Press of Harvard University Press, 2016), 334.
4. See the excellent article by Sylvie Aprile and Delphine Diaz, "Europe and Its Political Refugees in the 19th Century," *Books and Ideas*. April 18, 2016. http://www.booksandideas.net/Europe-and-its-Political-Refugees-in-the-19th-Century.html
5. On these examples see Konstantina Zanou and Maurizio Isabella, eds., *Mediterranean Diasporas: Politics and Ideas in the Long 19th Century* (London: Bloomsbury Academic,

Notes

2016). Also Andrew Robarts, *Migration and Disease in the Black Sea Region: Ottoman-Russian Relations in the Late Eighteenth and Early Nineteenth Centuries* (London: Bloomsbury Academic, 2017).

6. Tara Zahra, *The Great Departure: Mass Migration from Eastern Europe and the Making of the Free World* (New York: W.W. Norton, 2017), 24.

7. David Blackbourne, *The Long Nineteenth Century: A History of Germany, 1780-1918* (New York and Oxford: Oxford University Press, 1998), 201.

8. *Lloyd's Weekly Newspaper*, no. 1378, April 18, 1869. Darwin, *Unfinished Empire*, 90.

9. Victor Tissot, *De Paris à Berlin: Mes vacances en Allemagne* (Paris: Blériot, no date [1886]), 2-3 and 8.

10. [Eliza Lynn], "Passing Faces," in Charles Dickens, ed., *Household Words*, April 14, 1855. Edmondo De Amicis, *Studies of Paris*, trans. W. W. Cady, 3rd ed. (New York: G. P. Putnam's Sons, 1882), 3-4.

11. Charles Baudelaire, *Paris Spleen 1869*, trans. Louise Varèse (New York: New Directions, 1970), 20.

12. Ibid., 52-53.

13. From Balzac's 1834 novel *La Fille aux yeux d'or* cited in Patrice Higonnet, *Paris: Capital of the World* (Cambridge, MA and London: Belknap Press of Harvard University Press, 2002), 265.

14. Flora Tristin, *The London Journal of Flora Tristin 1842 or the Aristocracy and the Working Class of England*, trans. Jean Hawkes (London: Virago, 1982), 17.

15. These quotations from *L'Echo de la semaine* (1892) and Alfred Delvau's *Les plaisirs de Paris* (1867) are found in Vanessa Schwartz, *Spectacular Realities: Early Mass Culture in Fin-de-Siècle Paris* (Berkeley: University of California Press, 1998), 21. The quote from Emile Zola found in *The Ladies Paradise*, trans. Brian Nelson (Oxford: Oxford University Press, 1998), 28.

16. *Illustrated London News*, 1849. Image available at London Metropolitan Archives, Collage Collection.

17. See the powerful description of The City in Chapter Four of Jonathan Schneer, *London 1900: The Imperial Metropolis* (New Haven, CT: Yale University Press, 1999).

18. These statistics (found on page 173) and the list of major exports come from the remarkable documentation in Charles Capper, *The Port and Trade of London: Historical, Statistical, Local and General* (London: Smith & Elder, 1862). Also excellent is Thomas Baines, *History of the Commerce and Town of Liverpool, and of the Rise of Manufacturing Industry in the Adjoining Counties* (London: Longman, Brown, Green & Longmans, 1852).

19. Margaret Harkness, *In Darkest London* (Cambridge: Black Apollo Press, 2009), 12. Originally published as *Captain Lobe: A Story of the Salvation Army* (London: Hodder & Stoughton, 1889).

20. *Liverpool Mercury*, May 14, 1886.

21. Murray Steele, "Transmitting Ideas of Empire: Representations and Celebrations in Liverpool, 1886-1953," in Sheryllynne Haggerty, Anthony Webster, and Nicholas J. White, eds., *The Empire in One City? Liverpool's Inconvenient Imperial Past* (Manchester: Manchester University Press, 2008), 125-26.

22. William H. Sewell, *Structure and Mobility: The Men and Women of Marseille, 1820-1870* (New York: Cambridge University Press, 1985), 230-31.

Notes

23. Marina Cattaruzza, "Population Dynamics and Economic Change in Trieste and Its Hinterlands, 1850-1914," in Richard Lawton and Robert Lee, eds., *Population and Society in Western European Port Cities, C. 1650-1939* (Liverpool: Liverpool University Press, 2002), 176–211.
24. Judson, *The Hapsburg Empire, a New History*, 114.
25. Kohl, *Austria, Vienna, Hungary, Bohemia and the Danube*, 439.
26. See Faith Hillis, "Modernist Visions and Mass Politics in Late Imperial Kiev," in Jan C. Behrends and Martin Kohlrausch, eds., *Races to Modernity: Metropolitan Aspirations in Eastern Europe, 1890-1940* (Budapest and New York: CEU Press, 2014), 58–61.
27. Quote on page 389 in Peter J. Gurney, "'The Sublime of the Bazaar': A Moment in the Making of a Consumer Culture in Mid-Nineteenth Century England," *Journal of Social History* 40, no. 2 (2006): 385–405.
28. Thomas Onwhyn, *Mr. & Mrs. Brown's Visit to London to see the Grand Exposition of All Nations: How they were Astonished at Its Wonders!!, Inconvenienced by the Crowds, & Frightened Out of their Wits, by the Foreigners* (London: Ackermann & Co., 1851).
29. *Illustrated London News*, vol. 20, June 5, 1852, p. 441. See also Norman Davies and Roger Moorhouse, *Microcosm: Portrait of a Central European City* (London: Pimlico, 2002), 220–24.
30. *The Athenaeum*, no. 2541, July 8, 1876, p. 58.
31. See Hans Jürgen Teuteberg, "Urbanization and Nutrition: Historical Research Reconsidered," in Peter J. Atkins, Peter Lummel, and Derek J. Oddy, eds., *Food and the City in Europe since 1800* (Milton Park, Abingdon and New York: Routledge, 2016), 13–24.
32. Tristin, *The London Journal of Flora Tristin 1842*, 170–71, 175.
33. On Whitecross Street, see Peter T. A. Jones, "Redressing Reform Narratives: Victorian London's Street Markets and the Informal Supply Lines of Urban Modernity," *The London Journal* 41, no. 1 (2016): 66. See also Stephen Jankiewicz, "A Dangerous Class: The Street Sellers of Nineteenth-Century London," *Journal of Social History* 46, no. 2 (2012): 391–415.
34. James Stevenson Bushnan, *The Moral and Sanitary Aspects of the New Central Market, as Proposed by the Corporation of the City of London* (London, 1851), 15–16 as recounted in Patrick Joyce, *The Rule of Freedom: Liberalism and the Modern City* (London and New York: Verso, 2003), 79.
35. Descriptions of British markets, pp. 31–34 in James Schmiechen and Kenneth Carls, *The British Market Hall: A Social and Architectural History* (New Haven, CT: Yale University Press, 1999).
36. Ibid., 160–62.
37. Hermione Hobhouse, *A History of Regent Street: A Mile of Style* (Chichester, West Sussex: Phillimore, 2008), 79.
38. Ian Mitchell, "Innovations in Non-Food Retailing in the Early Nineteenth Century: The Curious Case of the Bazaar," *Business History* 52, no. 6 (2010): 884.
39. Benjamin, *The Arcades Project*, 42.873–74.
40. Asa Briggs, *Victorian Cities* (Berkeley, CA: University of California Press, 1993), 143, 171.
41. *Leeds Mercury*, July 24, 1889.
42. This figure from James Jefferys, *Retail Trading in Britain, 1850-1950* (Cambridge, 1954) is given in Frank Trentmann, *Empire of Things* (New York: Harper, 2016), 205.

Notes

43. On European department stores, see Geoffrey Crossick and Serge Jaumain, eds., *Cathedrals of Consumption: The European Department Store, 1850-1939* (Aldershot: Ashgate, 1999).
44. On the British department stores, see Chapter 2 "Luxury Democratized," in Bill Lancaster, *The Department Store: A Social History* (London and New York: Leicester University Press, 1995).
45. Quote from David Clay Large, *Berlin* (New York: Basic Books, 2000), 86.
46. First published as Leo Colze, *Berliner Warenhäuser* (Berlin & Leipzig Ostwald, 1908), reprinted in Iain Boyd Whyte and David Frisby, eds., *Metropolis Berlin* (Berkeley, CA: University of California Press, 2012), 96. On Russia, see William Craft Brumfield, Boris V. Anan'ich, and Yuri A. Petrov, *Commerce in Russian Urban Russian Culture, 1861-1914* (Baltimore, MD: John Hopkins University Press, 2001).

Chapter 5

1. Hartmut Kaelble, "Representations of Europe as a Political Resource in the Early and Late Twentieth Century," *Comparativ* 22 (2012): 14.
2. See the introductory essay by S. N. Eisenstadt, "Multiple Modernities," in Shmuel N. Eisenstadt, ed., *Multiple Modernities* (Abingdon and New York: Routledge, 2017).
3. See Sophie Forgan, "From Modern Babylon to White City: Science, Technology, and Urban Change in London, 1870-1914," in Miriam Levin, ed., *Urban Modernity: Cultural Innovation in the Second Industrial Revolution* (Cambridge, MA and London: MIT, 2010), 93.
4. Particularly useful is Chapter 1 "Maps, Numbers and the City: Knowing the Governed," in Joyce, *The Rule of Freedom*.
5. Recounted in Peter Hall, *Cities of Tomorrow: An Intellectual History of Urban Design in the Twentieth Century* (New York: Blackwell, 1998), 26–27.
6. Andrew Mearns, *The Bitter Cry of Outcast London* (London: J. Clarke, 1883) Available online at the Internet Archive.
7. A good summary of the sanitation movement is found in Chapter 4 of Andrew Lees and Lynn Hollen Lees, *Cities and the Making of Modern Europe, 1750-1914* (Cambridge and New York: Cambridge University Press, 2007).
8. Harold L. Platt, *Shock Cities: The Environmental Transformation and Reform of Manchester and Chicago* (Chicago and London: University of Chicago Press, 2005), 318–23. Stuart Hylton, *A History of Manchester* (Stroud: Phillimore, 2003), 173.
9. Patrick Kamoun, *Hygiène et morale: La naissance des habitations à bon marché* (Paris: L'Union sociale pour l'habitat, 2011), 37–44. Lees and Lees, *Cities and the Making of Modern Europe*, 116–17.
10. Joyce, *The Rule of Freedom*, 64.
11. On Hamburg, see Dirk Schubert, "The Great Fire of Hamburg, 1842. From Catastrophe to Reform," in Greg Bankoff et al., eds., *Flammable Cities* (Madison: University of Wisconsin, 2012), 212–34. Richard Evans, *Death in Hamburg: Society and Politics in the Cholera Years* (New York: Penguin Books, 2005) as well as Jennifer Jenkins, *Provincial Modernity: Local Culture and Liberal Politics in Fin-de-Siècle Hamburg* (Ithica, NY: Cornell University Press, 2003).
12. Boulevard de la Madeleine, Boulevard des Capucines, Boulevard des Italiens, Boulevard Montmartre, Boulevard Poissonnière, Boulevard Bonne-Nouvelle, Boulevard Saint-Denis,

Boulevard Saint-Martin, Boulevard du Temple, Boulevard des Filles du Calvaire, and Boulevard Beaumarchais.

13. Peter Sramek, ed., *Piercing Time: Paris after Marville and Atget, 1865-2012* (Chicago: University of Chicago Press, 2013), 16.

14. *Paris Guide 1867* quoted in Higonnet, *Paris: Capital of the World*, 289. Also James D. McCabe, *Paris by Sunlight and Gaslight* (Philadelphia: National Publishing, 1869), 111-12. Quote on the Boulevard des Italiens from Augustus J. C. Hare, *Paris* (London: G. Allen, 1887), 485. Quotes from George Montorgeuil, *La vie des boulevards* (1896) and Emile Bergerat, "Le boulevard," *L'Echo de la Semaine*, October 9, 1892 in Schwartz, *Spectacular Realities*, 20-21.

15. Cerdà (source not cited) quoted in Salvador Tarragó Cid, "The Development of Cerdà's Interways. Three proposals (1855, 1959 and 1963) for the founding of a new industrial city," Institut Ildefons Cerdà, *Cerdà Urba I Territori (Planning Beyond the Urban)* (Barcelona: Fondació Catalana per a la Recerca, 1996), 67.

16. H. Baden Pritchard, *The Photographic Studios of Europe* (London: Piper & Carter, 1882), 258. Stefan Zweig, *The World of Yesterday* (London: Cassell, 1947), 25.

17. Blau, "The City as Protagonist: Architecture and Cultures of Central Europe," in Eve Blau and Monika Platzer, eds., *Shaping the Great City: Modern Architecture in Central Europe 1890-1937* (Munich: Prestel, 1999), 12-13. Also see Chapter 2, "The City as Political Monument," in Ákos Moravánskzy, *Competing Visions: Aesthetic Invention and Social Imagination in Central European Architecture, 1867-1918* (Cambridge, MA: MIT Press, 1998). See also Gerhard Michael Dienes, ed., *Fellner & Helmer. Die Architekten der Illusion. Theaterbau und Bühnenbild in Europa anlässlich des Jubiläums "100 Jahre Grazer Oper"* (Graz: Stadtmuseum, 1999).

18. Julia Pardoe, *The City of the Magyar, or Hungary and Her Institutions in 1839-40*, vol. 2 (London: George Virtue, 1840), 41-42.

19. Zahra, *The Great Departure*, 29.

20. See Moravánskzy, *Competing Visions*, 21-22.

21. Péter Hanák, *The Garden and the Workshop: Essays on the Cultural History of Vienna and Budapest* (Princeton, NJ: Princeton University Press, 1998), 13-14.

22. Walter Crane, *An Artist's Reminiscences* (New York: Macmillan, 1907), 472. Frank Berkeley Smith, *Budapest, the City of the Magyars* (New York: J. Pott & Company, 1903), 18, 21.

23. See the description of Agai's Journey from Pest to Budapest in Gwen Jones, *Chicago of the Balkans: Budapest in Hungarian Literature, 1900-1939* (London: Legenda, 2013), 46-48.

Chapter 6

1. On the new industries of Lyon, see Fondation Berliet, "Les riches heures de l'automobile Lyonnaise," in Ville de Lyon, ed., "L'esprit d'un siècle: Lyon 1800-1914" (Lyon: Fage éditions, 2007), 150-59. An excellent overview is also given in *Lyon et la région lyonnais en 1906*, 2 vols., vol. 2 (Lyon: A. Rey, 1906).

2. Marc Bonneville, *Naissance et métamorphose d'une banlieue ouvrière: Villeurbanne: processus et formes d'urbanisation* (Lyon: Presses Universitaires de Lyon, 1978), 37-43. See a also Jean-Luc de Ochandiano, *Lyon à l'italienne. Deux siècles de présence dans L'agglomération lyonnais* (Lyon: Lieux Dits, 2013).

Notes

3. Leif Jerram, *Streetlife: The Untold History of Europe's Twentieth Century* (Oxford: Oxford University Press, 2011), 21.

4. Pierre de Peretti, "La fête comme enjeu politique," in Noëlle Gérome, Danielle Tartakowsky, and Claude Willard, eds., *La Banlieue en fête. De la marginalité urbaine à l'identité culturelle* (Saint-Denis: Presses Universitaires de Vincennes, 1988), 209.

5. Lees and Lees, *Cities and the Making of Modern Europe*, 218-19.

6. On the question of working-class respectability, see chapter 2 in Peter Bailey, *Popular Culture and Performance in the Victorian City* (Cambridge and New York: Cambridge University Press, 1998).

7. Friedrich Lenger, *European Cities in the Modern Era, 1850-1914* (Leiden and Boston: Brill, 2012), 104.

8. See Alain Faure, "Comment se logeait le peuple parisien à la Belle Epoque?" *Vingtième Siècle* 64, no. October-December (1999): 41-52 as well as Alain Faure and Claire Lévy-Vroelant, *Une chambre en ville. Hôtels meublés et garnis à Paris 1860-1990* (Paris: CREAPHIS, 2007).

9. Jean-Claude Farcy, "Banlieues 1891: Les enseignements d'un recensement exemplaire," in Alain Faure, ed., *Les premiers banlieusards. Aux origines des banlieues de Paris, 1860-1940* (Paris: Editions Créaphis, 1991), 52.

10. Henri Sellier, "Les aspects nouveaux du problème de l'habitation dans les agglomérations urbaines," *La vie urbaine* 19 (1923): 90-91. The second quote: Jules Romains, *Les hommes de bonne volonté*, vol. 1 (1932), chapter 28 in Marie-Geneviève Dezès, "L'image en négatif des communes suburbaines," in Gérome, Tartakowsky, and Willard, *La Banlieue en fête*, 50-51.

11. Renate Banik-Schweitzer, "Vienna," in M. J. Daunton, ed., *Housing the Workers, 1850-1914: A Comparative Perspective* (London and New York: Leicester University Press, 1990), 134.

12. Recounted in Hall, *Cities of Tomorrow*, 26.

13. These details are given in Roland Perényi, "Urban Places, Criminal Spaces: Policy and Crime in Fin de Siècle Budapest," *Hungarian Historical Review* 1, no. 1-2 (2012): 134-65. Quote from page 142.

14. Dominique Kalifa, "Les Lieux du crime: Topographie criminelle et imaginaire social à Paris au XIXe siècle," *Sociétés et représentations* 17 (March 2004): 139-41.

15. Cited in Judson, *The Hapsburg Empire, a New History*, 362.

16. Matthew Arnold, *Culture & Anarchy: An Essay in Social and Cultural Criticism* (New York: Macmillan & Co., 1883), 81.

17. See Despina Stratigakos, *A Women's Berlin: Building the Modern City* (Minneapolis: University of Minnesota Press, 2008). Also Scott Spector, *Violent Sensations: Sex, Crime, and Utopia in Vienna and Berlin* (Chicago: University of Chicago Press, 2016).

18. Karl Scheffler, *Berlin. Ein Stadtschicksal* (Berlin: E. Reiss, 1910) quoted in Hans Kollhoff, "The Metropolis as a Construction: Engineering Structures in Berlin 1871-1914," in Josef Paul Kleihues and Christina Rathgeber, eds., *Berlin/New York: Like and Unlike: Essays on Architecture and Art from 1870 to the Present* (New York: Rizzoli, 1993), 48. Mark Twain, "The Chicago of Europe," *Chicago Daily Tribune*, April 3, 1892.

19. On the boom years in Berlin, see Gerhard Masur, *Imperial Berlin* (New York and London: Basic Books, 1970), chapter 3. Also Alan Balfour, *Berlin: The Politics of Order, 1737-1989* (New York: Rizzoli, 1990). More recently Large, *Berlin*.

20. See Frederic Schwartz, *The Werkbund: Design Theory and Mass Culture before the First World War* (New Haven and London: Yale University Press, 1996). Also Joan Campbell,

The German Werkbund: The Politics of Reform in the Applied Arts (Princeton, NJ: Princeton University Press, 2016).

21. The research on the *mietskasernen* is extensive. See for example, Harald Bodenschatz, *Platz frei für das Neue Berlin! Geschichte der Stadterneuerung in der "Größten Mietskasernenstadt Der Welt" seit 1871* (Berlin: Transit, 1987). See also Nicholas Bullock, "Berlin," in Nicholas Bullock and James Read, eds., *The Movement for Housing Reform in Germany and France, 1840-1914* (Cambridge: Cambridge University Press, 1985).

22. First published as "Der Nordring: Ein Fahrt auf der Ringbahn," in *Berlin für Kenner: Ein Bärenführer bei Tag und Nacht durch die deutsche Reichshauptstadt* (Berlin: Boll und Pickert, 1913) quoted in Whyte and Frisby, eds., *Metropolis Berlin*, 125.

23. Amanda M. Brian, "Art from the Gutter: Heinrich Zille's Berlin," *Central European History* 46 (2013): 41.

24. Gábor Gyáni, "Budapest," in Daunton, ed., *Housing the Workers, 1850-1914*, 176.

25. Cited in Anders Henriksson, "Riga: Growth, Conflict, and the Limitations of Good Government, 1850-1914," in Michael F. Hamm, ed., *The City in Late Imperial Russia* (Bloomington: Indiana University Press, 1986), 180–81.

26. Sandra Halperin, *War and Social Change in Modern Europe: The Great Transformation Revisited* (Cambridge and New York: Cambridge University Press, 2004), 129–30.

27. Henry Vizetelly, *Berlin under the New Empire, Its Institutions, Inhabitants, Industry, Monuments, Museums, Social Life, Manners, and Amusements*, 2 vols., vol. 2 (London: Tinsley Brothers, 1879), 274.

28. W. Scott Haine, *The World of the Paris Café. Sociability among the French Working Class, 1789-1914* (Baltimore & London: John Hopkins, 1996), 3.

29. Vizetelly, *Berlin under the New Empire*, 2, 292.

30. Quote and translation in Mary Gluck, *The Invisible Jewish Budapest: Metropolitan Culture at the Fin De Siècle* (Madison, WS: University of Wisconsin, 2016), 22.

31. Matthew Solomon, "Fairground Illusions and the Magic of Méliès," in Martin Loiperdinger, ed., *Traveling Cinema in Europe: Sources and Perspectives* (Frankfurt am Main: Stroemfeld, 2008), 17.

32. H. E. Meller, *Leisure and the Changing City, 1870-1914* (London, Henley and Boston: Routledge & Kegan Paul, 1976), 213. See also Bailey, *Popular Culture and Performance in the Victorian City*.

33. Davies and Moorhouse, *Microcosm: Portrait of a Central European City*, 291. David Ciarlo, *Advertising Empire: Race and Visual Culture in Imperial Germany* (Cambridge, MA and London: Harvard University Press, 2011), 81–83.

34. John Hollingshead, *The Story of Leicester Square* (London: Simpkin, Marshall, Hamilton, Kent & Co., 1892), 75.

35. Among the many publications on Paris entertainment at the turn-of-the-century, see Schwartz, *Spectacular Realities*. As well as Charles Rearick, *Pleasures of the Belle Epoque: Entertainment & Festivity in Turn-of-the-Century France* (New Haven and London: Yale University Press, 1985).

36. Raymond Rudorff, *The Belle Epoque: Paris in the Nineties* (New York: Saturday Review Press, 1973), 41.

37. Rearick, *Pleasures of the Belle Epoque*, 189.

Notes

38. David Kirby, *The Baltic World 1772-1993: Europe's Northern Periphery in an Age of Change* (Abingdon: Routledge, 1995), 215.

39. Martin W. Rühlemann, *Varietés und Singspielhallen- Urbane Raume des Vergnügens. Aspekte der Kommerziellen Populären Kultur in München ende des 19. Jahrhunderts* (Munich: Martin Meidenbauer, 2012), 214.

40. Stephen Oettermann, *The Panorama: History of a Mass Medium* (New York: Zone Books, 1997), 214 and 30.

41. Joseph Garncarz, "The Fairground Cinema—A European Institution," in Loiperdinger, ed., *Traveling Cinema in Europe*, 82.

42. Richard Stites, *Russian Popular Culture: Entertainment and Society Since 1900* (Cambridge and New York: Cambridge University Press, 1995), 30. Vladimir P. Buldakov, "Mass Culture and the Culture of the Masses in Russia, 1914-1922," in Murray Frame et al., eds., *Russian Culture in War and Revolution, 1914-1922*, 2 vols., vol 1: Popular Culture, the Arts, and Institutions (Bloomington, Indiana: Slavica, 2014), 33.

43. Oleh Sydor-Hybelynda, "Film in Kiev, 1910-1916," in Irena R. Makaryk and Virlana Tkacz, eds., *Modernism in Kiev: Kyiv/Kyïv/Kiev/Kijów/Ḳiev: Jubilant Experimentation* (Toronto: University of Toronto Press, 2010), 153–54.

Chapter 7

1. Ivan Berend, *An Economic History of Twentieth-Century Europe* (Cambridge and New York: Cambridge University Press, 2006), 17.

2. Nathaniel D. Wood, *Becoming Metropolitan: Urban Selfhood and the Making of Modern Cracow* (DeKalb, IL: Northern Illinois University Press, 2010), 131.

3. Quoted in Peter Fritzsche, *Reading Berlin 1900* (Cambridge, MA: Harvard University Press, 1996), 109.

4. Luigi Barzini, *Pekin to Paris: An Account of Prince Borghese's Journey across Two Continents in a Motor-Car* (London: E. Grant Richards, 1907), 634–35.

5. *Utro*, May 10, 1911 as cited in Michael F. Hamm, *Kiev: A Portrait, 1800-1917* (Princeton, NJ: Princeton University Press, 1993), 168.

6. See Daniel Unowsky, "Staging Habsburg Patriotism. Dynastic Loyalty and the 1898 Imperial Jubilee," in Pieter M. Judson and Marsha L. Rozenblit, eds., *Constructing National Identities in East Central Europe* (New York and London: Berghahn 2005), 151.

7. Angela Bartie et al., "Performing the Past: Identity, Civic Culture and Historical Pageants in Twentieth-Century English Small Towns," in Luďa Klusáková, ed., *Small Towns in Europe in the 20th and 21st Centuries: Heritage and Development Strategies* (Prague: Karolinum, 2017), 32. For Strasbourg, see Detmar Klein, "Folklore as a Weapon: National Identity in German-Annexed Alsace, 1890-1914," in Timothy Baycroft and David Hopkin, eds., *Folklore and Nationalism in Europe During the Long Nineteenth Century* (Leiden and Boston: Brill, 2012), 177.

8. See David Harvey, *Paris, Capital of Modernity* (New York and London: Routledge, 2003), 212.

9. Albert Robida, *The Twentieth Century*, trans. Philippe Willems (Middletown, CT: Weslyan University Press, 2004), 50.

10. Josip Lavtižar, *Pri severnih Slovanih. Potopisne črtice s slikami* (Celovec, 1906) translated and quoted in Bracewell, ed., *Orientations*, 206–7.

Notes

11. Theodore Petermann, ed., *Die Grossstadt. Vorträge und Aufsätze zur Städteausstellung* (Dresden: Zahn & Jaensch, 1903), 182.

12. August Endell, "Die Schönheit der Großen Stadt," (1908) in Iain Boyd Whyte and David Frisby, eds., *Metropolis Berlin*, 122.

13. Otto Wagner, "The Development of the Great City," (1912) reprinted in *Oppositions* 17 (1979): 115. See also August Sarnitz, "Realism versus *Verniedlichung*: The Design of the Great City," in Harry Francis Mallgrave, ed., *Otto Wagner: Reflections on the Raiment of Modernity*, (Santa Monica, CA: Getty Center for the History of Art and the Humanities, 1993), 105. See also Charles C. Bohl and Jean-François Lejeune, eds., *Sitte, Hegemann and the Metropolis: Modern Civic Art and International Exchanges* (Milton Park, Abingdon and New York: Routledge, 2009).

14. Walter Besant, *All Sorts and Conditions of Men: An Impossible Story* (New York: Harper & Brothers, 1889), 37 and 77.

15. George Brandes, *Poland: A Study of the Land, People, and Literature* (London: William Heinemann, 1903), 171–72.

16. See George R. Collins and Christiane Crasemann Collins, *Camillo Sitte: The Birth of Modern City Planning* (Mineola, NY: Dover, 1986).

17. Georg Simmel, "The Metropolis and Mental Life," (1903) in Gary Bridge and Sophie Watson, eds., *The Blackwell City Reader* (Oxford and Malden, MA: Wiley-Blackwell, 2002), 18.

18. Oswald Spengler, *The Decline of the West*, trans. Charles Francis Atkinson (New York: Alfred A. Knopf, 1926), 32.

19. Max Weber quoted in Thomas Rohkrämer, "German Cultural Criticism: The Desire for a Sense of Place and Community," in Rajesh Heynickx and Tom Avermaete, eds., *Making a New World: Architecture and Communities in Interwar Europe* (Leuven: Leuven University Press, 2012), 33.

20. Peter Alterberg, *Telegrams of the Soul*, trans. Peter Wortsman (New York: Archipelago, 2005), 25.

21. T. W. H. Crosland, *The Suburbans* (London: John Long, 1905), 9.

22. See Robert Fishman, *Bourgeois Utopias; the Rise and Fall of Suburbia* (New York: Basic Books, 1987).

23. *Birmingham Daily Mail*, November 26, 1903 quoted in John R. Kellett, *The Impact of Railways on Victorian Cities* (London and New York: Routledge, 1969), 364.

24. W. Pett Ridge, *Outside the Radius: Stories of a London Suburb* (London: Hodder and Stroughton), 3–4 and 8–9.

25. Descriptive map of London poverty 1889 to accompany *Labour and Life of the People.* Appendix to volume II. Edited by Charles Booth (London & Edinburgh: William and Norgate, 1891).

26. Rosemary Wakeman, *Practicing Utopia: An Intellectual History of the New Town Movement* (Chicago: University of Chicago Press, 2016), 21–24. On the garden city movement, see Stanley Buder, *Visionaries and Planners: The Garden City Movement and the Modern Community* (Oxford: Oxford University Press, 1990). And Stephen V. Ward, ed., *The Garden City: Past, Present, and Future* (Abingdon, Oxon: Spon Press, 1992).

27. Andrew Lees, *Cities, Sin, and Social Reform in Imperial Germany* (Ann Arbor: University of Michigan, 2002), 56. See also Helen Meller, "Imagining the Future of Cities through Exhibitions," in Robert Freestone and Marco Amati, eds., *Exhibitions and the Development of Modern Planning Culture* (Burlington, VT: Ashgate, 2014), 19–34.

Notes

28. Suzanne Pouchier-Plasseraud, *Arts and a Nation: The Role of Visual Arts and Artists in the Making of the Latvian Identity, 1905-1940*, trans. Nick Tait (Leiden, The Netherlands: Koninklijke Brill NV, 2015), 29.

29. On Style Moderne in St. Petersburg and Moscow, see John E. Bowlt, *Moscow & St. Petersburg 1900-1920: Art, Life & Culture of the Russian Silver Age* (New York: Vendome, 2008).

30. On the cabaret, see Harold B. Segel, *Turn-of-the-Century Cabaret* (New York: Columbia University Press, 1987) as well as Lisa Appignanesi, *The Cabaret* (New Haven and London: Yale University Press, 2004). And Peter Jelavich, *Berlin Cabaret* (Cambridge, MA and London: Harvard University Press, 1993).

31. Mabel W. Daniels, *An American Girl in Munich: Impressions of a Music Student* (Boston: Brown, Little & Company, 1905), 179 and 187.

32. Rainer Metzger, *Munich 1900. La Sécession, Kandinsky et le Blaue Reiter* (Paris: Hazan, 2009), 203-28.

33. Alterberg, *Telegrams of the Soul*, 164.

34. See in particular Herbert Lederer, "The Vienna Coffee House: History and Cultural Significance," in Leona Rittner, W. Scott Haine, and Profess Leona Rittner, eds., *The Thinking Space: The Café as a Cultural Institution in Paris, Italy and Vienna* (Farnham: Taylor and Francis, 2013), 25-32. See also Käthe Springer, "Das Weiner Kaffeehaus- Ein Literarisches Verkehrszentrum," in Christian Brandstätter, ed., *Wien 1900: Kunst und Kultur*, 2 ed. (München: Deutscher Taschenbuch 2011), 335-42.

35. On Kraków, see David Crowley, "Castles, Cabarets and Cartoons: Claims on Polishness in Kraków around 1905," in Gee, Kirk, and Steward, *The City in Central Europe*, 107-9. See Richard Stites, *Russian Popular Culture: Entertainment and Society since 1900*, 22.

36. Appignanesi, *The Cabaret*, 60.

37. Gábor Gyáni, *Identity and the Urban Experience: Fin-De-Siècle Budapest*, trans. Thomas J. DeKornfeld (Boulder, CO: Social Science Monographs, 2004), 106-9.

38. Ernst Van Bruyssel, *L'Industrie et le commerce en Belgique. leur état actuel & leur avenir* (Brussels: C. Muquardt, 1868), 17-30.

39. Marcel Schmitz, *Figure de Bruxelles* (Dilbeek en Brabant: Editions Art et Technique, 1944), 20.

40. Deborah L. Silverman, "Art Nouveau, Art of Darkness: African Lineages of Belgian Modernism, Part I," *West 86th* 18, no. 2 (Fall-Winter 2011): 146. See also Franco Borsi, *Bruxelles 1900* (New York: Rizzoli, 1977).

41. See Silverman, "Art Nouveau, Art of Darkness," 139-81.

42. Jānis Krastiņš, *Art Nouveau Buildings in Riga: A Guide to Art Nouveau Metropolis* (Riga: Add Projekts, 2014), 19-21.

43. Berend, *Case Studies on Modern European Economy*, 184.

44. Franklin Hugh Adler, *Italian Industrialists from Liberalism to Fascism: The Political Development of the Industrial Bourgeoisie, 1906-1934* (Cambridge and New York: Cambridge University Press, 1995), 36.

45. Cristina Della Coletts, "Exposition Narratives and the Italian Bourgeoisie: Edmondo De Amicis's *Torino 1880*," in Stefania Lucamante, ed., *Italy and the Bourgeoisie: The Rethinking of a Class* (Madison and Teaneck: Fairleigh Dickinson University Press, 2009), 34-36.

46. See Alison Fleig Frank, *Oil Empire: Visions of Prosperity in Austrian Galica* (Cambridge, MA and London: Harvard University Press, 2005).
47. Alfred Döblin, *Journey to Poland* (London and New York: I.B. Tauris, 1991), 139–40, 44, 56. See Chapter 1 in Tarik Cyril Amar, *The Paradox of Ukrainian Lviv: A Borderland City between Stalinists, Nazis, and Nationalists* (Ithaca and London: Cornell University Press, 2015).
48. On the Galician General Provincial Exhibition, see Larry Wolff, *The Idea of Galicia: History and Fantasy in Habsburg Political Culture* (Stanford, CA: Stanford University Press, 2010), 286–94.
49. Robert Blobaum, "A City in Flux: Warsaw's Transient Populations During World War I," *The Polish Review* 59, no. 4 (2014): 26 as well as Blobaum's *A Minor Apocalypse: Warsaw During the First World War* (Ithica Cornell University Press, 2017), 232.

Chapter 8

1. This phrase is used by Large, *Berlin*, 157.
2. Henri Tajfel and John L. Dawson, *Disappointed Guests: Essays by African, Asian, and West Indian Students* (London and New York: Oxford University Press, 1965), 59.
3. Marc Matera, *Black London: The Imperial Metropolis and Decolonization in the Twentieth Century* (Berkeley, CA: University of California Press, 2015), 166. Also Judith Walkowitz, *Nights Out in Cosmopolitan London* (New Haven: Yale University Press, 2012), Chapter 1.
4. George Orwell, *Down and out in London and Paris* (San Diego and New York: Harcourt Brace, 1933), 71.
5. Michael Goebel, *Anti-Imperial Metropolis: Interwar Paris and the Seeds of Third World Nationalism* (New York: Cambridge University Press, 2015), 21, 28. See also Jennifer Anne Boittin, *Colonial Metropolis: The Urban Grounds of Anti-Imperialism and Feminism in Interwar Paris* (Lincoln and London: University of Nebreska Press, 2010).
6. Tyler Stovall, *Paris Noir: African Americans in the City of Light* (Boston and New York: Houghton Mifflin, 1996), 35–45.
7. Béla Tomka, *A Social History of Twentieth-Century Europe* (London: Routledge, 2013), 36. See also chapter 2 in Claudia Skran, *Refugees in Inter-War Europe: The Emergence of a Regime* (Oxford and New York: Oxford University Press, 1995).
8. Joseph Roth, *What I Saw: Reports from Berlin, 1920-33* (London: Granta, 2003), 96.
9. Dudley Kirk, *Europe's Population in the Interwar Years* (New York and London: Gordon & Breach, 1946), 32–3.
10. François Caron, Paul Erker, and Wolfram Fischer, eds., *Innovations in the European Economy between the Wars* (Berlin and New York: Walter de Gruyter, 1995), 14–18. Youssef Cassis, *Big Business: The European Experience in the Twentieth Century* (Oxford: Oxford University Press, 1997), 59. Rainer Karlsch, "The Chemical Industry in the Soviet Zone of Occupation (SBZ/GDR, 1945-1965," in John E. Lesch, ed., *The German Chemical Industry in the Twentieth Century* (Dordrecht: Springer Science+Business, 2000), 369–71.
11. Mathieu Flonneau, "Infrastructures et citadins: réflexions sur l'acceptance de l'impact de l'automobile à Paris au XXe siècle, " *Le Mouvement Social* 192 (2000): 106. See also his *Paris et l'automobile: un siècle de passions* (Paris: Hachette, 2005).

Notes

12. See James Laux, *The European Automobile Industry* (New York: Twayne, 1992), 100. Roy Church, *The Rise and Decline of the British Motor Industry* (Cambridge: Cambridge University Press, 1995), 31. Also Kathryn A. Morrison and John Minnis, *Carscapes: The Motor Car, Architecture and Landscape in England* (New Haven and London: Yale University Press, 2012), 22–30.

13. On the Baťa Company and the development of Zlín, see chapter 3 in Helen E. Meller, *European Cities, 1890-1930s: History, Culture, and the Built Environment* (Chichester and New York: Wiley, 2001), 129–48.

14. Franz Hessel, *Walking in Berlin: A Flaneur in the Capital* (Cambridge, MA and London: MIT Press, 2017), 29.

15. See Siegfried Kracauer, *The Salaried Masses: Duty and Distraction in Weimar Germany*, trans. Quintin Hoare (London: Verso, 1998).

16. Janet Ward, *Weimar Surfaces: Urban Visual Culture in 1920s Germany* (Berkeley, CA: University of California Press 2001), 107.

17. Roth, *What I Saw*, 149–50.

18. Michael W. Jennings, Howard Eiland, and Gary Smith, eds., *Walter Benjamin, Selected Writings*, vol. 2: 1927-1934 (Cambridge, MA and London: Belknap Press, 1999), 301–2.

19. Peter Jelavich, *Berlin Alexanderplatz: Radio, Film, and the Death of Weimar Culture* (Berkeley, CA: University of California Press, 2006), 24.

20. Véronique Parent, *Enquête sur les sièges de l'Info* (Paris: L'Arsenal/Hazan, 1994), 86.

21. Suzanne Lommers, *Europe—on Air: Interwar Projects for Radio Broadcasting* (Amsterdam: Amsterdam University Press, 2012), 93–94.

22. Karl Christian Führer, "A Medium of Modernity? Broadcasting in Weimar Germany, 1923-1932," *Journal of Modern History* 69, no. December (1997): 722.

23. George Grosz, *George Grosz: An Autobiography*, trans. Nora Hodges (Berkeley, CA: University of California Press, 1998), 113.

24. Diana Mishkova, "Balkans/Southeastern Europe," in Mishkova and Trencsényi, eds., *European Regions and Boundaries*, 148.

25. Ivan T. Berend and Györgi Ránki, *Studies on Central and Eastern Europe in the Twentieth Century* (Aldershot, Hampshire and Burlington, Vermont: Ashgate, 2002), V. 116–18.

26. Ferdynand Zweig, *Poland between Two Wars, a Critical Study of Social and Economic Changes* (London: Secker & Warburg, 1944), 21 and 31.

27. Kathryn Ciancia, "Borderland Modernity: Poles, Jews, and Urban Spaces in Interwar Eastern Poland," *Journal of Modern History* 89, no. September (2017): 539.

28. Polish National Exhibition Poznań. May–September 1929 oai:www.wbc.poznan.pl:2230

29. Hanna Grzeszczuk-Brendel, "Architecture of the Polish National Exhibition (1929) and Architecture in Poznań of the 1930s: Transfer of Modern Movement Ideas," in Maria Jolanta Sołtysik and Robert Hirsch, eds., *Modernism in Europe, Modernism in Gdynia: Architecture of the 1920s and 1930s and Its Protection* (Gdynia: Gdynia City Hall, 2009), 120.

30. On the growth of Warsaw, see Edward D. Wynot, "The Society of Interwar Warsaw: Profile of the Capital City in a Developing Nation, 1918-1939," *East European Quarterly* 6, no. 4 (1973): 504–19 as well as Anna Zarnowska, *Workers, Women, and Social Change in Poland, 1870-1939* (Aldershot and Burlington, Vermont: Ashgate, 2004), 296–8.

31. The descriptions of Warsaw before the First World War can be found in chapter 3, "The Faces of the City," in Stephen D. Corrsin, *Warsaw before the First World War: Poles and Jews*

Notes

in the Third City of the Russian Empire 1880-1914 (New York: Columbia University Press, 1989). The quotations are from pages 47-48.

32. The plans for Warsaw are recounted in chapter 5 of Edward D. Wynot, *Warsaw between the World Wars: Profile of the Capital City in a Developing Land, 1918-1939* (New York: Columbia University Press, 1983) as well as Piotr Marciniak, "New Towns and Cities in Reborn Poland between the Wars," in Helen Meller and Heleni Porfyriou, eds., *Planting New Towns in Europe in the Interwar Years: Experiments and Dreams for Future Societies* (Newcastle upon Tyne: Cambridge Scholars Publishing, 2016), 109-44. See also Martin Kohlrausch, "*Warszawa Funkcjonalna*: Radical Urbanism and the International Discourse on Planning in the Interwar Period," in Behrends and Kohlrausch, eds., *Races to Modernity*, 206-31.

33. On Warsaw's cultural life in the interwar years, see Ron Nowicki, *Warsaw: The Cabaret Years* (San Francisco: Mercury House, 1992). On the Warsaw cabarets, see Beth Holmgren, "Acting Out: *Qui Pro Quo* in the Context of Interwar Warsaw," *East European Politics and Societies and Cultures* 27, no. 2 (2012): 205-23.

34. An excellent description of public health in Moscow and St. Petersburg is given in James H. Bater, "St. Petersburg and Moscow on the Eve of Revolution," in Daniel H. Kaiser, ed., *The Workers' Revolution in Russia: The View from Below* (Cambridge and New York: Cambridge University Press, 1990), 50-53.

35. Quoted in Joseph Bradley, *Muzhik and Muscovite: Urbanizataion in Late Imperial Russia* (Berkeley, CA: University of California Press, 1985), 61.

36. R. Lockhart, and H. Bruce, *British Agent* (New York and London: G. P. Putnam's Sons, 1933), Book Two, chapter 1, http://www.gwpda.org/wwi-www/BritAgent/BA02.htm

37. David Goldfrank, ed. *Passion and Perception: Essays on Russian Culture by Richard Stites* (Washington DC: New Academia, 2010), 137-40.

38. See John Milner et al., *Revolution: Russian Art 1917-1932* (London: Royal Academy, 2017).

39. Walter Benjamin, *Moscow Diary*, trans. Richard Sieburth (Cambridge, MA and London: Harvard University Press, 1986), Quotes from pp. 18 and 22.

40. On the Soviet Communal House and the Narkomfin Building, see Victor Buchli, *An Archaeology of Socialism* (Oxford and New York: Berg, 2000).

41. "Introduction by Vladimir Tolstoy from *Street Art of the Revolution*," Jan Cohen-Cruz, ed., *Radical Street Performance: An International Anthology* (London and New York: Routledge, 1998), 19-20. See also Catherine Cook, *Russian Avant-Garde: Theories of Art, Architecture and the City* (London: Academy, 1995), 20-23. Matthew Gale and Natalia Sidlina, *Red Star over Russia* (London: Tate Modern, 2017).

42. Timothy J. Colton, *Moscow: Governing the Socialist Metropolis* (Cambridge and London: Harvard University Press, 1995), 283.

43. Sheila Fitzpatrick, *Everyday Stalinism: Ordinary Life in Extraordinary Times: Soviet Russia in the 1930s* (New York and Oxford: Oxford University Press, 1999), 67-70. Colton, chapter 4. See also Katerina Clark, *Moscow, the Fourth Rome: Stalinism, Cosmopolitanism, and the Evolution of Soviet Culture, 1931-1941* (Cambridge, MA: Harvard University Press, 2011), chapter 2.

44. *New Moscow* (1939), [Film] Dirs. Aleksandr Medvedkin, Aleksandr Olenin, USSR.

45. See Joe Nasr and Mercedes Volait, eds., *Urbanism, Imported or Exported?* (New York: John Wiley & Sons, 2003) as well as Alexandra Yerolympos, "Domesticating Modernity through City Building: New Plans for Balkan Cities, 1900-1922," in Andreas Lyberatos, ed., *Social*

Notes

Transformation and Mass Mobilisation in the Balkan and Eastern Mediterranean Cities, 1900-1923 (Crete: Crete University Press, 2013), 27.

46. Maria Todorova, "The Ottoman Legacy in the Balkans," in Carl L. Brown, ed., *Imperial Legacy: The Ottoman Imprint on the Balkans and the Middle East* (New York: Columbia University Press, 1996), 46.

47. See Kaloyan Stanev, "Railways, Regions and the Urban Network in the Balkans During a Century of Political Transformations 1900-2000," *Etudes Balkaniques* XLVII, no. 1 (2011): 5–37.

48. See the elegant descriptions of the Islamic urban heritage in Raina Gavrilova, *Bulgarian Urban Culture in the Eighteenth and Nineteenth Centuries* (Selinsgrove: Susquehanna University Press, 1999).

49. Joseph Roth, *The Hotel Years: Wanderings in Europe between the Wars*, trans. Michael Hofmann (London: Granta, 2016), 139. Henry Debraye, *Autour de la Yougoslavie* (Grenoble: Arthaud, 1931), 83–85.

50. Huntley Film Archives, "Yugoslavia in the 1930's Jugoslavia," Film 6371 and "Sarajevo 1939 in Color" (Filmschätze aus Köln - Vom Rhein - Welfilmerbe), youtube.com

51. Rebecca West, *Black Lamb and Grey Falcon. A Journey through Yugoslavia* (New York: Penguin, 20017, first published 1940), Quotations from pages 297 and 321. Holm Sundhaussen, *Sarajevo. Die Geschichte einer Stadt* (Vienna and Cologne: Böhlau, 2014), 60–61.

52. Elitza Stanoeva, "Architectural Praxis in Sofia: The Changing Perception of Oriental Urbanity and European Urbanism, 1879-1940," in Behrends and Kohlrausch, eds., *Races to Modernity*, 184–85, 89. See also Stanoeva's "Interpretations of the Ottoman Urban Legacy in the National Capital Building of Sofia (1878-1940)," in Eyal Ginio and Karl Kaser, eds., Ottoman Legacies in the Balkans and the Middle East (Jerusalem: European Forum at the Hebrew University, 2013), 209–30.

53. John Foster Fraser, *Pictures from Balkans* (London and New York: Cassell 1906), 18–19, 66.

54. Franjo Ksaverski Horvat-Kiš, *Viđeno iI neviđeno: Putničke crtice* (Zagreb, 1911) translated and quoted in Bracewell, ed., *Orientations*, 162. The second quote is from Lena Jovičić, *Peeps at Many Lands. Yugoslavia* (London: A & C Black, 1928), 11.

55. Pavle S. Zorić, "Lepa varoš," *Srpski knjiž glasnik* (1902) translated and cited in Dubravka Stojanović, "Unfinished Capital- Unfinished State: How the Modernization of Belgrade Was Prevented, 1890-1914," *Nationalities Papers* 41, no. 1 (2013): 19. See also Mirjana Roter Blagojević and Ana Radivojević, "Les Espaces publics et la vie publique à Belgrade au XVIIIe et au XIXe siècle et leur transformation au XXe siècle," *Etudes Balkaniques* 14 (2007). See also David A. Norris, *Belgrade, a Cultural History* (Oxford and New York: Oxford University Press, 2009).

56. Huntley Film Archives, "The Coronation of King Peter of Serbia, 1904," Film 11057.

57. Fraser, *Pictures from Balkans*, 19, 265.

58. Miloš Cosić, *Stenografske beleške Narodne skupštine* (1909) translated and cited in Stojanović, 27.

59. On the redevelopment of Ljubljana, see Breda Mihelić, "From Provincial to National Center: Ljubljana," in Blau and Platzer, eds., *Shaping the Great City*, 196–200. Anthony Alofsin, *When Buildings Speak: Architecture as Language in the Habsburg Empire and Its Aftermath, 1867-1933* (Chicago: University of Chicago Press, 2006), 173–75.

Notes

60. "Stari Beograd—1940," "Yugoslavia and Belgrade/Serbia 1930s" (Periscope), and "The Streets of Zagreb in the 1930s" (Croatian National Radio-Television), youtube.com.
61. Feda Vukić, ed. *Zagreb Modernost i Grad* (Zagreb: AGM, 2003), 51–52.
62. Sonja Briski Uzelac, "Visual Arts in the Avant-gardes between the Two Wars," in Dubravka Djurié and Misko Suvakovié, eds., *Impossible Histories: Historical Avant-Gardes, Neo-Avant-Gardes, and Post-Avant-Gardes in Yugoslavia, 1918-1991* (Cambridge, MA: MIT Press, 2015). See also Timothy O. Benson, *Central European Avant-gardes: Exchange and Transformation, 1910-1930* (Los Angeles and Boston: Los Angeles County Museum of Art/ MIT Press, 2002). See also, Marijeta Božović, "Zenit Rising. Return to the Balkan Avant-Garde," in Radmila Gorup, ed., *After Yugoslava: The Cultural Spaces of a Vanished Land* (Stanford, CA: Stanford University Press, 2013), 142. Dina Mishkova, "Balkans/Southeastern Europe," 151.
63. Translated and cited in Celia Hawkesworth, *Zagreb: A Cultural History* (London: Oxford University Press, 2008), 110. See also Eve Blau and Ivan Rupnik, eds., *Project Zagreb: Transition as Condition, Strategy, Practice* (Barcelona: Actar, 2007).

Chapter 9

1. See David M. Pomfret, "'Lionized and Toothless': Young People and Urban Politics in Britain and France, 1918-1940," in Axel Schildt and Detlef Siegfried, eds., *European Cities, Youth and the Public Sphere in the Twentieth Century* (Aldershot and Burlington, VT: Ashgate, 2005), 38.
2. Robert Wegs, *Growing up Working Class: Continuity and Change among Viennese Youth, 1890-1938* (Philadelphia: Penn State University Press, 1989), 26–27.
3. Mary Nolan, *Social Democracy and Society: Working Class Radicalism in Düsseldorf, 1890-1920* (Cambridge and New York: Cambridge University Press, 1981), 139–41. See also Stefan Berger, *Social Democracy and the Working Class in Nineteenth and Twentieth Century Germany* (Abingdon and New York: Routledge, 2013).
4. Katherine Milcoy, *When the Girls Come out to Play: Teenage Working-Class Girls' Leisure between the Wars* (London: Bloomsbury Academic, 2017), 66.
5. Françoise Cribier, "Le Logement d'une génération de jeunes Parisiens à l'époque du Front Populaire," Susanna Magri and Christian Toalov, eds., *Villes ouvrières 1900-1950* (Paris: Harmattan, 1989), 113.
6. Susanna Magri and Christian Topalov, "De la cité-jardin à la ville rationalisée. Un tournant du projet réformateur, 1905-1925: Etude comparative France, Grande-Bretagne, Etats-Unis," *Revue française de sociologie* 28, no. 3 (1987): 417–51. More recent, see Kamoun, *Hygiène et morale*.
7. Sheffield Labour Party, quoted in Tim Willis, "Politics, Ideology and the Governance of Health Care in Sheffield before the NHS," Robert J. Morris and Richard H. Trainor, eds., *Urban Governance: Britain and Beyond since 1750* (Abingdon and New York: Routledge, 2000), 128. See also Larry Bennett, *Neighborhood Politics: Chicago and Sheffield* (New York and London: Garland, 1997), 48.
8. Kamoun, *Hygiène et morale*, 148–53. See also Uwe Kühl, ed., *Der Munizipalsozialismus in Europa* (Munich: Oldenbourg, 2002).

Notes

9. Hannah Lewi and Christine Phillips, "The Modern Pool as a New Civic Space," *Architektúra & Urbanizmus* 3-4 (2010). Ken Worpole, *Here Comes the Sun. Architecture and Public Space in Twentieth Century European Culture* (London: Reaktion, 2000), 115-18.

10. Aude Chamouard, "La Mairie socialiste, matrice du réformisme (1900-1939)," *Vingtième siècle* 96, no. 4 (2007): 24.

11. Jean-Claude Duphil, *Toulouse socialiste, 1906-1940* (Portet-sur-Garonne: Empreinte, 2005), 76-82.

12. Conseil d'architecture d'urbanisme et de l'environnement de la Haute-Garonne and Ecole d'architecture de Toulouse, eds., *Toulouse 1920-1940: La Ville et ses architectes* (Toulouse: Ombres, 1991), 179. See also Laura Girard, "Jean Montariol et les artistes toulousains," *In Situ. Revue des Patrimoine* 32 (2017), http://journals.openedition.org/insitu/docannexe/image/14840/img-6.jpg

13. Bernard Vere, *Sport and Modernism in the Visual Arts in Europe, c. 1909-39* (Manchester: Manchester University Press, 2018), 150. See also Alain Vollerin, *Tony Garnier et Lyon: aux origines de la modernité* (Lyon: Mémoire des arts, 2011).

14. Anne-Sophie Clémençon, ed., *Les Gratte-ciel de Villeurbanne* (Besaançon and Paris: Les Editions de l'imprimeur, 2004), 75 and quote on page 81. See also Jean-Luc Pinol, *Espace social et espace politique: Lyon à l'époque du Front Populaire* (Lyon: Presses universitaires de Lyon, 1980).

15. Helmut Gruber, *Red Vienna: Experiment in Working-Class Culture, 1919-1934* (Oxford and New York: Oxford University Press, 1991), 15. See also the description in the *New York Times*, July 20, 1931.

16. The description of these festivals is given in Gruber, *Red Vienna*, 109-10.

17. See Eve Blau, *The Architecture of Red Vienna, 1919-1934* (London: MIT Press, 1999).

18. See chapter 5 on tuberculosis campaigns in Marjaana Niemi, *Public Health and Municipal Policy Making: Britain and Sweden, 1900-1940* (Aldershop and Burlington, VT: Ashgate, 2007).

19. Iain Boyd Whyte, *Bruno Taut and the Architecture of Activism* (Cambridge: Cambridge University Press, 1982), 97. See also Winfried Brenne, *Bruno Taut: Master of Colorful Architecture in Berlin* (Schweiz: Braun 2013). Most recently, Deutscher Werkbund Berlin, *Bruno Taut; Visionär und Weltbürger* (Berlin: Wagenbach, 2018) as well as their *Bauen und Wohnen: Die Geschichte der Werkbundsiedlungen* (Berlin: Wasmuth and Zohlen, 2016).

20. See Kenneth Frampton, *Modern Architecture, a Critical History*, 3rd ed. (London: Thames & Hudson, 1992), 124.

21. Richard Pommer and Christian F. Otto, *Weissenhof 1927 and the Modern Movement in Architecture* (Chicago and London: University of Chicago Press, 1991), 135.

22. On the Frankfurt Experiment, see Susan R. Henderson, *Building Culture: Ernst May and the New Frankfurt Initiative, 1926-1931* (New York: Peter Lang International Publishers, 2013) and also John Robert Mullin, "City Planning in Frankfurt, Germany, 1925-1932," *Journal of Urban History* 4, no. 1 (1977): 3-28. See also Wakeman, *Practicing Utopia*, 28-29.

23. On the *folkhemmet* ideal and social democracy, see Eva Rudberg, "Building the Utopia of the Everyday," in Helena Mattsson and Sven-Olov Wallenstein, eds., *Swedish Modernism: Architecture, Consumption and the Welfare State* (London: Black Dog, 2010), 152-59. See also Cecilia Widenheim, ed. *Utopia and Reality- Modernity in Sweden 1900-1960* (New Haven and London: Yale University Press, 2002).

Notes

24. See Eva Rudberg, *The Stockholm Exhibition 1930: Modernism's Breakthrough in Swedish Architecture*, trans. Paul Britten Austin and Frances Lucas (Stockholm: Stockholmia Förlag, 1999).

25. Grant Allen, *The European Tour* (New York: Dodd, Mead, & Company, 1899), 195.

26. Henri Béraud, *Ce que j'ai vu a Rome* (Paris: Editions de France, 1929), 22–23.

27. Simonetta Falasca-Zamponi, *Fascist Spectacle: The Aesthetics of Power in Mussolini's Italy* (Ann Arbor, Michigan: University of Michigan Press, 2000), 21–23. Among the abundant scholarship on fascist Rome, see Joshua Arthurs, *Excavating Modernity: The Roman Past in Fascist Italy* (Ithaca & London: Cornell University Press, 2012). Also Harald Bodenschatz, *Städtebau für Mussolini. Auf der Suche Nach der Neuen Stadt im Faschistischen Italien* (Berlin: DOM, 2011). Harald Bodenschatz, Piero Sassi, and Max Welch Guerra, eds., *Urbanism and Dictatorship: A European Perspective* (Berlin: Birkhauser, 2015).

28. Béraud, *Ce que j'ai vu à Rome*, 24.

29. See Aristotle Kallis, *The Third Rome, 1922-1943: The Making of a Fascist Capital* (New York: Palgrave Macmillan, 2014), 46–50. See also chapter 3, "Sports, Education, and the New Italians," in Borden W. Jr. Painter, *Mussolini's Rome: Rebuilding the Eternal City* (New York: Palgrave Macmillan, 2005), 39–57. On fascist architecture as spectacle, see D. Medina Lasansky, *The Renaissance Perfected: Architecture, Spectacle, and Tourism in Fascist Italy* (University Park, PA: Pennsylvania State University Press, 2004).

30. Ameury Duval quoted in Frank M. Snowden, *Naples in the Time of Cholera, 1884-1911* (Cambridge: Cambridge University Press, 1995), 18.

31. Joseph A. Buttigieg, ed., *Antonio Gramsci. Prison Notebooks, Volume I* (New York: Columbia University Press, 1992), 168. See also Jordan Lancaster, *In the Shadow of Vesuvius: A Cultural History of Naples* (London and New York: I.B. Tauris, 2005).

32. Giorgio Bertellini and Saverio Giovacchini, "Ambiguous Sovereignties: Notes on the Suburbs in Italian Cinema," in Peter Lang and Tam Miller, eds., *Suburban Discipline* (New York: Princeton Architectural Press, 1997), 90–91. See also Giuliana Bruno, "Streetwalking around Plato's Cave," in Laura Pietropaolo and Ada Testaferri, eds., *Feminisms in the Cinema* (Bloomington and Indianapolis: Indiana University Press, 1995), 147.

33. Giuseppe Galasso, ed., *Benedetto Croce. Un Paradiso abitato da diavoli* (Milan: Adelphi, 2006).

34. Walter Benjamin and Asja Lacis, "Naples," In Marcus Bullock and Michael W. Jennings, eds., *Walter Benjamin: Selected Writings. Volume 1, 1913-1926*, 5th ed. (Cambridge, MA and London: Belknap Press of Harvard University Press, 2002), 416–17.

35. See Benedetto Gravagnuolo, "From Schinkel to Le Corbusier, The Myth of the Mediterranean in Modern Architecture," in Jean-François Lejeune and Michelangelo Sabatino, eds., *Modern Architecture and the Mediterranean: Vernacular Dialogues and Contested Identities* (London and New York: Routledge, 2010), 16–39. Adolf Max Vogt, *Le Corbusier, Le Bon Sauvage: vers une archéologie de la modernité*, trans. Léo Biétry (Gollion, Switzerland: Infolio, 2003), 77.

36. Walter Benjamin and Asja Lacis, "Naples," Bullock and Jennings, eds., *Walter Benjamin*, 420.

37. Robert W. Carden, *The City of Genoa* (London: Methuen, 1908), v.

38. See Giuseppe Felloni, "The Population Dynamics and Economic Development of Genoa, 1750-1939," in Richard Lawton and Robert Lee, eds., *Population and Society in Western European Port Cities, C. 1650-1939* (Liverpool: Liverpool University Press, 2002), 74–90.

39. Kracauer, *The Mass Ornament*, 38.

Notes

40. Léon Abastado, *L'Orient qui meurt. (Salonique, ce qu'elle est)* (Salonica: Acquarone, 1918), 22. Second quote in Leon Sciaky, *Farewell to Salonica* (New York: A.A. Wyn, 1946), 39.

41. Chapter 3 in Régis Dargues, *Salonique au XXe siècle: de la cité ottomane à la métropole grecque* (Paris: CNRS, 2000). https://books.openedition.org/editionscnrs/1323. Abastado, *L'Orient qui meurt*, 24. On the history of Salonica, see Mark Mazower, *Salonica, City of Ghosts* (New York: Vintage, 2004).

42. Sciaky, *Farewell to Salonica*, 213.

43. Vilma Hastaoglou-Martinidis, "A Mediterranean City in Transition: Thessaloniki between the Two World Wars," *Facta Universitatis* 1, no. 4 (1997): 503. See also Alexandra Yerolympus, "Thessaloniki (Salonika) before and after 1917: Twentieth Century Planning Versus 20 Centuries of Urban Evolution," *Planning Perspectives* 3, no. 2 (1988): 141–66.

44. Evdoxios Doxiadis, *State, Nationalism, and the Jewish Communities of Modern Greece* (London and New York: Bloomsbury Academic, 2018), 126. See also Devin E. Naar, *Jewish Salonica: Between the Ottoman Empire and Modern Greece* (Stanford, CA: Stanford University Press, 2016).

45. *El Escándalo* quoted in Robert A. Davidson, *Jazz Age Barcelona* (Toronto: University of Toronto Press, 2009). Google Books. Henry de Montherlant, *La petite infante de Castille*. Paris: Grasset, 1929 quoted in Joan Ramon Resina, *Barcelona's Vocation of Modernity: Rise and Decline of an Urban Image* (Stanford, CA: Stanford University Press, 2008). Stanford Scholarship Online. See Resina's excellent chapter 3, "Like Moths to a Lamp," on the Barrio Chino.

46. See Nick Rider, "The New City and the Anarchist Movement in the Early 1930s," in Smith, ed., *Red Barcelona*, 74–75.

47. Antoni Castells Duran, "Revolution and Collectivization in Civil War Barcelona, 1936-9," in Smith, ed., *Red Barcelona*, 127–41.

48. George Orwell, *Homage to Catalonia* (London: Secker & Warburg, 1938). E-book available https://theanarchistlibrary.org/library/george-orwell-homage-to-catalonia. For a description of the May Days on the streets of Barcelona, see Robert J. Alexander, *The Anarchists in the Spanish Civil War*, vol. 2 (London: Janus, 1999), 902–13.

49. *Catalunya Martir* (1938), [Film] Dir. J. Marsillach [Laya Films], 3 parts. Laya Films was the production company for the Spanish Republic's Propaganda Division.

Chapter 10

1. Karl Schlögel, "Urbizid. Europäische Städte im Krieg," in Karl Schlögel, *Marjampole oder Europas Wiederkehr aus dem Geist der Städte* (Munich: Carl Hanser, 2005), 171–82.

2. George Kennan, *Memories 1925-1950* (New York: Pantheon, 1983), 280. Alfred Döblin, *Autobiographische Schriften und letzte Aufzeichnungen*, 397 quoted in Wolfgang Schivelbusch, *In a Cold Crater: Cultural and Intellectual Life in Berlin, 1945-1948*, trans. Kelly Barry (Berkeley: University of California Press, 1998), 5.

3. See for example, David F. Crew, *Bodies and Ruins: Imagining the Bombing of Germany, 1945 to the Present* (Ann Arbor: University of Michigan Press, 2017).

4. Stephen Castles, "Immigration and Asylum: Challenges to European Identities and Citizenship," in Dan Stone, ed., *The Oxford Handbook of Postwar European History* (Oxford: Oxford University Press, 2014), 205.

Notes

5. Mairie de Paris, *C'était Paris dans les années 50* (Paris: Ville de Paris, 1997), 116.

6. On reconstruction regional architecture, see chapter 2, "L'heure a-t-elle sonné pour une reconstruction régionaliste?" in Gilles Plum, ed., *L'architecture de la reconstruction* (Lassay-les-Châteaux: Nicolas Chaudun, 2011).

7. Peter W. Sattler, *Gießen. Stadt im Wandel, 1933-2007* (Erfurt: Sutton, 2008), 59. Another perspective is given in Karl D. Qualls, *From Ruins to Reconstruction: Urban Identity in Soviet Sevastopol after World War II* (Ithaca: Cornell University Press, 2009). See also Keith Lowe, *Savage Continent: Europe in the Aftermath of World War II* (New York: Picador, 2013).

8. Ivana Lazanja, "The Reconstruction of the Croatian Coastal City of Zadar," in Nicholas Bullock and Luc Verpoest, eds., *Living with History, 1914-1964: Rebuilding Europe after the First and Second World Wars and the Role of Heritage Preservation* (Leuven: Leuven University Press, 2011), 279-87. See also Jasna Galjar and Anđela Galić, "Kultura stanovanja u zadru 1950-Ih Godina u kontekstu afirmacije modernizma," *Ars Adriatica* 7 (2017) as well as Antonija Mlikota, "Četrnaest arhitektonskih i urbanističkih vizija povijesne jezgre zadra nastalih 1953. Godine," *Ars Adriatica* 5 (2015): 163-92.

9. Czesław Miłosz, *The Captive Mind*, trans. Jane Zielonko (New York: Vintage, 1990), 26.

10. David Crowley, "People's Warsaw/Popular Warsaw," *Journal of Design History* 10, no. 2 (1997): 210-12.

11. See chapter 6 in Anders Aman, *Architecture and Ideology in Eastern Europe During the Stalin Era: An Aspect of Cold War History* (New York and Cambridge, MA: Architectural History Foundation and MIT Press, 1992).

12. *Le Figaro*, March 19, 1951.

13. Katherine Pence and Paul Betts, eds., *Socialist Modern: East German Everyday Culture and Politics* (University of Michigan Press, 2008), 101, 104.

14. Nicholas Bullock, *Building the Post-War World. Modern Architecture and Reconstruction in Britain* (London: Routledge, 2002), 61. See also John R. Gold, *The Experience of Modernism: Modern Architects and the Future City, 1928-1953* (London: Spon, 1997), 210-14.

15. The scholarship on the housing estates is voluminous. On the British example of postwar modernism, see ibid. Stephanie Zeier Pilat, *Reconstructing Italy: The Ina-Casa Neighborhoods of the Postwar Era* (Abingdon and New York: Routledge, 2014), 3.

16. Linda Bendali, *Sarcelles, une utopie réussie?* (Nantes: Gulf Stream, 2006), 20.

17. Ibid., 28. Thibault Tellier, *Le Temps des HLM 1945-1975: La Saga urbaine des trente glorieuses* (Paris: Autrement, 2007), 85-86.

18. *Mon Oncle* (1958), [Film] Dir. Jacques Tati [Specta Films].

19. Bendali, *Sarcelles, une utopie réussie?*, 33.

20. Mary Nolan, "Negotiating American Modernity in Twentieth-Century Europe," in Per Lundin and Thomas Kaiserfeld, eds., *The Making of European Consumption: Facing the American Challenge* (London: Palgrave Macmillan, 2015), 18.

21. Cited in Dominic Sandbrook, *Never Had it So Good: A History of Britain from Suez to the Beatles* (London: Little, Brown, 2005), 596.

22. See Hartmut Kaelble, *A Social History of Europe, 1945-2000: Recovery and Transformation after Two World Wars*, trans. Liesel Tarquini (New York: Berghahn, 2013), 83-84.

23. British Pathé, *Drive In and Buy*, 1961 (youtube.com). Sarah Ryle, *The Making of Tesco: A Story of British Shopping* (London: Bantam Press, 2013). Google Books. See also Ralph Jessen

Notes

and Lydia Langer, eds., *Transformations of Retailing in Europe after 1945* (Farnham and Burlington, VT: Ashgate, 2012).

24. These statistics are given in James B. Jeffreys and Derek Knee, *Retailing in Europe: Present Structure and Future Trends* (London, 1962), 106 and Wolfgang Disch, *Der Grosse- und Einzelhandel in der Bundesrepublik* (Cologne, 1966), 60 as cited in Victoria de Grazia, "Changing Consumption Regimes in Europe, 1930-1970," in Susan Strasser, Charles McGovern, and Matthias Judt, eds., *Getting and Spending: European and American Consumer Societies in the Twentieth Century* (Cambridge: Cambridge University Press, 1998), 79. See also Victoria de Grazia, *Irresistible Empire: America's Advance through Twentieth Century Europe* (Cambridge, MA and London: Belknap Press, 2005), 394-96.

25. On postwar urban conditions, see Donald Filtzer, *The Hazards of Urban Life in Late Stalinist Russia* (Cambridge and New York: Cambridge University Press, 2010).

26. Shane Hamilton, "Supermarket USA Confronts State Socialism: Airlifting the Technopolitics of Industrial Food Distribution into Cold War Yugoslavia," in Ruth Oldenziel and Karin Zachmann, eds., *Cold War Kitchen: Americanization, Technology, and European Users* (Cambridge, MA and London: MIT Press, 2009): 137-59. See also Greg Castillo, *Cold War on the Home Front: The Soft Power of Midcentury Design* (Minneapolis and London: University of Minnesota Press, 2010).

27. Günter Grass, *Dog Years*, trans. Ralph Manheim (London: Minerva, 1997), 559.

28. Marion Leonard and Robert Strachan, eds., *The Beat Goes On: Liverpool, Popular Music and the Changing City* (Liverpool: Liverpool University Press, 2010), 18-19.

29. Dean Vuletic, "Generation Number One: Politics and Popular Music in Yugoslavia in the 1950s," *Nationalities Papers* 36, no. 5 (2008): 871.

30. Rosemary Wakeman, "European Mass Culture in the Media Age," in Rosemary Wakeman, ed., *Themes in Modern European History since 1945* (London and New York: Routledge, 2003), 148.

31. Sándor Horváth, "Patchwork Identities and Folk Devils: Youth Subcultures and Gangs in Socialist Hungary," *Social History* 34, no. 2 (2009): 177.

32. Gleb Tsipursky, *Socialist Fun: Youth, Consumption, and State-Sponsored Popular Culture* (Pittsburgh: University of Pittsburgh Press, 2016), 175.

33. Katarzyna Murawska-Muthesius, "Paris from behind the Iron Curtain," in Sarah Wilson, ed., *Paris: Capital of the Arts, 1900-1968* (London: Royal Academy of Arts, 2002), 250.

34. See the description of 1960s Berlin in Belinda Davis, "The City as Theater of Protest: West Berlin and West Germany, 1962-1983," in Gyan Prakash and Kevin M. Kruse, eds., *The Spaces of the Modern City: Imaginaries, Politics, and Everyday Life* (Princeton and Oxford: Princeton University Press, 2008), 248-56.

Chapter 11

1. V. Mykhnenko and I. Turok, *Cities in Transition: East European Urban Trajectories 1960-2005*, Working Paper No. 4 (Glasgow: Centre for Public Policy for Regions, 2007), 7-8. Kaelble, *A Social History of Europe, 1945-2000*, 274.

2. See Dematteis, "Spatial images of European urbanization," 52-53.

3. Kaelble, *A Social History of Europe, 1945-2000*, 185.

4. Stephen Castles, "Immigration and Asylum: Challenges to European Identities and Citizenship," in Stone, ed., *The Oxford Handbook of Postwar European History*, 206.

5. Astrid Kander, Paolo Malanima, and Paul Warde, eds., *Power to the People: Energy in Europe over the Last Five Centuries* (Princeton and Oxford: Princeton University Press, 2013), 253.

6. Roland Barthes, *Mythologies*, trans. Annette Lavers (New York: Noonday Press, 1972), 88. See also Wolfgang Sachs, *For Love of the Automobile: Looking Back into the History of Our Desires*, trans. Don Reneau (Berkeley: University of California Press, 1984).

7. Guilio Mazzocchi, "Come si viveva prima, durante e dopo," *I Problemi di Ulisse* 83–87 (1979): 74 as quoted in Stephen Gundle, *Between Hollywood and Moscow. The Italian Communists and the Challenge of Mass Culture, 1943-1991* (Durham and London: Duke University Press, 2000), 80.

8. *Epoca*, October 23, 1960, quoted in Arthur Marwick, *The Sixties: Cultural Revolution in Britain, France, Italy, and the United States, c. 1958-1974* (Oxford: Oxford University Press, 1998), 92.

9. These two films are discussed in Lewis H. Siegelbaum, *Cars for Comrades: The Life of the Soviet Automobile* (Ithaca & London: Cornell University Press, 2008), 225–30.

10. Laux, *The European Automobile Industry*, 207–11.

11. Luminita Gatejel, "The Common Heritage of the Socialist Car Culture," in Lewis H. Siegelbaum, ed., *The Socialist Car: Automobility in the Eastern Bloc* (Ithaca and London: Cornell University Press, 2011), 150. See also Valentina Fava, *The Socialist People's Car: Automobiles, Shortages, and Consent on the Czechoslovak Road to Mass Production (1918-64)* (Amsterdam: Amsterdam University Press, 2013).

12. Anna Funder, *Stasiland* (London: Granta, 2003), 92.

13. François Maspero, *Roissy Express*, trans. Paul Jones (London and New York: Verso, 1994), 20. Stephen Barber, *Extreme Europe* (London: Reaktion, 2001), 98.

14. Frank Schipper, *Driving Europe: Building Europe on the Roads in the Twentieth Century* (Amsterdam: Aksant, 2008), Chapter 7.

15. Massimo Moraglio, *Driving Modernity: Technology, Experts, Politics, and Fascist Motorways, 1922-1943*, trans. Erin O'Loughlin (New York and Oxford: Berghahn, 2017), 160.

16. Reiner Ruppmann, "The Development of the European Highway Network," in Ralf Roth and Colin Divall, eds., *From Road to Rail and Back Again? A Century of Transport Competition and Interdependency* (Farnham and Burlington, VT: Ashgate, 2015), 276–305. See also Peter Merriman, "Motorways and the Modernisation of Britain's Road Network, 1937-70" in the same volume. The M1 description is found page 325.

17. Michael Ignatieff, *Blood and Belonging: Journeys into the New Nationalism* (New York: Farrer, Straus & Giroux, 1993), 28.

18. On the history of town and regional planning in the Netherlands, see Coen Van der Wal, *In Praise of Common Sense. Planning the Ordinary: A Physical Planning History of the New Towns in the IJsselmeerpolders* (Rotterdam: 010 Publishers, 1997) as well as Hans Van der Cammen and Len De Klerk, *The Selfmade Land: Culture and Evolution of Urban and Regional Planning in the Netherlands* (Antwerp: Spectrum, 2012).

19. Cited in Cor Wagenaar, *Town Planning in the Netherlands since 1800: Responses to Enlightenment Ideas and Geopolitical Realities* (Rotterdam: 010 Publishers, 2011), 370.

20. This quote is cited in a number of planning histories. See Paul van der Laar, "Modernism in European Reconstruction-Policy and Its Public Perception: The Image of Rebuilding

Notes

Rotterdam, 1945-2000," in Georg Wagner-Kyora, ed., *Wiederaufbau Europäischer Städte/ Rebuilding European Cities* (Stuttgart: Franz Steiner, 2014), 216.

21. Lewis Mumford, "The Skyline: A Walk through Rotterdam," *The New Yorker*, October 12, 1957.

22. Michelle Provoost, *Automoviliteit in de Rotterdamse Stedebouw* (Rotterdam: Uitgeverij 010, 1996), 65–67. On the Randstad Development Scheme, see Van der Cammen and De Klerk, *The Selfmade Land*, 240–43.

23. Ronald Van Kempen and Jan Van Weesep, "Residential Dynamics of the Inner City: The Case of the Hague," *The Netherlands Journal of Housing and Environmental Research* 3, no. 3 (1988): 217.

24. Ed Taverne, "The Dream of Progress. The Netherlands during the Years of Reconstruction," in Anita Blom, Simone Vermaat, and Ben De Vries, eds., *Post-War Reconstruction the Netherlands, 1945-1965: The Future of a Bright and Brutal Heritage* (Rotterdam: 010 Publishers, 2016), 40.

25. Tim Pharoah and Dieter Apel, *Transport Concepts in European Cities* (Brookfield: Aldershot, 1995), 63, 65.

26. "Promotiefilm Hoog Catharijne 1970," Bouwput, published May 29, 2010, youtube. com. Tim Verlaan, "Producing Space: Post-War Redevelopment as Big Business, Utrecht and Hannover 1962-1975," *Planning Perspectives* 34, no. 3 (2019): 415–37 as well as Hans Buiter, "Constructing Dutch Streets: A Melting Pot of European Technologies," in Mikael Hard and Thomas J. Misa, eds., *Urban Machinery: Inside Modern European Cities* (Cambridge, MA and London, England: MIT Press, 2008). See also Aaron Betsky, "Hoog Catharijne: The Tomb of an Open Architecture," in Cor Wagenaar, ed., *Happy Cities and Public Happiness in Post-War Europe* (Rotterdam: NAi Publishers/ Architecturalia, 2004), 269–81.

27. Helena Mattson, "Where the Motorways Meet: Architecture and Corporatism in Sweden 1968," in Mark Swenarton, Tom Avermaete, and Dirk Van den Heuvel, eds., *Architecture and the Welfare State* (London and New York: Routledge, 2015), 155–75.

28. Sacha Craddock, "Tolmers United," in Astrid Proll, *Goodbye to London: Radical Art & Politics in the 70's* (Ostfildern, Germany: Hatje Cantz, 2010), 37.

29. Roger Karapin, *Protest Politics in Germany: Movements on the Left and Right since the 1960s* (University Park, PA: Pennsylvania State University Press, 2007), 65–74.

30. On Copenhagen, see René Karpantschof and Flemming Mikkelsen, "Youth, Space, and Autonomy in Copenhagen: The Squatters' and Autonomous Movement, 1963-2012," in Bart Van der Steen, Ask Katzeff, and Leendert Van Hoogenhuijze, eds., *The City Is Ours: Squatting and Autonomous Movements in Europe from the 1970s to the Present* (Oakland, CA: PM Press, 2014), 183–84. *Tolmers: Beginning or End?* (London, BSEFilms), written by Tolmers activist Nick Wate, who also published *The Battle for Tolmers Square* in 1976, reprinted as Nick Wate, *The Battle for Tolmers Square* (Abingdon: Routledge, 2013).

31. See Margit Mayer, "Social Movements in European Cities: transitions from the 1970s to the 1990s," in Bagnasco and Le Galès, eds., *Cities in Contemporary Europe*, 131–52. Also H. Bodenschatz, V. Heiser, and J. Korfmacher, eds., *Schluss mit der Zerstörung? Stadterneuerung und Städtische Opposition in West-Berlin, Amsterdam und London* (Giessen: Anabas, 1983).

32. *Cathy Coming Home*, produced by Tony Garnett, directed by Ken Loach, first aired on the *Wednesday Play* series, BBC1, November 16, 1966. On the West German squatter movement, see chapter 4 in Alexander Vasudevan, *The Autonomous City: A History of Urban Squatting* (London and New York: Verso, 2017).

Notes

33. Andrew O'Hagan, *Our Fathers* (New York: Houghton Mifflin Harcourt, 1999), 31 and 37.
34. The research on the housing estates is voluminous. On France, see Gérard Monnier and Richard Klein, eds., *Les Années ZUP. Architectures de la croissance, 1960-1973* (Paris: Picard, 2002). François Tomas, Jean-Noël Blanc, and Mario Bonilla, *Les Grands Ensembles, une histoire qui continue . . .* (Saint-Etienne: Université de Saint-Etienne, 2003). Also Kenny Cupers, *The Social Project: Housing Postwar France* (Minneapolis, MN: University of Minnesota Press, 2014). On the UK, John Robert Gold, *The Practice of Modernism: Modern Architects and Urban Transformation, 1954-1972* (London and New York: Routledge, 2007). Also Jamileh Manoochehri, *The Politics of Social Housing in Britain* (Berlin: Peter Lang, 2012). On the GDR, Christine Hannemann, *Die Platte: Industrialisierter Wohnungsbau in der DDR* (Berlin: Hans Schiler, 2005). For a global perspective, Florian Urban, *Tower and Slab: Histories of Global Mass Housing* (Milton Park, Abingdon, Oxon and New York: Routledge, 2012).
35. This term "idéologie du pré-fabrique" is used by Lydia Coudroy de Lille, "Une idéologie du pré-fabrique?" in Frédéric Dufaux and Annie Fourcaut, eds., *Le Monde des grands ensembles* (Paris: Editions CREAPHIS, 2004), 90–95.
36. "1968: Eerste bewoners Bijlmermeer, het huidige Amsterdam-Zuidoost- oude filmbeelden," Amsterdam—Verzamelde Historische Filmbeelden, published November 1, 2015, youtube.com. See also Marieke van Rooy, "The Bijlmer or Exercises in Giving Life to a Rigid Urban Plan," in Wagenaar," *Happy Cities and Public Happiness in Post-War Europe*, 154–62.
37. Alexander Vasudevan, *Metropolitan Preoccupations: The Spatial Politics of Squatting in Berlin* (West Sussex: Wiley Blackwell, 2015), 2. See also Forian Urban, "The Märkisches Viertel in West Berlin," in Swenarton, Avermaete, and Van den Heuvel, eds., *Architecture and the Welfare State*, 177–96.
38. Wagenaar, *Happy Cities and Public Happiness in Post-War Europe*, 394.
39. See R. W. Davies and Melanie Ilic, "From Khrushchev (1935-1936) to Khrushchev (1956-1964): Construction Policy Compared," in Jeremy Smith and Melanie Ilic, eds., *Khrushchev in the Kremlin: Policy and Government in the Soviet Union, 1953-64* (New York and Abingdon, Oxon: Routledge Press, 2011), 202–30. See also Steven E. Harris, *Communism on Tomorrow Street: Mass Housing and Everyday Life after Stalin* (Baltimore, MD: John Hopkins University Press, 2013) and Marina Balina and Evgeny Dobrenko, eds., *Petrified Utopia: Happiness Soviet Style* (London: Anthem, 2011).
40. Ivan Szelenyi, *Urban Inequalities under Socialism* (Oxford: Oxford University Press, 1983), 4–6. On East Germany, see Hannemann, *Die Platte*.
41. Slavenka Drakulić, *How We Survived Communism and Even Laughed* (London: Vintage, 1988), 91.
42. Timon Hoppe, *Rostock. Urbane Kulturlandschaft: Stadtbilder, Transformationen, Perspektiven ein Bericht mit Exkurionsführer* (Norderstedt: Books on Demand, 2008), 58–64. See also Joachim Palutzki, "Der standardisierte Wohnungsbau. Zur Entwicklung der Wohnungsbauprogramme der 1960er und 1970er Jahre in der DDR," in Bernfried Lichtnau, ed. *Architektur und Städtebau im Südlichen Ostseeraum Zwischen 1936 und 1980* (Berlin: Lukas, 2002), 420–33.
43. Kaelble, *A Social History of Europe, 1945-2000*, 275.
44. Marco Abram, "20th of October—Narratives of Identities in the Celebrations for Belgrade's Liberation Day (1945-1961)," *Histories of Communism in Europe* 3 (2012): 177–79. Danka Ninković Slavnić, "Celebrating Yugoslavia. The Visual Representation of State Holidays," in

Notes

Breda Luthar and Maruša Pušnik, eds., *Remembering Utopia: The Culture of Everyday Life in Socialist Yugoslavia* (Washington DC: New Academia, 2010), 68-69.

45. Brigette Le Normand, "The House that Socialism Built. Reform, Consumption, and Inequality in Postwar Yugoslavia," in Paulina Bren and Mary Neuburger, eds., *Communism Unwrapped: Consumption in Cold War Eastern Europe* (Oxford and New York: Oxford University Press, 2012), 356, 61.

46. Borislav Pekić, *The Houses of Belgrade*, trans. Bernard Johnson (Evanston, IL: Northwestern University Press, 1994), 9 and 166.

47. Wolfgang Thaler, Maroje Mrduljas, and Vladimir Kulic, *Modernism In-Between: The Mediatory Architectures of Socialist Yugoslavia* (Berlin: Jovis, 2012), 83.

48. Quote from E. Verhagen, *Van Bijlmermeerpolder tot Amsterdam Zuidoost* (Den Haag, 1987) in "Symbolic Gestures? Planning and Replanning Amsterdam's Bijlmermeer and New Town Almere since 1965," *Informationen zur modernen Stadtgeschichte* 1 (2013): 52.

49. This quote from *L'Express*, September 21-28, 1968 is given in Arthur Marwick, "Youth Culture and the Cultural Revolution of the Long Sixties," in A. Schildt and D. Siegfried, eds., *Between Marx and Coca-Cola: Youth Cultures in Changing European Societies, 1960-1980* (Oxford and New York: Berghahn, 2006), 51-52.

50. Richard Truman, *Mods, Minis, and Madmen: A True Tale of Swinging London Culture in the 1960s* (London: iUniverse, 2010).

51. Dick Hebdige, *Hiding in the Light* (London and New York: Routledge, 1988), 110-11.

52. See Susan E. Reid and David Crowley, eds., *Style and Socialism: Modernity and Material Culture in Post-War Eastern Europe* (Oxford and New York: Berg, 2000).

53. See the descriptions of the Centrum in Jürgen Hopfner, *Gleisverwerfung* (Halle-Leipzig: Mitteldeutscher, 1982).

54. Alexei Yurchak, *Everything Was Forever, until It Was No More* (Princeton and Oxford: Princeton University Press, 2005), 188.

55. Breda Luthar, "Shame, Desire and Longing in the West," in Luthar and Pušnik, eds., *Remembering Utopia*, 341-56. See also Francesca Rolandi, "Yugoslavia Looking Westward: Transnational Consumer Contact with Italy during the 1960s," in Dijana Jelača, Maša Kolanović, and Danijela Lugarić, eds., *The Cultural Life of Capitalism in Yugoslavia* (New York: Palgrave Macmillan, 2017), 191-207.

56. Radina Vučetič, "Džuboks (Jukebox)—The First Rock'n'roll Magazine in Socialist Yugoslavia," in Luthar and Pušnik, eds., *Remembering Utopia*, 146-47.

57. Uta G. Poiger, *Jazz, Rock and Rebels: Cold War Politics and American Culture in a Divided Germany* (Berkeley: University of California Press, 2000), 216.

58. William Jay Risch, "Only Rock 'n' Roll? Rock Music, Hippies, and Urban Identities in Lviv and Wrocław, 1965-1980," and Sándor Horváth, "The Making of the Gang. Consumers of the Socialist Beat in Hungary," both in William Jay Risch, ed., *Youth and Rock in the Soviet Bloc* (Lanham, MA: Lexington Books, 2015), 86 and 92, 107-8.

59. See Moritz Föllmer, "Cities of Choice: Elective Affinities and the Transformation of Western European Urbanity from the Mid-1950s to the Early 1980s," *Contemporary European History* 24, no. 4 (2015): 577-96.

60. Patrick Richardson, *In Search of Landfall: The Odyssey of an Indefatigable Adventurer* (UK: Ultima Thule, 2014). Google Books.

61. Vasudevan, *Metropolitan Preoccupations: The Spatial Politics of Squatting in Berlin*, 66.

Notes

62. Pekić, *The Houses of Belgrade*, 52.
63. Milan Kundera, *The Unbearable Lightness of Being*, trans. Michael Henry Heim (New York: Harper Collins, 1984), 26.

Chapter 12

1. Kundera, *The Unbearable Lightness of Being*, 249.
2. Vladimir Kulić, "Building Brotherhood and Unity: Architecture and Federalism in Socialist Yugoslavia," in Martino Stierli and Vladimir Kulić, eds., *Toward a Concrete Utopia: Architecture in Yugoslavia, 1948-1980* (New York: Museum of Modern Art, 2018), 104-11.
3. See Patrik Aker, "Ostankino TV Tower, Moscow: An Obsession with Space," in Staffan Ericson and Kristina Riegert, eds., *Media Houses: Architecture, Media, and the Production of Centrality* (New York: Peter Lang, 2010), 81-112.
4. Nevena Dakovic, "City Foxes/East-West Soap (Belgrade/New York)," in Sebastian M. Herrmann et al., ed., *Ambivalent Americanizations: Popular and Consumer Culture in Central and Eastern Europe* (Heidelberg: Universitätsverlag Winter, 2008), 109-10. The description of *Vruć vetar* from Patrick Hyder Patterson, *Bought and Sold: Living and Losing the Good Life in Socialist Yugoslavia* (Ithica: Cornell University Press, 2011), 276-77.
5. Peter Schneider, *The Wall Jumper*, trans. Leigh Hafrey (Chicago: University of Chicago Press, 1983), 56. Heather Gumbert, "Constructing a Socialist Landmark: The Berlin Television Tower," in Philip Broadbent and Sabine Hake, eds., *Berlin Divided City, 1945-1989* (New York and Oxford: Berghahn, 2010), 93.
6. Semezdin Mehnedinović, *Sarajevo Blues*, trans. Ammiel Alcalay (San Francisco: City Lights Books, 1998), 56. See also Peter Andreas, *Blue Helmets and Black Markets: The Business of Survival in the Siege of Sarajevo* (Ithaca and New York: Cornell University Press, 2008), 58-59.
7. See Gregory Andrusz, Michael Harloe, and Ivan Szelenyi, eds., *Cities after Socialism: Urban and Regional Change and Conflict in Post-Socialist Societies* (Oxford: Blackwell, 1996).
8. See Roch Sulima, "The Laboratory of Polish Postmodernity: An Ethnographic Report from the Stadium-Bazaar," in Monika Grubbauer and Joanna Kusiak, eds., *Chasing Warsaw: Socio-Material Dynamics of Urban Change since 1990* (Frankfurt and New York: Campus, 2012), 241-68.
9. Joanna Kusiak and Wojciech Kacperski, "Kiosks with Vodka and Democracy: Civic Cafés between New Urban Movements and Old Social Divisions," in Grubbauer and Kusiak, eds., *Chasing Warsaw*, 222.
10. BBC News online, December 5, 2002.
11. Milan Kundera, "The Tragedy of Central Europe," *The New York Review of Books* 31, no. 007 (April 26, 1984): 33.
12. György Konrád, "Is the Dream of Central Europe Still Alive?" in *Cross Currents: A Yearbook of Central European Culture* (Ann Arbor, MI: University of Michigan, 1986), 114.
13. See the excellent analysis in Balázs Trencsényi, "Central Europe," in Mishkova and Trencsényi, eds., *European Regions and Boundaries*, 174-76.
14. Eli Rubin, "Beyond Domination: Socialism, Everyday Life in East German Housing Settlements, and New Directions in GDR Historiography," *Imaginations* 8, no. 1 (2017): 38.

Notes

On Marzahn, see *Amnesiopolis: Modernity, Space, and Memory in East Germany* (Oxford: Oxford University Press, 2016) especially chapter 5 "Plattenbau Panopticon." See also Annemarie Sammartino, "The New Socialist Man in the *Plattenbau*: The East German Housing Program and the Development of the Socialist Way of Life," *Journal of Urban History* 44, no. 1 (2018): 78–94.

15. Mehdi Charef, *Tea in the Harem*, trans. Ed Emery (London: Serpent's Tail, 1989), 19–20.

16. This description is taken from Rosemary Wakeman, "Independent Filmmakers and the Invention of the Paris Suburbs," *French Politics, Culture & Society*, no. 1, 31 (Spring 2013): 86–87.

17. Tomka, *A Social History of Twentieth-Century Europe*, 38.

18. Hanif Kureishi, *The Buddha of Suburbia* (New York: Penguin, 1990), 7.

19. Stephen Castiles, "Immigration and Asylum: Challenges to European Identities and Citizenship," in Stone, ed., *The Oxford Handbook of Postwar European History*, 216.

20. Kaelble, *A Social History of Europe, 1945-2000*, 187–88.

21. Sonia Hirt, "Post-Socialist Urban Forms: Notes from Sofia," *Urban Geography* 27, no. 5 (2006): 464–88.

22. George Ritzer, *Enchanting a Disenchanted World: Revolutionizing the Means of Consumption* (Thousand Oaks, CA: Pine Forge Press, 2005), 41.

23. See Kiril Stanilov, "The Restructuring of Non-Residential Uses in the Post-Socialist Metropolis," in Kiril Stanilov, *The Post-Socialist City: Urban Form and Space Transformations in Central and Eastern Europe after Socialism* (Vienna: Springer, 2007), 73–99.

24. Ewan Morrison, *Tales from the Mall: Fact & Fiction from the Lost Age of Globalisation* (Glasgow: Cargo, 2012, digital edition 2017).

25. Owen Hatherley, *Trans-Europe Express: Tours of a Lost Continent* (London: Allen Lane, 2018), 136–39.

26. Antonio Font i Arellano and España, Ministerio de la Vivienda, eds., *La Explosión de la Ciudad: Transformaciones Territoriales en las Regiones Urbanas de la Europa Meridional [the Explosion of the City: Territorial Transformations in the South Europe Urban Regions]* (Madrid: Ministerio de la Vivienda, 2007).

27. European Environment Agency, *Urban Sprawl in Europe*, EEA Report No 11/2016 (Luxembourg: European Union, 2016), 65–67. OECD Territorial Reviews, *Madrid, Spain* (Paris: OECD, 2007).

28. Anne E. Gorsuch, *All This Is Your World: Soviet Tourism at Home and Abroad* (Oxford and New York: Oxford University Press, 2011), 59–60. Eva Näripea, "Medieval Socialist Realism: Representations of Tallinn Old Town in Soviet Estonian Features Films, 1969-1972," *Place and Location: Studies in Environmental Aesthetics and Semiotics* 4 (2004): 121–44.

29. Frank Moulaert, Arantxa Rodriguez, and Erik Swyngedouw, eds., *The Globalized City: Economic Restructuring and Social Polarization in European Cities* (Oxford: Oxford University Press, 2003). Gerardo Del Cerro Santamaría, ed., *Urban Megaprojects: A Worldwide View* (Bingly: Emerald, 2013).

30. See G. J. Ashworth and Brian Graham, "Heritage and the Reconceptualization of the Postwar European City," in Stone, ed., *The Oxford Handbook of Postwar European History*, 582–99.

31. Robert Broesi, "Euroscapes: Spatial Order in Twenty-First Century Europe," in Robert Broesi et al., eds., *Euroscapes* (Amsterdam: Must, 2003), 46.

Notes

32. Carl-Ludwig Holtfrerich, *Frankfurt as Financial Center: From Medieval Trade Fair to European Banking Centre*, trans. Karl Heinz Siber (Munich: C.H. Beck, 1999), 255.
33. Ibid., 96–97 and 275.
34. Michael H. Grote, "Frankfurt- An Emerging International Financial Center," in Daniel Felsenstein, Eike W. Schamp, and Arie Shachar, eds., *Emerging Nodes in the Global Economy: Frankfurt and Tel Aviv Compared* (Dordrecht: Springer Science+Business Media, 2002), 91–95.
35. See the museum catalog *Újváros Épül Miskolc 1945-1975* (Miskolc: Miskolci Galéria Városi Múvészeti Múseum, 2010). See also Zoltán Nagy, "The Development of Regional Centres in Hungary in the Past Two Decades," *European Integration Studies* 8, no. 1 (2010): 107–30.
36. Stefan Hertmans, *Intercities*, trans. Paul Vincent (London: Reaktion, 2001), 97 and 99.
37. OECD Territorial Reviews, *Vienna-Bratislava: Austria/Slovak Republic* (Paris: OECD, 2003), 36.

Conclusion

1. Lewis Dijkstra et al., *The State of European Cities 2016: Cities Leading the Way to a Better Future* (Luxembourg: European Commission & UN Habitat, 2016), 23–32. See also the online publication by Eurostat, *Urban Europe: Statistics on Cities, Towns and Suburbs*, 2016 Edition (Brussels: European Commission, 2016).

BIBLIOGRAPHY

General Studies

Benevolo, Leonardo. *The European City*. New York: Wiley, 1995.
Clark, Peter. *European Cities and Towns 400-2000*. Oxford, New York: Oxford University Press, 2009.
De Vries, Jan. *European Urbanization 1500-1800*. Cambridge: Harvard University Press, 1984.
Hall, Peter. *Cities in Civilization*. New York: Pantheon, 1998.
Hohenberg, Paul M., and Lynn Hollen Lees. *The Making of Urban Europe, 1000-1994*. Cambridge, MA: Harvard University Press, 1995.
Jerram, Leif. *Streetlife: The Untold History of Europe's Twentieth Century*. Oxford: Oxford University Press, 2011.
Lees, Andrew. *Cities Perceived: Urban Society in European and American Thought, 1820-1940*. New York: Columbia University Press, 1985.
Lees, Andrew. *The City: A World History*. Oxford and New York: Oxford University Press, 2015.
Lees, Andrew, and Lynn Hollen Lees. *Cities and the Making of Modern Europe, 1750-1914*. Cambridge and New York: Cambridge University Press, 2007.
Lenger, Friedrich. *European Cities in the Modern Era, 1850-1914*. Leiden and Boston: Brill, 2012.
Mumford, Lewis. *The City in History*. San Diego and New York: Harvest, 1989.
Pinol, Jean-Luc, ed. *Histoire de l'Europe urbaine*. Vol. 2. Paris: Seuil, 2003.
Schott, Dieter. *Europäische Urbanisierung (1000-2000): Eine Umwelthistorische Einführung*. Cologne: UTB/Böhlau Köln, 2014.

Recent Secondary Sources on European Cities

Abrams, Lynn. *Workers' Culture in Imperial Germany: Leisure and Recreation in the Rhineland and Westphalia*. London: Routledge, 2002.
Adler, Franklin Hugh. *Italian Industrialists from Liberalism to Fascism: The Political Development of the Industrial Bourgeoisie, 1906-1934*. Cambridge and New York: Cambridge University Press, 1995.
Agathocleous, Tanya. *Urban Realism and the Cosmopolitan Imagination in the Nineteenth Century: Visible City, Invisible World*. Cambridge, Cambridge University Press, 2013.
Alofsin, Anthony. *When Buildings Speak: Architecture as Language in the Habsburg Empire and Its Aftermath, 1867-1933*. Chicago: University of Chicago Press, 2006.
Aman, Anders. *Architecture and Ideology in Eastern Europe During the Stalin Era: An Aspect of Cold War History*. New York and Cambridge, MA: Architectural History Foundation and MIT Press, 1992.
Amar, Tarik Cyril. *The Paradox of Ukrainian Lviv: A Borderland City between Stalinists, Nazis, and Nationalists*. Ithaca and London: Cornell University Press, 2015.
Andreas, Peter. *Blue Helmets and Black Markets: The Business of Survival in the Siege of Sarajevo*. Ithaca and New York: Cornell University Press, 2008.
Appignanesi, Lisa. *The Cabaret*. New Haven and London: Yale University Press, 2004.

Bibliography

Arthurs, Joshua. *Excavating Modernity: The Roman Past in Fascist Italy*. Ithaca and London: Cornell University Press, 2012.
Auderbach, Jeffrey A., and Peter H Hoffenberg, eds. *Britain, the Empire, and the World at the Great Exhibition of 1851*. Aldershot and Burlington, VT: Ashgate, 2008.
Bade, Klaus J. *Migration in European History*. Translated by Alison Brown. Malden, MA and Oxford: Blackwell, 2003.
Baetens, Jan et al. *Europa! Europa?: The Avant-Garde, Modernism and the Fate of a Continent*. Berlin: De Gruyter, 2009.
Bagnasco, Arnaldo, and Patrick Le Galès, eds. *Cities in Contemporary Europe*. Cambridge: Cambridge University Press, 2000.
Bailey, Peter. *Popular Culture and Performance in the Victorian City*. Cambridge and New York: Cambridge University Press, 1998.
Balfour, Alan. *Berlin. The Politics of Order, 1737-1989*. New York: Rizzoli, 1990.
Ball, Michael, and David Sunderland. *An Economic History of London, 1800-1914*. London and New York: Routledge Press, 2001.
Barber, Stephen. *Extreme Europe*. London: Reaktion, 2001.
Bardet, Benoît, and Archives Municipales de Lyon. *L'esprit d'un siècle: Lyon 1800-1914*. Lyon: Fage éditions, 2007.
Barjot, Dominique, Rémi Baudouï, and Danièle Voldman, eds. *Les reconstructions en Europe, 1945-1949*. Paris: Complexe, 1997.
Bartetzky, Arnold, and Marc Schalenberg, eds. *Urban Planning and the Pursuit of Happiness. European Variations on a Universal Theme (18th-21st Centuries)*. Berlin: Jovis, 2009.
Bastéa, Eleni. *The Creation of Modern Athens: Planning the Myth*. Cambridge: Cambridge University Press, 2000.
Behrends, Jan C., and Martin Kohlrausch, eds. *Races to Modernity: Metropolitan Aspirations in Eastern Europe, 1890-1940*. Budapest and New York: CEU Press, 2014.
Beier, Dörte. *Kiel in der Weimarer Republik*. Kiel: Ludwig, 2004.
Beller, Steven. *Rethinking Vienna 1900*. New York: Berghahn, 2012.
Berend, Ivan. *Case Studies on Modern European Economy: Entrepreneurship, Invention, and Institutions*. London and New York: Routledge, 2013.
Berend, Ivan. *An Economic History of Nineteenth-Century Europe: Diversity and Industrialisation*. Cambridge: Cambridge University Press, 2013.
Berend, Ivan. *An Economic History of Twentieth-Century Europe*. Cambridge and New York: Cambridge University Press, 2006.
Berend, Ivan. *History Derailed: Central and Eastern Europe in the Long Nineteenth Century*. Berkeley: University of California Press, 2003.
Bergdoll, Barry. *European Architecture, 1750-1890*. Oxford History of Art. Oxford: Oxford University Press, 2000.
Berger, Stefan. *Social Democracy and the Working Class in Nineteenth and Twentieth Century Germany*. Abingdon and New York: Routledge, 2013.
Bernhardt, Christoph. *Environmental Problems in European Cities in the 19th and 20th Century [Umweltprobleme in Europäischen Städten des 19. und 20. Jahrhunderts]*. Münster: Waxmann, 2004.
Bernhardt, Christoph. *Städtische Öffentliche Räume: Planungen, Aneignungen, Aufstände 1945-2015 [Urban Public Spaces]*. Stuttgart: Franz Steiner Verlag, 2016.
Blau, Eve, and Monika Platzer, eds. *Shaping the Great City: Modern Architecture in Central Europe 1890-1937*. Munich, London and New York: Prestel, 1999.
Blau, Eve, and Ivan Rupnik, eds. *Project Zagreb: Transition as Condition, Strategy, Practice*. Barcelona: Actar, 2007.

Bibliography

Blobaum, Robert. *A Minor Apocalypse: Warsaw During the First World War*. Ithica: Cornell University Press, 2017.

Blom, Anita, Simone Vermaat, and Ben De Vries, eds. *Post-War Reconstruction the Netherlands, 1945-1965: The Future of a Bright and Brutal Heritage*. Rotterdam: 010 Publishers, 2016.

Bodenschatz, Harald. *Städtebau für Mussolini. Auf der Suche nach der Neuen Stadt im Faschistischen Italien*. Berlin: DOM, 2011.

Bodenschatz, Harald, Piero Sassi, and Max Welch Guerra, eds. *Urbanism and Dictatorship: A European Perspective*. Berlin: Birkhauser, 2015.

Bodnár, Judit. *Fin De Millénaire Budapest: Metamorphoses of Urban Life*. Minneapolis: University of Minnesota, 2001.

Bogdanović, Jelena, Lilien Filipovitch Robinson, and Igor Marjanović, eds. *On the Very Edge: Modernism and Modernity in the Arts and Architecture of Interwar Serbia (1918-1941)*. Leuven: Leuven University Press, 2014.

Bohl, Charles C., and Jean-François Lejeune, eds. *Sitte, Hegemann and the Metropolis: Modern Civic Art and International Exchanges*. Milton Park, Abingdon and New York: Routledge, 2009.

Boittin, Jennifer Anne. *Colonial Metropolis: The Urban Grounds of Anti-Imperialism and Feminism in Interwar Paris*. Lincoln and London: University of Nebreska Press, 2010.

Borsay, Peter, and Jan Hein Furnée, eds. *Leisure Cultures in Urban Europe, c. 1700-1870. A Transnational Perspective*. Manchester: Manchester University Press, 2016.

Borsay, Peter, and John K. Walton, eds. *Resorts and Ports: European Seaside Towns since 1700*. Bristol, Buffalo and Toronto: Chanel View, 2011.

Bowlt, John E. *Moscow & St. Petersburg 1900-1920: Art, Life & Culture of the Russian Silver Age*. New York: Vendome, 2008.

Boyer, Christine M. *The City of Collective Memory: Its Historical Imagery and Architectural Entertainments*. Cambridge, MA: The MIT Press, 1994.

Bracewell, Wendy, and Alex Drace-Francis, eds. *Balkan Departures: Travel Writing from Southeastern Europe*. New York and Oxford: Berghahn, 2009.

Bradley, Joseph. *Muzhik and Muscovite: Urbanization in Late Imperial Russia*. Berkeley: University of California Press, 1985.

Branczik, Márta, and Márkus Keller. *Korszerű Lakás 1960*. Budapest: Budapesti Történeti Múzeum, 2011.

Bren, Paulina, and Mary Neuburger, eds. *Communism Unwrapped: Consumption in Cold War Eastern Europe*. Oxford and New York: Oxford University Press, 2012.

Broadbent, Philip, and Sabine Hake, eds. *Berlin Divided City, 1945-1989*. New York and Oxford: Berghahn, 2010.

Broesi, Robert, Pieter Jannink, Wouter Veldhuis, and Ivan Nio, eds. *Euroscapes*. Amsterdam: Must, 2003.

Brown, Carl L., ed. *Imperial Legacy: The Ottoman Imprint on the Balkans and the Middle East*. New York: Columbia University Press, 1996.

Brumfield, William Craft, Boris V. Anan'ich, and Yuri A. Petrov. *Commerce in Russian Urban Culture, 1861-1914*. Baltimore: John Hopkins University Press, 2001.

Bullock, Nicholas. *Building the Post-War World: Modern Architecture and Reconstruction in Britain*. London: Routledge, 2002.

Bullock, Nicholas, and Luc Verpoest, eds. *Living with History, 1914-1964: Rebuilding Europe after the First and Second World Wars and the Role of Heritage Preservation*. Leuven: Leuven University Press, 2011.

Burdett, Charles, and Derek Duncan, eds. *Cultural Encounters: European Travel Writing in the 1930s*. New York and Oxford: Berghahn, 2003.

Burghard, Hermann et al. *Essen: Geschichte einer Stadt*. Bottrop and Essen: Pomp, 2002.

Bibliography

Bustee, Mervyn. *The Irish in Manchester*. Manchester: Manchester University Press, 2016.

Candoni, Jean-François, and Laure Gauthier, eds. *Les grands centres musicaux du monde germanique (XVIIe-XIXe siècle)*. Paris: Presses de l'Université Paris-Sorbonne, 2014.

Carmona, Michel. *Haussmann: His Life and Times, and the Making of Modern Paris*. Chicago: Ivan R. Dee, 2002.

Cassis, Youssef. *Big Business: The European Experience in the Twentieth Century*. Oxford: Oxford University Press, 1997.

Cattaneo, Claudio, and Miguel A. Martínez, eds. *The Squatters' Movement in Europe: Commons and Autonomy as Alternatives to Capitalism*. London: Pluto Press, 2014.

Chandler, James, and Kevin Gilmartin, eds. *Romantic Metropolis: The Urban Scene of British Culture, 1780-1840*. Cambridge: Cambridge University Press, 2010.

Chant, Colin. *European Cities and Technology: Industrial to Post-Industrial Cites*. Abingdon: Routledge, 2000.

Charle, Christophe. *Théâtres en capitales: Naissance de la société du spectacle à Paris, Berlin, Londres et Vienne, 1860-1914*. Paris: Albin Michel, 2008.

Chickering, Roger. *The Great War and Urban Life in Germany: Freiburg, 1914-1918*. Cambridge: Cambridge University Press, 2007.

Chomatowska, Beata. *Stacja Muranow*. Warsaw: Zarne, 2012.

Cioc, Mark. *The Rhine: An Eco-Biography, 1815-2000*. Seattle: University of Washington Press, 2002.

Clark, Katerina. *Moscow, the Fourth Rome: Stalinism, Cosmopolitanism, and the Evolution of Soviet Culture, 1931-1941*. Cambridge, MA: Harvard University Press, 2011.

Clark, Peter, Marjaana Niemi, and Catharina Nolin, eds. *Green Landscapes in the European City, 1750-2010*. Abingdon and New York: Routledge, 2017.

Clegg, Elizabeth. *Art, Design & Architecture in Central Europe 1890-1920*. New Haven: Yale University Press, 2006.

Clémençon, Anne-Sophie, ed. *Les gratte-ciel de Villeurbanne*. Besançon and Paris: Les Editions de l'imprimeur, 2004.

Cohen, Jean-Louis. *Scenes of the World to Come. European Architecture and the American Challenge, 1893-1960*. Paris and Montreal: Flammarion and the Canadian Center for Architecture, 1995.

Colton, Timothy J. *Moscow: Governing the Socialist Metropolis*. Cambridge, MA and London: Harvard University Press, 1995.

Conlin, Jonathan, ed. *The Pleasure Garden, from Vauxhall to Coney Island*. Philadelphia: University of Pennsylvania Press, 2013.

Cook, Catherine. *Russian Avant-Garde: Theories of Art, Architecture and the City*. London: Academy, 1995.

Corbin, A. *L'avènement des loisirs: 1850-1960*. Paris: Flammarion, 2001.

Cossick, Geoffrey. *Cathedrals of Consumption: The European Department Store 1850-1939*. London: Ashgate, 1999.

Costantini, Emanuela. *La Capitale Immaginata. L'evoluzione di Bucarest Nella Fasse di Costruzione e Consolidamento Dello Stato Nazionale Romeno (1830-1940)*. Rubbettino, 2016.

Crane, Sheila. *Mediterranean Crossroads: Marseille and Modern Architecture*. Minneapolis: University of Minnesota Press, 2011.

Crew, David F. *Bodies and Ruins: Imagining the Bombing of Germany, 1945 to the Present*. Ann Arbor: University of Michigan Press, 2017.

Crossick, Geoffrey, and Serge Jaumain, eds. *Cathedrals of Consumption: The European Department Store, 1850-1939*. Aldershot: Ashgate, 1999.

Crowley, David. *Warsaw*. New York: Reaktion, 2004.

Bibliography

Crowley, David, and Susan E. Reid, eds. *Socialist Spaces: Sites of Everyday Life in the Eastern Bloc.* Oxford and New York: Berg, 2002.
Cupers, Kenny. *The Social Project: Housing Postwar France.* Minneapolis: University of Minnesota Press, 2014.
Czaplicka, John, ed. *L'viv: A City in the Crosscurrents of Culture.* Cambridge, MA: Harvard University Press, 2005.
Daly, Nicholas. *The Demographic Imagination and the Nineteenth-Century City.* Paris, London, New York and Cambridge: Cambridge University Press, 2017.
Dargues, Régis. *Salonique au XXe siècle: de la cité Ottomane à la métropole grecque.* Paris: CNRS, 2000.
Davidson, Robert A. *Jazz Age Barcelona.* Toronto: University of Toronto Press, 2009.
Davies, Norman, and Roger Moorhouse. *Microcosm: Portrait of a Central European City.* London: Jonathan Cape, 2002.
Davis, Belinda Joy. *Home Fires Burning: Food, Politics, and Everyday Life in World War I Berlin.* Chapel Hill: University of North Carolina Press, 2009.
De Grazia, Victoria. *Irresistible Empire: America's Advance through Twentieth-Century Europe.* New York: Belknap, 2006.
Del Cerro Santamaría, Gerardo, ed. *Urban Megaprojects: A Worldwide View.* Bingly: Emerald, 2013.
Demetz, Peter. *Prague in Black and Gold: Scenes from the Life of a European City.* New York: Hill & Wang, 1998.
Dikec, Mustafa. *Badlands of the Republic: Space, Politics and Urban Policy.* New York: Wiley-Blackwell, 2007.
Dingsdale, Alan, ed. *Mapping Modernities: Geographies of Central and Eastern Europe, 1920–2000.* London and New York: Routledge, 2002.
Djurié, Dubravka and Misko Suvakovié, eds. *Impossible Histories: Historical Avant-Gardes, Neo-Avant-Gardes, and Post-Avant-Gardes in Yugoslavia, 1918–1991.* Cambridge, MA: MIT Press, 2015.
Dobrenko, Evgeny, and Eric Naiman, eds. *The Landscape of Stalinism.* Seattle and London: University of Washington Press, 2003.
Domaradzki, Krzysztof. *Prze-Strazeń Warszawy.* Warsaw: Muzeum Powstania Warszawskiego, 2016.
Domhardt, Konstanze Sylva. *The Heart of Our City. Die Stadt in den Transatlantischen Debatten der CIAM, 1933–1951.* Zurich: GTA Verlag, 2012.
Driver, Felix, and David Gilbert, eds. *Imperial Cities: Landscape, Display and Identity,* Studies in Imperialism. Manchester: Manchester University Press, 1999.
Dufaux, Frédéric, and Annie Fourcaut, eds. *Le monde des grands ensembles.* Paris: Editions CREAPHIS, 2004.
Duphil, Jean-Claude. *Toulouse socialiste, 1906–1940.* Portet-sur-Garonne: Empreinte, 2005.
Etienne-Steiner, Claire. *Le Havre: Auguste Perret et la reconstruction.* Paris: L'Inventaire, 1999.
Evans, Richard. *Death in Hamburg: Society and Politics in the Cholera Years.* New York: Penguin Books, 2005.
Falasca-Zamponi, Simonetta. *Fascist Spectacle: The Aesthetics of Power in Mussolini's Italy.* Ann Arbor: University of Michigan Press, 2000.
Filtzer, Donald. *The Hazards of Urban Life in Late Stalinist Russia.* Cambridge and New York: Cambridge University Press, 2010.
Fitzpatrick, Sheila. *Everyday Stalinism. Ordinary Life in Extraordinary Times: Soviet Russia in the 1930s.* New York and Oxford: Oxford University Press, 1999.
Flonneau, Mathieu. *Paris et l'automobile: un siècle de passions.* Paris: Hachette, 2005.

Bibliography

Föllmer, Moritz. *Individuality and Modernity in Berlin: Self and Society from Weimar to the Wall.* Cambridge: Cambridge University Press, 2013.

Font i Arellano, Antonio, and España. Ministerio de la Vivienda, eds. *La Explosión de la ciudad: Transformaciones Territoriales en las regiones urbanas de la Europa meridional [the Explosion of the City: Territorial Transformations in the South Europe Urban Regions].* Madrid: Ministerio de la Vivienda, 2007.

Forty, Adrian. *Concrete and Culture.* New York: Reaktion, 2002.

Freestone, Robert, and Marco Amati, eds. *Exhibitions and the Development of Modern Planning Culture.* Burlington: Ashgate, 2014.

Fritzsche, Peter. *Reading Berlin 1900.* Cambridge, MA: Harvard University Press, 1996.

Gauthier, Laure, and Mélanie Traversier, eds. *Mélodies urbaines. La musique dans les villes d'Europe (XVIe-XIXe siècles).* Paris: Presses de l'Université Paris-Sorbonne, 2008.

Gavrilova, Raina. *Bulgarian Urban Culture in the Eighteenth and Nineteenth Centuries.* Selinsgrove: Susquehanna University Press, 1999.

Gee, Malcolm, Tim Kirk, and Jill Steward. *The City in Central Europe: Culture and Society from 1800 to the Present.* Aldershot: Ashgate, 1999.

Ginio, Eyal and Karl Kaser, eds. *Ottoman Legacies in the Balkans and the Middle East.* Jerusalem: European Forum at the Hebrew University, 2013.

Gluck, Mary. *The Invisible Jewish Budapest: Metropolitan Culture at the Fin De Siècle.* Madison: University of Wisconsin, 2016.

Goebel, Michael. *Anti-Imperial Metropolis: Interwar Paris and the Seeds of Third World Nationalism.* New York: Cambridge University Press, 2015.

Gold, John. *Cities of Culture: Tourism, Promotion and Consumption of Spectacle in Western Cities since 1851.* Aldershot: Ashgate, 1999.

Gold, John. *The Experience of Modernism: Modern Architects and the Future City, 1928-53.* London: E & FN Spon, 1997.

Gold, John. *The Practice of Modernism: Modern Architects and Urban Transformation, 1954-1972.* London and New York: Routledge, 2007.

Gold, John Robert, and Margaret M. Gold. *Cities of Culture: Staging International Festivals and the Urban Agenda, 1851-2000.* Aldershot: Ashgate, 2005.

Goodman, David, ed. *The European Cities and Technology Reader: Industrial to Post-Industrial City.* London and New York: Routledge, 1999.

Gorup, Radmila, ed. *After Yugoslavia: The Cultural Spaces of a Vanished Land.* Stanford: Stanford University Press, 2013.

Gosseye, Janla, and Tom Avermaete. *Shopping Towns Europe: Commercial Collectivity and the Architecture of the Shopping Centre, 1945-1975.* London and New York: Bloomsbury Academic, 2017.

Grandits, Hannes, and Karin Taylor, eds. *Yugoslavia's Sunny Side. A History of Tourism in Socialism (1950s-1980s).* Budapest: Central European University Press, 2010.

Grubbauer, Monika, and Joanna Kusiak, eds. *Chasing Warsaw: Socio-Material Dynamics of Urban Change since 1990.* Frankfurt and New York: Campus, 2012.

Gunn, Simon. *The Public Culture of the Victorian Middle Class: Ritual and Authority and the English Industrial City, 1840-1914.* Manchester and New York: Manchester University Press, 2000.

Gunn, Simon, and James Vernon, eds. *The Peculiarities of Liberal Modernity in Imperial Britain.* Berkeley: University of California Press, 2017.

Gyáni, Gábor. *Identity and the Urban Experience: Fin-De-Siècle Budapest.* Translated by Thomas J. DeKornfeld. Boulder: Social Science Monographs, 2004.

Haggerty, Sheryllynne, Anthony Webster, and Nicholas J. White, eds. *The Empire in One City? Liverpool's Inconvenient Imperial Past.* Manchester: Manchester University Press, 2008.

Bibliography

Hajós, Géza, ed. *Stadtparks in der Österreichischen Monarchie, 1765-1918*. Vienna, Cologne and Weimar: Böhlau, 2007.

Hake, Sabine. *Topographies of Class: Modern Architecture and Mass Society in Weimar Berlin*. Ann Arbor: University of Michigan Press, 2008.

Hall, Peter. *Cities of Tomorrow: An Intellectual History of Urban Planning and Design in the Twentieth Century*. New York: Blackwell, 1998.

Hall, Thomas, and Thomas Hall. *Planning Europe's Capital Cities: Aspects of Nineteenth-Century Urban Development*. London and New York: E & FN Spon, 1997.

Hall, Thomas, and Martin Rèorby. *Stockholm: The Making of a Metropolis*. London and New York: Routledge, 2009.

Hanák, Péter. *The Garden and the Workshop: Essays on the Cultural History of Vienna and Budapest*. Princeton: Princeton University Press, 1998.

Hannemann, Christine. *Die Platte: Industrialisierter Wohnungsbau in der DDR*. Berlin: Hans Schiler, 2005.

Hapgood, Lynne. *Margins of Desire: The Suburbs in Fiction and Culture, 1880-1925*. Manchester: University of Manchester Press, 2009.

Hard, Mikael, and Thomas J. Misa, eds. *Urban Machinery: Inside Modern European Cities*. Cambridge and London: MIT Press, 2008.

Harding, Alan, Jon Dawson, Richard Evans, and Michael Parkinson, eds. *European Cities Towards 2000. Profiles, Policies and Prospects*. Manchester and New York: Manchester University Press, 1994.

Harris, Steven E. *Communism on Tomorrow Street: Mass Housing and Everyday Life after Stalin*. Baltimore: Woodrow Wilson Center Press/John Hopkins University Press, 2013.

Harris, W. V., ed. *Rethinking the Mediterranean*. Oxford: Oxford University Press, 2005.

Harvey, David. *Paris, Capital of Modernity*. New York and London: Routledge, 2003.

Hatherley, Owen. *Landscapes of Communism*. London: Allen Lane, 2015.

Hatherley, Owen. *Trans-Europe Express: Tours of a Lost Continent*. London: Allen Lane, 2018.

Healy, Maureen. *Vienna and the Fall of the Habsburg Empire. Total War and Everyday Life in World War I*. Cambridge: Cambridge University Press, 2017.

Herold, Stephanie, Benjamin Langer, and Julia Lechler, eds. *Reading the City: Urban Space and Memory in Skopje*. Berlin: Technischen Universität Berlin, 2010.

Herrmann et al., Sebastian M., ed. *Ambivalent Americanizations: Popular and Consumer Culture in Central and Eastern Europe*. Heidelberg: Universitätsverlag, 2008.

Hertmans, Stefan. *Intercities*. Translated by Paul Vincent. London: Reaktion, 2001.

Heynickx, Rajesh, and Tom Avermaete, eds. *Making a New World: Architecture and Communities in Interwar Europe*. Leuven: Leuven University Press, 2012.

Higgott, Andrew. *Mediating Modernism: Architectural Cultures in Britain*. London and New York: Routledge, 2007.

Higonnet, Patrice. *Paris: Capital of the World*. Cambridge and London: Belknap, 2002.

Hinze, Annika. *Turkish Berlin: Integration Policy and Urban Space*. Minneapolis: University of Minnesota Press, 2013.

Hofmann, Andrea, and Anna Weronika Wendland, eds. *Stadt und Öffentlichkeit in Ostmitteleuropa 1900-1939: Beiträge zur Entstehung Moderner Urbanität Zwischen Berlin, Charkiv, Tallin und Triest*. Stuttgart: Franz Steiner 2002.

Holtfrerich, Carl-Ludwig. *Frankfurt as Financial Center: From Medieval Trade Fair to European Banking Centre*. Translated by Karl Heinz Siber. Munich: C.H. Beck, 1999.

Hoppe, Timon. *Rostock. Urbane Kulturlandschaft: Stadtbilder, Transformationen, Perspektiven ein Bericht mit Exkurionsführer*. Norderstedt: Books on Demand, 2008.

Hurd, Madeleine. *Public Spheres, Public Mores, and Democracy: Hamburg and Stockholm, 1870-1914*. Ann Arbor: University of Michigan Press, 2000.

Bibliography

Hylton, Stuart. *A History of Manchester*. Stroud: Phillimore, 2016.
Jackson, James H., Jr. *Migration and Urbanization in the Ruhr Valley, 1821-1914*. New Jersey: Humanities Press, 1997.
Jackson, Lee. *Dirty Old London: The Victorian Fight against Filth*. New Haven: Yale University Press, 2014.
James, Kathleen. *Bauhaus Culture: From Weimar to the Cold War*. Minneapolis: University of Minnesota Press, 2006.
Jelača, Dijana, Maša Kolanović, and Danijela Lugarić, eds. *The Cultural Life of Capitalism in Yugoslavia*. New York: Palgrave Macmillan, 2017.
Jelavich, Peter. *Berlin Alexanderplatz: Radio, Film, and the Death of Weimar Culture*. Berkeley: University of California Press, 2006.
Jerram, Leif. *Germany's Other Modernity: Munich and the Making of Metropolis, 1895-1930*. Manchester: Manchester University Press, 2018.
Jones, Adrian. *Towns in Britain*. Nottingham: Five Leaves, 2014.
Jones, Colin. *Paris: Biography of a City*. New York: Viking, 2004.
Jones, Gwen. *Chicago of the Balkans: Budapest in Hungarian Literature, 1900-1939*. London: Legenda, 2013.
Joyce, Patrick. *The Rule of Freedom: Liberalism and the Modern City*. London and New York: Verso, 2003.
Judson, Peter. *The Hapsburg Empire, a New History*. Cambridge and London: Belknap Press of Harvard University Press, 2016.
Judt, Tony. *Postwar: A History of Europe since 1945*. New York: Penguin Press, 2005.
Kaelble, Hartmut. *A Social History of Europe, 1945-2000: Recovery and Transformation after Two World Wars*. Translated by Liesel Tarquini. New York: Berghahn, 2013.
Kähler, Gert. *Von der Speicherstadt Bis zur Elbphilharmonie Hundert Jahre Stadtgeschichte Hamburg*. Hamburg: Dölling und Galitz, 2009.
Kallis, Aristotle. *The Third Rome, 1922-1943: The Making of a Fascist Capital*. New York: Palgrave Macmillan, 2014.
Kamoun, Patrick. *Hygiène et morale: La Naissance des habitations à bon marché*. Paris: L'Union sociale pour l'habitat, 2011.
Kander, Astrid, Paolo Malanima, and Paul Warde, eds. *Power to the People: Energy in Europe over the Last Five Centuries*. Princeton and Oxford: Princeton University Press, 2013.
Karapin, Roger. *Protest Politics in Germany: Movements on the Left and Right since the 1960s*. University Park: Pennsylvania State University Press, 2007.
Kidd, Alan, and Terry Wyke, eds. *Manchester: Making the Modern City*. Liverpool: Liverpool University Press, 2016.
Killen, Andreas. *Berlin Electropolis: Shock, Nerves, and German Modernity*. Berkeley: University of California Press, 2006.
King, Charles. *The Black Sea: A History*. Oxford and New York: Oxford University Press, 2004.
King, Charles. *Odessa: Genius and Death in a City of Dreams*. New York: W.W. Norton, 2011.
Klemek, Christopher. *The Transatlantic Collapse of Urban Renewal: Postwar Urbanism from New York to Berlin*. Chicago: University of Chicago Press, 2011.
Klusáková, Lud'a, ed. *Small Towns in Europe in the 20th and 21st Centuries: Heritage and Development Strategies*. Prague: Karolinum, 2017.
Koter, Marek, Mariusz Kulesza, Wiesław Puś, and Stefan Pytlas. *Wpływ Wielonarodowego Dziedzictwa Kulturowego Łodzi na Współczesne Miasta*. Łódź: Uniwersytetu Łódzkiego, 2005.
Krastiņš, Jānis *Art Nouveau Buildings in Riga: A Guide to Art Nouveau Metropolis*. Riga: Add Projekts, 2014.
Ladd, Brian. *The Ghosts of Berlin*. Chicago: University of Chicago Press, 1997.

Bibliography

Lancaster, Jordan. *In the Shadow of Vesuvius: A Cultural History of Naples*. London and New York: I.B. Tauris, 2005.
Large, David Clay. *Berlin*. New York: Basic Books, 2000.
Large, David Clay. *The Grand Spas of Central Europe*. New York: Rowman & Littlefield, 2015.
Lawton, Richard, and Robert Lee, eds. *Population and Society in Western European Port Cities, C. 1650-1939*. Liverpool: Liverpool University Press, 2002.
Layton-Jones, Katy. *Beyond the Metropolis: The Changing Image of Urban Britain, 1780-1880*. Manchester: Manchester University Press, 2016.
Le Galès, Patrick. *European Cities: Social Conflicts and Governance*. Oxford: Oxford University Press, 2002.
Le Normand, Brigitte. *Designing Tito's Capital. Urban Planning, Modernism, and Socialism in Belgrade*. Pittsburgh: University of Pittsburgh Press, 2014.
Leboutte, René. *Vie et mort des bassins industriels en Europe*. Paris: L'Harmattan, 1997.
Lees, Andrew. *Cities, Sin, and Social Reform in Imperial Germany*. Ann Arbor: University of Michigan, 2002.
Lenger, Friedrich, ed. *Towards an Urban Nation: Germany since 1780*. Oxford and New York: Berg, 2002.
Leonard, Marion, and Robert Strachan, eds. *The Beat Goes On: Liverpool, Popular Music and the Changing City*. Liverpool: Liverpool University Press, 2010.
Leontidou, Lila. *The Mediterranean City in Transition: Social Change and Urban Development*. Cambridge: Cambridge University Press, 1990.
Lepetit, Bernard, and Christian Topalov, eds. *La ville des sciences sociales*. Paris: Editions Belin, 2001.
Levin, Miriam, ed. *Urban Modernity: Cultural Innovation in the Second Industrial Revolution*. Cambridge, MA and London: MIT Press, 2010.
Lichtnau, Bernfried, ed. *Architektur und Städtebau im südlichen Ostseeraum zwischen 1936 und 1980*. Berlin: Lukas, 2002.
Lisiak, Agata Anna. *Urban Cultures in (Post)Colonial Central Europe*. Indiana: Purdue University Press, 2010.
Lundin, Per, and Thomas Kaiserfeld, eds. *The Making of European Consumption: Facing the American Challenge*. London: Palgrave Macmillan, 2015.
Łupienko, Aleksander. *Kamienice Czynszowe Warszawy 1864-1914*. Warsaw: Instytut Historii PAN, 2015.
Luthar, Breda, and Marusa Pušnik, eds. *Remembering Utopia: The Culture of Everyday Life in Socialist Yugoslavia*. Washington DC: New Academia, 2010.
Lyberatos, Andreas, ed. *Social Transformation and Mass Mobilisation in the Balkan and Eastern Mediterranean Cities, 1900-1923*. Crete: Crete University Press, 2013.
Machedon, Luminiţa, and Ernie Scoffham. *Romanian Modernism: The Architecture of Bucharest, 1920-1940*. Cambridge, MA: MIT Press, 1999.
Maderthaner, Wolfgang. *Unruly Masses: The Other Side of Fin-de-Siècle Vienna*. Oxford: Berghahn, 2008.
Makaryk, Irena R., and Virlana Tkacz, eds. *Modernism in Kiev: Kyiv/Kyïv/Kiev/Kijów/Ḳiev: Jubilant Experimentation*. Toronto: University of Toronto Press, 2010.
Makas, Emily Gunzburger, and Tanja Damljanovic Conley, eds. *Capital Cities in the Aftermath of Empires: Planning in Central and Southeastern Europe*. London and New York: Routledge, 2009.
Manoochehri, Jamileh. *The Politics of Social Housing in Britain*. Berlin: Peter Lang, 2012.
Matera, Marc. *Black London: The Imperial Metropolis and Decolonization in the Twentieth Century*. Berkeley: University of California Press, 2015.

Bibliography

Mazower, Mark. *The Balkans from the End of Byzantium to the Present Day*. London: Phoenix, 2002.
Mazower, Mark. *Salonica, City of Ghosts*. New York: Vintage, 2004.
Mazur-Stommen, Susan. *Engines of Ideology: Urban Renewal in Rostock, Germany 1990–2000*. Münster: LIT, 2005.
McElligott, Anthony, ed. *The German Urban Experience, 1900–1945: Modernity and Crisis*. London and New York: Routledge, 2001.
Meighan, Michael. *Glasgow, a History*. Gloucestershire: Amberley, 2013.
Meller, Helen. *European Cities, 1890–1930s: History, Culture, and the Built Environment*. Chichester and New York: Wiley, 2001.
Meller, Helen. *Leisure and the Changing City, 1870–1914*. Hoboken: Taylor and Francis, 2013.
Meller, Helen, and Heleni Porfyriou, eds. *Planting New Towns in Europe in the Interwar Years: Experiments and Dreams for Future Societies*. Newcastle upon Tyne: Cambridge Scholars, 2016.
Metzger, Rainer. *Munich 1900. La Sécession, Kandinsky et le Blaue Reiter*. Paris: Hazan, 2009.
Mick, Christoph. *Lemberg, Lwów, L'viv, 1914–1947: Violence and Ethnicity in a Contested City*. West Lafayette: Purdue University Press, 2016.
Mishkova, Diana, and Balázs Trencsényi, eds. *European Regions and Boundaries*. New York and Oxford: Berghahn, 2017.
Morris, Robert J., and Richard H. Trainor, eds. *Urban Governance: Britain and Beyond since 1750*. Abingdon and New York: Routledge, 2000.
Moulaert, Frank, Arantxa Rodriguez, and Erik Swyngedouw, eds. *The Globalized City: Economic Restructuring and Social Polarization in European Cities*. Oxford: Oxford University Press, 2003.
Mumford, Eric Paul. *The CIAM Discourse on Urbanism, 1928–1960*. Cambridge, MA: MIT Press, 2000.
Mykhnenko, V., and I. Turok. *Cities in Transition: East European Urban Trajectories 1960–2005*. Glasgow: Centre for Public Policy for Regions, 2007.
Naar, Devin E. *Jewish Salonica: Between the Ottoman Empire and Modern Greece*. Stanford: Stanford University Press, 2016.
Nasiali, Minayo. *Native to the Republic: Empire, Social Citizenship, and Everyday Life in Marseille since 1945*. Ithaca and London: Cornell University Press, 2016.
Nead, Lynda. *Victorian Babylon: People, Streets and Images in Nineteenth-Century London*. New Haven: Yale University Press, 2005.
Neaman, Elliot and Timothy W. Luke. *Free Radicals: Agitators, Hippies, Urban Guerrillas, and Germany's Youth Revolt of the 1960s and 1970s*. Candor: Telos, 2016.
Nemes, Robert. *The Once and Future Budapest*. DeKalb: Northern Illinois University Press, 2005.
Niemi, Marjaana. *Public Health and Municipal Policy Making: Britain and Sweden, 1900–1940*. Aldershot: Ashgate, 2007.
Niezabitowski, Michal, ed. *Wolne Miasto Kraków: W Poszukiwaniu Nowoczesności*. Kraków: Muzeum Historyczne Miasta Krakowa, 2015.
Niney, François, ed. *Visions urbaines. Villes d'Europe à l'écran*. Paris: Centre Georges Pompidou, 1994.
Nolan, Mary. *Social Democracy and Society: Working Class Radicalism in Düsseldorf, 1890–1920*. Cambridge: Cambridge University Press, 1981.
Norris, David A. *Belgrade, a Cultural History*. Oxford: Oxford University Press, 2009.
North, Michael. *The Baltic: A History*. Cambridge, MA: Harvard University Press, 2015.
Ochandiano, Jean-Luc de. *Lyon à l'italienne. Deux siècles de présence dans l'agglomération Lyonnais*. Lyon: Lieux Dits, 2013.

Bibliography

Otter, Chris. *The Victorian Eye: A Political History of Light and Vision in Britain, 1800-1910.* Chicago: University of Chicago Press, 2008.

Paces, Cynthia. *Prague Panoramas: National Memory and Sacred Space in the Twentieth Century.* Pittsburgh: University of Pittsburgh Press, 2009.

Painter, Borden W. Jr. *Mussolini's Rome: Rebuilding the Eternal City.* New York: Palgrave Macmillan, 2005.

Palliser, D. M., Peter Clark, and M. J. Daunton. *The Cambridge Urban History of Britain.* 3 vols. Cambridge: Cambridge University Press, 2000.

Parkinson-Bailey, John J. *Manchester: An Architectural History.* Manchester: Manchester University Press, 2000.

Parsons, Deborah L. *A Cultural History of Madrid. Modernism and the Urban Spectacle.* Oxford and New York: Berg, 2003.

Patterson, Patrick Hyder. *Bought and Sold: Living and Losing the Good Life in Socialist Yugoslavia.* Ithica: Cornell University Press, 2011.

Penzo, Pier Paola. *La Città Italiana Prima Dell'unità. Milano, Torino, Genova (1700-1861).* Bologna: Cooperativa Libraria Univesitaria Editrice Bologna, 2000.

Peterson, Martin, and Martin Aberg, eds. *Baltic Cities: Perspectives on Urban and Regional Change.* New York: Coronet Books, 1998.

Petrie, Malcolm. *Popular Politics and Political Culture: Urban Scotland 1918-1939.* Edinburgh: Edinburgh University Press, 2019.

Pike, David. *The World beneath Paris and London, 1800-1945.* Ithaca: Cornell University Press, 2005.

Pillepich, Alain. *Milan capitale napoléonienne, 1800-1814.* Paris: Lettrage Distribution, 2001.

Pinon, Pierre. *Paris, Biographie d'une capitale.* Paris: Editions Hazan, 1999.

Platt, Harold L. *Shock Cities: The Environmental Transformation and Reform of Manchester and Chicago.* Chicago and London: University of Chicago Press, 2005.

Polasky, Janet L. *Reforming Urban Labor: Routes to the City, Roots in the Country.* Ithaca: Cornell University Press, 2010.

Polonsky, Antony, ed. *Jews in Łódź, 1820-1939.* Oxford: Littman Library of Jewish Civilization, 2004.

Pope, Ged. *Reading London's Suburbs: From Charles Dickens to Zadie Smith.* New York: Palgrave Macmillan, 2015.

Porter, Roy. *London: A Social History.* Cambridge, MA: Harvard University Press, 1995.

Prelorenzo, Claude. *Une Histoire urbaine: Nice.* Paris: Hartmann, 1999.

Prestel, Joseph Ben. *Emotional Cities: Debates on Urban Change in Berlin and Cairo, 1860-1910.* Oxford: Oxford University Press, 2017.

Prokopovych, Markian. *Habsburg Lemberg: Architecture, Public Space, and Politics in the Galician Capital, 1772-1914.* Indiana: Purdue University Press, 2009.

Ramet, Sabrina P., Gordana Crnkovic, and James A. Arieti, eds. *Kazaaam! Splat! Ploof! The American Impact on European Popular Culture, since 1945.* Lanham: University Press of America, 2003.

Reid, Susan E., and David Crowley, eds. *Style and Socialism: Modernity and Material Culture in Post-War Eastern Europe.* New York: Berg, 2000.

Reif, Heinz. *Berliner Villenleben: die Inszenierung bürgerlicher Wohnwelten am grünen Rand der Stadt um 1900 Berlin.* Berlin: Mann, 2009.

Resina, Joan Ramon. *Barcelona's Vocation of Modernity: Rise and Decline of an Urban Image.* Stanford: Stanford University Press, 2008.

Ring, Kristien, ed. *Emerging Identities- East!: Berlin, Bratislava, Budapest, Ljubljana, Prague, Riga, Tallinn, Vilnius, Warsaw.* Berlin: Jovis, 2005.

Rittner, Leona, W. Scott Haine, and Leona Rittner, eds. *The Thinking Space: The Café as a Cultural Institution in Paris, Italy and Vienna*. Farnham: Taylor and Francis, 2013.

Robarts, Andrew. *Migration and Disease in the Black Sea Region: Ottoman-Russian Relations in the Late Eighteenth and Early Nineteenth Centuries*. London: Bloomsbury Academic, 2017.

Rose, Michael E., Keith Falconer, and Julian Holder. *Ancoats: Cradle of Civilization*. Swindon: English Heritage, 2011.

Roth, Ralf, ed. *Städte im Europäischen Raum. Verkehr, Kommunikation und Urbanität im 19. und 20. Jahrhundert*. Stuttgart: Franz Steiner, 2009.

Rubin, Eli. *Amnesiopolis: Modernity, Space, and Memory in East Germany*. Oxford: Oxford University Press, 2016.

Rudolph, Nicole. *At Home in Postwar France: Modern Mass Housing and the Right to Comfort*. New York: Berghahn, 2015.

Ryckewaert, Michael. *Building the Economic Backbone of the Belgian Welfare State: Infrastructure, Planning, and Architecture 1945-1973*. Rotterdam: 010 Publishers, 2011.

Sattler, Peter W. *Gießen. Stadt im Wandel, 1933-2007*. Erfurt: Sutton, 2008.

Sayer, Derek. *Prague, Capital of the Twentieth Century. A Surrealist History*. Princeton: Princeton University Press, 2013.

Schildt, Axel, and Detlef Siegfried, eds. *European Cities, Youth and the Public Sphere in the Twentieth Century*. Aldershot: Ashgate, 2005.

Schipper, Frank. *Driving Europe: Building Europe on the Roads in the Twentieth Century*. Amsterdam: Aksant, 2008.

Schivelbusch, Wolfgang. *In a Cold Crater: Cultural and Intellectual Life in Berlin, 1945-1948*. Translated by Kelly Barry. Berkeley: University of California Press, 1998.

Schlör, Joachim. *Nights in the Big City: Paris, London, Berlin 1840-1930*. London: Reaktion Books, 1998.

Schmiechen, James, and Kenneth Carls. *The British Market Hall: A Social and Architectural History*. New Haven: Yale University Press, 1999.

Schneer, Jonathan. *London 1900: Imperial Metropolis*. New Haven: Yale University Press, 2001.

Schorske, Carl E. *Fin-De-Siècle Vienna: Politics and Culture*. New York: Random House, 2012.

Schröder, Karsten, ed. *Rostocks Stadtgeschiche von den Anfängen bis in die Gegenwart*. Rostock: Hinstorff, 2013.

Schwartz, Vanessa. *Spectacular Realities: Early Mass Culture in Fin-De-Siècle Paris*. Berkeley: University of California Press, 1998.

Scott, James C. *Seeing Like a State. How Certain Schemes to Improve the Human Condition Have Failed*. New Haven and London: Yale University Press, 1998.

Secchi, Bernardo. *La Città del Ventesimo Secolo*. Rome-Bari: Laterza, 2011.

Seigel, Jerrold. *Modernity and Bourgeois Life: Society, Politics, and Culture in England, France and Germany since 1750*. Cambridge: Cambridge University Press, 2012.

Smith, Angel, ed. *Red Barcelona: Social Protest and Labour Mobilization in the Twentieth Century*. London and New York: Routledge, 2002.

Snowden, Frank M. *Naples in the Time of Cholera, 1884-1911*. Cambridge: Cambridge University Press, 1995.

Soroka, Marina. *Summer Capitals of Europe, 1814-1919*. New York: Routledge, 2018.

Sparks, Mary. *Development of Austro-Hungarian Sarajevo*. London and New York: Bloomsbury Academic, 2014.

Spector, Scott. *Violent Sensations: Sex, Crime, and Utopia in Vienna and Berlin*. Chicago: University of Chicago Press, 2016.

Sramek, Peter, ed. *Piercing Time: Paris after Marville and Atget, 1865-2012*. Chicago: University of Chicago Press, 2013.

Bibliography

Stanilov, Kiril. *The Post-Socialist City: Urban Form and Space Transformations in Central and Eastern Europe after Socialism*. Vienna: Springer, 2007.

Steinberg, Mark D. *Petersburg Fin-De-Siècle*. Yale University Press, 2013.

Stierli, Martino, and Vladimir Kulić, eds. *Toward a Concrete Utopia: Architecture in Yugoslavia, 1948–1980*. New York: Museum of Modern Art, 2018.

Stobart, Jon. *The First Industrial Revolution: North-West England, C. 1700–60*. Manchester: Manchester University Press, 2004.

Stone, Dan, ed. *The Oxford Handbook of Postwar European History*. Oxford: Oxford University Press, 2014.

Stratigakos, Despina. *A Women's Berlin: Building the Modern City*. Minneapolis: University of Minnesota Press, 2008.

Sundhaussen, Holm. *Sarajevo. Die Geschichte einer Stadt*. Vienna and Cologne: Böhlau, 2014.

Swenarton, Mark, Tom Avermaete, and Dirk Van den Heuvel, eds. *Architecture and the Welfare State*. London and New York: Routledge, 2015.

Swope, Curtis. *Building Socialism: Architecture and Urbanism in East German Literature, 1955–1973*. London and New York: Bloomsbury Academic, 2018.

Tellier, Thibault. *Le Temps des HLM 1945–1975: La Saga urbaine des Trente Glorieuses*. Paris: Autrement, 2007.

Texier, Simon. *Paris contemporain de Haussmann à nos jours, une capitale à l'ère des métropoles*. Paris: Parigramme, 2005.

Thelle, Mikkel. *The Meat City: Urban Space and Provision in Industrial Copenhagen, 1880–1914*. Cambridge: Cambridge University Press, 2017.

Thompson, Victoria. *The Virtuous Marketplace: Women and Men, Money and Politics in Paris, 1830–1870*. Baltimore: John Hopkins University Press, 2000.

Thum, Gregor. *Uprooted: How Breslau Became Wroclaw During the Century of Expulsion*. Princeton: Princeton University Press, 2011.

Todorova, Maria. *Imagining the Balkans*. Oxford New York: Oxford University Press, 2009.

Toksoz, Meltem, and Biray Kolluoglu, eds. *Cities of the Mediterranean: From the Ottomans to the Present Day*. London: I.B. Tauris, 2014.

Umbach, Maiken. *German Cities and Bourgeois Modernism, 1890–1924*. Oxford: Oxford University Press, 2009.

Urban, Florian. *Designing the Past in East Berlin before and after the German Reunification*. Amsterdam and Boston: Elsevier, 2007.

Urban, Florian. *Tower and Slab: Histories of Global Mass Housing*. Milton Park and New York: Routledge, 2012.

Van der Steen, Bart, Ask Katzeff, and Leendert Van hoogenhuijze, eds. *The City Is Ours: Squatting and Autonomous Movements in Europe from the 1970s to the Present*. Oakland: PM Press, 2014.

Van Rahden, Till. *Jews and Other Germans: Civil Society, Religious Diversity, and Urban Politics in Breslau, 1860–1925*. Madison: University of Wisconsin Press, 2008.

Vasudevan, Alexander. *The Autonomous City: A History of Urban Squatting*. London and New York: Verso, 2017.

Vukić, Feda, ed. *Zagreb Modernost i Grad*. Zagreb: AGM, 2003.

Wagenaar, Cor. *Town Planning in the Netherlands*. Rotterdam: 010 Publishers, 2010.

Wagenaar, Cor, ed. *Happy Cities and Public Happiness in Post-War Europe*. Rotterdam: 010 Publishers/Architecturalia, 2004.

Wagner-Kyora, Georg, ed. *Wiederaufbau Europäischer Städte/Rebuilding European Cities*. Stuttgart: Franz Steiner, 2014.

Wakeman, Rosemary. *The Heroic City: Paris, 1945–1958*. Chicago: University of Chicago Press, 2009.

Bibliography

Wakeman, Rosemary. *Practicing Utopia: An Intellectual History of the New Town Movement.* Chicago: University of Chicago Press, 2016.
Walkowitz, Judith. *Nights out in Cosmopolitan London.* New Haven: Yale University Press, 2012.
Ward, Janet. *Post-Wall Berlin: Borders, Space and Identity.* New York: Palgrave Macmillan, 2011.
Ward, Janet. *Weimar Surfaces: Urban Visual Culture in 1920s Germany.* Berkeley: University of California Press, 2001.
Ward, Stephen V. *Planning the Twentieth-Century City: The Advanced Capitalist World.* West Sussex: John Wiley & Sons, 2002.
Ward, Stephen V. *Selling Places: The Marketing and Promotion of Towns and Cities, 1850-2000.* London and New York: Routledge Press, 1998.
Welter, Volker M. *Imaginationen des Urbanen: Konzeption, Reflexion und Fiktion von Stadt in Mittel- Und Osteuropa.* Berlin: Lukas, 2010.
Whyte, Iain Boyd, and David Frisby, eds. *Metropolis Berlin.* Berkeley: University of California Press, 2012.
Widenheim, Cecilia and Eva Rudberg, eds. *Utopia and Reality: Modernity in Sweden, 1900-1960.* New Haven: Yale University Press, 2002.
Willimott, Andy. *Living the Revolution: Urban Communes & Soviet Socialism, 1917-1932.* Oxford: Oxford University Press, 2017.
Wilson, Sarah, ed. *Paris: Capital of the Arts, 1900-1968.* London: Royal Academy of Arts, 2002.
Wolff, Janet, and Mike Savage, eds. *Culture in Manchester: Institutions and Urban Change since 1850.* Manchester: University of Manchester, 2016.
Wolff, Larry. *The Idea of Galicia: History and Fantasy in Habsburg Political Culture.* Stanford: Stanford University Press, 2010.
Zahra, Tara. *The Great Departure: Mass Migration from Eastern Europe and the Making of the Free World.* New York: W.W. Norton, 2017.
Zanou, Konstantina, and Maurizio Isabella, eds. *Mediterranean Diasporas: Politics and Ideas in the Long 19th Century.* London: Bloomsbury Academic, 2016.
Zarecor, Kimberly Elman. *Manufacturing a Socialist Modernity: Housing in Czechoslovakia, 1945-1960.* Pittsburgh: University of Pittsburgh Press, 2011.
Zeier Pilat, Stephanie. *Reconstructing Italy: The Ina-Casa Neighborhoods of the Postwar Era.* Abingdon and New York: Routledge, 2014.

INDEX

AEG (Allgemeine Elektricitäts Gesellschaft) 146–7, 170, 200
Alexanderplatz 105, 204, 269, 297, 304, see also Berlin
Amsterdam 13, 15, 80, 91, 165, 178, 277–9, 283–6, 289, 298, 320
amusement park 77, 143, 162–3, 186, see also entertainment
Ancoats 34–6, 46, 116, see also Manchester; slums
Andrássy Avenue 132–3, 143, 166, 181, see also Budapest
Angel Meadow 35–6, see also Ancoats
arcades 87, 101–3, 106, 122, 161, 184, 280, 312
art deco 205, 221, 228, 230–1, 242
art nouveau 179, 182–9
    buildings 106, 176, 184–90, 229, 245
    d'Aronco, Raimondo 182, 188
    exhibitions 182, 184, 188, 191
    Gaudi, Antoni 190
    Horta, Victor 184–5
Athens 53, 69–71, 220, 236, 244, 309
automobile 135, 153, 166, 175, 202, 207, 211, 214–15, 221–2, 278–85, 313, 323, see also industries
    brands 167, 188, 200, 223, 280, 300
    culture 171, 175, 188, 200, 202, 285, 311
    manufacturing 40, 45, 146, 207, 242, 293, 323

Balkans 6, 9, 81, 152, 198, 215–16, 244–5, 275, 282
    definition 2, 16, 54, 69, 207, 222, 307
Baltic 12–19, 29, 41, 61, 75, 91, 95, 105, 152, 168, 192, 206, 208, 254, 261, 292, 310
    definition 2–3, 16–17, 186, 197, 259
banking 28, 55–6, 61, 89, 91, 187, 202, 222, 284, 320–1, see also Frankfurt; London
Barcelona 30, 40, 72, 124–5, 153–4, 189–90, 247–9, 309, 315, 319, see also Cerdà; Eixample
Bauhaus 233–6
Belgrade 26, 193, 207, 216, 218–20, 251, 259, 282, 293–4, 297, 300, 303–4
Benjamin, Walter 8, 101, 161, 204, 212, 243–4
Berlin 4, 48, 85, 145–9, 154–7, 165–8, 171, 178, 197–9, 202–6, 223, 229, 271, 273, 286–91, 298–302, 304–7

commerce 87, 99–100, 105, 269, 297
culture 60, 142, 145, 149, 155–7, 162–3, 167, 173, 198, 202–6, 214, 298–9
housing 142, 148, 234, 263, 288–91, 307
industry 41, 145–7, 165–6, 170–1, 199, 321
migration 81–2, 148, 197, 277, 309
outskirts 146–7, 149, 155–6, 177
population 9, 80, 145, 325
protests 54, 137, 151, 154, 192, 195, 224, 272, 299–300, 305
wartime 192–3, 251, 253–5
Berlin Wall 2, 5, 7, 271, 273, 304
Bijlmermeer 289–91, 294, see also housing
Bilbao 125, 317
Black Sea 13, 20, 22–4, 50, 65, 70, 216, 261
Booth, Charles 114, 177
Brăila 23–5, 81
Bratislava (Pressburg) 302, 324
Breslau (Wrocław) 9, 56, 80, 92, 95, 106, 159, 324
Brno 45, 56, 182, 202
Brussels 80, 93, 95, 165, 183–6, 236, 299, 310, 319, 325
brutalism 278, 301
Bucharest 9, 25–6, 50–1, 110, 198, 216, 218, 220, 259, 262, 293, 311–12
Budapest 9, 26–7, 80–1, 83, 95, 117, 129–33, 165–6, 195–7, 251, 262, 271–2, 278, 303, 307
    commerce 99–100, 297, 306, 312
    culture 138, 144, 156, 162, 181–2, 228–9, 271, 298, 319
    housing 139, 142, 150
    industry 27, 31, 170, 199, 207
    outskirts 142–3

cabaret 156–7, 159, 163, 173, 179–1, 189, 205–6, 210, 212, see also entertainment
Caen 251, 257, 268
Catalonia 30–1, 40, 124, 190, 248–9
Cerdà, Ildefons 124–5
cholera 22, 24, 33, 44, 64, 66, 111–17, 120, 124, 223, 241
CIAM (Congrès Internationaux d'Architecture Moderne) 233, 236, 244, 254, 294
The City 87–9, 175, see also banks; London
coal 23, 31–5, 37–50, 61, 82, 91, 99, 135, 312, 323
    deposits 31–3, 37–8, 45, 47–9, 183, 207–8

Index

coffee house   12–13, 60, 71, 91–2, 132, 156, 174, 179–2, 188, 216, 220, *see also* entertainment
Cold War   2, 5, 262, 268, 273, 276, 288, 291, 293, 300, 307
Cologne   56, 60–3, 80, 84, 105, 147, 162, 254, 287
colonialism   6, 106, 184, 196, 307, 309, *see also* migration
concrete   202, 212, 264–5, 273, 288, 294, 308, 310
construction   147, 177, 230–1, 235, 258, 281, 288, 296
structures   281, 285–6, 290
Congress of Vienna   41, 45, 53–5, 64, 67
constructivism   213, 222
consumerism   79, 86, 92, 97, 103, 106, 173, 262, 268, 285, 295, 299, *see also* department stores; markets; shopping centers; youth
cotton mills   32, 34–8, 41, *see also* industries
Covent Garden   93, 97–8, *see also* London; markets
Crystal Palace   64, 92–5, 104, 168

dance halls   58, 60, 122, 156, 159, 196, 247, *see also* entertainment
Danube   11, 13, 23–7, 58, 81, 95, 99, 125–6, 129–2, 189, 193, 219–20, 232, 294, 307, 319, 324
ports   23, 25–7, 50–1, 70, 130–2, 216
Danzig (Gdansk)   15–17, 19, 45, 61, 68, 323
decolonization   7, 277, 287
department stores   8, 79, 86–7, 103–6, 132, 143–4, 162, 165, 170–1, 175, 199, 202–4, 211–12, 221, 225, 245, 268, 306, 311–12
Berlin   105, 203–4
Brussels   185, 296–7, 299
Budapest   297
London   101, 104, 299
Paris   86, 103–4, 136
Vienna   106, 126
Dickens, Charles   34, 84, 113, 149, 161
Döblin, Alfred   191, 204, 232, 255
Docklands   89–90, 137, 200, 253, 320, *see also* London
Canary Wharf   320

East Berlin   262–3, 269, 271, 304–5, *see also* Berlin
East End   89–90, 113, 138, 141, 149, 155, 172, 175, 192, 253, 264, 277, 320, *see also* London
Eixample   124–5, 190, 248, *see also* Barcelona; Cerdà
electricity   7, 169–70, 216, 232, 265, 278
cultural influence   169–70, 216
power   40, 135, 226, 232, 278
Engels, Friedrich   35, 37, 66, 112
entertainment   58, 64–5, 75–7, 100–4, 122, 126, 154–4, 168–9, 173–4, 202–3, 209, *see also* cabaret; coffee house; dance hall; movie

house; music hall; pageants; panorama; pub; theater
burlesque   156, 159
industry   210, 247–8, 285, 303, 312–13, 316
mass   163, 174, 198, 203
popular   126, 154–6, 168, 247, 303
epidemics   110–14, 124, 193, 211, 241, *see also* cholera
Essen   41–5, 178, 192, 268, 282
exhibitions, including expositions   8, 64, 75, 79, 86, 92–5, 131–2, 141, 146–7, 159, 162, 166, 168–71, 175–6, 178, 184, 191, 198, 208, 210–12, 221, 227, 235, 237, 239, 242, 262–4, 271, 301, 315, 319
Budapest Millennial   132
German Cities   179
Great Exhibition   93–4
Latvian Ethnographic   186
Liverpool Commerce and Manufacture   90
Paris   182
Paris Colonial   196
Stockholm   237
Turin   188
Urbanism & Habitat   163
Weissenhof   235
Wembley Imperial   196
Werkbund   147

festivals   54, 57–8, 61, 63, 68, 75, 168, 190, 260–2, 266
communist   225, 262, 297
fascist   238–9
Festival of Britain   264
music   60, 190, 271, 319
religious   10, 134, 154
street   8, 213, 286
World Youth   262, 298
film   175, 202–4, 207, 212, 214–15, 217, 220, 255, 261, 265, 289, 294, 296, 308, 316, 323, *see also* entertainment; movie house
early   153, 161, 163, 174
industry   198, 210, 213, 270–1
promotional   249, 283, 285, 288, 291
technology   200, 280, 287
Frankfurt   16, 60, 80, 151, 159, 162, 263, 299–300, 314
housing   235–6, 287
industry   56, 145, 170, 200, 320–2

Galaţi   23–5, 49, 81
Galicia   22, 24, 50–1, 66, 81, 91–2, 126, 172, 190–1, 197, 207
Garden City   45, 177–8, 202, 226, *see* Howard; Sellier
Garnier, Tony   230–1

377

Index

Geddes, Patrick 177–8
Genoa 9, 21, 67, 187, 244, 278, 325
Glasgow 37–40, 80–2, 88, 95, 111–12, 116, 165, 176, 182, 189, 224, 316, 322
   commerce 99, 104, 312–13
   housing 38–9, 140, 142–3, 288, 290
grain trade 14–15, 17, 19–20, 22–3, 26–7, 29
Gropius, Walter 147, 234–5

Hamburg 9, 56, 60, 80, 82, 105, 117, 127, 142, 145, 151, 159, 162, 287, 296
   commerce 13, 16–17, 19, 61, 91, 278, 321
   planning 58, 118–19, 318
   wartime 251, 254
Haussmann, Georges-Eugene 99, 103, 108, 110, 119–24, 139, 151, 155, *see also* Paris
Helsinki 17–19, 105, 179, 182, 206
heritage 50, 59–61, 67, 70, 75, 129, 246–7, 252, 261, 323
   cultural 18, 54, 77, 108, 214, 223
   urban 4, 54, 61, 168, 191, 238, 259, 311, 315–16
Hoog Catharijne 285, *see also* Utrecht
housing 44–6, 110–11, 124, 126, 139–48, 178, 184, 186, 202, 209, 211–13, 246, 248, 251, 257–8, 263–7, 276–7, 285, 288, 291, 294, 301, 308, 314–15, 321
   conditions 33, 117, 138, 141, 148, 223, 233, 248, 287, 292, 310–11
   demolition 107, 111, 140, 285, 287–8
   estates 5, 8, 141–2, 176, 230, 265–6, 269, 288–93, 294–5, 306–15, 323
   prefabrication 202, 233, 235, 263, 265, 278, 285, 288–92, 294, 307, 324
   public 6, 141, 223, 226–8, 230–2, 265, 267, 288
   reform 115–16, 136, 141, 224, 226–8, 231–7, 264
Howard, Ebenezer 177, 226, *see also* Garden City

IG Farben 199–200, 267
impressionism 123, 133
industries 10, 17, 30, 38–9, 61, 68, 72, 89, 96, 135–9, 145–6, 152, 183, 188, 192, 195, 199, 202, 207, 210, 241, 247, 277, 282, 292, 306, 314, 317, 319–20, 323–4, *see also* automobile
   advertising 87, 146–7, 165, 173, 198, 202–5, 237, 295, 305–6
   chemical 7, 32, 34, 38, 40–1, 46, 72, 90–1, 120, 135–6, 146, 153, 188, 199–201, 216, 230, 272, 324
   cotton 11, 30–4, 36–8, 40–1, 45–6, 89–90, 241
   engineering 33–4, 39, 42, 51, 115–16, 126, 135–6, 146, 188, 192, 199, 227, 244, 281, 285

food 6, 41, 51, 96–100, 210–11, 216, 247, 262, 267–8, 277, 306, 323–4
   putting-out system 29–33
   shipbuilding 17, 39, 90, 317
   steel 41–4, 47–8, 89, 136, 216, 227, 241, 262, 272, 322–3
infrastructure 6, 14, 29, 49, 51, 99, 107–9, 117, 119, 139, 172, 176, 207–8, 211, 215, 240, 247, 251, 261–2, 276, 278, 283, 285, 289, 319, *see also* automobile; railroad
   airports 251, 276, 296
   highways 8, 118, 281–5, 311–15, 320
   sewer systems 64, 75, 107, 109, 115–19, 120, 124, 139, 171
   water 64, 75, 107–9, 115–20, 124, 126, 139, 142, 148, 171, 226–7, 231
Iron Curtain 256, 258, 270–1, 276, 288, 291–2, 297, 305, 307

Jewish life 10, 15, 17, 20–1, 24, 26–7, 36, 46–7, 51, 60, 66–7, 69, 81, 83, 91–2, 96, 117, 130, 148, 150, 153, 181, 191, 195, 206–10, 218, 231, 245–7, 251, 254–5, 259, 324
   Kazimierz 66
   Muranów 251, 260
   Terézváros 156

Karl-Marx-Hof 232–3, *see also* housing
Katowice 48, 195, 205, 208
Kiel 57, 91, 192, 195, 254
Kiev 92, 157, 163, 167, 207, 214, 251, 303
Kraków 9, 15, 56, 64–7, 95, 166, 179, 181–2, 191, 205, 208, 210, 251, 324
Kreuzberg 148, 277, 287, 300, 309, *see also* Berlin
Krupp 42, 44–5, 178
Kurfürstendamm 105, 149, 163, 202–3, 206, 286, 305, 315, *see also* Berlin

labor 11, 20, 25–6, 29, 31–2, 43–5, 73, 82–3, 86, 90, 100, 112, 139–40, 151–5, 200, 221, 227, 236, 241–2, 248, 255, 258–9, 264, 276, 294, 309, *see also* working class
   Labor Party 137, 227–8
   manual 32, 35, 43, 136, 228
   skilled 33, 44, 136, 278
   unions 45, 137–8, 224–6, 231, 234, 256
La Défense 278, 320, *see also* Paris
Lancashire 31–7, 43, 76
Latin Quarter 58, 65, 196, 295, 300
Le Corbusier 235–6, 243
Leeds 30–1, 99, 101–2, 111, 115
Le Havre 82, 157, 251, 257–8
Leicester Square 159, 161–2, *see also* London
Lemberg (L'viv, Lwów) 56, 80, 168, 172, 182, 190–1, 197, 205, 208, 287, 298
Les Halles 97, 99–100, 120, 218, 286, *see also* Paris

Index

liberalism 7, 36, 55, 57, 107, 127
Lijnbaan 283-4, see also Rotterdam
Lisbon 72, 81, 144, 156, 314-15
Liverpool 31, 76, 80, 82, 84, 111, 115, 141-2, 154, 157, 165, 176-7, 226, 316
  commerce 23, 33, 36, 90, 99
  music 269, 296
Ljubljana 216, 220-1, 263, 282, 297-8, 300
Łódź 41, 45-7, 81, 91, 152-3, 205, 207-8, 210
London 1, 4, 53, 58, 83-90, 108-9, 111-16, 141, 157, 165-8, 172, 175-8, 196, 205, 282, 309, 319-21, see also markets; music halls; pubs
  commerce 13, 15, 86-90, 96-101, 104, 268
  culture 144-5, 155-3, 167-8, 225, 269-70, 295-7, 299
  housing 286-7, 290-1
  industry 192, 200, 205, 278, 320
  migration 81-2, 196, 277, 309
  outskirts 175-7, 198, 269, 311
  planning 115-16, 178, 264
  population 9-10, 80-1, 176, 325
  protests 113, 137-8, 151, 192, 277, 286-7
  slums 90, 113-14, 145
  wartime 192-3, 251, 253
Lyon 30-1, 68, 73, 82, 135-6, 139, 157, 161, 192, 199, 230-1, 251, 308, 310-11

Madrid 15, 55, 81, 93, 124-5, 167, 248, 309-10, 313-14, 325
Manchester 27, 40-1, 46, 76, 80, 88, 92, 111-13, 115-16, 119, 139, 165, 176, 322
  commerce 36-7, 104, 313
  industry 30-5, 200
markets 5, 11, 14, 20, 22, 28, 30, 54, 56, 70, 79, 86, 95-100, 106, 124, 139, 154, 165, 201, 259, 267, 271, 278, 297, 306, 325, see also arcades; supermarkets
  bazaar 22, 58, 69-71, 93, 99, 101, 103, 106, 139, 242, 245-6, 306
  halls 8, 11, 14, 87, 99, 120, 208, 228
  open-air 72, 97-8
  regulation 99
  street 36, 96-7, 142, 156, 175, 259
Märkisches Viertel 289, 290-1, 294, see also housing
Marseille 21, 23, 72-4, 81-2, 91-2, 117, 152, 157, 199, 229, 244, 251, 278, 287, 309-11
Marshall Plan 259, 262-3, 321
Mediterranean 3-6, 9, 13, 16, 20-1, 23, 29, 53-4, 69-5, 223, 241-8, 258, 278, 287, 311-13, 315
  cities 3-4, 13, 16, 21, 69, 71-2, 90-1, 216, 241, 244, 247-8, 278
Midlands 31, 37, 43, 83, 137, 200, 311, see also Manchester
mietskasernen 148, 290, see also housing

migration 14-16, 81-3, 197, 244, 277, 309, 314, 325
  emigration 130, 255, 259, 275
  immigration 6, 36, 277, 290, 308-9
Milan 9, 67-9, 105, 117, 187, 238, 251, 265, 325
Moabit 146-9, 154, see also Berlin
Mods 270, 279, 295-6, see also under youth
Montmartre 101, 123, 159, 163, 179-80, 196-8, see also Paris
Moscow 2, 21, 106, 153, 163, 165, 178, 181, 195, 198, 253, 293, 306, 313, 316, 325
  communist 210-15, 259, 262-3, 271, 280, 302-4
  industry 201, 211, 278
movie houses 163, 271
Munich 9, 60, 63-4, 70-1, 80, 95, 108, 127, 131-2, 155, 159-60, 162, 298, 319
  commerce 56, 105, 268, 321
municipal socialism 4, 223, 227-8, 231-2, 241
music 57-8, 65, 68, 87, 101-3, 121, 128-9, 132, 138, 143, 154, 156-3, 171, 175, 180, 186, 196, 198, 205-6, 210, 220, 225, 239, 261-2, 269, 270-1, 273, 296-8, 324
  choral 60-2, 168
  clubs 18, 57, 60-1, 269
  festivals 60-2, 190, 271, 319
  jazz 196-8, 205, 210-2, 225, 247, 269, 271
  rock 'n roll 269-71, 286, 296-300
music halls 143, 156-7, 160-3, 175, see also entertainment

Naples 9, 53, 67-8, 72, 82, 117, 161, 238, 241-4, 251
Napoleonic Wars 1, 19, 47, 53-4, 58, 61, 63-4, 67, 75, 81, 108, 117
newspapers 13, 18, 37, 48, 59-60, 73, 113, 137, 143-4, 155, 166, 171, 174-5, 181, 198, 204, 221, 225
nightclubs 196-8, 206, 295, see also music

Odessa 3, 20-3, 70, 95, 152, 157, 165, 179, 181, 193, 214
oil 50-1, 190, 207, 216, 278, 309, 321, 324
  production 49-51, 190, 207, 324
Olympic Games 232, 241
Ottoman Empire 1, 6, 9, 20-4, 26, 50, 67, 69-71, 81, 131, 181, 188, 207, 294
  towns 26, 70, 215-16, 218-21, 245-6, 301, 311

pageants 64, 87, 151, 168, 282
panoramas 159, 161-3, 316, see also entertainment
Paris 1, 4, 25, 75, 83-7, 108-9, 111-12, 116, 119-23, 167, 169-70, 174-5, 192-3, 196-200, 223, 228-9, 254, 256, 319,

379

Index

see also department stores; exhibitions; markets; panorama
boulevards   85–7, 100–1, 103, 110, 119–23, 132, 134, 159, 163, 179, 286
commerce   16, 73, 86, 96–7, 99–101, 103–4, 136
culture   85, 144, 155–6, 159–63, 179–82, 198, 271, 295, 298
housing   226, 263, 265–6, 277, 290, 308, 310
industrial districts   138–9, 199–200
industry   92, 95, 192, 199–200, 278–9, 320
migration   81, 196–7, 247, 277, 287, 309
outskirts   16, 140–1, 143, 151, 179, 226, 229, 263, 266, 290, 295, 308, 313
planning   108–9, 119–22, 124, 178, 286
population   9–10, 80, 119, 122, 196–8, 226, 325
protest   54, 151, 256, 299–300, 310
slums   140, 149, 287–8
tourism   54, 313, 315
traffic   110, 166, 281–2, 286
photography   38, 84, 110, 118, 128, 133–4, 136, 140, 174–5
 Annan, Thomas   38
 Atget, Eugène   140
 Daguerre, Louis   118, 133, 161
 Klösz, György   133
 Lumière Brothers   136
 Marville, Charles   121
 Stauda, August   128
pleasure gardens   58, 64, 154, 156
pollution   33, 35, 74, 115–16, 135, 149, 284, 286, 313, *see also* sanitation
 air   116, 284
 sewers   33, 43, 109, 111, 115, 121, 209, 273
post-industrial   316, 324
Prague   54, 91, 166, 168, 179, 181–2, 191–2, 201–2, 206, 262, 300, 302, 305, 307
Prater Park   58, 95, 126, 128, 162, 232, *see also* Vienna
prostitution   98, 142, 144, 155, 159, 209
protests   44, 63, 65, 67, 69, 81, 152, 155, 195, 224, 272, 285–7, 299, 304, 310, *see also* students
 1968 revolt   7, 286, 300
 anti-renewal   288, 320
 anti-tourism   55, 318
 housing   141, 150, 172, 290
 Prague Spring   300
 worker   112, 137, 151–3, 192, 225, 227, 300
public space   83, 101, 123, 304, 312, 317
pubs   34, 114, 143, 225, 297

railroad   28, 30–1, 41, 46–7, 56, 73–5, 83, 107, 111, 126, 132, 146, 149, 152–3, 184, 211, 215, 281

stations   37, 75, 79, 83, 94, 96, 151, 166, 184, 208
transport   14, 54, 67, 96, 157, 166, 169, 171, 175, 180, 216
Randstad   283–4, 325
reconstruction   5, 51, 107, 129, 207–8, 215, 256–7, 259–64, 264, 266, 275, 291–2, 309, 321
 Giessen   258
 Hamburg   118–19
 Le Havre   258
 Rotterdam   283
 Warsaw   259–61
 Zadar   257–8
refugees   23, 66, 72, 196, 198, 223, 246–7, 255, 259, 305, 310, *see also* migration
 political   10, 53, 67, 197, 244, 246, 257, 310
 war   19, 24, 81–2, 193, 197, 220, 223, 235, 245, 251
Regent Street   87, 101, 108, 112, 172, *see also* London
religion   21, 172–4, 181
revolutions   5, 16, 81, 113, 120, 324
 Bolshevik   195, 224, 244
 Hungarian (1848)   195, 224, 244
Rhineland   49, 61–2, 82
Rhine river   41–2, 61, 167
Riga   16–19, 56–7, 59, 61, 152–3, 165, 168, 179, 182, 186, 206–7, 302
Ringstrasse   127–8, 132, 168, 172, 179, 188–9, 191, 232, *see also* Vienna
Rochdale   32–4
Rome   9, 54, 64, 67, 72, 151, 170, 238–41, 244, 278, 290, 309
Rostock   192, 254, 261, 278, 292–4, 297
Rotterdam   43, 82, 91, 165, 251, 263, 277–8, 283–4, 287, *see also* Randstad
Ruhr   13, 40–5, 47–9, 61, 82, 139, 151, 154, 178, 192, 208, 321–2, 325

St. Petersburg   2, 21, 80, 95, 129, 144, 152–3, 163, 165, 170, 175, 179, 181, 183, 192–3, 197
 commerce   16–17, 106
 communist   195, 211–13, 293
 Leningrad   251, 253
Salonica   9, 69–70, 72, 92, 216, 220, 245–7
sanitation   4, 115–19, 211, 227, 254, *see also* epidemics; infrastructure
 Bazelgette, Joseph   116
 Chadwick, Edwin   115–16, 118
 Lindley, William   118
 Mayhew, Henry   113
Sarajevo   69, 216–18, 221, 297–8, 300, 305–6, 319
 siege of   305–6

Index

Sarcelles 265–6, *see also* housing
Schwabing 180, *see also* cabaret; Munich
secession movement 179, 188–9, 191, 219
Seine River 28, 99, 120, 151, 169, 286, 320
Sellier, Henri 140, 226, *see also* Garden City
Semper, Gottfried 118–19, 177
Sheffield 111, 227–8, 265, 270
shopping centers 265, 283, 296–7, 311–14, 320, 324
shrinking cities 323
Siemens 146, 166–7, 170, 267
Silesia 31, 39, 43, 45, 47–9, 65, 91–2, 95, 192, 195, 207–8, 210, 311, 322–4
Simmel, Georg 85, 173
Sitte, Camillo 129, 173, 177
Skopje 69, 216–17, 282, 301–2
slums 33, 35–6, 46, 84, 90, 120, 137, 152, 156, 211, 227, 237, *see also* London; Manchester; Paris
    clearance 38, 111, 140, 141, 184, 215, 265, 276, 287–8, 290
    industrial 29, 35, 91, 116, 147, 224
    literature 113, 144–5, 149
    rookeries 90, 112–15
socialism 4–6, 66, 212, 223, 227–8, 230–4, 237, 241, 271, 273, 276, 293–4, 305–6, 312, *see also* municipal socialism
socialist realism 260–1, 269, 292
Sofia 207, 216, 218, 220, 251, 298
Soho 196, 295–6, *see also* London
Speicherstadt 91, 318, *see also* Hamburg
sports 138, 171, 205, 225, 227, 232, 241, 306, 319, *see also* swimming pools
    clubs 138, 212, 225, 239
    facilities 186, 228–9, 230–2, 276, 288, 290, 306
    Olympiad 232, 248
    Olympics 232, 241, 302, 316, 319
sprawl 9, 31, 42–3, 50, 126, 189, 200, 211–12, 283–4, 311, 315, 323, *see also* suburbs
squatters 113, 209, 246, 259, 286–7, 290, 298–9, 315, 324
Stalinallee 261, 269, 272, 304, *see also* Berlin
Stettin (Szczecin) 17, 19, 45, 91, 192, 258
Stockholm 16, 93, 199, 236–7, 285, 310
strikes 33, 49, 69, 113, 137–8, 141, 151–3, 154–5, 160–1, 172, 176, 192, 195, 210, 224, 248, 256, 266, 272, 300
students 59, 65–6, 87, 129, 139, 180, 186, 287, 295, 298, 316, *see also* youth
    colonial 196
    protests 5, 152, 272, 286–7, 299–300
suburbs 17–18, 57, 80, 126, 145, 156, 177, 200, 229–31, 235, 251–2, 265–6, 268, 272, 278, 285, 288–90, 297, 302, 308–10, 314, *see also* housing; sprawl
    corporate 313–14, 324
    industrial 51, 126, 153, 199, 272
    middle-class 176–7, 295, 311–13
    model 45, 177–8, 186, 226, 263
    working-class 175–6, 189, 314, 319
subways 107, 132, 166, 169, 204, 242, 273
supermarkets 267–9, 296, 306, 311, *see also* markets
swimming pools 228–30, 232, 239, 241, 315

Tallinn 12, 17–19, 61, 161, 168, 206, 316
Taut, Bruno 167, 234–5
telephone 154, 165, 170, 199
television 205, 210, 265, 267, 271, 276, 287–91, 295–6, 298, 302–4, 307–8, 311, 321
    shows 287, 290, 303–4
television towers 30–4, 323
tenements 35, 40, 44, 46, 114–16, 126, 139, 142–3, 146, 149–50, 153–4, 209, 211, 223, 227–8, 238, 242, 269, 287–8, 323, *see also* housing
Thames River 9, 13, 58, 89, 115
theater 19, 22, 24, 48, 57–60, 64, 67, 75–7, 86–7, 93, 97, 103–4, 122, 126–8, 132, 156–7, 161–3, 167, 179–80, 189, 203, 210, 213, 221, 230–1, 256, 296, 298, 312, 320, *see also* entertainment
    commercial 87, 103, 157, 159, 160–1, 163, 180, 210, 296
    musical 60, 67, 103, 128
    public 59, 93, 132, 156, 206
Thessaloniki, *see* Salonica
Tirana 207, 216–17
Tolmers Square 286–7, *see also* housing; London
Toruń 15, 19, 205, 208
Toulouse 92, 157, 167, 229–30
    Montariol, Jean 230
tourism 54, 74, 95, 206, 242, 311
    over-tourism 318–20
    policy 242, 311, 315
Trieste 21, 23, 72, 80, 91–2, 258, 297
Turin 53, 59, 69, 102, 136, 168, 182, 187–8, 192, 200–1, 238, 251 265, 279–80

Uppsala 59
Utrecht 283 5

Via dell'Impero 239–40, *see also* Rome
Vienna 1, 10, 23, 53, 66, 125–9, 131, 133, 170–1, 197, 199, 206, 222, 231, 324
    commerce 68, 87, 91–2, 126
    culture 143–4, 162, 168, 174, 180–2, 188–9, 319
    housing 126, 142, 232–3, 307, 314
    migration 81, 83, 126
    outskirts 126, 198, 224
    planning 126–7, 129, 173, 178, 189

Index

population 9, 80, 189, 231
protest 54, 80, 192, 195, 224
Villeurbanne 136, 231
Vistula river 15, 19, 64, 260

Wagner, Otto 126, 129, 171–2, 189
Warsaw 4, 15, 45–6, 65, 80–1, 152, 165, 199, 205–10, 278, 296, 298, 306–7, 311, *see also* reconstruction
communist 262, 271–2, 300, 304–5
housing 139, 178
planning 259–61
population 9, 209, 259
wartime 193, 251–3, 255
welfare state 4, 6, 224, 267, 276
Werkstatte 180, 188–9
West Berlin 263, 269, 271, 273, 280, 286–7, 289, 298–90, *see also* Berlin
West End 100, 112, 196, 200, *see also* London
working class 33–5, 49, 51, 100, 105, 113–14, 120, 124, 144–5, 150–7, 159, 164, 188, 212, 224–8, 230–2, 237, 242, 247–9, 266, 270, 276, 319, 323

clubs 138, 269
districts 44, 74, 117, 139, 149, 152, 154–5, 184, 192, 222–3, 229, 287, 290
families 44–5, 94, 96, 104, 110, 137, 139–41, 154, 169, 175, 205, 224, 234, 287, 292, 315
neighborhoods 98, 120–1, 138, 142, 150, 223, 225, 228–30, 302, 310

youth 59, 173, 179–80, 239, 241, 267–71, 273, 275, 280, 282, 293, *see also* consumerism; music; students
clubs 271, 297
Mods 270, 279, 295–6
rebels 85, 179, 271, 297–8
Teddy Boys 270
World Youth Festival 262, 298

Zagreb 80, 196, 216, 221–2, 269, 271, 278, 282, 294, 297, 300
Zille, Heinrich 149–50
Zlín 202
Zola, Emile 86, 100, 104, 149

www.ingramcontent.com/pod-product-compliance
Ingram Content Group UK Ltd.
Pitfield, Milton Keynes, MK11 3LW, UK
UKHW021904220326
469204UK00008B/170